Teaching Reading

to Every Child

Teaching Reading

to Every Child

Diane Lapp

James Flood

Boston University

Macmillan Publishing Co., Inc.
New York
Collier Macmillan Publishers
London

Macmillan Publishing Co., Inc.
866 Third Avenue, New York, New York 10022

Collier Macmillan Canada, Ltd.

Library of Congress Cataloging in Publication Data

Lapp, Diane.
  Teaching reading to every child.

  Includes bibliographical references and index.
  1. Reading. I. Flood, James, joint author.
II. Title.
LB1050.L365   372.4'1   77-5093
ISBN 0-02-367610-8

Printing: 1 2 3 4 5 6 7 8   Year: 8 9 0 1 2 3 4

Dedicated to our favorite readers

Eric
Shannon
and Sharon

Preface

Regardless of the grade level or the content area, all teachers, are teachers of reading. This is true because the mastery of almost all information involves the integrated processes of language, reading, and thinking.

This book has been specifically designed to assist the prospective teacher of reading in understanding the integral processes of learning to read. We have divided the book into four parts: 1) Your Role as a Teacher; 2) Your Students; 3) The Reading Process; 4) Your Reading Program.

The first part, "Your Role as a Teacher," introduces the professional responsibilities of being a reading teacher. The teaching profession brings with it an enormous need for commitment. The teacher is asked to make many decisions about teaching role, students' needs, and curriculum.

The second part of the book, "Your Students," introduces current biological, psychological, and linguistic factors which affect the development of students. This section also includes a chapter on current trends in preschool reading programs. The importance of parental involvement in the education of the child and the effects of television as well as the affective aspects of reading are discussed. There is a chapter on activities for the preschool reading program, as well as language arts activities for the older child. Means of assessing students' attitudes and interests are discussed in detail.

The third part of the book, "The Reading Process," is divided into two sections: (a) perceiving and (b) integrating and evaluating. "Perceiving" will assist the teacher in instructing children in the beginning steps of reading: visual and auditory discrimination of sounds, letters, and words. We have included a chapter on activities to reinforce these early activities for beginning reading.

The second section, "Integrating and Evaluating," introduces topics of literal, inferential, and critical comprehension, study skills, and content area learning. A variety of activities that will help develop an effective reading program has also been included.

The fourth part of the book, "Your Reading Program," introduces methods of understanding and designing a diagnostic-prescriptive reading program.

The special needs of the bilingual student are also presented in this section, as is a discussion of the historical precedents of current instructional methods. This entire fourth part of the book is focused on the integration of theory and practice.

The reading teacher's task is a difficult one, a task among the most complex and important in any school. The teacher is the key to each child's success; with the teacher's help, students *will* learn to read.

D. L.
J. F.

Acknowledgments

We gratefully acknowledge the assistance of Michelle Sullivan, Lynne Thrope, Irene Fountas, Darlene Jones, Suzanne Driscoll, and Eric Freidman for their valuable contributions toward the publication of this book. We especially want to thank Linda Lungren and Sharon Ryan-Flood for their extensive work on this manuscript—their support was a mainstay in the completion of this book.

Contents

Your Role As a Teacher

The purpose of this section is to introduce you to the personal commitment you must be willing to make if you have chosen *teaching* as your profession. Your tasks will be extremely complex because you will be constantly making decisions about *your role as a teacher, your students,* and *your curriculum.*

Regardless of grade level or content specialization, you will be a *teacher of reading* because the mastery of all information involves the integrated processes of reading and thinking.

This text is designed to assist *you* in understanding the processes in learning to read. It will also introduce you to varied methods of teaching reading.

1

The teacher, the student, and reading

Have you ever rightly considered what the mere ability to read means? That it is the key which admits us to the whole world of thought and fancy and imagination? To the company of saint and sage, of the wisest and the wittiest at their wisest and wittiest moment? That it enables us to see with the keenest eyes, hear with the finest ears, and listen to the sweetest voices of all times?

James Russell Lowell

GOALS: To aid the reader in understanding
1. the purpose of this book.
2. the necessity for formulating an individual definition of reading.
3. the place of the teacher in society, in the school, and in the classroom.
4. the learner as an individual.
5. the existence of a variety of possible curricula.

> Do <u>you</u> like to share ideas?
> Are <u>you</u> willing to work long hours?
> Does the candor of youth appeal to you?

If you answer yes to all these questions, you should consider a career in teaching. Teaching requires all of these characteristics, as well as a dedication and enthusiasm that go far beyond an 8:00 AM to 3:00 PM schedule and your summers free. If you decide to answer yes, you may, as an education major or "teacher type" college student, be scorned by less pragmatic types who feel that teaching kindergarten, third, or sixth grade requires little more than a seventh-grade education and a bag full of tricks. Eventually you will be harassed by well-meaning parents who believe they know more about teaching than you do. After all, everyone has been to school, and many people believe their own experience is all that is required in order to teach. Isn't it peculiar that this "experience by going" philosophy does not apply to all professionals: doctors, dentists, clergy?

Begin your career as a teacher by accepting these social realities with a smile, and appreciate that your job is the most important one society has to offer: *the education of its young.* Take pride in knowing that tomorrow's future will be sitting before you each morning as you enter your classroom door. Yes, indeed, yours is a very important task. You are a *teacher*, and you will experience life in a way that no other professional person can. You will meet all kinds of people, some of whom you will cherish and always remember. You will touch the lives of hundreds of people, but be prepared to meet all kinds, all sizes, all shapes.

> I have taught school for ten years. During that time I have given assignments, among others, to a murderer, an evangelist, a pugilist, a thief, and an imbecile.
>
> The murderer was a quiet little boy who sat on the front seat and regarded me with pale blue eyes; the evangelist, easily the most popular boy in school, had the lead in the junior play; the pugilist lounged by the window and let loose at intervals a raucous laugh that startled even the geraniums; the thief was a gay-hearted Lothario with a song on his lips: and the imbecile, a soft-eyed little animal seeking the shadows.
>
> The murderer awaits death in the state penitentiary; the evangelist has lain a year now in the village churchyard; the pugilist lost an eye in a brawl in Hong Kong; the thief, by standing on tiptoe, can see the windows of my room from the county jail; and the once gentle-eyed little moron beats his head against a padded wall in the state asylum.

All of these pupils once sat in my room, sat and looked at me gravely across worn brown desks. I must have been a great help to these pupils—I taught them the rhyming scheme of the Elizabethan sonnet and how to diagram a complex sentence.

(White, 1937, pp. 151, 192)

The point of this passage is clear. We must attempt to make our curricula relevant to the lives and needs of our students. We must focus on their interests rather than hold true only to the old familiar requisites of a "classical" education. For, indeed, in the course of your career, *they* will *all be seated* before *you.*

Many children claim to dislike reading. Do they dislike reading because reading is perceived as a perennial bore to be equated with "Dick and Jane" stories? Many children who disclaim reading the basal reader are found reading baseball cards, comic books, and magazines during their free periods. It is easy to see that what they dislike is not reading but rather the materials and processes that are often used to teach reading.

Each summer, as September approaches, we hear many children saying negative things about the reopening of schools. Why does this happen? What do we do to children to make school such a disheartening place? Irrelevant curricula? Grumpy teachers? Strict rules? Lack of humor? Boredom?

What can you do about it? How do you plan to make school learning relevant to the life experiences of your students? How do you plan to engage them in a reading program that will make a difference?

Whatever you decide to do, you must base your decisions on the needs, interests, and abilities of your students because, as Durr (1967), a reading authority, cautions,

The best methods and wisest methods lose their effectiveness when we know too little about our pupils . . . . (p. 104)

Yes, as Durr tells us, the central focus of the curriculum must be the student. This text is designed to meet that need; its sole purpose is to help you to teach reading—to make sure that you will want to be part of all the educators who believe *Teaching Reading to EVERY Child* is the most important part of any curriculum.

Purpose of This Book

This book is designed for you, the teacher of reading, to plan learning experiences that will make a difference in the lives of students. If you are puzzled about being referred to as a "teacher of reading," remember that regardless of your content specialization, you will be required to teach reading. It is important to remember that all content subjects present students with facts to be learned and texts to be read. Students are required to read, and read, and reread. Your role is to provide children with the skills that will enable them to read for *information* and for *enjoyment*. *All* teachers at *all* grade levels in *all* content areas are teachers of reading.

To prepare you for this task, each chapter of this text deals with important issues in the field of reading, and presents current theoretical concerns and effective instructional applications. Our contention is that both teacher and students need to be prepared for reading. In a sense, then, this book is intended to ready you for the task of teaching children to read. For those of you who have become seasoned teachers of reading, this text will serve as an aid for reevaluating beliefs and reassessing curricular practices.

What Is Reading?

This seemingly simple question is filled with complexity. Educators, psychologists, linguists, and information scientists who are interested in the reading process have filled volumes with their definitions of reading. Frequently, these definitions are contradictory, each emphasizing a different component of the reading process. It would be counterproductive to present a long list of definitions here because each of you will have to develop your own definition of the process after you understand its components. It is this development that should be your end goal in reading this text. Your definition will continue to change and grow with new evidence from research. However, it is extremely important for you to formulate a definition of reading because you will be forced to develop an instructional program as soon as you enter the classroom. If you have not given any thought to the question, *"What is reading?,"* your program will probably suffer from a fragmented and incomplete notion of the reading process.

In general, all definitions of reading fall into two categories. First, there are those who view reading primarily as a *decoding process*, a breaking of a visual code. In a second view, *reading* for *meaning* is emphasized from the very earliest stages of instruction; in this view reading as a comprehension process is stressed.

Although there are differences of opinion about a precise definition of reading, most educators agree, at least, that the reading process includes:

1. letter and word perception/recognition
2. comprehension of the concepts conveyed by the printed word(s)
3. reaction and assimilation of the new knowledge with reader's past experience.

Every instructor of reading must decide for him-herself what reading is. Several authors have thought about the problem, have devised definitions, and have established an approach on the basis of their definition. These approaches, along with subsequent definitions of reading, will be presented in detail in Chapter 12, *Approaches and Methods of Teaching Reading.*

Although we will explore several of these approaches, we believe that reading is basically a process of *perceiving, interpreting,* and *evaluating* printed material. These concepts (perception, interpretation, and evaluation) will be thoroughly discussed throughout this text.

After exploring all of the presented definitions, it will be to your benefit to establish your definition of reading; once you have done so, you will be able to *evaluate* your classroom reading program to see if it meets your desired plan. We will provide you with more detailed information about an evaluative procedure in Chapter 15, "*Creating and Managing a Reading Program.*"

With these rudimentary notions of what reading is and what the reading process entails, we can begin to look at the most important elements in the reading process: teacher and learner. The act of teaching reading is a play with two main characters who are dependent on each other to produce a masterpiece. Each character is extremely important. Each receives his cues from the other before progress is made. Given this setting, let us then present some important ideas about the teacher and the learner.

The Teacher

The teacher has emerged as a variable of considerable importance and attention in many reading research studies. In fact, when Malmquist (1973) reviewed the massive federally funded study, "The Cooperative Research Program in First-Grade Reading Instruction," she stated: "Studies indicate that the teacher is a more important variable in reading instruction than are the teaching methods and instructional materials."

G. Spache (1973) also commented on the importance of the teacher after analyzing the results of these first-grade studies, which attempted to compare several methods of reading instruction. He stated:

> Our reading research into the effectiveness of various instructional methods in classroom or remedial situations is often pointless. Such comparative research tends to ignore the fact that the dynamic practices of the teacher and the kinds of teacher-pupil interaction she promotes are the most important determinants of pupil's achievements. The collected results of the large-scale First Grade Reading Studies . . . strongly reaffirm this fact. Hardly any real differences in pupil achievement were found in comparisons among a half-dozen different approaches in carefully equated populations. Rather, in almost every study, achievement varied more from one teacher's classroom to the next than it varied according to the methods of materials employed. (p. 43–44)

Tinker and McCullough (1975) maintain that experimental classes in experimental/control-group comparative studies usually show great achievements in reading scores because they reflect the teacher's drive and enthusiasm during the experimental stage, regardless of the teacher's knowledge of specific reading skills. They further maintain that the teacher is a greater factor in this achievement than specific methods or materials. King (1973), agreeing with Tinker and McCullough, stated that the differences in teaching styles and professional competencies among teachers have a definite effect on childrens' reading achievement. Goldbecker (1975) underscores the assertion that the teacher is an all-important part of the reading program when she states: "The salient point remains that no reading program operates by itself. The teacher is still the single catalyst who can determine success or failure of a reading program, no matter where its emphasis lies." (p. 4)

With the teacher as the prime factor in the learning encounter, it becomes incumbent on you to think through many of your values, to assess your philosophy of teaching, and to learn a great deal about the children who have been assigned to you. You need to consider theories of learning, as well as the physical, mental, psychological, and sociological developmental patterns of children. You also need to process this information and integrate it into a cohesive approach to teaching.

This book will provide you, the teacher, with a great deal of the background information essential to teaching reading. However, it cannot provide you with your philosophy of teaching, only you can do that.

The Teacher's Role

What is your role as *teacher* in the learning process?

How can you be sure that children who spend one year of their lives with you are aided in the development of knowledge that will help them become successful in life? Sometimes, at the end of an especially exhausting day, you may find yourself having the following, or similar, thoughts: "I didn't realize that Irene was having so much trouble reading her science book. I must spend extra time with her tomorrow. When she discussed her problem with me today, her eyes and voice were filled with anxiety. She really wants to succeed. How can this be solved?" The sources of difficulty are very complex.

As a teacher, your task is to identify your most effective style of relating to students in order to encourage comfortable teacher-student interaction and maximum learning. To determine your most effective teaching style, you first have to understand yourself, your values, your approach to people, your place in society, your school, and your classroom. Insights into self may be gained by exploring some of the following questions:

1. What is my view of the world and what purpose does education play in it?
2. Although students learn in many ways, how do I think they learn best?

3. What do "to learn" and "to teach" mean to me?

4. What are the value priorities that I may be transmitting to my students, consciously or unconsciously?

These are personal questions, the answers to which must be found within each individual; answers to them will emerge bit by bit. Teaching is a personal experience; one teacher's answers will reflect her educational individuality. In answering these questions, you will begin the development of that identity. "The teacher's understanding and acceptance of herself [are] the most important requirement[s] in any effort she makes to help students to know themselves and to gain healthy attitudes or self-acceptance." (Jersild, 1955, p. 3)

Once you have thought about your values and your social position in the world, you need to determine your feelings about your position in the school and in your classroom. You have to begin to develop a philosophy of teaching and begin to deal with the important question: What *is* my personal role as a teacher?

> Teachers have failed, or have been so classified because they: (1) have been too stern or too easy; (2) had too much book knowledge or too little common sense; (3) have dressed too well or too shabbily; (4) have taught too much (in that some prominent patron's son failed) or too little; and (5) have been too modern or too antiquated.
>
> *(Hunt, 1938, p. 176)*

One of the roles of the classroom teacher is to facilitate the learning process. In your relationship with students, never impose yourself. Your role is that of facilitator, providing a variety of educationally rich environments, confirming and encouraging each student by your positive regard. Whether limited to your own classroom or given responsibility in the entire school, you must strive to create learning environments that reflect the learning patterns of children.

The Learner

Once you, as the teacher of reading, have confronted some questions about yourself, you must come to appreciate many facts about your students. Essentially, you must begin with the attitude that you are educating the whole child. Educators (Rousseau, 1964; Drucker, 1957; Dewey, 1938) for decades have been espousing Gestalt psychology, that is, the development of the total child. As Dewey (1938) states:

In this period [ages four to eight] the connection of the school life with that of the home and neighborhood is, of course, especially intimate. The children are largely occupied with direct social and outgoing modes of action, with doing and telling. There is relatively little attempt made at intellectual formulation, conscious reflection, or command of technical methods. As, however, there is continual growth in the complexity of work and in the responsibilities which the children are capable of assuming, distinct problems gradually emerge in such a way that the mastery of special methods is necessary.

Hence, in the second period [from eight to ten], emphasis is put upon securing ability to read, write, handle numbers, etc., not in themselves, but as necessary helps and adjuncts in relation to the more direct modes of experience. Also, in the various forms of handwork and of science, more and more conscious attention is paid to the proper ways of doing things, methods of reaching results, as distinct from the simple doing itself. This is the special period for securing knowledge of the rules and technique of work.

In the third period, lasting until the thirteenth year, the skill thus acquired is utilized in application to definite problems of investigation and reflection, leading to recognition of the significance and necessity of generalizations. When this latter point is reached, the period of distinctly secondary education may be said to have begun. This third period is also that of the distinctive differentiation of the various line of work, history, and science, the various forms of science, etc., from one another. So far as the methods and tools employed in each have been mastered, so far is the child able to take up the pursuit [of] each by itself, making it, in some sense, really a study. If the first period has given the child a common and varied background, if the second has introduced him to control of reading, writing, numbering, manipulating materials, etc., as instruments of inquiry, he is now ready in the third for a certain amount of specialization without danger of isolation or artificiality. (pp. 53–4)

The teacher of reading, in educating the whole child, has to understand aspects of four different factors that affect the reading ability of the child:

1. Sensory and perceptual factors
2. Cognitive factors
3. Language factors
4. Socioeconomic factors

Sensory and Perceptual Development

A child's visual and auditory readiness to accommodate printed material is often the greatest initial concern for the teacher of reading. Silbiger and Woolf (1965) and many other educators have suggested that there is no one best age at which a child should begin a visual or auditory readiness program. It should be noted that perceptual development, as well as sensory development, is often very dependent on emotional, physical, linguistic, and home motivating factors. The specifics of readiness assessment are discussed in detail in Chapter 2.

Cognitive Factors

When discussing cognitive factors related to reading achievement, it is important to consider an array of mental processes and general intelligence.

Mental Processes. Cognitive processes can be described in different ways, and experts have developed whole schemas for sharing complex ideas about cognition. Thinking processes may be categorized under two broad headings that indicate two somewhat different mental processes. The first of these processes, *logical thinking*, deals with the formal, well-structured thought processes that are used in the ordered solving of problems. The second category, *creative thinking*, could be labeled informal and divergent. If the school is to nurture the individual, it most surely must concern itself with both of these thought processes.

Piaget (1962), Gordon (1961), and several other psychologists and educators deal in depth with the developmental stages of the mental processes. Most psychologists assert that a large portion of cognitive growth takes place in the early years; they view it, in part, as a biological function. This notion will be given considerable attention in Chapter 2, "The Developing Reader."

Intelligence

> After an Old Home Week in the school system, when those we flunked return in Rolls-Royces to patronize us, we are positive of one thing:
> Either it takes no intelligence to make money, and education is of comparatively little value, or teachers don't know a smart child when they see one.
>
> *(Preston, 1938, p. 176)*

Although many factors have been correlated with reading and language achievement, *intelligence* and reading have been closely entwined since earliest times. Two examples illustrate this point:

> And he who shall be said to be a sot and idiot from his birth, is such a person who cannot account of number twenty pence, nor can tell who his father or mother, or how old he is, etc., so as it may appear that he hath no understanding of reason what shall be for his profit, nor what for his loss. But if he hath such understanding, that he know and understand his letters, and do read by teaching or information of another man, then it seemeth that he is not a sot nor a natural "idiot."
>
> *(Fitzherbert, 1534, p. 18)*

In 1972, P. R. Lohnes and M. M. Gray, after reanalyzing the data from the First Grade Cooperative Study concluded: "The best single explanatory principle for observed variance in reading skills was variance in general intelligence. (p. 59)"

There are many definitions of intelligence in operation; we will define intelligence as a combination of biological factors and environmental experiences. Unfortunately, the computation of the IQ score, while considering MA (mental age) and CA (chronological age), gives little attention to the experiential background of the child. Generally, it focuses on a child's present level of intellectual functioning. Often, an IQ score is computed, the child is labeled "bright," "average," or "dull," and the case is closed. In so doing, the following questions remain unanswered:

1. Was the child ready to be tested?
2. Has he had experiences similar to those of the "average" child?
3. If his experiences have been different from the norm, which set of experiences should be tested?
4. Does the child need exposure to a specific set of experiences before he is given a particular test?

Many children entering first grade who score poorly on intelligence tests are erroneously labeled "dull" or "retarded" and are placed in the lowest reading group; they are abandoned there to mentally deteriorate for 12 years. Frequently, we misinterpret low IQ scores as a lack of potential and, thus, excuse ourselves from planning personalized programs for these children. The findings of Cohen and Glass (1968) are frightening; they state that there is no significant relationship between first-grade reading ability and IQ scores, but that there are significant relationships by grade four. Bond and Wagner (1966) suggest that:

> The correlation between mental age, as measured by individual Stanford-Binet tests, and reading comprehension at the end of the first grade is approximately .35; at the end of the fifth grade it is approximately .60; during the high school years it approaches .80. (p. 119)

The precise nature of the relationship between reading and intelligence is unknown. Much of the research is contradictory and sheds little light on this topic because the larger question of the efficacy of IQ tests is still unanswered. Durkin's study (1966) tells us an interesting bit of information related to this controversial question. Children with a range of IQ scores who began to read before first grade in New York and Oakland, California, scored consistently higher on standardized reading tests than their IQ counterparts who did not begin reading until formal instruction in first grade. From this data we can infer that intelligence is not particularly related to early reading; we can also infer that children who begin to read early stay ahead of children with comparable IQs.

Language Factors

Reading, which involves one's ability to interpret the printed symbol, is a language-related process. Bonney (1962) points out the following:

> In addition to being a more or less efficient instrument of semantic transfer, language is the individual's personal equipment by means of which he organizes the world around him into principles and concepts; it is his means of coping with external reality. He must be able to use this equipment with confidence, to use it freely so he can live and act freely. If you hedge in his language, you hedge in his development, because, as the psychologists point out, language behavior is not one among many, but an all-pervasive activity. The world—everything outside us—comes to us in a confusion of limitless numbers of impressions provoking endless associations. One of the ways man tries to achieve order out of the chaos is through his language. It is with words that the infant labels his environment. They serve him as handles with which he begins quickly to manipulate his environment. This gives him a hold . . . This verbalizing becomes internal and silent . . . but continues to be the process whereby the individual reduces reality to chunks he can manage. (p. 59)

The development of one's language, or linguistic skills, is a topic of constant research in education. Such theorists as Lenneberg (1970) stress the innate aspects of language acquisition, whereas others, such as Skinner (1972), emphasize behavioral *reinforcement* as a prime factor in language development. Still others, such as Piaget (1962), focus on the child's *interactions* within his environment as an essential factor in establishing concepts that will be communicated later through language. After reviewing, grouping, and labeling existing theories as nativistic, behavioristic, and cognitive, S. F. Wanat (1971) states:

> Group differences have generally been ignored in research on language development. Thus, dialect differences, possible ethnic differences in capacities and strategies for processing information, differences in thinking style, and emotionally related factors are not adequately taken under consideration. None of the theories reviewed (Nativistic, Behavioristic, Cognitive) gives an adequate explanation of the way a child acquires his language. Each of the theories is wrong in that each unjustifiably claims to provide a complete explanation. Yet, each of these theories is valuable in that each provides part of the information we need to understand language. (p. 147)

Although there is certainly a need for continued research involving larger sample populations with greater sociological and motivational controls, existing theories do offer much of what is needed in understanding the language base of the reading process. A child may enter school with a "private" language (dialect) as well as a "formal" (public) language. If the private language is better developed than the formal or public language, the child may find reading to be a difficult task, because most reading materials are written in formal or public language. Children from cultural backgrounds other than the teacher's may have difficulty with school experiences because their private language is often misunderstood or misinterpreted. *All* children must be encouraged to accept both their *private* and *public* languages while becoming aware of the phonological and grammatical variations that exist between these two languages. The child learns, respects, and applies the appropriate language at the appropriate time.

Because we believe that language refinement and growth are highly dependent on teacher acceptance, we encourage you, as reading teachers, to accept the language presented by the child and then through your examples provide further learning. For example, if your first-grader says, "I busted it!" you reply, "I see that you *broke* it. Delicate things *break* easily. *Broken* things are hard to repair, but let's try." Thus, you begin to aid the child in acquiring public language skills, while accepting his private language. If you can offer children such nonthreatening verbal interactions, they will continually *learn* language by *using* it.

Socioeconomic Factors

Many reading studies have shown high correlations between reading failure and low socioeconomic status. Rogers (1969) may have offered a possible explanation for this phenomenon when he pointed out that until quite recently educators:

> frequently failed[ed] to recognize that much of the material presented to students in the classroom has, for the student, the perplexing, meaningless quality that learning a list of nonsense syllables has for us. This is especially true for the child whose background provides no context for the material with which he is confronted. Thus, education becomes the futile attempt to learn materials which have no personal meaning.
>
> Such learning involves the mind only. It is learning which takes place "from the neck up." It does not involve feelings or personal meanings: it has no relevance for the whole person. (pp. 3–4)

And as educators we must ask:

> Does the public school select a range of mental problems and skills which is so narrow that the school fails to develop much of the mental potential of all the students?
>
> *(Davis, 1961, p. 89)*

These and similar questions need to be considered and studied before we can fully understand the impact of socioeconomic factors and reading. In Chapter 2, we will further discuss issues concerning the home and the preschool experiences of children who are beginning to learn to read.

Curriculum

What do I do to be an effective reading teacher? The role of the classroom teacher is extremely complex and will demand extensive treatment throughout the book. The "What Do I *Do*?" part of this question will be discussed in Chapter 12. The "effective reading teacher" part of the question will be discussed in depth in Chapter 15.

Both your philosophical and methodological beliefs will determine the curricular structures of your classroom. How will information be transmitted? What type of teacher-student interactions will you use? As an educational facilitator, you will be continuously reassessing existing curricula, methods, and materials as the strengths and needs of your students change. As a teacher of reading, you will be called on to make many curricular decisions.

Classroom Simulation

Together, let's construct a simulated classroom of your choice. You determine the age range, socioeconomic and geographical statistics. Can you picture the setting? It's a week or so before Labor Day and you're beginning to think about your children, colleagues, curriculum, and planning strategies.

You might be asking yourself the following types of questions concerning yourself as teacher, your students, and your curriculum.

Teacher

1. What is my role as the teacher? Who am I to my students? What descriptive word best describes my role: facilitator, expert, resource person, co-equal, confronter?
2. What is my world view? What societal values am I presently conveying to my students?
3. What is my view of man? What am I specifically doing through day-to-day interactions to produce the ideal, mature, human being?
4. What are my basic values? Do I encourage children to accept my value structure, or do I teach them a process for developing and selecting their own value system?
5. With what type of student-teacher interactions am I most comfortable? Is the flow of communication one-way or two-way, open-ended, or planned and determined?
6. To what types of motivational sources do I ascribe? Does the motivational source come from within the student, or does the class have a materialistic reward system? Does the motivational source distort the learning process or insert noneducational values into the educational process?
7. What types of discipline will I employ? How do I handle individual problems? Group problems? Total class problems? What are the emotional and educational results of my discipline?

Students

1. What will be the role of the student? What expectations do I have for my students? Who are these children? What do I know of their experiential readiness for learning? What word or phrase best describes their relationship to me and the learning process: receivers of the word, creators, individualists, technicians, obedient children?
2. How do children learn? How will they view my role in teaching them?
3. How are students evaluated? Do students have a clear understanding of the evaluative process? How are these children emotionally, socially, and cognitively affected by the evaluative processes of the classroom?

Curriculum

1. What will be the learning climate? Will it be quiet, active, friendly, individually oriented, teacher-dominated, task-oriented, almost unstructured, enthusiastic, altering in tempo, or even-paced? Will the atmosphere be friendly, fearful, respectful, "hard-at-work," or personal-growth oriented? What will be my role in determining the learning environment?
2. What will be the major purpose, or goal, of education in this classroom? What specific social, psychological, emotional, and cognitive learning will occur within the classroom?

Although the process of answering these questions may seem heavy and even a bit burdensome, we certainly encourage you to attempt to formulate answers which will help you in integrating your philosophical, psychological, and curriculum beliefs. This attempt at integration may best begin by describing the principles of your philosophy, the effects of these principles on the psychological development of your students, and the practical curricular implementation.

Once you have initially formulated or refined your educational beliefs, you can begin to plan a curriculum that will provide your students with the experiences and information needed to become a successful reader. Our role in this process is to provide *you* with a comprehensive view of reading literature and methods for implementing this theory. You will then be a *practitioner* as well as a *theoretician*.

QUESTIONS AND RELATED READINGS

If at this time you do not feel that you have attained adequate knowledge to successfully answer the following questions, we would like to suggest related readings.

1. What is your definition of reading?
2. What is the effect of the teacher in the learning process?
3. In what way is the theory of "learner as individual" important for the teacher of reading?
4. What are some possible curricula available to the reading teacher?

Goal 1: To aid the reader in understanding the necessity for formulating an individual definition of reading

Question 1: What is your definition of reading?

Smith, Frank. *Understanding Reading—A Psycholinguistic Analysis of Reading and Learning to Read.* New York: Holt, Rinehart and Winston, 1971.

Van Allen, Roach. "How a Language-Experience Program Works." *Elementary Instruction,* ed. by Althes Beery, et al. Boston: Allyn & Bacon, Inc., 1969.

Wallen, Carl J. *Word Attack Skills in Reading.* Columbus, Ohio: Charles E. Merrill Publishing Company, 1969.

Goal 2: To aid the reader in understanding the place of the teacher in society, in the school, and in the classroom

Question 2: What is the effect of the teacher in the learning process?

Feeley, Joan. T. "Teaching Non-English Speaking First-Graders to Read." *Elementary English* 47 (Feb. 1970), 199–208.

Hodges, R., and H. Rudorf, ed. *Language and Learning to Read.* Boston: Houghton Mifflin Company, 1972.

Klein, Howard, ed. *The Quest for Competency in Teaching Reading.* Newark, Del.: International Reading Association, 1972.

Goal 3: To aid the reader in understanding the learner as an individual

Question 3: In what way is the theory of "learner as individual" important for the teacher of reading?

Baratz, Joan C. "Linguistic and Cultural Factors in Teaching Reading to Ghetto Children." *Elementary English,* 46 (Feb. 1969), 199–203.

Harris, L. A., and C. B. Smith, (ed.) *Individualizing Reading Instruction: A Reader.* New York: Holt, Rinehart and Winston, 1972.

Ruddell, Robert B. "Attitudes Toward Language—What Value for the Classroom Reading Teacher?" Claremont Reading Conference, by Malcom B. Douglass. Thirty-Eighth Year-Book. Claremont, Calif.: The Conference, 1974, pp. 21–33.

Goal 4: To aid the reader in understanding the existence of a variety of possible curricula

Question 4: What are some possible curricula available to the reading teacher?

Aukerman, Robert C. *Approaches to Beginning Reading.* New York: John Wiley & Sons, Inc., 1971.

Bagford, Jack. "The Role of Phonics in Teaching Reading." *Reading and Realism,* ed. by J. Allen Figurel. Proceedings of the Thirteenth Annual Convention, 13, Part 1. Newark, Del.: International Reading Association, 1967, pp. 82–87.

Downing, John A., *The Initial Teaching Alphabet.* Rev. ed. New York: Macmillan Publishing Co., Inc., 1974.

BIBLIOGRAPHY

Bond, G. L., and F. B. Wagner. *Teaching the Child to Read.* New York: Macmillan Publishing Co., Inc., 1966.

Bonney, M. "An English Teacher Answers Mario Pei," *Saturday Review,* (Sept. 15, 1962), 58–60, 75.

Cohen, A., and G. G. Glass. "Lateral Dominance and Reading Ability." *The Reading Teacher,* 21 (1968); 343–48.

Davis, Allison. *Social-Class Influences Upon Learning.* Cambridge, Mass.: Harvard University Press, 1961.

Dawson, Mildred. "Developing Comprehension Including Critical Reading." Newark, Del.: *International Reading Association,* 1968.

Dewey, John. *Experience and Education.* New York: Macmillan Publishing Co., Inc., 1938.

Drucker, Peter. "The New Philosophy Comes to Life." *Harper's Magazine,* (Aug. 1957), 37–40.

Durkin, Dolores. *Children Who Read Early: Two Longitudinal Studies.* New York: Bureau of Publications, Teachers College, Columbia University, 1966.

Durr, William K. *Reading Instruction: Dimensions and Issues.* Boston: Houghton Mifflin Company, 1967.

Fitzherbert, Anthony Sir. *The New Natura Breuium.* England, 1534.

Goldbecker, Sheralyn S. "Reading: Instructional Approaches." Washington, D.C.: *National Education Association,* 1975.

Gordon, W. J. J. *Synectics: The Development of Creative Capacity.* New York: Harper & Row Publishers, 1961.

Hunt, R. L. "Why Teachers Fail," *The Clearing House,* 12 (April 1938), 176.

Jersild, A. T. *When Teachers Face Themselves.* New York: Bureau of Publication, Teachers College Press, Columbia University, 1955.

King, Ethel M. "The Influence of Teaching on Reading Achievement." *Reading for All,* edited by Robert Karlin. Proceedings of the Fourth IRA World Congress on Reading. Newark, Del.: International Reading Association, 1973, pp. 110–15.

Lenneberg, E. H. "On Explaining Language." *In Language and Reading—An Interdisciplinary Approach,* edited by D. V. Gunderson, Washington, D.C.: Center for Applied Linguistics, 1970.

Lohnes, P. R., and M. M. Gray. "Intelligence and the Cooperative Reading Studies," *Reading Research Quarterly,* 3 (Spring 1972).

Malmquist, Eve. "Perspectives on Reading Research." *Reading for All,* edited by Robert Karlin. Proceedings on the Fourth IRA World Congress on Reading. Newark, Del.: International Reading Association, 1973, pp. 142–55.

Patin, H. "Class and Caste in Urban Education." *Chicago School Journal,* 45 (1964), 305–10.

Piaget, Jean. *Plays, Dreams, and Imitation in Childhood.* New York: W. W. Norton & Company, Inc., 1962.

Preston, E. F. "Those We Flunked." *The Clearing House,* 12 (April 1938), 176.

Rogers, Carl. *Freedom to Learn.* Columbus, Ohio: Charles E. Merrill Publishing Company, 1969.

Rousseau, Jean-Jacques. *Emile, Julie, and Other Writings.* New York: Barron's Educational Series, Inc., 1964.

Silbiger, Francene, and David Woolf. "Perceptual Difficulties Associated with Reading Disability." *College Reading Association Proceedings,* 6 (Fall 1965), 98–102.

Skinner, B. F. *Beyond Freedom and Dignity.* New York: Alfred A. Knopf, Inc., 1972.

Spache, George D. "Psychological and Cultural Factors in Learning to Read." *Reading for All,* edited by Robert Karlin. Proceedings of the Fourth IRA World Congress on Reading. Newark, Del.: International Reading Association, 1973, pp. 43–50.

Tinker, Milis, and Constance M. McCullough. *Teaching Elementary Reading.* 4 ed. Englewood Cliffs, N.J. Prentice-Hall, Inc., 1975.

Wanat, Stanley F. "Language Acquisitions: Basic Issues." *The Reading Teacher,* 25 (Nov. 1971), 142–7.

White, N. J. "I've Taught Them All." *The Clearing House,* 12 (Nov. 1937), 151, 192.

Section **II**

Your Students

The purpose of this section is to provide you, the teacher, with the necessary background information related to the development of the young child and to discuss the potential effect of preschool programs for preparing young children to read. The development of the child from birth throughout his school program is both an internal and an external process.

All children, given minimal input, will acquire the language of their environment. Linguists and biologists studying cognition have come to some agreement about the internal development of the brain in the young child. This development follows the same pattern in all children. Piaget, among the most celebrated developmental psychologists, specifies chronological age correlates of cognition. The external development of the young child is often determined by the child's learning environment.

This section also deals with parental involvement in the prereading preparation of young children and it includes the specifics for helping the young child to prepare for reading. The merits of preschool and kindergarten programs are discussed in detail, and the historical and philosophical correlates of reading preparation are presented.

2

The developing reader

for I was no longer a speechless infant, but a speaking boy. This I remember; and have since observed how I learned to speak. It was not that my elders taught me words . . . in any set method; but I, longing by cires and broken accents and various motions of my limbs to express my thoughts, that so I might have my will, and yet unable to express all that I willed, or to whom I willed, did myself, by the understanding which Thou, my God, gavest me, practise the sounds in my memory. . . . And thus by constantly hearing words, as they occurred in various sentences, I collected gradually for what they stood; and having broken in my mouth to these signs, I thereby gave utterance to my will. Thus I exchanged with those about me these current signs of our wills, and so launched deeper into the stormy intercourse of human life . . . .

St. Augustine,

Confessions (c. A.D. 400)

GOALS: To aid the students in understanding:
1. cognitive stages of human development.
2. stages of language development.
3. the effect of the home environment, including parental involvement, on preparation for reading.
4. The effect of television on preparing a child for reading.

Before proceeding to the matter of teaching reading, it is extremely important for prospective teachers of reading to become acquainted with a large body of background information about children. We have designed this chapter as an information resource system for you; it is filled with important background information that is absolutely essential for you to think about before beginning to teach reading.

Information about the cognitive and linguistic development of the child, as well as home and family factors, contributes to a child's success in school. Such information is, therefore, the first required material that you need to know as you attempt to teach reading.

There are internal and external stimulants that shape the growth of the human organism. In this chapter, we will discuss two general aspects of internal growth: *cognition* and *language development*. Obviously, each of these is determined in part by outside factors, but in the growth pattern of "normal" children, cognition and language development occur roughly at the same time, suggesting that there is something innate in the biological composition of all children that causes the organism to grow at a determined rate. The external stimulants to human growth that we will discuss in this chapter are *family influences* and *environmental factors*, including the effects of television and educational materials on the prereading skills of young children.

Internal Stimulants of Human Development

The four internal stimulants of human development discussed in this chapter are:
1. Cognitive development.
2. Perceptual development.
3. Language development.
4. Human information processing.

Although there are innumerable other internal factors that affect human development, we have selected these four areas because they are thought to be the factors most closely related to later reading success.

Cognitive Development

When discussing the cognitive development of the child, it is important to begin with a detailed explanation of the mental processes operating in human beings. The mental processes, or thinking processes, can be categorized under *logical creative* [handwritten annotation]

two broad headings that indicate two somewhat different mental processes. The first of these processes is *logical thinking*; it deals with the formal well-structured thought processes that are used in the ordered solving of problems. The second category *creative thinking* is an informal, divergent kind of thinking. If the curriculum is designed to nurture the individual, the teacher must be concerned with both kinds of thought processes.

Concept + perception [handwritten annotation]

Imp — [handwritten annotation]

Logical Thinking. Under this broad heading, a number of processes will be examined: *concept formation and attainment*, the *generalizing process*, and *hypothesizing* and *predicting*.

Concept Formulation. A concept is a word or phrase that identifies or classifies a group of objects, events, or ideas. Given any group of objects, we tend to observe similarities and differences so that we classify the similarities under a concept label. A concept may be concrete: *dog* or *car*; or it may be abstract: *democracy* or *love*. The concept may be more or less inclusive as well. *Animal* is more inclusive than *mammal*; *mammal* is more inclusive than *dog*; and *dog* is more inclusive than *English Shepherd*. Authors sometimes focus on one element rather than another; thus, inclusiveness may be stressed by one author, whereas abstractness may form the base for another author's definition of a specific concept.

Concept formation is a mental state or process whereby we construct an understanding of objects and experiences, particularly in relation to other objects and experiences. Conception or concept formation denotes process, whereas concept denotes product. The designation of a concept in words is called a *term*.

Definition Concept formation [handwritten annotation]

The transition from perception, or mere awareness, to conception is complex, and much remains to be learned about it. In moving from perception to conception, Piaget observed that (1) the amount of redundant material decreases, (2) the amount of irrelevant information that can be tolerated without affecting the responses increases, and (3) the integration of the spatial and temporal separation over which the total information contained in the stimulus field increases. As a concept is formed, repetition becomes less essential, irrelevant information distracts less, and time and space separation can be greater without disturbing the learner.

Vygotsky (1962) studied the complex process of concept formation in some detail and concluded that a child, in his early years, associates a number of objects with a word; sometimes the association is based only on a chance impression—for example, *doggie* may equal *horse, cow, cat, donkey, oddly shaped chair,* and *teddy bear.* From this somewhat random collection of objects, the child improves the unorganized *congerie,* or "heap" (as Vygotsky calls them), in three ways: trial-and-error methods, organization of the visual field, and reorganization of the heaps by associating elements from different heaps with a new word. This tendency continues as the child matures; however, he begins to unite objects on the basis of more concrete or factual bonds. The child does not yet distinguish between the essential and the nonessential (relevant and irrelevant) attributes for object. The child may associate objects on the basis of similarities, contrasts, proximity in space or time, or on the basis of his own practical experiences. In this phase of concept formation, which Vygotsky refers to as thinking in complexes, the subjective associations are supplemented by more objective bonds, but the child still groups objects *in toto* with all of their attributes.

In the final stage of concept formation, the child isolates elements and is able to consider these elements apart from the concrete experience in which they were encountered. The application of a concept to new situations that must be viewed in these terms presents an even greater difficulty for the child. "When the process of concept formation is seen in all its complexity, it appears as a *movement* of thought within the pyramid of concepts, constantly alternating between two directions from the particular to the general and from the general to the particular." (Vygotsky, 1962, pp. 80–1)

Concept formation in its simplest form consists of three basic steps:

1. Differentiation of properties/elements of objects/events. This involves the breaking down of global wholes into specific criteria.

2. Grouping or collecting these specific elements. This necessitates a careful analysis of common characteristics; commonalities aid the process of pattern detection.

3. Elements are named, labeled, or categorized by the individual. Pattern recognition is involved as decisions about exclusion or inclusion of a new element in the category are made.

Because young children are growing both mentally and physically, they need to be given many opportunities to subject the concepts they have already developed to careful scrutiny, and they need to be provided with experiences that will expose them to new objects, events, and ideas.

Concept Attainment. Several factors affect concept attainment. The *kind* of concept (abstract or concrete) and the *developmental age* of the child are factors in concept attainment. The *number* and *degree* of intensity of *experiences* that the individual has will also affect the attainment of concepts. This suggests that there is time and a kind of experience that is appropriate for a child—the "*right kind* of experience at the *right time* for the developing organism." (Hooper, 1968, p. 423) Several of Piaget's concepts, which deal specifically with this idea, follow:

1. *Accommodation:* When the individual encounters something new, which does not fit his existing mental structure, he accommodates the new by modifying or reorganizing the present structure.

2. *Assimilation:* When the individual internalizes the change so that he can handle the new experience with ease, as a part of his own life space, he has been able to assimilate the new information. In dealing with children, some time must be allowed for the accommodation process. Ginsburg and Opper (1969) give a prime example of infant accommodation:

Suppose an infant of four months is presented with a rattle. He has never before had the opportunity to play with rattles or similar toys. The rattle, then, is a feature of the environment to which he needs to adapt. His subsequent behavior reveals the tendencies of assimilation and accommodation. The infant tries to grasp the rattle. In order to do this successfully he must accommodate in more ways than are immediately apparent. First, he must accommodate his visual activities to perceive the rattle correctly; then he must reach out and accommodate his movements to the distance between himself and the rattle; in grasping the rattle he must adjust his fingers to its shape; and in lifting the rattle he must accommodate his muscular exertion to its weight. In sum, the grasping of the rattle involves a series of acts of accommodation, or modifications of the infant's behavioral structures to suit the demands of the environment. (p. 19)

One can consider the accomodation/assimilation process by a single term: *adaptation*. The child adapts to the environment when the concepts of accommodation and assimilation are integrated.

Piaget suggests that the evolution of thought takes place in the following stages, which coincide roughly with age-developmental stages.

a. *Sensorimotor* stage, or preverbal intelligence—roughly birth to eighteen months or two years.

b. *Preoperational*, the stage in which children group and categorize on a functional basis: for example, pencil with paper. A child grouped a knife with a carrot and a potato because, "you peel them with it." This is common in young children of two to seven years of age.

c. *Concrete operations*, or thinking with objects and concrete events; this generally occurs between the ages of seven to eleven years.

d. *Formal operations* is the stage of conceptual or formal thought; this begins roughly at eleven years of age. At this stage the child likes to think in abstract terms and enjoys hypothesizing.

Piaget asserts that cognitive developmental changes are related to biological developmental processes. Each stage of cognitive growth with its concomitant changes, emerges logically, and inevitable connections stem from each of the preceding stages. The stages are not reversible, nor is a stage avoidable. "As Piaget suggests, every child must pass through the stages of cognitive development in the same order." (Wadsworth, 1971, p. 28) The child cannot go through the concrete operations stage and then the preoperational stage in reverse order. Piaget is a true developmental-stage theorist and postulates that one stage builds on another, that the child accomplishes certain learning tasks before proceeding to more complex tasks. Therefore, bypassing stages or reversing stages are not possibilities.

Although these stages are identified within certain age ranges, the ranges are not precise or binding, but are only approximations. The rate at which children pass through these processes is *not fixed*; it is an approximation that may be affected by intelligence, general health, social conditions, and other variables.

Generalizing. The generalizing process produces an end product that has required differentiation and synthesis of ideas. Poincaré (1952) says, "However timid we may be, there must be interpolation. Experiment only gives us a certain number of isolated points. They must be connected by a continuous line, and this as a true generalization." (p. 141) There are an incomprehensible number of facts about mankind, and these facts must be ordered and generalized if they are to have any meaning at all for the learner. The learner must be the primary agent in ordering and generalizing from many items of data in order that he may find meaning in his own collection of facts.

Predicting and Hypothesizing. Isolated facts alone are useless unless we can group them to generalize and, based on these generalizations, make predictions. A fact observed will never be repeated. All that can be affirmed is that under analogous circumstances an analogous fact will be produced. To predict we must, therefore, invoke the aid of analogy. We base our prediction on as large a number of facts as possible. "However solidly founded a prediction may appear to us, we are never absolutely sure that experiment will not prove it to be baseless if we set to work to verify it." (Poincaré, 1952, p. 144) Even so, it is far better to predict without complete certainty than not to hypothesize at all. It is important that students learn to hypothesize and then carry out experimentation that will verify or negate their hypotheses.

According to Piaget, there are several indications when a child is in transition between the concrete operations level of thinking and the formal thinking stage. One such indicator is the child's ability to transcend time and space via symbolic representation (sometimes this is symbolism). He sees the hypothetical consequences of a proposed solution, and he can suggest alternate solutions. The child goes beyond the time and space barriers and solves problems intellectually. Usually this occurs during adolescence, and the youth delights in considering "that which is not." The child is engaging in what is called antecedent/consequent thinking, in predicting what will happen. On the basis of this, the child selects the consequence that will be least hazardous and/or expensive to him.

Creative Thinking. We hope to stress the notion that "the mission of education is to persuade each child that he is a richer source of ideas than he suspects and to enable him to experience the exhilaration that is inherent in the creative use of mind." (Kagan, 1971, p. 4) As the mission of education, it becomes at least partly the teacher's responsibility to provide opportunities for creative thinking.

The teacher might best encourage creative uses of the mind by demonstrating his own interest in novel situations and curiosity about different and unique ideas. In a memorial to Robert Kennedy, Frank Mankiewicz (1968) said, "He was one of those rare men whose education continued after adulthood. He was learning all the time: from books, from his staff, his friends, the press, and from joyous participation in the public life of his country." (p. 52) Kennedy's delight in learning was obvious to many. The teacher, in the same way, must work at showing an interest in learning to the children in her or his classroom. Having shown this interest and delight in learning to a child, the teacher must provide the child with ample opportunity to develop and pursue these interests in learning. Some educators call this approach discovery learning.

There are several advantages to *discovery learning*:

1. It enables the child to identify problems and possible solutions.

2. It develops the learner's self-confidence and attitudes toward trying alternative solutions.

3. It encourages the student to discover broad principles and larger connections between different bodies of knowledge.

There may also be some disadvantages involved in the process of discovery learning:

1. It is not suitable for use in a classical curriculum because it does not lend itself readily to a structured approach.

2. There is a need for highly skilled teacher guidance in the discovery processes.

3. There can be an arbitrary nature about the ideas or knowledge gained this way. A sense of ownership emerges about the conclusions; that is, "Because I discovered it, it must be right." Continuous self-evaluation of one's ideas may be difficult.

Sometimes discovery is considered as though it were a completely creative thing. It should be noted, that some researchers believe that the function of discovery is specialized and limited, and that there are certain kinds of discovery within the realms of possibility in certain content areas:

1. Discovery involves *skill*, that skill required to complete the desired act. Pribram (1964) says, "Discoverers make their discoveries through what they already know: They match the unfamiliar against a thoroughly incorporated body of fact." He adds: "Novelty rises out of variations of the familiar." (p. 10). This means that a person does not create on a completely knowledge-less basis, but that he has probably already done considerable work in a field of endeavor.

2. A second requirement for creative thinking is the unique combination of a person's talents and background that is not reproducible. Some skills and information are necessary in order to be able to produce, but they will not guarantee a unique discovery in a field. "We need a balance between overinformation and freedom, a point between lack of information and the fettering of imagination by too much of it." (Peel, 1960, p. 171) The person who is truly creative seems to be able to detect that delicate balance and combine it with elements from his unique life space to produce a new product—a refining of his world view.

3. A third element necessary for discovery is the appropriate mind set of the person involved. Some persons are highly motivated, whereas others are determined, and still others believe that the job they set out to do requires a great deal of persistence. These qualities are mind set. It is obvious that the execution of the task involved in the discovery process usually requires determination; for example, an idea for the development of a new piece of jewelry or for a new curricular design may easily come to a person's mind rather quickly, but

the transformation of this idea into a product that others can share may be time-consuming, and it necessitates perseverance to task completion.

4. There is evidence of *emotional involvement* in the creative act. Persons indicate an unusual degree of satisfaction with a creative accomplishment because they have been emotionally involved in the production of the idea and/or product.

Psychologist W. J. J. Gordon (1961) discusses mental states that may help a person become better able to discover new relationships. He is interested in the area of scientific discovery and uses the term *synectics*, which means "the joining together of different and apparently irrelevant elements." Gordon delineates the mental states that are beneficial to the synectic process as follows:

1. Detachment-involvement: removing a problem from its familiar settings, seeing it differently; then becoming involved in order to produce a new insight
2. Deferment: resisting the first solution that comes along
3. Speculation: permitting the mind to run free to search for solutions
4. Autonomy of the object: crystallizing ideas into some kind of solution (p. 18, 19)

Gordon (1961) explains ways that persons may achieve these mental states. For example, he says that the use of *personal analogy* is one way in which a teacher can help a student to be more productive in solving a problem. In role-playing sessions, when we ask a child to assume the role of another and then ask, "How did you feel when you were Brian?" we are using personal analogy.

A second way that a person achieves problem-solving mental states is through *direct analogy*. We use direct analogy when we compare and contrast or use parallel facts, knowledge, or technology. We say, for instance, "You need to know how the people in the Fiji Islands solve their housing problem. Let's think about how the people in the Arctic solved their housing problems," or "You have studied the way baboons behave in groups. Can we find similar areas of behavior in human group behavior?"

The third way is through the use of *symbolic analogy*. One might use impersonal and objective objects to solve a problem. When using this thinking style, we are trying to discover the relationships between past knowledge and new information.

A fourth means of achieving these mental states is that of *fantasy analogy*. Gordon (1961) discusses the wild ideas that one thinks about. We say, "Wait a minute about saying, 'that is irrelevant,' let's look at the apparent irrelevancies—let's examine this idea again to see whether it does, in some situations, make sense." (p. 39–52)

J. J. Gallagher (1964), investigates the phenomenon of original thought, and he has suggested that the following procedures are useful in original, productive thinking:

1. *Preparation:* During this stage the problem is investigated from all directions. This is primarily a period of identification and fact gathering.
2. *Incubation:* The person does not consciously think about the problem. Perhaps some kind of internal process of association of new information with past information and some internal reorganization of the information may occur during this period.
3. *Illumination:* "Aha phenomenon" – it is this stage in which the creator finds the solution to the problem.
4. *Verification:* During this stage the idea is tested to determine its validity. (p. 359)

The following table lists some of the differences between Gordon and Gallagher's theories of discovery process:

DISCOVERY IDEAS COMPARED	
Synectics (W. J. J. Gordon)	Productive thinking (J. J. Gallagher)
detachment–involvement	preparation
deferment	incubation
speculation	illumination
autonomy	verification

Familiarity with the major issues and theories raised in the area of cognitive development is undoubtedly important for your consideration as a teacher of children. The degree to which you are able to integrate your awareness of the types and processes of thinking that can be expected of children will be reflected in your success in the classroom. The implication of much of this research on cognition is that by carefully assessing cognitive abilities, and by structuring learning activities where discovery can take place, teachers can accelerate and expand a child's mental growth.

Perceptual Development

The second factor to be discussed under the topic of internal stimulants of human development is the child's perceptual development. As we have emphasized throughout this chapter, there are many factors that influence a child's ability to cope with a learning situation. The child's visual readiness to accommodate printed material is a developmental task of great concern to the teacher of reading. Silbiger and Woolf (1965) suggest that there is no one best age at which a child should begin a visual readiness program for reading. While children may enter grade one with varying levels of *visual readiness*, visual readiness for reading involves the eye's ability to visualize the printed word or phrase units as wholes while using perceptual cues to add meaning to the utterances. A child's perceptual development, as well as sensory development, is extremely dependent on emotional, physical, linguistic, and home motivating factors. The topic of when to begin reading instruction is discussed in great detail in Chapter 3.

Perception and its relationship to the reading process has been a topic of research for decades. A child's perceptual ability involves the factors of *seeing* (visual), *hearing* (auditory), *smelling, tasting,* and *touching* (kinesthetic). Prime emphasis has been placed on visual and auditory perception in the studies investigating perception and reading.

Although perception of a stimulus may differ from individual to individual, Vernon (1962) suggests that the perceptual process as it pertains to the reading act consists of the following four points: (1) *discriminating* visual stimulus from its background characteristics or recognizing that sound patterns within words are separate entities; (2) *recognizing* essential similarities necessary for the general classification of sound patterns into a succession of word patterns; (3) classifying visual symbols within their broader class, which are reflected as sounds; and (4) *identifying words,* usually through naming.

Therefore, perception involves the process of associating meaning with a concept that previously has been isolated through experience. After successful identification and recognition, the perceptual process involves one's ability to modify and relate the previous association with the present situation. Here we see that the child has refined the factors of *identification* and *recognition, categorization, generalization, analysis,* and *synthesis.*

Until the child enters school, he has been involved primarily with the sounds of whole words and their symbolic representations. For example, the child has been exposed to concretes: the word *cookie* refers to the good-tasting chocolate chip treat given to him by his mother and the word *shoe* refers to the clothes he wears on his feet. Through exposure he learns that there are many categories of cookies and shoes. Because perceptual development is affected by emotional, physical, and socioeconomic factors, children entering first grade may have substantially different perceptual background and abilities. In view of potential differences, a wide variety of exposures must be offered to the beginning reader. It is not sufficient for a beginning reader to *see* letters and to hear words. He must be perceptually able to discriminate differences in the letter shapes in order to form words. Most young children need practice in perceiving word parts and whole words.

Language Development

The third major internal stimulant of human growth discussed in this chapter is language development. It is almost axiomatic to say that teachers who are preparing to instruct children in reading need to know a great deal about the language development of the child.

The relationship between the language development of young children and the reading process has become a major focus in linguistic and educational research in recent years. Psycholinguistics also has contributed considerably to our understanding of language acquisition and development of language in young children; efforts have been made in the field of reading to incorporate the findings of this research into a viable instructional approach to reading. For this reason, a brief overview of the current research on language acquisition will be presented in the following section.

Beginning of Language

From the field of physiology we have learned that the human infant is born with an immature nervous system. The central nervous system—the brain and the spinal cord—is more mature than the peripheral nervous system. Infants learn to control their muscles, and with this maturation of the system, they become more capable of discriminating between sets of sounds, shapes, and colors. Researchers have reported a time schedule at which certain types of linguistic performance occur. For almost all children the schedule looks something like this:

Age	Vocalization
At birth	Crying
1–2 mo.	Cooing and crying
3–6 mo.	Babbling, cooing, and crying
9–14 mo.	First words
18–24 mo.	First sentences
3–4 yr.	Almost all basic syntactic structure
4–8 yr.	Almost all speech sounds correctly articulated
9–11 yr.	Semantic distinctions established

When a child is born, he is incompletely equipped either to perceive or produce speech; he does not produce sounds directly related to those that will later be part of his language. Although there is a range when the stages in this table occur, Lenneberg (1966, 1967) has stated that they occur in the same sequential order for every child.

Based on what is known about language acquisition, Chomsky (1967) and others have forwarded the idea that humans possess an innate, specific language-acquisition device. They tell us that all infants acquire this language tool without overt teaching; every physiologically "normal" child learns to talk, given a minimal amount of language input. Even mentally retarded children with IQs of 60 learn to talk, often not as rapidly as the normal child, and often with a smaller vocabulary than the "normal" child.

Components of Language. Let us now look at the various components of language and the specifics of their acquisition in the young child. In discussing language, the basic components usually discussed follow:

1. Phonology: The sound system
2. Morphology: Inflections, tense markers
3. Syntax: The order of words in an utterance
4. Semantics: The meanings of words

Phonology. One of the major concerns of linguists is to examine the specific speech sounds that make up language. The study of these speech sounds is called phonology. Because the reading process includes the deciphering of speech transferred to print, it is important that teachers of reading understand some basic points about how the child acquires and uses the phonology of his language.

An interesting aspect of emerging sound systems in very young children is that during their first year, the direction of the development of consonant–like sounds is from back to front in the mouth, and for vowel–like sounds it is from front to back (Irwin 1947a, 1947b, 1947c; McCarthy, 1954); however, during the last part of the first year of life, the direction is switched.

R. Roman Jakobson, a linguist, (1941) asserts that the development of the phonemic system is the result of the child's attempts to establish a system of oppositions within a sound continuum. The first oppositions are maximal ones between a consonant and a vowel; usually they are the opposition between the most open central, farthest back vowel, /a/, and the farthest front, stopped consonant, /p/. Thus, /a/ is the "optimal" vowel, and /p/ the "optimal" consonant. There is great frequency of /papa/ as a first-syllable sequence in young children. Sometimes there is less than optimal control over the larynx and over the velum, which is the flap of skin at the back of the roof of mouth. In this case, the first syllable sequences are /baba/ or /mama/. Jakobson points out that this is why "papa," "baba," and "mama" are often the child's first-remembered or quoted sequences; it also explains why they are used as parental names/substitutes in many cultures.

Although the terminology of the English phonetics system is extremely complex, it is important for the teacher of reading to become totally familiar with the vocabulary. In the following charts, taken from M. Alyeshmerni and P. Tauber's *Working with Aspects of Language*, the positions of articulation for the consonants of English are described.

Positions of Articulation. Most of the contrasts in the sounds of speech are made by modifying the relation of the *lower jaw* and the *tongue* to the *upper jaw.* The generally stationary organs of the upper jaw are called points of articulation. They are the *upper lip* and *teeth,* the *alveolar ridge,* the (hard) *palate,* the velum (or soft palate), and the *uvula.* The uvula and the upper lip are the only organs in the upper jaw that move. The organs along the lower jaw are called articulators. They are the *lower lip* and *teeth,* and the *apex* (tip), *front,* and *dorsum* (back) of the tongue. There are six major positions of articulation made by the relation of the articulator to the point of articulation, and they are defined as follows:

Articulator	Point of articulation	Position of articulation	Examples
1. Lower lip	Upper lip	Bilabial	p, b, m
2. Lower lip	Upper teeth	Labiodental	f, v
3. Apex of the tongue and lower teeth	Upper teeth	Interdental	θ th as in thin ð as in then
4. Apex of the tongue	Alveolar ridge	Apicoalveolar	t, d, s, z, n, l, r
5. Front of the tongue	Palate	Frontopalatal	č (chip), ǰ (jet) š (ship), ž (azure) y (boy)
6. Dorsum of the tongue	Velum	Dorsovelar	k, g, ŋ (ring), w

A seventh position, the <u>glottal</u> position, is described as follows: when no organs other than the vocal folds are used in producing a sound, the sounds are called glottal. The <u>h</u> in <u>he</u> and the sound heard between the two parts of the colloquial negative <u>hunh-uh</u> are examples of this position in articulation.

Here is a brief exercise that may help you in learning the positions of articulation.

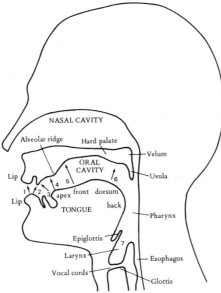

Figure 1. The positions of articulation. From *Working with Aspects of Language*, Second Edition, by Mansoor Alyeshmerni and Paul Tauber © 1975 by Harcourt Brace Jovanovich, Inc. and reprinted with their permission.

Exercise

Name the positions of articulation signified by numbers 1 through 7 in the preceding diagram.

1. _____

2. _____

3. _____

4. _____

5. _____

6. _____

7. _____

If you had difficulty completing this exercise Alyeshmerni and Tauber's (1975) phonetic chart, including vowels, (see page 35) is a further aid to your understanding of positions of articulation.

The following chart illustrates developmental distinctions between speech sounds and how and where they are formed in the mouth. It is an illustration of Jakobson's theory of distinctive features.

Consonants	Dental vs labial (/t/ vs /p/)
Vowels	Narrow vs wide (/i/ vs /a/)
Velar vowels	Rounded vs unrounded (/a/ vs /u/)
Consonants	Velopalatal vs labial and dental (/k/ vs /t/)
Consonants	Palatal vs velar (/s/ vs /k/)
Consonants	Rounded vs unrounded or pharyngealized vs nonpharyngealized

Manner of Articulation		Position of Articulation →	Bilabial	Labiodental	Interdental	Apicoalveolar	Frontopalatal	Dorsovelar	Glottal
Stop	Stop	VL	p (*pit*)			t (*tip*)		k (*kit*)	
		V	b (*bit*)			d° (*dip*)		g (*get*)	
(Continuant)	Affricate	VL					c (*chip*)		
		V					j (*jet*)		
	Fricative	VL		f (*fit*)	θ (*thin*)	s (*sit*)	s (*ship*)		h (*hit*)
		V		v (*vex*)	(*then*)	z (*zip*)	z (*azure*)		
(Resonant / Oral / Central)	Nasal	(V)	m (*moon*)			n (*noon*)		ŋ (*ring*)	
	Lateral	(V)				l (*loom*)			
	Semivowel	(V)				r (*bar*)	y (*boy*)	w (*bow*)	
	Vowel	(V)							

Vowel chart:

Tongue height ↕   Degree of Frontness →

	Front	Central	Back
High	i (beat)		u (boot)
Lower high	I (bit)	i ɜ	u (put)
Mid	e (bait)	ə ɜ	o (boat)
Lower mid	ɛ (bet)	ʌ (but)	ɔ (bought)
Low	æ (bat)		a (pot)

Note: The vowel qualities in the examples will not match those of every speaker. You will have to find examples in your own speech that fit the definition of the vowels.

° The flap sound [ð] appears in words such as butter and ladder in American speech and in very in British speech.

† This is similar in articulation to an aspirated voiceless vowel.

‡ The *r* is not pronounced in New England and much of the South. In this chart semivowel = semiconsonant.

The three reduced vowels *i* (*many*) ə, often called *shwa* (*sofa*), and I (*willow*) represent vowels usually found in unstressed positions in words.

Figure 2. The Phonetic Chart from *Working with Aspects of Language,* Second Edition, by Mansoor Alyeshmerni and Paul Tauber © 1975 by Harcourt Brace Jovanovich, Inc. and reprinted with their permission.

As the child continues to develop, so does his ability to use a wider variety of consonant sounds. Some linguists suggest rough age correlates for production of English consonants:

Age	Proficient consonant articulation
3½	b p m w h
4½	d t h g k y ŋ
5½	f
6½	v ĭ z̆ š̆ l
7½	s z θ f

Morphology. *Morphology* is the term linguists use to refer to the study of the smallest units of meaning in language; these units are called morphemes. Inflectional endings and tense markers, as well as the root words to which they are attached, all represent types of morphemes. In morphology study, the teacher is interested in looking briefly at how the child demonstrates a growth of understanding about the effect that inflectional ending and tense markers have on meaning in language.

In an important study on the acquisition of morphology, linguist Jean Berko-Gleason (1958) showed children a picture of a cartoon figure, telling the children in the study, "This is a *wug*." She then told the children that there were two animals, showed them a picture and said: "These are two _____," expecting the children to supply the plural "wugs"/ wugz/. She used nonsense words that elicited all three of the English plural morphemes into consideration (/-s/ as in *hats*; /-z/ as in *rugs*; and /-iz/ as in *doses*. Berko found that children in the age range of four years made 6 per cent errors with the /-iz/ forms, but only 25 per cent errors with /-z/ forms. She also found that the children have /-iz/ forms in their lexicons, for 91 per cent had the correct plural for *glass*. She concluded that at a relatively early age children are able to account for morphological changes in language.

Syntax. Linguists use the term *syntax* to refer to the arrangement of words in a meaningful order. The expansion of the child's language from single to multiple utterances suggests the need for consistency in ordering such utterances so that they will be sensible to others.

Telegraphic Speech and Pivot. The child produces his first word between nine and fourteen months of age; and then, within six months of that point, he has at least fifty items in his lexicon or vocabulary. At this point, the child begins to put these words together. Most of these early combinations are "telegraphic." According to Brown and Fraser (1963), articles, prepositions, and auxiliaries are not used. Here are some samples of telegraphic speech:

> Mommy glass
>
> Baby book

Shortly after this period, children begin to use some of their words as "pivots"—that is, some of these words are fixed and other words are attached to them. The following illustrations exemplify this phenomenon:

> byebye daddy
>
> byebye mommy
>
> byebye truck

or

> allgone milk
>
> allgone car
>
> allgone candy

Brown and Fraser (1963) further indicate that the child divides his lexicon into "function" words and "object" words. These divisions may be the basis of functional divisions that later become formal word classes—for example, nouns, verbs, and adjectives.

Slobin (1972) presents examples of some of these pivot structures:

Function	English
Modify, qualify	pretty_____
	my_____
	allgone_____
	all_____
Locate, name	there_____
	here_____
	see_____
	it_____
Describe act	_____away
	_____on
	_____off
	_____it
Demand	more_____
	give_____
Negate	no_____
	don't_____

syntax

Forming Questions. English has two ways of forming a question: (a) to begin the sentence with a verb or auxiliary (do, did)—for example, Does Big Boy have the salad? and (2) to begin the sentence with a "Wh-word" (*who, what, where, when, why, how*). The first type of question is called a yes/no question. Wh-questions are called information questions.

When children learn to ask questions, they do so by incorporating the rising intonation typical of English questions into the same sentences they used for statements and demands—for example, Ellen happy?

The second step in the acquisition process is the use of Wh-questions. When yes/no questions occur for the first time, the auxiliary *do* takes on a unique function in inverted questions and in negatives. The system is similar to an adult system, but auxiliaries are still not inverted in Wh questions—for example, Does Marty say why? There are no combinations of auxiliaries in the children's speech, like the following: He has had the operation. The auxiliary form of *be* does not usually appear in children's early speech—for example, Marion has been having a good time in New Orleans.

Relative Clauses. Chomsky (1969) showed that many children do not fully comprehend relative clauses until quite late; many eight-year-olds do not thoroughly understand such sentences as:

> "Tell Kelly when to water the plants."

> "Ask Pris which chair to sit on."

If pushed, some young children will say, "Pris, which chair to sit on?"

Chomsky, like Clark (1970), suggests that most children who are five to ten years of age regard the first noun phrase in a sentence as the subject and the second noun phrase as the object; thus, "The pie was eaten by Tom Murphy" is thought of as subject = pie, object = Tom Murphy.

Semantics. In its simplest form, semantics is the study of word meaning. Single words can have multiple meanings for the child and even "fixed" multiple meanings can be altered by syntactic and contextual constraints. A four-year-old child knows that a figurative meaning is being attached to the word *puppy* when his mother says: "Kevin, you're acting like a puppy." Furthermore, the child knows if "puppy" is being used in a good or bad sense by his mother's tone and by contextual considerations (for example, is the child chewing on the sofa?).

If we take this consideration one step further and the utterance is changed to "Kevin, you're acting like a zumtoadbat," the child can use his knowledge of syntax, intonation, and context to arrive at an acceptable synonym for "zumtoadbat." Semantics, then, is the study of word meaning, including phonology, syntax, and pragmatics, i.e. contextual usage.

Herb Clark (1970), a linguist who has examined semantics, has proposed a theory of semantic features, similar to the use of distinctive features in phonology, using Jakobson's notion of binary oppositions. He maintained that young children interpret *less* as though it meant *more*. Clark argued that, when children learn polar adjectives and comparatives, they first learn that *more/less*, *big/little*, *near/far* refer to the same concept: *having*. The child then realizes that dimension is involved and proceeds to use both words positively, therefore big = little. Then the child realizes that the dimension is polar and he begins to use the words correctly.

Clark's semantic feature theory may look like this:

	dog	horse
	+ animal	+ animal
	+ four legs	+ four legs
Later development:	+ little	+ big

In the earliest form of the language-acquisition device, Chomsky (1972) tried to minimize semantics, claiming:

> it has been found that semantic reference ... does not apparently affect the *manner* in which acquisition of syntax proceeds; that is, it plays no role in determining which hypotheses are selected by the learner. (p. 33)

However, E. V. Clark (1974), did not totally agree with Chomsky's theory, and she argued:

> semantic information *does* affect the manner in which the subject (or child) approaches the learning of syntactic rules, contrary to Chomsky's (1965) assumption. Without any semantic information, subjects simply tried to learn the relative positions of words. (p. 56)

Other researchers (Ferguson 1971; Berko-Gleason 1973; Shatz and Gelman 1973;) have contributed information that makes it clear that the language-acquisition-device theory has been reformulated to include mechanisms that will handle the acquisition of semantics as well as the acquisition of syntax.

Human Information Processing

In recent years, psychologists, educators, mathematicians, and linguists have begun to study the phenomenon of human information processing. They have begun to ask such questions as:

1. What is the role of perception in processing information?
2. What is the role of memory in processing information?
3. How much information can be processed in x number of seconds?
4. How much information can be stored in x number of seconds?
5. What is the best form of information to be presented in order for it to be processed and stored?

Their questions could fill an entire chapter, but to list them would exceed our needs here. The field of human information processing has added considerably to our understanding of perception, language processing, and reading. Therefore, it is extremely important for you to be exposed to this body of knowledge. Before beginning, it is important to point out that this is a relatively new field and that there has not been a great deal of research completed on the relationships between human information processing and reading. However, we do know that information processing has added considerably to what we know about the human capacity for reading. For example, psychologists have investigated what cognitively happens to simple visual materials, such as letters of the alphabet, over the course of a few seconds. One experiment was conducted in the following way: each subject was shown a *target* letter such as "A," followed immediately by a second letter or a *match* letter; this was a physical match, "A", or a name match "a," or neither, "Z," to the first letter. The subject was required to respond "same" or "different," either on the basis of physical or nominal identity.

Experiments of this type have provided a variety of interesting results. When the target letter and the match letter were presented at the same time, and when the instructions were to say "same" if the names were equivalent, subjects were able to identify a physically identical pair as the "same" more quickly (around 450 msec) than they could identify a nominally identical pair (around 525 msec). When they were given instructions to perform a physical-identity match, it took longer to identify a pair as "different" with the same name (especially when the upper- and lower-case forms were physically similar, as in *Cc* or *Kk*) than a pair that was physically and nominally different. When delay between the presentation of the target letter and match letter was increased, the difference in response times became smaller; it disappeared altogether after three seconds. The most obvious interpretation of these data is the following: During the initial stages of stimulus processing, a person is sensitive to *both* the physical and nominal characteristics of the stimulus, but within a few seconds all processing is complete. Prior to the completion of processing, the fastest judgments can be made when physical and name match codes are congruent, but when they are brought into conflict, the process is retarded.

This example provides an insight into Posner's work and the work of other researchers in the area of information science. The major conclusions from Posner's work are (1) that in the perception of the alphabet characters by a literate adult, both sensory (physical) and associative (nominal) coding occurs, (2) that both of these codes may be stored in the memory and processed separately, but (3) the sensory storage system is overloaded and deteriorates over time more quickly than the associative system.

In a similar study, Neisser (1967) found that literate adults could scan a list of stimulants for ten targets as quickly as they could for one. He found that subjects could scan a list of words for members from a particular class (for example, fruits) almost as fast as they could for a single item (for example, store). Scanning for items from other large, open classes such as animal or names was slower. Chase (1973) found that rate increases linearly with memory size, although it does *not* depend on the form of the task, preview, or the probability of a target.

In more recent studies on cognition, psychologists and educators have examined interactions among sensori-perceptual and attentional processes, short-term retention, and associative factors in memory. Most studies related to the reading process are the coding transformations that occur within a matter of seconds in most literate adults. There is presently evidence which supports the following: (1) these information-processing operations may entail both sensory and associative storage; (2) when subjects are given a few seconds to study a list of familiar items, memory rates are comparable for letters or numbers, words, or word categories (Smith, 1967); and (2) both memory and visual search rates depend heavily on the familiarity of the materials, the relative emphasis given to speed and accuracy, and the practice time.

Although this body of information may not seem particularly relevant or necessary to you as a teacher, it is important for you to be aware of current research in the field as well as new, and often varied, directions that researchers are investigating in order to find more efficient ways to help children learn to read.

External Stimulants of Human Development

Teachers of reading need to prepare themselves for the most difficult assignment in any of our educational settings. The job is tremendously difficult and the stakes are exorbitantly high; however, the results, if successful, are immeasurable. A child who learns to read has the promise of an exciting future; unfortunately, the child who is neglected, who never learns to read, has to face a life of exclusion and possible discrimination.

So beware! In addition to learning all about the internal composition of the child, you have to study the external factors that shape and mold the child. We hope here to introduce you to some of the possible external stimulants that have shaped the child who will sit before you as he or she tries to learn to read. We will examine external stimulants in three categories: family, home environment, and parent involvement. There are no simple answers to questions about how or why a child does or does not learn to read. All we can present here are the findings of current research which has examined some of these relationships and the reading achievement of the child.

Family

How early does the family begin influencing the child's attitude toward reading? Indirectly, this occurs as early as the child is able to respond to language. Oral language provides the foundation for success in reading. To encourage language development, parents need to talk to their child as soon as he is born in order to provide the child with a model of language development.

As the child matures, parents can begin reading to him, holding the book so that he can view the illustrations as well as the printed page. The intent here is not to initiate reading, but to establish and to reinforce an understanding of the relationship between the printed pages and spoken words. Parents should discuss the ideas in the material which they read to their children. Such interaction may introduce new words that the parents can help the child incorporate into his vocabulary. Parents can gain insight into their child's growth and maturity in this way.

Anecdotes and reminiscences abound when parents and teachers try to remember how they began to read. As adults, the most successful readers vividly remember parts of the process of their introduction to reading. For example, one teacher recalls the arrival of the daily newspaper and the fact that her father, an energetic and hard-working farmer, always read it before going to bed. She recalled her daily anticipation of crawling up into his lap to hear her favorite comic strips read and her motivation to learn to read so she could "read the paper" before he did. She also recalled a book of stories from which her mother read after tucking her into bed at night. Although she could not recall specific comic strips or stories that had been read to her, the pleasure of these situations remained with her and continued to influence her attitude toward reading. As the child observes his parent in the act of reading, he becomes involved with *imitative* and *identification* behavior. The child is aware of a complicated task (reading) that he wishes to accomplish, as he observes a master craftsman at work.

Modeling. Many studies have shown that children who view their parents reading, who are read to, and who have books and educational toys succeed at prereading tasks. Hess and Shipman (1966), Klaus and Gray (1968), Wilkart (1969) have found that modeling in all cases affects higher performance than when parental noninvolvement exists. However, most modeling research is not specifically related to readiness for reading. Durkin's studies (1966, 1972, 1972a) are the exceptions because she discovered that, in cases of early readers, modeling was an important predictor of reading success.

In the area of family factors, the verbal interaction betwen the parent and the child seems to be extremely important in understanding the current developmental level of the child.

Parent-Child Verbal Interaction Factors. McCarthy (1954) postulated that a degree of verbal and reading sufficiency was dependent on the frequency and quality of the parent's contact with the child. Also, Hess and Shipman (1965) suggested that a child's performance on cognitive tasks is associated with the "teaching style" of the mother. This maternal teaching style is particularly evident in reading episodes between parent and child.

Reading Episodes Between Parent and Child. There is an extensive body of normative literature suggesting that reading to young children enhances language development (Templin, 1957; MacKinnon, 1959; Durkin 1974; Bullock, 1975) and is related to reading success (Almy, 1942; Durkin 1974, 1974). Educators have urged frequent oral reading to young children in the belief that "language is as much caught as it is taught" (Durkin, 1974). Several methodological texts on the teaching of reading urge parents to read to young children because books and stories provide children with important "models of book language" (Durkin, 1974) and with models of "life-lifting language." (Martin, 1970)

There is also an historical body of normative literature suggesting that children should be read to during the school day. Chapparo (1975) maintains: "Story-time reading to children should be an integral part of every reading program—children need models." Durkin (1974) argues in favor of reading to young children on the premise that an oral reading episode "can be a vehicle for learning about children's readiness for reading."

Few educators will dispute the need for reading to young children, but even fewer educational researchers have investigated the most efficacious ways in which this reading should be done. Sir Allan Bullock's report, "A Language for Life" (1975) addresses the "how" of reading to young children by stressing the importance of the socioemotional implications of the child's first contacts with books. The report advised: "The best way to prepare the very young child for reading is to hold him on your lap and read aloud to him stories he likes—over and over again." (p. 28)

There has been limited empirical research on the effects of style of reading to young children and cognitive growth. One of the few studies in this area was reported by Swift (1970) when he explained the success of a parent training program called *Get Set* which took place in Philadelphia, Pennsylvania. His program first presented the value of reading to young children. The purpose of the program was to enable mothers to lengthen thoughts, elaborate on ideas, and improve observational skills. Parents were taught to retell certain parts of stories in order to extend their children's verbalization and communication skills; parents also were taught to develop their children's thoughts by asking experiential questions during the readings.

In a second study, Flood (1977) found that parents can enhance their children's experiences by following these four steps during a reading episode:

1. Prepare children for the story by asking warm-up questions.
2. Verbally interact with the child during the story by asking and answering many questions.
3. Positively reinforce the child during the episode.
4. Finish the episode by asking evaluative questions.

Reading episodes provide parents and teachers with unique opportunities for verbal interaction with young children. Some researchers believe that this interaction is directly related to language and reading success. It has been frequently reported that the interaction of adults and children creates an environment that fosters language growth in the child (Durkin, 1966, 1974). Durkin found that it was important for parents to talk with their children, and to answer their questions, thereby providing them with experiences that result in new vocabulary.

Home Environment

Educational Materials

In addition to the family influences and the interaction of the parent and the child, there is also an extensive body of normative literature suggesting that children need books and materials (toys, chalkboards, and magnetic letters for example) in order to prepare for reading (Bernstein, 1967; Beck, 1973; Durkin, 1974). In her analysis of environmental variables on the development of verbal abilities and reading, Jones (1972) found that the availability of materials and organizational opportunities for the child's use were important in the development of reading. Perhaps the single greatest home environmental influence on the child's later cognitive abilities, including reading ability, is the effect of television viewing.

Television

There is no longer a question of whether educational shows are effective, but rather to what degree they are effective. As early as the mid-1950s, M. Templin (1957) argued in favor of periodic children's language studies because of the influence of television on changing norms of language ability. In the introduction to *Certain Language Skills in Children* (1975), she states:

> The present study was begun after the introduction of television into many homes. Thus, it is likely that more adult language was present in the environment than would have been true earlier. ... It may be that the effect of such language stimulation in the child's environment would be even greater today than when the first data for this study were gathered just a few years ago. (p. vii)

Figure 3. The effect of TV on childrens' performance. "The Family Circus" by Bil Keane reprinted courtesy The Register and Tribune Syndicate, Inc.

Templin's warning for updated norms to account for the influence of television certainly has been heard, and there has been a great deal of television research. However, 17 years later, Leifer (1974) reports, "To date we understand little about the combined roles of television, the home, and the school in influencing child development." (p. 74) A great deal of research has been conducted on the social and cognitive effects of television, but few have studied the interrelationship between television and language learning and reading.

Furthermore, few studies have investigated the role of parents in the cognitive development of children via television. That parents are important in shaping attitudes toward television has been demonstrated by several researchers. Lyle and Hoffman (1972) report, "Mothers who watch television at least three hours per day are likely to have children who watch a great deal of television." (p. 70) Leifer (1974) also states: "Parents need to be especially active in limiting and guiding their young children's exposure to television." (p. 191) Unfortunately, researchers have found that only one third of parents state that they have definite viewing rules (Lyle and Hoffman, 1972). Leifer reports that parental interaction with children during and after television viewing "may influence the degree to which the child incorporates what has been seen."

Sesame Street. *Sesame Street* resulted from a joint venture of the Carnegie and Ford Foundations and the United States Office of Education. Extensive pretesting and observation of the viewer's responses were examined. As a result of this, the proposed format of the show underwent some changes. Vocabulary, letter names, and beginning sounds were taught through rhythm, puppetry, songs, stories, and direct instruction.

Although general television may or may not have a beneficial effect on children's language growth, there is a significant body of literature suggesting that educational television, in general, and the Children's Television Workshop, in particular, are beneficial for children. The Educational Testing Service's evaluation of *Sesame Street* conducted by Ball and Bogatz (1972) stated: "The facts are that the show was seen to have a marked effect, not only in the areas of rote learning of basic skills, such as counting, and in simple contiguity association learning, as in learning the names of letters and numbers, but also in higher areas of cognitive activity, such as sorting and classifying pictorial representations." (p. 7) Frequent viewing of *Sesame Street* seemed to be a better predictor of performance at post-test than was age. In this study, post-test frequency of viewing matched the pretest data. Ball and Bogatz maintain that the implication of this finding is that "we should think of beginning with younger than four-year-old children and perhaps raise our expectations of what these young children can learn."

According to them:

> The children who watched the most learned the most, and skills that received the most attention in the program were the best learned by the children. The goals of the program directly related to reading included recognizing, naming, and matching capital and lower-case letters, recognizing and matching letters in words, recognizing initial sounds and

reading words. ... The results from *Sesame Street* point up the importance of being specific about educational goals and directing the educational program toward these goals. (p. 18)

What are the specific goals of education television? How did they begin? What are the objectives? Blanton (1972) studied this question and listed the objectives of prereading programs, maintaining that these objectives were the basis for the educational television curriculum. These objectives seem to be comprehensive and appropriate in an early education program.

Blanton's Educational Television Prereading Objectives*

Letters

1. Matching: Given a printed letter, the child can select the identical letter from a set of printed letters.
2. Recognition: Given the verbal label for a letter, the child can select the appropriate letter from a set of printed letters.
3. Labeling: Given a printed letter the child can provide the verbal sound.
4. Letter sounds:
   a. For sustaining consonants (f, l, m, n, r, s, v), given the printed letter, the child can produce the letter's corresponding sound.
   b. Given a set of words presented orally, all beginning with the same letter sound, the child can select from a set of words another word with the same initial letter sound.
5. Recitation of the alphabet. The child can recite the alphabet.

Words

1. Matching: Given a printed word, the child can select an identical word from a set of printed words.
2. Boundaries of a word: Given a printed sentence, the child can correctly point to each word in the sentence.
3. Temporal-sequence/spatial-sequence correspondence: (Words and sentences are read from left to right.)
   a. Given a printed word, the child can point to the first and last letter.
   b. Given a printed sentence, the child can point to the first and last word.
4. Decoding: Given the first five words on the reading vocabulary list (ran, set, big, mop, fun), the child can decode other related words generated by substitutions of a new initial consonant. (Example: given the word ran, the child can decode man and can.)
5. Word recognition: For any of the words on the Sesame Street word list, the child can recognize the given word when it is presented in a variety of contexts.
6. Reading: The child can read each of the 20 words on the Sesame Street word list.

*From "How Effective is Sesame Street?" by William Blanton in the ERIC/CRIER column in the May 1972 issue of *The Reading Teacher*, p. 807. Reprinted by permission.

Blanton concludes that:

> the *Sesame Street* series has been accepted by the public and by many educators with some enthusiasm. The effectiveness of the series has been questioned, sometimes with more passion than objectivity. The educational community would be well advised to withhold judgment on the effectiveness of the series until additional evidence is offered.

The Electric Company. *The Electric Company* was designed to pick up where *Sesame Street* left off—that is, to supplement the reading of seven to ten-year-olds.

Roser (1972) noted that the show was designed to emphasize these curricular items:

1. The left-to-right sequence of print corresponds to the temporal sequence of speech.
2. Written symbols stand for speech sounds. They "track" the stream of speech.
3. The relationship between written symbols and speech sounds is sufficiently reliable to produce successful decoding most of the time.
4. Reading is facilitated by learning a set of strategies for figuring out sound-symbol relationships. (p. 684)

A study of the effectiveness of *Electric Company* was conducted by Ball and Bogatz (1972). They used a match-gains of classes design; pretest-post-test. Half of the classes (there was a total of 100 classes) viewed *Electric Company* in school; the other half was encouraged by the teachers to watch it at home. The results seemed to show that the classes that viewed *Electric Company* had significantly larger adjusted gain scores on the total than the nonviewing classes. Although most teachers generally liked the program, students' attitudes toward school and toward reading were not affected.

In summary, television cannot and should not be ignored as a vehicle of potential in children's learning. Even though there are those who are concerned only with reading via print, the world of television (and indeed it is here to stay) should be utilized, making it possible for children to respond more easily to print with greater understanding.

QUESTIONS AND RELATED READINGS

Let us return to the goals of this chapter listed on page 22 to assess your knowledge of the main components of the research on the young child as a developing reader.

If at this time you do not feel that you have attained adequate knowledge to successfully answer the following questions, we would like to suggest more related readings.

Goal 1: To aid the student in understanding cognitive stages of human development.

Question 1: Explain the cognitive development of the child.

Elkind, D., and J. H. Flavell. *Studies in Cognitive Development.* New York: Oxford University Press, Inc., 1966.

Gibson, E. J. "Learning to Read." *Science,* 148 (1965) 1066–70.

Gibson, E. J. *Principles of Perceptual Learning and Development.* In press.

Goal 2: To aid the student in understanding stages of language development.

Question 2: Explain the language development of the child.

Brown, R., and J. Berko. "Word Association and the Development of Grammar." *Child Development,* 31 (1960) 1–14.

Menyuk, P. "Syntactic Structures in the Language of Children." *Journal of Child Development,* 34 (1963) 407–22.

Slobin, D. *Psycholinguistics.* Glenview, Ill.: Scott, Foresman and Company, 1971.

Goal 3: To aid the student in understanding the effect of the home environment, including parental involvement, on preparation for reading.

Question 3: In what ways does the home environment affect prereading development?

Aftanas, M. S., et al. "A Study of the Psychological and Social Factors Related to Preschool Prediction of Reading Retardation." Paper presented at the Canadian Psychological Association Convention, 1970 Winnepeg, Manitoba.

Bullock, Sir Alan. "A Language for Life." Report for the British Government, 1975.

Goal 4: To aid the student in understanding the effect of television on preparing a child for reading.

Question 4: How is television affecting young children?

Ball, Samuel, and Gerry Bogatz. *Reading with Television: An Evaluation.* Princeton, N.J.: Educational Testing Service, 1973.

Becker, George J. *Television and the Classroom Reading Program,* Reading Aids Series. Newark, Del.: International Reading Association, 1973, pp. 5–6.

Lyle, J. "Television in Daily Life: Patterns of Use (overview)." In *Television and Social Behavior,* 4, edited by E. A. Rubenstein, G. A. Comstock, and J. P. Murray, Washington, D.C.: U.S. Government Printing Office, 1972.

Lyle, J., and H. R. Hoffman, "Children's Use of Television and Other Media." In *Television and Social Behavior,* 4, edited by E. A. Rubenstein, G. A. Comstock, and J. P. Murray, Washington, D.C.: U.S. Government Printing Office, 1972.

BIBLIOGRAPHY

Almy, M. "The Importance of Children's Experience to Success in Beginning Reading." In *Research in the Three R's,* edited by Hunnicutt and W. Iverson. New York: Harper & Row, Publishers, 1958.

Alyeshmerni, M., and P. Tauber. *Working with Aspects of Language.* New York: Harcourt Brace and Jovanovich, Inc., 1975.

Ball, S., and G. A. Bogatz. "Research on *Sesame Street:* Some Implications for Compensatory Education." Paper presented at the Second Annual Blumberry Symposium in Early Childhood Education, Johns Hopkins Press, 1972.

Beck, I. L. *A Longitudinal Study of the Reading Achievement Effects of Formal Reading Instruction in the Kindergarten: A Summative and Formative Evaluation.* Ph. D. dissertation, University of Pittsburgh, 1973.

Bernstein, B. "Elaborated and Restricted Codes: Their Social Origin and Some Consequences." In *The Ethnography of Communication*, edited by B. Gumperz and D. Mymes. American Anthropologist Publication, 1967.

Berko-Gleason, J. "The Child's Learning of English Morphology", *Word,* 14 (1958), 150–77.

Blanton, W. "How Effective is Sesame Street?" in the ERIC/CRIER column, *The Reading Teacher,* May 1972, p. 807.

Brown, R., and C. Fraser. "The Acquisition of Syntax." In *Verbal Behavior and Learning*, edited by C. N. Cofer and B. Musgrave. New York: McGraw-Hill Book Company, 1963.

Bullock, Sir A. "A Language for Life." Report for the British Government.

Chase, W. G., ed. *Visual Information Processing.* New York: Academic Press, Inc., 1973.

Chomsky, C. S. *The Acquisition of Syntax in Children from 5 to 10.* Cambridge, Mass.: The MIT Press, 1969.

Chomsky, N. *Syntactic Structures.* The Hague: Mouton, 1957.

"Phonology of Reading." In *Basic Studies in Reading,* edited by M. Levin and J. Williams. New York: Harper & Row, Publishers, 1970.

Language and Mind. New York: Harcourt Brace and Jovanovich, Inc., 1972.

Aspects of the Theory of Syntax. Cambridge, Mass.: The MIT Press, 1965.

Chapparo, J. "A New Look at Language Experience." In *A Successful Foundation for Reading in a Second Language Conference,* San Diego, California, February, 1975.

Clark, E. V. "On Acquisition of the Meaning of 'Before' and 'After,'" *Journal of Verbal Learning and Verbal Behavior,* 10 (1971), 266–75.

Clark, H. H. "The Primitive Nature of Children's Relational Concepts." In *Cognition and the Development of Language,* edited by J. R. Hayes. New York: John Wiley & Sons, Inc., 1970.

"Semantics and Comprehension." In *Current Trends in Linguistics.* vol. 12. *Linguistics and Adjacent Arts Sciences,* edited by T. A. Sebeok,The Hague: Mouton, 1974.

Durkin, D. *Children Who Read Early: Two Longitudinal Studies.* New York: Bureau of Publications, Teachers College Press, Columbia University, 1966.

Teaching Young Children to Read. Boston: Allyn & Bacon, Inc., 1976.

Teaching Them to Read. Boston: Allyn & Bacon, Inc., 1974.

Flood, J. "Parental Styles in Reading Episodes With Young Children," *The Reading Teacher.* May, 1977. Volume #30.

Hess, R. D., and V. C. Shipman. "Early Experience and the Socialization of Cognitive Modes in Children." *Child Development* 36 (1965), 869–86.

Gallagher, J. J. "Productive Thinking." In *Review of Child Development Research*, vol. 1, edited by M. L. Hoffman and L. W. Hoffman. New York: Russell Sage Foundation, 1964.

Ginsberg, H., and S. Opper *Piaget's Theory of Intellectual Development.* Englewood Cliffs, N.J.: Prentice Hall, Inc., 1969.

Gleason, J. B. "Language Development in Early Childhood." In *Oral Language and Reading,* edited by J. Walden. Champaign, Ill.: National Council of Teachers of English, 1969.

Gordon, W. J. J. *Synectics—The Development of Creative Capacity.* New York: Harper & Row, Publishers, 1961.

Jones, J. P. *Intersensory Transfer, Perceptual Shifting, Modal Preference, and Reading.* Newark, Del.: International Reading Association, 1972.

Jakobson, R. *Kindersprache, Aphasie, und Allegmeine Lautgesetze.* Uppsala: Almquist and Wiksell, 1941. (English translation: *Child Language, Aphasia and Phonological Universals*). The Hague: Mouton, 1968.

Kagen, J. *Change and Continuity in Infancy.* New York: John Wiley & Sons, Inc., 1971.

Klaus, R. A., and S. W. Gray. *The Early Training Project for Disadvantaged Children: A Report After Five Years.* Society for Research in Child Development Monographs, Serial no. 120, 1968, pp. 33–4.

Leifer, G. "Children's Theater Workshop." Harvard Educational Workshop, 1974.

Lenneberg, E. H. *Biological Foundations of Language.* New York: John Wiley & Sons, Inc., 1967.

Lyle and Hoffman, "Children's Use of Television and Other Media." In *Television and Social Behavior*, edited by E. A. Rubinstein, G. A. Comstock, and J. P. Murray. 4, Washington, D.C.: U.S. Government Printing Office, 1972.

MacKinnon, P. *How Do Children Learn to Read?* Montreal: The Copp Clark Co., 1959.

McCarthy, D. "Language Development in Children." In *Manual of Child Psychology.* 2d ed., edited by L. Carmichael. New York: John Wiley & Sons, Inc., 1954, pp. 492–630.

Mankiewicz, F. "Two Tributes." *Look Magazine Tribute to Robert Kennedy,* Special Issue (1968).

Martin, J. G. *Mediated Transfer in Two Verbal Learning Paradigms.* Ph. D. dissertation, University of Minnesota, 1960.

Neisser, U. *Cognitive Psychology.* New York: Appleton-Century-Crofts, 1967.

Peel, E. E. *The Pupil's Thinking.* London: Oldboume, 1960.

Piaget, J. *The Origins of Intelligence in Children.* New York: W. W. Norton & Company, Inc, 1963.

Poincaré, H. *Science and Hypothesis.* New York: Dover Publications, Inc., 1952.

Pribram, K. A. "Neurological Notes in the Art of Educating." In *Theories of Learning and Instruction,* National Society for the Study of Education. Chicago: University of Chicago Press, 1964.

Roser, Nancy L. Electric Company Critique: *Can Great Be Good Enough?* The Reading Teacher, Vol. 17, No. 7 April 1974 pp. 680–684.

Salus, P. *Psycholinguistics.* Englewood Cliffs, N.J.: Prentice–Hall, Inc., In press.

Smith, H. K. "The Responses of Good and Poor Readers When Asked to Read for Different Purposes." *Reading Research Quarterly,* 3 (1967), 53–83.

Spache, G. D., and E. B. Spache. *Reading in the Elementary School.* Boston: Allyn & Bacon, Inc., 1973.

Swift, M. "Training Poverty Mothers in Communication Skills. *Reading Teacher,* (Jan. 1970), 360–67. Volume #23.

Templin, M. *Certain Language Skills in Children.* Minneapolis: The University of Minnesota Press, 1957.

Vernon, M. D. "The Perceptual Process in Reading." *Reading Teacher,* 13 (Oct. 1959), 2–8.

Vygotsky, L. S. *Thought and Language.* Cambridge, Mass.: The MIT Press, 1962.

Wadsworth, B. J. *Piaget's Theory of Cognitive Development.* New York: David McKay Co., Inc., 1971.

3

Readiness for reading: preparation and programs

Children grow in mental maturity from the very beginning by the active process of discovering relationships regarding the school essentially as a laboratory where such discoveries may be made. (p. 11)

Mitchell, G., *The Young Geographers.* New York: Bank Street College of Education, 1971.

GOALS: To aid students in understanding

1. historical explanations for readiness practices in the United States.
2. the need for defining readiness as a child's existing capacity for completing a specific task.
3. components of a model prereading program in preschool and kindergarten.
4. reading teaching strategies in preschools and kindergarten.
5. assessment instruments that measure aspects of readiness.

When Is a Child Ready to Read?

Now that we have discussed the development of the human organism and some of the antecedents to reading, we must address an extremely controversial question: "When is a child ready to read?" This question is extremely complex and demands a brief historical overview in order to place it in proper perspective.

History of Beginning Reading Instruction at a Mental Age of 6.5 Years

Until 1931, educators in the United States seemed unconcerned about the accepted practice that beginning school, which occurred at about six years of age, meant simultaneously beginning to learn to read. Huey (1908) was one of the few who specifically spoke against the practice. He seemed to favor a more organic, spontaneous approach to the beginning of reading: "[the child] is concerned about the printed notices, signs that come his way, and should be told what these things say when he makes inquiry." (p. 28)

The "scientific" movement toward measurement and assessment in the 1920s brought with it a zealous concern for evaluation of children's achievement. Holmes (1927), and Reed (1927) reported large numbers of children who failed first grade because they were unable "to read." In an attempt to explain this failure, many researchers, including Deutsch and Holmes, concluded that children entering first grade were not ready to learn to read. The investigators, for the most part, did not examine other relevant variables, such as instruction (approach, materials), class size and the preparation of teachers. As a result of these findings, readiness programs began to emerge throughout the country.

Gesell was one of the greatest single forces contributing to the notion that children were not ready to learn to read at six years of age and, therefore, instruction should be postponed until they were "readied." Gesell, a medical doctor, was greatly interested in the phenomenon of neural maturation and looked for an explanation of biologically determined developmental stages from the point of view of intrinsic growth, neural ripening, and unfolding behaviors.

[handwritten margin note: Huey 1908 spoke against the practice]

[handwritten margin note: Gesell concerned with neural maturation]

He applied his theories to reading, convinced that the ability to read occurred at one of these stages. The reasons why his suggestions received such great support are unknown, but they may have been accepted because of the prevailing psychological thought in the 20s and 30s, which placed great importance on the "natural" development of the child.

Mental-Age Formula to Determine Reading Readiness. Because the times dictated exactness in measurement, not vague notions of stages, psychologists and educators sought to determine the exact age when reading instruction should begin. Group intelligence tests had recently become available to the educational community (1920s). Because these tests provided teachers with a numerical equivalent of the mental age for each child, they became the catalyst for pinpointing the moment at which a child would be able to begin reading instruction. The commonly accepted formula for mental age was

$$\text{Mental Age} = \frac{\text{Intelligence Quotient} \times \text{Chronological Age}}{100}$$

Many studies in the 1920s showed high correlations between reading achievement and intelligence. Arthur's (1925) study, for example, maintained that a mental age of 6.0 to 6.5 was "necessary for standard first-grade achievement." The most famous of these studies was conducted by Morphett and Washburne and was reported in 1931. Unequivocally, they declared that they had discovered that 6.5 was the proper mental age to begin reading instruction. This finding became the basis for reading readiness programs during the next thirty years. Their study was conducted on children using *one* method of instruction in *one* school system (Winnetka, Illinois); they concluded their report with: "Mental age alone showed a larger degree of correlation with reading progress than did intelligence quotient or the average of mental and chronological age." (p. 502)

Morphett + Washburne 6.5 proper mental age for beginning reading Instruction

Objections to Beginning Reading Instruction at 6.5 Years

As early as May 1936, objections to the mental-age concept of reading readiness were being raised. In his research report, "Reading Readiness: A Study of Factors Determining Success and Failure in Beginning Reading," Arthur Gates maintained:

> This study emphasizes the importance of recognizing and adjusting to individual limitations and needs ... rather than merely changing the time for beginning reading. It appears that readiness for reading is something to develop rather than merely to wait for ... (p. 681)

He stated further that, "the age for learning to read under one program with the method employed by one teacher may be entirely different from that required under other circumstances." In spite of such objections, there seem to be many reasons why the practice of starting young children to read at a mental age of 6.5 was maintained for so many years. Durkin (1972) suggests that psychologists were to blame: "they were the reason for too little change over too many years ... psychological conceptions of human growth and development changed very little from the 20s to the 50s." For example Gesell's (1946) views supported the popular notions that readiness for reading resulted from maturation—that is, the passing of time. Olson's (1949) concept of organismic age and Havighurst's (1953) "teachable moment" further supported the proponents of the mental-age theory.

Gesell

MacGinitie (1969) summarized Durkin's theory that readiness and beginning reading instruction should not be viewed as two separate entities in his concise statement: "when a child is taught a little, he is then ready for a little more." Along with Gates (1937), Durkin (1972) suggests that rather than inquire about the correct age for beginning instruction, the researcher should ask, "Is the child ready to succeed with this particular kind and quality of instruction?"

After examining the available studies on the age at which children should be admitted to school and, therefore, begin formal reading instruction, Calfee and Hoover (1973) stated: "Early admission of mentally advanced children seems to yield desirable outcomes, whereas early admission of children on a nonselective basis to programs without provision for individual difference is less effective." (p. 10) In short, programs and teaching methods that are not individualized to meet the needs of beginning readers will not be effective. Readiness, therefore, probably should not be defined solely as the property of the child. As we will explain later in this chapter, readiness is determined by many factors: the child's ability at the moment, the task the child is being asked to perform, the child's ability to respond to a specific method of teaching, and innumerable other factors.

imp

Criticism of Reading Readiness Tests. Readiness tests were developed and popularized throughout the 30s, 40s, and 50s. While many of these tests have been currently revised, they are often criticized because (1) the competencies measured by the tests are often only tangentially related to reading; (2) visual discrimination tasks are often too complex; (3) they do not adequately assess potential reading ability; and (4) total readiness programs are built on the results of diagnostic tests, the components of which may not have measured later reading success.

Alternatives to Readiness Testing: Predictors of Reading Success. Although no single reading readiness test may accurately assess a child's "ripeness" for formal reading instruction, there may be a series of short tests that will sensitively predict the potential of a child to be able to learn to read. These predictors may be used as alternatives to the standardized reading readiness tests that are often marred by the internal problems suggested in the preceding section. These predictors may help you to plan appropriately individualized programs for young children who are at high risk of failure or for those children who exhibit potentially serious reading problems.

Predicting Reading. Research in recent years has suggested that a sensitive prediction of children who will succeed at reading can be obtained by an assessment of several prereading skills: alphabet recognition, whole-word recognition, vocabulary, and visual discrimination.

Alphabet Recognition. Most researchers who have investigated the relationship between letter recognition and reading have reported that letter-name knowledge is highly predictive of reading achievement. Monroe (1935), Durrell (1958), Silvaroli (1965), and Silverburg (1968) all found that the ability to name letters at the beginning of first grade was highly predictive of reading achievement at the end of the school year. In their study, Weiner and Feldman (1963) found that letter recognition was more closely related to reading achievement (at the .01 level of significance) than matching printed words. Bond and Dykstra (1967) found that the letter-naming subtest of the Murphy-Durrell Readiness Test was the best single predictor of later reading. Jansky and DeHirsch (1972) also reported that letter naming was the single greatest predictor of later reading success.

From his study, Muehl (1966) found that letter knowledge was clearly an advantage for reading, but that the lack of letter-name knowledge was not causally related to reading difficulties. On the other hand, Olson (1958) found that knowledge of letter names was not causally related to high reading achievement, but that lack of this knowledge was usually associated with low achievement.

Samuels (1972) has reported that two separate experimental studies failed to support the assumption that letter-name knowledge facilitates reading. In partial replication of Samuel's study, Chisholm and Knafle (1975) found opposite results; they discovered that letter-name knowledge was highly predictive of reading achievement. They concluded that their study "supported the statement by Calfee, Chapman, and Venezky (1972): 'to read English a child must learn to isolate, differentiate, and identify the letters of the alphabet.'" (p. 145)

In summary, alphabet recognition is probably the quickest way to predict reading success and alphabet recognition and discrimination are probably essential for learning to read English; however, we can not assume that teaching the child the alphabet will automatically guarantee reading success. It should be noted again that these studies do *not* suggest that alphabet recognition or letter-name knowledge will cause a child to learn to read. Rather, the research indicates that most children who learn to read knew the alphabet before they began reading. Therefore, alphabet recognition can be used as a useful, efficient predictor of reading but not necessarily as an instructor of reading.

Word Knowledge. Several researchers have shown that word recognition is highly related to reading. Gavel (1958) and DeHirsch et al. (1966) found that recognition of words that the child had been taught was highly predictive of reading at the first-grade level. Examples of these words include a child's full name (for example, Barbara Elizabeth Scott) or a date (July 4, 1776) or words with special meaning for the child (Big Bird, monster, candy).

Vocabulary Knowledge. Vocabulary has been found to be the most frequently occurring component of IQ tests, which, in turn, have been extremely predictive of later reading success. Lohnes and Gray (1972), after reanalyzing Bond and Dykatra's massive study, *The Cooperative Research Program in First Grade Reading Instruction,* attempted to discover *the* best method of teaching reading, concluded: "The best single explanatory principle for observed variance in reading skills was variance in general intelligence." (p. 60) Lohnes and Gray concluded that differences in children's ability to read were related more to their general intelligence than the method of instruction they received.

Vocabulary tests have been used as effective predictors of later reading achievement. When children were given picture-recognition tasks as a vocabulary subtest, Morgan (1960) found a significant correlation between performance on a picture-vocabulary test and reading achievement. DeHirsch *et al.* (1966) found that achievement on the Peabody Picture Vocabulary Test correlated significantly with second-grade achievement.

Analyzing student performance on an oral vocabulary task, Artley (1948) stated that "any limitation in word meaning ... would have a bearing on reading ability." Loban (1963) concluded that kindergarteners who had the most extensive vocabulary continued to exceed other children's performance as they progressed through grades 1–6. Robinson (1963) found vocabulary to be related to prediction of reading success.

DeHirsch *et al.* (1966) used categorization, a third type of vocabulary task, which directed children to provide a generic name for a cluster of words. She found that this test significantly correlated with second-grade reading achievement. Jansky and DeHirsch (1972) also found categorization to be related to later reading achievement.

Visual Discrimination. Visual discrimination has been an extremely controversial predictor of reading. Although most researchers now agree that visual discrimination of nonalphabetic shapes and forms is probably not a worthwhile method of prereading instruction, the question of the predictive value of visual discrimination ability continues to be debated.

Goins (1958) and DeHirsch et al. (1966) found that matching two- and three-letter sequences is highly predictive of reading achievement. For example

		bd		
bp	pd	db	bd	pq

The directions for this test might state: "Color the box in the second line which contains the same letters as the box on the first line."

Barrett (1965) found that scores on word matching tests correlated very closely with reading achievement, but he also suggested that visual perception was unable to "bear the entire burden of prediction." Many researchers (Wilson and Fleming, 1960; Bryan, 1964; Barrett, 1965) have found that visual discrimination ability in young children correlates extremely well with later reading achievement. DeHirsch et al (1966) maintained that primitive and poorly integrated visual discrimination skills are characteristic of children with reading disabilities. In her study, she found that visual discrimination correlated highly with reading achievement at the end of the second grade. In his study, Buktenica (1969) found that visual discrimination ability was a far more reliable predictor of reading achievement than intelligence.

However, Calfee, Chapman, and Venezsky (1972) were unable to demonstrate that visual discrimination was an adequate predictor of reading achievement. Olson and Johnson (1970) also found that visual discrimination, as measured by the Frostig Developmental Test of Visual Perception, was the least effective predictor of the five readiness predictors (spatial relations, position in space, form constancy, figure ground, eye-motor coordination) that they investigated.

In summary, these four components of reading—alphabet recognition, word knowledge, vocabulary knowledge, and visual discrimination—*may* be used as useful predictors of later reading success. As predictors, they *may* serve as instruments for selecting appropriate children for early reading programs.

Early Programs

With some historical and theoretical information in mind, two questions arise: The first echoes our query at the beginning of this chapter: "When is a child ready to read?" The second question is "What is an appropriate curriculum design for a reading preparation program?" Let's try to answer each of these questions.

1. *When* implies a time, an age. This part of the question seems most easily answered: When the child indicates an interest in printed material. Some might find this to be a simplistic answer, but it makes the most sense in a number of ways. In order to explain this answer, we have to agree on the meanings of the other words in the original questions.

2. *Taught* means exposed to visual symbols which represent concepts and instructed in the correspondence between the graphemes (letter symbols) and the sound (phoneme) uttered.

3. *To read* is to match internalized concepts with graphemic representations that have been auditorially transmitted. For example, the word

     C–A–T

represents the class to which a specific animal belongs.

     P–U–F–F

is the animal's name which further describes a specific animal within the general class.

With these simple notions in mind, it becomes clear that a very young child who asks his mother, "*What does that say?*" is asking for reading instruction. When he can say, "That says *Wheaties*," he is indeed reading. Certainly, such a simple answer to the important question, "When should a child be taught to read?", avoids the question to a degree. If we are talking about formal instruction, using phonics or whole-word strategies, then a more sophisticated answer seems necessary. We need to ask, "What is readiness?"

What Is Readiness?

In the past, the purpose of readiness tests was to determine when the child would be mentally capable of benefiting from reading instruction. Unfortunately, the historical times gave too much attention to the comprehensive score on a standardized readiness test and too little attention to the individual needs of the child. Ausubel (1959) suggested that readiness is "the adequacy of existing capacity in relation to the demands of a given learning task." In other words, he suggested that the "when" of reading instruction depends on the child, the instruction, and the specific components of what is being taught. Some very young children of the same chronological age may be "ready" to learn that their name begins with *A*, whereas others may be ready to learn to "read" the following sentence:

> The cat is yellow.

This second group of children has already learned to decode these four words and have committed them to their sight vocabulary. As classroom teachers, you must not infer from these differences that children in the second group are any more intelligent than the children in the first group. Their readiness preparation is simply at a different stage of development. Such differences may be the result of many of the external stimulants of human development which were discussed in Chapter 2.

Readiness is different for every child. There simply is no single age at which all children should be taught to read. In fact, in many countries of the world, children begin formal instruction before the age of six. In the United Kingdom, for example, children generally begin reading at five years of age, and in Israel some children begin formal instruction at four years of age. There have been several programs in the United Kingdom that have proven to be fairly successful in teaching reading to preschoolers who are four years of age.

There are many myths surrounding the initial instruction of reading in the United States. Many educators have researched the phenomenon of early readers and have evaluated the effect of these early starts. It seems appropriate, at this point, to review several research studies and reports of early reading programs in order to determine whether early reading is a help or a hindrance to the young child.

Early Reading

Perhaps the most prominent study of the phenomenon of early reading was conducted for six years by Durkin in Oakland, California, and New York City in 1966. In her results, she reported that some children read before they entered first grade and before they received formal reading instruction. She concluded that early reading was not necessarily a function of socioeconomic status, ethnicity, or intelligence. Furthermore, she found that early readers achieved higher reading scores than their nonearly reading counterparts during their entire elementary school careers.

However, in her latest research, reported in "A Six-Year Study of Children Who Were Taught to Read in School at the Age of 4," *Reading Research Quarterly*, vol. X, (1974–75), Durkin did not reach the same conclusion. In this study, conducted in Illinois, she found that early readers who had been trained in a special two-year preschool language arts/reading program scored significantly higher than their nonearly reading classmates on standardized reading tests in grades 1 and 2, but the differences between the two groups were not statistically significant in grades 3 and 4. "One very likely explanation for the reversal," she maintains, "is that the characteristics of a family that fostered preschool reading ability would continue to foster achievement, with or without an instructional program in school."

An alternate explanation for the reversal may be offered by reexamining the data. Durkin analyzed her data in such a way that the phenomenon of increased variance in the scores of the upper-grade students was not taken into consideration. If this reanalysis of the data is performed, it may show that the early readers really did outperform the nonearly readers even in the later grades.

Several other researchers in the last few years have investigated the effects of early reading, but few have investigated its causes. Despite the fact that some educators and researchers have acknowledged the existence of early reading, for example, Durkin (1966, 1970, 1974), there has been little systematic research into these important questions: What factors in the home contribute to the success of early reading? Is there an environment that is conducive to early reading? What is the role of the parent-child relationship in early reading?

These questions remain seriously underinvestigated, but folk wisdom abounds. Some parents and some educators have favorite anecdotes about young children who have learned to read "on their own." Durkin (1966, 1972) asserts that young children *do not* learn to read by themselves. Through interviewing, she discovered that parents of early readers had spent a great deal of time conversing with their young children, that it was characteristic of early readers to ask many questions, and that parents had taken time to answer these questions. Among her early readers, Durkin found "What's that word?" to be a very common question.

Effects of Early Reading Programs.   Although it seems obvious, it is important to reemphasize that parents of early readers spent a great deal of time preparing their children for reading. Children simply do not learn to read spontaneously. Someone has to "break the code" for them in order to start them on their way.

Research findings, while often seriously marred by design problems and faulty analyses, show that early reading generally produces successful readers. McKee, Brzienski, and Harrison (1966) found that kindergarteners who were taught to read in the Denver Public Schools were able to sustain their early achievement "when the reading program in subsequent years capitalized upon their early starts."

Shapiro and Willford (1969) reported that children who were taught the Initial Teaching Alphabet (ITA) approach to reading in kindergarten performed better at the end of the second grade than children who were not taught to read until first grade, using the same approach. Gray and Klaus (1970) found excellent results at the end of the first grade for high risk children who had participated in intervention programs; however, they found no continued growth after first grade. Unfortunately, this study did not take into account the instruction which each child had received after first grade.

King and Freisen (1972) found that early readers who were selected in kindergarten outperformed nonearly readers at the end of first grade. However, intelligence was not taken into consideration—the mean intelligence score was 11 points higher for early readers than non-early readers (115 to 104).

Beck (1973) found early readers had significantly higher intelligence scores than nonearly readers. Adjusting for intelligence, she found that children who started to read in kindergarten outperformed their nonearly reading classmates in grades 1 through 5. The selection process for early readers in this study was unique—*teachers* selected them as being "ready" to read. She suggests that her results should be interpreted very cautiously because of her unusually small sample, which dwindled to only eight early readers by fifth grade.

Although there are some flaws in the design and analysis of these studies, it can be concluded that early readers score higher than their nonearly reading counterparts in many cases. However, objections to early reading still seem to occur in many parts of the country. It might be useful to list traditional objections and to analyze their validity in light of current research findings.

Objections to Early Reading

Objections	Comments
1. Early reading will hurt the child's vision.	There is little evidence to support this claim. In fact, it may be argued that a child's vision is ready for reading because many children are writing by four or five years of age.
2. Parents cannot teach reading.	Parents may not have taken formal reading courses, but there are many activities they can do with their children. These activities are presented in Chapter 4.

3. Children who learn to read early will be bored in school.	Children will only be bored with reading if they have to begin again. However, with personalized programs that give individual attention to each child, there seems no logical or inherent reason for boredom.
4. Early childhood is a time for play, not academics.	Reading can be a playful, enjoyable activity for young children. If children have as much reading activity as they seem to want, then the concern about introducing too much academe seems unwarranted.

Early Intervention and Need for Prereading and Early Reading Programs

Need for Early Intervention. Some educators will argue that prereading or early reading programs are unnecessary and are often counterproductive. They argue that these programs will frustrate young children and will have the effect of making reading distasteful to them. Such claims have not been substantiated. In fact, as the preceding review of research indicates, early programs are often quite successful. In fact, there may be a greater need for early programs now than ever before in our history. Many researchers argue that high-risk, potentially handicapped children need to be identified when they are very young so that appropriate programs can be established to remediate their problems before they are overwhelming. We have entered an age of prevention in medicine and in education. Early concern and good care have significantly reduced medical problems in many areas. Educators are also examining preventive measures to avoid serious educational problems later in a child's life. The wise remark "Get them when they're young," seems entirely appropriate in this context.

As early as 1966, Money said the early identification of high-risk children was a major problem and challenge in efforts to alleviate childhood learning disabilities. *The Report of the 1969 Task Force on Dyslexia and Reading Related Disorders* (U. S. Department of Health, Education and Welfare) also stated that the early identification of children who may have potential reading problems is urgently needed to protect children from the psychological trauma of reading failure and to ensure appropriate intervention to prevent this failure.

Research Supporting Early Intervention Programs. Researchers who favor early intervention often assert that the causes of reading failure can be found in germinal stages in a child's first few years of life (Hallgren, 1950; DeHirsch et al., 1966; Ingram, 1970; Owens et al., 1968; Silver, 1971; Satz and Von Nostrand, 1973).

Based on these and other research findings, educators have supported a concept of timely intervention, arguing that very young children are often more sensitive and receptive to remediation than older children. Caldwell (1968) stated: "There is some evidence to suggest that the child may be more sensitive to environmental stimulation (for example, remedial intervention) during that period in which maturation of the brain is evolving and when behavior is less differentiated." (p. 220) Satz and Van Nostrand (1973) affirmed Caldwell's position on the potential efficacy of early identification and intervention when he reported that early childhood is a time when the central nervous system is more plastic and subject to rapid growth (Lenneberg, 1967), and a time when the child is generally free of personality disorders (Gates, 1968).

In the last few years, a broader knowledge base regarding the general development of language ability in children has also developed. The research indicates that basic language ability develops between birth and the age of five or six (Menyuk, 1963). Such evidence suggests that amelioration of reading difficulties in elementary school children might best be accomplished through intervention during the preschool years.

J. McV. Hunt (1961), in *Intelligence and Experience*, presented a well-developed rationale for early intervention programs. During the past decade programs such as Head Start have been developed as a result of Hunt's theories of cognitive development in young children. Based on continuous evaluation data these early intervention programs have been modified in an attempt to further their effectiveness. Program modifications have included (1) starting intervention earlier and incorporating parent involvement as an integral part of the intervention (Parent and Child Centers; Home Start), (2) extending the intervention support into the primary grades (Follow Through), (3) coordinating services to children and their families over an extended period of time (Child and Family Resource Centers), and (4) supporting the development of innovative educational programs (Planned Variation).

While the development of early intervention programs is obviously justified, we encourage you to be prepared to dispel one objection to early reading programs to which you may often be exposed: This objection is: There is a developmental, biologically determined CRITICAL PERIOD for the acquisition of reading. To tamper with this biological clock is unnatural and will create adverse effects in the child.

Critical Period for Language Acquisition. The educators who argue in this way have probably based their concept of critical period on the linguistic theory of critical period in the language acquisition of human beings. Let us first examine the linguists' theory of critical period in language acquisition in order to understand the possible origins of a similar concept in reading. Then, we will examine the appropriateness of such a theory for reading.

The notion of critical period for language acquisition may be a convenient fiction for creating a facile label that is an inadequate explanation for the phenomenon it proposes to define. A suitable definition of critical period is the following: a non-chronological period or stage in which the human organism is especially sensitive to the specifics of language development (phonology, syntax, morphology, semantics, and pragmatics). Furthermore, it is possible that there are certain periods that are extremely propitious for the development of each of these components. These periods of heightened sensitivity might parallel psychophysiological theories (1972) of the rate of growth in the human brain, which, in turn, closely parallel Piaget's (1963) stages of cognitive development—for example, the first growth spurt between two and four years of age *might* be the most sensitive period for phonological development. It should be pointed out that the sensitive stage/critical period means that there are periods of sensitivity to language development and not terminal points after which language development will not occur.

It seems important to investigate several determinants of language that will affect sensitivity to development. Three of the major determinants are: *neurophysiology, psychology* and *environment.*

Neurophysiology. The notion of a critical period derives from behavior observed in geese, dogs, and other animals. It states that a particular behavior is acquired at a specific time. This biological concept of critical period has been applied by some researchers to the acquisition and development of language. Lenneberg (1966, 1967) and others have claimed that language cannot be learned after the completion of the lateralization of the brain, a phenomenon that Lenneberg thought occurred at puberty. Geschwind (1972, 1974), while suggesting a much earlier functional assymetry, maintained that lateralization is vital to speech. Although some neurolinguists claim lateralization is complete by age five, they allow that transfer may still continue into puberty.

Others think lateralization occurs even earlier than five. Kinsbourne suggests that lateralization may be a neonatal phenomenon. These positions are attractive because they parallel Piaget's sensorimotor stage and may lead researchers to an investigation of the relationship between the critical period of language development and the sensorimotor period.

Psychology and Environment. A second determinant of language development is the psychological composition of the individual. Psychology includes such factors as cognition, intellectual functioning, experience, attitude, motivation, and culture. A composite of these factors must be taken into account when proposing a theory to explain a sensitive stage of development. In some ways, the biological growth of the brain can be observed in the unfolding of Piaget's developmental cognitive stages.

When explaining a specific stage of language development one must also consider environmental influences. Included in this category are auditory input/ stimulation and semantic and syntactic input. The case of Genie, a fictitious name, demonstrates the profound effect of environment on language. Genie was a thirteen-year-old girl who was brought to Children's Hospital in Los Angeles in November 1970, after having been virtually "locked in a closet" for most of her life. The actual details of the case are unknown for the most part. But at the time of her entry into Children's Hospital, she had no speech, limited signs of nonverbal language, and was barely able to control her vocal muscles, which would have allowed her to produce speech or to chew and swallow. After several years of life in a normal foster home and work with educators, psychologists, and speech pathologists, Genie exhibited an incredible amount of growth. She comprehends speech, uses expressive speech, and understands cognitive relationships far beyond the expectations of many researchers who would hold to a strict theory of critical period development.

Although her phonology is far from perfect, her syntax, in general, far exceeds the normal expectations of a typical five- or six-year-old who has been learning English for that period of time. Genie's language acquisition, which began with the onset of puberty, certainly contradicts Lenneberg's theory of the critical period for language acquisition, which he suggested occurs between birth and puberty.

Although it is true that neurophysiology, psychology, and environment are determinants affecting an individual's sensitivity to language development, it should be pointed out that there is always an interaction among them. One determinant may affect the others; it is simply not clear which single factor occurs first or is most significant for the acquisition of language.

Critical Period for Acquisition of Reading. Because it is not generally agreed that there is a critical period for the acquisition of language, there are few educators who would hold to a theory of a critical period for the spontaneous acquisition of reading. Yet, there is a tangentially related theory suggesting that there may be a critical period for the beginning of reading instruction. This theory suggests that initial reading instruction should take place between four and six years of age, a time when the child is rather sophisticated, having acquired most of the rules of English syntax.

When studying cognitive development processes, it seems that there is a limited relationship between cognition, using Piaget's terminology, and the acquisition of beginning reading. Kohlberg (1968) has stated:

> Learning the mechanics of reading and writing need not depend heavily upon the development of new levels of cognitive structure (categories of relation), although it may depend on the development of perceptual structure. ...Compared with cognitive-structural transformations required for development of spoken language at age two or five; the cognitive-structural requirements in tying together spoken and written signs seems modest. ... Because reading and writing (especially reading) are relatively low-level sensorimotor skills, there is nothing in the cognitive structure of the reading task which involves any high challenge to the older child. In contrast, the identification of letters and words ... may be challenging fun for younger children. (pp. 103–108)

Teachers who have tried in vain to instruct a child to read may refute Kohlberg's conclusions. However, the point is clear: learning to speak is, in principle, a less difficult task than translating the spoken form to a written form of language. In fact, almost all children learn to speak, but many children experience great difficulty when trying to learn to read. Certainly, part of the problem may be a mismatch between the child's cognitive development and beginning reading instruction. Reading has traditionally been taught when the child is six to eight years of age. This is the time, according to Piaget, when the child is engaged in "concrete operations." The repetitive drills involved in beginning reading may be interruptive. Therefore, we agree with those who propose beginning reading instruction at an earlier age, particularly if researchers discover that there is a lacuna in cognitive development instruction at the age of four to five.

Many researchers already have reported a major change in cognitive behavior at five or six—the age at which American children enter school. White (1965) states: "four contemporary points of view concerning cognitive development have held the five–seven period to be important, each on its own evidence and in its own terms". (p. 210) These four positions are (1) Piaget, (2) the Russian researchers, typified by Luria, (3) stimulus-response behaviorists such as the Kendlers and Reese, and (4) Freud.

Among the psychologists whose efforts relate directly to this research are E. Gibson, White, and Kagan. Gibson's work on the nature of visual form perception is summarized in Gibson and Levin's *Psychology of Reading* (1975). By using novel letterlike forms, Gibson's research has provided insights into the development of perceptual processes. Gibson et al. (1962) showed that letter-like forms remained perceptually invariant under specific transformations (for example, a change in perspective) but not under other transformations (rotation or reversal). There were fairly dramatic changes in the degree of perceptual invariance around the ages of four to five; four-year-olds accepted rotations and reversals as equivalent to a standard about half the time; at five years of age these confusions only occurred about one-fifth of the time. The results of this research indicate that young children are able to abstract distinguishing features and separate them from the context of a visual perceptual task.

It seems important to emphasize the fact that there is a major change in skill performance between the ages of five and seven. The following factors may account for this change: general, level of intellectual functioning and/or language, improved organizational abilities, and changes in attention (duration and fixation). In fact, an argument can be made that impulsive, rapid action is optimal for a child whose ability to record complex action is limited. For such a child, the longer he waits, the less likely he is to retain the primary sensory information. The proper training for this kind of child may not be to restrain him forcibly from responding, but rather to teach him cognitive skills, which are essential to efficient storage of information. However, the question of when to begin reading instruction is still complex. The best answer seems to come from Gates (1937) and Calfee and Hoover (1973), when they suggest that instruction should match the needs of the child.

What is An Appropriate Curriculum Design for a Preparatory Program?

Before describing a model prereading program, it seems important to reiterate Ausubel's (1959) definition of readiness: "the adequacy of existing capacity in relation to the demands of a given learning task." It should be pointed out that the existing capacity has to be evident before a teacher proceeds to give instruction in readiness activities; the child should exhibit readiness for preparatory activities. A word of caution: The child will exhibit his degree of interest in each preparatory activity. The observant teacher will individualize the instruction to meet each child's needs.

Let us present a hypothetical case:

> Asia, aged three years, is sitting with Charles (three years), Robert (four years), Amy (four and one-half years), Darlene (five years), and Gigi (five years). Sharon, the volunteer teacher, decides to read the story *The Cat in the Hat* to the group. Asia listens to two pages and wanders away. After the story, Gigi and Robert beg to be allowed to hold the book for themselves, pouring over the pictures. Darlene starts enacting the story for the inattentive group, and Charles tells Sharon, "I have a cat. It's name's Ella and she knocked over her dish this morning. My mother yelled at her ... "

Although this reading session may have been beneficial for all the children, which of them do you think would be ready for a follow-up language experience activity? What individualized activities could you plan for the children?

What Should a Prereading Program or Early Reading Program Look Like?

There are many preschool and kindergarten programs in existence at the present time that incorporate various language and prereading activities. If they meet the needs of the children, then each is a model program. If they allow children to progress at their own rate, with gentle nudges, and if they provide a rich language environment, then they are probably doing an excellent job in preparing the young child for reading.

Any model prereading program must take into consideration certain factors about the ways in which children learn. Piaget (1963) suggests that children learn by abstracting features from a stimulus and integrating these features into an existing cognitive framework. He, and other cognitively-oriented psychologists and educators, believe children learn by generating hypotheses and testing them against the input they have received. This theory is consistent with the views of many linguists (Menyuk, 1971) who maintain that children acquire language by generating rules, testing them, and reformulating them. This language acquisition theory was explained in detail in Chapter 2.

If we hold a view of learning that is consistent with Piaget's, then we must make the learning of reading an accessible adventure for children. Children will be able to abstract letter-sound correspondences only when materials are available to them. They must see books, hear the words read over and over. When this is done, they will be able to generate hypotheses about letter-sound correspondences which they will be able to test.

Reading As a Prop for Play

Children also need to interact with reading as a real, "true-to-life" phenomenon. This can be done by creating environments in which children need "to read" to play. "Reading Props" can enhance play, for example, if you include empty cereal boxes and juice containers in your housekeeping corner, children will begin to play with these props. Children will begin to distinguish between *Cheerios* and *Wheaties*, *Apple Juice* and *Orange Juice* because these distinctions will become important to their play situation.

Wherever possible, you should try to incorporate reading into children's play. Some examples may illustrate this point:

1. Housekeeping Corner
   A. Include empty boxes, cartons, and cans. You can intervene in children's play by asking, "I wonder what the baby wants to eat?" Go to the empty containers and start to read, "I wonder if she wants peaches, pears, or apple sauce?" Children will begin to model this behavior.
   B. Include menus that have been made by the children for their restaurant play.
   C. Create little homemade books for the children to read to their dolls.

2. Block Area
   A. Include many different kinds of signs in this area. If your children are building a city or town, intervene in their play by asking them: "Is this the drugstore?" If they say, "Yes," ask them: "Do you want to make a sign?" You can attach signs to the blocks by using paper and toothpicks. In this way the signs can be saved.

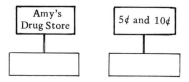

   B. Sometimes children enjoy building "cars" and "airplanes" out of blocks. This seems like a perfect opportunity for including signs (reading props) in the play situation. Signs can be made that are interchangeable; they can be saved and used in many different situations.

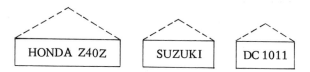

3. Dramatic Play Corner
   A. "Doctor/Hospital" is a perfect situation in which reading can be incorporated into children's play. Signs can be made to enhance the play, e.g.:

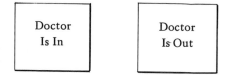

Forms can be made that children will have to complete

Name ___NANCY___
Date _____
Illness _____

B. "Store" is also an excellent opportunity for incorporating reading into play. Children can "make" money and use it to buy groceries. A grocery list can also be prepared by the children before they begin their "shopping."

Elements of a Prereading or Early Reading Program

In addition to incorporating reading into play, there are many elements that are necessary for a successful prereading program. In the next few pages, we will present some of the highlights of what we consider the most important elements in a prereading program. First, the general objectives of a prereading program should be comprehensive. In the following chart, we have presented a list of fourteen objectives we consider absolutely necessary in a good prereading program. These objectives can be implemented in any preschool or kindergarten classroom by selecting and using appropriate teaching strategies. Objectives and strategies are presented in the following chart.

GENERAL OBJECTIVES AND STRATEGIES FOR A PREREADING PROGRAM

Objectives

1. Improvement of general language ability: phonology, morphology, syntax, semantics, and pragmatics. For bilingual children and non-English speaking children, support language development in the child's native language and provide opportunities for the acquisition of English as a second language where appropriate.

2. Enjoyment of books and an understanding of books as resources. Books represent a wide variety of cultural and linguistic backgrounds. Children whose first language is not English should have the opportunity to be read stories in their own languages.

Strategies

Language-experience approaches. Children who show interest in beginning reading instruction will be afforded the opportunity to begin a personalized language-experience reading program. These children can make word cards and will be taught to "read" single words.

Reading to children individually and in small groups, in other languages (where appropriate) and in English. Asking questions relating to the story and encouraging children to retell it in their own words.

Picture books readily available to children in a reading corner.

Films of familiar stories.

Trips to libraries and museums and other neighborhood places of interest.

3. Comprehension of material related orally such as in understanding simple directions or a story that has been read.

Listening experiences via records and tapes of stories, songs, and nursery rhymes. Listening experiences that result in following simple directions. Musical listening, singing and movement experiences.

4. Appreciation of the relationship between oral and written language.

Language-experience approaches. Children who show interest in beginning reading instruction will be afforded the opportunity to begin a personalized language-experience reading program. These children can make word cards and can be taught to "read" single words.

5. Confidence in their ability to create written materials—for example, stories dictated to a teacher.

Taking down children's dictated stories and helping children make their own books.
Opportunities for dramatic play.

6. Recognition of the alphabet.

Games and other manipulative materials (felt letters and felt board; magnetic letters and magnetic board; alphabet bingo) that develop alphabet recognition and letter-sound associations.

7. Sight vocabulary that is familiar and important to the child, such as the child's name and the names of frequently used classroom materials (for example, door, a window).

Use of labels in the classroom to indicate names of things and places for their storage.
Use of children's names on lockers, or tote boxes, and art work.

8. Letter-sound associations, particularly initial phonemes, consonants, and recognition of familiar sounds.

Phonics training for those children who show interest and who, it appears, will profit from such a program.

9. Recognition of rhyming words.

Phonics training for some children who show interest and who, it appears, can profit from such a program.

10. Introduction to and/or development of effective viewing of educational television.

Use of educational television in selected classrooms.

11. Ability to communicate about concrete objects.

Use of referential communication games.

12. Recognition of sequence.

Use of recipe charts for cooking activities.
Use of sequencing materials—for example, puzzles, stories (some without endings), and picture cards.

13. Simple categorization.

Work with children on visual discrimination skills (for example, matching letters, shapes, and designs).

14. Acquisition of directionality.

Exercises and games on directionality.

Lesson Plan

If you were actually to use these strategies to complete one of your objectives, an appropriate lesson would resemble the following. This lesson plan could be used to teach letter-sound association (Objective 8).

Objective/goal:
Improvement of letter-sound associations

Behavioral objective:
Given an array of several letter shapes, the child will be able to select the letter shape that represents the /d/ phoneme in English

Materials:
dough, baking pans, a stove

Strategies:
Using a multisensory approach
1. The child will form the letter shape "d" out of prepared dough.
2. The child, aided by the teacher, will deep fry the dough on the stove.
3. The teacher will prepare and bake several other letter shapes—for example, x, m, and o.
4. After allowing time for cooking, the teacher will present the letter shapes to the child and ask the child to select the letter shape that matches the phoneme /d/.
5. The child will put sugar on the dough.
6. The teacher will explain to the child that his product is sometimes called a doughnut or donut, emphasizing the initial phoneme /d/.
7. The child will serve the donuts for dessert.

There is a great deal of controversy in the field of reading concerning the effectiveness of training children in visual and auditory discrimination when shapes and sounds are used that are not the letters and sounds of the English alphabet. Durkin (1972) and others have argued that there is little transfer of the ability to visually and auditorially discriminate non-alphabetic shapes and the ability to read. Researchers and educators who agree with Durkin argue that children should be taught to discriminate visually and auditorially actual letters and sounds, introducing them to graphemes and their corresponding phonemes at a very early age.

Instructional Program.   The instructional program which you may use in your preschool must be based on clearly defined goals and objectives. If you followed the objectives outlined in the previous section, your instruction would include activities in four areas: letter recognition, whole word techniques, phonics techniques, and language experiences.

Letter Recognition.   Children can learn to begin to read as soon as they exhibit some interest in it. The earliest strategies teachers should use to ready children for reading are letter-recognition activities. Most children three years of age, after having been exposed to *Sesame Street*, are quite capable of recognizing the alphabet. Frequently, these same children often become early readers. There are many ways to present the task of letter recognition, depending on the needs of the children. Some children *need* to begin by matching the same letter shapes from two groups of letters. Other children can learn through an auditory modality, and a third group can learn by being taught the letters of their own names. Children can be given magnetic letters as a stimulus for learning letters. To reinforce letter recognition, they can trace letters in sand, in clay, or with water on the blackboard and watch them "mysteriously" disappear.

Whole-Word Techniques. Children will probably commit certain personal words to memory rather quickly—for example, their own names: *Erin, Jay.* In order to develop this whole-word recognition, children may have their names put on their lockers or cubicles. If lockers or cubicles are not available, you can use empty milk cartons for the same purpose.

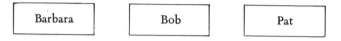

You might teach lessons on the *weather, dates,* or *time* in order to encourage whole-word recognition. For example, you may have a sign where the child is asked to choose the correct day and put it in the slot;

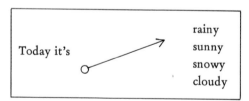

or you may have a chart describing the daily weather with a spinwheel:

Each child may take a turn pointing the arrow to the weather for each day.

Birthdays are always useful for helping children with sight words. You may make a display like this one:

January Birthdays

Another useful technique is to label many things in the classroom. Labeling, which helps children to categorize, is especially useful for beginning reading. You may label boxes where specific toys are kept:

Frisbies	Dolls	Puzzles

Special areas of the room may be labeled:

Records   Painting   Library

Signs are useful for teaching sight words:

It's lunch time.		It's snack time.		It's milk time.
Doctor is in.		Mailbox		Toy Department

Phonics Techniques. Some initial phonics may be introduced in the preschool or kindergarten. First, you may want to prepare children for work with sounds by practicing rhyming. Ask children to rhyme as many words as they can with the following:

cat   rope   brother

You may then begin another activity with the following introduction: "Betty is the name for today. Who has a name that begins with the same sound as Betty?" This might be a good time to do some careful observations to determine which children seem prepared to continue with more phonics activities. Other activities appropriate for phonics instruction are included in Chapter 4.

Language Experience Techniques. For some children who seem to be ready for reading instruction, you may begin your instruction by using a language experience approach. The base of this approach is the actual language of the child. After you and your class have had a shared experience—for example, a trip to the zoo—get a large piece of construction paper and give the child some magic markers. You can begin the story in the following way:

We went to the zoo today. We saw the animals.

Next you should elicit specific animals from the children by asking: "Tana, what animal did you see?"

> Tana saw a giraffe.
> Willie saw a monkey.
> Kevin saw a penguin.

Then add something like:

> We all had fun.

These charts can be illustrated by the children or you can cut out pictures from magazines. Language experience charts like the next one can be constructed for special occasions:

> We are going to have a Halloween party.
> We will wear costumes.
> Jimmy is going to be a ghost.
> Robin is going to be a clown.
> Frank is going to be a pirate.
> Margaret is going to be a farmer.
> Lena is going to be a rabbit.
> Michael is going to be an owl.
> Tony is going to be a cowboy.
> Sharon is going to be a swan.
> Anthony is going to be a monster.
> We will have candy and cookies.

Again, these charts can be illustrated and decorated as elaborately as you think appropriate. Sometimes the illustrations alone create great interest for the children. At first, the teacher reads the entire chart to the children, then she asks the children to read their entries. Eventually, the children will read the entire story.

Assessment of Progress

With any discussion of the "right" or "best" prereading program to use in a preschool, the inevitable question arises "How do we assess the child and the program to determine growth?" You will probably want to assess some children's readiness with a diagnostic measure. You will also want to assess your program. In the next few pages we will present some examples of assessment instruments that may be useful in the preschool.

Assessing Beginning Reading Readiness

Essentially, there are two ways to assess readiness for reading: (1) observation of children throughout the entire day, using a *checklist* of characteristics that are important for success in reading and (2) reading readiness tests. The best evaluation involves a combination of both.

Observations and Checklists

A teacher checklist of characteristics related to reading success can be extremely important in any classroom. After observations, the teacher should take a moment to record some notes about each child's progress. We will present three useful checklists in the next few pages: (1) Russell's Checklist, (2) the Prereading Rating Scale, (3) an informal teacher checklist. We will also present one observation instrument, The Santa Clara County Inventory of Developmental Tasks.

Russell's Checklist. Russell's checklist can be used to help teachers better organize the knowledge they have acquired about a child or a group of children Russell (1967) developed the following list:

Checklist for Reading Readiness*

Physical Readiness

		Yes	No
1. Eyes			
a. Does the child seem comfortable in the use of his eyes (does not squint, rub eyes, hold materials too close or too far from eyes)?	1.	☐	☐
b. Are the results of clinical tests or an oculist's examination favorable?	2.	☐	☐
2. Ears			
a. Is it apparent through his response to questions or directions that he is able to hear what is said to the class?	3.	☐	☐
3. Speech			
a. Does he articulate clearly?	4.	☐	☐
b. Does he speak in a group with some confidence?	5.	☐	☐
c. Does he speak without gross errors in pronunciation?	6.	☐	☐
d. Does he respond to suggestions for speech improvement?	7.	☐	☐
4. Hand-eye coordination			
Is he able to make his hands work together in cutting, using tools, or bouncing a ball?	8.	☐	☐
5. General health			
a. Does he give an impression of good health?	9.	☐	☐
b. Does he seem well nourished?	10.	☐	☐
c. Does the school physical examination reveal good health?	11.	☐	☐

Social Readiness

1. Cooperation			
a. Does he work well with a group, taking his share of the responsibility?	12.	☐	☐
b. Does he cooperate in playing games with other children?	13.	☐	☐
c. Can he direct his attention to a specific learning situation?	14.	☐	☐
d. Does he listen rather than interrupt?	15.	☐	☐

2. Sharing

a. Does he share materials, without monopolizing their use?   16. ☐ ☐
b. Does he offer help when another child needs it?   17. ☐ ☐
c. Does he await his turn in playing or in games?   18. ☐ ☐
d. Does he await his turn for help from the teacher?   19. ☐ ☐

3. Self-Reliance

a. Does he work things through for himself without asking   20. ☐ ☐
the teacher about the next step?
b. Does he take care of his clothing and materials?   21. ☐ ☐
c. Does he find something to do when he finishes an assigned   22. ☐ ☐
task?
d. Does he take good care of materials assigned to him?   23. ☐ ☐

Emotional Readiness

1. Adjustment to task

a. Does the child seek a task, such as drawing, preparing?   24. ☐ ☐
b. Does he accept changes in school routine calmly?   25. ☐ ☐
c. Does he appear to be happy and well adjusted in school-   26. ☐ ☐
work, as evidenced by relaxed attitude, pride in work,
and eagerness for a new task?
d. Does he follow adult leadership without showing resent-   27. ☐ ☐
ment?

2. Poise

a. Does he accept a certain amount of opposition or defeat   28. ☐ ☐
without crying or sulking?
b. Does he meet strangers without displaying unusual shy-   29. ☐ ☐
ness?

Psychological Readiness

1. Mind set for reading

a. Does the child appear interested in books and reading?   30. ☐ ☐
b. Does he ask the meanings of words or signs?   31. ☐ ☐
c. Is he interested in the shapes of unusual words?   32. ☐ ☐

2. Mental maturity

a. Do the results of the child's mental test predict probable   33. ☐ ☐
success in learning to read?
b. Can he give reasons for his opinions about his own work   34. ☐ ☐
or the work of others?
c. Can he make or draw something to illustrate an idea as   35. ☐ ☐
well as most children his age?
d. Is his memory span sufficient to allow memorization of   36. ☐ ☐
a short poem or song?
e. Can he tell a story without confusing the order of events?   37. ☐ ☐
f. Can he listen or work for five minutes without rest-   38. ☐ ☐
lessness?

3. Mental habits

a. Has the child established the habit of looking at a suc-   39. ☐ ☐
cession of items from left to right?
b. Does his interpretation of pictures extend beyond mere   40. ☐ ☐
enumeration of details?

    c. Does he grasp the fact that symbols may be associated   41. ☐ ☐
       with spoken language?
    d. Can he predict possible outcomes for a story?   42. ☐ ☐
    e. Can he remember the central thought of a story as well   43. ☐ ☐
       as the important details?
    f. Does he alter his own method to profit by another child's   44. ☐ ☐
       example?

4. Language Patterns
    a. Does he take part in class discussions and conversations?   45. ☐ ☐
    b. Is he effective in expressing his needs in classroom situa- 46. ☐ ☐
       tions?
    c. Are the words used in the preprimers and the primer   47. ☐ ☐
       part of his listening and speaking vocabulary?
    d. Does he understand the relationship inherent in such   48. ☐ ☐
       words as up and down, top and bottom, big and little?
    e. Does he listen to a story with evidence of enjoyment and   49. ☐ ☐
       the ability to recall parts of it?
    f. Is he able to interpret an experience through dramatic   50. ☐ ☐
       play?

Not all the foregoing items will be pertinent to any one child. However, in general, the primary teacher will help children make a good start if she watches carefully their behavior related to the overlapping categories of their physical, social, emotional, and psychological readiness.

Prereading Rating Scale. To use the prereading rating scale, place a check in the appropriate box in front of the following questions. The test manual describes the use and interpretation of this scale in detail.

I.   Facility in Oral Language

Yes No
☐   ☐   1. Does the child take part in class discussions and conversations?
☐   ☐   2. Is he effective in expressing his needs in classroom situations?
☐   ☐   3. Can he tell a story or relate an experience effectively?

II.   Concept and Vocabulary Development

☐   ☐   4. Is he familiar with the words and concepts related to his environ-
          ment: for example, people, places, things, and activities?
☐   ☐   5. Does he have a knowledge of nursery rhymes and traditional chil-
          dren's stories and can he talk about them?
☐   ☐   6. Has he travel experiences within the community and to other places
          and can he describe them?

*Reprinted from pages 55–7 of the Manual for Teaching the Reading Readiness Program rev. ed. Ginn Boston, 1967 by David H. Russell, Odille Ousky, and Grace B. Haynes.

III. Listening Abilities

☐ ☐ 7. Is the child able to understand directions read or told to him?

☐ ☐ 8. Does he possess the ability to recall stories heard by providing the essential information and a sequence of events?

☐ ☐ 9. Is he able to memorize a short poem or story?

☐ ☐ 10. Is he a retentive and responsive listener?

IV. Skills in Critical and Creative Thinking

☐ ☐ 11. Does the child's interpretation of pictures extend beyond mere enumeration of details?

☐ ☐ 12. Can he predict possible outcomes for a story?

☐ ☐ 13. Does he express unique ideas about personal experiences, classroom happenings, and stories he has heard?

☐ ☐ 14. Does he demonstrate flexibility in his thinking patterns or does he have a "one-track mind"?

V. Social Skills

☐ ☐ 15. Is the child accepted by other children?

☐ ☐ 16. Can he play competitively with others?

☐ ☐ 17. Does he listen rather than interrupt?

☐ ☐ 18. Does he await his turn for help from the teacher?

VI. Emotional Development

☐ ☐ 19. Can the child accept some opposition or defeat?

☐ ☐ 20. Is he eager for new tasks and activities?

☐ ☐ 21. Can he accept changes in routine?

☐ ☐ 22. Does he appear to be happy and well adjusted in schoolwork?

VII. Attitude Toward and Interest in Reading

☐ ☐ 23. Does the child ask questions about letters, words, and numbers?

☐ ☐ 24. Has he grasped the fact that "writing is talk written down?

☐ ☐ 25. Is he enthusiastic about beginning to learn to read?

VIII. Work Habits

☐ ☐ 26. Can the child work by himself?

☐ ☐ 27. Can he see a task through to completion?

☐ ☐ 28. Can he find something to do when he finishes an assigned task?

Most vision problems are detected by the alert classroom teacher, who observes her students very closely during the act of reading. Some educators suggest that facial contortions, books held too closely to the face, tension during visual work, tilting of one's head, thrusting the head forward, body tension while observing distant objects, poor sitting positions, excessive hand movements, frequent rubbing of eyes, avoidance of close visual work, and loss of place while reading are clues that the reader is experiencing visual difficulty.

Informal Teacher Checklist

Student's name: _____

Date: _____

Skill	Definitely Yes	To a Degree	No	Comment
a. Can recognize letters				
b. Can rhyme				
c. Has memorized alphabet				
d. Can describe actions & pictures				
e. Can sound out words				
f. Can tell story about picture				
g. Can hold a pencil				
h. Can match objects that are the same or different				
i. Knows that written words mean spoken words				
j. Can put pictures in order				
k. Can write letters of alphabet				
l. Knows numbers				
m. Can write numbers				
n. Can name the colors				
o. Knows words about time (before, after, until)				
p. Can "read" simple stories				
q. Knows abstract words (happy brave)				
r. Knows words about space (front, back, above)				
s. Knows common nouns (dog, lake)				

Before assessing specific cognitive competencies, teachers should be certain that the child's vision and hearing are adequate for the task of reading. Auditory and visual acuity may often be initially assessed through observation.

Vision. Although there are many factors involved in the reading process, the subject of vision is certainly of prime importance because reading is basically a visual act. Seeing is central to reading because the printed stimulus enters the mind through the eye.

Spache (1973) describes the visual aspect of the reading process:

> his eyes hop or glide from one stop to the next, from left to right. He does not read in a smooth sweep along the line but only when the eyes are at rest in each fixation. During the sweeps or swings from one fixation to the next, the reader sees nothing clearly, for his eyes are temporarily out of focus. Each fixation, during which reading actually occurs, lasts from about a third of a second in young children to about a quarter of a second at the college level. In all probability most of the thinking that occurs during reading is done during this fractional part of a second, for a number of studies show that the duration of the fixation often lengthens if the reading material is very difficult. The fixations are the heart of the visual reading act, for they occupy about 90 per cent of the time for reading, while interfixation and return sweeps account for the rest.
>
> If the reader fails to recognize what he sees in a fixation, or to understand the idea offered, he tends to make regression. That is, he makes another fixation at approximately the same place or he swings backward to the left to read again. He may regress several times until the word is recognized or the idea comprehended before resuming the normal left-to-right series of fixations. Then near the end of each line he makes one big return sweep to a fixation close to the beginning of the next line. (p. 9)

Hearing. The development of *hearing* acuity precedes vocabulary development and may be viewed as a reading readiness base. Even the smallest impairment of auditory ability *may* cause problems with both language development and reading. Because research in this area is inconclusive, it is not obvious to what degree the reading process may be hindered by lack of auditory ability. Auditory discrimination relates to reading because a child's ability to hear small sound units and add meaning to the units is a word-analysis skill that is essential in reading. Readiness programs must provide tasks that help children perceive partial word utterances as well as whole word utterances.

The classroom teacher needs to be alert in order to detect symptoms that might suggest that a child is having hearing difficulty. Some common symptoms are *slurred or inaudible language, turning one's ear toward the speaker, interchanging words with similar sounds, inability to discriminate like or unlike sounds, cupping one's ear when listening, requesting that statements be repeated, earaches, frequent colds, and unnatural tonal quality of the voice.*

Santa Clara Unified School District Inventory of Developmental Tasks

Here is an example of a comprehensive inventory checklist, designed by the Santa Clara Unified School District, Santa Clara, California to assess vision and hearing and language/thought development. It has been used to assess certain aspects of readiness.

The following extremely comprehensive instrument has been described by its creators in terms of sequential and hierarchical skills. Before using this instrument, it is important to point out the taxonomic approach used in its creation. If you look at the scoring sheet first, the ordering will be quite clear.

Santa Clara Unified School District

Name   *Jim N.*   Date _____

Birthdate _____ School _____

Teacher _____ Grade/Type of Class _____

INVENTORY
of
DEVELOPMENTAL TASKS
An Observation Guide

0   1   2   40

Conceptual

| | 9.9 assign number value | | 9.10 identify position | | 9.11 tell how 2 items are alike | | 9.12 sort objects 2 ways |

0   1   2

Language

| | 8.8 give personal information | describe simple objects 8.9 | relate words and pictures 8.10 | define words 8.11 | use correct grammar 8.12 |

0   1   2

Auditory Memory

| | 7.7 perform 3 commands | repeat a sentence 7.8 | repeat a tapping sequence 7.9 | repeat 4 numbers 7.10 | recall story facts 7.11 | repeat 5 numbers 7.12 |

0   1   2

Auditory Perception

| | 6.6 discriminate between com. sound | identify common sounds 6.7 | Locate source of sound 6.8 | match beginning sounds 6.9 | hear diff. between words 6.10 | match rhyming sounds 6.11 | screen sounds 6.12 |

0   1   2

Visual Memory

| | 5.5 recall animal pictures | name objects from memory 5.6 | recall 3 color sequence 5.7 | recall 2 picture sequence 5.8 | reproduce design from memory 5.9 | recall picture sequence 5.10 | recall 3 part design 5.11 | recall word forms 5.12 |

0   1   2

Visual Perception

| | 4.4 match color objects | match form objects 4.5 | match size objects 4.6 | match size and form on paper 4.7 | match numbers 4.8 | match letter forms 4.9 | match direction on design 4.10 | isolate visual images 4.11 | match words 4.12 |

0   1   2

Visual Motor

| | 3.3 follow target with eyes | string beads 3.4 | copy a circle 3.5 | cut with scissors 3.6 | copy a cross 3.7 | copy a square 3.8 | tie shoes 3.9 | copy letters 3.10 | copy sentence 3.11 | form patterns 3.12 |

0   1   2

Coordination

| | 2.2 creep | walk 2.3 | run 2.4 | jump 2.5 | hop 2.6 | balance on one foot 2.7 | skip 2.8 | balance on walking beam 2.9 | show left and right 2.10 | jump rope assisted 2.11 | jump rope alone 2.12 |

0   1   2

| 1.1 | 1.2 | 1.3 | 1.4 | 1.5 | 1.6 | 1.7 | 1.8 | 1.9 | 1.10 | 1.11 | 1.12 |

| | Level 1   Pre-School | | | | | Level II 5–5½ yrs | | Level III 6–6½ yrs | | Level IV 7– yrs |

Each of the skills from coordination to conceptualization is ordered by ascending difficulty. Each of the tasks on the horizontal axis (2.2 creep to 2.12 jump rope alone) are also ordered by ascending difficulty. The complete list of tasks is presented with a model page from the *Santa Clara Guide*. This example page demonstrates the scoring procedure for each task; task 5.8, 5.9, and 5.10 are presented as examples.

Instructional Activities

Level

1. Attending Behavior

2. Coordination

I.
- 2.2 Can creep—crawling in homolateral, then cross-pattern
- 2.3 Can walk—timed: Rooster walk, Elephant Walk, Bear Ostrich
- 2.4 Can run—3-legged race, Bird run, Crab run, Dog run, Horse gallop
- 2.5 Can jump—chairs, blocks, hopscotch
- 2.6 Can hop—height, time
- 2.7 Can balance on one foot

II.
- 2.8 Can use hands and arms—right/left: Follow the Leader, Simon Says, Twister, teach body parts
- 2.9 Can skip and play skip-ball tag, lean while skipping

III.
- 2.10 Can balance on walking beam—hands behind back
- 2.11 Can jump rope, assisted

IV.
- 2.12 Can jump rope, unassisted

I.
3. Visual motor
- 3.3.1 Walking—A sitting student watching is able to follow a teacher walking around the room
- 2 Skipping—A sitting student watching is able to follow another child skipping around the room
- 3 Object focus — Look at _____ until I count to 5
- 4 Ball roll count aloud until ball stops
- 5 Gliders
- 6 Thumb focus
- 7 Pencil tracking—Practice directional objects
- 3.4 String beads, thread needles, sorting tasks (timed) make chains of colored strips (own patterns)
- 3.5 Can copy circle—Simple forms, complex forms, mazes

II.
- 3.7 Can copy cross—Follow numbers (dot-to-dot)
- 3.8 Can copy square—The Clock Game

III.
- 3.6 Can use scissors—Zigzag strips, geometric forms
- 3.10 Can copy letters—Copy-speed tests
- 3.11 Can copy simple words, then cut up and rearrange
- 3.12 Form Patterns—Tinker Toy construction projects (Play Tiles) ball and jacks, drawing people, catching the ball (see Bayne Hackett and Robert Jenson, A Guide to Movement Exploration. Peck Publications, Palo Alto, Calif.: 1966.
  Can copy diamond

Level

I. 4. <u>Visual perception</u>

    4.4 Can match color objects—Color-code typing
    4.5 Can match form objects—Use shape to make pictures
         Child has to match shapes to build the picture:

tree

    4.6 Can match size objects—Parquetry blocks to have child work a design
         on top of a marked paper
    4.7 Can match Size and Form on Paper—have child match a shape on
         on paper

II. 4.8 Can match numbers
     4.9 Can match letters

III. 4.10 Can match direction of design—Toy card (same direction?) Mirror
          patterns (see <u>Frostig's Manual</u>, pp. 149–150) Play camera, obstacle
          course

IV. 4.11 Can isolate visual images—Cloud pictures
     4.12 Can match words

I. 4. <u>Visual memory</u>

    5.5 Recalls animal pictures
    5.6 Can name objects from memory—Chalk, button
    5.7 Reproduce a visual sequence of three colors from memory, five color
         chips, three color flash cards: tell child to reproduce the order you
         just gave him/her
    5.8 Can recall a picture sequence
         One tachistoscope for building visual memory in one frame:
         in one frame:

    5.9 Can reproduce design from memory
         Draw from memory:

| c | a | t | Have children put one letter in a square

III. 5.10 Can reproduce a sequence of three pictures from memory
     5.11 Can recall impart design

IV. 5.12 Can recall word forms:

| Arzo | | Arpo Arno Arzo |

Expose target word for five seconds
Internal design
Match words in a list

Level

6. Auditory perception

    6.6　Can discriminate between common sounds
          Have children close eyes and listen for familiar sounds.
    6.7　Can identify common sounds—Cross the Road game
    6.8　Can locate source of sounds
    6.9　Can match beginning sounds
        1　I'm going to the _____ and I'm taking _____
        2　Rissen-Act game (aural version of Simon Says)
        3　Come Letter game
        4　Shopping at the Supermarket game
        5　Lost Squirrel game

III.   6.10　Can hear fine differences between similar words
          Badder-Lantern/Sheep Sleep/Cub Cup
IV.   6.11　Can match ending sounds

7. Auditory memory

    7.7　Can perform three commands
II.   7.8　Can repeat a sentence—Play Echo, rote poem
    7.9　Can repeat a tapping sequence
        Worksheet .　. . .　.　. .　. .　.
III.   7.10　Child repeats a series of four numbers:
          6　　2　　9　　7　forward, backward
    7.11　Can recall story facts—(Simple comprehension)
    7.12　Can repeat five numbers:
IV.   2 – 4 – 2 – 7 – 8　or　A – R – C – K – L

II. 8. Language

    8.8　Can give personal information—Who am I?
    8.9　Can describe simple objects
        The gift box
        Who was it?
        Come and find it
        What do I have in my hand?
        Feel box
        The Mystery box
III.   8.10　Can relate words and pictures—Giraffe/tall　　Rabbit/hop
    8.11　Can define words
IV.   8.12　Can use correct grammar
        Improve usage of see/saw
        (see And to Think I Saw It on Mulberry Street, Dr. Seuss)
        Improve usage of was/were

II. 9. Conceptual

    9.9　Can assign number value
        Which is bigger? 5 or 8
III.   9.10　Can identify first, last, or middle
    9.11　Can tell how two things are alike
        Riddles
        Grouping/card-sorting tasks

Find identical objects in a room

Subclasses—e.g., animals, dogs, collies

Complete functional sentences—e.g., Knives are to cut with.

9.12 Can sort objects two ways:

Place things in categories

Learning-to-think series

Sample Sheet from Guide

Visual Memory   Level II   Task 5.8

5.8 Reproduce a sequence of two pictures from memory.

Material: Five picture cards, three flash cards

Procedure: Show child a flash card for five seconds. Say: "First this, then this." Remove card from view. Say: "Make one just like mine." Child reproduces the sequence seen on the flash card by arranging two pictures in the proper order.

Scoring Procedure

Scoring:

0	1	2
Child has two or more errors.	Child has one error.	Child has all correct.

Visual Memory   Level II   Task 5.9

5.9 Reproduce designs from memory   ←—o   o—⌐   ⋈

Material: Three picture flash cards

Procedure: Say: "I'm going to show you a card with a drawing on it. After I turn the card over, you draw one just like the one on the card." Show child the card for five seconds.

Scoring:

0	1	2
Child cannot reproduce two or more designs.	Child fails to reproduce one design.	Child can reproduce the three forms accurately.

Visual Memory   Level III   Task 5.10

5.10 Reproduce a sequence of three pictures from memory.

Material: Five picture cards and three picture flash cards.

Procedure: Show child a flash card for five seconds. Say: "First this, then this, then this." (point left to right.) Remove card from view. Say: "Make one just like mine." Child reproduces the sequence seen on the flash card by arranging three pictures in the proper order.

Scoring:

0	1	2
Child has two or more errors.	Child has one error.	Child has them all correct.

Reading Readiness Tests

You may wish to use standardized readiness tests as well as informal checklists and subjective observations to assess beginning student competencies.

Some readiness tests that may prove useful include the Clymer-Barrett Pre-reading Battery, Gates-MacGinitie Readiness Skills Test, Harrison–Stroud Reading Readiness Profiles, Macmillan Reading Readiness Test, and the Metropolitan Readiness Test. Generally, these contain subtests designed to check visual and auditory discrimination, vocabulary, hand-eye coordination, and knowledge of letters of the alphabet. Either directly or indirectly, attention span and ability to listen to and follow directions can be evaluated through the child's performance on these tests.

First-grade intelligence tests may also be used. These are group tests and are in many ways similar to readiness tests. However, readiness tests are believed to provide a better prediction of beginning reading success than the intelligence tests.

Most formal reading readiness tests include some items similar to the following:
1. Associating pictures with the spoken word. The child has a series of four

   pictures. He is asked to circle the shoe.
2. Visual discrimination.
3. Sentence comprehension.
4. Drawing a human figure.
5. Counting and writing numbers.
6. Word recognition
7. Copying.
8. Auditory discrimination.

A language readiness test which may be of help to you is the Illinois Test of Psycholinguistic Ability (ITPA). Its results provide a comprehensive check of language development; the test is designed to check development in receptive, associative, and expressive processes; visual, auditory and motor channels of communication; and automatic/sequential and representational levels of organization. The test is administered individually; considerable practice is required for effective administration and scoring because of time considerations and the complexity of the test. It is more feasible to use this test with special cases that require individual testing than all children.

QUESTIONS AND RELATED READINGS

If at this time you do not feel that you have attained adequate knowledge to successfully answer the following questions, we would like to suggest related readings.

Goal 1: To aid students in understanding historical explanations for readiness practices in the United States.

Question 1: Why did readiness factors become fixed in school curricula?

Ausubel, David P. "Viewpoints from Related Disciplines: Human Growth and Development," *Teachers College Record,* 60 (Feb. 1959), 245–54.

Durkin, Dolores. "When Should Children Begin to Read?" *Innovation and Change in Reading Instruction*, Sixty-seventh Yearbook of the National Society for the Study of Education, Part II. Chicago: University of Chicago Press, 1968, Chap. 20

Gates, Arthur I., and Guy L. Bond. "Reading Readiness: A Study of Factors Determining Success and Failure in Beginning Reading." *Teachers College Record* XXXVII (March 1936), 679–85.

Goal 2: To aid students in understanding the need for defining readiness as a child's existing capacity for completing a specific task

Question 2: What are the various ways that one can define a child's readiness for completing a specific task?

Aukerman, Robert C., ed. *Some Persistent Questions on Beginning Reading.* Newark, Del.: International Reading Association, 1972.

Durkin, Dolores. "When Should Children Begin to Read?" In *Innovation and Change in Reading Instruction,* edited by Herman G. Richey. NSSE Yearbook, Part II. Chicago: University of Chicago Press, 1968.

Hymes, James L., Jr. *Before the Child Reads.* New York: Harper & Row, Publishers, 1964.

Goal 3: To aid students in understanding the components of a model prereading program in preschool and kindergarten.

Question 3: What are the various teaching strategies used in preschool and kindergarten?

Howes, Virgil M., and Helen F. Darrows. *Reading and the Elementary School Child.* New York: Macmillan Publishing Co., Inc., 1968.

Karlin, Robert, ed. *Perspectives on Elementary Reading.* Part III. New York: Harcourt Brace Jovanovich, Inc., 1973.

Robinson, Helen M., ed. *Sequential Development of Reading Abilities.* Proceedings of the Annual Conference on Reading. Vol. 22. Chicago: University of Chicago Press, 1960.

Goal 4: To aid students in understanding reading teaching strategies in preschools and kindergarten

Question 4: What are some of the ways of teaching reading strategies in preschools and kindergarten?

Chappel, Bernice M. *Listening and Learning.* Belmont, Calif.: Fearon Publishers, 1973.

Dorsey, Mary E. *Reading Games and Activities.* Belmont, Calif. Lear Siegler, Inc./Fearon Publishers, 1972

Merrick, Virgin E., and Marcella Nerbovig. *Using Experience Charts with Children.* Columbus, Ohio: Charles E. Merrill Publishing Company, 1964.

Goal 5: To aid students in understanding the assessment instruments that measure aspects of readiness

Question 5: Name various instruments with which aspects of readiness are measured.

Boland, Mary Ellen, and David Trachtenberg. *Handbook of Reading Readiness Activities.* Middletown, N.Y.: City School District Board of Education, 1969.

Platts, Mary E. *LAUNCH: A Handbook for Early Learning Techniques for the Preschool and Kindergarten Teachers.* Stevensville, Mich.: Educational Service, Inc., 1972.

Tinker, Miles A. *Preparing Your Child for Reading.* New York: Holt, Rinehart and Winston, 1971.

BIBLIOGRAPHY

Arthur, G. "A Quantitative Study of the Results of Grouping First Grade Children According to Mental Age." *Journal of Educational Research,* 12 (Oct. 1925), 173–85.

Artley, A. Sterl. "A Study of Certain Factors Presumed to be Associated with Reading and Speech Difficulties." *Journal of Speech and Hearing Disorders,* 13 (1948) 351–60.

Ausubel, D. P. "Viewpoints from Related Disciplines: Human Growth and Development." *Teachers College Record,* 60 (Feb. 1959), 245–54.

Almy, M. "The Importance of Children's Experiences to Success in Beginning Reading." In *Research in the Three R's,* edited by R. Hunnicutt and W. Iverson. New York: Harper & Row, Publishers, 1958.

Ball, S., and G. A. Bogatz. "Research on *Sesame Street*: Some Implications for Compensatory Education." Paper presented at the Second Annual Blumberg Symposium in Early Childhood Education, 1971. Johns Hopkins Press.

Barrett, T. C. "Visual Discrimination Tasks as Predictors of First Grade Reading Achievement." *Reading Teacher,* 18 (1965), 276–82.

Beck, I. L. *A Longitudinal Study of the Reading Achievement Effects of Formal Reading Instruction in the Kindergarten: A Summative and Formative Evaluation.* Ph. D. dissertation, University of Pittsburgh, 1973.

Bellugi, U., and R. Brown, eds. *The Acquisition of Language.* Chicago: University of Chicago Press, 1971.

Bond, G. L., and R. Dykstra. "The Cooperative Research Program in First Grade Reading Instruction." *Reading Research Quarterly,* 2 (1967), 5–142.

Bryan, Q. "Relative Importance of Intelligence and Visual Perception in Predicting Reading Achievement. *California Journal of Educational Research,* 15 (1964), 44–8.

Buktenica, N. "Group Screening of Auditory and Visual Perception Abilities: An Approach to Perceptual Aspects of Beginning Reading." Paper Presented at the American Education Research Association Convention, April 1969, Washington, D.C.

Caldwell, B. M. "The Usefulness of the Critical Period Hypothesis in the Study of Filiative Behavior." In *Contemporary Issues in Developmental Psychology,* edited by N. D. Endler, L. R. Boulter and H. Osser. New York: Holt, Rinehart and Winston, 1969, pp. 213–23.

Calfee, R., R. Chapman, and R. Venezky. "How a Child Needs to Think to Learn to Read." In *Cognition in Learning and Memory,* edited by L. Gregg. New York: John Wiley & Sons, Inc., 1972, 139–82.

Calfee, R., and K. Hoover. "Policy and Practice in Early Education Research." Paper presented at the California Council for Educational Research, November 1973, Los Angeles, California.

Chisholm, D., and J. Knafle. "Letter-Name Knowledge as a Prerequisite to Learning to Read." Paper presented at the American Education Research Association Convention, April 1975, Washington, D.C.

DeHirsch, K., J. J. Jansky, and W. S. Langford. *Predicting Reading Failure.* New York: Harper & Row, Publishers, 1966.

Durkin, D. *Children Who Read Early: Two Longitudinal Studies.* New York: Bureau of Publications, Teachers College Press, Columbia University, 1966.

———. "A Language Arts Program for Pre-First Grade Children: Two-Year Achievement Report." *Reading Research Quarterly,* 5 (Summer 1970), 534–565.

———. *Teaching Them to Read.* Boston: Allyn & Bacon, Inc., 1974.

———. *Teaching Young Children to Read.* Boston: Allyn & Bacon, Inc., 1972.

Durrell, D. D. "First-Grade Reading Success Story: A Summary." *Journal of Education,* 140 (1958), 2–6.

Fromkin, V., and R. Rodman. *An Introduction to Language.* New York: Holt, Rinehart and Winston, 1974.

Gates, A. I. "The Necessary Mental Age for Beginning Reading." *Elementary School Journal,* 37 (1937), 497–508.

———. "The Role of Personality Maladjustment in Reading Disability." In *Children with Reading Problems,* edited by G. Matchez. New York: Basic Books, Inc., Publishers, 1968, pp. 80–6.

———. and G. L. Bond. "Reading Readiness: A Study of Factors Determining Success and Failure in Beginning Reading." *Teachers College Record,* 37 (May 1936), 679–85.

Gavel. S. R. "June Reading Achievements of First-Grade Children." *Journal of Education,* 140 (1958), 37–43.

Gesell, A. *The First Five Years of Life.* New York: Harper & Row, Publishers, 1940.

———. and Ilg, F. *"The Child From Five to Ten."* New York: Harper & Row, 1946.

Gibson, E. and H. Levin, *Psychology of Reading.* Cambridge, Massachusetts: MIT Press, 1975.

Gibson, E. J., J. J. Gibson, A. D. Pick, and H. A. Osser. "A Developmental Study of the Discrimination of Letter-Like Forms." *Journal of Comparative and Physiological Psychology,* 55 (1962), 897–906.

Goins, J. T. "Visual Perception Abilities and Early Reading Progress." *Supplementary Educational Monograph,* 87 (1958), 116–128.

Gray, W. S., and R. Klaus. "The Early Training Project: A Seventh-Year Report." *Child Development,* 41 (Dec. 1970), 900–24.

Hallgren, B. "Specific Dyslexia: A Clinical and Genetic Study." *Acta Psychiatrica et Neurologia,* 65 (1950), 1–287.

Havighurst, R. *Human Development and Education.* New York: Longman, Inc., 1953.

Holmes, M. C. "Investigation of Reading Readiness of First Grade Entrants." *Childhood Education,* 3 (Jan. 1927), 215–21.

Huey, E. B. *The Psychology and Pedagogy of Reading.* New York: Macmillan Publishing Co., Inc., 1908.

Hunt, J. M. *Intelligence and Experience.* New York: The Ronald Press Company, 1961.

Ingram, T. T. S. "The Nature of Dyslexia." In *Early Experience and Visual Information Processing in Perceptual and Reading Disorders,* edited by F. A. Young and D. B. Lindsley. Washington, D.C.: National Academy of Sciences, 1970, 405–44.

Jansky, J. and K. DeHirsch. *Preventing Reading Failure.* New York: Harper & Row, Publishers, 1972.

King, E. M., and D. T. Friesen. "Children Who Read in Kindergarten." *Alberta Journal of Educational Research,* 18 (Sept. 1972), 147–61.

Kohlberg, L. "Early Education: A Cognitive-Developmental View." *Child Development,* 39 (Dec. 1968), 1013–62.

Lenneberg, E. H. *Biological Foundations of Language.* New York: John Wiley & Sons, Inc., 1967.

Loban, W. D. *The Language of Elementary School Children.* Champaign, Ill.: National Council of Teachers of English, 1963.

Lohnes, P. R., and M. M. Gray. "Intelligence and the Cooperative Reading Studies." *Reading Research Quarterly,* 3 (Spring 1972).

MacGinitie, W. N. "Evaluating Readiness for Learning to Read: A Critical Review and Evaluation of Research." *Reading Research Quarterly,* 4 (Spring 1969), 396–410.

McKee, D., J. Brzinski, and L. Harrison. "The Effectiveness of Teaching Reading in Kindergarten." Cooperative Research Project No. 5-1371. Denver Public Schools and Colorado State Department of Education, 1966.

McNeill, D. "Developmental Psycholinguistics." In Smith, F. and Miller, G. A. (eds.) *The Genesis of Language.* Cambridge, Mass.: MIT Press, 1966.

Menyuk, P. "Syntactic Structures in the Language of Children." *Journal of Child Development,* 34 (1963), 407–22.

Menyuk, P. *The Acquisition and Development of Language.* Englewood Cliffs, New Jersey.: Prentice-Hall, 1971.

Money, J. "On Learning and Not Learning to Read." In *The Disabled Reader: Education of the Dyslexic Child,* edited by J. Money. Baltimore: The Johns Hopkins University Press, 1966, pp. 21–40.

Morphett, M. and Washburne, C. "When Should Children Begin to Read?" *Elementary School Journal* XXXI (March, 1931), 496–503.

Morgan, E. "Efficacy of Two Tests in Differentiating Potentially Low From Average and High First Grade Readers." *Journal of Educational Research,* 53 (1960), 300–4.

Muehl, S. and Kremenack, S. "Ability to Match Information Within and Between Auditory and Visual Sense Modalities and Subsequent Reading Achievement," *Journal of Educational Psychology* 57 (4), 1966, 230–239.

National Task Force on Dyslexia and Related Reading Disorders. U. S. Department of Health, Education and Welfare, 1969.

Olson, A. V. "Growth in Word Perception Abilities as It Relates to Success in Beginning Reading. *Journal of Education,* 140 (1958), 25–36.

——. and C. Johnson. "Structure and Predictive Validity of the Frostig Developmental Test of Visual Perception in Grades One and Three." *Journal of Special Education,* 4 (1970), 49–52.

Olson, W. C. *Child Development.* Boston: D. C. Heath & Company, 1949.

Owens, F., P. Adams, and T. Forrest. "Learning Disabilities in Children: Sibling Studies." *Bulletin of the Orton Society,* 18 (1968), 33–62.

Reed, M. M. *An Investigation of Practices in First Grade Admission and Promotion.* New York: Bureau of Publications, Teachers College Press, Columbia University, 1927.

Robinson, H. M. "Vocabulary: Speaking, Listening, Reading and Writing." In *Reading and the Language Arts,* edited by H. A. Robinson. Chicago: University of Chicago Press, 1963.

Russell, D. *Manual for Teaching the Reading Readiness Program.* Lexington, Massachusetts: Ginn and Company, 1967.

Satz, P. and Van Nostrand, G. "Developmental Dyslexia: An Evaluation of a Theory." Part II *The Disabled Learner,* 1973, 121–148.

Samuels, S. J. "The Effect of Letter-Name Knowledge on Learning to Read." *American Educational Research Journal,* 9 (1972), 65–74.

Schickendanz, J., M. York, I. Stewart, and D. White. *Strategies for Teaching Young Children*. Englewood Cliffs, N.J.: Prentice-Hall, Inc., 1977.

Shapiro, B., and R. Willford. "ITA. Kindergarten or First Grade?" *Reading Teacher*, (Jan. 1969).

Silvaroli, N. J. "Factors in Predicting Children's Success in First Grade Reading." In *Reading and Inquiry International*, Reading Association Conference Readings, edited by J. A. Figurel, Vol. 10, 1965, pp. 296–298, Newark, Delaware: IRA Publications.

Silver, L. B. "Familial Patterns in Children with Neurologically Based Learning Disabilities." *Journal of Learning Disabilities*, 4 (1971), 349–58.

Silverberg, N., et al. "The Effects of Kindergarten Instruction in Alphabet and Numbers on First Grade Reading." Final Report. Minneapolis: Kenny Rehabilitation Institute, 1968.

Spache, G. D., and E. B. Spache, *Reading in the Elementary School*. Boston: Allyn & Bacon, Inc., 1973.

Suppes, P. "Mathematical Concept Formation in Children." *American Psychologist*, 21 (1966), 139–50.

Weiner, M., and S. Feldman. "Validation Studies of a Reading Prognosis Test for Children of Lower and Middle Socio-Economic Status." *Educational and Psychological Measurement*, 23 (1963), 807–14.

White, B. *First Three Years*, Englewood-Cliffs, N. J.: Prentice Hall, 1975.

Wilson, F. T., and C. W. Fleming. "Grade Trends in Reading Progress in Kindergarten and Primary Grades." *Journal of Educational Psychology*, 31 (1960), 1–13.

4

Activities for preschool

If we provide a game situation for the child, and his/her winning or doing well in the game depends largely on being able to apply new learnings to the game, the learning *does* become important. Now the child *wants* to remember what was just learned. He or she is caught up in the excitement of competing and there is a pay-off for remembering. The child enjoys the informality and socialness of the game situation and is eager to prove his capabilities to his peers. In brief, children love playing games.

A Practical Guide to Creating Reading Games. (Cambridge, Mass.: EDCO, Reading and Learning Center, 1974).

In this chapter several activities and games are presented for teachers who are preparing young children for reading.

Directionality

According to Spache (1972) discriminations of forms and shapes are based fundamentally on the bodily hand-and-eye experience of each child. These discriminations (left-right, up-down) are first learned in the muscles. During the early years, a child gradually learns to transfer these muscular cues into visual cues. Then he is ready to apply these visual cues to reading.

Not every child needs training in this area. Even the children who do need extra practice will vary in the amount of time they need. The following section offers some practical games that a classroom teacher might find helpful when attempting to aid children in developing skills in directionality.

1. Run the Obstacle Course

Goal: Body coordination

Grade level: K–1

Construction: Set up a small obstacle course in the gym or outside, using inner tubes, balance beam, and hoola hoops, for example. Put up charts showing the course to follow, using such illustrations as "walk across the beam," "jump through the tires," "hop on one foot," and "twirl the hoop five times."

Utilization: Students go through the course as quickly and as accurately as possible.

2. Help

Goal: Working from left to right

Grade level: Preschool

Construction and utilization: Give the children a worksheet divided into various sections. Each section is a separate story, with each story consisting of the same direction from left to right. Ask the children to trace the dotted arrow leading from left to right.

Example:

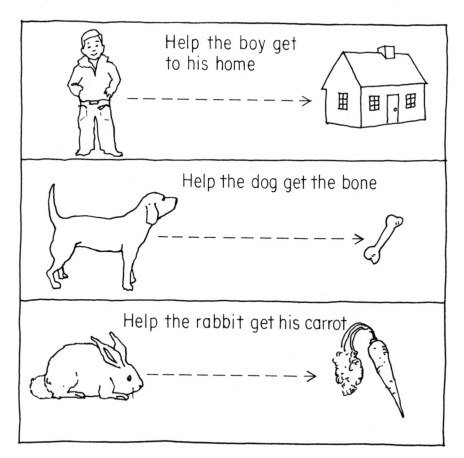

Help the boy get to his home

Help the dog get the bone

Help the rabbit get his carrot

3. Sewing Cards

Goal: Left to right—alphabet recognition

Grade level: Preschool

Construction: Make large cards out of oak tag. On the left, make capital letters going from top to bottom. Punch a hole to the right of each capital letter. On the right side of the card make corresponding small alphabet letters with holes punched to the left of the letters.

Utilization: The child then takes colored yarn and "sews" the capital letters to the corresponding small letter, by threading left to right. A variation of this activity might be to use pictures instead of letters.

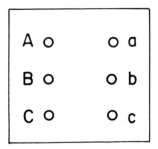

4. Labeling

Goal: Left and right discrimination

Grade level: K +

Construction and utilization: If the child has an individual desk, label the upper left-hand corner with an "L" and the upper right hand corner with an "R." At various times during the day, instruct the children to "put your papers on the left side of your desk" or to "rest your head on the right side of your desk." Refer to left and right frequently during the day, using their labeled desks as reference points.

5. Patterns

Goal: Left to right

Grade level: Preschool +

Construction: The teacher should cut long strips of paper. The paper should be divided in the center. Using a stamp pad and stamps of various shapes or pictures, the teacher stamps several designs in a row on the left of the paper.

Utilization: The child then follows the pattern and duplicates the design.

Visual Memory and Discrimination

Research related to the development of visual skills is controversial. Durkin (1974) strongly recommends dealing with visual skills through letters and words. Spache (1976) argues the opposite, suggesting that the first developmental stage of form discrimination is followed by three-dimensional materials and, finally, by the use of paper and pencil in two-dimensional reproduction and matching. She feels that shapes and forms *are* closely related to the hand-eye movements of writing and the visual movements of reading.

The New York City *Guide to Understanding and Fostering Intellectual Development in Young Children* (1965) also states that a child is first able to distinguish an object of one shape from that of another through his/ or her contact with the environment.

Whichever view one adopts, it is clear that some children entering school have not reached the stage of development whereby certain visual cues can be applied to reading. In the following section the classroom teacher is provided with some useful games to help the child who needs visual skills development.

6. A Lotta Lotto

Goal: Visual discrimination

Grade level: K-1

Construction: Using oak tag or cardboard, design a small lotto board of three or four columns with three different shapes drawn in each. The shapes should be different in size and color. Make matching cards for the shapes drawn on the boards.

Utilization: Cards are spread face down on the floor and each player in turn draws a card and tries to match it to an identical shape on his board. If he cannot, the card must be passed to the person on his right who then gets a chance to match it to his lotto board. If he cannot use it either, it is passed to the right until someone can use it. The first player to fill his card wins.

7. Read My Mind

Goal: Color, size, and shape discrimination

Grade level: K-1

Construction: Use attribute blocks of various colored and sized triangles, circles, and squares.

Utilization: The teacher tells the class, "I am thinking of an object. You must guess which object I am thinking about by asking me questions that can only be answered with yes or no. For example, you may ask if it is blue, or if it is small, or if it is a triangle." Put out simple objects first, such as circles. When the children get the idea of identifying the selected object, progress to more varied blocks, like triangles and squares.

8. I Saw That . . .

Goal: Visual memory

Grade level: K-1

Construction and utilization: The teacher walks around the room and touches three objects. In turn, each child touches the same three objects but adds another to the series. Play continues until someone forgets to touch an object.

9. Matching Shapes, Sizes, and Colors

Goals: Visual discrimination: Shapes, colors, and sizes

Grade level: K-1

Construction: Prepare a collection of geometric shapes of graduated sizes in the basic colors. (Or prepare wooden shapes that can be painted.) This collection might include circles, squares, rectangles, triangles, hexagons, and octagons.

Utilization: Numerous uses can be made of these:
1. All objects of the same color can be grouped.
2. All objects of the same shape can be grouped.
3. All objects of the same shape and color can be grouped. These also can be arranged in order of size.

Note: It is not necessary for children to be able to name the different geometric forms in order to play or benefit from this game. However, the names can be taught as directions are given and games are played.

10. Finding the Relationship

Goal: Visual discrimination: matching pictures that are the same or have some common element

Grade level: K-1

Construction: Collect and mount individually on cards:
1. Several pairs of identical pictures
2. Several pictures having different content but some similar element
3. Series of pictures that tell a story

Utilization: Suggested uses for each of the collections:

1. Identical picture pairs:
   a. An individual is given the set and asked to match all pairs.
   b. Individuals in a group are given a card. Then each player matches his card to the identical card of another player.
2. Having several pictures to examine, the player is asked to choose those having: (a) something green, (b) a house, (c) people, (d) animals, (e) a country setting, (f) a city setting. The possibilities are limitless.
3. The player is given a set of cards portraying a story and is asked to arrange them in the correct order.

Variation: The player is given one picture that does not belong or he is asked to tell the story shown by the cards.

11. Finding Similarities and Differences

Goal: Visual discrimination: letters

Grade level: K-1

Construction: This can be played with plastic or styrofoam letters, construction paper letters, or letters on work sheets. Directions here are for using plastic letters.

Utilization:

1. Arrange groups of letters, all of which are identical except for one which is strikingly different. Ask players to find and remove the different letters.

   Example: A   A   A   C   A   A

   b   b   b   b   w   b

2. Arrange groups of letters that are <u>more</u> similar. Again, have the different letter found.

Example: H   R   H   H   H   H
          c   c   o   c   c   c

3. Give each player several letters and have him group the ones that are the same.
4. Make a pattern with letters and let players copy with their letters. Your design may or may not spell a word.

12. Match the Word

<u>Goal</u>: Visual discrimination: word forms

<u>Grade level</u>: K–1

<u>Construction</u>: Mark a piece of heavy chart paper off in word-sized squares. Using a magic marker, fill the blocks with word forms. Make a set of word cards.

call	Dan	see
town	music	father
house	boat	school

<u>Utilization</u>: Ask players to match word pairs by placing their word cards on the square having the same word. This can be made for an individual game or, if larger charts are made, it can become a group activity with children taking turns matching word cards that have been distributed to them.

<u>Variation</u>: Children may select a card from the face-up (or face-down) cards to match with a chart word.

13. Connect the Pairs

<u>Goal</u>: Visual discrimination: word forms

<u>Grade level</u>: K–1

<u>Construction</u>: Prepare word cards or work sheets having three-word clusters. If word cards or work sheets are used, they should be similar to the following:

	saw			come
man			came	
	man			came
	hand			brother
hand			mother	
	yellow			mother
	ball			time
ball			time	
	bell			team
	see			about
sun			apple	
	sun			apple

<u>Utilization</u>: Players should be asked to draw a line to connect the words that look the same. Or, if word cards are used, they can put the matching words together.

Auditory Memory and Discrimination

The relationship between auditory memory and discrimination ability and success in beginning reading is an area of importance to reading educators who continue to debate which sounds a child should be able to auditorially discriminate in order to succeed in reading. Durkin (1972) feels that discrimination tasks should focus on real words because the children will be working with these words in reading. Spache (1976), on the other hand, feels that this ultimate goal of having children discriminate letter sounds in different words is founded on *many* types of listening exercises. She claims that the child must first be able to discriminate loudness, rhythmic patterns, and pitch, for example. These skills, she feels, are directly related to phonics and structural analysis, for it is here that the child is asked to discriminate the pitches of letter sounds, the loudness that determines accent, and the comparative duration of the sounds of vowels and consonants.

Since auditory discrimination is an important skill, the following section may prove useful to you in your teaching endeavor.

14. Musical Medials

<u>Goal</u>: Auditory discrimination of medial sounds

<u>Grade level</u>: K-1

<u>Construction and utilization</u>: This is a good activity to use right before music class. Pass out various instruments such as tambourines, shakers, triangles, bells, and two sticks. Say pairs of words, some of which will have medial sounds that are the same. As soon as the children hear two words with the same medial sound, they may make noise with the instruments.

15. Can You Tell Which?

<u>Goal</u>: Auditory discrimination: heightened awareness and perception of sound.

<u>Grade level</u>: K-1

<u>Construction</u>: Secure a piano or a xylophone (or you may want to use your own voice for this).

<u>Utilization</u>: Play (or sing) two series of notes and have the children tell you (1) which note was higher or lower and (2) which note was louder or softer.

<u>Variations</u>: Play (or sing) two series of notes and have the children tell you (1) whether the two were the same or different and (2) whether one series was faster or slower. Choose a familiar song and play it (or hum the melody) with varying tempos to suggest different moods. Have children decide how the changes made them feel. For example, "Mary Had a Little Lamb" played with a fast, rollicking rhythm might make them feel like dancing. A slow, heavy rhythm might make them feel tired. To extend the use of this, the children might express their interpretations through facial expressions or body movements.

16. Picture Match: Beginning Sounds

<u>Goal</u>: Auditory discrimination: initial sounds

<u>Grade level</u>: K-1

<u>Construction</u>: Develop a file of picture cards, each of which has pairs of objects and most of which have names beginning with the same sound. Objects pictured should be things the children using the game will recognize quickly and easily.

<u>Utilization</u>: Individuals may play this game alone, placing cards having pictures of objects beginning with the same sound in one stack and those that do not in another. The stacks may be checked by the teacher or by another player with the teacher as consultant if there is any disagreement about categorization.

<u>Variation</u>: Prepare picture cards having only one object on each card. Seat a group of children around a table or in a circle on the floor. Deal three cards to each child in the group. Place additional cards in a stack in the center of the group. Each player checks to see if he has any matching sound cards. If he does, he places them on the table. Beginning with a designated student, one player draws a card from the hand of the player on his left and makes any matches he can. The person from whose hand a card was drawn may pick up a new card from the stack, but he cannot place any cards on the table until it is his turn to play. Proceed around the circle until the stack of cards has been used. Then players having cards left may check

around the circle as their turn to play comes, in order to see who has a matching card. He may then claim it. When the cards have all been matched, each player in turn must call the names of his pairs while others listen to determine if he is correct.

Note: In this exercise, players must listen to and follow directions, they must cooperate, and they must articulate the names of the pictured objects.

17. Which Words Begin Alike?

Goal: Auditory discrimination: initial sounds in words

Grade level: K-1

Construction: Develop lists of word pairs (similar to those listed here), most of which have the same beginning sound. It may be helpful to work with words that begin with single consonants before including words beginning with consonant blends.

bat	go	loose
bell	get	lump
car	help	toy
come	half	tan
dog	jello	man
danger	jack	mat

Utilization: To use this game with a group and gain some assurance that each child is thinking for himself, the teacher may ask children to close their eyes or put their heads on their desks. When children hear a pair of words that sound alike at the beginning, they may raise their hands. When words do not have the same beginning sound, children should make no response.

18. Rhyming Words

Goal: Auditory discrimination:

Grade level: K-1

Construction: Prepare lists of word pairs, the majority of which rhyme. Decide before preparing your list how many sounds you wish to use with your particular group at one time.

call	bed	hot
ball	fed	not
man	met	pat
tan	fret	pet
land	tan	make
sand	Sam	take
father	come	box
brother	some	rocks

Utilization: If the game is to be played with an individual, the words should be pronounced distinctly and correctly but without exaggeration. The student indicates whether the pair of words sound alike (rhyme).

To use the game with a group, give each player several blue and yellow tokens or pieces of construction paper. Have each player select a blue token if the words rhyme and a yellow token if they do not. These may be arranged in a straight row across the player's desk. When the list is completed, the teacher may quickly check each child's arrangement of tokens to determine if he is succeeding or having difficulty. The teacher may need to remind children of color coding as the game is being played: "If these words rhyme, place a blue token in the line; if they do not, place a yellow token in the line." If some children have difficulty with some of the pairs or if additional reinforcement would be helpful, the teacher can repeat the list and let children respond orally while they check their own arrangements of the tokens.

A circular seating arrangement is not advisable for this game. Children should be seated so that what other players are doing is not distracting.

19. Name An Object

Goal: Auditory discrimination: beginning or rhyming sounds

Grade level: K-1

Construction: This game requires no specially prepared materials. It should be be played in a setting having many objects that children can identify.

Utilization: Have children name pairs of objects found in the playing area that either begin with the same sound or that rhyme. Examples: cabinet, corner; window, wall; chalk, chair; wall, ball; chair, hair; blocks, box.

Variation: One player may name an object or simply give a word that the player on his right must match. Occasional exchanging of positions in a circle is helpful if the game continues very long.

20. Hearing Middle Sounds

Goal: Auditory discrimination: medial sounds

Grade level: K-1

Construction: As is true for many such activities, this game has many possibilities for variation. To begin, one might develop lists of words such as the following:

Type I

bad	pop	come	ham
bed	pep	came	hum
pet	hat	mouse	stump
pit	hot	moose	stomp

Type II

child	came	note	sum
mind	raise	soak	buck
split	hand	pond	fuse
thin	fat	boat	funnel
same	sent	cat	tune
floor	tell	bond	pure

Utilization: With words such as those in Type I, the players can indicate whether the sounds they hear in the middle of the words are the same or different. In these words, the only sound differences are those found in medial positions.

With Type-II words, the same information is desired, but the player does not get the support that comes when all other sounds are the same.

21. Matching Middle Sounds

Goal: Auditory discrimination: medial sounds in words

Grade level: K-1

Construction: Develop clusters of words similar to those listed here:

cat	set	feet	reed	sit	met
	slap		road		fit

Utilization: Pronounce the words in each cluster asking the child to listen for the word that has the same middle sound as in the first word.

Variation: This same technique can be applied to beginning and ending sounds.

22. Supply the Ending

Goal: Listening and interpretation

Grade level: K-1

Construction and utilization: Select a story and begin reading the story until the major facts have been revealed. Stop and let the listeners finish the story. Accept any reasonable ending.

Oral Expression and Concept Building

Most educators would agree that what cannot be understood when spoken cannot be understood when written. Simply stated, all of the different aspects of language are interrelated and interdependent. The teacher who cares about reading generally plans a program which extends her children's language learning through their everyday experiences. The need for continuous language learning is stressed by Brown (1958) when he says:

> The usefulness of being able to sound a new word depends on the state of the reader's speaking vocabulary. If the word that is unfamiliar in printed form is also unfamiliar in spoken form the reader who can sound it out will not understand the word any better than the reader who cannot sound it. . . . The real advantage in being able to sound a word that is unfamiliar in print only appears when the word is familiar in speech.   (p. 69)

A teacher's goal should be to help children grow in the ability to use language. There is so much that can be done with every young child. The following section provides some games that may be useful in accomplishing this goal.

23. "Month" Words

Goal: Increase oral vocabulary

Grade level: Preschool +

Construction and utilization: Place the name of each new month on chart paper. Then have the class think of as many words as they can that have to do with that month. Children can use these words later to create their own stories.

Examples:

March

St. Patrick's Day
birthdays (children in the room)
pinwheels
spring
windy
kites
lion
lamb

24. Tell the Story

Goal: Oral interpretation

Grade level: K-1

Construction: Collect, mount, and laminate pictures of scenes or situations to which prereaders can readily relate.

Utilization: Choose a picture. Allow children in a small group to study the picture for a minute while they decide what story the picture tells. Then let them take turns telling their stories to the class. Encourage reticent children to tell all they can about the picture.

25. I See . . .

Goal: Listening and using concept-loaded words

Grade level: Preschool +

Construction and utilization: The teacher or another child looks around and finds an object in the room. The child then gives the other children clues such as "I see something that is big and green. Do you see it?" The other children must keep guessing from these clues.

26. Eat a Letter

Goal: Letter formation

Grade level: K-1

Construction and utilization: For reinforcement of letter formation, use a cookie or bread recipe to make a dough. Have children form the dough into letter shapes and then bake. If the child needs practice in forming particular letters, they could be handed cards that say which letters they are to form.

27. Color Collage

Goal: Color identification

Grade level: K-1

Construction and utilization: Each child selects from a hat the name of a color. The teacher can read the name for the child if necessary. The students then look through magazines to find pictures of the color. Pictures should be cut and made into a collage. The teacher should display the collages in the room for the entire class to see.

28. Let's Share

Goal: Social readiness: sharing

Grade level: K-1

Construction: Select two children. Plan secretly with them a role-playing situation where they are to share crayons for work they are doing. (This can be incorporated into regular class activities.) One of the two children uses more than his part of the crayons and refuses to share them. The other student snatches and runs away with the crayons. Then he refuses to share.

Utilization: Have the situation played as naturally as possible. Then reveal to the rest of the class that this was "make believe." Lead them to discuss how they felt about the whole situation. Ask them to consider whether they have ever behaved in a similar manner and how such behavior might be changed. Work for suggestions of self-discipline.

29. Work or Shirk

Goal: Social readiness: accepting responsibility

Grade level: K-1

Construction: Plan a role-playing situation by asking two people to be responsible for keeping the bookshelves and chalkboards clean for the day. One person works diligently, but the other plays around watching the fish, and puttering with clay and various other things.

Utilization: Have role players enact the situation. Have the rest of the group discuss:
1. How they think the worker felt
2. Why they think the other person did not do his job
3. What the worker could or should have done

30. Troublesome Tongue Twisters

Goal: Taking turns

Grade level: K-1

Construction and utilization: Teacher states a tongue twister and selects a child to repeat it. Each speaker selects another person to repeat the tongue twister.

Listening

Children are subjected daily to endless numbers of sounds, yet they do not always know what to listen for or how to listen. For this reason, there has been an emphasis placed on the teaching of listening as a necessary skill to be developed in the classroom.

The importance of teaching listening was stressed in a study conducted by the Central New York Study Council (1957). They drew the following conclusions:

1. Elementary aged children gain certain information through listening.
2. Preschool children get directions better from listening than reading.
3. Listening results do not necessarily parallel reading achievement.
4. The listening abilities of males and females are similar from kindergarten through sixth grade.

Pratt (1963) also found that even a short training period of five weeks can be helpful in raising the general level of listening ability. This result reinforces the idea that listening can be taught.

But why train one to listen? Is it so necessary? Our answer is an emphatic yes! Listening is an important skill for group living. The young child needs to listen to and be able to follow directions, enjoy stories, and share the experiences of others. It helps the child develop the types of thinking that are demanded in reading. According to Smith (1973), children who listen well seem to stand a much better chance of developing an extensive oral vocabulary. As a result, it is the good listener who often speaks exactly and creatively. The good listeners have more words at their command.

Because young children are usually very active and talkative, they are regarded as poor listeners and, therefore, need listening activities that are simple and short. In the following section some listening games are included that you may find helpful for classroom utilization.

31. Silence (Montessori Technique)

Goal: Attentive listening

Grade level: Preschool

Construction and utilization: Have the children close their eyes and listen while the teacher whispers a child's name. When that child hears his name, he may then whisper the name of another child. This can continue until all of the children have had a chance to whisper a name.

32. Word Clap

Goal: Attentive listening for a specific word

Grade level: 1

Construction and utilization: The teacher or a child picks a special word. The class is then instructed to clap every time they hear that word used in a sentence. Set a time limit.

Example:
   Every time you hear the word table, you should clap. This game will last until recess.

33. 1-2-3 Follow Me

Goal: Listening and following directions

Grade level: Preschool +

Construction and utilization: The teacher gives three simple directions such as "Clap your hands once, touch your head, blink your eyes." The children must follow the directions, using the presented sequence. Later the children may take turns giving the three simple directions.

Parent Activities

Some parents may ask what they can do to prepare their children for reading. Here is a list of activities you might suggest.

34. Reading Circles and Squares

Goal: Recognition of simple geometric shapes and reading labels of geometric shapes.

Grade level: Preschool

Construction and utilization: Discuss with the child the shapes of objects in his environment. For example, cookies, donuts, coins, some table tops, cushions, plates, teething rings, car tires, steering wheels, and eyes can all be described as circles. Windows, television screens, pictures (photographs), sidewalk slabs, a sandbox, and block patterns on clothes, can be described as squares. This can be discussed with the very young child in an informal manner. As the child gets older, pictures can be drawn of objects such as snowmen, balls, houses, and boxes and the shapes discussed in more detail. Make labels for these objects. Ask the children to read the labels.

Variation: Count the sides of the objects. Cut shapes out of magazines. Play circle games such as Ring-Around-the-Rosie and Here We Go Round the Mulberry Bush.

35. Reading Numerals

Goal: Recognition of numerals

Grade level: Preschool

Construction and utilization: The child sees numerals constantly. Names can be attached to them very informally. House numbers, numerals on the telephone, and numerals on the television can be "named" as the parent uses them. There are many colorful books with large numerals and corresponding numbers of objects. Songs such as "Ten Little Indians" and "One-Two Buckle My Shoe" can be sung showing the appropriate numerals.

36. Identifying Colors

Goal: Association of color name with colors

Grade level: Preschool

Construction and utilization: Talk about objects in terms of color. Color surrounds the child. "Let's put on your blue shirt today." "Would you like some orange sherbet?" Take a walk with your child and have him/her notice the green trees and the red and yellow flowers. Children love to be helpers. Encourage the child to do such things as "Take Daddy his brown shoes." Opportunities for using color words are plentiful, and even if using them sounds silly to an adult, the child is learning from them.

37. Sorting into Groups

Goal: Simple classification

Grade level: Preschool

Construction and utilization: A simple sorting activity is done with an egg carton and different shaped and colored buttons. The child can sort the buttons by putting them into the different "cups" of the container. Sorting can be done by size, shape, color, or texture. Different material fabrics are also good sorting materials for texture. Informally, a child can help put away silverware, since the compartments of the drawer are often used for specific pieces of silverware. Playing cards may also be sorted into number, color, or picture categories. Children may also be encouraged to hypothetically sort their foods, toys, and clothes, into appropriate categories.

38. Listening to Sounds

Goal: Recognition of environmental sounds

Grade level: Preschool

Construction and utilization: Talk about different sounds in a very informal manner. Animal sounds are usually of particular interest to most children. Games such as Old MacDonald also are useful here. Everyday sounds from cars, trucks, toaster popping, food cooking, and a tea kettle whistling should be pointed out and discussed. Have your child close his/her eyes and listen to a familiar sound. Then have the child guess what it is. Make two familiar sounds and have the child tell you how they are the same or different.

39. Using the Public Library

Goal: Stimulating interest in library facilities

Grade level: Preschool

Construction and utilization: There is no better way to interest the child in using the public library than to use it frequently yourself and have your child accompany you. Most public libraries offer preschool activities such as story time, puppet shows, movies, and plays. Children can learn that it is fun to be in the library. As soon as your child reaches the correct age, he should obtain his own library card.

40. Use of Rhymes

Goal: Recognition of rhyming words

Grade level: Preschool

Construction and utilization: Read to your children a list of rhyming words or the beginning of a nursery rhyme which contains words with similar sound patterns. (Hickory Dickory Dock). As a child listens to such patterns he learns that words may sound alike yet not be the same word.

41. Read to Your Child

Goal: Fostering an interest in reading

Grade level: Preschool

Construction and utilization: One of the most important things you can do to foster a love of and an interest in reading is to read to your child. It motivates the child to learn to read so that he can read his favorite books to himself or a sibling. Imitating adult behavior is the way a child learns most things, and reading is no exception.

42. Left and Right

Goal: Recognition of the left and right

Grade level: Preschool

Construction and utilization: Games such as Loop-de-loo and Hokey-Pokey are excellent activities for practicing left and right. Also, when reading to a child, exaggerate the left-right swing. Identify to the child the name of the hand with which he writes or eats. Even encouraging the child to underline using a left-to-right motion is good practice in developing this concept.

43. Reading Labels

Goal: Recognition of words in everyday experiences

Grade level: Preschool

Construction and utilization: The very young child can be made aware of the fact that labels are words that name or tell something. A trip to the supermarket can be a very rich reading experience. All of the packages being placed into the grocery basket say something. We select a certain package because it says something to us. Driving in the car presents a wealth of experiences: reading street signs, traffic signs, billboards, and store fronts. (Most children "read" the Mc-Donald's sign.) The kitchen is another world of labels that can be verbalized and used with the child.

BIBLIOGRAPHY

1. Brown, R. *Words and Things.* New York: The Free Press, 1958, p. 69.
2. Burns, P., and B. Broman, *The Language Arts in Childhood Education.* Shokie, Ill.: Rand McNally & Company, 1975.
3. Croft, D. R. *An Activities Handbook for Teachers of Young Children*, (2nd Ed.). Boston: Houghton Mifflin Company, 1975.
4. Central New York Study Council. *Some Helps for Building Guides for Skill Development in the Language Arts: Listening.* Report no. 7. Syracuse, N.Y.: Syracuse University Press, 1957.
5. Durkin, D. *Teaching Young Children to Read,* Boston: Allyn & Bacon, Inc., 1972. Chap. 7.
6. ____ . *Teaching Them to Read*, 2 ed. Boston: Allyn & Bacon, Inc., 1974.
7. "Let's Look at First Graders—A Guide to Understanding and Fostering Intellectual Development in Young Children." New York, N.Y.: Board of Education, 1965.
8. Pratt, L. E. "The Experimental Evaluation of a Program for the Improvement of Listening in the Elementary School." Ph. D. dissertation, State University of Iowa, 1963.
9. Russell, David, and Etta Karp. *Reading Aids Through the Grades.* New York: Bureau of Publications, Teachers College, Columbia University, 1956.
10. Smith, James. *Creative Teaching of the Language Arts in the Elementary School.* Boston: Allyn & Bacon, Inc., 1973.
11. Spache, E. *Reading Activities for Child Involvement.* Boston: Allyn & Bacon, Inc., 1972.
12. ____ . *Reading Activities for Child Involvement.* 2 ed. Boston: Allyn & Bacon, Inc., 1976.

5

Developing a student's interest in reading

Instead of teaching young people as if we were feeding them pack-aged prescriptions, we should inspire them and challenge them to invest their efforts and ideas in learning to read.

Roma Gans, 1963

Roma Gans, *Common Sense in the Teaching of Reading* (New York: 1963), p. vi.

GOALS: To aid students in

1. understanding what teachers and parents can do to motivate children to read.

2. understanding children's attitudes toward reading and their interests in reading.

3. assessing children's most effective style of learning.

4. providing stimulating and appropriately motivating reading materials for their students.

THE PUNCTUATION PROCLAMATION*

Characters

HARK ⎰
HO ⎱ *heralds*

KING PISH-POSH

ROYAL TUTOR

ROYAL STORYTELLER

ROYAL SCRIBE

ROYAL TREASURER

ROYAL COOK

TWO BOY COURTIERS

TWO GIRL COURTIERS

OTHER COURTIERS

SETTING: *The throne room of King Pish-Posh, in the kingdom of Bosh.*

AT RISE: KING PISH-POSH *is snoring noisily on his throne.* HARK *is patrolling the stage from right;* HO *is patrolling from left, and they meet at center.*

HARK: Come on, now. It's your turn to waken him, HO.

HO: Oh, no. I distinctly remember that I woke him the last time, HARK.

HARK: Go on. It's half past the hourglass. He'll miss his reading lesson.

HO: That reading lesson! He's always in such a fearful temper when he has to read. Here, let's toss a coin. (*He takes coin from pocket, tosses and catches it and puts it on the back of his hand.*)

HARK: Heads.

HO: Tails. (*Looks at his hand*) Whew! It's tails. Go ahead, Hark. I'll stay right behind you to catch you when he flattens you. (ROYAL TUTOR *enters timidly from left, with easel, large lesson pad, and book.*)

HARK: Wait. Here's the Royal Tutor. Let him have the honor of telling the King it's time to read. (*Heralds tiptoe down right, sit on stools, and watch.*

TUTOR *places easel, with lesson pad on it, up left, near throne. He opens book, crosses to throne, and pulls gently at* KING's *sleeve.*)

TUTOR: Your Majesty.

KING (*Snoring*): Bluhuhuh

TUTOR (*A little louder*): It is time for your daily reading lesson, King Pish-Posh. (*KING sits bolt upright.*)

KING: Humph! Reading, is it? I knew there was some reason why this was a bad day.

TUTOR: If Your Majesty would only relax. Reading is fun.

KING: Fun! I'd rather be boiled in green, gurgling oil. All those letters huddling together, staring at me like black cats—

TUTOR: The letters are trying hard to mean something to you, Sire. Here— (*He uncovers sentence written on the lesson pad. It reads "I am the King."*) Here is the sentence we have been trying to read for the last three months. Do let us see now how well you can read it.

KING (*Scowling*): Tutor, that sentence is too hard. There are (*counts on fingers*) ten letters in that sentence. Why can't I have a sentence with *one* letter? I could read that.

TUTOR (*Sighing*): Impossible, Sire. Come now, please. I know you can read this. I beg you to try.

KING: Botheration! (*He thrusts out his lip as he glares at sentence.*) Um-um-um.

TUTOR: The first word is—(*Points to himself*)

KING: The first word is "you." There. I read a word.

TUTOR: No, no, Majesty. The word is "me"—I mean, "I."

KING: I knew that. I was jesting with you. Let me read it, now. "I"—

TUTOR: Sound it out, Gracious Highness.

KING: A-M. A-M. Aha! I have it. LALLAPALOOZA!

TUTOR (*Throwing up his hands*): No, Sire—"am." Now, try the next word. And I suggest that you really *look* at the word.

KING: You never let a poor king rest, do you? Very well, I'll look. I'll stare a hole through the paper. (*He stares at easel. He rises, takes a step closer, and stares again. Then he goes up and tries to brush the period off the paper.*)

TUTOR: What is the matter, Majesty?

KING: There is some sort of beetle on the paper. (*Slaps easel*) There! I got it! No, I didn't. He's still there.

TUTOR (*Coming to easel*): Let me see. Oh, I beg to differ with you, Sire. That is not a beetle. That is a "period."

KING (*Walking back to throne*): I don't care what kind of insect it is. It doesn't belong in my nice, neat palace. (KING *sits on throne*)

TUTOR: But a period is a punctuation mark. It is part of the sentence.

KING: What? Do you mean to tell me that, in addition to twenty-six letters of the alphabet, I shall have to remember an inky blob?

TUTOR: There are many punctuation marks, Sire. There are commas, exclamation marks, question marks, colons, and apostrophes.

KING (*Holding his ears*): Enough! Stop! I won't have it. No. Twenty-six letters are troublesome enough.

TUTOR: But there is nothing I can do, Sire. Punctuation was part of the language before we were even born.

KING: Well, *I* can do something about it. I shall abolish it.

TUTOR (*Wringing his hands*): That is not possible!

KING: Am I, or am I not the King? I am the King! (*Pompously*) There. That's a good sentence. You ought to have that sentence on the easel: "I am the King." I can abolish anything I wish. (*To the heralds*) Heralds! Heralds! (*They rise and run to* KING.)

HARK: Front and center, Sire!

HO: At your service, Majesty!

KING: Draw up a proclamation of abolishment. (*Heralds cross to table with scrolls and quill pens, and prepare to write proclamation.*—Ahem. (KING *dictates.*) "His Royal Highness, King Pish-Posh, of the kingdom of Bosh—" Do you have that?

HARK: Yes, Sire.

KING: "Hereby proclaims that all punctuation marks shall be abolished throughout the land, forever and ever and a day." Seal it with the Royal Seal, and proclaim it immediately.

HO: Immediately, Your Majesty. (*Heralds bow and exit with scrolls,* HARK *at left,* HO *at right.*)

KING: There. That is that. Now, let us be done with reading. It is time for the court to assemble. Tutor, bid my courtiers and the Storyteller enter. (*The* TUTOR *goes off right and returns with* COURTIERS.) Now, we must have a jolly story. Where *is* my Storyteller? (COURTIERS *sit on chairs to left and right of throne.* ROYAL STORYTELLER *runs in from right with large book under his arm.*)

STORYTELLER: The Royal Storyteller begs to announce his presence in the court of King Pish-Posh.

KING: Humph. Very good. Let us have a story.

TUTOR (*Aside*): I do hope it isn't "Goldilocks and the Three Bears" again.

COURTIERS (*Groaning*): Oh, no!

1ST BOY COURTIER: Please, Sire, not that story today.

1ST GIRL COURTIER: Please, Sire, we have heard that story three hundred sixty-five times.

KING: Humph. I suppose it is the fashion to be democratic. Very well. What other story would you like to hear?

2ND BOY COURTIER: Might we hear about Robin Hood?

COURTIERS: Yes, yes!

KING: Robin Hood? That's a frightful story. Think what that outlaw did to good King John. Some other tale, think of some other tale.

2ND GIRL COURTIER: Then, Your Majesty, may we hear the story of Sleeping Beauty? We ladies would enjoy it so much.

KING: Would you?

GIRL COURTIERS: Yes, yes!

KING: Does it have a bad fairy in it?

2ND GIRL COURTIER: Oh, yes. She is most dreadfully wicked.

KING: Then we shan't have it. Bad fairies make me nervous.

GIRL COURTIERS (*Sadly*): Oooh.

KING: It is my turn. Royal Storyteller, open your book to the story of Goldilocks and the Three Bears. (*As* STORYTELLER *opens book,* HO *enters from right, and* HARK *enters from left, to announce proclamation. They read from scrolls.*)

HO: Hear ye! Hear ye! His Royal Highness, King Pish-Posh, of the kingdom of Bosh, hereby proclaims—

HARK: That all punctuation marks shall be abolished throughout the land, forever and ever and a day. (*Heralds exit,* HARK *left and* HO *right.*)

STORYTELLER: What? No more punctuation?

KING: Never mind. It doesn't concern you. Continue.

STORYTELLER: Very well, Your Highness. (*He begins to read in a singsong fashion with no pauses. As he reads the* COURTIERS *yawn, and fall asleep, and the* KING *grows more puzzled.*) "Once upon a time there lived a little girl named Goldilocks she was an adventurous child she lived in a great wood her parents said do not go into the forest alone but she said pooh pooh I am old enough to take care of myself—"

KING: Stop!

STORYTELLER: This is impossible, Your Majesty. There are no commas or periods. It is like being in a wilderness with no signposts.

KING (*To* TUTOR): Is this true?

TUTOR: It is true, Sire. I tried to warn you. (HARK *enters from left with* ROYAL SCRIBE *and* ROYAL COOK, *who carries large menu and wooden spoon.* HO *enters from right with* ROYAL TREASURER, *who carries small abacus.*)

HARK: Your Highness! There is terrible chaos in the land. The people clamor for you to restore punctuation. Thousands of requests are pouring in. The Royal Scribe is desperate.

SCRIBE (*Bowing*): Honored King, the records of the kingdom are snarled and confused. We need our apostrophes urgently. Without apostrophes we do not know what belongs to whom, or whose things are which.

HO: The Royal Treasurer is in a tizzy. He cannot figure out the taxes.

TREASURER (*Bowing*): Moneyed Majesty, I must have periods in abundance. We use them by the carton for decimal points. (*Holding up abacus*) I cannot tell now whether you have one million gold ducats or only one millionth of a ducat.

KING: My treasury is in danger? This *is* serious.

HARK: What's more, Your Majesty, the Royal Cook is frantic.

COOK (*Tartly*): Highness, I demand that you put commas back.

KING: Humph. I see no need for commas. I don't eat commas.

COOK (*Advancing to* KING *and thrusting menu under his nose*): Look at this menu. Does this sound appetizing? Beef soup salad creamed chicken ice cream coffee cigars.

KING: Coffee cigars? Blah. Very well. I declare a state of emergency. I seem to have made a mistake. Kings do make mistakes.

TUTOR: Sire—

KING: You shouldn't interrupt in the middle of my mistake.

TUTOR: But, I merely wanted to tell you that you *can* put things right again. (*In stage whisper, as he points to heralds*) The heralds.

KING: I can? Yes, yes, of course I can. Heralds. (*They bow.*) Punctuation is in again. Go spread the word.

ALL: Hooray! (*Heralds exit.*)

KING: And now we can get on with our story.

ALL: UGH.

KING: On second thought, ever since I heard that story without the punctuation, I am not nearly so fond of it. (*To* 2ND GIRL COURTIER) What was the title of that tale you declared was so interesting?

2ND GIRL COURTIER: "Sleeping Beauty," Your Majesty.

KING: "Sleeping Beauty" it shall be, then. After all—(*He stares at the easel.*) I-AM-THE-KING. Period! I read it. I read the sentence. There was nothing to it. It was fun!

ALL: Hooray for King Pish-Posh!

KING: I'm a Royal Reader! Why didn't someone tell me it was fun?

TUTOR: We tried, Sire. We certainly did try! (*curtain*)

The End

Why Read?

Before you read any farther, think of the King's various reactions to reading and then answer the following items:

1. Can you think of five feelings that describe your attitude toward reading?
2. Can you explain why you described reading the way you did?
3. Why do you read?
4. Given the following choices, indicate by number the order in which you would choose them as ways to spend your free time.

_____ Talking with friends
_____ Watching TV
_____ Participating in sports
_____ Reading
_____ Napping

What Were Your Responses?

A number of college seniors who were preparing to be elementary teachers were asked to answer Item #4. Some said reading was enjoyable, a pleasure: "fun" was listed by 71 per cent of the students; 52 per cent stated that reading was a necessity. In response to item 4, "talking with friends" was the first choice of 69 per cent of the students. Reading was the second choice of 42 per cent and 33 per cent listed reading as a third choice.

Neither the King in the preceding play nor the students responding to the preceding items were a widely representative group. They were in a situation that required a considerable amount of reading for information, and they freely selected that situation and their responses reveal this interest in reading.

Let us consider the reasons why people read. Essentially, there are two: for *information* and for *enjoyment*.

Motivation

An individual's motivation to read can be summarized in the following ways:
1. to learn how to do something
2. to gain understanding of a concept or a person
3. to satisfy curiosity
4. to prove a point
5. to be entertained
6. to experience new things vicariously
7. to relax
8. to fill time

You might be very much like the King and find yourself asking, "But why read? All of the reasons for reading which are listed here can be fulfilled through other media. There are recordings, video tapes, filmstrips, movies, radio, and television, and all of them are much easier than reading." Many, many children have such attitudes. If you plan to be a teacher, how do you plan to excite students to read while enabling them to gain an understanding of the worth of reading? Russell (1961) gives us an appropriate and inspiring answer.

> The acid test of any reading program is whether or not the children in it or graduated from it read for themselves. There is little value in developing competent reading ability unless it is voluntarily put to use. One of the aims of any modern program, . . . is the development not only of skills but of habits of reading and positive attitudes toward it. The best means of evaluation of the success of a school program is not a score on a standardized test, but rather the amount and quality of the materials children read. The development of worthwhile interests and tastes may be regarded as the crowning achievement of any reading program. A good program creates the desire to read and develops habits of reading not only for recreation but as a means of personal development.
>
> The development of a permanent interest in reading seems to have a number of social and personal values. . . . the health of a democracy is dependent upon a citizenry equipped with some knowledge of the problems faced by the total group. Unless these problems are known to all, and unless possible solutions are communicated through the printed word, without this unifying influence the democracy may become an oligarchy, an anarchy, or a fascist state. One of the personal values in the habit of wide reading during the school years is the favorable effect on reading ability itself. One of the best ways of becoming a competent reader, as measured by a standardized test or any other instrument, is to do much reading of different kinds of materials. Probably more important, the habit of reading can contribute to the child's knowledge of himself, his acquaintances, and his world in a way few other activities can. (pp. 362–3)

Rationale for Influencing Student's Activities

"Children learn best when they *want* to learn. If they want to learn they can and will . . ." (Allen, 1965). As teachers, we should take this statement as a directive: "Make children want to read." The desire to do something involves one's *attitude* or predisposition toward a given task. Attitude has been defined by Thurstone (1928) as the "sum total of man's inclinations and feelings, prejudice or bias, preconceived notions, ideas, fears, threats and convictions about any specified topic." Allport (1935) defined attitude in both cognitive and physioneural terms as "a mental and neural state of readiness, organized through experience, exerting a direct or dynamic influence upon the individual's responses to all objects and situations in which he is related." Dobbs (1947) defined attitude as a predisposition to respond to a specified object. Fishbein (1967), building on these earlier definitions, suggested that the predisposition to respond remains *consistent*. For example, if a child is predisposed to dislike reading he will *probably* display negative behaviors *each time* he is engaged in the act of reading. While these reactions may demonstrate a negative attitude toward the act of reading, only the behaviors not the attitude, would be visible to the observer. An attitude exists within the self as a personal unobservable construct. Therefore, one's expressions, responses, and attitudes are believed to be indicative of one's attitude.

As you think about these statements, the difficulty of accurate measurement probably becomes quite obvious because there is difficulty in assessing the *attitudes* of students simply by observing their behavior. Thurstone cautioned us about the major problem existing in assessing attitude; one's outward expression and his actual attitude may not always be congruent. Dobbs (1947) illustrated a second problem in assessing student attitude when he suggested that it may be possible for several people to possess the same unobservable attitude but may not always be possible to recognize this similarity because their behavioral responses may be different. For example, three children in your classroom may have negative attitudes toward reading; one may feign illness, one may misbehave, and the third student, who also has a negative attitude toward the act of reading, may be attentive to reading because he realizes that the act of reading is important to you. As a teacher you may be perplexed. You may wonder what actually determines one's behavioral response. Perhaps it is a combination of the *cognitive* (development of intellect) *affective* (development of emotions or attitudes), and *conative* (development of volition) domains.

Conation

Conation, defined by McDougall (1911, p. 325), denotes "the active or striving side of our nature, as the equivalent of will in its widest sense, as comprehending desire, impulse, craving, appetite, wishing, and willing." The conation is the original impulse which "supplies the motive power to all the activities that are only means to the attainment of the desired end. The train of activity, supported by any one of the instinctive impulses, may become indefinitely prolonged and incessantly renewed, it may take the predominantly intellectual form of thinking out means for the attainment of the end." (McDougall, 1921, p. 181).

While it appears that one's observable behavior may be a display of *conation* rather than *attitude*, a great deal of literature exists which makes no mention of conation. For example, Rowell (1967) attempted to determine the relationship between achievement and change in attitudes toward reading of 40 elementary and junior high school students; all of these students were considered disabled readers. It was discovered that negative attitudes toward reading were more closely related to reading achievement than to other factors, like socioeconomic status or age.

Similar findings were reported by Gardner (1972), and Puryear (1975) when studying the attitudes and achievement of fourth graders. A follow-up study of remedial reading instruction was reported by Buerger (1968). The focus of this study was an investigation of the effect of remedial reading instruction on long-term progress and attitude. Seventy-two, third to seventh grade students received fifty hours of remedial instruction; they were compared with seventy-two achievers who had not received long-term remedial instruction. Post-remedial findings indicated that the remedial reading itself had no significant effect upon mental ability, vocabulary, reading comprehension or attitudes toward reading.

The effects of selected reporting practices upon reading achievement and reading attitude was investigated by Fanning (1969). Pupils from grades three to six, designated by their classroom teacher as reading at least one-half year below grade level were grouped by four systems: (1) D-grades, (2) narrative report with supportive comments, (3) regular report with below average reading grade or (4) regular report with supportive comments. It was discovered that no single reporting system significantly affected the reading attitude of less competent readers. Fowler (1972) found that even when the negative attitudes of a group of sixth graders were positively influenced, the achievement levels of these children remained the same. Similar findings were presented by Koch (1974) when working with fourth and sixth grade students.

As you can see, the data on the relationship between attitude and achievement provides us with inconclusive answers. These studies seem to offer little guidance as to what might profitably be practiced so that we can "Make children want to read!" This remains a constant challenge for us in our classrooms. If further research is to provide greater insights, educators need to construct useful instruments which measure attitudes. Johnson (1964) discussed the construction of an inventory, *An Inventory of Reading Attitude*, to assess children's attitudes toward reading in the elementary school. He found that the lower the grade level of the child, the better his attitude was toward reading.

The Reading Apperception Test, developed by O'Connor (1968), explored relationships between attitude toward reading and reading achievement. He concluded that attitude toward reading was related to reading ability within a *specific* reading situation. An older study of special interest was conducted by McKillop in 1952. The study investigated the relationship between the reader's attitude and specific types of reading response. McKillop concluded: ". . . any specific response is the product of the interaction of three factor groups: general reading skill, experience, and attitude." She also found that questions which required an evaluative judgment were significantly influenced by the attitude of the subject.

Johnson (1959) investigated the reading behavior, achievements, and attitudes of 101 first grade boys. These boys were divided into two groups of readers with equal reading readiness test scores, intelligence, and reading test scores. One group was called "eager readers" and they reported the following:

1. I have a specific role in learning to read, and I look for the specific materials and methods involved in my program.
2. I get anxious in reading situations.
3. In reading, I accept the teacher's opinions and tools; someday I will be rewarded.
4. Reading situations remind me of the harshness in the world around me.
5. I like books.

The second group, called "the reluctant readers" reported that:

1. Reading makes me fall behind or isolates me.
2. Reading is unpleasant.
3. Reading brings punishment.
4. Reading interferes with fun.

Both groups reported that:

1. The teacher is likely to add to one's discomfort.
2. Reading involves classroom routines.
3. Reading situations involve certain minor misbehavior.
4. Reading involves unfriendliness between children.
5. Showing off reading achievement is a pleasure.

All of these studies were presented in order to offer insight into the relationship between attitude development and reading. Some seem less productive than others; however, all raise further questions to be investigated and answered if we are to be able to influence our students' attitudes toward reading.

You are probably perplexed in your efforts to understand how children's attitude toward reading affects their ability to learn to read. If you are confused, you are not alone. For decades, educators who have been interested in human psychology and communication have explored theoretical and empirical issues in an attempt to understand attitude formation, change, and its relationship to learning.

In one of the most recent studies, the 1976 National Assessment of Reading Progress, researchers have again sought an answer to these questions. They found answers to the cognitive issues: "Students of all ages demonstrate little difficulty in comprehending basic, literal, straightforward written material. But comprehension drops off quickly as soon as the reading tasks become more difficult." These results do not provide answers for pertinent questions about the relationship between reading achievement and attitude. While reasons such as increased funding, managed reading programs, and better educated parents have been forwarded to account for the successes, we must also account for the declines. In attempting to do so, we might find some answers in negative attitudes toward reading. If we polled the participants we might find that students:

1. are very much like the king in the preceding play, in that they are uninterested in reading.

2. are unaware of a reason for reading.

If the second reason appears to be a prime factor, American children may be like The Little Old Man Who Could Not Read.

THE LITTLE OLD MAN WHO COULD NOT READ

by Irma Simonton Black
published by Reader's Digest Services, Inc., Pleasantville, N.Y., 1968

> Once there was a little old man who could not read. He just never wanted to learn. His wife went to the store and bought the food but the little man stayed home and made beautiful toys out of wood. Children all over the world loved his toys, and many wrote to tell him so. But still the little old man never wanted to learn to read. One day his wife decided to go on a visit. "You will need to go to the store," she said. "Get a can of soup, and a big can of spaghetti sauce and some spaghetti. Get some sugar and some milk and some oatmeal. Eat well!" And she kissed the old man and left. The old man went to the store. There

were rows and rows of cans with pictures on them. And there were rows and rows of cans and boxes without pictures. What were they? The little man did not know, and he didn't like to ask. He bought a middle-sized can. It looked like the cans of soup his wife brought home. He bought a long box that looked like a sphaghetti box and a big can that looked like a spaghetti sauce can. He bought a blue box that looked like a sugar box. He bought a round box that looked like an oatmeal box. And, last of all, he bought a square carton. It looked like the milk cartons his wife brought home. "Ah!" said the little old man when he got home. "That walk made me hungry. I shall have some hot soup for lunch." He opened the middle-sized can. It was onion soup. The little old man hated onions of any kind—and onion soup worst of all. "Fiddle," he said. "Onion soup. I shall save it for my good wife." At dinnertime, the little old man rubbed his hands with pleasure and took down the long box that looked like a spaghetti box and the great big can that looked like a spaghetti sauce can. Beaming, he opened the long box. But the box did not have spaghetti in it. It had waxed paper. "Fiddlesticks and fish fur!" said the little old man. "Who wants to eat wax paper—even with sauce on it? Not I, for one. But I can eat the sauce all by itself." He reached for the big can. For the first time, he noticed that it had a plastic top on it, so he took that off. "That's funny," he said to himself. "I never saw a plastic top on a sauce can. I do hope this isn't a coffee can!" He opened the big can. It <u>was</u> a coffee can. The coffee smelled delicious, but it wasn't much good for a hungry little old man. "Shall I have my oatmeal and milk and sugar instead?" he asked himself. Then he answered himself. "No, I'll have a cup of coffee and go to bed. In the morning, I'll have a nice big breakfast." By the next morning, he was very, <u>very</u> hungry. "Oatmeal!" said the old man as he jumped out of bed. "I shall put lots and lots of milk and sugar on it. Ah!" The little old man got the round box and the blue box and the square carton. He put them all on the table. Then he opened the round box. There was no oatmeal in it. It was full of something grainy and white. The old man tasted it carefully. Salt! "Fiddles and flutes," said the old man. "Who wants milk and sugar on salt?" He opened the blue box and got a spoon to have a sweet taste of sugar. But there was no sugar in the box. It was full of little white flakes. "Soap!" said the old man sadly. "Who wants soap even with milk? Oh, oh, how hungry I am!" He opened the square carton to get a drink of milk. But the milk in the carton smelled funny. It was buttermilk, sour <u>sour</u> buttermilk. The old man hated buttermilk, but he was so hungry that he drank every drop of it. The old man hated onion soup. But at noon he was so hungry that he ate onion soup. At night the wife came back. The old man was very glad to see her. "Wife," he said, "I had a bad time." He told her how he got all mixed up with the cans and cartons and boxes. "The long box was not spaghetti. It was wax paper! The blue box was soap flakes! The round box was salt! Wife, please teach me to read!" "Very well, I shall," said his good wife. First the old man learned to read the word spaghetti. Next he learned to read the word milk. Then he learned to read the words for everything in the big store. And then he learned to read the words for everything in the world. But he still made his beautiful toys out of wood, and now he could read the letters the children sent to him. And he never—no, never—went hungry again.

If we believe that American students are like the king in that they *do not like reading*, or like the little old man, in that they *see no purpose for reading*, we may be called upon to investigate a dimension of human behavior other than the *cognitive* and *affective* domains of learning. We may need to explore the *conative* or *will* domain. Success in reading may be dependent upon the *conation* or *will* to read.

You may find that some children have a view of reading as pleasurable, because of early encounters with books they may have shared with a loved one in an interaction of enjoyment. But some of these children who enter school having had pleasurable reading experiences find that school reading is an arduous task involving basal readers, worksheets, and constant teacher reprimands. Many of these children quickly develop negative attitudes toward reading. Within this group of children there may be those who view reading as a means of becoming more like the adult they aspire to model, and they may realize that reading is necessary for later pleasure. But there may also be students who are unable to see the purposes of reading and their negative behaviors may manifest this lack of purpose.

A study by Mager (1969) that assessed student attitudes toward academic subjects demonstrated a correlation between a positive attitude toward a subject area and (1) success (2) ability, and relationships with significant others. Many successful readers may be found in your classroom precisely because of "conative tendencies upon the course of mental process and of behavior." (McDougall, 1911, p. 327). You can have a profound effect upon reading achievement by providing specific purposes for reading.

One of the most significant factors to be considered in the process of motivating students to read is the teacher. Wilson and Hall (1972) maintain:

> The key to developing a personal love of books is a teacher who communicates enthusiasm and an appreciation of literature through his attitudes and examples. Knowing children and their interests, and knowing literature are of great importance in promoting personal reading. Significant as these are, however, the success or failure of the personal reading program in the elementary school rests with the classroom teacher. In those classrooms where encounters with literature are an integral part of the school experience, children are more likely to become avid readers. The teacher's responsibility, then, is to provide motivation, time, and materials to stimulate personal reading.

Let us consider these points further. How does a teacher communicate enthusiasm and appreciation for literature? Does she instruct students in appreciation? Does she behave in some particular way to convey this? The answer is yes to both. She discusses her interest in reading with her students. A testimonial is more effective when it is supported with evidence. In this case, the evidence comes from anecdotes about the books the teacher has read.

There are many things teachers do that strongly influence a student's interest in reading. These relate to the kinds of instruction provided and the manner in which they are provided. The teacher who creates a cheerful, encouraging atmosphere, who chooses appropriate and appealing material as a basis for instruction, and who has accurately gauged a student's level of development has cast a strong, silent vote for student interest in reading. The teacher who is hypercritical of students and who openly criticizes them, who designs a program and molds children to it, has done just the opposite. One does not harangue a child about a problem and expect him to jump back into the situation with eagerness.

What the Teacher Can Do in the Classroom

Teachers can do a great deal to help children enjoy reading by reading to them. Dawson (1972) endorses this philosophy when she says, "Teachers should read to children every day from books that are worthwhile, appropriate in level of interest, but probably too hard for them to read themselves." (p. 37) The perceptive teacher will find numerous opportunities to read aloud to children. Many students have been "hooked on reading" through this method. Reading to children provides the teacher with an opportunity to choose and help develop a taste for good literature. The following books are only a sample of a myriad of materials that you can share with children.

1977 Winners

Newberry:
    Winner: *Roll of Tundu, Hear My Cry,* Mildred D. Taylor (Dial)
    Honor Book: *Abel's Island,* William Steig (Farrar)
    Honor Book: *A String in the Harp,* Nancy Bond (Atheneum)/A Margaret K. McElderry Book)

Caldecott:
    Winner: *Ashanti to Zulu: African Traditions* by Margaret Musgrove, ill. by Leo & Diane Dillon (Dial)
    Honor Book: *The Amazing Bone* written & ill. by William Steig (Farrar)
    Honor Book: *The Contest* retold & ill. by Nonny Hagragian (Greenwillow)
    Honor Book: *Fish for Supper* written & ill. by M. B. Goffstein (Dial)
    Honor Book: *The Galom* written & ill. by Beverly Brodsky McDermott (Lippincott)
    Honor Book: *Hawk, I'm Your Brother* (Scribner)
                Text by Byrd Baylor
                Illustrated by Peter Parnall

1976 Winners

Newberry:
    Winner: *The Grey King* (Atheneum) by Susan Cooper
    Honor Book: *Dragon Wings* (Harper) by Lawrence Yep
    Honor Book: *The Hundred Penny Box* (Viking) by Sharon Bell Mathis

Caldecott:
    Winner: *Why Mosquitoes Buzz in People's Ears* (Dial)
                Text by Verna Aardemi
                Illustration by Leo & Diane Dillon
    Honor Book: *Streda Nona* by Tomie dePaola (Prentice-Hall)
    Honor Book: *The Desert Is Theirs* (Scribner)
                Text by Byrd Baylor
                Illustrated by Peter Parnall

1975 Winners

Newberry:

      Winner: *M. C. Higgins, The Great* by Virginia Hamilton
                      (Macmillan Publishing Co.,) 1974
  Honor Book: *Figgs & Phantoms* by Ellen Raskin (Dutton)
  Honor Book: *My Brother Sam Is Dead* by James Lincoln Collier (Four Winds)
  Honor Book: *The Perilous Guard* by Elizabeth Marie Pope (Houghton Mifflin)
  Honor Book: *Philip Hall Likes Me. I Reckon Maybe* by Bette Greene (Dial)

Caldecott:

      Winner: *Arrow to the Sun* by Gerald McDermott (Viking Press)
  Honor Book: *Jambo Means Hello: Swahili Alphabet Book* (Dial)
                   Text by Muriel Feelings
                   Illustrated by Tom Feelings

Building Reading Interests

Suggestions for the Teacher

1. Set aside a particular time of each day to read to children.

2. Choose a variety of contents to read to students. Try to choose something related to the special interests of each child. This has a twofold value: reading is enhanced for the child whose interest is tapped and for other children because they often discover a new interest.

3. Try to involve students in magazine and newspaper reading. Have room subscriptions for newspaper and magazines. Frequently, local newspaper publishers or the PTA will donate subscriptions.

4. Have informal discussions about interesting information gleaned from magazine or newspaper articles. Do not make this a current events activity only. Let it include human interest stories.

5. Establish a reading center or corner. This can be as simple as putting a throw rug in a quiet corner or it can be an elaborate adventure, depending on the space available. It is very important to make the space warm and inviting. Guidelines for the use of the corner should be designed by the teacher and the students together. The following language/reading games might be examples of materials found in this reading center.

Games

   Phonics We Use, learning games kit (Lyons & Carnahan)
   DiGraph Hopscotch, 1 game board (Educational Board Games)
   Consonant Lotto, first-grade (Garrard Publishing Co.)
   Faculty Cards, Elementary to adult (ACO Games Division, Allen Co., Inc.)
   The Happening Game, Elementary to junior high (Community Makers, Inc.)
   Matrix Games, elementary (New Century)
   People in Action, preschool to elementary (Holt, Rinehart and Winston)

Games, A Treasury of 600 Delightful Games for Children of All Ages (Jessie H. Bancroft, Macmillan, New York: 1973.

Contemporary Games, vols. 1 and 2 (Compiled by Jean Belch. Detroit. Gale Research Co., 1974)

6. Encourage children to include variety in their reading selections. There are many suggestions for this; you may want to have shelves labeled with different types of literature, such as biography, science-fiction, history, science, fairy tales, and humor.

7. Start a recommended book file. In a small metal file, place dividers labeled with various types of literature. Invite children to write brief recommendations for books that they have read and enjoyed. The size of the file and the cards included in the file will determine the maximum length of the recommendation. Standards for these recommendations should be set up so that the content will be adequate for the potential reader to get an idea about the book without "giving away" the whole story.

8. Work out situations in which children can read something that they have enjoyed to other children.

9. Work cooperatively with the art teacher to plan National Book Week festivities. Children can plan and develop bulletin boards, murals, and paper sculpture to display the books which they have read.

10. Organize children who have read the same book. Have them dramatize their book or portions of it. They can do this simply for their own satisfaction or to share with others.

11. Purchase collections of children's drama and organize a reader's theater for children. Reader's Theater will be discussed in greater detail at the end of this chapter. Some excellent collections include:

Burger, Isabel. *Creative Play Acting: Learning Through Drama*. Cranbury, N.J.: A. S. Barnes & Co., Inc., c-1950.

Carlson, Bernice Wells. *Act It Out*. Illustrated by Laszlo Matulay. Nashville, Tenn.: Abington Press, 1956.

Chambers, Dewey W. *Storytelling and Creative Drama*. Dubuque, Iowa: William C. Brown Company, 1970.

Durrell, Donald D. *Favorite Plays for Classroom Reading*. Plays, Inc., c-1965.

Fontaine, Robert. *Humorous Skits for Young People: A Collection of Royalty-free Short Plays and Easy-To-Perform Comedy Sketches*, Boston Plays, Inc., c. 1965.

McGee, Cecil. *Drama for Fun*. Nashville, Tenn.: Broadman, 1969.

Kamerman, Sylvia E., ed. *Fifty Plays for Junior Actors*. Boston: Plays, Inc., 1966.

12. Build students' enjoyment of poetry by selecting a variety of poems to read to them. Provide them with copies so there can be choral reading. Make a variety of poetry anthologies accessible to children.

13. Purchase many paperback books. If teachers coordinate the purchase of books, it is often possible to build an elaborate classroom collection through bonus books; the agency from which books are published might contribute free books for every 15th or 25th class purchase.

14. Plan focus weeks for different authors who have written books that children enjoy. Learn and share information that will make the author familiar to the children.

15. Prepare crossword puzzles about books and authors and about the content of a particular book.

Animal Crossword Puzzles, grades 2–3, Wonder, Wonder Treasure Books, Inc., Division of Grosset & Dunlap, Inc., 51 Madison Ave., New York 10010

Beginner's Crossword Puzzles, grades 4–9, Doubleday & Co., Inc.

Crackerjack Crosswords, grades 4–9, Doubleday & Co., Inc., Orders to: 501 Franklin Ave., Garden City, NY 11530

Crossword Puzzles, grades 1–2, Wonder

Crossword Puzzles, grades 2–3, Wonder

Crossword Puzzles, grades 3–4, Wonder

Crosswords for Kids, grades 2–4, by Low White, Fawcett World, Fawcett World Library, 1515 Broadway, New York, NY 10036

Junior Crossword Puzzle Books, grades 4–8, Platt, Platt & Munk Publishers, Division of Questor, Educational Products, 1055 Bronx River Ave., Bronx, NY 10472

X-Word Fun, grades 7–9, School Book Service, Scholastic Book Services, Division of Scholastic Magazines, Orders to: 906 Sylvan Ave., Englewood Cliffs, NJ 07632

16. Prepare collections of riddles about books, characters, and authors who are familiar to the students. These can be organized with self-correction so that they can be enjoyed by individuals, or they can be played by pairs or teams of players.

Riddle Book

Black Within & Red Without: A Book of Riddles. Compiled by Lillian Morrison. New York: (Thomas Y. Crowell Company).

Riddle Me, Riddle Me, Ree. Maria Leach, New York: The Viking Press, Inc., c. 1970.

Riddles, Riddles, Everywhere. Ernie Rees, New York: Abelard, c. 1964.

Ask Me Another Riddle. Ralph Underwood. New York: Grosset and Dunlap Inc., c. 1964.

The American Riddle Book. Carl Withers, New York: Abelard-Schuman, 1964.

What the Parent Can Do at Home

Parent-child interactions in reading should be encouraged throughout the elementary school years. As the child matures beyond the beginning reading stages, parents can continue to provide the basis for a good attitude toward reading by reading themselves and by making good material available for children to read. They can encourage children to discuss things they have read, and they can discuss with each other and their children some of the interesting things that they have read.

Most young children enjoy jingles and nursery rhymes, as well as the action and need for attentiveness that go with them. Picture books are designed for the young child. Parents can acquaint themselves and their children with the children's division of the library. The young child who visits the library with a parent and watches as the parent selects books for himself is acquiring the "library habit." Magazine and newspapers that are available in the home make a worthwhile contribution to the child's background or foundation for being a reader. The following suggestions are ones that you may want to share with the parents of your students.

1. Help young children realize the fun to be found in reading; select humorous poems, short stories, or magazine articles (on the child's level). Read some of the following books to your child and enjoy the humor with him.

Humorous Short Stories and Poems

Fenner, Phyllis R. *Fools and Funny Fellows.* Illustrated by Henry C. Pitz. New York: Alfred A. Knopf, Inc., 1947. Fifth and sixth grade

Fenner, Phyllis R. *Fun, Fun, Fun* Stories of Fantasy and Farce, Mischief and Mirth, Whimsy and Nonsense. Illustrated by Joseph Zabinski. New York: Franklin Watts, Inc. Fifth and sixth grade

Smith, William J. *Laughing Time.* Illustrated by Juliet Kepes. Boston: Atlantic-Little Brown Books, Toronto 1953. K–third grade

Riley, James W. *Joyful Poems for Children.* Illustrated by Charles Geer. Indianapolis: The Bobbs-Merrill Co., Inc., 1960. Third-sixth grade

Fenner, Phyllis R. *Giggle Box.* Illustrated by William Steig. New York: Alfred A. Knopf, 1953. Third-seventh grade.

Wiggins, K. D. and N. A. Smith, *Tales of Laughter.* Garden City, New York: Doubleday & Company, Inc., 1954. Fifth-eighth grade

2. Help the child increase his vocabulary by choosing a book or story that has a reasonable number of words unfamiliar to him. When the child hears an unfamiliar word, ask him to say "I don't know that word." You can record the word and then return to an appropriate stopping place. The word and its meaning should be discussed. Some interesting books are:

O'Dell, Scott. *Island of the Blue Dolphins.* Boston: Houghton Mifflin Company, 1960.

L'Engle, Madeline. *A Wrinkle in Time.* New York: Farrar, Straus & Giroux, Inc., 1962.

Hall, Marie. *Nine Days to Christmas, A Story of Mexico.* New York: ETS and Aurora Labratiola. The Viking Press, Inc., 1959.

Harder, Berta and Elmer, *The Big Snow.* New York: Macmillan Publishing Co., Inc., 1958.

Lofting, Hugh. *The Voyages of Doctor Dolittle.* Philadelphia: Lippincott Company, Inc., 1922.

Mukerji, Dhan Gopal. *Gay-Neck: The Story of a Pigeon.* New York: E. P. Dutton & Co., Inc., 1927.

Kelly, Eric P. *The Trumpeter of Krakow.* New York: Macmillan Publishing Co., Inc., 1928.

3. Help the child develop interest in reading by selecting picture books that have illustrations of the story. Have the child look at the pictures, telling the story he sees. Some appropriate titles are listed below.

Lifton, Betty Jean. *The Many Lives of Cio & Goro.* New York: W. W. Norton & Company, Inc., 1968.

Olds, Helen D. *What Will I Wear?* New York: Alfred A. Knopf, Inc., 1961.

Lindgren, Astrid. *Mischievous Meg.* New York: The Viking Press, Inc., 1960.

Hauff, Frans and Doris Orgel. *Dwarf Long-Nose.* New York: Random House, Inc., 1960.

Kraentzel, Margaret. *Rain Cloud, the Wild Mustang.* New York: Lothrop Lee & Sheperel Company, 1962.

Freeman, Don. *Penguins of All People!* New York: The Viking Press, 1971.
Elkin, Benjamin. *Why the Sun Was Late.* New York: Parent's Magazine Press, 1966.

4. When your child has enjoyed a story, choose characters you can portray. As you and your child go about your chores, act as you think the characters would act in your situation. Here are some useful references:

Balet, Jan. *Jango.* New York: Delacorte Press, 1965.
Buckley, Helen E. *Too Many Crackers.* New York: Lothrop, Lee & Shepard Company, 1966.
Cowles, Ginny, *Nicholas.* New York: The Seabury Press, 1975
Duncan, Lois. *Giving Away Suzanne.* New York: Dodd, Mead & Company, 1963.
Hill, Lorna. *Masquerade of the Ballet.* New York: Holt, Rinehart and Winston, 1952.
Levitin, Sonia. *Journey to America.* New York: Atheneum Publishers, 1970.
Ness, Evaline. *Do You Have the Time, Lydia?* New York: E. P. Dutton & Co., Inc., 1971.
Newman, Robert. *Merlin's Mistake.* New York: Atheneum Publishers, 1970.
Newman, Shirlee Retkin. *Yellow Silk for May Lee.* New York: The Bobbs-Merrill Co., Inc., 1961.

5. Set aside a family reading time; the material can be recreational or informative.

6. Try to interest your child in some of the following magazines:

Co-ed	Illinois History
Cricket	Jack & Jill
Curious Naturalist	Junior Scholastic
Current Events	Kansas School Naturalist
Ebony, Jr.	Man & His Music
Kids for Ecology	Maryland Conservationists
News Explorer	Maryland Magazine
My Weekly Reader Eye	Model Airplane News
Highlights for Children	Nature Canada
Horn Book	Popular Science
Humpty Dumpty's Magazine	Ranger Rick's Nature Magazine
for Little Children	Wee Wish Tree
Read	Wisconsin Trails
Roots	World Traveler
Science World	The New Yorker
Senior Scholastic	Young Miss
Senior Weekly Reader	Young World
Texas Historian	Zoonooz
Wee Wisdom	

7. Try to acquire some of the following records and "read along" editions of good books for readers.

European Folk and Fairy Tales CMS Records 1968 (K–6)

Drummer Hoff Barbara Emberley (K–3)
  Film, Morton Schindel, 1969, 16mm 5 min, color
  Filmstrip, Weston Woods, 34 grames, color w/record or cassette

Light in the Forest Conrad Richter
  Film, Buena Vista, 16mm color

The Mouse that Roared Leonard Wibberley (7–8)
  Film, Columbia, 1959, 16mm color
  Record, CMS Records, 1970 (by the author)

Mother Mother I Feel Sick Send for the Doctor Quick Quick Quick Remy Charlip (K–3)
  Filmstrip, Look/Listen & Learn, 43 frames, b/w

Where Does the Butterfly Go When It Rains? Mary Garelick
  Filmstrip, Weston Woods, 20 frames, color w/cassette or record

The Wisest Man in the World retold by Benjamin Elkin (K–6)
  Film, Thomas Sand, 1970, 16mm, color

The Witch of Blackbird Pond Elizabeth George Spetre
  Record or cassette, Miller-Brody Production, 1970

Evan's Corner Elizabeth Starr Hill (K–6)
  Film, Stephen Bosustow, 16 mm, color

Poetry Parade
  Record or cassette, Weston Woods, 1967

8. Help children develop the library habit. Take them to the library and let them help select books to read.

9. Use books as gifts. Ownership has been found to be one of the most important factors in encouraging reading. Some interesting books for gifts are:

Hoban, Lillian. *Arthur's Honey Bear.* New York: Harper & Row, Publishers, 1974, grades 1–3. PSM $2.95; PLB $3.43

Byars, Betsy. *After the Goat Man.* New York: The Viking Press, Inc., 1974, grades 4–6 PLB $5.95

Williams, Barbara. *Albert's Toothache.* New York: E. A. Dutton & Co., Inc., 1974, grade 2, PLB $4.95

Scott, Jack D. *Loggerhead Turtle: Survivor from the Sea.* New York: G. P. Putnam Sons, 1974, grades 4–7, CSM $6.95

Preston, Edna. *Squawk to the Moon, Little Goose.* New York: The Viking Press, Inc., 1974, preschool-grade 1, PLB $5.95

Snyder, Zilpa. *The Truth About Stone Hollow.* New York: Atheneum Publishers, 1974, grades 4–7, PLB $6.25

Determining a Student's Self-Concept

Krathwohl Taxonomy

Several researchers have attempted to present the components of the affective domain of the human intellect in a hierarchical array similar to the taxonomies presented by Bloom (1954) and Barrett (1968). Krathwohl (1969), among others, has attempted to demonstrate the relationship between affective processes and reading ability. The Krathwohl taxonomy is presented here:

1.0   Receiving (attending)
    1.1   Awareness
    1.2   Willingness to receive
    1.3   Controlled or selected attention
2.0   Responding
    2.1   Acquiescence in responding
    2.2   Willingness to respond
    2.3   Satisfaction in response
3.0   Valuing
    3.1   Acceptance of a value
    3.2   Preference for a value
    3.3   Commitment (conviction)
4.0   Organization
    4.1   Conceptualization of a value
    4.2   Organization of a value system
5.0   Characterization by a value or value complex
    5.1   Generalized set
    5.2   Characterization (p. 95)

Utilizing this taxonomy many researchers have demonstrated the relationship between the child's self-concept and his reading ability. In the past, educators have successfully attempted to intervene in a child's life by developing his or her self-concept. They had hoped that an increase in a positive self-concept would result in increased reading ability.

Before you set up an intervention problem, it is important to adequately assess the self-concept of each child. There are many instruments that have been developed to assess self-perceptions; for example, Gordon's (1966) *How I See Myself Scale.* The first six items from this scale are presented below:

1. Nothing gets me too mad   1 2 3 4 5   I get mad easily and explode
2. I don't stay with things and   1 2 3 4 5   I stay with something till I
   finish them   finish
3. I'm very good at drawing   1 2 3 4 5   I'm not much good at drawing
4. I don't like to work on   1 2 3 4 5   I like to work with others
   committees, projects
5. I wish I were smaller (taller)   1 2 3 4 5   I'm just the right height
6. I worry a lot   1 2 3 4 5   I don't worry much

Determining a Student's Attitudes Toward Reading

Analysis of a child's attitude toward reading tells us if he *likes* or *dislikes* to read. Like the king in the play on page 116–119, many children develop a negative attitude toward reading because they have been required to read materials for which they do not have the needed competencies. They often have had an unsuccessful reading experience. Once the child encounters failure, it is difficult to convince him that reading is either fun or important. The following measures may help you determine your students' attitudes toward reading.

The first measure is especially appropriate for young children.

Reading Attitude Inventory
Paul Campbell, 1966

Name _____   Grade _____   Teacher _____

1. How do you feel when your teacher reads a story out loud?

2. How do you feel when someone gives you a book for a present?

3. How do you feel about reading books for fun at home?

4. How do you feel when you are asked to read out loud to your group?

5. How do you feel when you are asked to read out loud to the teacher?

6. How do you feel when you come to a new word while reading?

7. How do you feel when it is time to do your worksheet?

8. How do you feel about going to school?

9. How do you feel about how well you can read?

10. How do you think your friends feel about reading?

11. How do you think your teacher feels when you read?

12. How do you think your friends feel when you read out loud?

13. How do you feel about the reading group you are in?

14. How do you think you'll feel about reading when you're bigger?

Below is an alternate form of the first measure.

Reading Interest/Attitude Scale
Right to Read Office, Washington, D.C. 1976

Date _____   Grade _____   Name _____

Directions: Read each item slowly twice to each child. Ask him/her to point to the face which shows how he/she feels about the statement. Circle the corresponding symbol. Read each item with the same inflection and intonation.

A	B	C
Strongly Agree	Undecided	Strongly Disagree
(Makes me feel good)	(OK or don't know)	(Makes me feel bad)

A	B	C	1. When I go to the store I like to buy books.
A	B	C	2. Reading is for learning but not for fun.
A	B	C	3. Books are fun to me.
A	B	C	4. I like to share books with friends.
A	B	C	5. Reading makes me happy.
A	B	C	6. I read some books more than once.
A	B	C	7. Most books are too long.
A	B	C	8. There are many books I hope to read.
A	B	C	9. Books make good presents.
A	B	C	10. I like to have books read to me.

This second measure can be used with older students. You can read some of the following statements to your students in order to assess their attitudes toward reading.

Reading Attitude Inventory
by Molly Ransbury, 1971

Yes   No

_____   _____   1. I visit the library to find books I might enjoy reading.

_____   _____   2. I would like to read a magazine in my free time.

Yes   No

_____   _____   3. I cannot pay attention to my reading when there is even a little noise or movement nearby.

_____   _____   4. I enjoy reading extra books about topics we study in school.

_____   _____   5. I would like to read newspaper articles about my favorite hobbies or interests.

_____   _____   6. I feel I know the characters in some of the comic books I read.

_____   _____   7. My best friend would tell you that I enjoy reading very much.

_____   _____   8. I would like to belong to a group that discusses many kinds of reading.

_____   _____   9. I would enjoy spending some time during my summer vacation reading to children in a summer library program.

_____   _____   10. My ideas are changed by the books I read.

_____   _____   11. Reading is a very important part of my life. Every day I read many different types of materials.

_____   _____   12. I read magazines for many different reasons.

_____   _____   13. My friends would tell you that I'd much rather watch T.V. than read.

_____   _____   14. When I listen to someone read out loud, certain words or sentences might attract my attention.

_____   _____   15. I would only read a book if my teacher or my parents said I had to.

_____   _____   16. Magazines, comic books and newspapers do not interest me.

_____   _____   17. I do not enjoy reading in my free time.

_____   _____   18. I would enjoy talking with someone else about one of my favorite books.

_____   _____   19. I might go to the library several times to see if a special book had been returned.

_____   _____   20. I am too busy during vacations to plan a reading program for myself.

Yes   No

_____ _____   21. Sometimes the book that I'm reading will remind me of ideas from another book that I've read.

_____ _____   22. If my only reading was for school assignments, I would be very unhappy.

_____ _____   23. Reading is not a very good way for me to learn new things.

_____ _____   24. I think reading is boring.

_____ _____   25. If I see a comic book or magazine I would usually just look at the pictures.

_____ _____   26. I sometimes read extra books or articles about something that we have discussed in school.

_____ _____   27. I enjoy going to the library and choosing special books.

_____ _____   28. I do not read during any of my vacations from school.

_____ _____   29. I would not want to help set up a book exhibit.

_____ _____   30. It would be very, very nice for me to have my own library of books.

_____ _____   31. I don't try to read many different kinds of books.

_____ _____   32. If I do not read many things when I'm an adult, I will miss many important ideas about life.

_____ _____   33. I read because the teacher tells me to.

_____ _____   34. I read only because people force me to.

_____ _____   35. I must shut myself in a quiet room in order to read almost anything.

_____ _____   36. I never do extra reading outside of school work because reading is so dull.

_____ _____   37. I only read extra books if my parents say I have to.

_____ _____   38. Reading certain newspaper articles might make me happy, or sad, or even angry.

_____ _____   39. I should spend some of my time each day reading so that I can learn about the world.

Yes   No

_____   _____   40. Before I make up my mind about something, I try to read more than one writer's ideas.

_____   _____   41. When I read, I sometimes understand myself a little better.

_____   _____   42. Some characters I have read about help me to better understand people I know.

_____   _____   43. Reading is a very important part of my life. I read nearly every day in books or newspapers and I enjoy doing so.

_____   _____   44. I would like to read some of the novels my teacher reads to the class.

_____   _____   45. I would like to read more books if I had the time.

_____   _____   46. I might keep a list of the books that I wish to read during the next few months.

_____   _____   47. My parents force me to read.

_____   _____   48. If people didn't tell me that I had to read, I would probably never pick up a book.

_____   _____   49. Sometimes I think ahead in my reading and imagine what the characters might do.

_____   _____   50. I wish I could buy more books for myself.

_____   _____   51. Sometimes I wish the author of the book had written the story a different way.

_____   _____   52. Much of my free time is spent in reading, library browsing and discussing books.

_____   _____   53. I read lots of different newspaper articles so that I can learn more about the world.

_____   _____   54. Reading is as much a part of my life as eating, sleeping and playing.

_____   _____   55. A story that I see on television might also be interesting to read in a book.

_____   _____   56. Even a little reading makes me feel tired and restless.

_____   _____   57. I try to read many different types of materials in my free time.

Yes   No

_____ _____ 58. I would always rather talk about things, than to read about them.

_____ _____ 59. I have never wanted to read a book twice.

_____ _____ 60. When I am an adult and work all day, I will not read.

_____ _____ 61. I would feel disappointed if I could not find a book that I was very interested in reading.

_____ _____ 62. I have sometimes told my friends about a really good book that they might like to read.

_____ _____ 63. I look for some main ideas that the writer presents when I read a magazine article.

_____ _____ 64. Reading is a very important part of my life when I am not in school.

These are only a few of the many available instruments which purport to measure reading attitudes. Others which may be of interest to you include:

Powell, A., Primary Attitude Reading Index with Administrator's Directions, 1971, (Grades 1-3)

Powell, A., Intermediate Attitude Reading Index with Administrator's Directions, 1971, (Grades 4-6)

Estes, Thomas H., "Assessing Attitudes Toward Reading," _Journal of Reading_, November, 1971

Koch, R. E., "What Do You Think About Reading?", 1974, (Grades 4-6)

Huntington, Betty, "Scales To Measure Attitudes Towards Reading," 1975, (Grades 1-6)

Determining Student's Interests in Reading

Witty (1963, p. 331) defined interest as:

> . . . a disposition or tendency which impels an individual to seek out particular goals for persistent attention. The goals may be objects, skills, knowledges, and art activities of various kinds. The behavior patterns in seeking these goals may be regarded as particular interests such as collecting objects or viewing TV. They should be looked upon as acquired, although they are based upon such factors as the constitutional nature of the individual and his personality structure as affected by his unique experiences and his particular environment.

This quote suggests that the development of student's positive interest in reading may depend upon the success with which you are able to know and understand the child's background and the experiences that have led him to his present state. It also suggests that some understanding of individual personality is required. How are such understandings acquired?

As you attempt to implement a reading program, you may wish to talk to the child about the things he enjoys doing. Ask him to explain what he does in his free time. You should observe the things which hold his interest and the things which seem to have little impact on him. It may also be useful to assess a student's reading interests by collecting information from an informal survey. Two surveys which may help you to collect this information are presented in the following pages. The first is a "complete the sentence" type of survey, and the second is a reading/responding survey.

Interest Inventory

Name _____ Age _____

Date _____

1. My favorite day of the week is _____ because

   _____ .

2. The television programs I like the most are _____

   _____ .

3. The most fun I ever had was when _____

   _____ .

4. The person I would most like to meet is _____ because

   _____ .

5. My favorite course in school is _____ .

6. The one course in school I don't like is _____ .

7. I dislike it because _____ .

8. On a sunny day I like to _____ .

9. Reading is _____ .

10. The things I like to read are _____ .

11. The best story I ever read was _____ .

12. In my spare time I like to _____ .

13. The chores I do at home are _____ .

14. My brothers and sisters _____ .

15. My hobbies are _____ .

16. I get really mad when _____ .

17. When I grow up I'd like to be _____

    because _____ .

18. Poetry makes me _____ .

19. Music is _____ .

20. Places I'd like to visit are _____ .

21. My favorite sport is _____ .

22. Libraries are _____ .

23. During the summer I like to _____ .

24. On a winter day I like to _____ .

25. I wish my parents would _____ .

26. Animals are _____ .

27. I'd like to have a _____ for a pet because

    _____ .

28. The best food in the whole world is _____ .

29. My favorite color is _____ .

30. Right now I'd like to _____ .

The following survey calls for direct verbal interaction between the student and the teacher. The child listens as the teacher reads each of these items and then responds to them orally.

Interest Inventory

Name _____ Age _____

Date _____

1. What do you like to do when you have free time?
2. How do you usually spend your summers?
3. How much reading do you do on your own?
4. How much television do you watch each day?
5. What are your favorite TV programs?
6. What movies have you seen that you really liked?
7. Do you ever read a book after you have seen the television or movie version?
8. Have you ever visited any of these places?

Art Museum	Circus	Theater
Science Museum	National Park	Library
Concert Halls	Zoo	

9. What other countries have you visited or lived in?
10. What other cities or states have you visited or lived in?

Circle the school subjects you like, cross-out the subjects you don't like:

Arithmetic	Science	Gym
Spelling	Social Studies	Health
Reading	Music	English
Art	Other languages	

Circle the kinds of books and stories you like, cross-out the books and stories you don't like:

Adventure	Mystery	Magazines
Animal stories	Motorcycles	Comic books
Hobby stories	Love and romance	Ghost stories
Biography	Science fiction	Family stories
Autobiography	Car magazines	Riddles and jokes
Science	Fables and myths	Horse stories
Western stories	Sports	Humor
Art and music	Religion	Fantasy
Fairy tales	People of other lands	History
Poetry	Newspapers	Geography

11. What is it that you do well?
12. What is it that you do not do well?

Determining Learning Style

Educational researchers direct a great deal of their attention to the learning style of the child. Each of us has a preferred learning style for every task we undertake. Some of us will say: "I'm a graphic-visual learner. I can only study by writing out the information." Others will say: "I'm an auditory learner, I need to have things spoken before I can learn." Although these statements may be true for a specific situation, they probably do not carry over to all situations. In other words, as competent adults we use several different learning styles despite the fact that we have a preferred style.

Our students, however, may not have acquired an array of styles. The following instrument will help us to assess students' perceptions of their "best" style, and then we can decide if we want to teach to this one style or build an array of effective styles.

Learning Style Indicator

DIRECTIONS: Read each pair of statements and mark the box next to the statement that <u>most closely</u> describes you.

1.	I understand things better from a picture.	☐	☐	I understand things better from someone telling me or reading about them.
2.	I look at charts and diagrams before I read the written part.	☐	☐	I read the written part before I look at the charts and diagrams.
3.	I memorize things by writing them out.	☐	☐	I memorize things by repeating them aloud.
4.	I like examples first, rules later.	☐	☐	I like rules first, examples later.
5.	I usually get more done when I work alone.	☐	☐	I usually get more done when I work with others.
6.	I enjoy doing a number of things at the same time.	☐	☐	I prefer doing things one at a time.
7.	I usually ask "why" questions.	☐	☐	I usually ask about facts.
8.	I prefer working quickly.	☐	☐	I prefer to work slowly.
9.	I answer questions quickly.	☐	☐	I answer questions carefully and slowly.
10.	I take chances at making mistakes.	☐	☐	I try to avoid making mistakes.

High Interest Materials

In an attempt to reverse negative reading attitudes, it is of utmost importance that you select reading materials that stimulate the children's interest while complementing their level of reading competency. A text selection can be made from the following resources.

Materials Lists

1. Tolman, Lorraine E., and Thomas E. Culliton. High-Interest-Low Vocabulary Reading Materials. *Journal of Education* (April 1967).
2. White, Marion E., ed. *High-Interest Easy Reading for Junior and Senior High School Students.* New York: Citation Press, 1972.
3. Spache, George. *Good Reading for Poor Readers.* Champaign, Ill.: Garrard Publishing Company, 1974.

The following texts serve as an example of high-interest/low-vocabulary materials.

1. Bamman, and Whitehead. *Beneath the Sea* (one of six titles in the World Adventure Series). Chicago: Benefic; 1964. RL*, 4 (Spache) IL*, 4 up
2. Corbett, Scott. *Cop's Kid.* Boston: Little, Brown and Company. RL 4–5 IL 4–up
3. Ojigbu, Okion. *Young and Black in Africa.* New York: Random House, Inc., 1971. RL 5–6 IL 6–up
4. Fejes, Claire. *Enuk, My Son.* New York: Pantheon, 1969. RL 3–9 IL 3–7
5. Aliki. *The Story of William Penn.* Englewood Cliffs, N.J.: Prentice-Hall, Inc., 1964. RL 3 IL up
6. Hearn, Emily. *Around Another Corner.* Champaign, Ill.: Garrard Publishing, 1971. RL 1–8 IL 1–3
7. DeJong, Meindert. *The Singing Hill.* New York: Harper & Row, Publishers, 1962. RL 3 IL 3–5
8. Klimo, Joan. *What Can I Do Today?* New York: Pantheon Books, Inc., 1971. RL 4–5 IL 4 up Series Books
9. *Big Treasure Books.* New York: Watts (RL, grades 2–4; IL, grades 2 up)
10. *First Books.* New York: Watts (RL, grades 2–6; IL, grades 4 up)

High interest games also need to be part of your classroom materials. For example:

1. Alcoch, Dorthen, *Blendograms,* Covina, Calif.: Alcoch Publishing, RL K–3 IL 3 up
2. Balinger, Willeta R., *You and Your World,* Palo Alto: Fenem, 1964, RL primary IL Jr. and Sr. High.

*RL = reading level; IL - Interest level

Astrology

The following list of people born under each sign should produce some interest among your students. Astrology, like magic, has delighted and involved audiences throughout the ages. This list can be a high-interest motivator for several reading lessons.

Ask your students to

1. Determine their sign.
2. "Read" about the characteristics of their sign.

Several more advanced reading and reference skills lessons could be developed around the theme of "astrological signs." Ask students to find other famous people who were born under their sign.

Aries

Pearl Bailey
Robert Frost
Charlie Chaplin
Gloria Steinem
Johann Sebastian Bach

Taurus

Harry Truman
Willie Mays
Peter Tchaikovsky
Barbara Streisand
Karl Marx

Gemini

Marilyn Monroe
John F. Kennedy
Paul McCartney
Joe Willie Namath
Bob Hope

Cancer

Nelson Rockefeller
Arthur Ashe
Bella Abzug
Ernest Hemingway
The United States

Sagittarius

Walt Disney
Ludwig von Beethoven
Jane Fonda
Shirley Chisholm
Mark Twain

Capricorn

Jesus
Muhammed Ali
Martin Luther King, Jr.
Joan Baez
Howard Hughes

Leo

James Baldwin
Casey Stengel
Jackie Kennedy
Mike Douglas
Napoleon Bonaparte

Virgo

Lyndon Johnson
Queen Elizabeth
Leonard Bernstein
Sophia Loren
Henry Ford

Libra

Johnny Carson
Pope Paul VI
John Lennon
Dwight Eisenhower
Ed Sullivan

Scorpio

Chang Kai-Shek
Billy Graham
Robert F. Kennedy
Pablo Picasso
Spiro Agnew

Aquarius

Leontyne Price
Ronald Reagan
Clark Gable
Thomas Edison
Hank Aaron

Pisces

Sidney Poitier
Sly Stone
W. E. B. Dubois
Albert Einstein
Barbara Gordon

As a cross-cultural unit, you may want to ask students to find out the symbol for the year of their birth in the Chinese calendar. Ask them to cross-reference the people born under their sign with their Chinese character symbol. Are there any discrepancies.

Reader's Theater

In the last few years, teachers have been effectively using Reader's Theater in the classrooms to encourage and motivate students to read. Before examining the effect of Reader's Theater, let us explain what it is. In Reader's Theater the student hears literature spoken but must *imagine* the scenery, action, and characters.

Reader's Theater differs from conventional theaters because all the characters have copies of the scripts in their hands. The audience does not have copies of the script during the performance. The people taking the parts of the character are not becoming that character, they are suggesting the character to the audience. The character has to be developed in the minds of the members of the audience. Generally, in Reader's Theater, the actors do not interact or look at one another. Usually there are no sets, costumes, or lights and there is little or no movement on the stage. The goal of Reader's Theater is to establish scenes, characters, and actions for the audience, forcing them to conjure or imagine the action. The effect is dramatic because our imaginations can be much more effective than what is produced by the reader-actors.

This is an excellent type of reading assignment for many students. First, most students are incapable of acting out parts in a play. Reader's Theater does not demand physical portrayal; it asks for oral interpretation. Second, the student who is part of the audience has to visualize the spoken word. Reader's Theater is a good exercise for helping students with their listening skills. Third, less capable readers can become involved in this form of reading because they have the opportunity to prepare the script. In the beginning, they can take the roles that demand less reading.

This form of drama is very experimental; it allows students to be creative. They can use music or any other audiovisual aid that they think will be effective. There should be no limit to what can happen to the audience's minds. Extensive rehearsal and memorization usually are unnecessary. But, as with any dramatic presentation, familiarity with the material enhances the production considerably.

Reader's Theater can be used effectively in team-teaching situations. A class can research the life of a famous scientist, mathematician, or literary figure and write biographical Reader's Theater scripts about him or her. The script can include sections from their journals, letters, and diaries and news clippings and personal documents.

Finally, students can rewrite literature into dramatic plays and use plays that have already been written. The stories and novels that are best for Reader's

Theater are those in which there is a great deal of dialogue. Actions that are visually important but unspoken are inappropriate for Reader's Theater—for example, Desdemona's dropping of the handkerchief.

In working with students in a Reader's Theater production, it is important to stress their role as an interpreter. This is often difficult for them, particularly for young children because they want to look at each other. It is important to discuss with students that the most important *sense* played to in Reader's Theater is not the audience's eyes, but their ears, as well as their minds and imaginations.

Characters can be arranged on the stage—that is in a selected part of your classroom—in a number of ways. Students should be seated on stools or chairs, and holding their script in front of them. A change in scene can be narrated by a student. Entrances and exits are handled by the characters standing or sitting, stepping forward or backward, dropping their eyes, or by any other methods that seem appropriate for a particular script. There are no rules in the Reader's Theater, but the audience should not *see* the action on the stage. There should be one guiding principle: Make the audience do the work in their minds.

Here are some scripts that are useful for Reader's Theater classroom productions.

WINNIE-THE-POOH: In Which Pooh Goes Visiting and Gets Into a Tight Place

A. A. Milne

NARRATOR
WINNIE-THE-POOH
RABBIT
CHRISTOPHER ROBIN

NARRATOR: Edward Bear, known to his friends as Winnie-the-Pooh, or Pooh for short, was walking through the forest one day, humming proudly to himself. He had made up a little hum that very morning as he was doing his Stoutness Exercises in front of the glass: Tra-la-la, tra-la-la, as he stretched up as high as he could go, and then Tra-la-la, tra-la-oh, help!—la, as he tried to reach his toes. Well he was humming this hum to himself and walking along gaily, wondering what everyone else was doing and what it felt like, being somebody else, when he came to a sandy bank, and in the bank was a large hole.

POOH: Aha! If I know anything about anything, that hole means Rabbit, and Rabbit means Company, and Company means Food and Listening-to-Me-Humming and such like. Rum-tum-tum-tiddle-un.

NARRATOR: So he bent down, put his head into the hole and called out:

POOH: Is anybody at home?

NARRATOR: There was a sudden scuffling noise from inside the hole and then silence.

POOH: What I said was "Is anybody at home?"

RABBIT: No. You needn't shout so loud. I heard you quite well the first time.

POOH: Bother! Isn't there anybody here at all?

RABBIT: Nobody.

POOH: There must be somebody there because somebody must have said "Nobody." Hello, Rabbit, isn't that you?

RABBIT: No.

POOH: But isn't that Rabbit's voice?

RABBIT: I don't think so. It isn't meant to be.

POOH: Well, could you tell me very kindly where Rabbit is?

RABBIT: He has gone to see his friend Pooh Bear, who is a great friend of his.

POOH: But this is Me!

RABBIT: What sort of me?

POOH: Pooh Bear.

RABBIT: Are you sure?

POOH: Quite, quite sure.

RABBIT: Oh well. Then, come in.

NARRATOR: So Pooh pushed and pushed and pushed his way through the hole and at last he got in.

RABBIT: You were quite right. It is you. Glad to see you.

POOH: Who did you think it was?

RABBIT: Well, I wasn't sure. You know how it is in the Forest. One can't have anybody coming into one's house. One has to be careful. What about a mouthful of something. Would you like honey or condensed milk with your bread?

POOH: Both. But don't bother about the bread, please.

NARRATOR: For a long time after that he said nothing until at last humming to himself in a rather sticky voice, he got up, shook Rabbit lovingly by the paw and said that he must be going on.

RABBIT: Must you?

POOH: Well, I could stay a little longer if it—if you—

RABBIT: As a matter of fact I was going out myself directly.

POOH: Oh well then I'll be going on. Good-bye.

RABBIT: Well good-bye—if you're sure you won't have any more.

POOH: Is there any more?

RABBIT: No, there wasn't.

POOH: I thought not. Well goodbye. I must be going on.

NARRATOR: So he started to climb out of the hole. He pulled with his front paws and pushed with his back paws and in a little while his nose was out in the open again and then his ears and then his front paws and then his shoulders and then . . .

POOH: Oh help! I'd better go back. Oh bother! I shall have to go on. I can't do either! Oh help and bother!

NARRATOR: Now by this time Rabbit wanted to go for a walk too and finding the front door full he went out by the back door and came round to Pooh and looked at him.

RABBIT: Hello, are you stuck?

POOH: No, just resting and thinking and humming to myself.

RABBIT: Here, give me a paw.

NARRATOR: Pooh Bear stretched out a paw, and Rabbit pulled and pulled and pulled.

POOH: OW! You're hurting!

RABBIT: The fact is, you're stuck.

POOH: It all comes of not having front doors big enough.

RABBIT: It all comes of eating too much. I thought at the time, only I didn't like to say anything, that one of us was eating too much, and I knew it wasn't me. Well, well. I shall go and fetch Christopher Robin.

NARRATOR: Christopher Robin lived at the other end of the forest and when he came back with Rabbit and saw the front half of Pooh, he said in a loving voice:

C. ROBIN: Silly old bear.

POOH: I was just beginning to think that Rabbit might never be able to use his front door again. And I should hate that.

RABBIT: So should I.

C. ROBIN: Use his front door again? Of course he'll use his front door again. If we can't pull you out Pooh, we might push you back.

NARRATOR: Rabbit scratched his whiskers thoughtfully and pointed out that once Pooh was pushed back, he was back, and of course nobody was more glad to see Pooh than he was, yet still there it was—some lived in trees and some lived underground and

POOH: You mean I'd never get out?

RABBIT: I mean that having got so far it seems a pity to waste it.

C. ROBIN: Then there's only one thing to be done. We shall have to wait for you to get thin again.

POOH: How long does getting thin take?

C. ROBIN: About a week. I should think.

POOH: But I can't stay here for a week!

C. ROBIN: You can stay here all right silly old Bear. It's getting you out which is so difficult.

RABBIT: We'll read to you. And I hope it won't snow. And I say old fellow—you're taking up a good deal of room in my house—do you mind if I use your back legs as a towel horse? Because I mean there they are—doing nothing—and it would be very convenient just to hang the towels on them.

POOH: A week! What about meals?

C. ROBIN: I'm afraid no meals because of getting thin quicker. But we will read to you.

NARRATOR: Bear began to sigh and then found he couldn't because he was so tightly stuck; and a tear rolled down his eye as he said:

POOH: Then would you read a Sustaining Book such as would help and comfort a Wedged Bear in Great Tightness?

NARRATOR: So for a week Christopher Robin read that sort of book at the North end of Pooh and Rabbit hung his washing on the South end and in between Bear felt himself getting slenderer and slenderer. And at the end of a week Christopher Robin said:

C. ROBIN: Now!!

NARRATOR: So he took hold of Pooh's front paws and Rabbit took hold of Christopher Robin and all Rabbit's friends and relations took hold of Rabbit and they all pulled together ... and for a long time Pooh only said:

POOH: OW! OW!

NARRATOR: And then, all of a sudden, just as if a cork was coming out of a bottle, he said:

POOH: Pop!

NARRATOR: And Christopher Robin and Rabbit and all Rabbit's friends and relations went head-over-heels backward ... and on the top of them came Winnie-the-Pooh—free! So, with a nod of thanks to his friends, he went on with his walk through the forest humming proudly to himself. But Christopher Robin looked after him lovingly and said to himself:

C. ROBIN: Silly old Bear!

THE GIVING TREE

Shel Silverstein

(Elementary 3–6)

NARRATOR 1
NARRATOR 2
TREE
BOY

NARRATOR 1: Once there was a tree ... and she loved the little boy. And every-day the boy would come and he would gather her leaves and make them into crowns and play King of the Forest.

NARRATOR 2: He would climb her trunk and swing from her branches and eat apples.

NARRATOR 1: And they would play hide and seek.

NARRATOR 2: And when he was tired he would sleep in her shade. And the boy loved the tree very much.

NARRATOR 1: And the tree was happy.

NARRATOR 2: But time went by and the boy grew older.

NARRATOR 1: And the tree was often alone. Then one day the boy came to the tree and the tree said,

TREE: Come boy, come and climb up my trunk and swing from my branches and eat apples and play in my shade and be happy.

BOY: I am too big to climb and play. I want to buy things and have fun. I want some money. Can you give me some money?

TREE: I'm sorry, but I have no money. I have only leaves and apples. Take my apples, Boy, and sell them in the city. Then you will have money and you will be happy.

NARRATOR 2: And so the boy climbed up the tree and gathered her apples and carried them away.

NARRATOR 1: And the tree was happy.

NARRATOR 2: But the boy stayed away for a long time. And the tree was sad. And then one day the boy came back and the tree shook with joy and she said,

TREE: Come boy, climb up my trunk and swing from my branches and be happy.

BOY: I am too busy to climb trees. I want a house to keep me warm. I want a wife and I want children and so I need a house. Can you give me a house?

TREE: I have no house. The forest is my house, but you may cut off my branches and build a house. Then you will be happy.

NARRATOR 1: And so the boy cut off her branches and carried them away to build his house.

NARRATOR 2: And the tree was happy.

NARRATOR 1: But the boy stayed away for a long time and when he came back, the tree was so happy she could hardly speak.

TREE: Come, boy,

NARRATOR 1: She whispered,

TREE: Come and play

BOY: I am too old and sad to play. I want a boat that will take me far away from here. Can you give me a boat?

TREE: Cut down my trunk and make a boat. Then you can sail away and be happy.

NARRATOR 2: And so the boy cut down her trunk and made a boat and sailed away.

NARRATOR 1: And the tree was happy ... but not really.

NARRATOR 2: And after a long time the boy came back again.

TREE: I am sorry boy, but I have nothing left to give you—my apples are gone.

BOY: My teeth are too weak for apples.

TREE: My branches are gone. You cannot swing on them.

BOY: I am too old to swing on branches.

TREE: My trunk is gone. You cannot climb ...

BOY: I am too tired to climb.

TREE: I am sorry (sigh). I wish that I could give you something but I have nothing left. I am just an old stump and I am sorry.

BOY: I don't need very much now. Just a quiet place to sit and rest. I am very tired.

TREE: Well,

NARRATOR 1: Said the tree, straightening herself up as much as she could.

TREE: Well, an old stump *is* good for sitting and resting. Come, boy, sit down. Sit down and rest.

NARRATOR 2: And the boy did.

NARRATOR 1: And the tree was happy.

POOR OLD LADY

1: Poor old lady, she swallowed a fly.
   I don't know why she swallowed a fly.

2: Poor old lady, I think she'll die.

3: Poor old lady, she swallowed a spider.
   It squirmed and wriggled and turned inside her.

1: She swallowed the spider to catch the fly.
   I don't know why she swallowed a fly.

2: Poor old lady, I think she'll die.

4: Poor old lady, she swallowed a bird.
   How absurd! She swallowed a bird.

3: She swallowed the bird to catch the spider.

1: She swallowed the spider to catch the fly,
   I don't know why she swallowed a fly.

2: Poor old lady, I think she'll die.

5: Poor old lady, she swallowed a cat.
   Think of that! She swallowed a cat.

4: She swallowed the cat to catch the bird.

3: She swallowed the bird to catch the spider,

1: She swallowed the spider to catch the fly,
   I don't know why she swallowed the fly.

2: Poor old lady, I think she'll die.

6: Poor old lady, she swallowed a dog.
   She went the whole hog when she swallowed the dog.

5: She swallowed the dog to catch the cat.

4: She swallowed the cat to catch the bird.

3: She swallowed the bird to catch the spider,
1: She swallowed the spider to catch the fly,
   I don't know why she swallowed the fly.
2: Poor old lady, I think she'll die.

7: Poor old lady, she swallowed a cow.
   I don't know how she swallowed the cow.
6: She swallowed the cow to catch the dog,
5: She swallowed the dog to catch the cat,
4: She swallowed the cat to catch the bird,
3: She swallowed the bird to catch the spider,
1: She swallowed the spider to catch the fly.
   I don't know why she swallowed a fly.
2: Poor old lady, I think she'll die.

8: Poor old lady, she swallowed a horse.
All: She died, of course.

GERTRUDE McFUZZ

By Dr. Seuss

(Elementary)

Characters

NARRATOR 1
NARRATOR 2
GERTRUDE
LOLLA-LEE-LOU

NARRATOR 1:	"Gertrude McFuzz."
NARRATOR 2:	By Dr. Seuss.
NARRATOR 1:	There once was a girl-bird named
GERTRUDE:	Gertrude McFuss.
NARRATOR 2:	And she had the smallest plain tail there ever was.
GERTRUDE:	One droopy-droop feather.
NARRATOR 1:	That's all that she had.
NARRATOR 2:	And, oh! That one feather made Gertrude so sad!
GERTRUDE:	(echoes "So sad!")
NARRATOR 1:	For there was another young bird that she knew
LOLLA-LEE-LOU:	A fancy young birdie named Lolla-Lee-Lou.
NARRATOR 1:	And instead of one feather behind, she had
LOLLA-LEE-LOU:	Two!
NARRATORS 1 & 2:	Poor Gertrude!
NARRATOR 2:	Whenever she happened to spy Miss Lolla-Lee-Lou flying by in the sky,
LOLLA-LEE-LOU:	She got very jealous.
NARRATOR 1:	She frowned.
NARRATOR 2:	And she pouted.
NARRATOR 1:	Then one day she got awfully mad

NARRATOR:	And she shouted.
GERTRUDE:	This just isn't fair! I have *one*! She has *two*!
	I must have a tail just like Lolla-Lee-Lou!
NARRATOR 1:	So she flew to her uncle, a doctor named Dake,
	Whose office was high in a tree by the lake
	And she cried.
GERTRUDE:	Uncle Doctor. Oh, please do you know
	Of some kind of a pill that will make my tail grow?
NARRATOR 2:	Tut Tut!
NARRATOR 1:	Said the doctor.
NARRATOR 2:	Such talk! How absurd!
	Your tail is just right for your kind of a bird.
NARRATOR 1:	Then Gertrude had tantrums. She raised such a din
	That finally her uncle, the doctor, gave in
	And told her just where she could find such a pill.
NARRATOR 2:	On a Pill-Berry vine on the top of the hill.
GERTRUDE:	Oh, thank you!
NARRATOR 1:	Chirped Gertrude McFuzz, and she flew
	Right straight to the hill where the Pill-Berry grew.
GERTRUDE:	Yes! There was the vine!
NARRATOR 2:	And as soon as she saw it
	She plucked off a berry.
NARRATOR 1:	She started to gnaw it.
GERTRUDE:	It tasted just awful.
NARRATOR 2:	Almost made her sick.
NARRATOR 1:	But she wanted that tail, so she swallowed it quick.
NARRATOR 2:	Then she felt something happen!
NARRATOR 1:	She felt a small twitch
NARRATOR 2:	As if she'd been tapped, down behind, by a switch.
NARRATOR 1:	And Gertrude looked 'round, and she cheered!
NARRATOR 2:	It was true!
GERTRUDE:	*Two feathers*!
NARRATOR 1:	Exactly like Lolla-Lee-Lou!
NARRATOR 2:	Then she got an idea!
GERTRUDE:	Now I know what I'll do . . .
	I'll grow a tail *better* than Lolla-Lee-Lou!
	_____ feathers are working just fine.
NARRATOR 1:	So she nibbled another one off of the vine!
NARRATOR 2:	She felt a new twitch.
NARRATOR 1:	And then Gertrude yelled.
GERTRUDE:	Whee!
	Miss Lolla has only just *two*! I have *three*!
	When Lolla-Lee-Lou sees this beautiful stuff,
	She'll fall right down flat on her face, sure enough!
	I'll show *her* who's pretty! I certainly will!
	Why, I'll make my tail even prettier still!
NARRATOR 2:	She snatched at those berries that grew on that vine.
NARRATOR 1:	She gobbled down four,

GERTRUDE:	five,
NARRATOR 2:	six,
NARRATOR 1:	seven,
NARRATOR 2:	eight,
GERTRUDE:	nine!
NARRATOR 1:	And she didn't stop eating,
NARRATOR 2:	Young Gertrude McFuzz,
NARRATOR 1:	Till she'd eaten three dozen!
GERTRUDE:	That's all that there was.
NARRATOR 1:	Then the feathers popped out!
GERTRUDE:	*With a zang!*
LOLLA-LEE-LOU:	With a *zing!*
NARRATOR 2:	They blossomed like flowers that bloom in the spring.
LOLLA-LEE-LOU:	All fit for a queen! What a sight to behold!
NARRATOR 1:	They sparkled like diamonds
NARRATOR 2:	And gumdrops
LOLLA-LEE-LOU:	And gold!

PROLOGUE TO MORNING

Dorothea Parfit

(Intermediate 4–8)

EVERYMAN.	Watchman, what of the night?
WATCHMAN.	The night has no stars and the winds are rising.
EVERYMAN.	Watchman, what of the sea?
WATCHMAN.	The sea is wild, and the shores are strewn with ships.
EVERYMAN.	Watchman—
WATCHMAN.	I hear.
EVERYMAN.	What of the hearts of men?
WATCHMAN.	They are as the night, and as the sea.
EVERYMAN.	Watchman, I am Everyman, and I am troubled. Where is my hope?
WATCHMAN.	Your hope is where it *has* been.
EVERYMAN.	Watchman, your answer is dark.
WATCHMAN.	To your mind, but not to your heart. Let the heart Listen and it will hear, Though the winds cry and the seas break.
EVERYMAN.	My heart is open.
WATCHMAN.	What does it hear?
EVERYMAN.	Storm.
WATCHMAN.	What else?
EVERYMAN.	A crying, as of a child lost in the dark.
WATCHMAN.	A crying?
EVERYMAN.	A fury, as of a child destroying his toys.
WATCHMAN.	No more?
EVERYMAN.	A Voice.
WATCHMAN.	A Voice?
EVERYMAN.	A Voice that cries, Think!
WATCHMAN.	What else?
EVERYMAN.	A Voice that calls, Aspire!

WATCHMAN.	What more?
EVERYMAN.	A Voice that whispers, Believe!
WATCHMAN.	Bow down, and hear!
EVERYMAN.	A Voice that commands, Dare!
WATCHMAN.	Lift up your eyes!
EVERYMAN.	Watchman, what have I heard?
WATCHMAN.	You have heard God speaking to Moses and to Socrates;
	To Jesus in the lonely places,
	To Isaiah and Amos and Micah,
	And Peter and John and Paul and Francis and Joan.
	You have heard God speaking to all His saints
	Who have fought for the recognition of His glory,
	And for liberation, and the expansion of the imprisoned, the dwarfed spirit.
	You have heard God speaking to the men who dared the seas to build a new nation,
	To Franklin and Washington and Jefferson
	And all the makers of the immortal Declaration
	That utters the hunger for life, for liberty, and the right of man to be free of the chain, the bars, and the whip.
	You have heard God speaking to Abraham Lincoln—
	And to you.
EVERYMAN.	To me? What am I that the God Who spoke to these
	Should speak to me?
WATCHMAN.	What does the Voice say, the Voice in the heart?
EVERYMAN.	The Voice says, You are of the great succession.
	Men have torn down, men have broken, men have destroyed.
	It is yours to build, says the Voice, yours to build.
	Out of the disaster of hate to bring the miracle of love.
	Out of the fury of destruction to bring a new creation.
	By men has the world been brought low.
	By men shall the world again be lifted up.
	By men and the Voice of God.
WATCHMAN.	The Voice of God is calling through the world!
EVERYMAN.	It is calling to me.
	I hear!
WATCHMAN.	What does the Voice say, the Voice in the heart?
EVERYMAN.	The Voice says, Everyman,
	I have a burden for you and a splendor.
	You are the end of things—
	Or a new world.
	Think!
	Believe!
	Aspire!
	Dare!
WATCHMAN.	What more?
EVERYMAN.	The Voice says, Day and night, let your heart listen.
WATCHMAN.	What is your answer, Everyman?
EVERYMAN.	My heart is listening . . . .
WATCHMAN.	Then the new world is born.

*"Prologue to Morning" is included here by permission of Mrs. Dorothea Parfit, 1207 North Western Avenue, Hollywood, Calif. 90029.

If at this time you do not feel that you have attained adequate knowledge to successfully answer the following questions, we would like to suggest related readings.

> Goal 1: To help students to understand what teachers and parents can do to motivate students to read.

> Question 2: What can the classroom teacher and parents do to make children want to read?

Arth, Alfred A., and Judith D. Whittemore. "Selecting Literature for Children that Relates to Life, The Way It is." *Elementary English*, 50 (May 1973) 726–8, 744.

Huus, Helen. "Developing Interest and Taste in Literature in the Elementary Grades." In *Elementary Reading Instruction* edited by Althea Berry et al. Boston: Allyn & Bacon, Inc., 1969, pp. 282–9.

Ryan, Florence H., "Taking Boredom Out of Book Reports." *Elementary English*, 51 (Oct. 1974), 987–9.

> Goal 2: To aid students in providing input into children's individual attitudes toward reading, as well as specific interests in reading.

> Question 2: Describe the ways in which you can assess children's attitudes toward reading and their reading interests.

Huck, Charlotte S. "A Comprehensive Literature Program." In *Elementary Reading Instruction*, ed. by Althea Berry et al. Boston: Allyn & Bacon, Inc., 1969, pp. 289–8.

Pillar, Arlene M., "Individualizing Book Reviews." *Elementary English*, 52 (April 1975), 467–96.

Smith, Richard J. "The Intermediate Grade Reading Program: Questions Teachers and Principals Ask." *Elementary English*, 49 (March 1972), 364–8.

> Goal 3: To aid students in assessing children's most effective learning styles.

> Question 3: What procedures would you employ to assess the learning styles of your children?

Criscuolo, Nicholas P. *Improving Classroom Reading Instruction*. Worthington, Ohio: Charles A. Jones, Publishing Co., 1973, Chap. 8.

Karlin, Robert, ed. *Perspectives on Elementary Reading*. New York: Harcourt, Brace, Jovanovich, Inc., 1973, Part 8.

Koe, Frank T. "Attitudes Toward Reading." *Elementary English*, 52 (March 1975), 342, 366.

> Goal 4: To aid students in providing stimulating and appropriately motivating reading materials for children.

> Question 4: List materials that have motivating appeal for children.

Bingham, Jand, and Grayce Scholt. "The Great Glass Slipper Search: Using Folktales with Older Children." *Elementary English*, 51 (Oct. 1974), 990–8.

Schulte, Emerita S. "Today's Literature for Today's Children." *Elementary English*, 49 (March 1972), 366–63.

Swynehardt, Mary, and Carolyn Hattlestad. "Extending Children's Appreciation of Book Illustration Through Creative Activity." *Elementary English*, 49 (Feb. 1972), 235–9.

BIBLIOGRAPHY

Allen, R. V. *Attitudes and the Art of Teaching Reading*. Washington, D.C.: National Education Association, 1965.

Arbuthnot, M. H. *Children and Books*. Chicago: Scott, Foresman and Company, 1957, p. 2.

Ausubel, D. P. "The Use of Advance Organizers In The Learning and Retention of Meaningful Verbal Material." Journal of Educational Psychology, 1960, 51, 267–272.

Bandura, Albert and Huston, A. C. "Identification as Accidental Learning'" *Journal of Abnormal and Social Psychology,* 63 (1961), p. 311.

———. and Frederick J. McDonald. "Influences of Social Reinforcement and the Behavior of Models in Shaping Children's Moral Judgements." *Journal of Abnormal and Social Psychology,* 67 (1963), 274–281.

Barrett, T. "The Barrett Taxonomy of Cognitive and Affective Dimensions of Reading Comprehension" in T. Clymer "What is 'Reading'?" Some Current Concepts," Innovation and Change in Reading Instruction. 67th Yearbook of the National Society for the Study of Education, 1968, pp. 7–29.

Bloom, B. S. "The Thought Process of Students in Discussion," in S. J. French, ed. *Accent on Teaching*. New York: Harper & Row, Publishers, 1954.

Boiko, Claire. *Children's Plays for Creative Actors*. Boston: Plays, Inc., 1967.

Buerger, T. A. "A Follow-Up of Remedial Reading Instruction" *Reading Teacher*. 1968, 21, 329–334.

Campbell, P. *Reading Attitude Inventory,* Livonia Public Schools. Livonia, Michigan, 1966.

Combs, A. W. and D. W. Soper. "The Self, Its Derivative Terms, and Research," *Journal of Individual Psychology*. 1957, 13, pp. 134–145.

Combs, A. W., D. W. Soper, and C. C. Courson. "The Measurement of Self-Concept and Self-Report," *Educational and Psychological Measurement,* 1963, 23, 493–500.

Dawson, Mildred A. "Developing Interest in Books," in Howard A. Klein, ed., *The Quest for Competency in Teaching Reading*. Newark, Delaware: International Reading Association, 1972, 36–41.

Dole, E. "Instructional Resources," in J. L. Goodlad, ed. *The Changing American School* (Sixty-Fifth Yearbook of the National Society for the Study of Education, Part II). Chicago: University of Chicago Press, 1966, p. 108.

Doob, L. W. *The Behavior of Attitudes*. Psychological Review 54: 135–156, 1947.

Estes, Thomas H. "Assessing Attitudes Toward Reading." *Journal of Reading*, 25, 1971, 135–138.

Fanning, J. F. "Effects of Selected Reporting Practices on Reading Achievement, Reading Attitude, and Anxiety of Below Average Readers in Grades 3 through 6." Unpublished Doctoral Dissertation, University of Maryland, 1969.

Fishbein, M. "Attitude and the Prediction of Behavior." in M. Fishbein, ed. *Readings in Attitude Theory and Measurement*. New York: John Wiley and Sons, 1967.

Fowler, F. C. "The Development of the 'Like to Read' Program and on Appraisal of its Effect Upon Student Attitudes Toward Reading and Upon Their Reading Achievement." Unpublished Doctoral Dissertation, University of Tennessee, 1972.

Gans, R. *Common Sense in the Teaching of Reading*. New York: The Bobbs-Merrill Company, 1962, p. vi.

Gardner, R. C. A. "The Relationship of Self-Esteem and Variables Associated with Reading for Fourth Grade Prima Indian Children." Doctoral Dissertation, University of Arizona, 1972.

Gordon, I. J. *Studying the Child In School.* New York: John Wiley and Sons, 1966.

Greenwald, Anthony, T. C. Brock, and T. M. Ostrom, *Psychological Foundation of Attitudes.* New York: Academic Press, Inc., 1968.

Gruber, J. "Exercise and Mental Performance." Addressed to the American Association for the Advancement of Science, Dallas, Texas, Sept. 27, 1968.

Heathington, B. S. "The Development of Scales to Measure Attitudes Towards Reading." Unpublished Doctoral Dissertation, University of Tennessee, 1975.

Jersild, A. T. *In Search of Self.* New York: Bureau of Publications, Teachers College, Columbia University, 1952.

Koch, R. E. "Relationships Between Reading Interests and Reading Comprehension Among Fourth Grade and Sixth Grade Students." Unpublished Doctoral Dissertation, University of Illionis, Urbana, 1974.

Krathwohl, D. R., B. S. Bloom, and B. B. Masia. *Taxonomy of Educational Objectives - Handbook II: Affective Domain.* New York: David McKay Company, Inc., 1969.

Labov, W. "The Logic of Non-Standard English," in De Stefano, *Language Society and Education.* Worthington, Ohio: Jones, 1973, p. 18.

McDougall, William. *Body and Mind.* New York: Macmillan Publishing Co., Inc., 1911.

_____. *An Introduction to Social Psychology.* Boston: John W. Luce and Co., 1921.

McKillop, A. *The Relationship Between the Reader's Attitude and Certain Types of Reading Response.* New York: Columbia University Press, 1952.

Mager, Robert. *Developing Attitudes Toward Learning.* Palo Alto, Calif.: Fearon Press, 1969, p. 37.

Miller, Neal E. and J. Dollard. *Social Learning and Imitation.* New Haven, Connecticut: Yale University Press, 1941.

O'Connor, W. F. "The Reading Apperception Test: An Exploration of Attitudes Toward Reading." Unpublished Doctoral Dissertation, Oklahoma State University, 1969.

Peifer, J. E. "The Development of An Attitude Scale to Measure Students' Attitudes Toward Reading in the Secondary Schools." Unpublished Doctoral Dissertation, Pennsylvania State University.

Puryear, Charles. "An Investigation of the Relationship Between Attitudes Toward Reading and Reading Achievement." Unpublished Doctoral Dissertation, University of South Carolina, 1975.

Ransbury, M. "Critical Factors in the Development of Attitudes Toward Reading As Defined by Individual Perceptions of Students, Their Teachers and Parents." Unpublished Doctoral Dissertation, Indiana University School of Education, Bloomington, Indiana, 1971.

Roswell, C. G. "Change in Attitude Toward Reading and its Relationship to Certain Variables Among Children with Reading Difficulties." Unpublished Doctoral Dissertation, George Peabody College for Teachers, 1967.

Rotter, Julian B. *Social Learning and Clinical Psychology.* Englewood Cliffs, N.J.: Prentice-Hall, Inc., 1954.

Russell, David H. *Children Learn to Read.* Lexington, Mass.: Ginn and Company, 1961.

Schroeder, H., M. Driver, S. Streufert, *Human Information Processing.* New York: Holt, Rinehart, and Winston, Inc., 1967.

Skinner, B. F. *Science and Human Behavior,* New York: MacMillan Publishing Co., Inc. 1953.

Smith, J. A. *The Nature of Creative Teaching.* Boston: Allyn & Bacon, Inc., 1975.

Stephens, J. *The Crock of Gold: Irish Fairy Tales.* New York: Macmillan Publishing Co., Inc., 1960.

Thorndike, Robert L. "Children's Reading Interests," in A. J. Harris, ed., *Readings on Reading Instruction.* New York: David McKay Company, Inc., 338–371.

Thurstone, L. L. "Attitudes Can Be Measured." *The American Journal of Sociology.* 33, pp. 529–554, 1928.

Wilson, Robert M. and Maryanne Hall. *Reading and the Elementary School Child.* New York: Van Nostrand Reinhold Company, 1972.

Witty, Paul and Associates, "Studies of Children's Interests—A Brief Summary," in Harris, A. J., ed., *Readings on Reading Instruction.* New York: David McKay Co., Inc., 330–337.

Yeatts, P. P. *Developmental Change in the Self-Concept of Children Grades 3–12.* Gainesville, Florida: Florida Educational Research and Development Council Research Bulletin, 1967, 3(2), Whole.

6

The integrated language arts

All the world's a stage
And all the men and women merely players;
They have their exits and their entrances;
And one man in his time plays many parts,
His act being seven ages.

Shakespeare

GOALS: To aid students in understanding:
1. the processes involved in developing listening skills.
2. the processes involved in developing speaking skills.
3. the processes involved in developing reading skills.
4. the processes involved in developing writing skills.
5. the interrelatedness of the language arts.

The term *language arts* describes a major portion of the elementary curriculum and includes the *communication processes* of *listening*, *speaking*, *reading*, and *writing*. The development of these interrelated communication processes is indispensible for the learner when he is acquiring or dispensing information.

Think for a minute about situations when you are listening, speaking, reading, and writing. Do you ever engage in two or more of the language arts simultaneously? Yes. More often than not, you are using more than one of these processes at a time. In this way, it is natural to view the act of communication as an interrelated process. Loban's (1976) research findings support this view; he states that students who have low abilities in oral language also have difficulty in reading and writing. He further suggests that the inverse of this interrelationship is true. He found that students with adequate language abilities show little, if any, difficulty in acquiring other communication skills.

As a classroom teacher, your task will be to integrate the language arts with each other and with the entire content curriculum. When a student engages in a science, mathematics, or social studies activity, he can be using all of the language arts. He listens to instructions; he is involved in verbal discussions; he is involved in reading content materials, and he writes detailed reports to express his ideas. Throughout the curriculum, students use the language arts; therefore, it is quite unrealistic to believe that for forty minutes each day you can have a single, separate period devoted to the communication processes.

You are probably wondering:
1. Which communication skills are appropriate for students at a particular stage of development.
2. What specific information you will need to know about each of the language arts.
3. How you can teach all of the language arts and all of the content area skills in an integrated fashion.
4. What you should do first.

This chapter is designed to serve two purposes: First, you will be introduced to information related to extending listening, speaking, and writing skills within your classroom. A discussion of the language art of *reading* will not be a prime focus of this chapter since it is the central focus of this text. Second, you will explore a simulated curriculum that illustrates the integration of the language arts within content areas of study.

PART I THE LANGUAGE ARTS

Listening

For many years, classroom teachers and parents have praised themselves for developing silent children—children who were seen and not heard; children who *listened* and obeyed. These young children were involved in listening to the language of adults. In more recent years, children are still involved in listening; however, the message sender has been broadened to include the TV, radio, record player, telephone, and teaching machines. This phenomenon is extremely important because children need to develop listening skills which will enable them to function in a highly complex world. The sobering question we have to ask is: "Are silent children listening children?"

The Beginning Years

From the very earliest moments of life, children are exposed to sound. The earliest listening patterns are developed in the home and the degree of listening activity reinforcement supplied by the home affects the development of beginning listening skills (Feltman, 1967). Listening activity reinforcement encourages the child to *hear* information, *process* information, *reflect* on the information, and *respond*, rather than simply hear and obey. The development of early listening skills is closely related to verbal interactions because the young child, by the age of four, is silent for only nineteen minutes of his waking day (Brandenburg, 1915). Although hearing involves the intake of information, the listening process encourages one to *process* and *reflect* on the information and, through language, respond to what has been heard.

Brown (1954) refers to this listening/language process as auding.

> "Auding is to the ears what reading is to the eyes." If reading is the gross process of looking, recognizing, and interpreting written symbols, auding may be defined as the gross process of listening to, recognizing, and interpreting spoken symbols. (p. 86).

Brown's contention is further explained by the following formula:

Seeing is to Hearing

as

Observing is to Listening

as

Reading is to Auding

(Russell, 1959, p. 3)

Parents and caretakers are extremely important in the early development of listening skills. The role of the parent and suggestions for parent activities have been discussed in Chapter 2.

The School Years

Because of the varied early home experiences children have had with listening, they enter school with a wide range of auding abilities. As you attempt to strengthen these skills, you must determine if there are any children with hearing disabilities in your classroom. Detecting these problems is not always an easy task; however, through observation you may notice that a child:

1. strains to hear what is being said around him
2. ignores a speaker with whom he does not have direct eye contact
3. uses many gestures to convey his ideas
4. has difficulty relating sequences to which he has listened
5. evidences unclear language patterns
6. has difficulty repeating long, detailed sentences
7. may be unable to reproduce consonant phonemes
8. evidences voice production (pitch, stress, rhythm) difficulties

If you detect any of these difficulties, refer the child to a speech and hearing specialist or school doctor. If, after a check-up, the child is diagnosed as having no hearing loss, you will have to plan curricula to facilitate the progress of these underdeveloped listening skills. Duker (1968) encourages the development of such curricula because he believes that listening skills can be effectively taught.

Be cautious in your diagnostic attempts, and do not confuse linguistic variations in speech patterns with hearing impairment in children. Some of the omissions, additions, distortions, and substitutions you may observe in the speech patterns of your students may not be a function of hearing difficulty; rather, they may be a natural outgrowth of dialect. If you are working with children who have dialects other than your own, be careful not to incorrectly diagnose their listening/language needs.

In addition to language variations, attitudes toward listening may vary depending on a child's culture, for example, some cultures prohibit the male from listening to female commands; others restrict the singling out of an individual for the purpose of a compliment; and still others may limit the frequency of child-adult conversations.

As you begin to select from commercially prepared programs or as you begin to develop your own curricula, be careful to remember the following developmental and environmental constraints:

> it is not uncommon for children to be expected to listen far beyond the time of their attention span with lawn mowers going or children playing outside the window, with noise-amplifying flooring, sweltering weather (unairconditioned), or overheating—every imaginable kind of inhibition to attention.
>
> *(Lundsteen, 1971, p. 28)*

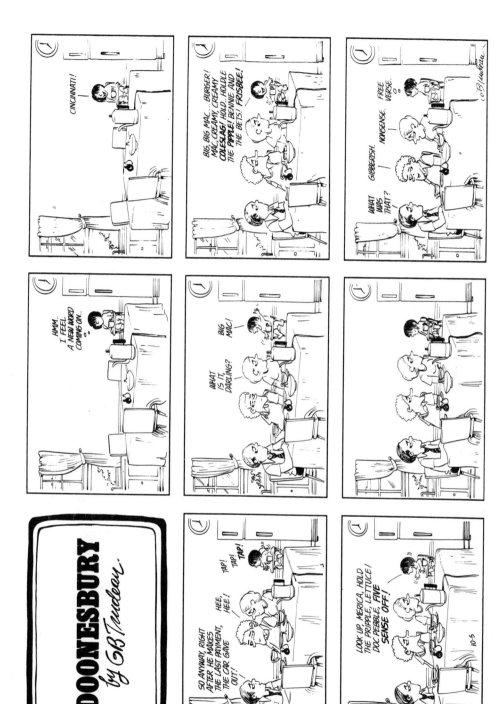

Classroom Programs

You should include the following factors in your classroom program:

Developing positive listening attitudes. The development of a positive attitude toward listening is accomplished by:
  a. discussing with your children the importance of listening
  b. beginning each lesson by establishing a specific purpose
  c. encouraging children to listen and share ideas
  d. reinforcing good listening habits
  e. being a good listener yourself

Listening to the sound of one's personal world. Who are the children you are teaching? Where do they come from each morning? With these considerations in mind, ask your students to:
  a. listen to and share the sounds they hear on their way to school
  b. describe the most pleasant sound they hear in their personal environment
  c. describe the sounds of seasons
  d. share the sounds of tears and laughter
  e. describe the sounds of home
  f. discuss the sounds that remind them of school
  g. share the sound of the voice of someone who they love

Creating sounds. Children of all ages enjoy producing sounds from such objects as metal lids, water taps, paper, and other materials that are easy to collect. Provide a large cardboard box where "sound machine makers" may be stored. Each time a child devises a new sound, encourage him to share it with others. Keep your curriculum flexible enough to accommodate new developments.

Listening for a definite purpose. Hearing a sound is simply not enough; the child must be able to infer meaning from it. If, for example, the child turns and looks at a ringing phone but does not attempt to answer it, he may not have inferred what the ringing sound means. You may encourage the development of comprehensive listening by planning lessons that:
  a. illustrate *sequencing* (numbers, directions, musical patterns)
  b. encourage the child to listen and anticipate what may follow. For example, read the children a story or poem and leave out some obvious words. Encourage the children to listen for context clues that will enable them to supply missing information.

> Harold was riding his new _____. He _____ up streets and _____ alleys.
> He rang the _____ on his bicycle. Harold _____ a very _____ boy.

  c. encourage children to infer meaning. This may be accomplished by reading a passage similar to:

> Beverly and Ronnie were playing with their new toys. Ronnie's new skates were broken. Ronnie got very angry with Beverly. Ronnie took all of his toys and went home.

After reading the passage you can ask:

    1. Why was Ronnie angry?
    2. How were Ronnie's skates broken?
    3. Did Beverly break Ronnie's skates?
    4. Why did Ronnie take his toys home?

As the children answer these questions, be sure to encourage their awareness of how their answers were formed. Was the information for their answers text-explicit or was it from their own past experience?

    d. Encourage children to answer questions. This may be accomplished by reading a passage similar to:

> Mary and Colleen were spending the summer with Grandmother. Mary awakened early one morning and tiptoed into Grandmother's kitchen. As she crept around the corner of the pantry feeling for the cookie jar, she jumped with fright! A shadow! Someone else was in the kitchen. She momentarily forgot about the cookie jar and groped for the light. There was Colleen also inching her way toward the cookie jar.

After reading the passage ask:

    1. At what time do you think the story occurred?
    2. How did Mary know Colleen was in the kitchen?
    3. How many girls stayed at Grandmother's?
    4. What were the girls doing in the kitchen?

It is important to ask a wide range of questions because answering them encourages the student in various thinking activities.

Evaluating listening competencies. Encourage your students to evaluate their strengths as a listener. They may do this by observing if they:
a. direct their attention toward the speaker
b. listen until the speaker has completed his statement
c. think carefully about the message being sent
d. listen for the organizational style of the speaker
e. determine the validity of the statement
f. think of appropriate responses
g. weigh the value of their response

As you plan lessons which encourage children to evaluate their listening capabilities, it may be important for you to answer the following questions:

    1. Do I sequence my verbal instructions?
    2. Do I present clear explanations?
    3. Do I use a well-modulated voice?
    4. Am I an adequate model of good listening habits?

Additional classroom activities have been provided at the end of this chapter. These activities will enable you to develop adequate listening practices for your classroom.

Speaking

> When Confucius was asked what he would do if he had the responsibility for administering a country, he said that he would improve language. "If language is not correct he stated, then what is said is not what is meant, then what ought to be done remains undone; if this remains undone, morals and acts would deteriorate; justice will go astray; if justice goes astray, the people will stand about in helpless confusion."
>
> *Confucius (c. 551–479 B.C.)*

It is obvious from the quote that one of man's *continuous problems* is a problem of communication. This problem continues because parents and teachers tend to emphasize "correct" communication rather than determine the extent to which correct communication encourages effective communication.

Curricula emphasizing language or communication processes have tended to stress the memorization of "correct" syntactical rules and applications of these rules. Although such rule knowledge may provide a general understanding of the syntax of written communication, it cannot serve as a total program because some cultural contact must be experienced before the intended message can be communicated. In order for the receiver to receive the intended message, there must be as little semantic interference as possible. It should be noted that increased cultural exposure decreases the potential for interference.

Sender	Message	Receiver

Writings by Smith, Goodman, and Meredith (1970) suggest that, within a cultural setting one can observe the language development of children approximating adult language; as this occurs, more effective communication between sender and receiver occurs. In this way, language serves as a means of transmitting what is understood about culture.

Language, which is the creative activity of each person, is characterized by certain basic structures. Most of these structures are learned by the age of five or six. Once language habits, which are determined by age, socioeconomic group, and geographical region, have been acquired, they are very difficult to alter. The concept of "correct" language is impossible because of pronunciation, word collection, phrasing, and construction variations.

Most children come to school with language and the desire to communicate. So inherent is the desire to communicate that, throughout history, language has been developed wherever man has congregated. Given this potential, why is there so often a communication breakdown in the classroom? Perhaps as we observe the child entering school we must ask: Are the structure of language symbols in use within the classroom highly correlated with those of the child's culture? Studies by Loban (1976) suggest that if there is a large language discrepancy between the language of the child and the language of the school, when the child enters school, inflexible teaching practices will only encourage increased discrepancy. This discrepancy is an inevitable prelude to school failure.

The Early Years

As suggested in Chapter 3, from the very earliest days of life, the child is encouraged to speak by the doting adult hovering over the crib. During this early stage, the child listens to sounds, attempts sounds, combines and experiments with the production of speech sounds. The child eventually strings these unintelligible sounds together, continually receiving ample positive reinforcement from the doting adults and siblings of his extended family. Eventually, the words and word strings acquire comprehensibility. These early language patterns soon begin to include sentences so that:

> After the age of six there is relatively little in the grammar or syntax of language that the average child needs to learn, except to achieve a school imposed standard of speech or writing to which he may not be accustomed in his home environment.
>
> *(Carroll, 1971, pp. 200–11)*

Speech, another of the most commonly used communication processes, is believed by some to begin as early as five months after conception (Wilkinson, 1971), whereas others believe it begins with the child's first cry at birth. Regardless of the age of acquisition, the child progresses through stages of cooing, babbling, single words, word commands, phrases, sentences, and the mastery of grammatical rules. Although the basics of language are learned long before the child enters school, you as a teacher can continue to encourage language experience and language expression within the classroom setting.

The School Years

The elementary school curriculum provides programs that attempt to build on the early language structures of children. As you attempt to implement such curricula within your classroom, it is important for you to understand the comprehensiveness of any individual's language usage.

For every person, language is a means of *expressing the self*. Our earliest attempts at self-expression may take the form of a grunt or cry; however, as time progresses, we begin to use more sophisticated forms of language to convey our desires, feelings, and emotions. The language of self-expression is seldom neutral because it conveys our ideas, love, humor, hate, anger, excuses, and other human sensations. As classroom teachers, you must encourage the use of language as self-expression through a climate of self-acceptance because one of life's functions is the continual identification of self in a constantly altered environment of social interaction.

One's ability to use language as a process through which extended thinking is shared is heavily dependent on an ever-increasing vocabulary. Your classroom, therefore, must be rich with exposure to language. See the activities sections of Chapters 7 and 8 for many examples of ways to accomplish vocabulary development.

Time is an important factor in the development of self-expressive speech. One must *try* sharing a small amount of information; *weigh* the results and consequences of giving oneself through language; and perhaps, if the consequences are not too harsh, *try again*. If a teacher rejects these early attempts at self-expression, the student will be very cautious before trying again—perhaps even to the point of altering his own ideas and expressing ones that will receive the teacher's positive acceptance.

Egocentrism in young children's language is very common. Egocentric language lessens, as the child is engaged in situations where he must listen to others to complete a task or to be part of a group situation. As the child engages in many sender-receiver exchanges, his language becomes less egocentric and more *expository* which ultimately enables him to receive a wider variety of messages. As well as being a means of self-expression, language is also a means of acquiring information. Alone, a person is unable to totally understand the world around him; however through language interchanges, a person continually experiences larger segments of the universe. Many of these interchanges are verbal. How do I get to city hall? What are your views regarding ... ? Have you read ... ? Such interchanges supply us with topics of discussion as well as bits of valuable information.

A second means of acquiring information is through *gestures, graphics,* and *mechanical codes.* Children may become familiar with the interpretation of *gestures* through role-playing and pantomime activities. Graphic messages are received by interpreting traffic signs, advertisements, books, and other printed materials. The interpretation of mechanical messages can come to the receiver through traffic lights, flashing lights on a police car or ambulance, and train crossings. These unspoken expositions of language offer a wide range of facts and ideas.

If students are to develop and refine their speaking skills, they need many opportunities to talk. Students in your classroom may represent a variety of speaking styles and dialects. The beginning speaker should be given every opportunity for oral expression, with little, if any, attention directed toward the addition of an alternate dialect.

Teacher Attitudes

Children from many races and ethnic backgrounds will be in your classrooms. You must confront prejudices:

> That people speak different dialects, in no way stems from their intelligence or judgement. They speak the dialect which enables them to get along with the other members of their social and geographical group.
>
> *(Shuy, 1967, p. 5)*

Think for a moment about some of the stereotypes that you have heard about people. Are they true; do they have any grounding in the real world? Confront these stereotypes, analyze them, and deal with any residue you may have that may interfere with your teaching.

Language Styles

Experiences with language continually enable the student to accommodate each encounter with the appropriate language style. As Joos (1967) suggests, *informal* situations shared with intimate friends allow us to exhibit our private language styles. This style is often comprised of one-word or one-phrase utterances. The receiver is so well aware of our thinking patterns that he can anticipate what we will say almost before it is said. *Casual* situations shared with friends who are not quite as intimate may still allow us to use our private language; however, our utterances may need to be more explanatory. The *consultative* style of language is one that is used to convey factual information. The speaker may use this style when he is expressing his ideas to an audience comprised of people who are not members of his private community. The need arises for an alternate style of language, a more public language that will be shared and understood by most of the audience. Certain contexts require *frozen* styles of language, such as written messages or speeches to colleagues, which are often heavily dependent on the use of an extremely formal language. It will become obvious that the development of various dialects must receive some attention in your classrooms if you are to prepare students to accommodate the multilanguage interactions that they will experience throughout their lives. Additional activities are provided at the end of this chapter to help you accomplish this task.

Writing

Writing, like speaking, provides the student with an outlet for the expression of ideas. Written expression may appear in many forms: compositions, letters, poems, reports, and short stories. Initial writing involves inventing, devising, selecting, eliminating, and arranging one's ideas. Proofreading, editing, and correcting one's ideas are laborious but critical tasks in the writing process.

Many educators distinguish between "creative" and "practical" writing experience by referring to stories and poems as acts of creativity. Although we understand their rationale, we believe that anytime a person conveys his thoughts through written language, regardless of the form, he has engaged in an act of creativity. Throughout this chapter, we will avoid a distinction between creative and practical writing.

The Primary Years

During the beginning school years you will find that children love to listen to and to create stories. When encouraged, young children will freely engage in storytelling. While many of the stories focus on their environmental experiences, you will find that children delight in playing with words. If you capitalize on these situations by recording their stories, your students can listen to these own stories and tales while creating illustrations for them. An activity such as this may serve as the basis for an entire writing curriculum.

What you do as an early primary teacher may definitely influence your students' attitudes toward writing. Be flexible with your assignments, remembering that there are many ways to complete any task. Through early language discussions, you will be able to encourage students to believe that they have many things to write about. Correct style, form, and spelling may need to receive secondary attention during these early writing attempts. Any device that encourages children to *talk*, and eventually to turn that talk to *writing*, can be viewed as a positive motivational device.

During the early primary grades, your language and writing programs should be closely intertwined. Many successful writing experiences have evolved in the following ways:

1. Young children encounter various sensory experiences.
   A. touching soft textures
   B. smelling a variety of things: onions, apples, perfume
   C. looking at a series of pictures

2. After the sensory exposure, children are encouraged to share their reactions verbally.

3. Recordings are made.

4. Children listen and then illustrate their thoughts.

5. With the help of the teacher, word or word phrase descriptions are added.

6. After the children complete the writing experience, they are encouraged to edit their work.

7. When the work is completed, it is verbally shared with peers. In some instances, children share the text with their family by writing a note or letter to accompany the text.

Activities such as this demand an integration of listening, speaking, reading, and writing in many different forms: story, poem, letter, and note.

As you listen to the text that your students created, you will observe that the best stories are often shared accounts of in-depth perceptions. It is very important to plan activities that will heighten sensory awareness among your students. You may accomplish this by

1. Having children close their eyes and listen to a variety of sounds. Have them describe the sounds.

2. Asking children to describe the face of a person they love.

3. Blindfolding the children and having them feel around in several bags, each of which contains something different—melted fudge, raw liver, or a small piece of burnt toast. Ask them to describe what they feel.

4. Asking children to describe pleasant or frightening odors.

Activities such as these encourage children's awareness of their world, and extend language development.

The Intermediate Years

There are many excellent opportunities in the intermediate classroom for engaging students in writing processes. The importance of extending writing activities throughout the middle years cannot be minimized because such activities (1) provide students with an opportunity for self-expression, (2) provide a means for extending language development, and (3) arouse students' interest in literary materials.

All of your students may not always be anxiously awaiting an opportunity to participate in a written exchange. For the child who has difficulty with writing, you may need to provide (1) word lists and basic language activities, (2) alternate assignments, and (3) areas of interest that can be pursued through writing.

One excellent activity that you may want to use in your writing curriculum is sentence-combining.

Teaching Sentence Combining

Several researchers in the field of written composition have reported successful attempts at having students manipulate sentences in order to expand their ability to organize. This device of manipulating sentences organizationally is called combining.

Mellon (1965) and O'Hare (1973) were among the first to create sentence-combining activities for children. Here are some examples from Mellon's NCTE monograph.

Fact Clause*

    A. SOMETHING seemed to suggest SOMETHING.
        Bill finished his lessons in less than an hour. (T: fact)
        He had received special help from another student. (T: fact)
    B. The fact that Bill finished his lessons in less than an hour seemed to suggest that he had received special help from another student.

Question Clause

    A. In her letter Mrs. Browning demonstrates SOMETHING.
        So much feeling may be conveyed by a few words. (T: wh)
    B. In her letter Mrs. Browning demonstrates how much feeling may be conveyed by a few words.

WH–Infinitive Phrase

    A. The instruction manual did not say SOMETHING.
        Someone overhauls the engine sometime. (T: wh+inf)
    B. The instruction manual did not say when to overhaul the engine.

*From John C. Mellon, *Transformational Sentence-Combining: A Method for Enhancing the Development of Syntactic Fluency in English Composition.* Copyright © 1965 by the National Council of Teachers of English. Reprinted by permission of the publisher.

Infinitive Phrase

    A. SOMETHING would be almost unbearable.

        The rocket fails in its final stage. (T: infin)

    B. For the rocket to fail in its final stage would be almost unbearable.

General Problems

    A. SOMETHING meant SOMETHING.

      The boy realized SOMETHING. (T: der-NP)

      He would have to find a dog. (T: fact)

        The dog would be courageous enough to bay the bear.

      He would have to look beyond the hounds. (T: fact)

        The hounds were loyal but ordinary.

        The hounds were living on the Major's plantation.

    B. The boy's realization that he would have to find a dog courageous enough to bay the bear meant that he would have to look beyond the loyal but ordinary hounds living on the Major's plantation.

    A. SOMETHING used to anger Grandfather no end. (T: exp)

      SOMETHING should be so easy. (T: fact–T: exp)

        The children recognized SOMETHING. (T: infin)

          SOMETHING was only a preliminary to SOMETHING sometime. (T:wh)

          He insisted SOMETHING. (T: gerund)

            They had had enough peppermints. (T: fact)

          He gave them still another handful. (T: gerund)

    B. It used to anger Grandfather no end that it should be so easy for the children to recognize when his insisting that they had had enough peppermints was only a preliminary to his giving them still another handful.

Sentence combining will help students who are engaged in most types of writing activities, especially in editing compositions. However, it is important to encourage students' awareness that sentence combining may be inappropriate when writing poetry, musical creations, or tall tales.

You will notice how inappropriate it would be during haiku writing because haiku writing, like all poetry, uses a different language base than prose. It does not use the sentence as its basic element.

Haiku is extremely enjoyable for children to write; it is a form of Japanese poetry which has three lines containing a total of seventeen syllables. The first and third lines contain five syllables and the second line has seven syllables. All your students can write haiku; these poems are usually written about nature.

    Flowers are growing
    Very near my window pane
    I think it is spring.

Activities to further encourage student interest in writing can be found at the end of this text.

PART II THE LANGUAGE ARTS CURRICULUM

Although the language arts (listening, speaking, reading, and writing) may be separated for discussion, it is very difficult to separate them when teaching. This part of the chapter includes a simulated curriculum that illustrates the integration of all of the language arts within content areas of study.

The Theme

As you begin to consider the development of your language arts curriculum, you must select a central focus through which all the communication skills can be explored. Select such topics as
1. Literature
2. Poetry
3. Music

For the purpose of this simulated unit, we will select the *literature* strand of the curriculum for use as our central point. *Do not stop reading if you are a primary grade teacher.* Through the study of literature, children of all ages can explore:
1. their cultural heritage.
2. people of all times.
3. self through others.
4. the vicarious experiences of others.
5. listening skills.
6. various writing styles.
7. numerous reading materials.
8. language.

The exploration of literature encourages students to learn the wonders of self through the vicarious explorations of others. The following literary texts will show you how literature exists for all ages.

Ages 2-6

1. Ets, Marie Hall. *Gilberto and the Wind.* New York: The Viking Press, Inc., 1963.
2. Barrett, Judi. *Animals Should Definitely Not Wear Clothing.* New York: Atheneum Publishers, 1970.

Ages 6-9

1. Miles, Miska. *Nobody's Cat.* Boston: Little, Brown and Company, 1969.
2. Lightfoot, Gordon. *The Pony Man.* New York: Harper & Row, Publishers, 1972.

Ages 10–14

1. Larrick, Nancy. *On City Streets.* Evans, 1968.
2. Colum, Padraic. *Roofs of Gold: Poems to Read Aloud.* New York: Macmillan Publishing Co., Inc., 1964.

The Scope and Sequence

Once you have decided on a central focus, or *thematic* area, it is necessary to determine the: (1) general unit goals, as well as (2) the specific skills you want to develop.

Because our topic is the exploration of literature, our goals might include

1. Developing an understanding of the organization of a given literary work:
   a. Form (story, poem, drama)
   b. Main theme
   c. Plot
   d. Characters
   e. Author's writing style
2. Developing an understanding of the possibility of self-exploration through literature
3. Introducing students to a variety of reading and writing styles
4. Increasing listening skills through reading and sharing ideas about a given literary work
5. Increasing students' awareness of the variety of social values evidenced by literary characters
6. Acquainting students with the scientific progress made throughout history

These are only a few of the goals that might be explored through the study of literature. The six goals listed have incorporated all of the language arts and several areas of content study. Once you are satisfied with your overall goals, you need to list the specific skills that you want to cover in each of the language arts and content areas that have been incorporated in your thematic unit

Reading

1. Vocabulary extension
2. Comprehension of a wide variety of writing styles

Writing

1. Practice with cursive writing
2. Self-expression through writing

Listening

1. Following directions through listening
2. Developing listening skills as the basis for good conversational practices

Speaking

1. Exhibiting organizational skills in language
2. Increasing language fluency

Social Studies

1. Understanding others through their writings
2. Understanding self through story characters

Science

1. Exploring new environments described through literature
2. Exploring social awareness regarding the environment through statements made by literary characters

Math

1. Developing basic skills: addition, subtraction, and division
2. Developing logical thinking skills

After defining the list of skills you want to develop, you must decide which skills can approximately be incorporated within the given unit of study. Any one unit cannot serve as the means for covering all of the skills and objectives you have for *all* of the content and language arts areas of the curricula. This unit can be given a separate time slot in the curricula, or it can become part of the already existing English and reading program.

Objectives and Assessment

Now that you have generally decided on the amount of time that will be allotted to this unit, as well as the specifics regarding skill development, you will need (1) to *develop specific behavioral objectives* and (2) to assess your children to determine their existing competencies within this area of study. Once you have determined your students' competencies, as related to the stated behavioral objectives, you can begin to determine the composition of your study groups. Consider these behavioral objectives for this literary unit:

1. After the children have read *Henny-Penny*, they will be able to state the reasons why Henny-Penny and her friends never come out of Foxy-Loxy's den.

2. After being read a dramatic selection, the children will write a detailed description of the reasons they are like or unlike the main character.

3. After reading or listening to *Across Five Aprils*, the student will be able to state at least one of the reasons that led the families to war.

Compare these objectives with the general unit goals as well as the general skills to be taught. As you can see, they attempt to integrate all of these areas. For example, behavioral objective #3 includes the development of listening, reading, and social studies skills. When developing specific behavioral objectives, you must always refer to your general goals and skills in an attempt to plan a comprehensive unit. If you are not familiar with the development of behavioral objectives, please refer to Chapter 15.

After determining specific behavioral objectives, you need to adjust the program to the students' needs. This can be accomplished through formal and informal assessments of your students. Informal assessment might include an analysis of:

1. the reading levels of the texts to be read
2. which children can easily read the texts; who will require minimal help; and who needs a great deal of help
3. the writing, listening, and speaking skills required to complete each task
4. the types of abilities each child has as they relate to each area
5. the content area concepts being explored
6. what the children know about the content areas that are being explored.

Procedures for informal assessment might include: (1) a general class discussion, (2) knowledge from previous assignments, or (3) a game, worksheet, or reading assignment. After determining the relationship between the goals to be accomplished and the skills and information possessed by each child, you can begin to determine *basic grouping patterns*.

Planning Lessons

Unit lessons should reflect (1) thematic information, (2) skills to be mastered, and (3) content areas to be explored. Because of varying degrees of student competency, more than one lesson may need to be operating simultaneously. When you are planning your lessons, be sure not to make yourself the central focus of each one. Incorporate media, games, and student-directed activities into your lessons. In this way, each lesson will be able to function even when you are not there. Classroom management is an arduous task, and one that will need your constant attention.

Lesson Unit Evaluation

Evaluation is a continuous process that is needed throughout the planning and implementation stages of your unit. When you are assessing student competencies in order to plan your groups, you are involved in an evaluative process.

After the lesson is implemented, you must determine who has successfully completed it. For those children, you will plan a lesson related to the next unit objective, remembering again to engage in the diagnostic assessment process you used during the planning of the initial lesson. For the children who have not mastered the lesson, you will need to ask: "Why?"

Begin by asking yourself:

1. Was the lesson successfully implemented?
2. Did the children possess the skills necessary to master the lesson?
3. Was the lesson too involved? Did it convey too much information?

Once you have determined why the lesson was not successfully mastered, you will be better able to continue instruction with each group.

Can You Do It?

In this chapter an attempt has been made to introduce you to the various components of a language arts program, as well as to acquaint you with the classroom management procedures involved in implementing integrated units. The task may seem complicated, but, once you begin, the process becomes very clear. Children do not *learn* language arts in isolation, nor do they *use* them in isolation; therefore, it is more realistic to learn them in an integrated curriculum. Although this type of classroom management is probably unlike the one under which you learned your language arts skills, we encourage you to try to implement this model. It attempts to *individualize* as well as to *integrate* the language arts curriculum. The following activities are included to further enable you to develop a language arts curriculum.

LANGUAGE ARTS ACTIVITIES

1. What Are They Really Thinking?

Goal: Interpreting and using nonverbal communication

Grade level: 1–8

Construction: Discuss with your class the different ways people show their true feelings without using words. Describe differences between how a person might act and what he really thinks. Design situations for the students to act out, utilizing nonverbal communication. Situations may be written on 3x5 index cards.

Utilization: Two or more students select a card and act out the situation. The remainder of the group must guess what the person using nonverbal communication is really thinking and name the techniques he or she is using.

2. Telephone Know-how

Goal: Developing telephone skills

Grade level: 1–4

Construction: Set up a pretend telephone system using string and tin cans. If possible, contact your local phone company to borrow a Teletrainer (two phones that plug into a box). With this set, someone can press buttons that will cause the phone to ring or give a busy signal. Make up index cards giving such situations as, "You just saw a building on fire, what is the proper way to phone for help?" Before enacting the situations, review with the class how to make collect, person-to-person, and direct long-distance calls; how to take messages, how to interpret the different signals; and how to call for information.

Utilization: Each student draws a card and demonstrates the proper way to use the telephone. Two people may be needed for some situations.

3. Asking Around

Goal: Developing interviewing skills

Grade level: 3–8

Construction: Students are responsible for selecting a parent or community person to interview on a specific topic. They can talk to someone in a career they are interested in or someone who can add enrichment to subjects the class is studying. For example, if the class is doing a unit on "Our Community" they can talk to an elderly person who has lived there for many years.

Utilization: Students prepare a form for the questions they plan to ask, leaving space for a brief outline of the answers. If possible, the student can tape record the interview. A preliminary exercise could involve dramatizing a short interview in class.

4. A How-to-Do-It Demonstration

Goal: Developing skills for giving directions

Grade level: 1–8

Construction: Have students choose a how-to-do-it topic for which they will give the class directions. The topic can be one with which the children are either familiar or unfamiliar. Suggested topics are dialing a phone, tying a shoe, and brushing teeth.

Utilization: After each student has given instructions, have the class discuss the strengths and weaknesses of each attempt at direction giving.

5. Move to the Music

Goal: Developing skills in body movement

Grade level: 1–8

Construction: Discuss with the class the role of body movement in the communication process. Ask children if different types of music ever make them feel a certain way: happy, sad, or afraid, for example.

Utilization: Play music capable of evoking emotions in young children and encourage them to sway, jump, hop, shake, twist, or move in whatever way the music makes them feel.

6. Make Your Own Movie

Goal: Developing words from a standard Latin or Greek base

Grade level: 4–8

Construction: Secure a large cardboard box and make a slit in two sides. Also secure a roll of white shelf paper and several colored magic markers.

Utilization: Have children select Latin or Greek word bases from the dictionary and list several words containing the bases.

Example: centum   cele
             century   celebrant
             centurion   celebrate
             centuple   celebration
             bicentennial celebrity

Have the children write a story, play, or script incorporating several of the derived words. The meanings of the words should be understood through the events in the story. Have the children illustrate their script on the shelf paper. Pull one end of the paper through the slits of the cardboard box and then roll it around a paper towel tube.

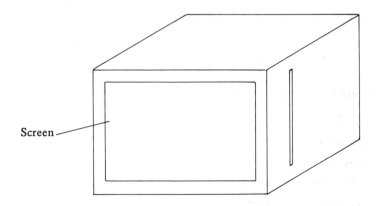

Screen

7. Complete the Family Tree

Goal: Tracing word histories

Grade level: 4–8

Construction: Prepare a ditto or laminated sheet making a large tree with many branches. On the trunk write the original Latin or Greek derivative.

Utilization: Have the child complete the family tree by writing on the branches words that developed from Latin or Greek. If centum was written on the trunk, the child would label the branches with century, centennial, etc.

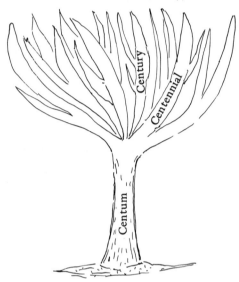

8. Mystery Sounds

Goal: Developing listening sounds

Grade level: 3–8

Construction: Tape record various sounds from the student's environment, such as a faucet dripping, paper crumbling, a door slamming, and a telephone ringing. Pictures identifying these sounds can be collected.

Utilization: The students try to identify the sounds or match the pictures provided by the teacher with the sounds.

9. What Sounds Do Your Ears Like?

Goal: Developing skills in listening appreciatively

Grade level: 1–8

Construction: Prepare a tape of various sounds from the environment: a siren, a baby crying, a dog growling, music, and people laughing, for example.

Utilization: Have students complete a chart divided into two sections: "Sounds I Like" and "Sounds I Don't Like." After they have exhausted the sounds from the tape, have them supply others of their own. The teacher can write the suggestions of young children on a large chart to reinforce the language experience.

10. Painting to Music

Goal: Developing skills in listening appreciatively

Grade level: 1–4

Construction and utilization: Provide each child with finger paints and finger painting paper. Select music capable of evoking emotion. Selections should differ in volume and tempo throughout the recording. Before the finger painting begins, have the children explore moving their bodies according to how the music makes them feel. Play the music a second time, encouraging the children to express their feelings using the finger paint.

11. Quiet Sounds and Loud Sounds

Goal: Developing skills in listening attentively

Grade level: 1–8

Construction: Tell the class that they are going to compare sounds from different locations. First, take the class for a short walk down a city street and have them make a list of the sounds they hear. Younger children can just make a mental note of them. Next, take the class to a wood or other quiet place and again have them take note of the sounds they hear.

Utilization: When back in the classroom, make an experience chart listing city sounds on one side and country sounds on the other. Have the class discuss the differences and initiate a discussion of why the differences exist.

City Sounds	Country Sounds

12. Can You Finish It?

Goal: Developing skills in listening appreciatively

Grade level: 4–8

Construction: Make up 4–6 line poems or limericks, preferably that rhyme. Leave out one word at the end that the student must fill in. The student should be able to guess the word using context clues or rhyming words.

Utilization: The student fills in the correct word. Examples of rhymes and limericks can be found in May Hill Arbuthnot, et al. The Arbuthnot Anthology of Children's Literature. 3rd ed. (1971).

13. Break the Listening Code

<u>Goal</u>: Developing skills in interpretive listening

<u>Grade level</u>: 4–8

<u>Construction</u>: Prepare a code formula substituting letters for numbers. For example, A = 1, B = 2, C = 3, etc. Translate a secret message from letters to the code numbers. Prepare dittos consisting of 10 to 15 lines of numbers in random order.

3	5	8	10	15	4	6
9	11	12	18	4	2	1

Prepare directions for the student to circle one of the numbers in each line. For example: "Mark the number that is fourth from the end," or "Mark the second number after 18." When all of the numbers are circled, tell the students the secret formula.

<u>Utilization</u>: The student changes the numbers to letters and figures out the coded message.

14. How Do You Feel?

<u>Goal</u>: Developing skills in interpretive listening

<u>Grade level</u>: 4–8

<u>Construction</u>: Choose any story that is capable of evoking emotion in young children (a pet dying or trouble in school). Before reading it aloud, discuss with the group different kinds of feelings that people have—happiness, sadness, surprise, and fear, for example.

<u>Utilization</u>: After reading the story, give each child a chance to tell how the story made him feel.

15. Using Your Mind and Ears

<u>Goal</u>: Developing skills in critical listening

<u>Grade level</u>: 4–8

<u>Construction</u>: Together with the class, choose a speaker to give a controversial talk to the class or the entire school. First, the class must determine the speaker's qualifications; then a letter of invitation must be written.

<u>Utilization</u>: After the speaker has finished, evaluate his or her persuasion techniques; look for reasons for any bias; and decide if the person supported his or her statements.

16. With Whom Do You Agree?

<u>Goal</u>: Developing skills in critical listening

<u>Grade level</u>: 4–8

Construction: Prepare, with a helper, a tape cassette imitating two historical people having an argument. You could be Aaron Burr and Alexander Hamilton, Stephen Douglas and Abraham Lincoln, two people currently running for president, or a rock musician and a conductor of classical music.

Utilization: Have the students listen to the tape offered by each speaker as many times as necessary and write down the supporting statements. They should determine which person they agree with most and state the reasons.

17. Determined Debaters

Goal: Developing skills in listening and speaking

Grade level: 4–8

Construction: Review with students the techniques and procedures of debating. Assist them in selecting topics. Choose four volunteers, two for each team. The topic that will be debated is called the proposition, which is stated in the affirmative. For example, Resolved: Students should be allowed to set up a student lounge in the school. The affirmative team is in favor of the proposition, and the negative team is against it. Traditionally, constructive speeches prepared in advance are given first, followed by rebuttal speeches, in which the students disagree with the content of the other team's speeches and defend their own stances. The order in which the team members give their speeches is usually:

Constructive speeches	Rebuttal speeches
1. First affirmative	5. First negative
2. First negative	6. First affirmative
3. Second affirmative	7. Second negative
4. Second negative	8. Second affirmative

Utilization: A chairman reads the topic and introduces the team members. A time-keeper makes sure they do not go over the established time limit (15 minutes). The remaining members of the class serve as judges. They should decide which team performed better with regard to supporting statements, speaking clearly, and holding interest.

18. Improvisational Theater

Goal: Developing skills in listening and speaking

Grade level: 4–8

Construction and utilization: Have an improvisational type of theater performance in which the audience makes suggestions as to what the actors must improvise. The actors can ask for the name of a song, place, or a short plot from the viewers; the actors then develop a skit based on the audience's suggestions.

19. Listening for Your Homophones

Goal: Developing skills in listening, speaking, and writing

Grade level: 4–8

Construction: Review with the class the meaning of homophones. Divide the class into two groups and ask them to make up five to ten sentences, each containing two homophones. For example: I had to go by your house on my way to buy the groceries. Students should try to include as many decoys as possible.

Utilization: In turn, the players read a sentence to a player on the other team. The other player must then state the two words that are homophones; if correct, he scores one point for the team. Whichever team has the most points when everyone's sentences have been read, wins the game. This can also be done with compound words or antonyms.

20. Constructive Arguing

Goal: Developing skills in listening, speaking, and reading

Grade level: 4–8

Construction and Utilization: Have a small group prepare an oral report on a controversial book all members of the group have read. Possible topics are smoking, drugs, and Women's Liberation. The group should begin by outlining the subcategories of the topic being discussed. Members of the group should take different stands on the issue, defending points of view after listening to the others. Time should be allotted for questions from the audience.

21. Write Your Own Stage Play

Goal: Developing skills in listening, speaking, reading, and writing

Grade level: 4–8

Construction: Read aloud a favorite story

Utilization: Have students redesign the story, changing it to a play using a narrator and dialogue. Students could also specify the scenery and costumes to be used. After practicing, they can perform the play for the rest of the class.

22. Speaking at the O-K "Chor-al"

Goal: Developing skills in listening, speaking, reading, and writing

Grade level: 3–8

Construction: Assist the class in writing a poem for choral speaking. Either the refrain or the lines of the poem should be repetitive. Perhaps the teacher could read other poems used for choral speaking to give the children some idea of what choral speaking is.

Utilization: Six to ten students read the main lines of the poem, and the remainder of the class listens in order to know when to join in with the refrain.

23. How to Find Timbuktu

Goal: Developing skills in listening, speaking, reading, and writing

Grade level: 4–8

Construction: Display a large map of the world in front of the room. Divide the group into two teams and have each member locate a specific place on the map. Each member should then write five steps of directions, using cardinal directions, latitude, and longitude.

Utilization: In turn, a player from team A reads his directions to player B. If player B finds the location using the five steps, player B gets the point for the team. The team with the most points, after everyone has had a turn finding a location, wins.

24. Guessword

Goal: Developing skills in listening, speaking, reading, and writing

Grade level: 4–8

Construction: Provide students with a list of 20 to 25 vocabulary words. Divide the class into two teams and have them make up clues for a part of one or two words on the list. For example, if one of the words is catastrophe, the student could make up a clue for "cat" or "trophy."

Utilization: In turn, a player from one team reads a clue for one of the words to a player on the other team. That person must try to guess the complete word after he has guessed the clue. Score five points for each word guessed correctly. The first team to reach 75 points wins.

QUESTIONS AND RELATED READINGS

If at this time you do not feel that you have attained adequate knowledge to successfully answer the following questions, we would like to suggest related readings.

Goal 1: To aid students in understanding the processes involved in developing listening skills.

Question 1: What processes would you as a classroom teacher employ to develop students' listening skills?

Bryant, J. E. "Listening Centers: A Second Investment in Education?" *Journal of Learning Disabilities*, 3 (1970), 156–9.

Devine, T. G. "Reading and Listening: New Research Findings." *Elementary English*, 45 (1968), 346–8.

Lundsteen, S. W. *Listening: Its Impact on Reading and the Other Language Arts*. NCTE/ERIC Studies in the Teaching of English. Urbana, Ill.: National Council of Teachers of English, 1971.

Goal 2: To aid students in understanding the processes involved in developing speaking skills.

Question 2: What processes would you as a classroom teacher employ to develop students' speaking skills?

Britton, J. *Language and Learning*. Coral Gables, Fla.: University of Miami Press, 1970.

Stewig, J. "Instructional Strategies: The Owl, The Pussy-Cat and Oral Language." *Elementary English*, 50 (1973), 325–30.

Wilkinson, A. "The Concept of Oracy." *English Journal*, 59 (1970), 71–7.

Goal 3: To aid the students in understanding the processes involved in developing reading skills.

Question 3: What processes would you as a classroom teacher employ to develop students' reading skills?

Allen, Roach Van, and Claryce Allan. *Language Experiences in Reading*. Chicago: Encyclopedia Britannica Press, 196 .

Reid, Virginia. *In The Dynamics of Reading,* edited by Robert B. Ruddell. Waltham, Mass.: Blaidsell Press, 1970, p. 23.

Trace, Arthur. *What Ivan Knows That Johnny Doesn't*. New York: Random House, Inc., 1961.

Goal 4: To aid the students in understanding the processes involved in developing writing skills.

Question 4: What processes would you as a classroom teacher employ to develop students' writing skills?

Burrows, A. T. et al. *They All Want to Write: Written English in the Elementary Classroom*. New York: Holt, Rinehart and Winston, 1965.

Carlson, Ruth K. *Writing Aids Through the Grades*. New York: Bureau of Publications, Teachers College Press, Columbia University, 1970.

Petty, Walter T. *Slithery Snakes and Other Aids to Children's Writing*. New York: Appleton-Century-Crofts, 1970.

Goal 5: To aid the students in understanding the interrelatedness of the language arts.

Question 5: What is meant by the "interrelatedness" of the language arts?

Herman, Wayne J. "The Use of Language Arts in Social Studies Lessons." *American Educational Research Journal,* 4 (March 1967), p. 117–24

Lundsteen, S. W. "Language Arts in the Elementary School." In *Teaching for Creative Behavior*, edited by W. B. Michael. Bloomington, Ind.: Indiana University Press, 1968, pp. 131–61.

Reddin, Estoy. "Listening Instruction, Reading and Critical Thinking." *The Reading Teacher*, 21 (April 1968), 654–8.

BIBLIOGRAPHY

Bradenburg, Robert. "The Language of a Three-Year-Old Child." *Pedagogical Review,* 21 (March 1915), 89.

Brown, Dave. "Auding as the Primary Language Ability." Ph. D dissertation, Stanford University, 1954.

Burrows, Alvina T. et al., *They All Want to Write.* New York: Holt, Rinehart and Winston, 1964, p. 88.

Carroll, John B. "Language Development." In *Child Language,* edited by Aaron Bar-Adon and F. Leopold Weiner. Englewood Cliffs, N. J.: Prentice-Hall, Inc., 1971, pp. 200–211.

Colum, Padraic. *Roofs of Gold,* New York: Macmillan Publishing Co., Inc., 1964.

Duker, Sam. *Listening Bibliography,* 2nd ed. (Metuchen, N. J.: The Scarecrow Press, Inc., 1968.

Feldman, Arlene K. "The Effect of Reinforcement of Listening Skills of the Culturally Deprived." Master's thesis, The Ohio State University, Columbus, 1967.

Hunt, Irene. *Across Five Aprils,* Chicago: Follett, 1964.

Jacobs, Joseph, *Time for Fairy Tales Old & New.* Putnam.

Joos, Martin. *The Five Clocks.* New York: Harcourt Brace Jovanovich, Inc., 1967.

Larrick, Nancy. *On City Streets.* New York: Evans, 1968.

Loban, Walter. *The Language of Elementary School Children.* Champaign, Ill.: National Council of Teachers of English, 1976.

Lundsteen, W. W. *Listening: Its Impact on Reading and the Other Language Arts.* NCTE/ERIC Studies in the Teaching of English. Urbana, Ill: National Council of Teachers of English, 1971.

Russell, D. H., and E. J. Russell. "Listening Aids Through the Grades." New York: Bureau of Publications, Teachers College Press, Columbia University, 1959.

Sager, Carol. *Improving the Quality of Written Composition Through Pupil Use of Rating Scale.* Unpublished Ed. D. dissertation, Boston University School of Education, Boston, Massachusetts, 1972.

Smith, Goodman, Kenneth and Meredith, Robert. *Language and Thinking in the Language Arts in the Elementary School.* New York: Holt, Rinehart and Winston, 1970.

Wilkinson, Andrew. *The Foundations of Language.* London: Oxford University Press, Inc., 1971.

Section

The Reading Process

The purpose of this section is to isolate the components of reading in an attempt to fully explore this integral process.

Comprehension is the process whereby meaning is constructed from a language that is represented by graphic symbols. In order to construct meaning from language, a child must have an understanding of *graphophonic* cues, which help him in decoding words; *syntactic cues*, which allow him to understand word arrangements in passages; and *semantic cues*, which enable him to understand the meaning of texts.

The areas of initial reading instruction that need to be transferred to content-area programs also are examined in this section. Despite excellent basal programs, provisions for helping children to master the complexities of content area materials are often overlooked. The material in this section attempts to present an effective methodology for teaching reading in content areas.

A variety of activities that will help you in implementing an effective reading program are included in this section.

7

Understanding and implementing word analysis strategies: phonics

æ	b	c	d	ꜯ
face	bed	cat	dog	key

f	g	h	ie	j	k
feet	leg	hat	fly	jug	key

l	m	n	œ	p	ɹ
letter	man	nest	over	pen	girl

r	s	t	ue	v	w
red	spoon	tree	use	voice	window

y	z	ʒ	wh	ch
yes	zebra	daisy	when	chair

th	th	ʃh	ʒ	ŋ
three	the	shop	television	ring

a	au	a	e	i	o
father	ball	cap	egg	milk	box

u	ω	ꙍ	ou	oi
up	book	spoon	out	oil

The difference between the right word and the almost right word is the difference between lightning and the lightning bug.

Mark Twain

GOALS: To aid students in understanding
  1. the processes involved in visual perception and discrimination.
  2. the processes involved in auditory perception and discrimination.
  3. the content of phonics.
  4. how to provide instruction in phonics strategies.

When you begin to teach children to read, you need to help them build a reading vocabulary by helping them to understand the origins of their spoken language. Unfortunately, we sometimes ask children to tuck away their spoken language and to begin to decode a printed language that may seem to them to be entirely different from their spoken language. The child may not see the relationship between the two languages, and a situation is created whereby the transition from spoken to written language becomes an extremely complicated process.

Educators have argued that children have a *spoken* as well as a *listening, writing,* and *reading* vocabulary. It should be noted that a knowledge of the language of one of these vocabularies does not necessarily insure transfer to knowledge of any other vocabularies. The first vocabulary that a child acquires is a listening vocabulary, followed closely by the development of a spoken vocabulary. One's auditory capabilities generally exceed one's spoken vocabulary. Most individuals auditorially comprehend a far greater range of language patterns than they use in their spoken text. Listening vocabulary also exceeds one's early writing and reading vocabularies.

As we discussed in Chapter 2, most children have acquired a sophisticated understanding of the syntax of the English language by the age of four. By the time children begin formal instruction in reading, they have also acquired a substantial listening and speaking vocabulary, and they can discriminate between most of the sounds of the English language. As teachers of reading, our task is to help children decode the written symbolic representations of a language that they already know. In some ways it must seem to be an extremely easy task, but the intricacy of this perceptual job becomes an overwhelming burden for many teachers.

In this chapter we intend to describe the process of beginning reading by explaining the phenomenon of decoding. A great deal of background information and implementation strategies are presented here in order to help you teach children to read.

Reading is a two-part perceptual process: *visual* and *auditory.*

Visual Perception

By the time the normal child is four years old, he or she can perceive visual objects and is able to discriminate between fine details.

Letter Discrimination

mn   bd   oc   qg   and   QO   JT   EF   RP

These sets of letters look enough alike to us, as competent readers, that we can easily understand why children may not always see the differences between them. Difficulty with visual discrimination of letters becomes even more obvious when one reads the following sentences quickly:

Dan ran to the dam and sat on the sand.

Did Dan run to the damp dam in the sand?

Did Dame Dann run with Dan to the dam?

Sam sat in the sand in front of the dam; did Dame?

Did you have any difficulty in discriminating between letters as you read these sentences? Gibson (1974) has researched the ways in which children identify abstract visual symbols, and she suggests that they use a set of distinctive features to discriminate between these symbols. The four distinctive features that children attend to are the following:

1. Straight-Line Segments. In the Roman alphabet there are several letters that are made up of this type of visual symbol:

    E   F   H   I   L   T

2. Curved Segments. In the Roman alphabet the following letters are examples of curved segmental visual symbols.

    C   O

3. Symmetries. The following alphabetic letters constitute examples of symmetries.

    M   W   X

4. Discontinuities. Several   alphabetic   letters   are   examples   of discontinuities:

    K   B   G   J

Children process these features in order to arrive at a solution. For example, one child might look at the letter *J* and see straight-line segments and curved segments. A second child may see only the top part of the letter *J*, which looks like *T*; he may fail to perceive the curved line segments and to attend to both stimulants. In order to avoid initial difficulties, teachers can instruct children in letter discrimination using a developmental plan similar to one described below:

STEP 1:   Ask children to look at single letters.

1. a d

2. d b

3. b a

4. b b

STEP 2: Ask children if the letters are the same or different.

STEP 3: Ask children to look at sets of letters and to determine if the sets are the same or different.

ad   ba   db   ad

STEP 4: Ask children to examine sets of words and determine if they are the same or different.

| tan   man | ran   man | mad   dam |

After children have completed this assignment, it is important to explain to them that one word can be written in at least four different forms. You may want to progress to:

STEP 5: Ask children to examine the following set of words and to determine if they are the same or different.

TAN   tan   *tan*   Tan

Letter-Name Knowledge

Many teachers and researchers have asked the important question: Is letter-name knowledge important in the acquisition of reading skills?   Durkin (1972) argues convincingly that knowledge of letter names is helpful in carrying out initial reading instruction. Murphy and Durrell (1972) use a letter-naming system for initial phonics instruction.

D:	Initial	Medial	Final
	dean	audience	lady
	decent	comedian	speedy
	decide	radio	tidy

With the creation of *Sesame Street,* most middle-class children arrive in kindergarten knowing the names of the letters of the English alphabet. The child who begins first grade knowing the letter names is more likely to succeed in learning to read than the child who has not acquired this knowledge. This is correlation, not causality. Several studies have shown that teaching the letter names in isolation does not have much effect on later success in reading (Jenkins, Bausel, and Jenkins, 1972; Silberberg, Silberberg, and Iverson, 1972). Knowledge of letter names is an indicator of the student's readiness for reading. The student who has learned the alphabet before coming to school most probably has been exposed to other elements of reading. It does not hurt a child to learn the letter names. These are relatively easy to acquire, certainly easier than letter-sound associations. This experience may, through general transfer, make it easier for the child to learn the letter-sound associations at a later time.

Auditory Perception

Children are capable of perceiving almost all of the sounds of their environment by the age of four. As was suggested in Chapter 2, children may not be capable of producing all of the sounds of English until they are eight or nine years old. However, an inability to produce sounds does not interfere with the ability to begin reading.

Auditory Discrimination

Young children are capable of discriminating between the sounds of English; they can discriminate adequately between minimal pairs of sounds, e.g., *mit* and *pit* and *man* and *pan*. They can also match sounds, e.g., box begins with a /b/ sound. Which of the following words begin with the same sound?

wall   paw   ball   saw

Your task as a teacher is to introduce the child to the correspondence between letters and sounds. In other words, you must help the child to "break the code." The child has language—*phonology, syntax,* and *vocabulary*—and he can visually discriminate between many different symbols. He often knows the names of the letters of the alphabet and can discriminate between them. All he needs now is the knowledge of the code, the link between letters and sounds.

Letter-Sound Correspondence (grapheme-phoneme correspondence)

The following charts contain consonant and vowel correspondences in various positions within a word. These charts can be extremely useful to you in teaching students how to analyze words. The lists represent most of the sounds of the English language. If a child is able to read all of these correspondences within meaningful contexts, he can probably be considered a competent decoder.

CONSONANT CORRESPONDENCE IN VARIOUS POSITIONS

Letter-Sound (Grapheme-Phoneme) Relationships

Phoneme	Grapheme	Phoneme In Initial Position	Phoneme In Medial Position	Phoneme In Final Position
/b/	b	bake baby	cabin	tub
/k/	c	cat	become	tick
	k	kite	making	work
	ck		tracking	back
	x		complexion	
	ch	charisma	anchor echo	monarch
	qu	queen	raquet	bisque
	cc		account	
/s/	s	suit	insert	porous
	ss		massive possessive	miss possess
	c	cite	pencil glacier	face
	st		gristle listen fasten	
	ps	pseudonym		
	sc	scissors	Pisces visceral	
/c/	ch	cherry	lecher	such
	t		picture nature virtue	
/d/	d	dish	body	hard
	dd		middle	odd
/f/	f	fish	safer	knife
	ff		raffle	muff
	ph	phonograph phrase	telephone cephalic	graph
	gh			tough
/g/	g	good	rigor	bag
	gh	ghetto ghost		ugh
	gg		trigger	egg
	gu	guest	beguile unguent	rogue
/j/	g	gin	wager	
	du		schedule	

Phoneme	Grapheme	Phoneme In Initial Position	Phoneme In Medial Position	Phoneme In Final Position
	j	jug	prejudice	
	dg		dredger	hedge
			badger	
/h/	h	horse	behead	
	wh	who		
/l/	l	long	bailer	stale
	ll		falling	doll
/m/	m	moon	hamper	game
	mb		tombstone	dumb
	mm		drummer	
/nj/	n	nest	diner	pin
	nn		thinner	
	gn	gnat		
	kn	knight		
/n/	ng		stinger	song
	n		think	
/p/	p	point	viper	hip
	pp		hopping	
/r/	r	rat	boring	tear
	rr		merry	
	wr	write		
	rh	rhyme	hemmorhage	
/š/	sh	shadow	crashing	dish
	s	sure		
	ci		precious	
	ce		ocean	
	ss		obsession	
			assure	
	ch	chic chevron	machine	
	ti		motion	
/t/	t	test	water	cat
	tt		letter	putt
	pt			receipt
	bt		debtor	debt
/o/	th	thin	either lethal	wreath
/d/	th	then	either	bathe
/v/	v	violet	hover	dove
/w/	w	will	throwing	how
	ui		sanguine	
/ks/	x		toxic	box
	cc		accent	
/y/	y	yarn	lawyer	day

Phoneme	Grapheme	Phoneme In Initial Position	Phoneme In Medial Position	Phoneme In Final Position
/z/	z	zipper	razor	blaze
	s		visit	logs
			amuser	
	zz		drizzle	fizz
			nozzle	
	x	xanthippe		
		xylophone		
/ž/	z		azure	
	su		treasure	
	si		allusion	
	ss		fissure	
	g	genre		decoupage
/gz/	x	xeroxes	exhibit	
			exert	
			exact	
	gs			digs

VOWEL CORRESPONDENCES

Sound Label	Vowel	Letter Label	Example
Unglided or short		a	an
		au	laugh
Glided or long	/ey/	a.e	pane, bake
		ai	rain
		ea	steak
		ei	feign
		ay	tray
		ey	obey
		ua	guaze
Unglided or short	/e/	e	pen
		ea	lead
		eo	jeopardy
		ei	heifer
		ai	stair
		ie	friendly
Glided or long	/iy/	e.e	mete
		e	he
		ea	heat
		ee	tree
		ei	conceive
		ie	believe
Unglided or short	/i/	i	hit
		ui	guild

Sound Label	Vowel	Letter Label	Example
		y	gym
		u	business
Glided or long	/ay/	i.e.	write
		uy	buyers
		ie	tries
		ai	aisle
		ia	trial
		y	spy
		i	find
		ei	sleigh
		igh	night
Unglided or short	/a/	oo	not, fought, thought
Glided or long	/ow/	o.e	shone
		oa	goat
		ow	snow
		o	no
		ew	sewing
		ough	dough, through
		oo	floor
		eau	beau, bureau
		oe	hoe, doe
		jo, yo	fjord
Unglided or short	/ə/	u	nut
		oo	flood
		ou	enough, curious, pretentious
		ough	rough
		o	hover, cover, come
Glided or long	/yuw/	u.e	yule
		eau	beauty
		ew	dew
		ieu	lieu, lieutenant
Unglided or short	/u/	oo	good
		u	putt
		ew	grew
		ui	fruit
Unglided or short	/ɔ/	a	walk
		au	maul
		o	frog
		aw	saw
Unglided or dipthong	/aw/	ow	down
		ou	cloud
Glided or dipthong	/ɔy/	oy	boy
		oi	loin
		ai	stair
Note: an unglided	/ar/, /er/	ar, ea	art, pear
or short vowel	/ir/, /ɔr/	ea, oa	tear, boar

Sound Label	Vowel	Letter Label	Example
followed by -r is some-	/ur/, /yur/	oo, u.e	poor, cure
times referred to as an	/ər/	e	her
r-controlled vowel		i	sir

Word Discrimination

A Chinese woman studying in the United States for the first time, quipped, "All words in English look alike." Most first graders who are beginning to read might quickly agree with her. As competent adult readers of English, we might argue with her that all words in Chinese look the same to us. If you were beginning to learn to read in Chinese, you would probably see sentences like these:

日 日 有 明 月

秋 季 末 森 林 內 村 人 採 木 材

Do the words in each of these sentences look alike to you? This is what happens to the young child when he first sees written words in English. We have to be extremely patient with the child to make sure that he can distinguish each separate word.

In English the two Chinese sentences mean:

Every day the moon is bright.

At the end of autumn, the villager gathers wood in the forest.

We have no difficulty in distinguishing each word in the English translation. This proficiency is the result of a great deal of exercise, practice, and experience. Most children in the first grade are able to distinguish the letters of the English alphabet in a relatively short period of time and with little practice, but it is not uncommon to hear a young child say, "I have trouble reading the little words." This might mean that young children have difficulty in quickly identifying little words like *in, and, on, an, or, for, from, form, foam.* Test yourself again by quickly reading these "little" words aloud.

inn	in	on	and
ache	ate	ace	atom
to	too	toe	tow
it	in	it	if
of	off	oft	often
for	from	form	foam
each	eat	ear	earn
here	her	hear	heart

Now read this brief passage as quickly as possible.

Ira went to the inn in Innsbrook in December. It was there that he saw her on a seesaw in the inn. He kicked her with his toe to see if she saw him there. This was their meeting ritual.

After the child learns to identify letters by processing visual and/or auditory stimuli, he acquires the ability to discriminate between words. The next step in the process is the *decoding* of written words for meaning—children attach these written symbols to concepts. One of the first decoding strategies which children use is a phonics strategy. An explanation of the content of phonics and its application to reading will be presented throughout the remaining part of this chapter.

Phonics Strategies

The Sound System of English

Let us thoroughly examine the sound system of English. Educators have extracted information about this sound system from a body of knowledge which is called *phonetics*. The phonetician studies speech sounds in their most subtle physiological and acoustical variations. The educator has taken the most useful parts of this knowledge for the teaching of reading and has attempted to develop a body of knowledge called *phonics*. This subset, phonics, includes the most common sounds of English and the most frequently used letter or strings of letters which record these sounds.

The Origin of Phonics Instruction

The history of teaching reading through instruction in phonics dates back to the 1890s, when the reading program in most American schools was a synthetic phonics method. Before this time, children spent a great deal of time learning and drilling the alphabet. Emphasis began to shift from exercises in naming letters to exercises in naming the sounds of the letters. Phonics exercises were unrelated to meaning. Children would recite "phonics," e.g., they would practice the following drill:

da	ra	pa	sa	la	na	ma
di	re	pi	si	li	ne	me

Rebecca Rollard's *Synthetic Method* was introduced to schools in 1890. In this method she advocated the following practices:

1. Articulation drills in single letters before reading instruction began.
2. Drills for each consonant; each consonant had the sound of a syllable: /bə/, /kə/, /də/, /fə/, /gə/, /lə/, /mə/, /nə/, /pə/, /rə/, /sə/, /tə/.

3. Drills on phonograms (word families): *bill, pill, mill, drill, trill, back, pack, sack, track.*
4. Drills on diacritical markings in sentences: The lamb̸ ate the grass̸ at nig̸h̸t.
5. Drills on phrases in sentences: The dog/sat/on his tail,/and/he yelped.

Syllable Generalizations

You may want to begin phonics instruction with the introduction of the syllable. This position seems reasonable because reading researchers have found that teaching vowels without reference to syllables is a futile process. But what is a syllable? As Groff (1970) points out in his discussion of the syllable, English is "stress-timed language"; therefore, it is easy to identify the number of syllables in a given word, but it is very difficult to determine syllable boundaries. The syllable presents a problem similar to that of a cartographer deciding exactly how much of the valley between the two hills belongs to each hill.

Syllable boundaries are usually determined by the existence of a vowel, and the phonological features which exist within a syllable are a vowel and consonant; together they result in emphasis on one part of the syllable. Gibson and Levin (1975) found that some children use such units rather automatically when they are decoding; instruction in the visual recognition of larger letter units facilitates many children's word recognition abilities. It should also be noted that the visual identification of letter sequences for pronunciation can facilitate the decoding process.

Knowledge of syllables and stress in English will also be helpful for you when you are structuring an application of phonics strategies. It is therefore important to remember that the following generalizations are subject to scrutiny and exception.

1. All syllables have a vowel sound: pen - cil, why.
2. When a second vowel appears in a word, the final *e* usually does not add another sound: tale.
3. When two consonants exist between two vowels, a division takes place between the consonants: spar - tan.
4. When a consonant exists between two vowels, a division takes place between the first vowel and the consonant: o - dor.
5. If the single consonant preceded and followed by vowels is *x*, the *x* and the preceding vowel are in the same syllable: ex - it.
6. When a word ends in *le*, and it is preceded by a consonant, the consonant and *le* make up a new syllable: bun - dle, can - dle.

Stress Rules

English is a time-sequence language; it contains stress points. Knowledge of these stress rules of English may help children learn how to decode unknown words. The following brief set of rules may help you when you are structuring your phonics program:

1. If a root has two syllables, the first is *usually* stressed: mother, battle, summer.

2. If a root has two syllables and the second syllable contains a long vowel, the syllable with the long vowel is stressed: precede, canteen.

3. If the first vowel in a multisyllabic root is a short vowel and it precedes two consonants, the first syllable is stressed: permanent, latitude, sacrosanct.

4. If the first vowel in a multisyllabic root is a long vowel and it precedes two consonants, the syllable which contains the long vowel is stressed: alliance.

5. If a final syllable contains *le*, it is not stressed: table, preamble.

Although stress is an important component in learning to read, it is extremely difficult to write an exhaustive list of rules that do not have a long list of exceptions. Most children, however, who have heard a word spoken will be able to find the stress pattern while they are decoding the constituent parts of the word. If the child decodes con. sti. tu. tion, he will be able to match the stress to his knowledge of the spoken word.

Before beginning our discussion of consonant and vowel sounds, it seems important to present the total array of English phonemes with a transcription key, using the symbols of the International Phonetic Alphabet. This key will help you to aid children in deciphering words that they are unable to pronounce. For example, if a child did not know how to pronounce *treasure*, he might say /tri . sur/ instead of /trEžr/. The phoneme list is presented below.

ENGLISH PHONEMES WITH KEY FOR PRONUNCIATION

Consonants

Phoneme Symbol	Key Word (Target underlined)	Transcription of Key Word
/p/	pin	/pIn/
/b/	bin	/bIn/
/t/	tile	/taIl/
/d/	dime	/daIm/
/k/	cope	/kop/
/g/	goat	/got/
/č/	church	/črč/
/ǰ/	judge	/ǰəǰ/
/f/	find	/faId/
/v/	vine	/vaIn/
/θ/	thin	/θIn/
/ /	that	/ðae/
/s/	sin	/sIn/
/z/	zip	/zIp/
/š/	shoot	/šut/
/ž/	treasure	/trEžr/
/l/	lid	/lId/
/r/	rid	/rId/
/m/	mean	/min/

Phoneme Symbol	Key Word (target underlined)	Transcription of Key Word
/n/	neat	/nit/
/n/	sing	/slŋ/
/w/	wit	/wIt/
/y/	yelp	/yElp/

Vowels

Phoneme Symbol	Key Word (target underlined)	Transcription of Key Word
/i/	seat	/sit/
/I/	sit	/slt/
/e/	gait	/get/
/E/	get	/gEt/
/æ/	rat	/ræt/
/a/	top	/tap/
/ /	bought	/b∂t/
/o/	coat	/kot/
/U/	put	/pUt/
/u/	root	/rut/
/∂/	but	/b∂/
/ol/	toy	/tol/
/aU/	cow	/kaU/
/al/	kite	/kalt/

Consonants

It is important to understand the phonetic principles which govern articulation of consonants in English. Several consonants have only one sound in English, while others have a variety of sounds. In the next few pages we will introduce you to a series of rules which govern consonants.

The beginning sounds in the following words are representative of the most common consonant sounds. Each of these 16 graphemes (letters) has only one sound in the initial position in English; the sound is always the same.

b	baby	n	not
d	doll	p	pipe
f	fan	r	ran
h	home	s	saw
j	juice	t	took
k	kit	v	very
l	lady	w	was
m	me	z	zoo

As you have noticed, words beginning with the consonants *c*, *g*, *q*, and *x* were not included in the list. *C* and *g* were not included because they have two sounds: *hard* and *soft* sounds.

C

For example, the hard sound of c is heard in words such as cat, candy, cape, coat, cuff, cough, calf, fabric, and picnic. The hard sound of c is heard as /k/.

The soft sound of c is heard in words such as city, cell, cent, cigar, and cyst. The soft sound of c is heard as /s/.

Hard C Sound	Soft C Sound
cat	city
candy	cell
coat	cent
cuff	cigar

When the consonant c is followed by a, o, or u, the sound of /k/ is often heard. When c is followed by e, i, or y, the sound of /s/ is often heard.

G

The hard sound of g is heard in words such as game, give, get, gate, goat, good, gulp, and guest and in the final position in words like bag, and gag. The hard sound of g is heard as /g/.

The soft sound of g is heard in words such as gym, gentle, gender, and gent and in the final position in badge and rage. The soft sound of g is heard as /j/.

Hard G Sound	Soft G Sound
game	gender
good	gentle
guest	gym

In many words when the consonant g is followed by e, i, or y, the sound of /j/ is heard; and when g is followed by a, o, or u, the hard or /g/ sound is heard. This principle is not as reliable in its application to g as it is in application to c.

Q

The consonant q always appears with the vowel u. Together they make the following sounds:

qu as the /k/ sound: antique, queue

qu as the /kw/ sound: quack, quail, quarrel, queen, quiz, quote

X

The letter x, like the letters c and q, has sounds that are represented by other letters:

x as the / z / sound: xylem, xylophone, Xavier, Xenia

x as the / ks / sound: sox, taxi

x as the / gz / sound: exist, exotic

W and Y

The letters w and y are unique because they can function as both consonants and vowels.

The letters w and y function as consonants only when they appear as the initial letter in a syllable.

yard	yellow	you	war	wilt	went
yawn	canyon	yelp	walnut	wallow	wonder
young					

Consonant Clusters (sometimes called blends)

When two or more consonants appear in succession in a word, they are referred to as consonant blends. The following examples represent a sample of consonant blends in the initial position:

bl	bloom	fl	flee	pr	prize	scr	screw
br	bright	fr	free	sc	scout	str	straight
cl	clown	gl	glad	sk	skate	st	stop
cr	cradle	gr	grape	sl	sled	sw	sweep
dr	draw	kr	kraut	sm	smile	tr	train
dw	dwarf	pl	plum	sn	snap	tw	twinkle

The following words represent examples of consonant blends in the final position:

−st	−sk	−sp	−nt	−nd
must	ask	crisp	went	bend
fast	desk	grasp	spent	sent
rest	brisk	clasp	want	sand
coast	task	wisp	ant	hand
most	dusk	rasp	bent	wind
last	risk		elephant	hind
best	mask			blind
toast	tusk			
chest	flask			

-mp	-ft	-lm	-nk	-lt
limp	left	calm	bunk	felt
skimp	lift	balm	sunk	melt
lamp	loft	film	brink	belt
clamp	graft		sink	malt
lump	raft		honk	salt
dump			spunk	bolt
bump				silt
				hilt
				pelt

-lp	-ld
help	held
gulp	hold
kelp	old
scalp	mold
	told
	cold

Consonant Digraphs

When two consonants appear together in a word in a *combination* sound which differs from each of the individual sounds, it is referred to as a *consonant digraph*. The following words contain examples of consonant digraphs:

gh	ghost	ng	rung	sh	short
gh	laugh	ph	photo		

The following consonant digraph has more than one sound:

chef
character
chomp

In the case of the /th/ sound, it is necessary to distinguish between the voiced sound and voiceless sound.

voiced sound /ɤ/	voiceless sound /θ/
they	thigh
them	thimble
bathe	bath
breathe	breath

In English we also have three consonants which, when they are combined, are read or spoken as one sound:

chr	chrome	phr	phrase	sch	school	spl	splash	thr	through
	/kr/		/fr/		/sk/		/spl/		/ʒr/

The following list contains examples of consonant digraphs in the initial position:

ch	sh	th	th (th)	wh
chin	ship	this	thin	whip
chip	shall	those	thank	whistle
chop	shop	that	thick	whale
chuck	shell	there	thump	whisper
chill	shut	then	thorn	whack
chest	shot	them	thumb	wheel
chair	shout	these	thing	white
chick	shed	the	thunder	when
chain	shoe	than	thud	where
cherries	shine	their	thermometer	why

The following lists contain consonant digraphs in the final position:

ch	sh	th (th)	nk	ng	ck
much	wish	tooth	bank	bang	back
rich	mash	both	rank	sang	sack
lunch	dash	health	sank	sing	sick
such	dish	math	tank	ring	pick
crunch	crush	with	link	song	dock
march	flash	breath	mink	strong	lock
branch	fresh	wealth	pink	rung	luck
ranch	fish	myth	sink	hung	duck
bunch	wash	bath	junk	gang	pack
pinch	rash	path	sunk	wing	kick

Some additional terminology may be useful for you when you are implementing your reading program:

Voiced Consonants

The consonants /b/, /d/, /g/, /j/, /l/, /m/, /n/, /r/, /v/, /w/, /th/ (this), and /z/) are referred to as voiced consonants. When these consonants are articulated, they cause the vocal chords to vibrate.

Voiceless Consonants

The consonants /p/, /f/, /h/, /k/, /s/ (sand), /t/, /th/ (thin), /sh/, /ch/, and /wh/ are referred to as voiceless consonants. When these consonants are articulated the vocal chords do not vibrate.

Stops or Continuants

The consonants /b/, /p/, /d/, /t/, and /g/ are referred to as stops. They must be pronounced instantaneously; they cannot be held like the phoneme /m/.

Vowels

It is important to understand the phonetic principles which govern the articulation of vowel sounds. The vowel sounds of English are often complex for children learning to read because there are multiple sounds for each vowel. In the next few pages we will introduce you to the rules of articulation for English vowels. It is extremely important for you to familiarize yourself with these rules in order to adapt these theoretical principles to your reading instruction program.

The following letters represent vowel sounds in English:

a   e   i   o   u   (y and w)

Every vowel has a long and a short sound:

long vowel sound	short vowel sound
a able	apple
e evil	elephant
i ice	igloo
o ocean	octopus
u universe	umbrella

The long vowel sounds can be marked with a macron (–):

ā āim	ē ēat	ī īce	ō ōld	ū ūse
gāme	bēlow	bīke	hōme	fūse
bāit	bēat	tīe	bōat	mūse

If you are assisting children who need work on vowel sounds, the following systematic list of long and short vowels in the initial and medial position may be of some help to you. You could make flash cards or word charts of these lists to help your children who are having trouble with these sounds.

LONG VOWEL SOUND IN THE INITIAL POSITION

ā	ē	ī	ō	ū
able	evil	ice	ocean	universe
ache	even	ivy	okay	unicorn
ace	evening	ivory	Oklahoma	unite
acre	equal	item	over	use
age	equation	icing	obey	useless

ā	ē	ī	ō	ū
acorn	Egypt	identify	oh	usual
ape	ecology	idea	old	ukelele
	ego	I	open	Utah
Asia	eve	Irish	oval	uniform
April	Edith	iodine	oboe	unicycle

LONG VOWEL SOUND IN THE MEDIAL POSITION

ā	ē	ī	ō	ū
cake	Pete	like	cone	cube
race	Steve	nine	stove	mule
game	beet*	white	note	cute
place	tree*	ride	home	fume
cage	feet*	bike	nose	mute
gate	seed*	kite	smoke	dune
face	meet*	mile	hope	fuse
save	sweet*	wipe	stone	flute
snake	green*	line	vote	duke
lake	wheel*			tune

The short vowel sounds can be marked with a breve (˘):

ă	ĕ	ĭ	ŏ	ŭ
at	egg	if	odd	us
bat	set	kit	flop	run
		mistake	position	function

SHORT VOWEL SOUNDS IN THE INITIAL POSITION

ă	ĕ	ĭ	ŏ	ŭ
apple	elephant	igloo	octopus	umbrella
as	Eskimo	it	ox	uncle
astronaut	enter	is	on	us
after	exit	if	ostrich	under
ant	edge	invade	olive	umpire
alligator	eggs	ill	October	ugly
actor	enemy	itch	object	up
am	engine	improve	odd	unlucky
afternoon	escape	ignore	otter	until
anniversary	energy	insect	opera	usher

*ee

SHORT VOWEL SOUNDS IN THE MEDIAL POSITION

ă	ĕ	ĭ	ŏ	ŭ
bad	pet	big	pot	bus
bat	ten	ship	fox	tub
black	fell	tin	block	puppy
cap	bed	hill	box	jump
cat	help	sit	top	much
can	step	stick	doll	sun
clap	red	pig	sock	cup
dad	sled	kit	mop	duck
fan	spell	win	hot	cut
map	yes	pin	shop	rug
rag	west	dig	rock	drum
tan	tent	hid	lock	club
sad	hen	bit	drop	fun
man	well	will	spot	but

When you are introducing vowel usage, the following rules may be extremely useful.

Short Vowels

1. A vowel grapheme represents a short vowel when it is followed by a consonant unit, e.g. fat, crab, pet, pit, sin, put, rat.
2. A vowel grapheme represents a short vowel when it is followed by a compound consonant unit, e.g., -dg/dj or -x/ks/: badge, existence
3. A vowel grapheme represents a short vowel when it is followed by a cluster of consonants, e.g., tt or st as in fast.
4. A vowel grapheme represents a short vowel when it is followed by a double consonant, e.g., little, ball, bottle.

Long Vowels

1. A vowel grapheme represents a long vowel sound when it is followed by a consonant, which in turn is followed by l or r and another vowel, usually a final e, e.g., cradle, table.
2. The vowel graphemes oi and oy represent the long vowel sound /y/ in boil and boy. The vowel graphemes ou and ow represent the long vowel sound /aw/ in bout and how.
3. When the vowel grapheme occurs as the last unit of a syllable and when it is preceded by a consonant unit, the grapheme will represent the long vowel sound, e.g., Jimmy, tree, knee.

Schwa Sound

The schwa symbol /ə/ appears often in unaccented syllables of polysyllabic words, and in many recent dictionaries it also appears in some accented syllabes. The schwa (ə) is illustrated in the following words:

about	(əbout')
April	(ā'prəl)
arrogant	(ar'əgənt)
taken	(tāk'ən)
lemon	(lem'ən)
circus	(sər'kəs)
upon	(əpon')

As you can see, the schwa sound may appear as any vowel letter if the vowel is found in an unaccented syllable. It may also represent the short *u* sound and the vowel sound in *er, ir,* and *ur.*

Y As a Vowel

The letter *y* generally represents the short *i* sound when it appears within a syllable not containing a vowel letter.

myth   system   lymph

The letter *y* generally represents the long *ī* sound when it appears as the final sound in a one-syllable word.

by   cry   my

The letter *y* generally represents the long *ē* sound when it appears as the final letter in a multisyllabic word.

fairy   dairy   berry   briskly

The letter *y* generally represents the long *ī* sound when it appears as the final letter of a syllable that is not the last syllable in a multisyllabic word.

cycle   dynamo   asylum

Vowel Digraphs

A vowel digraph is a combination of two vowel letters which represent the equivalent of *one* vowel sound.

treat	bread	read	read
through	touch	cough	soup
shook	wood	cool	
receive	weigh		
bait			
caught			
loan			

Burmeister (1968) examined the frequency of adjacent vowel pairs which act as vowel digraphs, and she found that certain vowel pairs consistently acted as digraphs and certain vowel pairs rarely acted as digraphs:

Grapheme	Example	Pronunciation	Frequency	Percent
ay	gray	/ā/	132/137	96.4
oa	road	/ō/	129/138	93.5
ai	villain	∂	9/309	2.9
ea	sergeant	∂	3/545	0.5

Source: Based on information reported in Lou E. Burmeister, "Vowel Pairs," *The Reading Teacher*, 21, 5 (February 1968), 447–448. Reprinted by permission of the International Reading Association and the author.

Burmeister's work suggests that teachers should be extremely cautious when they use phonics as their principal mode of instruction. Many of the rules of phonics are consistent and extremely useful, but some phonics principles need constant re-examination.

Vowel Diphthong

A vowel diphthong consists of two vowel letters in one syllable, *both* of which are sounded. The first vowel is strongly sounded, while the second becomes a glided or semivowel sound.

Examples of vowel diphthongs in English are:

Diphthong	Example
oi	soil
oy	toy
ou	pout
ow	howl

Burmeister (1968) also researched the frequency of adjacent vowel pairs which act as diphthongs and found similar patterns of consistency and inconsistency:

Grapheme	Example	Pronunciation	Frequency number of cases	Percent
oi	moist	oi	100/102	98.0
au	auction	o	167/178	93.8
oy	coyote	oi	1/50	2.0
oo	blood	ou	7/315	2.2

When reviewing this information, it becomes obvious that phonics rules may need consistent re-examination.

Additional Vowel Rules

The following generalized rules may be of help to you when you introduce your students to the concept of vowel sounds:

1. When a single vowel in a syllable is followed by the letter r, the letter r is the dominant sound recorded and the vowel sound is affected or influenced by it.

chart	dollar	fir	for	work
cart	her	first	fort	curl

2. When the letter a is followed by ll or lk in a syllable, the a represents the sound of ou or au.

all	wall	enthrall	walk
ball	call	chalk	talk

3. When the letter combinations gn, gh, ght, ld, or nd follow the single letter i in a syllable, the i represents a long vowel sound.

sign	tight	mild
sigh	light	mind

4. When the letter combination ld follows the single letter o in a syllable, the letter o generally represents a long vowel sound.

cold	fold	mold
told	old	behold

5. When the letter combination re follows a single vowel in a syllable, one generally hears an r sound.

core	tire	bore	lure
here	tore	cure	

6. E's at the end of a monosyllabic word usually make the first vowel a long sound. This is sometimes called the Magic E Rule.

cape	time	dote	vane	note
hate	wine	cube	Pete	code
made	bite	cute	dime	hope
pane	ripe	dude	hide	rode
rate	pine	tube	kite	robe

Clymer (1963), Bailey (1967), and Emans (1967) published comprehensive views of the overall usefulness of traditional phonics rules. Do you recognize these rules? As children, many of you had to memorize these rules in isolation. Were they valuable to you in learning to read? Perhaps some of them were useful and some of them confused you. The figures which are presented below explain the usefulness of most of the rules of phonics and the frequency with which these rules apply in English. The rules with high frequency (about 75 percent) are especially helpful when you are teaching children how to decode. The rules with low frequencies should not be taught because they are not useful in learning decoding skills; no phonics rule should ever be taught in isolation. These rules are only useful in applied contexts.

FORTY-FIVE PHONIC GENERALIZATIONS

	Percentage of Utility		
	Clymer	*Bailey*	*Emans*
	Grades 1-3	Grades 1-6	Grades 4-
1. When there are two vowels side by side, the long sound of the first vowel is heard and the second vowel is usually silent. (leader)	45	34	18
2. When a vowel is in the middle of a one-syllable word, the vowel is short. (bed)	62	71	73
3. If the only vowel letter is at the end of a word, the letter usually stands for a long sound. (go)	74	76	33
4. When there are two vowels, one of which is final e, the first vowel is long and the e is silent. (cradle)	63	57	63
5. The r gives the preceding vowel a sound that is neither long nor short. (part)	78	86	82
6. The first vowel is usually long and the second silent in the digraphs ai, ea, oa, and ui. (claim, beau, roam, suit)	66	60	58
ai		71	
ea		56	
oa		95	
ee		87	
ui		10	
7. In the phonogram ie, the i is silent and and the e is long. (grieve)	17	31	23
8. Words having double e usually have the long e sound. (meet)	98	87	100
9. When words end with silent e, the preceding a or i is long. (amaze)	60	50	48
10. In ay, the y is silent and gives a its long long sound. (spray)	78	88	100
11. When the letter i is followed by the letters gh, the i usually stands for its long sound and the gh is silent. (light)	71	71	100
12. When a follows w in a word, it usually has the sound a as in was. (wand)	32	22	28
13. When e is followed by w, the vowel sound is the same as that represented by oo. (shrewd)	35	40	14
14. The two letters ow make the long o sound. (row)	59	55	50
15. W is sometimes a vowel and follows the vowel digraph rule. (arrow)	40	33	31
16. When y is the final letter in a word, it usually has a vowel sound. (lady)	84	89	98
17. When y is used as a vowel in words, it sometimes has the sound of long i. (ally)	15	11	4
18. The letter a has the same sound (o) when followed by l, w, and u. (raw)	48	34	24
19. When a is followed by r and final e, we expect to hear the sound. (charge)	90	96	100
20. When c and h are next to each other, they make only one sound. (charge)	100	100	100
21. Ch is usually pronounced as it is in kitchen, catch, and chair, not like ah. (pitch)	95	87	67
22. When c if followed by e or i, the sound of s is likely to be heard. (glance)	96	92	90

23. When the letter c is followed by o or a, the sound of k is likely to be heard. (canal)	100	100	100
24. The letter g is often sounded as the j in jump when it precedes the letters i or e. (gem)	64	78	80
25. When ght is seen in a word, gh is silent. (tight)	100	100	100
26. When a word begins kn, the k is silent. (knit)	100	100	100
27. When a word begins with wr, the w is silent. (wrap)	100	100	100
28. When two of the same consonants are side by side, only one is heard. (dollar)	100	100	100
29. When a word ends in ck, it has the same last sound as in lock. (neck)	100	100	100
30. In most two-syllable words, the first syllable is accented. (bottom)	85	81	75
31. If a, in, re, ex, de, or be is the first syllable in a word, it is usually unaccented. (reply)	87	84	83
32. In most two-syllable words that end in a consonant followed by y, the first syllable is accented and the last is unaccented.	96	97	100
33. One vowel letter in an accented syllable has its short sound. (banish)	61	65	64
34. When y or ey is seen in the last syllable that is not accented, the long sound of e is heard.	0	0	1
35. When ture is the final syllable in a word, it is unaccented. (future)	100	100	100
36. When tion is the final syllable in a word, it is unaccented. (notion)	100	100	100
37. In many two- and three-syllable words, the final e lengthens the vowel in the last syllable. (costume)	46	46	42
38. If the first vowel sound in a word is followed by two consonants, the first syllable usually ends with the first of the two consonants. (dinner)	72	78	80
39. If the first vowel sound in a word is followed by a single consonant, that consonant usually begins the second syllable. (china)	44	50	47
40. If the last syllable of a word ends in le, the consonant preceding the le usually begins the last syllable. (gable)	97	93	78
41. When the first vowel element in a word is followed by th, ch, or sh, these symbols are not broken when the word is divided into syllables and may go with either the first or second syllable. (fashion)	100	100	100
42. In a word of more than one syllable, the letter v usually goes with the preceding vowel to form a syllable.	73	65	40
43. When a word has only one vowel letter, the vowel sound is likely to be short. (crib)	57	69	70
44. When there is one e in a word that ends in a consonant, the e usually has a short sound. (held)	76	92	83
45. When the last syllable is the sound r, it is unaccented. (ever)	95	79	96

Now that you have been introduced to the theoretical principles of phonics, you are probably asking some of the following questions:

1. How do I teach children each of these strategies?
2. When should I use a particular strategy?
3. When should I introduce a new strategy?

The answers to these questions will be determined by your unique situation. Every teacher and every child is different, and what is effective for one child may not be effective for every child. We hope to answer some instructional questions which teachers of reading often ask, re-emphasizing the fact that *every situation is different*. The instructional answers which will be provided here are only guidelines for you as a teacher. You will have to implement the teaching of phonics in your own particular manner to meet the specific needs of your students.

Phonics is one of the most difficult and important strategies for the student to learn. It should be noted that not every child can or should learn phonics. There is no one strategy that meets the needs of all of your students. Phonics, like each of the other components of word analysis, is merely a means to the goal of comprehension. If we lose sight of comprehension as the end of reading instruction and we begin to emphasize only isolated phonics strategies, we may never reach our goal. Phonics strategies are to be viewed only as decoding aids that assist the student with comprehension.

Instructional Questions and Answers

The question which is asked most frequently when one is teaching phonics strategies is: "What should I teach first?" This question implies an effective introductory sequence for teaching consonant and vowel correspondences. The answer to this involved question is complex, but recent research has offered us a number of reasonable suggestions;

Suggestion #1: Introduce children to vowels early in the program.

Many teachers and publishers of packaged programs have delayed teaching the vowels because they believed that all the consonants needed to be taught first. They argued that the regularity of the letter-sound correspondence of the consonants helped the child learn to read. This view failed to consider the high correlation between the letter-sound correspondences of many vowels and the importance of the ability to decode vowels in order to read independently without adult guidance. Most children can clearly articulate vowels by the ages of four or five, and most children have had some experience in decoding vowels, such as when they memorize certain sign words like Emma or Happy Birthday. The early introduction of vowels will help children to become involved independently in the reading process from the beginning of instruction.

Suggestion #2: Sequence vowel instruction by decibel rating.

A logical question follows: Which vowel sounds should be introduced in the early stages of instruction? Fairbanks' (1966) work may provide us with some meaningful answers. He found that the vowels in the following words have different decibel levels:

Vowel		Decibel Level
cap	/ae/	4.5
talk	/ɔ/	3.8
shop	/a/	3.7
choke	/ow/	3.0
check	/e/	2.2
coop	/yu/	1.9
cup	/ɔ/	1.1
cheek	/iy/	1.0
cook	/u/	0.3
pit	/i/	0.0

These findings suggest that children can discriminate vowel sounds with the highest decibel ratings. This natural phenomenon should dictate the sequence of instruction.

Suggestion #3: Introduce children to visually contrastive pairs (d and b) very early in the program.

In the past teachers have been encouraged not to simultaneously introduce two letters which are easily confused with one another, such as d and b. However, the current opinion is that the introduction of contrastive pairs like d and b, q and p, m and n has instructional value because the child has to focus on the distinctive features of each of the letters within a specific context (dog, bog). Researchers argue that this initial struggle will reduce later confusion for the child.

Suggestion #4: Teaching the /f/, /s/, /v/, /m/ sounds in words

Coleman (1967) maintains that children find continuants, consonants which are produced by the constant release of air, like /s/, easier to blend with other sounds than consonants which are formed by stopping the air flow, like /t/. He suggests that the continuants are easily learned and should be among the first consonants which are taught to the beginning reader. Continuants include:

    /s/   sat
    /f/   fat
    /v/   vat
    /m/   mat

Suggestion #5: Introduce children to variations in letter-sound correspondences.

One criticism of the linguistic method of reading instruction, which is described in detail in Chapter 12 is that children begin to expect one-to-one letter-sound correspondence (pan, man, can), and they find it difficult to transfer their phonics strategies to new words which do not fit the pattern. These findings suggest that children should be introduced to variations in letter-sound correspondence from the very beginning, such as <u>tap</u> and <u>tape</u>, in order to prepare them for later reading.

Suggestion #6: Capitalize on children's natural order strategies.

Marchbanks and Levin (1965) maintain that it is also important to note that children use definite <u>order</u> strategies when they are decoding. First they look at the initial letter(s), then they look at the final letter(s), then the middle letter(s), then the configuration of the word. This phenomenon underlines the need for children to learn independent phonics strategies so that they will be able to cope with new and unfamiliar words.

Suggestion #7: Introduce children to word families through phonograms.

Teachers often use word families to teach phonics. These word families are sometimes called phonogram lists. Teachers can use these lists to create games or activities for children. A game might look like this:

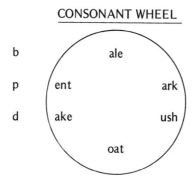

CONSONANT WHEEL

Ask the children to write as many words as they can with b, p, and d as the initial letter. Lists may look like this:

dark	bark	park
	bush	push
	boat	
	bake	
dent	bent	pent

Another way in which phonograms may be used is to have children brainstorm. Write *an* on the board and have them tell you as many words as they can which have this sound. Then change *an* to *ane* and do the exercise again. Similar substitution exercises can be devised for final consonants.

cat   I put the butter in the _____.

ban   Michael hit the ball with the _____.

pit   She sat on a _____.

The vowel correspondence can be introduced in a similar manner—the child can learn to substitute b*an* for b*in*.

There's a _____ on buying cigarettes.

"A Vocabulary of Rhyme," *Webster Collegiate Dictionary*, is a very useful list of phonograms that may help you in developing students' early reading vocabularies. Examples from that list are included below:

ace   brace, face, grace, lace, place, race, space
eal   deal, heal, meal, real, seal, veal
ig   big, dig, fig, jig, pig, rig, wig
oat   boat, coat, float, goal, throat

Based on these suggestions, the following questions and answers will help you develop a sequential, effective phonics teaching program.

1. Q. Should consonants or vowels be introduced first?

   A. They should be introduced simultaneously, taking into consideration the information we have acquired about continuants /f/, /s/, /v/, and /m/; visually similar graphemes b and d; and decibel loading for certain vowel sounds.

2. Q. Should short vowels or long vowels be introduced first?

   A. Short vowels should be introduced in the order presented in the decibel loading chart. Long vowel sounds should be introduced as contrasts to short vowel sounds, using words which have become part of the child's sight vocabulary, such as cap and cape. When you are introducing graphemes and graphemic patterns, you should tell the children that graphemes represent sounds, not that graphemes make phonemes.

3. Q. Should I reinforce vowel correspondence by teaching vowels within words, such as cat, bat, rat?

   A. Definitely. Children should be introduced to the concept of syllable and word meaning from the beginning of their reading programs.

4. Q. Should I be concerned about dialect variations in my children's pronunciation?

   A. Dialect variation will result in different sounds for letter-sound correspondences. However, this should not concern you because your students will develop letter-sound equivalents which reflect their own dialect.

After reviewing the answers to such questions, a more immediate question arises: How do I teach an introductory phonics strategy lesson implementing all of the phonics information I have acquired? First, you must decide upon an appropriate sequence for your instructional program. The following steps may be helpful in establishing an effective instructional sequence:

Consonants should be introduced within CVC words, for example:

> pin
>
> bin
>
> sin

When teaching initial consonants, do not stress sounds; instead, emphasize each sound within the context of the word.

The following lesson plan illustrates *one* way of presenting an introductory lesson on the topic of letter-sound correspondence of the grapheme *b*.

Lesson Plan

Goal: To introduce the grapheme b and its corresponding phoneme /b/.

Grade/Grade Level: Primary

Construction and Utilization:

1. Write b on the board. Ask children if they can name words that begin with /b/.

2. Assess the degree to which children need this exercise. If some children have difficulty naming words, continue using this lesson. The other children who have already mastered this information or who are not yet ready to pursue this lesson should be provided with activities to meet their needs.

Procedure:

1. List on the board the words which children have named:

   > birthday
   > Bobby
   > bumblebee
   > Bonny
   > Buddy
   > bunny

2. To reinforce this skill, divide an oaktag board into four sections. In section one, draw a picture of a ball; in section two, a boy; in section three, a bat; and in section four, a boat. Ask children to name the picture, then write the words ball, boy, bat, and boat under each of the pictures. Have the children copy the same pictures and words on their own papers. When the children seem to have grasped the idea, have them present their pictures and help them write their own words under each picture.

   Evaluation: Put another b on the board and ask children to draw pictures and write words under each one.

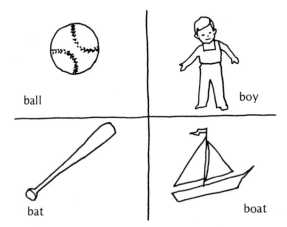

ball   boy

bat   boat

This lesson can be followed by a lesson on *d*. Point out the similarities of these two letters to children and ask them to explain the differences. The *d* board may look like the following:

dog   doll

door   dress

Another method of introducing initial consonants is by using substitution practices. Children can be introduced to patterned substitution drills in which they can infer that there are relationships between words. For example, in the following exercise the child must fill in the appropriate word by changing the first letter of each word.

fan   The ___man___ sat on the chair.

tan   He ___ran___ to the store.

sit   He _____ the ball.

kit   I want a little _____ of the cake.

tone   Feed the dog the _____ .

lone   I want an ice cream _____ .

Using the same CVC words, you may want to introduce short vowel sounds within the context of a word. Using the same or similar CVC words, you may introduce the final consonant sounds. Once the consonants and vowels have been introduced in the context of words, you may wish to develop word family charts to be on display in your classroom. In this manner, the words are continually reinforced through sight word strategies. An example of a word family chart is the following:

ba̲t
ca̲t
fa̲t
ha̲t
ma̲t
na̲t
ra̲t
sa̲t

Short vowels may also be introduced through patterned exercises in which children substitute both initial and final consonants as well as the medial vowel within a word. For example, children have these three options:

bat	bat	bat
↓	↓	↓
cat	bad	bit

or

sip	sip	sip
↓	↓	↓
dip	sir	pip

Consonant blends (digraphs) may come before or after your lessons on short vowels. Blends should be taught in the same way that the initial and final consonants were taught; they should be taught within the context of a word family:

car	scar
tar	star
par	spar

Long vowels may be introduced by contrasting CVC words and CVC-e words. for example:

mat	māte
kit	kīte
not	nōte

Teaching Syllables

As we pointed out earlier in the chapter, some researchers will argue that vowel sounds should not be taught except within a syllable. Whether you agree with this position or not, it seems extremely important to teach children some rules of syllabication. In some ways, this is an easy task because children already understand the principles of syllabication. An inductive method of teaching can be used by asking children to "break" apart words which they have in their sight vocabulary, such as *hap · py* and *birth · day*. Then ask them to read words like:

hap · pen	Mon · day	birth · place
mis · hap	day · time	re · birth

The following rules may be helpful to you when you are teaching your children the principles of syllabication:

1. Look at the word. Ask yourself if it is a compound word. If it is, name the parts which make up the word, such as base · ball.

2. Look for affixes in the words and look for tense markers like *-ed* and *-ing*. Look for word parts within the word with which you are familiar such as *-ness*. If there are word parts which you know, separate them from the word and read the rest of the word—this will be the root word. For example, good/ness. Now put the stress on the root, *góod*, and read the whole word: góodness.

3. Look in the midst of the word for a cluster of consonants or for a consonant digraph. If there is a cluster of two consonants, try to separate the word into two parts between the two letters of the cluster: ras · cal. If the cluster has three consecutive consonants, separate after the second of the three consonants: shing · le. If there is a consonant digraph, divide the word after the digraph. Put the stress on the first syllable: thatch · er.

4. If no cluster of consonants exists within the middle of the word, you might want to try the following: Separate the word after the consonant which comes after the first vowel in the word and read the word by making the vowel in the first syllable a short vowel and putting the stress on the first syllable: can · ard. Vowel sounds in the second syllable will usually be a schwa sound /ə/. If you still do not know the word, separate the first vowel after the first vowel digraph, such as *ai* in raisin, and read the first syllable as a CV word. Give the vowel a long sound and put the stress on this syllable.

When Do I Use Phonics Strategies?

You may want to ask one final question: When do I use phonics instruction with children who have mastered most of the phonics strategy rules? This is an extremely difficult question because children may have mastered the rules of phonics without being able to use them accurately all the time. For example, if the child looks at this sentence:

Philip Ryan threw the soccer ball to the end of Boylston Street.

and reads:

Philip Ryan threw the _____

and stops, you might say: "Let's break the word apart; you know the parts of the word: soc-cer." Then you might tell him to read the next word, "ball," and ask him to guess the preceding word. When he has succeeded in decoding the word, he may continue the sentence:

ball to the end of

and stop again. You may continue with the same technique:

Boy - l - ston (Boylston)

One final suggestion may be crucial in establishing an effective reading pro-gram: If a child reads the sentence "*Senator Lawrence Darrell of California* voted in favor of the bill" as "*Senator Lawrence Dar of Connecticut* voted for the law," and answers the comprehension question "*Did Senator Darrell oppose the legislation?*" with a "*no,*" then understanding may have taken place and further phonics instruction may not be necessary for this sentence.

In fact further phonics instruction may be counterproductive; it may interfere with the student's progress. However, the child must be encouraged to read carefully, since word substitution *may* result in comprehension errors.

In conclusion, you may want to remember the following general guidelines when you are establishing your reading program:

1. Phonics is a means of decoding. If it is too confusing for the child, try another strategy.

2. Try to break the words into parts for the child, using the syllabication rules which were presented in the preceding section.

3. If the child cannot decode the word and you sense that frustration is overwhelming him, tell him the word.

4. Phonics is a means to an end: comprehension. When phonics decoding hinders comprehension, it is no longer useful. Decide just how many words the child can struggle through in each sentence before there is serious comprehension loss and structure your teaching accordingly.

This chapter intended to introduce you to visual and auditory perception and to the content of phonics strategies. If at this time you do not feel that you have attained adequate knowledge to successfully answer the following ques-tions, we would like to suggest related reading.

Goal 1: To aid students in understanding the process involved in visual perception and discrimination.

Q. Explain the developmental processes of visual perception and letter/word discrimination.

Boyden, M. "Auditory-Visual and Sequential Matching in Relation to Reading Ability." *Child Development,* 43, 824–832.

Chase, W. (ed). *Visual Information Processing.* New York: Academic Press, 1973.

Gibson, E. and H. Levin. *The Psychology of Reading.* Cambridge, Mass.: MIT Press, 1975.

> Goal 2: To aid students in understanding the process involved in auditory perception and discrimination.
>
> Q. Explain the relationship between auditory processing and reading.

Jensen, A. R. "Individual Differences in Visual and Auditory Memory." *Journal of Educational Psychology,* 62, 123–131.

McNinch, G. "Auditory Perceptual Factors and Measured First Grade Reading Achievement." *Reading Research Quarterly,* 6, 472–492.

Smith, F. *Understanding Reading.* New York: Holt, Rinehart and Winston, 1971.

> Goal 3: To aid students in understanding the concept of phonics.
>
> Q. List and explain the basic components of phonics.

Durkin, S. *Phonics and the Teaching of Reading.* New York: Teachers College Press, Columbia University, 1965.

Heilman, A. *Phonics in Proper Perspective.* Columbus, Ohio: Charles Merrill Co., 1976.

> Goal 4: To aid students in understanding how to use phonics strategies.
>
> Q. Explain some effective ways of teaching children how to decode by using phonics principles.

Durkin, D. *Teaching Them to Read.* Boston: Allyn and Bacon, 1974.

Heilman, A. *Phonics in Proper Perspective.* New York: Charles Merrill Co., 1976.

Ruddell, R. *Reading-Language Instruction.* Englewood Cliffs, N.J.: Prentice-Hall, Inc., 1974.

In the next few pages, we will present several activities that you might find useful for your reading program.

Letter and Word Discrimination Activities

1. Hopscotch

Goal: Letter discrimination

Grade level: Primary

Construction: Draw a hopscotch game using chalk on the playground or masking tape on the classroom floor. Choose ten different letters to put into the squares. Shape the letters from tape or tape down old letter cards. Make small index cards with a series of four to five letters on each—preferably those that are usually confused by children: b, d, p, and q.

Utilization: The child must jump on each of these letters in the correct order without stepping on any other letters. Score one point for each series performed correctly.

2. Round the World

<u>Goal</u>: Letter recognition

<u>Grade level</u>: K–3

<u>Construction</u>: Make large flash cards showing frequently confused letters such as b, d, g, p, q (one letter per card).

<u>Utilization</u>: Have the children sit in a circle on the floor. One child begins by standing behind the person on his right. Hold up a flash card while both children attempt to name the correct letter. Whoever is first (or correct) gets to continue around the circle. The child who beats everyone wins by going around the world.

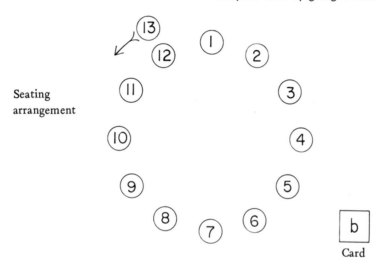

Seating
arrangement

Card

3. Old Dragon

<u>Goal</u>: Visual discrimination of beginning or ending letters

<u>Grade level</u>: K–3

<u>Construction</u>: Make a deck of 25 cards containing 12 pairs of various words that begin or end with the same letter. Write one of the 12 words on each card. Also design one card for the Old Dragon, which is a word that can't be paired with any of the other cards.

<u>Utilization</u>: Have all the cards dealt out and have each take turns drawing a card from the person on his left. If he gets a pair he puts it down on the table, saying the two words and whether they end or begin with the same letter. The game ends when all the cards are paired and someone is left with the Old Dragon.

4. Letter Bingo

<u>Goal</u>: Recognition of frequently confused letters

<u>Grade level</u>: K–1

<u>Construction</u>: Make a bingo board with the following letters:

B	Q	C	O	F
b	q	c	o	f
D	G	J	T	E
d	g	j	t	e
R	r	N	n	m

Utilization: Play this game with the regular bingo rules. The caller names a letter (for example, "capital B, small b"), and the players have to cover the correct letter.

5. Roll Your Word

Goal: Discriminating between letters and their use in spelling words

Grade level: K-3

Construction: Construct two piles of index cards representing each letter of the alphabet. One pile contains the vowels; the second pile, the consonants. Make at least five cards for each vowel.

Utilization: Each child rolls the dice and is allowed to pick up the number of cards he has rolled on the dice. He is allowed to select from either the consonant or vowel pile. The child receives one point for each letter of the word he has created. The object of the game is to collect points.

Phonics Activities

6. Blind Man's Bluff

Goal: Visual-auditory discrimination of beginning and ending sounds

Grade level: K-3

Construction: Construct 6- x 4-inch letter cards.

Utilization: Blindfold a child and have him choose a letter card. After the blindfold is removed, he must say a word that begins or ends with the letter on the card. If correct, the child gets to keep the card. Whoever has the most cards at the end of the game wins.

7. Clip the Clothespins

Goal: Discriminating long vowel sounds

Grade level: K–3

Construction: Construct a large cardboard circle. The circle should be subdivided into five sections. Collect pictures that represent the long vowel sounds of a, e, i, o, u. Pictures can be taken from discarded workbooks. Paste pictures containing the same vowel sounds in each section. On the reverse side of each section, write the letter sound being represented by the pictures. Secure six clothespins with clips. With paint or nail polish write one letter on each clothespin leg. The same letter should be written on both legs of one clothespin.

Utilization: Have the child name the pictures in the first section. He selects the clothespin bearing the letter heard in the words he has just pronounced. He checks his answer by looking at the back side of the cardboard circle.

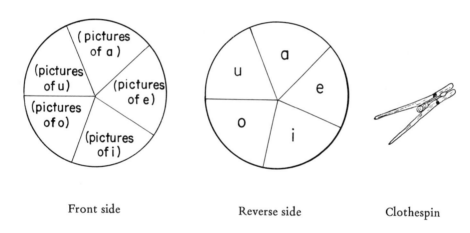

Front side   Reverse side   Clothespin

8. In Whose House Do I Live?

Goal: Discriminating short vowel sounds

Grade level: 1–3

Construction: Construct a large chart. The chart should be large enough to be subdivided into five columns. At the top of the first column write an a. On the tops of columns 2 through 5, write the letters e, i, o, u. Write one letter on the top of each column. Draw several rectangles in each column. Design 40 to 50 rectangular cards. On each card write one word containing a short vowel sound.

Utilization: Word cards are placed in a deck. The first child selects a card and pronounces the word without exposing it to the other players. The child beside him identifies the column containing the correct vowel sound heard in the word. If the child is correct, he places the card in the correct column (the proper "house") and scores one point. The game continues until all of the cards have been placed in their proper houses.

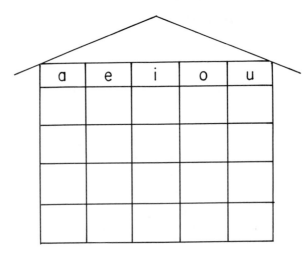

9. Find the Animal

<u>Goal</u>: Visual and auditory discrimination of words that have the same vowel sound.

<u>Grade level</u>: 1–3

<u>Construction</u>: Draw an outline of an animal in puzzle form on a ditto master. Label the pieces that make up the animal with words containing a vowel sound different from those on the pieces surrounding the animal. All of the words surrounding the animal should contain the same vowel sound. Give the child a lead word (which has the same vowel sound as those words surrounding the animal).

<u>Utilization</u>: Instruct the child to color in the pieces on the puzzle that have the same vowel sound as the lead word. If done correctly, the animal will appear.

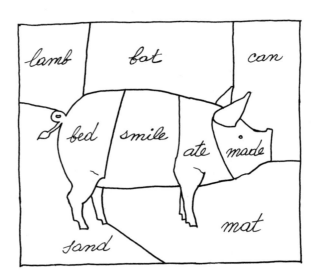

10. Hang a Word

Goal: Using consonant clusters (blends) to make words

Grade level: 1–3

Construction: Make a "blend board" from a piece of wood you have painted or decorated. Pound six columns of nails into the board. Cut several cards from thick paper. Punch holes into the tops of all of the cards. Write various blends on half the number of cards and word endings on the other half. Hang blends on the first two columns. Leave columns 3 and 5 blank. Hang word endings on columns 4 and 6.

Utilization: Have the child hang blends in front of the endings, making as many different words as possible. He then writes down the word and uses it in a sentence.

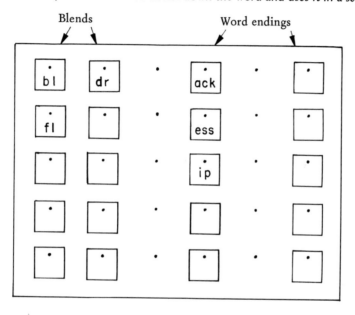

11. Listen and Write

Goal: Practice in identifying consonant digraphs.

Grade level: 1–3

Construction: Prepare a cassette tape of sentences that contain words spelled with consonant digraphs. Make up an accompanying ditto master or laminated sheet containing pictures of the words and the part of the word without the digraph.

Utilization: The child listens to the tape and follows along on the paper, filling in the consonant digraphs. If desired, he can then make his own cassette tape, using the words in a story.

12. Finish the Story

Goal: Recognizing consonant digraphs

Grade level: 1–3

Construction: Write a short story on a ditto master or laminated paper. Replace some of the words containing consonant digraphs with a picture. At the bottom of the page show the pictures again, along with part of the word, omitting the consonant digraph.

Utilization: The student must insert the correct consonant digraph. This activity also gives good practice in using contextual clues.

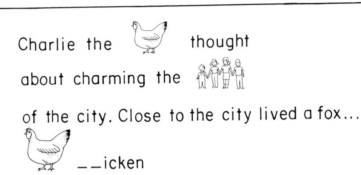

13. Color the Ice Cream Cones

Goal: Distinguishing vowel digraphs

Grade level: 1–3

Construction: On a sheet of paper, list several rows of words containing the same vowel digraphs. Each row should contain three words. Although each row should contain words having the same vowel digraph, it is not necessary that all words within a row have the same digraph sound (touch). At the end of each row, draw the outline of a small ice cream cone.

Utilization: Instruct the child to pronounce the words in each row. If all the words have the same vowel digraph sound, the ice cream cone should be colored yellow. If all of the words do _not_ have the same vowel digraph sound, the ice cream cone should be colored blue. Example:

ou	ŭ	ou		
couch	touch	ouch		(Cone colored blue)
mean	seal	team		(Cone colored yellow)

Traffic lights could be substituted for the ice cream cones. The child would then be instructed to color the traffic light green if all of the words <u>do</u> have the same vowel digraph sound, and to color the traffic light red if all of the words <u>do not</u> have the same vowel digraph sound.

14. The Diphthong Book

<u>Goal</u>: Recognition of vowel diphthongs

<u>Grade level</u>: 1–3

<u>Construction</u>: A loose-leaf book may be made by cutting out two 8- x 10-inch cardboard covers. Place two holes along the end of each cover. Several pieces of 7- x 9-inch colored construction paper are placed between the cardboard covers. The paper should contain the same holes as the cover. Tie yarn through the holes to secure the book and decorate the cover with wallpaper or children's art designs.

<u>Utilization</u>: Children should be asked to cut pictures from magazines or draw pictures that represent words containing vowel diphthongs. The children paste the pictures into the book, label each picture, and draw a line under each vowel diphthong.

15. Diphthong Jotto

<u>Goal</u>: Recognition and use of words containing vowel diphthongs.

<u>Grade level</u>: 1–3

<u>Construction</u>: All that is needed for two players is paper and pencil.

<u>Utilization</u>: Each player thinks of a word containing a vowel diphthong and tells how many letters are contained in the word. The object is to guess the other person's word. Player A suggests a word containing the same amount of letters that player B said his word contained. Player B must then say how many letters of that word are in his word, without indicating <u>which</u> letters or in what position they are. For example, if player B's word was <u>shoulder</u>, and player A suggested <u>pleasing</u>, player B would answer "three." Then it is player B's turn to say a word. It is helpful if the player guessing writes down the word he guessed, along with the number of letters found in the other player's word. Player A would write: pleasing—3. The first one to guess his word wins.

16. Crazy Eights

Goal: Practice in matching final endings

Grade level: 1-3

Construction: Make a deck of 40 cards with words containing five different word endings (eight cards for each ending—for example, <u>ite</u>, <u>ood</u>, <u>eigh</u>). Make five extra cards with the number 8 on them.

Utilization: This game is played like the card game Crazy Eights. Five cards are dealt to each player. One card is turned face up in the center. Players in turn try to get rid of their cards by putting down a card with the same ending as the word card turned up (saying the word orally as it is placed down). If the player doesn't have a card, he can play an 8, or he can draw a card from the deck. If he does have an 8 he can also place it in the center and begin another ending. If the player does not read the word card correctly, he must keep the card and lose his turn.

17. Cut and Paste the Syllables

Goal: Syllabication of given words

Grade level: 4-6

Construction: Make several 3- x 10-inch word cards containing multisyllable words. Construction paper and glue will also be needed.

Utilization: Have the child cut up word cards into correct syllables and paste them on construction paper in any design he chooses. Accent marks should also be added. If desired, the child can then illustrate the word on the piece of construction paper.

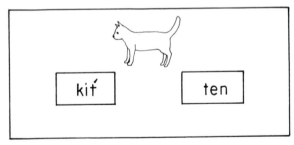

18. Syllable Match Game

Goal: Practicing syllabication

Grade level: 4-6

Construction: Prepare a list of words, identifying the proper syllables.

Examples: turkey   tur / key
           ball   ball
           alphabet   al / pha / bet

Utilization: Divide the class into teams of five players each. An "MC" (master of ceremonies) calls out a word from the list, and each player writes its syllabicated form. Teams may score ten points for each player who divides the word correctly. A bonus of five points is given if two players on a team are correct, and two additional points are given for other team members with correct answers. The team earning the most points wins.

BIBLIOGRAPHY

Baily, M. "The Utility of Phonic Generalizations in Grades One through Six". *The Reading Teacher"*, XX (February 1967), 412–18.

Burmeister, L. "Vowel Pairs." *The Reading Teacher,* 21 (February 1968), 447–498.

Clymer, T. "The Utility of Phonics Generalization in the Primary Grades." *The Reading Teacher,* XVI (January 1963), 252–258.

Dolch, E. "A Basic Sight Vocabulary." *Elementary School Journal,* XXXVI (February 1936), 456–460.

Durkin, D. *Teaching Them to Read.* Boston: Allyn and Bacon, 1974.

Emans, R. "The Usefulness of Phonics Generalizations Above the Primary Grades." *The Reading Teacher,* XX (February 1967), 419–25.

Ernst, M. *Words.* 3rd ed. New York: Knopf, 1955.

Fries, C. *Linguistics and Reading.* New York: Holt, Rinehart and Winston, 1963.

Gibson, E. and H. Levin. *The Psychology of Reading.* Cambridge, Mass.: MIT Press, 1975.

Gleason, J. "Language Development in Early Childhood," *Oral Language and Reading,* ed. by Jas. Walden. Champaign, Ill.: NCTE, 1969. Ruddell p. 303.

Groff, P. *The Syllable: Its Nature and Pedagogical Usefulness.* Portland, Ore.: Northwest Regional Educational Laboratory, 1971.

Guszak, F. *Diagnostic Reading Instruction in the Elementary School.* New York: Harper and Row, 1972.

Heilman, A. *Principles and Practices of Teaching Reading.* Columbus, Ohio: Charles Merrill Co., 1972.

Hoover, K. *The Effect of Sequence of Training in Kindergarten Children.* Unpublished Ph.D. thesis, Stanford University, 1975.

Jenkins, J., R. Bausel, and L. Jenkins. "Comparison of Letter Name and Letter Sound Training as Transfer Variables," *American Educational Research Journal,* 9 (1972), 75–86.

Murphy, H. and D. Durrell. *Speech to Print Phonics.* New York: Harcourt Brace Jovanovich Inc., 1972.

Pollard, Rebecca S. *Pollard's Synthetic Method.* Chicago: Western Publishing House, 1889.

Ruddell, R. *Reading-Language Instruction.* Englewood Cliffs, N.J.: Prentice-Hall, 1974.

Silberberg, N., M. Silberberg, and I. Iverson. "The Effects of Kindergarten Instruction in Alphabet and Numbers on First Grade Reading." *Journal of Learning Disabilities,* 5 (1972) 254–261.

Spache, G. and E. Spache. *Reading in the Elementary School.* Boston: Allyn and Bacon, 1973.

Thorndike, E. *The Teaching of English Suffixes.* New York: Bureau of Publications, Teachers College, Columbia University, 1932.

8

Understanding and implementing word analysis strategies: sight word analysis, structural analysis, contextual analysis

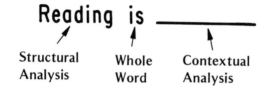

Without word analysis skills a person cannot learn to read, but reading involves much more than word analysis.

Burmeister, L. E. Words—From Print to Meaning.
Reading, Mass.: Addison-Wesley, 1975.

241

GOALS: To aid students in understanding:
1. sight word strategies for analyzing unknown words.
2. the role of structural analysis strategies in word recognition.
3. the role of contextual analysis strategies in word recognition.

In addition to phonics skills and strategies, you will want to instruct your children in three other word analysis strategies which will help them to decode unknown words. In this chapter we will present additional word analysis strategies in these areas: *sight word skills, structural analysis skills,* and *contextual analysis skills,* and we will present some instructional principles which may help you implement your word analysis knowledge.

Sight Word Strategies

Most basal programs begin by teaching high-frequency sight words. The rationale for this method of teaching, which is sometimes called a *whole-word method* or a *look-say method,* is that children are able to participate immediately in the reading process.

Children are able to recognize many words prior to beginning reading instruction. These words are usually highly meaningful for the child. Sometimes they can

read words affecting their daily activities:	Happy Birthday
	Merry Christmas, Chanukah
read words naming frequent interactions:	McDonald's, toys, gum
read signs:	stop, go

Some children can recognize and write about their own names when they enter first grade: *Jo-Ann, Sylvia, Adam, Candy, Jeffrey, Marge, Denny, Bob, Kate.*

One way of increasing this list is to use Sylvia Ashton-Warner's ideas about personal, secret words. In her book *Teacher,* she explains how she taught the Maori children in New Zealand to read without any books or materials. She asked the children to tell her a word; she wrote it on a card and gave it to them. Using her example, you may want to ask children to tell you a secret word, then write it on an index card and let the children keep the cards in their special files. Words may look something like this:

crocodile	dragon
Halloween	television
monster	castle

Review these words periodically with the children. Perhaps these words can serve as catalysts for storytelling, language experience charts, or play productions. A language experience method of teaching reading, which will be explained in detail in Chapter 12, begins instruction with the child's experiences, which are expressed by the words the child already knows and uses. Some of these words are recognizable as sight words for the child.

Basal programs which begin with the introduction of sight words introduce new words in such ways that they can be compared and contrasted with the words which have already been presented. For example, initial stories might introduce a phonogram (a word family like *an*) and then introduce the following words: *man, can, Dan, ran, pan.*

As competent adult readers, we tend to identify many clues when we are reading. Among these clues are configuration clues; for example, if the following array is presented to us and we are told that the answer will be a football cheer, we examine the word configurations to arrive at an answer:

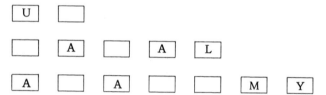

In the following pattern we are told that the answer is the name of a college:

We use configuration clues to arrive at our two answers, "Hip, hip, hooray" and "U.S. Naval Academy."

Shapes of words also offer configuration clues for children; for example, bed is different in shape from puppy. Children often attend to and depend upon configuration when they are decoding. One concern which has been voiced about the introduction of the phonogram is the child's dependence upon the configuration and a phenomenon called "first letter guessing." The child realizes ran means ran; he is introduced to man and is told this says *man.* What sometimes happens is the following: The child internalizes this information: ran = *ran.* When he sees the word "run" in a sentence, he recognizes the "r" and *guesses* that the word says "ran." In other cases, the child who has learned ran = *ran* might even say "ran" when he comes across words like rooster, rabbit, rye, or rough.

The selection of appropriate words to be taught as sight words needs to be examined carefully by teachers so that children's memories do not become overtaxed; for example, children may not be able to learn long words like *nightingale* or *superintendent* as sight words. An appropriate starting point is the child's own name. Color names and numeral names are also useful because of their convenient visual referents, such as *black, gray, 4 (four).*

The next step is to determine appropriate criteria for introducing sight words. The best single criterion seems to be to select high-frequency functional words, like *the*, e.g.:

(The) cat (in) (the) hat .

The following is an extended list for use as a sight word vocabulary.

THE DALE LIST OF 769 EASY WORDS

A	beautiful	build	coming	E	finger	grew
a	because	building	company	each	finish	ground
about	bed	built	cook	ear	fire	grow
above	bee	burn	cool	early	first	guess
across	been	busy	corn	earth	fish	
act	before	but	corner	east	fit	H
afraid	began	butter	cost	easy	five	had
after	begin	buy	could	eat	fix	hair
afternoon	behind	by	count	edge	floor	half
again	being		country	egg	flower	hall
against	believe	C	course	eight	fly	hand
ago	bell	cake	cover	either	follow	hang
air	belong	call	cow	else	food	happy
all	beside	came	cried	end	foot	hard
almost	best	can	cross	England	for	has
alone	better	cap	crowd	English	forget	hat
along	between	captain	crown	enough	fourth	have
already	big	car	cry	evening	found	he
also	bill	care	cup	ever	four	head
always	bird	careful	cut	every	fresh	hear
am	bit	carry	D	everything	friend	heard
American	black	case	dance	except	from	heart
an	bless	catch	dark	expect	front	heavy
and	blind	cause	day	eye	fruit	help
animal	blood	cent	dead	F	full	here
another	blow	center	dear	face	G	herself
answer	blue	chair	deep	fair	game	hid
any	board	chance	did	fall	garden	high
anything	boat	change	die	family	gate	hill
apple	body	chief	different	fancy	gave	him
are	bone	child	dinner	far	get	himself
arm	book	children	do	farm	gift	his
around	born	choose	doctor	farmer	girl	hold
as	both	Christmas	does	fast	give	hole
ask	bottom	church	dog	fat	glad	home
at	bow	circle	done	father	glass	hope
away	box	city	don't	feed	go	horse
B	boy	class	door	feel	God	hot
baby	branch	clean	double	feet	going	house
back	brave	clear	down	fell	gold	how
bad	bread	clock	draw	fellow	golden	hundred
bag	break	close	dream	felt	gone	hunt
ball	breakfast	cloth	dress	fence	good	hurry
band	bridge	clothes	drink	few	got	hurt
bank	bright	cloud	drive	field	grain	I
basket	bring	coal	drop	fight	grass	I
be	broken	coat	dry	fill	gray	ice
bear	brother	cold	dust	find	great	if
beat	brought	color		fine	green	in
	brown	come				

Indian
instead
into
iron
is
it
its

J
jump
just

K
keep
kept
kill
kind
king
kiss
knee
knew
know

L
lady
laid
lake
land
large
last
laugh
lay
lead
learn
leave
left
leg
lesson
let
letter
lie
lift
light
like
line
lion
lips
listen
little
live
load
long
look
lost
lot
loud
love
low

M
made
mail
make
man
many
march
mark
market
matter
may
me
mean
measure
meat
meet
mean
met
middle
might
mile
milk
mill
mind
minute
miss
money
month
moon
more
morning
most
mother
mountain
mouth
move
Mr.
Mrs.
much
music
must
my
myself

N
name
near
neck
need
neighbor
neither
nest
never
New York
next
nice

night
nine
no
noise
none
noon
nor
north
nose
not
note
nothing
now
number

O
oak
ocean
of
off
office
often
old
on
once
one
only
open
or
other
our
out
outside
over
own

P
page
paint
pair
paper
part
party
pass
path
pay
pen
people
pick
picture
piece
place
plain
plant
play
please
point
poor

post
pound
present
press
pretty
pull
put

Q
quarter
queen
quick
quiet
quite

R
race
rain
ran
rather
reach
read
ready
real
reason
red
remember
rest
rich
ride
right
ring
river
road
rock
roll
roof
room
rose
round
row
run

S
said
sail
salt
same
sand
sat
save
saw
say
school
sea
season
seat
second

see
seed
seem
seen
self
sell
send
sent
serve
set
seven
several
shake
shall
shape
she
sheep
shine
ship
shoe
shop
short
should
shoulder
show
shut
sick
side
sign
silk
silver
sing
sir
sister
sit
six
size
skin
sky
sleep
slow
small
smile
smoke
snow
so
soft
sold
soldier
some
something
sometime
song
soon
sound
south
space

speak
spot
spread
spring
square
stand
star
start
station
stay
step
stick
still
stone
stood
stop
store
storm
story
straight
street
strike
strong
such
sugar
suit
summer
sun
suppose
surprise
sweet

T
table
tail
take
talk
tall
taste
teach
teacher
tear
tell
ten
than
thank
that
the
their
them
then
there
these
they
thick
thin
thing

think
this
those
though
thought
thousand
three
through
throw
tie
till
time
tire
to
today
together
told
tomorrow
tongue
too
took
top
touch
town
trade
train
tree
true
try
turn
twelve
twenty
two

U
uncle
under
until
up
upon
us
use

V
valley
very
visit

W
wait
walk
wall
want
war
warm
was
wash
waste

watch	well	where	whose	wing	word	year
water	went	whether	why	winter	work	yellow
wave	were	which	wide	wish	world	yes
way	west	while	wild	with	would	yesterday
we	what	white	will	without	write	yet
wear	wheat	who	win	woman	wrong	you
weather	wheel	whole	wind	wonder	XYZ	young
week	when	whom	window	wood	yard	your

Repetition of sight words is essential for the child who is beginning to read. Dolch (1936) prepared a list of 220 words which constitute nearly half of the words which a mature reader encounters in print. Many of the words which are included on this list almost literally defy phonics generalizations. Therefore, it seems sensible to teach these words as sight words.

THE DOLCH BASIC SIGHT VOCABULARY OF 220 WORDS

a	call	from	jump	on	sing	under
about	came	full	just	once	sit	up
after	can	funny		one	six	upon
again	carry		keep	only	sleep	us
all	clean	gave	kind	open	small	use
always	cold	give	know	or	so	
am	come	go		our	some	very
an	could	goes	laugh	out	soon	walk
and	cut	going	let	over	start	want
any		good	like	own	stop	warm
are	did	got	little			was
around	do	green	live	pick	take	wash
as	does	grow	long	play	tell	we
ask	done	had	look	please	ten	well
at	don't	has		pretty	thank	went
ate	down	have	made	put	that	were
away	draw	he	make		the	what
	drink	help	many	ran	their	when
be		her	may	read	them	where
because	eat	here	me	red	then	which
been	eight	him	much	ride	there	white
before	every	his	must	right	these	who
best		hold	my	round	they	why
better	fall	hot	myself	run	this	will
big	far	how			those	wish
black	fast	hurt	never	may	three	with
blue	find	I	new	saw	to	work
both	first	if	no	say	today	would
bring	five	in	not	see	together	write
brown	fly	into	now	seven	too	yes
but	for	is	of	shall	try	you
by	found	it	off	she	two	your
	for	its	old	show		

Contractions

It is also important to teach contractions as sight words because of the inconsistency of their formation patterns. An easy rule for children to remember as an aid for recognizing contractions is the following: when two or more words combine to form a new, shorter word, an apostrophe (') is substituted for one or more letters in the new word. The following is a list of contractions:

I have	I've	she is	she's	have not	haven't
I am	I'm	has not	hasn't	it is	it's
I will	I'll	are not	aren't	will not	won't
he will	he'll			of the clock	o'clock
I am	I'm	it is	it's	would not	wouldn't
she is	she's	he is	he's	there is	there's
she will	she'll	he will	he'll	I will	I'll
did not	didn't	cannot	can't	is not	isn't
was not	wasn't	do not	don't	should not	shouldn't
did not	didn't	had not	hadn't	could not	couldn't
does not	doesn't	has not	hasn't	have not	haven't
will not	won't	must not	mustn't	you are	you're
they are	they're	they have	they've		

Whole words, as well as contractions, need to be taught at every level, not just during initial reading instruction. This occurs because of the lack of correspondence between spelling and prononciation which the student encounters throughout his school years. More difficult and less frequently used words which may be effectively taught as sight words include: *pneumonia, phlegm, mnemonic.*

Certain borrowings from other languages which have entered English have unusual spellings which children may find difficult. Some of these words may be taught effectively as sight word. Ruddell (1974) provides us with the following list:

Language Source	Plants and Animals	Food	Culture	Miscellaneous
American Indian	sequoia catawba cayuse	supawn pemmican	manitou kayak	chautauqua
French	caribou	brioche a la mode parfait sazarac	bureau bateau pirogue	Cajun charivari rotisserie
Spanish	mesquite marijuana mosquito palomino	frijol tequila enchilada	sombrero serape lariat pueblo	conquina hombre savvy
German		blutwurst schnitzel zwieback	pinochle rathskeller turnverein	katzenjammer phooey spiel
Italian		spaghetti ravioli	duet opera piano virtuoso	granite balcony
Persian	lilac lemon	sherbet	caravan khaki borax	paradise check
Greek			acrobat barometer catastrophe	tactics tantalize elastic
Russian		vodka	ruble droshky	steppe

Regardless of the grade level or the content which you are teaching, you will be introducing and reinforcing sight word skills. As you observed in the Dolch or Dale Word Lists and the list of contractions, many of the words which you will be teaching as sight words do not lend themselves to visual representations, such as *the* and *I'm.* Therefore, they must be taught in context. The following rules may aid you to help your children to develop their sight word vocabularies:

Rules for Teaching Sight Words

1. When it is appropriate, show a picture of the word or concept being introduced. Present a sentence containing the sight words you wish to introduce or reinforce. Encourage your students to study the picture and the number of words on the page and try to guess what will be said in the passage. You can also ask the child to guess the word by first reading the sentence context. If the child has difficulty, provide him with a riddle: The _____ was the tallest animal on Mr. Hess's farm. After the child incorrectly guesses giraffe because of the contextual information "tallest," make him reread "on Mr. Hess's farm." Then you may want to provide a riddle: This animal has four legs and has black and white stripes all over his body.

2. Ask the students to look at the words as you read them. This helps the children to decide if their guesses are correct.

3. Point to the picture and reread the passage while the children follow the story visually.

4. Encourage the children to read the passage with you.

5. Ask individual children to read the sentences while the other children follow the story visually.

6. After reading the sentence, point out the individual words you are introducing.

7. Discuss the meaning of each word. Explain that some words serve as helpers to complete sentences, such as *the, is,* and *am.*

8. "Tell" children certain words which have extremely irregular patterns: *sight, of, who, laugh, though, the, should.*

9. While framing each word, assist students in recognizing the length and configuration, initial letter(s), and ascending letter features.

10. Finally, encourage students to reread the sentence with you.

Exercises for Reinforcing Sight Words

In addition to the activities section at the end of the chapter, the following vocabulary exercises are provided as aids:

1. Putting Scrambled Sentences Together

Ask children to rearrange this sentence:

| brown | | The | | the | | grass. | | eats | | green | | cow |

You can include the upper case *T* in [The] and the period after [grass.] to give students clues.

You could also ask students to assemble sentences which have many possibilities:

> Suddenly the car stopped.
> The car stopped suddenly.
> The car suddenly stopped.

Such exercises tend to encourage students to focus on meaning. They are reinforcing these words as part of their sight repertoire. This same activity can be conducted with words printed on dice. The dice can be thrown and students will have to assemble a sentence. In order to prepare the dice, you print items of a particular class, either grammatical or semantic, on each die.

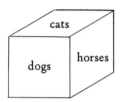 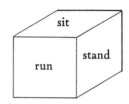 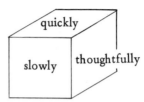

On the other three sides:

bears	jump	joyfully
cows	fly	sadly
rabbits	kneel	pensively

Students can roll as many dice as you decide to keep in the cup at one time. When the dice have been rolled, the children would have to make sentences from the words which appear on each die.

> Cats jump quickly.
> Horses kneel sadly.
> Thoughtfully cows fly.

2. Completing Sentences

The same principle is in use in this exercise. When you encourage students to focus on comprehension, they will be reinforcing their sight vocabulary. Ask students to complete the following sentences:

> The deer in the forest was frightened by _____.
> The _____ smelled of _____.

3. Categorizing/Classifying

For beginning readers, it is sometimes useful to give them the opportunity to organize their ideas by classifying them into appropriate categories. Ask students to name a category and then ask them to name examples of the category:

Animals	Names	Cars
dog	Joan	Volvo
horse	Paul	Saab
zebra	Doris	Toyota

4. Building on Words

It also helps beginning readers to show them how compound words are built. Write the words which are part of their sight vocabulary on the board and ask the children to read the cognates:

ice	cream
pop	corn
honey	moon
blue	berry
under	wear
up	stairs
back	ward

5. Configurations

Teachers of reading need to provide children with a great deal of practice in visual discrimination of word configurations as a basis for developing sight word skills. Durrell (1963) suggests that young children need a great deal of practice and training to be able to recognize and quickly distinguish between words with very similar configurations. Here are some examples:

come	purpose	ran	over
some	suppose	run	oven

write	house	dog	paint
wrote	horse	day	point

When teachers say to the children, "What do you think the word looks like?" they are actually helping children to use configuration analysis as a strategy for decoding a word by sight; for example, the configurations of the following words are quite different.

little   bed   play

However, relying too heavily on configurations has obvious limitations, as demonstrated by the following list of words which have similar configurations:

little   bed

battle   bud

bottle   bad

6. First Letter

Some children rely on the first letter as a clue to meaning; for example, they see *d* and read *don't* for *doesn't*. They may need continued instruction in analyzing all of the letters before they try to read the word. A useful example may be to cover the first letter and have children guess the word:

—oy   —unt   —alk

After you have taught several sight words, you may wish to evaluate your students' competence in reading sight words. One effective way of doing this is to select certain words from the Dolch list or the contraction list and write them on a piece of paper. Put a dash in front of each word. If you are working with an individual, you can ask the child to read each word. You may want to check the words which the child reads correctly. If you are using this format with a group of students, ask the children to number the words as you call them out. An example of this format is presented below:

_____ the	_____ this
_____ of	_____ had
_____ and	_____ not
_____ to	_____ are
_____ a	_____ but

This becomes a useful record-keeping system as well as a diagnostic base for effective teacher decision-making.

Structural Analysis Skills

While skills in sight word strategies are useful in word recognition, the reader also needs *structural analysis* skills as a further word analysis process. When you are able to help children break words down into their smallest parts, you are helping them to decode the word *and* to unlock its meaning. Children who can unravel the parts of a word like *un · sports · man · like* by knowing that the prefix *un* = *not* and the suffix *like* = *as* will be able to say the word and know that it means "not as a sportsman." A thorough knowledge of all the rules of morphology will be helpful for you in establishing the structural analysis segment of your word analysis program.

When linguists discuss the contents of structural analysis, they usually include a description of the following:

<u>Morphology</u>

affixes (suffixes and/or prefixes)

<u>Variants</u>

inflectional endings
  plural(<u>s</u>)
  tenses (<u>ed</u>)
  comparatives (<u>est</u>)
grammatical usage
compound words

As you begin to develop your students' structural analysis skills, it is important for you to become acquainted with a description of morphology.

Morphology

The morpheme is the smallest structural unit of meaning in any language. The morpheme should not be confused with a word. A word may be a single morpheme or it may be composed of several morphemes: *back* or *back · ward*. Morphemes may be free, such as the word *back*, or bound, like *ing*, in *back · ing*. The following chart illustrates examples of bound and free morphemes.

Bound Morpheme	Free Morpheme	Bound Morpheme
pre	view	
re	view	
	view	er
	view	ing
pre	view	er
re	view	ing
pre	test	
re	test	
	test	er
	test	ing
pre	test	ing
re	test	ing

Free morphemes are sometimes called *root words* or base words. Examples of root words are presented below.

word	play	sleep	agree	fear
boy	box	cover	part	

Can you add bound morphemes to these root words to create new words? Ernst (1955) gave us an insight about root words:

> Words are interesting.... When you begin to know which ones belong to the same families and who their forefathers were, they become fascinating.

It is extremely important to teach children about the construction of words in order to help them unlock word meanings. To do so, children must be introduced to the affixes of English. Affixes are called bound morphemes, and they include prefixes and suffixes. The following chart illustrates the affixes of the English language.

Word Class	Affix	When Affix Is Added To	Example
ADVERB	-ly	ADJ	hardly, slowly
		derived ADJ	carelessly
			stereotypically
			advantageously
			relatively
	-wise	N	otherwise
	-wards	N	frontwards
	a-	N	aside, ahead
		V	afloat
		ADJ	alive, afresh, aloud
		STEM	aghast
	al-	ADV	almost
			already
	-fore	ADV	therefore
	-most	N	foremost
ADJECTIVE	-y	N	lengthy
		STEM	pretty
	-al	N	functional
		STEM	terminal
			integral
	-ible	V	reversible
		STEM	fallible
			visible
	-able	V	adorable
		STEM	viable
			durable
	-ful	N	careful
	-less	N	guileless
	-en	N	wooden
	-ive	V	possessive
		N	defective
		STEM	native
	-ar	N	particular
		STEM	regular, linear
	-ary	N	honorary
		STEM	ordinary
	-ic	N	aromatic
		STEM	arctic
			analytic

	-ish	N	foolish
		STEM	squeamish
	-ous	N	mischievous
		STEM	fabulous
	-ent	V	abhorrent
		STEM	resident
			expedient
	-ose	ADJ	grandiose
		STEM	morose
	-ed	N	spotted
		V	determined
	-id	STEM	morbid, lucid
	-ing	N	conflicting
		V	hanging
	-ate	N	proportionate
		STEM	literate
	-ile	STEM	mercantile
			juvenile
	-ory	V	contradictory
		STEM	illusory
	-ant	N	concordant
		STEM	rampant
			verdant
	-some	V	meddlesome
VERB	-ate	N	fabricate
		STEM	separate
	-ize	N	idolize
		ADJ	vitalize
		STEM	emphasize
			mesmerize
	-ify	N	citify
		ADJ	simplify
			clarify
		STEM	liquify
			modify
	-ish	STEM	finish, polish
	-en	N	hasten
		ADJ	moisten
		STEM	glisten
	en-	N	engulf, enjoy
		V	enliven, enjoin
		ADJ	embitter, enrich
		STEM	endure, endow

	-le	N	handle
		STEM	amble
	-er	V	loiter, saunter
NOUN	-age	V	spoilage
	-ance	V	condonance hindrance perserverance
	-cy	N	hyprocrisy agency
		ADJ	obstinacy consistency
	-ee	V	employee refugee
	-er	N	boxer biographer
		V	skier
		STEM	tailor, matter
	-ian	N	historian
	-ile	N	projectile
	-ism	N	despotism
		STEM	paroxism
	-ist	V	typist
		N	pianist
		ADJ	socialist
	-ive	N	objective
		V	relative
		STEM	missive
	-ity	STEM	animosity
		ADJ	generosity
	-ment	V	payment amusement
	-ness	ADJ	goodness liveliness
	-old	N	cuckold
	-ship	N	citizenship
		ADJ	hardship
	-ster	N	gangster roadster
		ADJ	oldster
		STEM	monster
	-um	V	continuum
		ADJ	ultimatum
		STEM	curriculum

-us	N	modulus
	STEM	stimulus
		animus
-tion	derived V	solution
	V	eruption
		vibration
-hood	N	statehood
		motherhood

New affixes are constantly being added to English. Many of these pass quickly from the English language, but some of them remain in the general language usage:

Examples: from *hamburger*, we derive *burger*, and *cheeseburger* can be created.

sandwich	wich	fishwich
panorama	orama	foodorama
marathon	thon	telethon

Prefixes

Some of the most frequently recurring prefixes and their meanings in English are listed below:

dis (not, a part)	em (in)
in (not)	de (from)
mis (wrong)	inter (between)
anti (against)	ex (out, from)
non (not)	en (in)
com (with)	op, ob (against)
con (with)	pro (in front of)
pre (before)	per (fully)
super (over)	im (not, in)
tri (three)	un (not, opposite of)

Suffixes

When the meaning of a word is modified by the addition of a *new ending*, a suffix has been added to the root word. Thorndike's text *The Teaching of English Suffixes* (1932) allows us some insight into the frequency with which some suffixes appear. For example, the five most common suffixes in English are:

ion	decoration
er	harder
ness	awareness
ity	purity
y	rainy

Other suffixes which appear frequently are:

able	objection<u>able</u>
ant	pleas<u>ant</u>

More examples of recurring English suffixes include:

ness (being)	wise (ways)
ment (result of)	ling (little)
ward (in direction of)	ty (state)
our (full of)	ity (state)
ious (like, full of)	ure (denoting action)
eous (like, full of)	ion (condition or quality)
et (little)	ian, or, ist, er (one who does)
able, ible, ble (capable of being)	en (made of, to become)
ic (like, made of)	ly (similar in appearance or manner)
ish (like)	full (full of)
ant (being)	ness (quality or state of being)
ent (one who)	less (without)
age (collection of)	y (like a, full of)
ance (state of being)	al (pertaining to)
ence (state or quality)	man (one who)

In addition to affixes, including prefixes and suffixes, certain other elements of the English language add meaning to words and are also called bound morphemes. These elements include inflectional endings (plurals, possessives, and markers for third person singular verbs), tense markers, and pronoun markers (number, case, and possession).

Inflectional Endings

Since English is a word-order language, it does not have many inflectional endings. All of the commonly used endings are included in the following chart:

1. Plural, Possessive, and Third Singular Verb Markers

A. If the word ends in any of these phonemes (/s, z, c, j/), the inflectional ending is /z/.

mass	/mez/	masses	/mezəz/
barage	/bəraj/	barages	/bərajəz/

B. If the word ends in a voiceless consonant, the appropriate ending is /s/.

bit	/bɪt/	bits	/bɪts/
sip	/sɪp/	sips	/sɪps/

C. If the word ends in either a voiced consonant or a vowel, the appropriate ending is /z/.

crib /krIb/   cribs /krIbz/
rid /rId/   rids /rIdz/

2. Tense Markers

A. Past Tense and Past Participle

Both of these forms use the same rules to produce their appropriate endings.
1. If the verb ends in /t/ or /d/, the ending is /əd/.

rate /ret/   rated /retəd/

2. If the verb ends in a voiceless consonant, the ending is /t/.

dip /dIp/   dipped /dIpt/

3. If the verb ends in a voiced consonant or a vowel, the ending is /d/.

rib /rIb/   ribbed /rIbd/

B. The Progressive

When the progressive is used, i.e. ing, as in "He is going," /Iŋ/ is added to the verb form, following the BE.

he will sell   /hi wIl sel/
he will be selling   /hi wIl bi selIŋ/

3. Pronouns
Pronouns in English are also inflected for number, case, and gender:

Singular			Plural		
Subject	*Object*	*Possessive*	*Subject*	*Object*	*Possessive*
1st I/aI/	me/mi/	my/maI/ mine&maIn/	1st we/wi/	us/əs/	our/aUr/ ours/aUrz/
2nd you/yu/	you/yu/	your/yor yours/yorz/	2nd you/yu/	you/yu/	your/yor/ yours/yorz/
3rd he/hi/	him/hIm/	his/hIz/	3rd they/ðe/	them/ðEm/	their/ðEr/ theirs/ðErz/
she/si/	her/hr	her&hr/ hers/hrz/			
it/It/	it/It/	its/Its/			

Compound Words

As part of structural analysis, children need to be made aware of their innate knowledge of compound words. In doing this, children are able to extract meaning quickly from compound words. Gleason (1969) conducted a study of children's definitions of compound words. She offers the following definitions for the words *airplane*, *breakfast*, and *Friday*.

> They knew what the words referred to and how to use them, but their ideas about the words were rather amusing. One little boy said that an airplane is called an airplane because it is a plain thing that goes in the air. Another child said that breakfast is called breakfast because you have to eat it fast to get to school on time. Several subjects thought that Friday is called Friday because it is the day you eat fried fish.

During beginning reading programs children may be taught to identify many compound words as sight words.

policeman	mailman
grandmother	football
grandfather	doghouse
thanksgiving	toothpick
breakfast	seaweed
outcome	filmstrip

Because many of these words will be part of the spoken vocabularies of your children, they can be used as a base for drawing generalizations about other compound words. The following is a list of compound words that are frequently used in basal programs:

township	anthill	anyway	toothache
wheelbarrow	countryside	something	marksman
policeman	peppermint	whenever	spellbound
soapstone	grasshopper	himself	sharpshooter
teenage	flagpole	snowman	beeswax
nighttime	peacetime	windshield	rowboat
marblehead	lifejacket	toothbrush	drawbridge
needlepoint	Northwest	toothpaste	raincoat
understatement	downpour	motorcycle	hatbox
gentlemen	fingertip	broadcast	bathtub
wristwatch	shortstop	aircraft	chessboard
overpower	houseboat	anyone	doormat
airplane	floodlight	afternoon	sailboat
baseball	eyeball	evergreen	bellhop
basketball	otherwise	airport	cowboy
football	pigtail	sandbox	eyeglass
skydive	classmate	railroad	clothesline
underground	slowpoke	bookcase	wishbone
fireman	blacksmith	horseshoe	doghouse
sweatshirt	notebook	lighthouse	sidewalk
eiderdown	pushpin	upset	pocketbook
uptown	taxpayer	salesman	cookbook
downtown	riverbank	lifetime	faraway
classroom	undersize	without	bedroom
homework	birthday	clubhouse	nowhere
lunchbox	weatherman	typewriter	barefoot

Structural analysis is an extremely useful tool for you as a teacher of reading. When you translate this knowledge into an instructional program, your children will be able to use the rules of morphology to unlock the meanings of words. When you are implementing your structural analysis program, you may want to follow some of these rules:

1. Encourage children to analyze the ending of each word, such as *s*, *ed*, as tense markers, *s* as possession, and *s* as a plural marker.

2. Encourage children to split words into parts with which they are already familiar; e.g. re/*view*/ing.

3. Encourage children to guess the pronunciation of a new word by looking at the parts of the word which are familiar to them.

4. Encourage children to make their own "new" compound words. This will help them better understand how compound words are formed.

An understanding of structural analysis will help your children deal with many new words. Structural analysis, like phonics and sight word strategies, is only one way of helping children learn to decode words. Each strategy is useful only as an aid to learning—no strategy can substitute for learning.

Contextual Analysis

The process of word recognition also involves the analysis of the printed language within a given context.

> All language . . . concerns itself with meanings. Or, perhaps, we should say rather that human beings are basically concerned with meanings and use language as their tool to grasp, to comprehend, and to share meanings. It is the linguist's business to turn the spotlight on the tool-language-itself in order to examine the physical material of which it is composed and to determine the ways this material has been selected and shaped to accomplish its function of mediating meaning.
>
> *—Fries (1963), p. 97*

As we have pointed out in the preceding chapter and the first part of this chapter, new readers have to be helped with an application of phonic strategies, sight word strategies, structural analysis strategies, and contextual analysis strategies in order to unlock the meaning of the printed word. Statements which contain definitions, synonyms, summaries, similies, examples, apposition, antonyms, groupings, are often embedded within the contextual structure of sentences, passages, and stories. It is very important for students to be introduced to these additional clues to meaning. Because children learn to read in many different ways, we, as teachers, have to help them by exposing them to *all* of the available clues within a text. Students can extract meaning from sentences and passages by learning about context clues. Each of these clues is extremely important and needs to be taught. Before we suggest instructional activities for each of these clues, it is important that we understand them thoroughly.

Definition

As children's materials are being written, authors closely monitor the introduction of new words. One common way of providing children with an understanding of the new word is to *introduce* and *define* it within the same context:

> The cornea is the transparent outer coating of the eyeball.

Synonym

Another contextual clue for the reader is the incorporation of *synonyms* within the printed text.

> a. I hanker to visit California. This restless longing never ends.
> b. It was an accident, since it occurred as happenstance.

Summary

Through a *statement of summary* the reader is offered a detailed account of the happening.

> a. Mary is a student who is interested in intellectual inquiry as well as research. She has a curious, creative mind. Mary is believed by many to be inquisitive.
> b. And now, in sum, let me pinpoint the specific characteristics of this chair.
>   1. beauty
>   2. price
>   3. durability

Simile

The words *as* and *like* are used to introduce a *simile* to the reader.

> a. Her hair was as blond as harvested wheat.
> b. Her lips were as taut as a steel pipe.
> c. The boy's eyes glistened like bright stars in the sky.

Examples

Another contextual clue which offers the reader word understanding is the *example*.

> a. Linda is an ambitious girl. For example, she spends every evening doing extra work for her assignements.
> b. The words running, going, doing, and crying are examples of the incorporation of the suffix ing to root words.

Apposition

A statement of *apposition* is also a contextual clue that is provided by authors to enable the reader to become familiar with the word in its contextual setting.

> a. The dictionary, a book which contains an alphabetic arrangement of the words of one language, was of help to the child.
> b. Dickens, an English novelist, wrote A Christmas Carol.

Antonym

An *antonym*, a word opposite in meaning from another, is often provided in printed material as a contextual clue.

> a. Lynne is often calm. Anxiety is a characteristic that cannot be ascribed to her.
> b. We stood silently watching the raucous waves.

Groupings

When an unfamiliar word is classified in context with other words to depict similarities, the meaning of the word is often more readily recognized by the reader.

> a. His tie was a combination of many colors: yellow, red, and chartreuse.
> b. I bought a chamois, sponges, wax, and detergent on my way home from school.

Spache clearly delineates the importance of teaching children contextual analysis strategies when he explains the relationship between contextual analysis and inferential thinking skills:

> Apparently most context clues demand some degree of inferential thinking. As a result, some teachers assume that contextual analysis is not much more than guesswork and therefore should not be promoted. The truth is that such inferential thinking is an essential part of the reading process at all maturity levels and should be strongly encouraged. Pupils should not be burdened with learning the technical terms which might

be employed to describe the types of context clues. Rather the emphasis should be placed upon helping the reader use the sense of the sentence or the surrounding sentences as an aid in identifying the probable meaning of a difficult word. The goal of contextual analysis is not always an exact recognition of a word or its pronunciation. These may be approached by other means such as phonic or structural analysis. But when these techniques are successful, they do not necessarily result in the derivation of the meaning of the word, for it may not be encompassed in the reader's auditory vocabulary. Thus contextual analysis takes the reader beyond pronunciation to meaning, which in many situations is more significant for his ultimate comprehension. (1973), p. 497)

It should be noted that there are other contextual clues which may also benefit the reader: *italics, footnotes, capitalization, boldface type, quotation marks,* and *parenthetical statements.* Teachers can encourage children to use contextual clues in order to extract meaning from the printed word.

Teaching children contextual analysis strategies will not insure the effective reading of every word, but it may provide the child with an added possibility for decoding the unknown word. You can instruct children in contextual analysis strategies by calling their attention to the following: picture clues, lexical clues (word and sentence meaning of clues) relational clues (word order clues in sentence), interpretation clues. You can do this by instructing children through the use of cloze exercises like the following:

1. Deleting words from sentences

   > Lena Valentino, elected Senator from Massachusetts, _____ for the Equal Rights Amendment.

2. Deleting words from language experience stories

   > We went to the zoo.
   > Mary Fredericks liked the gorillas.
   > Jim Hill liked the _____.

Additionally, contextual clues can be taught using some of the following strategies:

Picture Clues

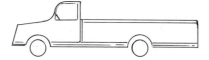

1. Annie drove the _____ down the highway.

2. It's sometimes difficult to build a _____.

Lexical Clues

_____, the rich and creamy white substance, is made of egg yolks and oil.

Relational Clues

1. The bright, yellow _____ chirped with enthusiasm when I began to feed her.
2. The girl in the green bathing suit dove in the _____ with her arms stretched above her head.

Interpretive Clues

1. The dazzling light was like a _____ in the darkened sky.
2. The spider spun its ensnaring _____ in the corner of our room.

Contextual analysis may be viewed as another aid in developing reading comprehension. When the child uses contextual analysis strategies as a process to further his understanding of the printed page, he is using another set of clues which will help him to decode and acquire meaning. The mature, competent reader greatly depends upon context clues to help him accelerate his reading and increase his comprehension of difficult and unfamiliar texts. It is important for you to encourage your children to pay attention to the context of a passage. When your students are unable to continue in a passage because they are stumped by an unfamiliar word, tell them to ask themselves the following questions:

1. Are there clues to the meaning of this word in the surrounding words?
2. Will I understand this word if I continue to the end of the sentence?
3. Have I examined the pictures for clues to the meaning?

In the next few pages, we will present several activities that may be useful reinforcements for your word analysis program.

SIGHT–WORD STRATEGIES

1. Word Puzzle

<u>Goal</u>: Discrimination of sight words with similar configurations

<u>Grade level</u>: Primary

Construction: Divide a piece of oak-tag board into four sections. Cut each section into a puzzle pattern. On each piece write a matching pair of sight words, one below and one above the cut.

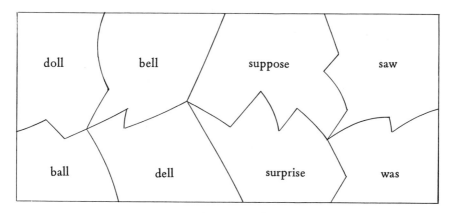

Utilization: Children have to read each word correctly before they can match it with the appropriate puzzle pieces. As a team children can take turns and put the puzzle together.

2. Sight–Word "Go Fish"

Goal: Discrimination of function sight words.

Grade level: K–3

Construction: Write a list of function sight words on separate index cards. Write sentences leaving out one word spaces. Ask the children to supply the correct sight words.

Function words:

Sentences:

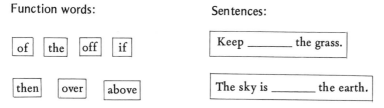

Utilization: This game can be played like Go Fish. Deal each player seven cards and put the rest of the deck in the middle of the table. The object of the game is to match two cards, | Keep _____ the grass | and | off | . If a player cannot make a match, he asks the player to his right: "Do you have an off card?" If he does not have it, he tells the original player to Go Fish!

3. Sight-O

Goal: Recognizing sight words

Grade level: K–3

Construction: Draw a Bingo card using the word S I G H T - O. Write sight words in each of the boxes.

S	I	G	H	T	O
of	every	off	sight	how	would
the	is	FREE	might	should	where
each	as	from	what	who	when

Utilization: The caller draws the sight words from a pile of prepared sight words. He names the card as each student examines his board to see if he has the word. If he has, he covers it with a chip. The first to have all the spaces covered wins the game.

4. Word Puzzles

Goal: Developing word-recognition skills by reinforcing the visual structure of words

Grade level: Pre-K–3

Construction: Select a series of words that have a distinctive visual structure. Words should be those that can be combined into meaningful sentences. Write each word on a piece of oak tag. Cut the oak tag to emphasize the visual structure.

Utilization: Each child selects a series of words and from these forms a sentence.

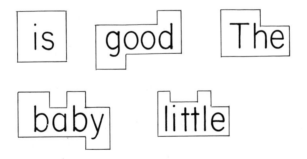

5. Baseball

Goal: Recognizing sight words

Grade level: K–3

Construction: Draw on a large piece of oak tag a baseball field showing four bases and a pitcher's mound. Make word cards containing sight words in the shape of baseball players.

Utilization: Divide the class into two teams. Show the sight-word card for the pitch; the child must then pronounce the word in order to take his base. (Only singles can be earned.) If the child is unable to pronounce the word, he loses his turn at bat. When three players have lost their turn at bat, the other team is up. The team with the most runs scored (or just hits) wins.

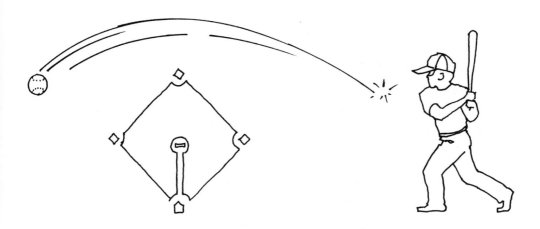

6. Word for the Day

Goal: Practice in word recognition

Grade level: K–3

Construction: Design or acquire a calendar with large daily squares. Construct cardboard number squares for each day of the month. On each page of the calendar write the name of the month; on each cardboard square write the number of the day and a sight word.

November						
Sun.	Mon.	Tues.	Wed.	Thurs.	Fri.	Sat.
1	2	3	4	5	6	7
8	9	10	11	12	13	14
15	16	17	18	19	20	21
22	23	24	25	26	27	28
29	30					

15
saw

26
the

Utilization: In turn, each child draws a cardboard number card. He must then pronounce the corresponding word appearing on the calendar for that day. If correct, the child receives the number of points appearing as the number of the day on the cardboard card. Whoever has the most points when all of the cards are drawn wins.

7. Checkers

Goal: Recognition of sight words

Grade level: K–3

Construction: Draw a checker board on oak tag. In each square write a sight word twice, having it face both directions. Also needed are checkers or chips (or lima beans).

Utilization: In order to jump a piece or land on a square, the child must pronounce the word on the space he is moving to. The rules for checkers are followed.

to		am		were
oʇ		ɯɐ		ǝɹǝʍ
	it		saw	
	ʇı		ʍɐs	
		the		
		ǝɥʇ		

8. The Choice is <u>Yours</u>

<u>Goal</u>: Forming plurals

<u>Grade level</u>: 3–6

<u>Construction</u>: Attach three envelopes to a bulletin board. Label one envelope for 5 points, one 10 points, and one 15 points. On small 3×5-inch cards, write the singular form of the words. Place the words in the envelopes. Five-point words should be less difficult than 10- or 15-point words.

<u>5</u>	<u>10</u>	<u>15</u>
cat	box	wolf
apple	match	child
game	baby	goose

<u>Utilization</u>: Divide the class into two teams. In turn, players from each team select an envelope. A word is then drawn. The team has 15 seconds to spell the plural form of the word. If the team can supply the correct word form, it is given the number of points appearing on the envelope. If the team cannot supply the plural form, it must subtract the number from its existing score. The team first earning 75 points wins.

9. Magnetized Words

<u>Goal</u>: Forming compound words

<u>Grade level</u>: 4–6

<u>Construction</u>: Write parts of compound words on two pieces of masking tape and affix each to a paper clip. A horseshoe magnet is also needed.

<u>Utilization</u>: Children pick up two words with a horseshoe magnet that, when they are joined together, form a compound word. The child writes the word and tries to form as many different words as possible.

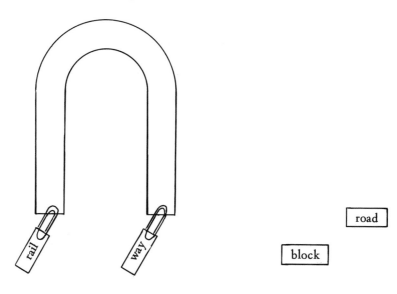

10. Concentration

<u>Goal</u>: Forming compound words

<u>Grade level</u>: 4–6

<u>Construction</u>: Make 3-x 5-inch word cards so that when two are combined they form a compound word.

<u>Utilization</u>: Sixteen cards are placed down and children take turns turning over two cards. If a compound word is formed from the two that are turned up, the child gets to keep it as a "match." If the two cards do not make a match, the cards are returned to their face-down positions, and another child tries to find the match. Whoever has the most pairs when all the cards are used wins.

11. Park My Car

<u>Goal</u>: Matching contractions with the original two words

<u>Grade level</u>: 3–6

<u>Construction</u>: On an oak-tag board draw a large parking lot with lines for parking spaces. The parking lot could have a store in the background. In each parking space write a contraction. Make up cards in the shape of automobiles and write the two words that form the contractions on the cars.

<u>Utilization</u>: The child must park the car by matching the two words with the proper contraction. A point is given each time a car is parked.

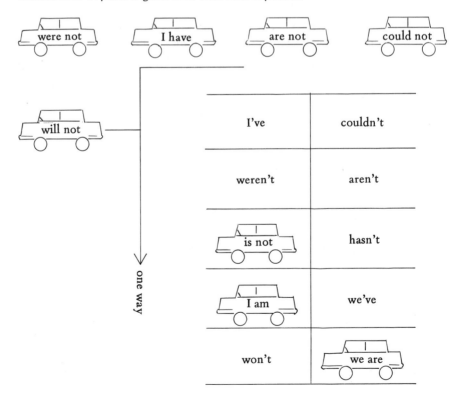

12. Listen and Contract

Goal: Making a contraction out of two spoken words

Grade level: 3-6

Construction: Record on cassette tape sentences containing words that could be made into contractions.

Utilization: The student writes on paper the proper words in contraction form.

13. Help! The Story Isn't Finished!

Goal: Completing stories by selecting appropriate root words and prefixes

Grade level: 3-6

Construction: Write a short story, leaving out several words that contain prefixes. The story could be written on a piece of oak tag, with slits cut into the blanks. Two decks of small cards should be designed, one set containing all of the root words and one set containing all of the prefixes. To facilitate a large group of children, the root words and prefixes could also be listed in two separate columns at the bottom of the printed story.

Utilization: A child selects the missing root word and prefix and inserts them into the proper blank.

14. Make a Connection

Goal: Matching appropriate suffixes with a root word
Grade level: Primary

Construction: Design pairs of puzzle pieces out of heavy cardboard. On some pieces write root words, and on connecting pieces write appropriate suffixes (there may be more than one suffix for each root word).

Utilization: The child connects word pieces to appropriate suffix pieces to make new words. If the suffix is incorrect, he will not be able to connect them.

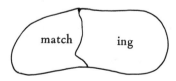

15. Supply the Suffix

Goal: Adding suffixes to given root words
Grade level: Primary

Construction: You will need to secure an overhead projector, blank transparencies, and a felt-tip pen.

Utilization: Divide the group into two teams. The first member of team A writes a word on the transparency, to which a suffix could be added. The first member of team B must attach an appropriate suffix, making all the necessary changes in the root word. If team B's player is correct he writes a root word, and the second member of team A attempts to add a suffix. A point is scored for each correct suffix. If a player is unable to add the correct suffix, the next team member on the opposing team makes an attempt. The team having the most points after a 20-minute time period is the winner.

16. Derivative Relay

Goal: Making new words by adding a suffix

Grade level: Primary

Construction: All that is needed is a chalkboard and chalk.

Utilization: Divide the class into two teams. Write two words on the board to which endings could be added to make new words. The first member of each team goes up to the board and writes a new word, using the derivative. They run back and give the chalk to the next team member, who must then add a new ending. Whichever team writes the most words in one minute wins.

Examples:

explore
explores
explored
exploring
exploration

17. The Word–Making Octopus

Goal: Adding prefixes and suffixes to root words

Grade level: 3–5

Construction: Draw an octopus on a bulletin board, blackboard, or ditto master. The body of the octopus should contain a root word. On the arms of the octopus write various prefixes and suffixes.

Utilization: Each child writes as many different word combinations as possible. Whoever makes the most words wins.

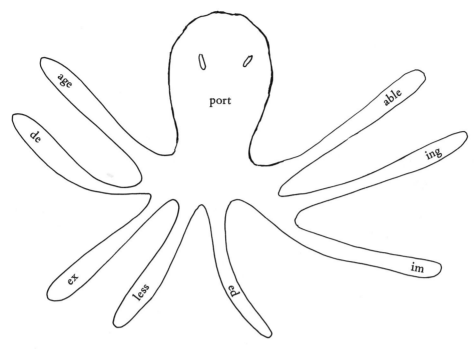

18. Can of Words

<u>Goal</u>: Adding prefixes and suffixes to root words

<u>Grade level</u>: 3–6

<u>Construction</u>: Secure three coffee cans and label them <u>prefixes</u>, <u>root words</u>, and <u>suffixes</u>. Construct several 3- x 5-inch cardboard backed cards. On each card write a prefix, suffix, or root word.

<u>Utilization</u>: The child draws a card from each can and attempts to make a word using all three pieces.

Example: | pre | | tend | | ing |

If the prefix or suffix does not apply, only one need be used. The child tries to make as many different words as possible.

19. Changes with Clay

<u>Goal</u>: Understanding and identifying inflectional changes within adjectives as they relate to tangible objects

<u>Grade level</u>: 4–6

<u>Construction</u>: Supply several children with equal amounts of clay. Design word cards with each card containing a series of adjectives with inflectional endings.

| big, bigger, biggest |

| tall, taller, tallest |

| long, longer, longest |

Give each child a word card.

Utilization: Each child reads a card and designs clay objects to illustrate the concept shown on the card. For example, the child could design three balls:

<u>big</u> ball
<u>bigger</u> ball
<u>biggest</u> ball

20. Make a Match

Goal: Modification of word forms through inflectional endings

Grade level: 4–6

Construction: Design an oak-tag game board. On the surface of the board paste a plain sheet of paper that has been subdivided into 3-x 5-inch squares. In each square write a base word. In a square close by, write a word partner that has been altered by an inflectional ending. In some 3-x 5-inch squares add pictures; in other squares write:

go back to beginning
penalty—move back six squares
reward—advance two squares

Also needed are a set of dice and four or five small objects to serve as playing pieces.

Utilization: In turn, players roll the dice and move the appropriate number of spaces. When a player lands on the appropriate square, he is to identify the word and also the very next word partner appearing on the board. If the child makes the correct identification, he may move his playing piece to the word partner. For example, if the child lands on <u>boy</u>, he should move to either <u>boys</u> or <u>boy's</u>, depending on which appears first. The first player to move around the board is the winner.

Make a Match Diagram:

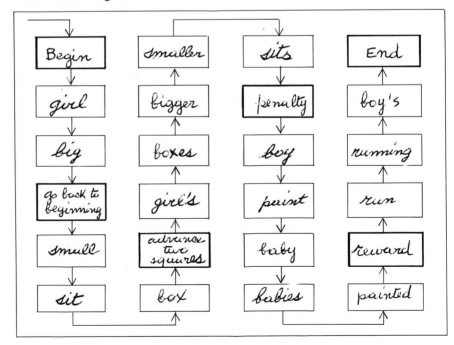

21. Let's Go Fishing

<u>Goal</u>: Altering word structures with inflectional endings

<u>Grade level</u>: 4–6

<u>Construction</u>: Make up 4-x 5-inch word cards from oak-tag board. Four cards from the same family comprise a "book."
Examples:

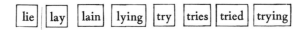

<u>Utilization</u>: Players are dealt four cards and the rest are scattered face down on the table. In turn, each player asks any other player for a card that could help to make a "book." If he receives it he can ask again; if the person does not have the card he says, "Fish" and the asker must draw a card. If he draws the card he was asking for, he gets another turn. Whoever has the most books when there are no more cards wins. Each player then must say the words in his books.

22. Switch a Story

<u>Goal</u>: Changing nouns to pronouns, and vice versa

<u>Grade level</u>: 4–6

<u>Construction</u>: Write a short story on a chart or ditto. Underline all nouns and pronouns.

<u>Utilization</u>: Have children replace all of the nouns in the story with pronouns and all of the pronouns with nouns. Children should recopy the story on another sheet of paper and tell which story sounds better to them and whether the original meaning of the story is still the same.

23. Slap Jack

<u>Goal</u>: Distinguishing between nouns and pronouns

<u>Grade level</u>: 4–6

<u>Construction</u>: Design a deck of cards that contain a variety of nouns and pronouns.

<u>Utilization</u>: Deal out all the cards and keep them face down. Instruct the children to slap only the words that are pronouns. Players in turn place a card in the center of the table. If it is a pronoun, the first to slap it gets to keep the card. When all of a player's cards are used up, he is out of the game. Whoever has the most cards at the end wins.

24. Possessive Jeopardy

<u>Goal</u>: Forming possessives of nouns and pronouns

<u>Grade level</u>: 4–6

<u>Construction</u>: Design a question board by securing a large square piece of oak tag. The board should be divided into four columns: <u>nouns, pronouns, possessive nouns,</u>

and <u>possessive pronouns</u>. Cut several squares from cardboard or material. Staple five squares to each cardboard column, leaving enough slack for the cardboard squares to be used as pockets. Squares within each column should be labeled 5, 10, 15, 20, and 25, respectively. Question cards, of increasing difficulty, dealing with the title of the column should be placed in the pockets. For example, use the question: How do you spell the possessive form of children?

<u>Utilization:</u> In turn, players choose a category (noun, pronoun, possessive noun, possessive pronoun) and the pocket number from which they want to draw their question. If the player answers correctly, he gains the score listed in the pocket from which his card was drawn (5, 10, 15, 20, 25). If the player cannot answer the question, he forfeits his turn. The player accumulating the most points is the winner.

<u>Possessive Jeopardy Diagram</u>

Nouns	Pronouns	Possessive nouns	Possessive pronouns
5	5	5	5
10	10	10	10
15	15	15	15
20	20	20	20
25	25	25	25

CONTEXTUAL ANALYSIS STRATEGIES

25. Crosswords

<u>Goal</u>: Utilizing contextual <u>definitions</u>

<u>Grade level</u>: 3-6

<u>Construction</u>: Design a crossword puzzle in which students have to choose a word from a list to complete a sentence. The selected word is to be defined within the context of the sentence.

<u>Utilization</u>: The child completes each sentence and then writes the correct letters in the appropriate puzzle boxes.

Example: <u>censor</u>   <u>candy</u>   <u>car</u>

   1. A _____ is an official who examines a book.

   2. A piece of _____ is a sweet treat made with sugar.

   3. An automobile is often defined as a _____.

```
                    1.
                  ┌───┐
                  │ c │
                  ├───┤
                  │ e │
            ┌───┬─┼───┼───┬───┐
        2.  │ c │ a │ n │ d │ y │
            └───┴─┼───┼───┴───┘
                  │ s │
                  ├───┤
                  │ o │
            ┌───┬─┼───┤
        3.  │ c │ a │ r │
            └───┴───┴───┘
```

26. What's My Job?

<u>Goal</u>: Utilizing contextual <u>groupings</u>

<u>Grade level</u>: 4-6

<u>Construction</u>: Design a series of groupings that describes the uses of one instrument or the tasks of an occupation. The end of the sentence that tells the name of the instrument or occupation is omitted. Clickers or some sort of noisemaker will also be necessary.

<u>Utilization</u>: Divide the class into teams each consisting of five players. Each team is given a noisemaker to be used for signaling. The Master of Ceremonies reads the description and calls on the team who signals first with the noisemaker. The player must supply the missing word. If the player is correct, the team scores five points. If he is incorrect, the other team is allowed to answer. The team with the most points at the end of the game wins.

Examples:

> I water my cattle, feed my ducks, milk my cows, and gather my chicken eggs.
> I am a (farmer) .
>
> I read music, practice the piano, perform in public, and polish my flute. I am
> a (musician) .
>
> I am used to plow fields, pull wagons, plant seeds, and mow large fields.
> I am a (tractor) .

27. Don't Do What I Do

Goal: Utilizing contextual antonyms

Grade level: 1–3

Construction: Make up descriptive sentences that contain antonyms.

Utilization: Read a sentence containing antonyms and have members of the class act out the sentence at the same time showing opposite actions. For example: She laughed so hard she cried. One child would pantomime laughter and another child would pantomime crying.

28. Synonym Selection

Goal: Utilizing contextual synonyms

Grade level: 3–6

Construction: Design sentences that utilize synonyms to introduce or define unfamiliar words. Do not include the new word in the sentence context. Instead, construct a chart consisting of missing words and deceptive letters mixed vertically, horizontally, and diagonally.

Example:

1. I _____ to visit California. This restless longing never ends.
2. The old _____ is a tired female horse.
3. My grandmother is my mother's _____.

o	m	o	t	h	e	r
h	a	n	k	e	r	t
z	r	l	j	a	m	l
l	e	s	q	t	o	p

Utilization: Each child is given a dittoed copy of the sentences and word chart. The child reads the sentence and then looks to the chart and selects the missing synonym. The child circles the synonym and also writes it in the sentence.

29. Help the Mouse Find the Cheese

<u>Goal</u>: Utilizing contextual <u>summaries</u>

<u>Grade level</u>: 3–6

<u>Construction</u>: On a large piece of oak tag, draw a game board with small squares. At one end of the board draw a mouse, and at the opposite end draw a piece of cheese. Design a set of 3-x 5-inch cards that offer detailed, descriptive statements. A summary of each statement is written in various squares on the board. Secure buttons, beans, or other desired playing pieces.

<u>Utilization</u>: In turn, each player draws a descriptive card. After reading the descriptive statement, the student moves his playing piece to the square on the board that offers a summary statement. If the player cannot identify the summary statement, he returns his playing piece to "mouse" and awaits his next turn. The first player to reach the "cheese" wins the game. If a student selects a descriptive card, the summary of which would move him in reverse, he remains where he is if he can identify the summary square. If he cannot identify the summary square, he should be aided in doing so and returned to "mouse."

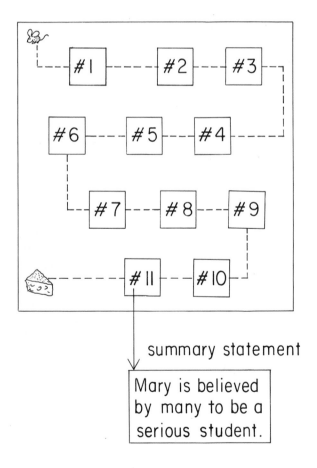

30. Add An Example

Goal: Utilizing contextual examples

Grade level: 4–6

Construction: Prepare a list of introductory sentences. One sentence should appear at the top of a blank sheet of paper.

Utilization: One paper, with an introductory sentence, is given to the first person in each row or at a learning center. The paper is passed throughout the group or row and each child adds an example that clarifies the introductory statement. When all groups have finished, the statements are read and one point is given for each acceptable example. The team receiving the most points wins.

Example:

> Linda is an ambitious girl.
> Linda has red hair.
> Linda does all her homework.
> Linda has read two books today.

31. Show Me

Goal: Utilizing contextual similes

Grade level: 2–5

Construction: Divide large pieces of drawing paper into sections. Design a series of sentences using similes with one word omitted.

Example: His voice sounded like the roar of a _____.

Utilization: A child selects a sentence and mentally fills in the blank. He then illustrates the sentence on a piece of drawing paper and labels the picture with the completed sentence.

32. Complete the Elephant

Goal: Utilizing contextual appositions

Grade level: 2–4

Construction: On the board, draw two outlines of an elephant's body minus trunk, tail, feet, and legs.

Utilization: Divide the class into two teams. In turn, a member from each team is given a sentence that contains a word in apposition. However, the main word has been replaced by a blank line. Each time a player is correct, he may add a new part of the elephant. Whichever team completes the elephant first wins. Later, more complicated animals could be used.

Example:

The _____, an instrument used in a baseball game, was thrown by the pitcher. (ball)

The _____, a soft sweet mixture, began to drip from the cone. (ice cream).

QUESTIONS AND RELATED READINGS

If at this time you do not feel that you have attained adequate knowledge to successfully answer the following questions, we would like to suggest related readings.

Goal 1: To aid students in understanding sight word strategies for analyzing unknown words.

Question: What are the appropriate ways to begin sight word instruction?

Durkin, D. *Teaching Them To Read.* Boston: Allyn and Bacon, 1974.

Heilman, A. *Principles and Practices of Teaching Reading.* Columbus, Ohio: Charles Merrill, 1972.

Ruddell, R. *Reading–Language Instruction.* Englewood Cliffs, N.J.: Prentice-Hall, 1974.

Goal 2: To aid students in understanding the role of structural analysis strategies in word recognition.

Question: Explain what is meant by structural analysis strategies.

Dallman, M. et al. *The Teaching of Reading*. New York: Holt, Rinehart and Winston, 1974.

Spache, G. and E. Spache. *Reading in the Elementary School*. Boston: Allyn and Bacon, 1973.

Thorndike, E. *The Teaching of English Suffixes*. New York: Bureau of Publications, Teachers College, Columbia University, 1932.

Goal 3: To aid students in understanding the role of contextual analysis strategies in word recognition.

Question: Explain contextual analysis strategies.

Biemiller, A. J. "The Development of the Use of Graphic and Contextual Information as Children Learn to Read." *Reading Research Quarterly*, 6 (1970), 75–96.

Guszak, F. *Diagnostic Reading Instruction in the Elementary School*. New York: Harper and Row, 1972.

Winagrad, T. "Understanding Natural Language." *Cognitive Psychology*, 3 (1972), 1–191.

BIBLIOGRAPHY

Burmeister, L. *Words—From Print to Meaning*. Reading, Mass.: Addison–Wesley, 1975.

Coleman, E. *Collecting a Data Base for an Educational Technology, Parts I and III*. El Paso, Texas: University of Texas, 1967.

Ernst, M. *Words*. 3rd edition, New York: Knopf, 1955.

Fairbanks, G. *Experimental Phonetics: Selected Articles*. Urbana, Ill.: University of Illinois Press, 1966.

Fries, Charles C. *Linguistics and Reading*. New York: Holt, Rinehart and Winston, 1963.

Gleason, Jean B. "Language Development in Early Childhood." In *Oral Language and Reading*, edited by James Walden. Champaign, Illinois: National Council of Teachers of English, 1969.

Guszak, F. *Diagnostic Reading Instruction in the Elementary School*. New York: Harper and Row, 1972.

Kucera, H. and W. Francis. *Computational Analysis of Present-Day American English*. Providence, R.I.: Brown University Press, 1967.

Marchbanks, B. and H. Levin. "Cues by Which Children Recognize Words." *Journal of Educational Psychology*, 56 (1965), 57–61.

McHugh, J. "Words Most Useful in Reading." Compiled at California State University, Hayward, 1969.

Murphy, H. and D. Durrell. *Speech to Print Phonics*. New York: Harcourt, Brace, Jovanovich Inc., 1972.

Murphy, H. and D. Durrell. *Letters in Words*. Wellesley, Mass.: Curriculum Associates, Inc., 1970.

Ruddell, R. *Reading-Language Instruction*. Englewood Cliffs, N.J.: Prentice-Hall, 1974.

Shuy, R. "Some Relationships of Linguistics to the Reading Process," *Teachers' Edition of How It Is Nowadays,* by T. Clymer and R. Ruddell of the Reading 360 Series, © copyright 1973, by Ginn and Company. Used with permission.

Spache, George D. and Evelyn Spache. *Readings in the Elementary School*. Boston: Allyn and Bacon, 1973.

Webster Collegiate Dictionary. "Vocabulary of Rhymes." Springfield, Mass.: G. & C. Merriam Company, 1970.

9

Comprehending written discourse

A learned fool is one who has read everything, and simply remembered it.

Josh Billings

GOALS: To aid the reader in understanding:
1. processes involved in reading comprehension.
2. comprehension as a thinking process.
3. the role of questioning in the development of reading comprehension.
4. the need for rethinking current theories of comprehension.
5. the various types of classroom practices that aid children in developing comprehension skills.

Reading is comprehension; if you have not comprehended, you have not read. We should not ask a person to read for reading's sake, but rather, we should ask that someone read for some purpose, some goal. In order to accomplish this goal, the reader has to extract meaning from the text. The meaning which the reader extracts may be acquired from explicit text information and/or from his knowledge and experience of the world.

Figure 1. "I want a book that starts out, 'Once upon a time' and ends with, "They lived happily ever after." (Reprinted by permission of the artist.)

As Stauffer (1969) and many other reading educators have suggested, reading is a thinking process in which the reader has to be an active participant. Passivity and successful reading comprehension are mutually exclusive. Jenkins (1974) maintains that reading comprehension is closely linked with memory; memory is an integral part of comprehending. He suggests that what is best remembered is that which has been experienced:

> I think we will eventually conclude that the mind remembers what the mind *does*, not what the word does. That is, experience is the mind at work, not the active world impinging on a passive organism—and experience is what will be remembered. (p. 11)

The proficient reader processes written material by performing many operations during reading. Some of these operations are performed on the text and
some of them relate to his knowledge of the world. It has been demonstrated
that readers must process (infer) before they can extract meaning from texts
(Flood and Lapp, 1977). This processing, an interaction between the reader's
knowledge and the text, is an indivisible whole. The proficient reader knows
from the text and from his world knowledge that the following operations must
be performed to extract meaning:

> The text says: The duck is ready to eat.
>
> Operation #1:   The reader must resolve the ambiguity of this sentence.
>
> Operation #2:   Word knowledge (experience)
> 1. The reader enumerates the possibilities of the meaning of the
>   sentence.
>   a. The duck is ready to eat corn, his supper, a worm . . . .
>
> OR
>
>   b. Andy has finished cooking and the duck is ready to be eaten.
> 2. The reader waits for more contextual information from the
>   passage. Keep reading.
>
> The text says: The duck is ready to eat. He always squawks to announce to the
> farmer that he is hungry.
>
> Operation #3:   The reader extracts the implicit meaning of the first sentence, i.e.,
> the duck is ready to eat something.

All of this happens in a moment. The time it takes is not the critical element; however, the active participation of the reader in the process is absolutely
critical for comprehension. Thorndike (1917) discussed the importance of
recognizing reading as an active, participatory process:

> Understanding a paragraph is like solving a problem in mathematics. It consists in
> selecting the right elements of the situation and putting them together in the right
> relations, and also with the right amount of weight or influence or force for each. The
> mind is assailed as it were by every word in the paragraph. It must select, repress, soften,
> emphasize, correlate and organize, all under the influence of the right mental set of
> purpose or demands. (p. 329)

Theories of Reading Comprehension

Although we know that reading comprehension has to be an active process—
the reader must work—we still do not have a totally adequate explanation of
how reading comprehension works. In recent years, many researchers have
attempted to explain the processes involved in comprehending written discourse.
In the next few pages we will present some current theories. It is extremely
important for us to attempt to understand as much as we can about the nature
of reading comprehension in order to plan appropriate reading curricula. Too

frequently, we permit the curriculum to dictate our instructional program. It would be far better for you, the teacher, to decide for yourself what is involved in the reading comprehension process and to plan appropriate instruction based on your own findings. In this way, your teaching of reading will become focused and efficient.

One engages in the act of reading when one comprehends written thoughts. This is not a new concept. As early as 1920, reading educators defined the process of reading as "thought-getting" (Farr, 1971). Kingston (1961) further extended our understanding of reading comprehension when he stated, "Reading comprehension can best be understood as a product of communications that result from interaction between the reader and writer (p. 10). Even more recently, Trabasso (1972) and Chase and Clark (1972) present comprehension as information processing, while Dawes (1966) and Frederikson (1972) have generated reading comrpehension theories which illustrate the analysis of connected logical discourse. Other researchers such as Gough (1972), La Berge and Samuels (1974), Goodman (1968), Smith (1971), and Rumelhart (1976) have also developed theories which explicate the reading process.

As you read each of the following theories of comprehension you should ask yourself:

1. Has the designer of the theory established his reader's purposes for reading? Purpose will dictate the style of reading and the strategies that will be used to extract the desired information. For example, when we open a telephone book to get a number, we do not want to know the number of every person on the page. We just want one piece of information.

2. Has the designer of the theory discussed the differences in types of texts? The reader probably uses different strategies for reading a poem than he uses for reading the newspaper. For example, we know that stories have identifiable episodic structures that consist of particular categories of propositions. Propositions, which will be explained later in this chapter, are statements that contain a single idea; for example, Daryl has a son can be broken down into several propositions:

   Daryl is a male.
   Daryl is a father.
   Daryl has a child.
   The child is male.

   In a story these propositions have temporal (time) and spatial (space) constraints. We also know that stories usually contain information that is directly relevant to human experience and to the resolution of internal conflict. Readers who have this knowledge of stories approach them with well defined expectations and specific strategies that are different from the strategies they use when reading non-narrative materials. Readers have strategies for non-story forms of discourse that are acquired as a result of their knowledge about the purposes of these kinds of discourse: exposition, persuasion, instruction, description.

3. Has the designer of the theory described the reader: his age, his reading experience, and so on?

Reading As Information Processing

Trabasso's Theory (1972)

Trabasso defines comprehension as:

> . . . a set of psychological processes consisting of a series of mental operations which process linguistic information from its receipt until an overt decision. Two main operations are noted: (1) encoding the information into internal representations and (2) comparing these representations. . . . Comprehension may be said to occur when the internal representations are matched. The overt response (true) is an end result of the act of comprehension. (1972, p. 113)

Trabasso's definition clearly presents a stage theory which assumes that the sequence of information processing on the part of the reader is not instant, since he manipulates the surface structure (subject and matching referential event) of a sentence, which affects the encoding and comparison processes. An operative example of this stage theory is provided by Trabasso through a sentence verification task, in which the reader is directed to compare either the sentence

The ball is red.

OR

The ball is not red.

with a picture of a ball which is either red or blue. The time it takes to process the information in this sentence can be predicted, since it depends on the number of encoding, matching, and recoding operations required of the reader.

Stage 1. encodes the sentence in the form of an internal representation. A sentence expressed as a negation may involve the encoding of "false" as a separate property.

Stage 2. encodes the picture and then compares the graphic and pictorial representations to determine if they match. If they do not match, the reader may have to recode.

Stage 3. formulates a "true" or "false" response.

A breakdown in the comprehension process is believed by Trabasso to be possible whenever a link in this sequence of stages is missed by the reader.

Chase and Clark's Theory (1972)

Further understanding of comprehension as information processing has been provided through the research of Chase and Clark (1972) in which a reader was asked to match the sentence:

The cross is above the star.

with a picture having a negative or positive correspondence. A picture might look like:

The researchers concluded that (1) encoding, comparing, and recoding were the stages involved in this information processing; (2) a negative correspondence required a longer process of encoding than positive correspondences; and (3) comprehension of both pictures and sentences is depicted in the exact mental symbolic system.

Rumelhart's Theory (1976)

Rumelhart has generated a computer theory based on what he calls interactive stages. The representation is given in Figure 2.

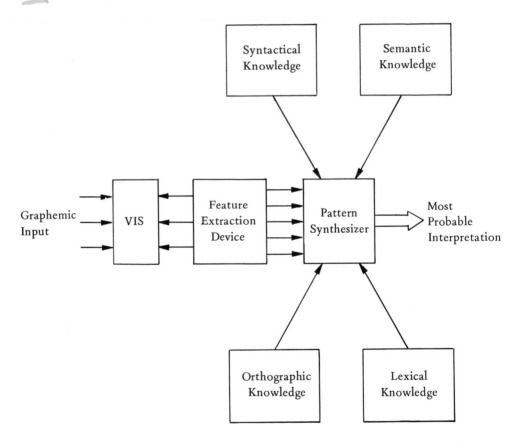

Figure 2. Rumelhart's Theory

The unique factor about Rumelhart's theory is that is provides for both top-down and bottom–up processing. The theory predicts that a reader begins with graphemic input to guide the extraction of meaning. The reader can assume features and proceed with meaning first and then move to verification of features and word patterns.

Rumelhart (1976) presents five implications of his theory:

1. Perception of letters depends on the surrounding letters.
2. Perception of words depends on the syntactic environments in which they are encountered.
3. Perception of words depends on the semantic environments in which they are encountered.
4. Perception of syntax depends on semantic context in which word strings are encountered.
5. Interpretation of meaning of the material depends on the general context in which the text is encountered.

As Rumelhart (1976) has pointed out, his theory is not as strict as Gough's model because the bypassing of some stages does not make it a total serial processing (element by element; each element is received in order) model. However, it does not have "top-down" capabilities as a theory.

Reading As Analysis of Connected Logical Discourse

Dawes' Theory (1966)

Dawes (1966) in a study of reading comprehension suggested that declarative statements assert set relationships. Such relationships that primarily exist between subject and predicate class involve identity, exclusion, inclusion, and disjunction. Set relations which include the message of a passage may be expressed in multiple ways. Therefore, memory for the relations need not be specified verbal units of grammatical structures. Dawes believed that by testing recall or recognition of a set relationship one could better understand memory or distortion of presented information. He suggested that two sets of information could have a structured or *nested* relationship if knowledge of one set provided information regarding a second set. He used the following sentences to illustrate a structured or nested relationship:

> All men wear trousers.
> Some girls wear trousers.

Knowledge that someone is a man allows the reader to instantly identify him with trousers, whereas knowing that someone is a female does not provide this instant knowing. Therefore, sentence one is nested, whereas sentence two is disjunctive or semantically independent of the first premise, *some* girls. Dawes believes that the reader will optimize structure, thereby reducing information. However, if a reader remembers a disjunctive relationship as a nested one, he has incorrectly *overgeneralized.* Dawes believes that readers made more errors of this type than the error of remembering a nested relation as disjunctive (pseudodiscrimination). Both types of error related to the semantic structure of the passage.

Frederiksen's Theory (1972)

A second theory of comprehension based on connected logical discourse is that of Frederiksen. Frederiksen's theory of discourse analysis is based on an analysis of propositions; it has evolved from an application of Fillmore's case grammar theory. Case grammar, developed by Charles Fillmore (1968), presents an interesting alternative. Grimes (1975) has taken the principles of case grammar and has extended them to the discourse of a paragraph, not just words and sentences as is done by the transformational grammarians. Semantics and syntax are tied together in case grammar, using terms like *agent of the sentence, patient,* and *instrument.* It reflects some of our traditional notions of subject verb, and object. Throughout, syntax is viewed as an aid to meaning. Fillmore states:

> The case notions comprise a set of universal, presumably innate concepts which identify certain types of judgments human beings are capable of making about the events that are going on around them, judgments about such matters as who did it, who it happened to, and what got changed. (1968, p. 24)

The following sentence, for example, would be described in this manner:

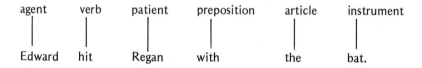

agent	verb	patient	preposition	article	instrument
Edward	hit	Regan	with	the	bat.

Explanation of Frederiksen's theory involves the study of the following content units:

1. Concept—the smallest element of semantic content.
2. Relation—the second element of content, which involves simple, compound, or nested relationships between two or more concepts.
3. Implication—the third element of content, which is defined as two or more propositions ("if . . . then" relations).
4. Semantic structure—the fourth element of content, which is composed of implications and systems of relationships.

These four content units are necessary as the reader attempts the following processing events: *input and production, verification, transformation, storage, and retrieval and output.*

Alternative Models of Reading

Gough's Model (1972)

Gough proposed a serial model with a set of linear, independent stages of processing. The diagram in Figure 3 illustrates his model. Gough suggests that

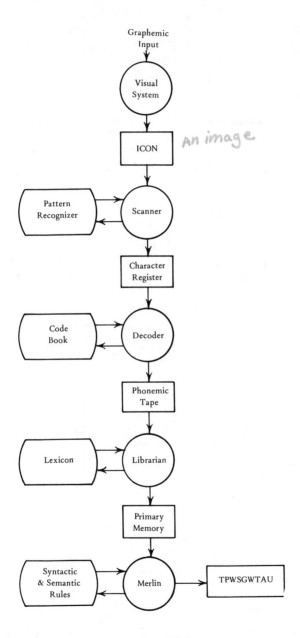

Figure 3. Gough's Model (1972)

reading proceeds letter-by-letter to word formation and phonemic representations. Lexical meanings are grouped into sentential units and interpreted by
the individual's processing mechanism of syntactic and semantic information.
Sentences are stored in TPWSGWTAU. Most of Gough's discussion focuses on
word recognition and lexical interpretation of Figure 3. visual system, pattern
organizer, phonemic tape. Higher level comprehension processes are not discussed because they are not sharply defined *outside* of the reading process. He
rejects the notion of "top down" processing which suggests beginning to teach
reading with the childs existing knowledge of the world. His model is prototypic
of the "bottom-up" type which suggests beginning to teach reading from the
graphic representation of the orthography. He does not believe that readers
use any guessing strategies to facilitate reading.

In Gough's model there are no immediate implications for comprehension
research *in reading*. What must be done is to investigate both the "individual
processing mechanism" and the TPWSGWTAU storage. Gough's model seems
to be useful only as a model of what skilled readers do. The early processing
stages are quite precise, but comprehension stages are rather imprecise.

LaBerge and Samuels' Model (1974)

This model is one of the first models to use automaticity. Automaticity
theory assumes that reading is divided into two general skills: decoding and
comprehension. It further assumes that attention is required to perform either
of these skills. In this model the authors suggest that only a fixed amount of
attention is available during processing. Until decoding is "automated," comprehension suffers. They maintain that extra attention can be diverted to comprehension when decoding is mastered. A representation of the model is given
in Figure 4.

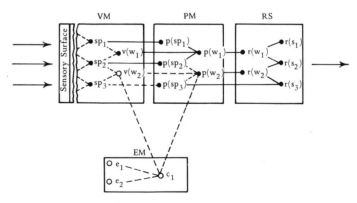

Figure 4. LaBerge and Samuels' Model (1974)

There are three stages that are strictly relevant to reading: (1) Visual feature
detectors and recognizers, (2) phonological interpreters, and (3) semantic interpreters. Units are processed individually or in groups in each of these stages.

This too is a "bottom–up" model. It assumes that *all* reading must begin with a visual input and end with a semantic interpretation.

What implications are there in this model for research in comprehension? One implication is the manipulation of decoding ability; comprehension should vary directly with this ability if the model is accurate and episodic cues should facilitate semantic interpretation. Semantic interpretation, however, should not have any effect on visual feature identifications.

This model is useful except for the top–down processing capabilities of competent readers. However, it falls short on precision when it deals with attention allocation and sufficient rules for bypassing processing stages.

Goodman's Model (1968)

This model is included for the sake of comparison. It consists of three "proficiency levels" which correspond to skills levels of the readers. At the highest level of proficiency, Goodman claims that the focus is on meaning; decoding is automatic, and reading is structured by oral language. A representation of this model is illustrated in Figure 5 on page 294.

In this form, Goodman's model is almost a strict "top–down" process. There is virtually no cue usage from the graphic input. Goodman's model is limited because almost any finding can be accounted for in the model, i.e., he views oral language as the basis for meaning in reading and, therefore, he contends that errors in reading can almost always be interpreted as "miscues" rather than mistakes. An example of this phenomenon which illustrates that his model is a "top–down" model is the acceptance of the lexical item "mommy" for "mother" in an oral reading situation. It is viewed as a miscue based on the assumption that the child may not have "mother" in his lexicon or that "mommy" is his preferred lexical item for this concept.

Smith's Model (1971)

In Smith's model of reading, he rejects the notion that reading is a decoding of printed words to spoken language. He rejects the theory:

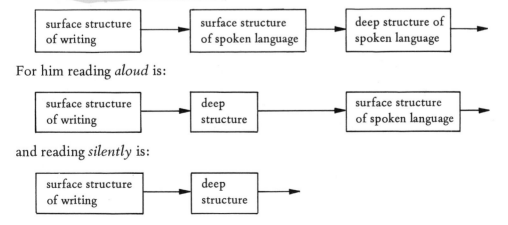

For him reading *aloud* is:

and reading *silently* is:

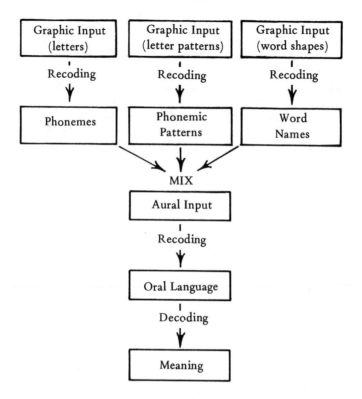

Proficiency Level 1

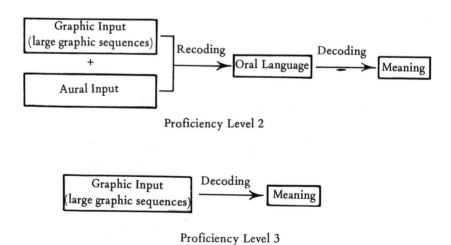

Proficiency Level 2

Proficiency Level 3

Figure 5. Goodman's Model

Smith

He believes comprehension must precede the identification of individual words. As an example of this phenomenon, he uses the following sentence: "We should *read* the *minute* print on the *permit*." None of the underlined words can be articulated until they have been understood in context. He explains that we have acquired information from an average span of four to five words ahead of and behind the actual words which we are reading in order to read aloud with comprehension and comprehensibility. He points out that experimental findings have reported that there is an eye–voice span of approximately four to five words, such that if the lights are extinguished on an oral reader, the reader will be able to recite the next four to five words of the text that he is reading. This occurs, he believes, because the reader had sampled words beyond the word which he was pronouncing when the lights went out.

Smith also believes that only a small part of the information necessary for reading comprehension comes from the printed page. He states: "The more that is known behind the eyeball, the less that is required to identify a letter, word, or meaning from the text." Conversely, when the material is more unfamiliar and the language is more complex, the reader may be unable to comprehend what he has read. In short, he is relying heavily upon the visual stimuli of the passage.

The actual process of reading for the competent adult reader is illustrated in the following diagram:

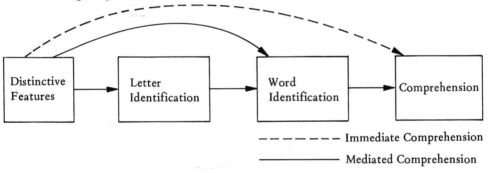

The main limitation of this view, however, is that it does not account for three well known phenomena:

1. The child who has never seen most of the words that he knows.
2. The fluent reader who encounters words he has never before seen.
3. The second language learner whose aural/oral repertoire exceeds his visual repertoire.

Throughout the presentation of these models, have you been attempting to answer our original query, which was: What are the processes involved in affective, mature reading comprehension? As you have observed from your attempts, the answering of this question is not easy since there are many theories which have been generated in an attempt to provide insights into reading processes. Understanding and integrating all of these theories is an undertaking that you cannot master by an introductory reading of this chapter; however, you have begun the task. Let's continue our study by discussing the historical development of several educators' understandings of comprehension processes.

Literal, Inferential, Critical Reading Comprehension

The preceding models illustrate some of the most current theories of reading comprehension. Many of these theories have been translated into practices based on the idea that there are 3 levels of comprehension; these levels are usually called *literal* (on the line) comprehension, *inferential* (between the lines) comprehension, and *critical* (beyond the lines) comprehension. This distinction was sometimes useful because it divided the whole world of comprehension into three manageable categories. However, many problems arose from this design because educators began to think linearly about these three levels, assuming that they represented three levels of difficulty. It was assumed that these three levels were hierarchically ordered, and that literal comprehension was easier than inferential comprehension, which in turn, was easier than critical comprehension.

This idea was probably the function of reading educators' attempts to model comprehension processes in a manner similar to the way that Bloom modeled levels of cognitive functioning. Figure 6 illustrates the way reading educators attempted to create a taxonomy of reading objectives based on Bloom's notions:

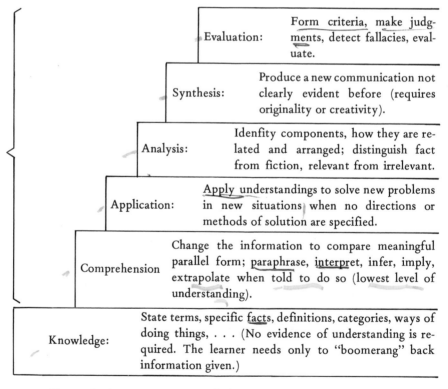

Evaluation:	Form criteria, make judgments, detect fallacies, evaluate.
Synthesis:	Produce a new communication not clearly evident before (requires originality or creativity).
Analysis:	Idenfity components, how they are related and arranged; distinguish fact from fiction, relevant from irrelevant.
Application:	Apply understandings to solve new problems in new situations when no directions or methods of solution are specified.
Comprehension	Change the information to compare meaningful parallel form; paraphrase, interpret, infer, imply, extrapolate when told to do so (lowest level of understanding).
Knowledge:	State terms, specific facts, definitions, categories, ways of doing things, . . . (No evidence of understanding is required. The learner needs only to "boomerang" back information given.)

Figure 6. Bloom's Taxonomy of educational objectives.

Bloom's taxonomy presents learning as a developmental process in which each category of the hierarchy became progressively more difficult. Mastery of one category may be dependent upon the preceding category.

According to Bloom, which category of thinking would a child be dealing with if he were asked to

1. _____ interpret data given in a graph? (comprehension)

2. _____ determine relevant data for a persuasive argument? (synthesis)

3. _____ state the seasonal elements needed to harvest corn? (knowledge)

4. _____ detect untrue statements in a newspaper selection? (evaluation)

As a classroom teacher, you can select a topic (e.g., consumerism, prey–predator relationships) and prepare a series of activities that will aid children in developing the evaluative thinking abilities that Bloom suggests are important to learning.

Some reading educators have suggested that Bloom's taxonomy of educational objectives is closely related to the hierarchy of learning that encompasses the comprehension processes. In the past, researchers in reading have based reading comprehension taxonomies on Bloom's taxonomy. These schemata were like the following:

Levels of cognitive development	Reading comprehension
	Text Explicit Information
Knowledge (recall)	(literal comprehension)
	Identification of
	sounds
	letters
	phrases
	sentences
	paragraphs
	Recognition and recall of
	details
	main ideas
	sequence
	comparison
	cause-and-effect relationships
	character traits
	patterns
Comprehension (understanding)	Translation of ideas or information explicitly stated:
	classifying
	generalizing
	outlining
	summarizing
	synthesizing
	Text Implicit Information
Application (abstracting)	(inferential comprehension)
	Realization of one's experiences and Textual exposures

Inferring:
  details
  main ideas
  sequence
  comparisons
  cause-and-effect relationships
  character traits

Analysis   →   Predicting outcomes
(analyzing)

Synthesis   Interpreting figurative language,
(production)   Imagery, character, motives, and
                                 responses
                               Synthesizing:
                                  convergently
                                  divergently

                        →   World Knowledge Information

Evaluation   (critical comprehension)
(judging)
                             Making evaluative judgments of
                                reality or fantasy
                                fact or opinion
                                adequacy and validity
                                appropriateness
                                worth, desirability, and
                                acceptability
                             Valuing
                           Propaganda detection:
                                euphemism
                                fallacy of reasoning
                                statistical fallacy (maps, charts)
                                stereotyping
                                oversimplification

                         Appreciation

                         Emotional response to content
                         Identification with characters or incidents
                         Reactions to the author's use of language
                         Reactions to the author's word pictures

---

Sources of Reading Comprehension

Because the three-part division of literal, inferential, and critical comprehension is still used by many publishers of reading comprehension tests and reading texts, it may be useful for you to think of this categorization scheme as an attempt to divide the sources of reading comprehension into three very important components:

> Literal comprehension—extracted from text explicit information
> Inferential comprehension—extracted from text implicit information
> Critical comprehension—extracted from world knowledge (experience)

There are two major objections to a three-level (literal, inferential, and critical comprehension) classification scheme:

1. It is assumed that there is a linear progression of difficulty in these three levels of comprehension, and it is assumed that tasks that measure comprehension can be correctly labeled as literal, inferential, or critical.

2. This scheme only takes the source of comprehension into consideration. It does not take into account the dynamic, active process of comprehension in which the reader participates. The operations of the learner during the reading process are ignored in this three-level scheme.

The first objection, the assumption that there is a linear progression of difficulty in these three levels of comprehension which can be labeled literal, inferential, or critical, stems from certain current discoveries. Let us try to determine the level that each of the following questions are measuring:

Text

(1) Zoe and Zeke, two talented masons, were building an internal fireplace for a cantankerous architect. (2) The architect was inflexible with his prints, insisting that the measurements had to be absolutely perfect despite his annoying habit of altering the plans every 20 minutes. (3) After three hours of utter frustration, Zoe and Zeke thought they understood the plans. (4) As they started to lay the foundation, the architect decided he wanted an external fireplace and announced: "I think your work is unprofessional. You're fired." (5) Zoe and Zeke, quite flabbergasted, said: "Sir, you are a poor excuse for an architect and the bane of all craftsmen. Your sense of professionalism is a sham."

L, I, C

_____ 1. How many times did the architect alter the plans while Zoe and Zeke were working?

_____ 2. Why did the architect tell the masons that they were unprofessional?

_____ 3. What was the masons' reaction to being fired?

_____ 4. When did the masons understand that the architect was troublesome?

The entire passage is straightforward and comprehensible. The details of the story are explicit and the characterizations of the architect and the masons are direct and thorough (for interpreting the author's point of view). However, the four questions, while easily answered, are quite difficult to label as literal, inferential, or critical. The source for the answer to each question is in the text, thereby making the question appear to be a test of literal comprehension, but the exact answer is not in the text. For example:

> Question: How many times did the architect alter the plans while Zoe and Zeke were working?

Text source: The architect was inflexible with his prints, insisting that the measurements had to be absolutely perfect despite his annoying habit
of altering the plans every 20 minutes. After three hours of utter
frustration, Zoe and Zeke thought they understood the plans.

Operation: Convert 3 hours into 180 minutes. Divide 20 minutes into 180
minutes to arrive at the answer: 9 times.

The answer is not explicitly stated in the text; the reader is called upon to
perform certain arithmetic operations beyond the text. Therefore, you may be
tempted to label the question inferential. However, it is clear that the reader
has to operationalize his previous knowledge (arithmetic computation) to
answer the question. Does this straying from the text qualify the question for
the label critical comprehension?

The difficulty of assigning the correct label is at once apparent and unnecessary. We have carefully explained the entire process of answering the question
without giving the question a label. This strongly suggests that we should be investigating the *processes* involved in answering the question (in comprehending)
and that we may be wasting our time by fighting over inappropriate and misleading labels.

Operations During Reading Comprehension

A second objection to a three-level classification scheme proposed by some
reading educators is that it only takes the source of comprehension into consideration. This is a reasonable objection because this scheme does not account
for the multiplicity of operations in which the reader participates. Let us
illustrate this point by analyzing several operations that are involved in answering these seemingly literal questions:

Question: What did Zoe and Zeke do for a living?

Text source: two talented masons

Operations: a. The reader has to understand apposition, i.e., Zoe and Zeke, two
talented masons means that Zoe and Zeke are two talented masons.
b. The reader has to process synonymy: Step 1, "do for a living" =
occupation/job; Step 2, occupation/job = masons.

While the question is easily answered, the sophistication and complexity of
the operations suggests that a facile label like "literal comprehension" is an inadequate descriptor for the entire process of comprehension. Rather, it seems
important to examine each of the steps involved in the processing of the original
story, the processing of the question, and the formulation of a correct answer.

It is extremely important to begin to unravel some of the processes involved
in proficient comprehension. An appropriate way to begin this unraveling is to
examine the operations of the reader during reading episodes. We know the
following facts about readers:

(1) Reader processes propositions and not sentences. A proposition is a
relational structure established by a predicate term and one or more argument
terms; e.g., in the sentence *Kirk's son, Jake, is an intelligent boy*, there are at
least six propositions:

Kirk is a father.
Kirk has a son.
The son is Jake.
Jake has a father.
Jake is a boy.
Jake is intelligent.

These propositions are not consciously articulated by the reader, but unconsciously the reader attends to these as propositions. In this model of reading, it is suggested that the reader is ready to accept anything that follows logically from these propositions—e.g., Jake can count backwards—but the readers is also prepared to carefully examine new information which does not logically follow from these propositions—e.g., Jake is a girl.

(2) All readers process (infer) regardless of memory demands (Flood and Lapp, 1977).

(3) Readers attend to certain semantic and/or syntactic elements in the initial proposition of texts (Flood, 1978; Clements, 1976; Trabasso, 1972). An example of this phenomenon was reported by Flood (1978) when he asked proficient readers to supply the second sentence for two passages which began in the following ways:

Passage A	Passage B
Christmas always meant going to Grandma's house.	One of the oldest drinks to man is milk.

In Passage A, all readers wrote in a similar personal, narrative (reminiscent) style, supplying a second highly descriptive sentence about the event of Christmas. In Passage B, all readers supplied a data-filled sentence using a formal non-narrative style.

All proficient readers seem to participate in similar operations during comprehension. Most proficient readers, after being exposed to the following two sentences:

Mary is crying, shaking, and trembling.
Her bicycle is on the ground.

will probably infer something like: "Mary is upset because she fell off her bicycle." The operations in which the reader participates can be described in the following way:

OPERATIONS

Type	Example
1. Clarification of anaphoric referent.	her bicycle - Mary's bicycle
2. Superordination of strings of lexical items.	crying, shaking, and trembling = upset
3. Inferring causality	Mary is crying, shaking, and trembling BECAUSE SHE FELL OFF HER BICYCLE WHICH IS on the ground.

Frederiksen (1977) suggests that there are 26 types of operations, which he calls inferences. These inferences are important for proficient reading, and there are certain conditions that elicit these operations. Some of the conditions that elicit processing (operations) in reading are the following:

Type	Example
1. Ambiguity in sentences and clauses.	Flying planes can be dangerous. I like her cooking. She fed her dog biscuits.
2. Unclear anaphoric referents.	Zoe and Zeke were masons. They were paid by Vera and Velma. They were inflexible.
3. Unclear cataphoric referents.	It was a day in spring. The month when Jim lost his job.
4. Unclear deictic referents. (person, place, time).	Paula and Patrick were meeting in the afternoon for food. Patrick was so late that Paula left.
5. Unclear topical referents.	It was always this way. They had so much fun when they went there that they decided to return again.
6. Partial lexicalization.	The set disappeared.
7. Missing connective.	Tony drove too fast. The police didn't care about the emergency.
8. Unclear segmentation.	Maria went to the fire station. Bernard and Maria lived happily ever after. They got the firemen to help them put out the fire.
9. Need for reduction.	Tom was whining, coughing, vomiting, crying, tossing.
10. Need for extensions	Emma lost her tooth. Her father put her quarter in her piggy bank.
11. Pragmatic considerations.	The house was 80 years old and the crew arrived.

Although we are only at the threshold in our understanding of reading comprehension, we are coming to some agreement that we need to specify the operations that the reader must perform if he is to read with proficiency. Frederiksen (1976) has offered us a first step over the threshold by specifying 26 types of operations as shown on pages 303 and 304.

While Frederiksen's approach has been extremely helpful, there are certain limitations to his system. The following system, designed by Flood (1977), is an attempt to create a scheme that is based directly on data collected from reader's processing of texts. These data were collected from readers of three age ranges (12 years old to adulthood, cf. Flood and Lapp, 1977). Chart I consists of nine operations that were used by readers and observed by researchers in each of these studies. Chart II specifies subcategories for each of the nine categories.

TYPE OF OPERATION	DEFINITION	EXAMPLE	
		Actual Text	Recalled Text
Lexical Operation			
1. Lexical expansion	Expanding a concept into one or more propositions	The child is sick.	The child is vomiting, sore, feverish.
2. Lexicalization	Replacing a proposition with a lexical concept	The child is vomiting, sore, feverish.	The child is sick.
Identification Operation			
3. Attribute inference	Specifying an attribute	The boy has a bicycle.	The boy has a big bicycle.
4. Category inference	Classifying an object or action	Joan is buying an outfit.	Joan is buying a skirt and sweater outfit.
5. Time inference	Specifying a time	She is watering the roses.	She was watering the roses.
6. Locative inference	Specifying location	She is watering the roses.	Mary is watering the roses in the garden.
7. Part structure	Specifying part of an object	She is watering the roses.	She is watering the roots of the roses.
8. Degree inference	Specifying the degree of an attribute, e.g., very	We'll put them in a vase.	We'll put them in a nice vase.
Frame Operation			
9. Act inference	Filling in an action	Father will be sad.	Father will feel sad.
10. Case inference	Inferring agent or instrument	a. Agent—Now the junk is all put away	a. Agent—Karen was putting away the party favors.
		b. Instrument—Tom hit the boy.	b. Instrument—Tom hit the boy with the bat.
11. Instrumental inference	Generating a cause of an event	Paula got well.	Dr. Ryan made Paula well.
12. Result inference	Generating the result of an action	Take some of mine.	Sadie, you can have some of mine.
13. Source inference	Inferring a prior state	Jimmy, you don't have a soda.	Take some of mine.
14. Goal inference	Generating a goal for an action	Bobby cleaned his room	Bobby cleaned his room so his father wouldn't get mad.

	Operation	Description	Example	Result
15.	Theme inference	Generating a theme	Let's fix the mistake.	Mitchell rebuilds the structure.
16.	Frame transformation	Transforming a frame of one type into a frame of another type	NVN_1—John bought shoes.	VN_2N_1—Buy shoes, John.
17.	Disembedding operation	Removing a proposition from an event frame	He wants to take a vacation.	He . . . went to New England.
18.	Embedding operation	Inserting a proposition into an event frame	This is Pearl. She is buying a boat.	Pearl want to buy a boat.
	Macrostructure Operation			
20.	Superordinate inference	New, more general proposition	He is sick.	He is vomiting, feverish, and cranky.
21.	Subordinate inference	More specific propositions	He is vomiting, feverish, and cranky.	He is sick.
	Event Generation			
19.	Event inference	10 subtypes, corresponding to the different slots (processive and resultive event frames).	The parade was held on Tuesday.	The parade of the clowns was postponed until Tuesday because it rained on Monday.
	Algebraic Operation			
22.	Algebraic inference	Metric (degree) or nonmetric	A little boy was watering the flowers and then he ran down the lane.	A little boy watered the flowers and ran down the lane
	Dependency Operations			
23.	Causal inferences	Connect unconnected events with causal relations	Tony was washing the windows and crashed and broke the vase.	Because Tony was washing the window carelessly, he fell and broke the window.
24.	Conditional inferences	Specify antecedent conditions for an event	Now Sara thinks that Bootie will be sad. She wants to hug him.	She thought he might be sad.
25.	Logical inferences	Specify the logic of the inferences	It's lightning outside.	It's lightning outside; it must be raining.
	Truth Value Operation			
26.	Truth value operation	Qualification or negation	Peter hurt Amy.	He thought she might be mad.

CHART I

Operations of Readers	Text	Example Recall
I. generating text identical information identical recall of information written in the text	Jason was a lawyer.	Jason was a lawyer.
II. generating macro or microstructures creating larger or smaller units to accommodate text information	animals	bears, tigers, horses
III. generating cause establishing preceding or succeeding information that can place an event within a framework that the reader can tolerate	Jason left Chicago.	A perennial quitter, Jason left Chicago because his law practice was failing.
IV. generating dimension creating a temporal, spatial, manner framework for an event	Jason left.	Jason quickly left Chicago in 1970.
V. accommodating referents establishing appropriate referents for ambiguous text elements	Jason was an engineer. His fellow architects praised him.	Jason was an architectural engineer.
VI. generating case frames creating case frameworks for text elements	Jason said, "I hit the wall."	Jason said to his fellow architects: "I hit the wall with a bulldozer."
VII. generating attributes creating modifications for actors, events, places or dimensions	Jason was an engineer.	Jason was a very enthusiastic engineer.
VIII. generating text erroneous information making incorrect inferences	Jason, once a lawyer, became an accountant.	Jason studied architecture, but practiced nothing.
IX. generating text external information using established conventions for recall that do not convey information	Jason was a lawyer.	I don't know why Jason was what he was.

Each category has several subcategories. The generic category and each of its subsets with explanations and examples are presented below:

CHART II

Complete Scoring System	Text	Recall
		Example
	Text	*Recall*
I. generating text identical information	soda	soda
II. generating macro/micro structures	couch	sofa
1. synonymy-a narrowly defined category; traditionally acceptable synonyms. This category assumes a high degree of rater reliability. Synonyms can be conventionally acceptable like couch/sofa (Thesaurus) or text specific		
2. colloquial (figurative)synonym-acceptable synonym within a specific context	dollar	buck
3. superordinate recall of the larger unit to which text element belongs	bear	animal
4. subordinate recall of smaller unit of which text element is a part	flower	daisy
5. categorization generation of larger concept that encompasses several text elements	uniforms, drums, batons, marching people	parade
III. generating cause		
1. text proactive extracting previous information from text that explains events as effects of causes	Jason was a lawyer. He became a dentist.	Jason realized he made a mistake.
2. text retroactive extracting subsequent information from text that explains an event as a cause	Jason liked Chicago. Jason moved to Cheyenne where he enjoyed his business.	Jason moved from Chicago to Cheyenne because he didn't like his job in Chicago.

Complete Scoring System

	Text	Recall
		Example
3. experience proactive presumptions about events that preceded and caused the existing event	Jason's business was successful.	Jason's family gave him a great deal of money.
4. experience retroactive assumptions about events that succeeded the existing event	Jason's business was successful.	Jason was successful as a lawyer after he sold his business and converted his business assets into client contacts.
IV. generating dimension		
1. space placing an event in space (metric or nonmetric)	Jason practiced law.	Jason's business was transcontinental, stretching from urban to rural communities.
2. time placing an event in time (metric or nonmetric)	Jason studied law.	In the autumn, Jason studied.
3. motion recalling movement	Jason's business was trans-continental. Jason studied.	Jason flew from coast to coast to help his business.
4. manner recalling specifiable characteristics		Jason studied assiduously.
V. accommodating referents		
1. conjunctive joining two elements	Jason was an architect. His fellow engineers praised him.	Jason was a lawyer and a dentist.
2. syncretic merging diverse elements into a single element	Jason was an architect. His fellow engineers praised him.	Jason was an architectural engineer.
3. disjunctive recall of one selected element	Jason was an architect. His fellow engineers praised him.	Jason was an engineer.
4. episodic sequencing events in a temporally fixed, irreversible order	Jason was an architect. His fellow engineers praised him.	Jason was a lawyer, but stopped being a lawyer. Then he became an engineer.

Complete Scoring System

Example

	Text	Recall
5. additive creating two sources to accommodate diverse information	Jason was an architect. His fellow engineers praised him.	One Jason was a lawyer. Another Jason was an engineer.
6. anaphoric establishing a referent.	They praised him.	The engineers praised him.
VI. generating case frames (traditional case grammar relations)	Jason learned law.	Jason was taught law by the faculty of Tulane Law School.
VII. generating attributes 1. actors	Jason studies law.	Mild-mannered Jason, the bookworm, studied law
2. events attributing qualifications to events	Jason led the parade.	The parade was the grandest show in Dublin.
3. places adding specificity to places	Jason studied in Louisiana.	Jason studied in the humidity of the South.
4. dimension attributing characteristics to dimensions	He moved to Chicago.	He moved very far from Tulane.
VIII. generating text erroneous information	Jason, once a lawyer, became an accountant.	Jason studied architecture, but practiced nothing
IX. generating text external information	Jason was a lawyer.	I don't know why Jason was what he was.

Instruction in Developing Reading Comprehension

At this point, you are probably asking, "What can I do to help children develop reading comprehension skills?" First, we suggest that you analyze the text for difficulties that your children may encounter. Ask yourself, "Is the passage clearly written; does it make sense?" If there are severe problems, you can do the following: (1) abandon the text and select an alternate text that is more clearly written, or (2) rewrite the text, correcting it to clarify potentially troublesome areas. For example, if the text says "Dan and Dee are playing basketball, but Don is not. Don and Del are roller skating," you may want to:

1. Change the names to avoid confusion.
2. Make the unclear reference to Don in the second sentence less ambiguous. The reader could rightly wonder if the Don in the second sentence is the Don in the first sentence.

A corrected, more readable version of the text that adheres closely to original intent might be: "Jay and Dee are playing basketball, but Jeffrey is not because he is roller skating with Marge."

Questioning Strategies

In addition to clarifying unclear texts, you can direct students' reading by developing comprehension tasks. The most frequently used task is *questioning*. There is an extensive body of research literature that demonstrates the importance of directing and focusing students' reading through teacher questions. It is absolutely critical for you to understand that a question is a useful tool, a stimulant for learning.

Too often in the past, teachers have fallen into the trap of thinking that a question automatically produces a certain type of thinking (a specific mental operation). The operation is done by the reader in his thinking processes, not by the question; the question is merely a device that may or may not stimulate the type of thinking that is desired by the teacher. We have spent a great deal of time and effort labeling questions as literal, inferential, and critical (evaluative). Much of this time and effort has been futile; we should turn our attention to examining the processes/operations that are involved during reading, remembering that questions can merely serve as stimulants to thinking, not as substitutes for it.

Because questions are sources for thinking, it seems obvious that we should ask our students many different types of questions in order to stimulate many different mental operations. It seems equally obvious that students interpret questions in many different ways; it is possible that a question that the test maker intended to elicit recall of explicitly stated information may not serve that purpose for some students. For example:

Ken Baxter, who was fifteen years old, wore a costume that was far too young for him. He came as a bunny rabbit.

Question:	What costume did the boy wear?
Intended answer:	A bunny rabbit costume.
Possible answers:	1. He wore a babyish animal costume.
	2. A costume that is only appropriate for young children to wear at parties.
	3. He was the laughingstock of the party.

Each of the possible answers is relatively correct; each strays farther from the text and the actual question, but we must be ready for interpretive answers like number 3, "He was the laughingstock of the party," if we want to fully understand the way our students make sense of texts.

Questions As Stimulants for Thinking

A second way to look at questioning as a stimulant for thinking is to think of questions as a tool for ordering thinking, for putting the pieces of a puzzle together. When a student misinterprets or miscomprehends, as demonstrated by getting the single crucial question wrong, what do we know? We only know from his answer that something went awry; we need to go back to the passage and discover, with the child, the pieces of the puzzle that he does not understand. This retracing procedure can be done through systematic questioning that is based on the logical propositions within the text or story. The following example is based on the beginning of the children's book, *Where the Wild Things Are:*

1. The night Max wore his wolf suit and made mischief of one kind
2. and another
3. his mother called him "Wild Thing!"
4. and Max said "I'll eat you up!"
5. so he was sent to bed without eating anything.

Let us suppose that you asked your readers to answer this question: Why did Max's mother send him to bed without eating? The answer that you might expect from your students would be similar to the following:

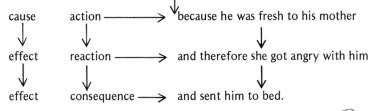

In order to arrive at the desired response, the reader has to (1) attend to the text and (2) perform numerous mental operations simultaneously.

Figure 7, on page 312, illustrates the complexity of the question by listing some of the operations (processes) that the child must perform and the text source for extracting the information needed to answer this question: If the child is unable to answer the question correctly, you, as the teacher, can retrace the reader's steps by asking logically ordered questions that require fewer operations than the original text. This set of questions may aid you to assist the reader in reconstructing the text:

Question 1: What did Max's mother call him on the night he made mischief of one kind and another?
 Text source: 1. The night Max wore his wolf suit and made mischief of one kind
  2. and another
  3. his mother called him "Wild Thing!"
 Operation: syntactic transformation of question to subject-verb-object sentence, i.e., Max's mother called him "Wild Thing!"

Question 2: Why did Max's mother call him Wild Thing?
 Text source: 1. The night Max wore his wolf suit and made mischief of one kind
  2. and another
  3. his mother called him "Wild Thing!"
 Operations: syntactic deletion—. . . Max . . . made mischief of one kind and another
  inferred causality—(so) his mother called him "Wild Thing."

Question 3: What did Max say to his mother when she called him Wild Thing?
 Text source: 4. and Max said "I'll eat you up!"
 Operation: elongation—I'll eat you up (to her)

Question 4: What do you think Max's mother thought of that?
 Text source: 5. so he was sent to bed without eating anything.
 Operation: extracting Max's purpose/tone
  application of world knowledge

Question 5: Then what did Max's mother say/do?
 Text source: 5. so he was sent to bed without eating anything.
 Operations: passive to active transformation—he was sent $\longrightarrow$
  _____ sent Max to bed. syntactic substitution
  (elongation——Mom sent Max to bed.
  world knowledge of (rule)—Mom's turn to talk—"I send you to bed without dinner"
  deleted imperative—Go to bed.)

There are additional tasks for the child. He must extract that dialogue is occurring, and he must know the rules of dialogue:

Mom: "Wild Thing!"
Max: "I'll eat you up!"
Mom's turn: "Go to bed without eating"

Operation	Text Source	Explicit	Implicit	World Knowledge
1. Synonymy "fresh" means the reader has extracted 1. tone (Max's intent) 2. dialogue rules 3. mother's intention in her reply	and Max said "I'll eat you up!"			x
2. conjoining and = so, therefore (cause effect)	his mother called him Wild Thing and (so, therefore) Max said		x	
3. transformational grammar deletion rule	"I'll eat you up" → (to her)	x	x x	
4. clarifying anaphoric referent	→ (his mother)		x	
5. generating retroactive causality	(so his mother said "Go to your room without eating anything") so he was sent to bed without eating anything			x

Figure 7

Leading students through the text in this step-by-step manner may be a productive procedure for helping them to understand the interrelatedness of the entire text.

Narrow and Broad Questions

You can provide the opportunities for your students to engage in many and varied operations, to engage in different types of cognition through your questions. But you must acknowledge the fact that we cannot guarantee that our students will engage in a single, specific, logical operation as a result of the questions we ask. Rather, you must remember that it is important to constantly assess your student's responses in order to evaluate the effect of the questions that you are asking. Are your questions stimulating your students to think in a variety of ways? Do your questions elicit only one logical operation?

The task of stimulating your children's thinking is comprehensive, but you can begin by constructing appropriately challenging questions along a continuum similar to the continuum by Cunningham (1971). An illustration of the continuum is presented below:

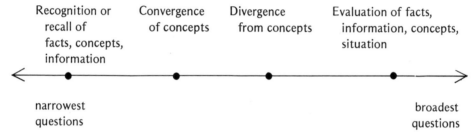

A second dimension of questioning strategies is the difficulty index of individual questions. Difficulty may shape a reader's response; there are easy narrow questions and difficult narrow questions; for example, after the student read: "Jason rarely moved in springtime, but he moved to Minneapolis without warning one April morning," you asked: "To which city did Jason move?" This would be an easy question, but the question "What is the eighth word in the original sentence?" is a difficult question. If a reader was unable to answer the second question, we could not conclude that he was unable to comprehend explicitly stated information. Rather, we would say that the question was extremely difficult (and absurd).

It should also be pointed out that readers need to be prepared to answer certain question types. If we always ask, "What was the eighth word . . .?", students can become attuned to this kind of question and can actually become quite capable of answering it. But they may be less successful in answering broader, more important questions if they have only had practice in answering a narrow memory type of question.

Therefore, it might be productive and useful to examine the types of questions we ask when we are encouraging comprehension in our classrooms. It may be informative to evaluate these questions along the dual dimensions we have established: ease/difficulty and narrowness/broadness. It may also be interesting for you to compare your in-class discussion questions with your test questions. You can do this by tape recording your classes and then by examining your end-of-unit test questions. You may want to plot your questions on a graph similar to the following one:

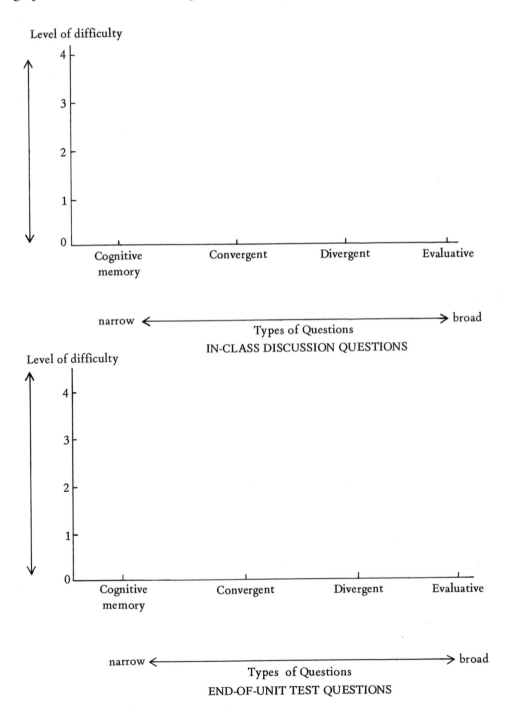

Level of difficulty

Types of Questions
IN-CLASS DISCUSSION QUESTIONS

Types of Questions
END-OF-UNIT TEST QUESTIONS

Level of Difficulty

In order to determine level of difficulty, you may use your own judgment by assigning each question a numerical measure of difficulty (1–4) and/or you may collaborate with a colleague in order to avoid serious misjudgments about degrees of difficulty. However, it should be noted that the individual teacher is the best judge of complexity because only she knows the degree to which the concept or the material was covered in the classroom.

You may notice some discrepancies between your in-class discussion questions and your test questions, and your set of graphs may look like this:

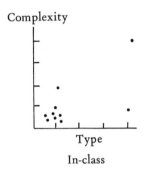

In-class

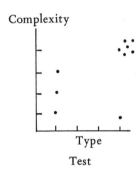

Test

This graph may tell you that you are asking mostly easy, recall-of-fact questions in class while on your tests you are asking mostly difficult, evaluative questions. This discrepancy may account for some students' poor performance.

It should be pointed out that one type of question is not necessarily better than any other type of question. You have to establish your own purposes for your questions. One type of question may be more appropriate than another for a specific purpose. If your purpose is to ask only one type of question for a period of time, this instrument may help you to determine if you have accomplished your goals. The singlemost effective purpose of this instrument is to assist you in gathering evidence that will affirm or reject your individual perceptions about the nature of your classroom questions. It may help to alter questioning strategies from time to time, and it may help to gain needed information for interpreting students' performance.

Concept Formation*

In addition to remembering that asking questions is a means for helping children to develop their comprehension skills and strategies, it is also important

---

*A *concept* is a word or phrase that identifies or classifies a group of objects or events or ideas. Given any group of objects, one is concerned with determining similarities and differences for purposes of classification. A concept may be described as concrete: *cat* or *bicycle*, or it may be described as abstract; *patriotism* or *hate*. The concept may be more or less inclusive, as well: as *animal* is more inclusive than *mammal; mammal* is more inclusive than *cat*; and *cat* is more inclusive than *Persian*. Thus, concept formation is a mental state or process that means, or refers to, more than one object or experience or to one object in relation to others. Conception or concept formation denotes process, whereas concept denotes the product. The designation of a concept in words is called a *term*.

for you to remember that reading comprehension is an interactive process that takes place as the reader interprets the text. This interpretation by the reader must necessarily be based on the reader's experience and background. It is important that you help your students to develop knowledge, background, and experience that will enhance their reading. One way to develop this background is through instruction in concept formation. This is one of several *cognitive factors* affecting the child's reading comprehension. In helping children learn how to form concepts, you are helping them to develop their critical thinking skills. Obviously, the development of critical thinking skills is an extremely important part of your curriculum.

In Taba's *Handbook* (1967) it is suggested that the teacher should engage children with an initial broad experience, such as taking a walk around the school or watching a film or some slides in order to help children form a concept. This can then be followed by organizing the many details of the experience into a workable grouping of research topics. The following process will help you to develop strategies for grouping details.

1. As students, "What did you see? hear? notice?" Students will begin to enumerate items to answer this question. While they are listing these items, they are also engaged in differentiating items.

2. After they have generated these lists, ask, "Which of these items go together?" As students begin to group the items, they will be engaged in the process of identifying common properties. They are beginning to engage in abstraction processing.

3. After they have established categories, ask students, "How would you label these groups?" As students begin this labeling process, they are involved in hierarchial ordering of superordinates and subordinates.

The acquisition of each of these processing skills is an extremely important element in the development of reading comprehension skills.

Concept formation can begin with the listing of discrete items. For example, after viewing a film on the Pilgrims, one group of students listed the following items:

Pilgrims	Massachusetts	furs
churches	utensils	tobacco
meeting houses	fireplaces	lumber
houses	slaves	schools
gardens	plantations	haystacks
farmers	Indians	shoes
clothing	water wheels	rock walls
maps	goats	mills
ships	canoes	ministers

To actually get the list on the board, a number of subquestions may be necessary. Children sometimes get stuck on a category and name many similar items. Look at the preceding list for an example. The students had listed meeting houses and houses. If they had continued with sheds or houses for the cattle, it would have been a good idea to shift their thinking by saying: "Did you see any other things in the film that interested you?" This questioning strategy often breaks the imitative responses. All students should be encouraged to participate. Everyone has seen something worth recording.

The students categorized the preceding list under the following concept headings:

people	travel, transportation
buildings	tools
industries	things to wear

Some of the items did not fit into any of these broad categories. The students then reexamined the list to determine what other labels would be needed to include the disparate items.

A second technique for developing concepts is called question-initiating. When this technique is used, an "opener," or introductory broad experience, is provided. Following this opener the student is asked to work in a small group or choose a partner and list all the questions that occurred to him as he watched the film or took the walk. What questions does he have for which he would like to find answers? A long list of 20 or 25 questions can be generated by brainstorming in this way. A separate slip of paper should be provided for jotting down each question. After the questions have all been jotted down, sorting and grouping into categories follows.

Using either one of the techniques suggested will help students determine the specific, concrete details that are subsumed under the category label, for example, the concepts of industries. Once the category has been formed it will be necessary to reexamine the variation within the category so that a general statement can be developed about the concept. It will be important now for the student to gather a large fund of information about the category he has chosen so that he can organize the data and, on the basis of his organized information, develop some general statements. Stauffer (1969) explains:

> The principal outcome of all this is the plea that the children be required to do their own learning. Teachers must present children with reading situations in which the children experiment by trying out ideas to see what happens, by manipulating things and ideas, by positing questions and seeking answers, by reconciling what they find at one time with what they find at another, and by comparing their findings with each other. Children must be active and required to act on material things as well as hypothetical ideas, and they should do this in social collaboration or in a group effort. Such children are required to communicate with each other. Intelligent functioning—which equilibrium obtains—requires a fine balance between a person and his milieu and stresses the paramount importance of interaction, so that a realistic and a meaningful support is secured, and so that a child can acquire the rationality and objectivity which only a multiperspective view can offer. Then he can sort particulars into a set of classes to order their diversity and form a concept. (p. 351)

Functional Literacy

After you have instructed your students in concept formation, you have begun to ready them for the task of reading. However, the demands of comprehension are so complex and varied in today's world that it is important for you to go beyond this preparatory process. Let us presume that you have effectively introduced your students to a new concept and that you have prepared appropriate questions for stimulating thinking. Now it is your task to help them through new, varied, lifelike materials that require the transfer of the reading strategies that they have acquired.

The 1976 National Assessment of Educational Progress* surveyed the reading strengths of American students. The findings may suggest that we as teachers need to expand our curriculum to include the teaching of comprehension strategies through materials that are relevant to older readers. The importance of such a curriculum expansion becomes obvious because we are surrounded daily by discussion of literacy. What is literacy? Who is literate? How is literacy related to reading comprehension?

Let's begin by defining *functional literacy*. Because of the many journal articles and national surveys which have described functional literacy as a dominant issue in American homes and schools, anyone who asks this question may appear to be somewhat naive. It is obvious to most of us, as teachers, that a person considered literate by the standard of one culture may be unable to meet the literary demands of another culture. Therefore, literacy tests must be suitable to assess the competencies of the general population with regard to life-coping tasks rather than only being applicable to a small part of the population. Once this issue has been addressed, it becomes necessary to ask, "Literacy for what purpose?"

The *advancement of literacy* is a basic goal of American education. The success of achieving this goal is often questioned as America continues to become an ever more *visual* nation, where films often replace rather than supplement books, and television supplants general newspapers and journal reading. At this time, when Americans appear to be spending less time with reading materials, we are witnessing an increase in both political propaganda and marketing advertisements. Everyday consumers are required to make decisions regarding insurance, taxes, applications, credit loans, personal purchases, and government organizations. Can a person be considered literate if he can perform only academic tasks? If the answer is *yes*, one wonders why so many students have evidenced success in school subjects, yet seem to have difficulty with high-level comprehension tasks.

*The National Assessment of Educational Progress (NAEP) is an information-gathering project that surveys the educational attainments of 9-year-olds, 13-year-olds, 17-year-olds, and adults (ages 26–35) in ten learning areas; art, career and occupational development, citizenship, literature, mathematics, music, *reading*, science, social studies, and writing. Information regarding any such surveys may be obtained by writing to NAEP, Suite 700, 1860 Lincoln Street, Denver, Colorado 80203.

A program which is designed to foster literacy may have dual complexity because it must include the development of language arts and computational skills, and it must also provide application strategies which are necessary in making decisions in life-coping situations. The following outline is presented in an attempt to further explain this duality:

I. Do you have the academic skills of literacy?
   A. Language arts
      1. Spoken language
        Are you able to communicate in the dominant language of the culture?
      2. Written language
        Can you express yourself through the written language of the dominant culture? (syntax, semantics, spelling)
      3. Reading
        Can you critically comprehend the printed materials of the dominant culture? (perceive, infer, evaluate, apply)
   B. Computation
     Can you add, subtract, multiply, divide, compute fractions and percentages, interpret graphs and thermometers?
II. Can you apply these skills to life-coping situations?
   A. Personal
      1. Restaurant functioning
      2. Driver's license application
      3. Transportation schedules
      4. Instructional manuals
      5. W2 forms
      6. Grocery slips
      7. Bank slips
      8. Insurance forms
      9. Savings accounts
      10. Home purchases
   B. Career
      1. Employment ads
      2. Pension plans
   C. Health
      1. Medications
      2. Health care
   D. Civic responsibilities
      1. Community resources
      2. Consumer economics
      3. Environmental issues

A curriculum designed to produce literate citizens must stress the *application* of basic academic skills to life-coping situations. In order to accomplish this task, students must be introduced to a common set of materials which are used by all people when they are involved in their daily functions. When this occurs, we begin to develop academic competence as well as life-coping competence. Such materials involve those listed under the personal, career, health, and civic responsibility sections of the outline. Strategies which need to be used to teach literacy skills are similar to those suggested in Chapter 11, "Reading: Key to Content Area Learning."

The issues of developing minimal competencies of literacy through appropriate curricula are being discussed by educators everywhere. As a result, many states are beginning to develop literacy assessment instruments to be administered to all students during their early high school years so that teachers will have appropriate time to develop remedial programs for the needs of these students. These literacy assessments are becoming a necessity in today's world of high-powered advertising, because children must be guided in developing the ability to evaluate critically what they read and hear.

As early as 1910, Dewey stressed the need for critical evaluation, and he discussed the five processes involved in critical evaluation as it relates to reflective thinking:

1. A felt difficulty
2. Its location and definition
3. Suggestion of a possible solution
4. Development by reasoning of the bearings of the suggestion
5. Further observation and experimentation leading to its acceptance or rejection; that is the conclusion of belief or disbelief

Kottmeyer (1944) emphasized the need for reflective, or critical, thinking when he suggested that the reader must be encouraged to "project his own judgments, attitudes, and appreciations into juxtaposition with the reading material."

Russell's (1956) six suggested steps add further clarity to the processes involved in critical thinking:

1. The child's environment stimulates mental activity.
2. The orientation of initial direction of the thinking is established.
3. The search for related materials takes place.
4. There is a patterning of various ideas into some hypothesis or tentative conclusion.
5. The deliberative, or critical, part of the thinking process is developed.
6. The concluding stage of the thinking process takes place when the hypothesis selected above is subjected to the test of use. (pp. 15–16)

As Vinacke (1952) states: The process of critical thinking is a process of problem solving that involves

apprehension or recognition of the problem, together with effort to deal with it; some manipulation or exploration of the situation; some degree of control or direction or performance; the understanding or mastery of intermediate requirements or steps; and emotional responses representing some degree of personal involvement in the situation. (p. 182)

Although the processes involved in critical thinking have been clearly outlined for decades, many people still make faulty evaluations, exhibit a lack of problem-solving strategies, and are unable to detect propaganda. In a world of consumer affairs, we must *all* possess critical reading/thinking/listening skills if we are to be considered literate.

The following discussion of *persuasion* as a technique used to influence consumers is presented to (1) further instruct you in the *necessity* of developing your students' functional reading skills and to (2) provide you with some curricular ideas that may aid you in accomplishing this task.

Persuasion

The theme of persuasion, the art of persuasion, and the art of persuading are certainly not new to any of us. Throughout history people have attempted to *influence*, or persuade, others. Persuasion, which can be accomplished through a variety of techniques, often utilizes forms of *propaganda* to promote products, ideas, and people. Propaganda involves one person or group's deliberate attempts to persuade another person or group of people to accept a differing point of view or action. The base of propaganda is heavily laden with syllogism.

Syllogistic Reasoning

A *syllogism* is an argument whose conclusion is supported by two premises. One of these premises, the major premise, contains the *major* term, which is the *predicate* of the conclusion. The other, the *minor* premise, contains the *minor* term, which is the subject of the conclusion. Common to both premises is the *middle* term, which is excluded from the conclusion.

A common example of syllogistic, or deductive, reasoning is the following:

> A is B
> B is C
> therefore
> A is C

In this instance,

> A is B   (Major premise)
> ↓
> (Major term)
> B is C   (Minor premise)
> ↓
> (Minor term)
> B   (Middle term)
> A is C

Now let's consider:

A. All people are human.
B. Mildred Cunningham is a person.
C. Therefore, Mildred Cunningham is a human.

Is this conclusion true? *Yes*, when the *major* and *minor* premises are true, the conclusion is true.

Now let's consider

A. All people who live in the Eastern United States are highly intelligent.
B. Lynne Thrope lives in the Eastern United States.
C. Therefore, Lynne Thrope is highly intelligent.

Why is this considered syllogistic reasoning? Statement *A* contains the major premise, and statement *B* contains the minor premise. However, the major premise is false; therefore, the conclusion is false. It is important for a critical reader or listener to distinguish between *valid reasoning* and *truth*.

In trying to influence one's intended audience, it is a common device for the producer to present an argument in a manner that is *valid* but then to use *major* and *minor* premises that are false. If one is not a critical *thinker, reader,* and *listener*, it is quite easy to be fooled by what appears to be a logical argument or syllogistic reasoning.

Now let's consider:

A. Anyone who opposes increased welfare payments for the poor is antidemocratic.
B. Harold Lee opposes increased welfare payments for the poor.
C. Therefore, Harold Lee is antidemocratic.

OR

A. Anyone who is opposed to girls playing hockey is a sexist.
B. Gertrude Hill opposes girls playing hockey.
C. Therefore, Gertrude Hill is a sexist.

OR

A. Reading a novel is an enjoyable hobby.
B. Linda Lungren is reading a book.
C. Therefore, Linda Lungren is engaged in an enjoyable hobby.

Are these conclusions true? The answer to this question can be determined only after you have decided if the major premise is true.

Remember that *all* persuasion is not *negative*, nor does it all contain *falsehoods*. Some persons or groups may be interested in persuading us to do good, happy, enjoyable, and morally sound things. Therefore, the reader or listener must be trained to detect the underlying *message within the message*. The critical reader or listener engages in an evaluative process that makes possible the determination of written or spoken propaganda. As readers and listeners, we are daily confronted with persuasion, or propaganda, from newspapers, magazines, textbooks, radio, movies, and television.

Let's consider

> Things Go Better with Coke.
> See the USA in Your Chevrolet.
> You Can't Do Better than Sears.

Aren't the statements in these advertisements the major premises or syllogisms? For example:

A. See the USA in Your Chevrolet.
B. I want to see the USA.
C. I ought to buy a Chevrolet.

OR

A. You Can't Do Better than Sears.
B. I want to do better.
C. I'll shop at Sears.

The basic line of each of these advertisements is a *major* premise within syllogistic reasoning. The reader/listener must be alerted to propaganda's appeal to his emotions, interest, needs, desires, fears, and prejudices. The questions posed by the critical reader are virtually the same as those needed for propaganda detection. Critical reading involves students posing and answering such questions as:

A. <u>What</u> do you think happened next?
B. <u>Why</u> do you think this happened?
C. <u>What</u> other things might have happened?
D. <u>How</u> would you have acted differently?

The act of critical thinking demands that one address the many ways in which other persons or groups attempt to influence our thinking. Propaganda techniques are easily detected in advertisement. The following are common forms of propaganda that are used to influence consumers. We have selected one product, cereal, to illustrate how a noncritical thinker/reader/listener can be influenced to buy a particular product. Although these examples are designed to exert positive influence, the same techniques can be used to effect negative outcomes. You may wish to present these techniques to your students because they are the primary audience for whom cereal commercials are designed.

Propaganda Techniques

Bandwagon

MORE MOTHERS PREFER <u>ZOOMIES</u> CEREAL THAN ANY OTHER

Although the bandwagon approach attempts to convince you that the vast majority of consumers prefer a particular product, it fails to alert you to the options.

Prestige

BOB GOMBAR, ACE GOALIE, EATS ODIES CEREAL

The prestige approach implies that you might be more like this famous personality if you were to use this product.

Testimonial

BILLIE JEAN RING, TENNIS PRO, SAYS, "I EAT CIRCLES CEREAL EVERY MORNING AND YOU SHOULD, TOO."

The testimonial approach not only implies that you will be like the tennis pro, but it also tells you what this famous personality believes is good for you.

Repetition

POPPY CEREAL IS NOT ONLY GOOD FOR BREAKFAST, BUT ALSO YOU'LL WANT TO <u>MUNCH</u>, <u>MUNCH</u>, <u>MUNCH</u> POPPIES FOR YOUR <u>LUNCH</u>, <u>LUNCH</u>, <u>LUNCH</u>.

Repetition creates a catchy jingle that is easily repeated.

Plain Folks

THE PRESIDENT OF STARTERS CEREAL WAS ONCE A CABBIE. SHE STILL ENJOYS COFFEE CLUBS WITH NEIGHBORHOOD MOTHERS.

This type of propaganda implies that the president is just one of the family; therefore, she would never cheat or sponsor an unreliable product.

Snob Appeal

ALL THE FAMILIES IN HIGHTOWN VILLAGE EAT CHUNK-UMS. DO YOUR KIDS EAT CHUNK-UMS?

Snob appeal suggests that if you want to be considered a member of the upper class, your children must be *Chunk-ums* eaters.

Emotional Word Appeal

GOOD MOTHERS BUY TARTIES CEREAL FOR THEIR CHILDREN.

This approach certainly implies the criterion necessary for successful motherhood.

Authority

> MOST DOCTORS AGREE THAT FILLERS CEREAL IS BETTER FOR YOUR HEALTH

Not only are you not informed as to what *Fillers* is better than, but you are also influenced by the fact that physicians have attested to its value.

Transfer

Although words may not be used to influence you, a picture is presented of a healthy child holding a box of *Fillers* cereal. You are encouraged to draw the conclusion that your child can be just like this if she eats *Fillers*.

Labeling

A catchy label such as *Wow* cereal easily becomes part of your vocabulary. You look for it at the grocery store.

Ego Building

> ARE YOU BRIGHT ENOUGH TO BUY SYSTEMS CEREALS?

Is there anyone of us who is not anxious to be labeled bright? We have the incentive to be readily persuaded.

Image Building

> YOU'LL BE LIKE ATLAS IF YOU EAT MUSCLES CEREALS

Again for the many, many people who wish to be a powerhouse of physical or emotional muscles, this becomes the perfect persuasive gimmick.

Oversimplification

> GURGLES MAKES EVERY BREAKFAST EATER FEEL HEALTHIER

How easy life is if only one follows the reasoning presented in this method of persuasion.

Buckshot

This persuasive method utilizes many approaches in a direct attempt to strike as many individuals as possible.

Smith (1963) suggests that, in an attempt to help children learn to analyze propaganda, they should be trained to ask and answer the following questions:

1. Who is the propagandist?
2. Whom is he serving?
3. What is his aim in writing on this subject?

4. To what human interests, desires, emotions does he appeal?

5. What technique does he use?

6. Are you or are you not going to permit yourself to be influenced through the tactics of this propagandist? (pp. 276-7)

One procedure that acquaints children with types of propagandists, as well as aids them in developing a questioning habit regarding propaganda, is to designate a specific wall, chart, scrapbook, or bulletin board as a propaganda center. Children then collect propaganda statements found in ballads, public speeches, posters, leaflets, journals, reports, newsletters, pamphlets, textbooks, newspapers, novels, radios, conversations, and button slogans. Categorizing statements by propaganda type will provide students with practice in answering the questions posed by Smith. Eventually this process of analysis will become automatic.

In addition to asking high-level questions and alerting children to propaganda techniques, you may need to offer demonstrations that will supply children with needed conceptual information. Experimenting with manipulating liquids, clay, and beads often encourages intellectual developmental processes. The selection of activities is dependent on the developmental stages of your students. Demonstrations may aid learning for some children who have reached a particular developmental stage, but it may be ineffective for those without sufficient "readiness." You must be *sensitive* to the developmental stages at which your students are operating.

Although many sociopsychological factors affect a child's learning, studies by Crassen (1948), McKillop (1952), Groff (1962), Johnson (1967), and Schnayer (1967) have emphasized that the child's *attitude* toward a particular topic effects his ability to draw inferences from the materials. Merritt (1967) suggests that it is the primary job of the classroom teacher to sequence instruction in reading in order to elicit desired comprehension behaviors. Merritt further cautions us that competency in reading comprehension can be developed *only* when materials are used in sequence according to the experiential readiness of the student. Examples of sequential instruction are provided in Chapter 15.

As suggested by Merritt, one's ability to read is affected by many factors; cognitive, socioeconomic, sensory, perceptual, language, school and the teacher. The totality of such factors results in one's *background experience,* by which reading comprehension may be affected; thus, we are again faced with the complexity of the literacy issues.

As you attempt to implement any type of instruction designed to further the development of your students' reading/literacy and comprehension skills, keep in mind the following points:

1. Children must be able to decode and understand the words in context before they can critically evaluate the validity of their content.

2. Children must be able to gain needed information through interpretation of *all* graphic aids pertaining to the material which they are being asked to read.

3. Children cannot critically evaluate beyond their experiential and reasoning capacities.

4. Children must be encouraged to suspend judgments based on personal experience until they fully understand the presentation of the reading passage.

5. Children may need to be introduced to prereading activities that will expand their experiential backgrounds. Such expansions may be a must if you are asking children to draw conclusions which rely heavily on personal experiences.

6. Children are better able to accomplish a reading task if the objectives of the task have been clearly defined.

7. Children may be better able to react critically to a written passage if the author is somehow similar to the child, in age or ethnic background.

Guidelines for Lessons on Comprehension

When you actually plan a lesson that is intended to encourage comprehension development, you must:

1. *Establish a purpose*: Ideally, the purpose of the lesson should be closely tied to the children's lives (planning the arrangement of the classroom, selecting a new game, discussing a classroom activity) Although your topic cannot always be totally related to the children's lives, it can be presented so that it establishes a new interest or capitalizes on an existing interest. Plan questions that will tap appropriate types of comprehension.

2. *Select materials*: The materials being selected should lend themselves to the teaching of a specified skill. Fiction, nonfiction, games, workbooks, high interest—low vocabulary materials are only a few examples of the extensive resources which are available to you. Remember that the selected materials should help you accomplish the purpose of the lesson.

3. *Plan experiences*: Through questions, materials, and follow-up activities, you will need to provide the child with opportunities to develop skill in finding main ideas, finding supporting details, detecting the organization plan of the material, detecting sequential arrangements, adjusting his reading rate, and critically evaluating work.

The ability to comprehend printed material involves a myriad of skills that are not acquired as a once-and-for-all process. To learn and continue to comprehend requires continuous attention. As classroom teachers you must continuously supply activities and questions that help children in the developmental process of comprehension.

Measurement

Many psychologists and educators, including Gibson and Levin (1974), have suggested that one of the greatest needs for future research in reading is for a comprehensive and precise theory of comprehension which will enable us to specify discernible and measurable units of comprehension. Only when we fully understand the nature of comprehension can we develop an exacting instrument that will adequately measure this phenomenon.

Pearson (1977) suggests a new view of comprehension which he calls "comprehensive comprehension clusters." From this view appropriate measures may be developed. He maintains:

> The proposed comprehension classification scheme is best modeled by a three dimensional cube. The first dimension . . . specifies the size of the linguistic units that must be manipulated in order to solve the task: a concept (usually expressed as a word), a proposition (expressed as a clause or sentence), and larger units (expressed as paragraphs or passages).
>
> The second dimension . . . specifies the type of logical relation that obtains between the linguistic unit. At present there are (several) relations, but we are not satisfied that this dimension is complete.
>
> The first relation is superordinate (given a class label, can one find a member of that class of things, e.g., dog → collie). We use the mnemonic, *Ruleg* . . ., borrowing a term from programmed instruction.
>
> The second relationship is subordinate (given an example of a class of things, can one find a class to which it belongs, e.g., collie → dog).
>
> The third relation is co-ordinate (given a member of a class of things, can one find another member, e.g., collie → spaniel (two dogs) or dog → cat, (two mammals or pets)). This relation also accounts for alleged synonomy (crate → box). The mnemonic can be either *Eg eg* or *Rule rule*, which turn out to be synonomous.
>
> The fourth relation we call attributional, characterizing the fact that at times we give a concept as a stimulus and ask for an attribute as a response, e.g., dog → bark. The mnemonic is Rulatt.
>
> The fifth relation is the inverse of four; that is we can give an attribute and ask for the concept to which it is related, e.g., bark → dog. Not surprisingly it is called *Attrule*.

A view of reading comprehension, similar to Pearson's view, may ultimately lend itself to the conception and construction of new instruments for adequately measuring both the current reading comprehension ability and the growth of this ability in each student. To date, our measures can only be used as indicators of comprehension ability; they are imprecise and must be used with sensitivity and thoughtfulness.

As we suggested earlier, we strongly believe that the prime goal of all reading instruction is *comprehension*. Within this chapter you have been introduced to both the theory and implementation strategies of reading comprehension. In order to be a successful reading teacher, you must understand the intricacies of reading comprehension, as demonstrated in the models of reading presented in the beginning of this chapter, as well as the appropriate strategies for teaching comprehension.

COMPREHENSION ACTIVITIES

1. Where and When?

<u>Goal</u>: Developing an understanding of time and place

<u>Grade level</u>: 3–6

<u>Construction</u>: On a sheet of paper, type a series of short stories that involve various times and places. On another sheet, make up a crossword puzzle, asking questions involving time and place. For example, "The third story takes place in the season of _____ ." If desired, provide a separate answer sheet for self-correcting.

<u>Utilization</u>: The student completes the crossword puzzle after reading each story.

2. Post Office

<u>Goal</u>: Identifying declarative and interrogative sentences

<u>Grade level</u>: 4–6

<u>Construction</u>: Get an empty carton with dividers that has been used to hold bottles. Divide the box into two parts by putting a long piece of colored tape down the middle of the side with dividers. Label one side with a card saying "declarative" and one side with "interrogative." Then, using masking tape, label each on the declarative side with "command," "statement," "narrative," etc. Label the slots on the interrogative side with "asking information," "disbelief," etc. On envelopes write sentences that could fit under one of the preceding categories, but do not use punctuation.

<u>Utilization</u>: A student inserts the envelopes into the appropriate slot, using the word clues in the sentence.

<u>Note</u>: To make it easier, include the punctuation.

3. The Hunting Game

Goal: Following instructions

Grade level: 1–3

Construction: Choose one object the players are to find and hide it somewhere in the classroom. Make up a series of clues that the children have to follow exactly in order to find the object, such as "on the left side of the drawer you will find ... , walk ten feet and turn right," etc. Place the clues accordingly around the classroom.

Utilization: There should be only two players for each object hidden. Tell them they are to find a certain object without mentioning its name. Then just tell them where to find the first clue.

4. Organize These "Books"

Goal: Classifying ideas

Grade level: 1–3

Construction: Put together shelves using cinder blocks and pieces of wood, or use red milk carton containers. Otherwise, shelves available in the classroom can be utilized. Books can be made from blocks of wood or small cardboard boxes. Write titles on the side. An alternative is to use a supply of books already in the classroom. Label each shelf for different ideas; for example, Places to Visit, Things to Make, Science Experiments, etc. This can be an ongoing activity if the class has a revolving library.

Utilization: Children place the books on the proper shelf according to title or subject.

5. Spin the Meaning

Goal: Understanding how punctuation affects meaning

Grade level: 3–4

Construction: Make up a folder of laminated sheets of paper that contain sentences with no punctuation. Construct a spinner with five sections: surprise, sadness, humor, disbelief, command, or whatever is desired.

Utilization: A student spins the dial and punctuates the sentence to show the emotion indicated by the spinner.

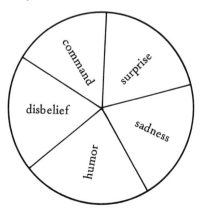

Alternative Game: Change the Meaning

Grade level: 4–6

Construction: On sheets of paper write sentences twice, using certain punctuation on one of them. Laminate the paper so that it can be reused.

Utilization: Using a felt-tip pen, students must punctuate the second sentence so that the meaning is changed. For example,

> "Joe," said Jim, "isn't here."
> Joe said, "Jim isn't here."

6. Figure Out the Funnies

Goal: Understanding sequences

Grade level: 5–8

Construction: Laminate and cut into sections several comic strips—the longer the better.

Utilization: Each child must arrange the comic strip sections in the proper order on a desk or table.

7. Tie Me Together

Goal: Inferring cause and effect

Grade level: 2–6

Construction: Cut out a large piece of cardboard and label one side with phrases that could be "causes" and the other side with phrases to serve as "effects." Label each side with the appropriate heading. Punch holes along the side of each cause and each effect card and attach a shoe string or piece of yarn to each hole on the cause side.

Utilization: Student must thread the yarn into the effect side holes, matching cause with the appropriate effect.

8. Synthesize and Generalize

Goal: Inductive reasoning

Grade level: 6–8

Construction: On a cassette tape, record paragraphs that give detailed information concerning any subject from which a generalization can be made.

Utilization: After the child listens to the paragraph he must state two generalizations that can be inferred.

9. Who's the Greatest?

Goal: To generalize from given information.

Grade level: 4–6

Construction: Between two sheets of clear contact paper, place six to eight baseball cards. Place these in a folder, along with a laminated paper on which questions that require generalizations are written, such as "Who appears to be the best all-round pitcher? From these player's records, which team would you predict to win the World Series?"

Utilization: On another sheet of paper, the student writes his answers to these questions and then makes a short generalization concerning the ability of each player.

10. Make Your Own Comic Book

Goal: Distinguishing narrative from conversation

Grade level: 4–6

Construction: Have students make a comic book using manilla paper for the inside pages and shiny shelf or finger paint paper for the cover. Fold it over and staple it.

Utilization: Tell students to make up any story and characters they wish, and to illustrate their work accordingly. The only criterion is that the narrative parts must be written with red pen and the conversation in blue.

11. Don't Laugh Your Head Off

Goal: Making inferences about figurative language

Grade level: 3–6

Construction: On large index cards, write stories using figurative expressions. Here are some suggestions of figurative expressions:

frog in my throat	keep your chin up
on pins and needles	take the floor
spill the beans	take the cake
money to burn	beat around the bush
drop me a line	eat his words
put your best foot forward	chip on your shoulder

Utilization: The student rewrites the story, replacing the figurative language with literal expressions. The student can then make up his own stories, using figurative expressions and exchanging them with a friend.

12. What Happens Next?

Goal: Predicting outcomes

Grade kevel: 3–8

Construction: Make up short stories on large laminated index cards or record them on cassette tape. Leave out the endings, but give clues as to how they could end.

Utilization: The students read or listen to the story and write down an ending and illustrate it. (Accept any reasonable response.)

13. Help: Analogies in Jeopardy:

Goal: Evaluating analogies

Grade level: 4–6

Construction: On a large piece of oak tag or cardboard attach 25 small envelopes in five rows each. On each envelope write $5, $10, $15, $20, or $25 down the column. Then attach headings to each column, such as movies, sports, and food, for example. In each envelope, insert cards with an analogy involving the words that fit under each category. The correct answer is written on the back.

Example: A dog is to a puppy as a cat is to a _____ . (kitten)
Bread is to a sandwich as _____ is to pie filling. (crust)
A conductor is to an orchestra as a _____ is to a football team. (coach)

Movies	Sports	Food	Animals	People
$5	$5	$5	$5	$5
$10	$10	$10	$10	$10
$15	$15	$15	$15	$15
$20	$20	$20	$20	$20
$25	$25	$25	$25	$25

Utilization: The student is the MC and there can be two or three players. Students take turns choosing which envelope they want to answer. The MC reads the analogy and if the player can complete it correctly, he accumulates that amount of money and gets another turn. If he is wrong, another player gets to answer. Whoever has the most money when all the envelopes have been chosen wins.

14. Are You for Real?

Goal: Evaluating fact and fantasy

Grade level: 4-6

Construction: Make 30 (or more) cards with "Fact" written on 15 of them and "Fantasy" written on the other 15.

Utilization: Two players, in turn, draw a card and make up a sentence stating a fact or fantasy, according to the card he draws. The other players must guess which word was on the card; they score one point for each correct answer. Players should make sentences that are not easily distinguishable, thus eliminating the chance of accumulating many points.

15. Why Should I Buy This?

Goal: Evaluating the differences between fact and opinion

Grade level: 4-6

Construction: Gather a collection of goods for sale from magazines or newspapers, and mount it on cardboard.

Utilization: Instruct each student to choose a picture and make up a television or radio advertisement for it. The paragraph-length advertisement should contain information about what the product can be used for, what it's made of, and why a person should buy it. Of course the truth can be stretched, as in the real world of advertising. Then each student should go back and underline those sentences that are only opinion.

QUESTIONS AND RELATED READINGS

If at this time you do not feel that you have attained adequate knowledge to successfully answer the following questions, we would like to suggest related reading.

1. What are the various processes involved in reading comprehension?
2. What are the relationships between comprehension and thinking skills?
3. What is the role of questioning in the development of reading comprehension?
4. Why is there a need to rethink existing theories of comprehension?
5. What type of classroom practices would you design to aid children in developing comprehension skills?

Goal 1: To aid the reader in understanding processes involved in reading comprehension.

Question 1: What are the various processes involved in reading comprehension?

Davidson, Roscoe. "Teacher Influence and Children's Levels of Thinking." *Reading Teacher,* 9 (Sept. 1944), 185-97.

Pearson, David P. "The Effects of Grammatical Complexity on Children's Comprehension, Recall, and Conception of Certain Semantic Relations." *Reading Research Quarterly,* 10 (1974-75), 155-92.

Goal 2: To aid the reader in understanding relationships between comprehension and thinking skills.

Question 2: What are the relationships between comprehension and thinking skills?

Braun, Jean S. "Relationships Between Concept Formation Ability and Reading Achievement at Three Developmental Levels." *Child Development,* 34 (1963), 675–82.

Cleland, Donald T., and Isabella Touissant. "The Interrelationships of Reading, Listening, Arithmetic, Computation, and Intelligence." *Reading Teacher* 15 (1962), 228–31.

Guilford, J. P. "Frontiers in Thinking That Teachers Should Know About." *Reading Teacher,* 13 (Feb. 1960), 176–82.

Goal 3: To aid the reader in understanding the role of questioning in the development of reading comprehension.

Question 3: What is the role of questioning in the development of reading comprehension?

Ascher, M. A. "Asking Questions to Trigger Thinking." *NEA Journal,* 50 (1961), 44–6.

Clegg, Ambrose A., Jr., Farley, G. M., and R. J. Curras, *Training Teachers to Analyze the Cognitive Level of Classroom Questioning,* Research Report no. 1 University of Massachusetts, (Applied Research Training Program, 1967).

Goldern, Sister Mary Laurentia. "Reading Guided by Questions Versus Careful Reading Followed by Questions." *Journal of Educational Psychology,* 33 (Sept. 1942), 463–8.

Goal 4: To aid the reader in understanding the need for rethinking comprehension.

Question 4: For what reasons does the student need to rethink existing theories of comprehension?

Betts, Emmett A. "Guidance in the Critical Interpretation of Language." *Elementary English,* 27 (Jan. 1950), 9–18, 22.

Gray, William S. "New Approaches to the Study of Interpretation in Reading." *Journal of Educational Research,* 52 (Oct. 1958), 65–7.

Putnam, Lillian. "Don't Tell Them to Do It ... Show Them How." *Journal of Reading,* 18 (Oct. 1974), 41–3.

Goal 5: To aid the reader in understanding the various types of classroom practices that aid children in developing comprehension skills

Question 5: What type of classroom practices would you design to aid children in developing comprehension skills?

Axelrod, Jerome. "Getting the Main Idea is Still the Main Idea." *Journal of Reading,* 18 (Feb. 1975), 383–7.

Dennison, Paul E. "Reading Programs Are Means—Not Ends!" *The Reading Teacher,* 28 (Oct. 1974), 10–12.

Goodman, Kenneth S. "Effective Teachers of Reading Know Language and Children." *Elementary English,* 51 (Sept. 1974), 823–8.

BIBLIOGRAPHY

Althick, Richard D. *Preface to Critical Reading.* Rev. Ed. New York: Holt, Rinehart and Winston, 1951.

Bloom, Benjamin S., ed. *Taxonomy of Educational Objectives Handbook I: Cognitive Domain.* New York: David McKay Co., Inc., 1956.

Chase, W. G. and H. H. Clark. "Mental Operations in the Comparison of Sentences and Pictures." *Cognitive in Learning and Memory,* edited by L. W. Gregg. New York: John Wiley & Sons, 1972.

Clements, Paul. "The Effects of Staging on Recall." Unpublished Ph.D. Dissertation, Cornell University, 1976.

Crossen, Helen J. "Effects of the Attitudes of the Reader upon Critical Reading Ability," *Journal of Educational Research,* (1948), 289–98.

Cunningham, Roger. "Developing Question-Asking Skills," *Developing Teacher Competencies,* J. Weig and (ed)., Englewood Cliffs, New Jersey: Prentice Hall, Inc., 1971.

Dawes, R. M. "Memory and Distortion of Meaningful Written Material." *British Journal of Psychology,* 57 (1966), 77–86.

Dewey, John. *How We Think.* Lexington, Mass.: D. C. Heath & Company, 1910.

Farr, R. "Measuring Reading Comprehension: An Historical Perspective." *Reading: The Right to Participate,* edited by Frank Green. National Reading Conference, 20th Yearbook, 1971.

Fillmore, Charles. "Some Problems For Case Grammar." Georgetown University Monograph Series in Language and Linguistics, 1971.

Fillmore, Charles. "The Case for Case" *Universals in Linguistic Theory.* Edited by Bach and Harms. New York: Holt, Rinehart and Winston, 1968.

Flood, James. "Inference: A Scoring System for Operations Performed by Readers in Text Recall." Paper presented at National Reading Conference, December 1977.

Flood, James. "The Effects of First Sentences on Reader Expectations in Prose Passages." *Reading World,* May 1978.

Flood, James and Diane Lapp. "Prose Analysis and the Effects of Staging on Prose Comprehension. Paper presented at the Second Annual Reading Association of Ireland Conference, Dublin, Ireland, 1977.

Frederiksen, C. H. "Discourse Comprehension and Early Reading. "Washington Basic Skills Group, National Institute of Education, 1976.

Frederiksen, C. H. "Effects of Task-Induced Cognitive Operations on Comprehension and Memory Processes." *Language Comprehension and the Acquisition of Knowledge,* edited by J. B. Carrol and R. O. Freedle. Washington, D.C.: V. H. Winston, 1972.

Frederiksen, C. H. "Inference and the Structure of Children's Discourse." Paper for the Symposium on the Development of Processing Skills, Society for Research in Child Development Meeting, New Orleans, 1977.

Gibson, E., and H. Levin. *The Psychology of Reading.* Cambridge, Mass.: The MIT Press, 1974.

Goodman, Kenneth S. "The Psycholinguistic Nature of the Reading Process." *The Psycholinguistic Nature of the Reading Process,* edited by K. S. Goodman. Detroit: Wayne State University Press, 1968.

Gough, Phillip B. "One Second of Reading." *Language by Eye and Ear,* edited by J. F. Kavanaugh and I. G. Mattingly. Cambridge, Mass.: MIT Press, 1972, 331–358.

Grimes, J. E. *The Thread of Discourse.* Mouton: The Hague, 1976.

Groff, P. J. "Children's Attitudes Toward Reading and Their Critical Reading Abilities in Four Content Type Materials." *Journal of Educational Research,* 55 (1962), 313–317.

Guilford, J. P. "The Three Faces of Intellect." *American Psychologist,* 14 (1959), 469–79.

Jenkins, J. J. "Can We Have a Theory of Meaningful Memory." *Theories in Cognitive Psychology: The Loyola Symposium,* edited by R. L. Solso. Hillsdale, N.J.: Earlbaum, 1974.

Johnson, J. C., II. *A Study and Analysis of the Relationships at the Intermediate Grade Levels Between Attitude as Reflected in Certain Thematic Content and Recalled Comprehension of that Content.* Ph. D. dissertation, University of California, Berkeley, 1967.

Kingston, Albert. "A Conceptual Model of Reading Comprehension." Edited by Emery P. Bliesmer and Albert J. Kingston, Jr. Phases of College and Other Adult Reading Programs. Tenth Yearbook of the National Reading Conference, 1961.

Kottmeyer, W. "Classroom Activities in Critical Reading." *School Review,* 52 (1944), 557–64.

LaBerge, David and S. Jay Samuels. "Toward a Theory of Automatic Information Processing, in Reading." *Cognitive Psychology,* 6 (1974), 293–323.

Lapp, Diane and Robert Tierney. "Reading Scores of American Nine Year Olds: NAEP's tests." *The Reading Teacher.* 30:7, April, 1977, p. 756–760.

Merritt, John E. "Developing Competence in Reading Comprehension," in *Reading Instruction: An International Forum,* Proceedings of the First World Congress on Reading. Newark, Del.: International Reading Association, 1967.

McKillop, Anne S. *The Relationship Between the Reader's Attitude and Certain Types of Reading Responses.* New York: Bureau of Publications, Teachers College Press, Columbia University, 1952.

National Assessment of Educational Progress, *Reading in America: A Perspective on Two Assessments.* Denver, Colo.: 1976.

Pearson, David. IRA Symbosium on Issues in Research on Reading Comprehension. "Operationalizing Terms and Definitions in Reading Comprehension." Miami, Florida, May 1977.

Piaget, Jean. *The Language and Thought of the Child.* 3rd ed. New York: The Humanities Press, Inc., 1959.

Robinson, Helen M. "Developing Critical Readers" in *Dimensions of Critical Reading.* Edited by Russell G. Stauffer. Newark, Del.: University of Delaware Reading-Study Center, 1964 pp. 1–12.

Rumelhart, David E. "Toward an Interactive Model of Reading" Technical Report No. 56, Center for Human Information Processing, University of California–San Diego, 1976.

Russell, David. *Children's Thinking.* Lexington, Mass.: Ginn and Company, 1956, pp. 15–16.

Schnayer, S. *Some Relationships Between Reading Interests and Reading Comprehension.* Ph.D. dissertation, University of California, Berkeley, 1967.

Smith, Frank. *Understanding Reading.* New York: Holt, Rinehart and Winston, Inc., 1971.

Smith, Nila B. *Reading Instruction for Today's Children.* Englewood Cliffs, N.J.: Prentice-Hall, Inc., 1963, pp. 276–7.

Spache, George, and Evelyn Spache. *Reading in the Elementary School.* Boston: Allyn & Bacon, Inc., 1973.

Stauffer, Russell G. *Directing Reading Maturity as a Cognitive Process.* New York: Harper & Row, Publishers, 1969.

Taba, Hilda. "The Teaching of Thinking." *Elementary English,* 52 (May 1965), 534–42.
—— et al. *Teacher's Handbook for Elementary School Studies.* Educational Series. Reading, Mass.: Addison–Wesley Publishing Co., Inc., 1967.

Thorndike, E. L. "Reading as Reasoning: A Study of Mistakes in Paragraph Reading." *Journal of Educational Psychology,* 8 (1917), 323–332.

Trabasso, Thomas. "Mental Operations in Language Comprehension." *Language Comprehension and the Acquisition of Knowledge.* Washington, D.C.: V. H. Winston, 1972.

Vinacke, W. Edgar. *The Psychology of Thinking.* New York: McGraw-Hill Book Company, 1952, p. 182.

10

Reading study skills

Every individual must be prepared to meet new developmental tasks. Each must be able to read, listen, and view critically and thoughtfully. Each must be able to use a library of books... Each must have methods of study and attitudes that will enable them to learn...

Edgar Dale

GOALS: To help the student

1. define "reading study skills."
2. develop an awareness of the variance in skills required for successful study at different maturational levels.
3. consider ways to help children learn to use study skills effectively.

In order to determine the meaning of *reading study skills* it may be helpful to determine the meaning of *study*. A possible definition might include some of the following factors:

1. When we think about a problem or situation, we look at it from as many vantage points as possible, we can say we have *studied* the problem.
2. When we see someone sitting deep in thought, we say that person is in deep *study*.
3. When we have a room set aside for reading and writing, we refer to it as a *study*.
4. When students go to college and major in history, we say their area of *study* is history.

The connotation of the term *study* in the last example probably comes closer than do the others to the meaning of study which we will use in this chapter. As the term is used in example 4, it implies that one is going to be giving concentrated attention to the acquisition of knowledge in the field of history. To do this most effectively, one needs many well-developed skills that will help him obtain this knowledge. If one is studying college-level materials, background information and preparation will be needed.

It should be pointed out that the topic of study skills will be analyzed twice in this text. In this chapter we will define and generally discuss those study skills which are needed by elementary school children in order to experience success in learning. Topics in Chapter 11 will explore the interpretation of these same study skills within specific content areas of study (math, science, social studies) and will also provide you with *methods* for classroom implementation. For example, the process of reading graphic data will be discussed generally in this chapter as a generic study skill because it pertains to all content area reading in both the primary and intermediate grades. In Chapter 11 the processes involved in reading graphic data will be discussed in relation to reading specific science, math, and social studies materials.

GENERIC STUDY SKILLS *first group of skills*

Selection–Evaluation–Selection

The process of selection-evaluation-selection is not only related to study situations, but it is basic to every choice in life. In making a decision one has to identify and select from many possible choices, evaluate the choices according to predetermined criteria, and then make a refined selection. The complexity of the use of the skill of evaluation depends on the complexity of selections to be made and the bases for those selections. If the user finds himself in a situation where he must choose a reference, he may need to examine several possibilities, weigh or evaluate their content as it relates to his need, and make a final choice or selection based on his evaluations. An individual who is asked a direct question needs to sift through possible answers that occur to him, evaluate their potential worth, and make a choice for a response. The child who is given an opportunity to choose a way to use a segment of time will need to consider all possibilities and make his choice accordingly. One might say selection and evaluation are basic to the decision to get up and start each new day.

This skill does not lend itself to the primary-intermediate breakdown as readily as several of the other common study skills. It is, however, basic to the use of each of the others.

Organization

Primary Years

Children develop a sense of order or organization at an early age which needs considerable encouragement and cultivation as the child matures. Success in the use of organizational skills depends on one's ability to see relationships.

Beginning activities for developing organizing skills usually include the grouping of objects of the same color or shape. Organizational skills can be refined by grouping items of varying shades of the same color or arranging objects of the same shape but different sizes in order from largest to smallest, or vice versa. This skill may also be developed by grouping objects or pictures which have some common elements. For example, in kindergarden, children might be asked to select and group a collection of pictures; for example, grouping the pictures which show people working or all those which have something orange in them.

Categorizing. After using such basic exercises, first-grade children can advance to the organization of words which have the same beginning, ending, or medial sounds. They can categorize or group words which have related meanings, for example, all the words which name toys or all the words which name actions.

In writing, composing, or relating ideas, the order of organization is quite significant. When primary school aged children are beginning to develop group stories, they may volunteer suggestions as soon as they think of them; however, the teacher may want to read the sentences over with them, guiding them in organizing the sentences according to sequence. Once the story has been composed and recorded on a chart, it may be cut into sentence strips so that children can read the sentences and then reconstruct the original story.

In a similar manner, children can be helped to see relationships among ideas. After they have heard or read a story that took place in a specific country, they might be asked to identify the things in the story that indicate the setting of the story. Another approach is to have them write ideas about two characters (Robin Hood and Little John) from a story they have heard, then mix them up, and ask the children to regroup the ideas that relate to each character.

The setting in which primary children study should have a good collection of books and other instructional materials. These areas need to be arranged and kept in some orderly fashion while the children are learning and while they are practicing their learning. Through classroom discussions, children can help to plan the organization and placement of these materials. They can also be involved in keeping the materials in some specified order.

Summarizing. Another organization skill which primary and intermediate children can be helped to develop is the skill of summarizing. This requires the ability to select the most significant points in a story, incident, or report and to relate them in a sequential order. Although the skill of sequencing becomes refined during the intermediate grades, it can be initiated quite early by asking children to tell about some event or story in their own words. Even at these early levels, you can begin building organizational skills with children through examples and discussions:

1. Encourage children through questioning to observe the structure of the material being read.
   a. Am I reading an essay within a book or a total book?
   b. What clues do the pictures give me?
   c. Title clues
   d. Subtitle clues
   e. Summary
2. Survey lessons with children to determine the language clues that enable one to better understand the author's organizational structure.
   a. Are there clue words that add to the total idea?

in addition	since	moreover
and	furthermore	too
another	otherwise	as well as
also	likewise	plus
again	besides	after all

   b. Are there clue words that emphasize the concluding idea?

finally	in conclusion
in sum	consequently
in brief	hence
thus	then
in the end	at last

   c. Are there clue words that emphasize reversing, qualifying, or modifying ideas?

but	on the other hand
nevertheless	either–or
still	conversely
in contrast	however
even if	opposed to

d. Are there clue words that indicate thought emphasis?

because	as
like	for instance

e. Are there clue words that indicate relationships in time, space, or degree?

last	here	many
now	there	more
later	close	little
after	for	some
previously	by	best
following	away	all
meanwhile	under	fewer
at the same time	above	greater
before	across	above all
immediately	beneath	worst

3. Encourage awareness of the headings and subheadings of the material being read.
   a. Position on page
   b. Type of print
4. Discuss the informational clues offered through headings, subheadings, and organizational pattern.
5. Read materials with students and ask questions that focus on organizational structure.
   a. What are the major headings? Subheadings?
   b. Were time relationships evidenced through headings?
   c. Were irrelevant subheadings included?
   d. Were more subheadings needed?
   e. Was a summary provided?
6. Develop note-taking skills.
   a. Begin reading a story.
   b. Stop when the emphasis of the story shifts.
   c. Write a sentence that summarizes what was read.
   d. Write a phrase containing the main points of the sentence.
   e. Continue reading, and repeat this process each time the emphasis of the story shifts.

Activities 1 and 2 at the end of this chapter are designed to help you to implement specific organization skills in your primary classroom.

Intermediate Years

At the intermediate level, there is a need to *extend* the development of organization skills which include advanced classification, grouping, sentence and story arrangement, and summarizing. Advanced classifying and grouping might involve dealing with more complicated ideas. Advanced sentence and story arrangement could suggest work with more complex sentences and longer paragraphs, as well as with sentences and paragraphs with more difficult content. The development of organizational skills helps the student to realize relationships among facts. Once the student has identified the organizational structure of the material, he has an operational base from which he can synthesize, compose, and evaluate newly learned facts.

Through the development of this study skill, the reader follows the author's plan by recognizing organizational patterns, major ideas, and details. The organizational patterns commonly used by authors include time orders, enumeration, comparisons, contrasts and cause-and-effect relationships.

Outlining. Outlining can be a difficult skill to master if children are not taught to understand purpose and organization throughout the primary levels. The basis for success in outlining lies in being able to understand the content that one is trying to outline and in being able to grasp the relationships among the ideas involved. The foundation for development of this skill is found in the primary skills: classifying (grouping ideas) and summarizing. The concept of outlining can be developed easily and naturally by children if the teacher makes a list of related ideas into a simple outline format. These lists may have the more important ideas set off by numerals and the supporting ideas indicated by letters. Move first into the use of major ideas, with supporting ideas indented, and then add letter and number designations. The use of such listings continually lends itself to the teaching of this skill.

As more formal outlining is practiced, a few basic principles of outlining should be taught. They are illustrated in the following outline form.

Topic

I. A Major Idea
   A.
      1.
        a.
          (1)
            (a)
            (b)
          (2)
        b.
      2.
   B.

The preceding outline form illustrates a relatively simple seven-level outline that does not exhaust the limits of delineating or analyzing information in outline form. It does go as far, and perhaps farther, than the majority of elementary children will be able to go in understanding and outlining material. Ultimately, the child needs to understand that the purpose of outlining is to help one identify main ideas and supporting ideas in some body of information. Children must be helped to understand that the author has already designed an outline for the material; the child has to interpret and use the outline as a clue for comprehension.

Students can easily obtain an understanding of topics and subtopics if they are provided with a text excerpt and a partial text outline which contains the topics. Then they need to be asked to supply the missing topics and subtopics. For example, present your students with a text excerpt like the following:

Census figures show many people are leaving the central parts of big cities for the more open spaces of the suburbs

Uncle Sam is now bringing out the first of many census reports. They are put together from the answers on the millions of census forms filled out by Americans last April. The first reports give population figures.

The story of how the U.S. is changing can be read from the figures. They show which states are growing fastest in population, which are growing slowly, and which are losing or gaining people. In short, the census reports show changes that have taken place during your lifetime—since 1960.

From Cities to Suburbs

One change to be read from the figures is that Americans are leaving the cities for the suburbs. About 15 million more people now live in the suburbs than in 1960. More people live in the suburbs around big cities than in-

(Please turn to p. 2)

(Continued from p. 1)

side the cities. Some big cities have fewer people than they had in 1960.

To the South and West

Many people have moved to sunshine states like Florida, Texas, and California. The mild climate drew some. Also, those states had space industries. Many people moved there for jobs.

Florida became one of the fastest-growing states. Its population went up by more than a million and a half. The number of people there is a third higher than in 1960. The movement of people to California made it the "most populous state." That title was held for a long time by New York.

The West in general attracted people from other states. Pacific states (Oregon, Washington, Alaska, Hawaii) and some mountain states were among the fastest-growing. Nevada's population increased by more than a half during the ten years—the biggest population change of any state. The state's total, however, is still under a million.

More Reports Coming

More reports of information taken off the census forms will be made in the coming months. Some will give a population count by age-groups, race, and sex. Other reports will show the kinds of jobs people have and the kinds of places they live in. The reports will also show the kinds of things people have, such as applicances and plumbing.

When the reports are completed, we will have a picture of the U.S. as the 1970s began.

REASONS FOR OUTLINING

Special permission granted by My Weekly Reader, Grade 5, published by Xerox Education Publications, 1970, Xerox Corp.

After the students have finished reading the excerpt, ask them to complete an outline similar to the following:

Census Shows Changes in the U.S.

Topic	I.	Americans are leaving the cities for the suburbs.
Subtopic	*(A.	Fifteen million more people now live in suburbs.)
Subtopic	(B.	Some big cities have fewer people than they did in 1960.)
Topic	II.	Many people moved to the South and West
Subtopic	(A.	Florida became one of the fastest-growing states.)
Subtopic	(B.	California became the "most populous state.")
Subtopic	(C.	Nevada showed the biggest population change of any state.)
Topic	III.	More information from the census forms is available.

*Information in parentheses should be eliminated when you use this format with your children.

These are other activities that enable children to understand the relevancy of main heading and subheading:

1. After children have read only chapter headings and subheadings, ask them to discuss the information which should be contained in each.

2. Encourage children to write a story summary using only the information provided in story headings and subheadings.

3. Ask children to read several paragraphs and develop a heading for each paragraph.

4. Select several newspaper articles. Remove the titles. Ask children to read the articles and select the appropriate title.

As children engage in independent study, they experience difficulty because of their inability to understand the relationships presented in the organized text structure. In addition to understanding main topics and subtopics, students need to understand that, in an outline, one does not use a *I* unless he has information for *II*. One may continue on through *III, IV, V,* and so on, but unless the information with which he is dealing can be broken into at least two parts of equal importance, he does not break the idea away from the preceding heading of greater importance. Therefore, if he has *I*, he needs *II*; if he has *A*, he needs *B*; if he has *1*, he needs *2*, and so on. He also needs to understand that, in some cases, a brief phrase or word outline will fulfill his needs, whereas on other occasions, he may want to prepare a sentence outline.

New Neighbors

Sentence Outline

 I. Daryl Chou is my new neighbor.
   A. Daryl is ten years old.
   B. Daryl is in my class at school.

 II. Daryl's mother owns many nice things.
   A. His mother has three cars.
   B. His mother's sailboat is in the backyard.
   C. Daryl's mother owns six televisions.

 III. Daryl's father is very smart.
   A. He is a teacher.
   B. His father owns many books.

New Neighbors

Brief Outline

I. Daryl Chou
   A. Ten years old
   B. Same class at school

II. Daryl's mother owns
   A. Three cars
   B. Sailboat
   C. Six televisions

III. Daryl's father
   A. Teacher
   B. Books

Decisions about the most appropriate outline form to use may depend on your use of it and the time in which the student is going to use it. If a great deal of time is going to elapse between development and use, the student may want to use the sentence form because it will be easier to remember the written selection of more information. The word or phrase outline is very useful for study purposes, or when giving an oral review of printed materials. If the outline is to be shared with others who have not read the information, the sentence format may be more effective.

It is usually recommended that the different forms not be mixed. When outlining is first being learned, it is advisable to adhere to this principle. However, as the outliner becomes more skilled and as he prepares outlines for his personal use, he may find a mixture more satisfactory.

When preparing outlines with your students, remember to emphasize these additional points:

1. Italicized or underlined words may indicate a foreign term.

2. Chapter introductions may provide them with an understanding of what can be anticipated within the text.

3. Chapter summaries may enable them to gain a complete understanding of the relationships which have been explored within the text.

Note Taking. Note taking is another skill that requires careful and continuous teaching. Children often resort to paragraph lifting in the name of note taking. It is important to help students, make use of different clues and cues as he takes notes. For instance, he needs to focus attention on topics and subtopics. Subsequently, he needs to read the material accompanying these topics and subtopics and make his notes in a form that he can understand and reuse. The notes should include in paraphrase the most significant information which is read in the material. If the individual is taking notes from either an oral or written presentation, he must:

1. be able to pick out the important points and related ideas.

2. realize the value of listening and reading before summarizing or paraphrasing.

3. list notes in his own words.

4. list brief notes.

5. develop notes that give structural clues: _first_, _most important_, _finally_.

6. invent his own abbreviation code.

7. be consistent.

8. develop a topical note filing system that includes a bibliographic reference to topic, date, and purpose of notes.

Read a selection with your students and then discuss

1. the ideas that should be recorded as notes.

2. the best form of notes for the intended purpose.

   a. outline

   b. list

   c. chart

   d. time line

   e. parallel columns

3. the need for notes to include:

   a. Who?

   b. What?

   c. When?

   d. Where?

   e. Why?

   f. How?

During the intermediate grades, students need to be helped to develop skill in preparing summaries. This may be accomplished by reading a newspaper or text selection with them and then

1. stating the main theme.

2. selecting the sentence that best summarizes each paragraph.

3. combining these sentences to summarize several paragraphs.

If students appear to be having difficulty in selecting main ideas you may present a passage and several sentences from the selection, and discuss the main idea of the selection with them and look for clue words and phrases. Once the topic becomes clearer, difficulties in selecting main ideas will diminish.

   1. Have the main ideas been included?

   2. Are the major details highlighted?

   3. Is the primary theme obvious to the reader?

   4. Have all unnecessary words been eliminated?

If students appear to be having difficulty in selecting main ideas, present them with a passage and several sentences from the selection; discuss the main idea of the selection with them and look for clue words and phrases. Once the topic becomes clearer, difficulties in selecting main ideas will diminish.

Summarizing and Synthesizing. Synthesizing and restating information gathered from various sources may require as much in the way of locational skills as it does in ability to organize. It provides an opportunity for the use of note taking, outlining, and summarizing skills. It requires considerable skill to be able to identify and to use a number of sources in gathering information on a topic and to be able to synthesize the information into a meaningful, logically ordered whole. As a student becomes competent in the use of a few sources, the number can be gradually increased. Another requirement for effective use of this skill is knowledge of suitable sources from which information may be gathered. If the individual does not know direct sources, then he must learn ways of identifying and locating such sources.

A statement of synthesis or summary is very similar to an outline because it contains the major and minor story details stated in one's own words. A summary presentation may take the form of a paragraph, a listing of events, or a record of procedural steps. In an attempt to develop these skills you might introduce students to a text excerpt that contains a summary, and after reading the excerpt and summary you may ask students to

1. list the main ideas and important details.
2. discuss their rationale for listing the major ideas and details.
3. determine if these bits of information are contained in the summary.
4. analyze the different styles used to present major and minor points in story and summary text.

Preparing Graphic Aids. A great deal of information can be presented in tabular or chart form. Children can learn to use and to develop this means of conveying information. In order to effectively prepare a chart or graph which uses symbols to represent quantities, students need to be instructed in abstract reading skills. For example, if children were trying to prepare a graph portraying the population in their home area since 1900, they would have to decide which years to chart or graph, the type of symbol to use, and the number of people each symbol should represent. They would also have to select a general format for the chart and they would need to prepare a legend explaining their use of symbols so that others could use the information. Examples of social studies and science graphs emphasizing these details are presented in Chapter 11. These examples will serve to emphasize the need to (1) read graphs with understanding, and (2) allot ample time for developing graph-reading skills.

When introducing students to graphic aids, you ought to read the materials with them, explaining in detail the illustrated concepts. Once the students have been introduced to graphic aids, you may want to use the following procedures in order to demonstrate issues related to their life functioning.

1. Develop a chart illustrating the height and weight of each student.
2. Design a map which depicts the home location of each student.
3. Construct diagrams showing how to use classroom AV equipment.
4. Develop pictures describing each child's hobbies.

Your continuous use of pictorial aids will encourage the reader to use these same aids when attempting to understand the printed text.

Recall

Primary Years

It is difficult in many cases to separate skills of comprehension when one is trying to help children to develop a specific study skill or when trying to assess the extent to which one has been developed. Frequently, attempts to check comprehension are actually checks of recall, and each of us has at some time realized that recall can occur with little or no comprehension or interpretation.

At the primary level, as well as at the intermediate level, teachers help children to develop skill in remembering by helping them set purposes for reading, listening, and viewing films to gain information. These purposes usually need to be stated in broad terms so that children do not focus their attention on small details and thereby fail to extract the larger meaning of the text.

One of the oldest and most frequently used means of checking recall is through *question asking*. The focus here is not on the question-asking technique, except as it is related to the ways answers can be given. Answers may be given orally or through demonstration, the carrying out of some direction, or role playing. Answers may also be shared through media, art, music, and dance.

As an aid to accuracy, as well as recall, it is helpful to let children verify points which they have recalled, particularly if there is a difference of opinion among "recallers." Too often the teacher becomes the arbitrator, as well as the "fountain of knowledge" when he or she simply supplies the correct answer. True, it often seems the most economical use of time, but even that argument may be questionable. When these instances arise, let the children with differences of opinion reexamine their sources and discuss their differences.

Intermediate Years

At the intermediate levels, refinement of the skills which were introduced at the primary levels should be continued. Much of our ability to function satisfactorily in our daily lives depends on our ability to recall specific information. Techniques that help us store some information so that it is ours are sometimes referred to as memorizing techniques. It is true that many people rise up in protest at the mere suggestion of memorizing. The contention to be made here is that there are acceptable and unacceptable ways of memorizing information. If one is to sing with a choir, he may find that he needs to know the words of some musical composition so that he can sing them without the aid of written material. He may also find that the choir director talks through the song, discussing with the choir the ideas the song intends to convey. When this is followed by practice in singing with the group, he may suddenly realize that he knows the words and the melody to the composition. Probably, they crept up on him unaware. First there was understanding, then there was practice and utilization, and then the composition was "memorized."

Using Memorizing Techniques.

SQ3R. Have you ever noticed that people who are organized seem to get much more accomplished than those who let things happen haphazardly? Organized people use certain steps that are essential in order to get things done. The first clue is to identify the steps. This is also true in reading.

A good way to really understand what we read is to follow the SQ3R method (survey, question, read, recite, review) because it helps us to become organized. There are certain steps to follow, and if we follow them, we will be able to accomplish our goals while we are reading.

Let us suppose that you have given your students an assignment to read an article from a magazine and report on it to the class the next day. The following instructions might help them in completing the task.

> The article you choose must be about business. While looking at the table of contents of a national magazine, you come across the title "Economy & Business." You turn to that section and you notice several articles:
>
> Resources
> Airlines
> Autos
> Mergers
> Retailing
> Beverages
>
> Step 1. You decide to do your report on "Autos." Now, what you have really been doing while searching for your article is Step 1 of the SQ3R method; that is, surveying. Everytime you are given an assignment, you should begin it by reading the title and noting the major headings and subheadings in the chapter you are reading.
>
> When you continue to survey the section you have chosen for your report, you will notice the heading "Autos," the title "Foreign Autos Are Fun."

Surveying involves glancing over the introductory sentence, main headings, and graphs and reading the summary, if one is provided. This sets the stage, or provides a framework, for subsequent steps.

> Step 2. Your next step is to question. To what does the term foreign autos refer? What are some other questions that come to your mind as you look at that title?

Questioning relates to the major headings. Beginning with the first main heading, the reader uses it to provide a purpose for reading—a question to answer. Teacher aid in developing these questions may at times be needed.

> Step 3. Now you are ready to read the section "Foreign Autos." Remember that you are not simply reading words. You are reading to find the answers to your questions. Ask yourself what the main idea is in this article. How does the author support his point of view? In other words, does the author support his statement, "Not since World War I ... has the French auto industry seen bigger trouble."?

Do your answers make sense? Do you have any personal thoughts on the subject? For example, there is a quote by the head of one of France's car companies. Do you agree with his feelings?

(Step 4) Now, recite the answers to yourself. Do your answers make sense? If they don't, you will want to go to another source to check the same information. Also, can you use this information in a new way? For example, can you compare what has happened in the auto industry with a similar occurrence in some other industry?

It's your turn now. Follow the same procedure with the second paragraph, "Unsold Autos"; that is, question, read, recite.

(Step 5) Finally, review what you have read. Reviewing is surveying, but with the details filled in. Make an outline in your mind; or, if you are new at the SQ3R method, make an outline on paper. Now you have acquired some important skills on how to read and study materials. If you read carefully using the SQ3R method, you will decrease substantially the time spent in memorizing facts.

After finishing the article, the student may find it helpful to review the points previously recalled. Notes that have been taken during the short recall periods may be used to facilitate recall of the whole article. If your students are systematically aided in this procedure, they can soon develop the habit of approaching study reading in this way.

Using Psychological Aids. The use of psychological aids suggests that there are certain things we can do to help our minds absorb and retain information. If we can see the relationships or logical connection between a number of ideas, it is often possible to link them and recall them better than we can recall them separately.

Association. Acquaint children with the concept of association as a process that will enable them to relate and synthesize information. For example, if your students are reading a text that discusses Indiana limestone, you might want to develop questions that will emphasize the following associations.

Facts found in the text:

1. Location of Indiana
2. Primary ingredient of limestone
3. Corals and tiny shells turn to minerals.
4. Limestone is found in caves and quarries.
5. Indiana has many quarries.

After highlighting these facts, ask a question which encourages association of the facts. For example, you might ask:

"Why is so much limestone found in Indiana?"

Association is only one method of aiding recall. The *delayed recall technique* is another memory helper. It might better be called the continued review technique. It means that one studies and checks his own recall and reviews it periodically until he has the information instantly available. You may develop this technique by periodically asking children to make reference to some body of data which they have already learned.

The *whole* and *parts methods* of recall is also a useful tool. The length of the material to be memorized plays an important part in determining which of these techniques is most effective. In all cases the initial focus should be on the "whole." Parts of the total material to be memorized should be studied until they are understood in total. Students should be introduced to all of these methods of review and encouraged to use them whenever appropriate.

Locating Information

Primary Years

If your primary goal is to provide students with the skills they need to become independent learners, then the development of *locational skills* will be one of your major concerns. Locational skills provide children with the necessary means of securing sources of information. One of the very basic skills a child needs is the ability to *alphabetize*.

Alphabetizing. Because alphabetical arrangement is used for storing and locating information, it is viewed as a locational skill. It is a prerequisite for using dictionaries, encyclopedias, and other reference books. Perhaps the logical way to begin teaching the skill of alphabetizing is to

1. Introduce the letters of the alphabet in sequential order.
2. Write the alphabet on the board and ask students to supply the missing parts.
   a, b,__, __, e, __, g, h, __, __, __, __, l, __, n, __, p, q, __, __, __, u, __, w, x, y, __ .
3. Supply word lists and ask children to alphabetize them.

any	run	see
car	the	boy
toy	is	girl
bat	we	mother
dog	us	top

4. Supply word lists that will have to be alphabetized by the second letter.

and	boy	cat	fun
all	big	city	father

5. Supply word lists that will have to be alphabetized by the third and fourth letters.

and	baby	ran	hail	them
ant	bat	rang	hair	these

Using the Dictionary. The picture dictionary is an excellent tool for reinforcing alphabetizing skills while introducing dictionary usage. Single-picture dictionaries catalogue words according to some common relationship: animals, clothing, food. Words in the groups may be alphabetized and illustrated with pictures. There is a wide variety of dictionaries available, and children may begin with these simple dictionaries and gradually advance to using standard dictionaries. Activity 3, at the end of this chapter, is designed to aid you in developing very basic alphabetizing and dictionary skills.

Table of Contents. After the young child has developed a thorough knowledge of alphabetization and a basic understanding of the dictionary, he is ready to learn the very first step in using a book. There are many things that are introduced at the primary levels and continued through the intermediate levels. One example is use of the *parts of books*.

At the primary level, children should be taught the purpose of the cover of a book and its title. They should be introduced to the table of contents to quickly locate major parts of the book. They need to realize that, although it may not contain a complete listing of all headings and subheadings, what is listed in the table of contents is in numerical order from beginning to end. Children need to begin finding pages by number as soon as they can read numbers. Within the text, children also need to learn to locate a specific bit of information or material quickly, such as words, phrases, or sentences.

Children will gain an understanding of a table of contents by using one. The following table of contents and questions are provided as an example of an exercise that you may want to use with your students.

Music in America

Table of Contents

Chapter

This table of contents provides a vast amount of information about the text. Ask your students to answer the following questions:

1. Where would you look for information about music and art? (Chapter VII)
2. Where would you find an explanation about the contents of the entire book? (Chapter I)
3. If you wanted to sing a sea chanty, where could you find an example? (Chapter II, section B)
4. Where would you look in order to find out what a hammer dulcimer is? (Glossary)
5. How could you tell on what page "On Top of Old Smokey" is located? (Index)
6. Your special assignment is to learn a cowboy song. Where could you find one in this book? (Chapter V, section A)
7. Spirituals were very popular in the south. In what section of the book are spirituals located? (Chapter III, section C)
8. Where would you look to see how many Christmas songs are printed in this book? (Chapter VI, section B)
9. Farming is very important in the middle west. If you wanted to sing a song about the corn harvest, where might you find one? (Chapter IV, section C)
10. What is the topic of this book? (American music)
11. How many chapters are in this book? (Seven)
12. How could you find out what kind of a song Mary Ann is? (Look in alphabetical listing and then turn to that page.)
13. Where could you find out about colonial art? (Chapter VII, section A)
14. Where could you find information about playing an instrument? (Chapter I)
15. Where could you find a Navaho Indian song? (Chapter V, section B, number 2)

When answering questions such as these, students are required to (1) locate page numbers, (2) find words, phrases, or sentences in context, and (3) use titles and chapter headings. Children benefit from this and similar activities that require them to make decisions about the information contained in a text. Be sure always to ask children to support their answers with facts.

After introducing the table of contents, which is the very basis for text usage, children should be introduced to other available classroom resources: encyclopedia, atlas and almanac.

Reference Materials. Although very few young children will be able to use encyclopedias, atlases, and almanacs independently, many may be ready to profit from hearing material read to them. Wanting to be able to use these resource texts is an extremely strong motivation for learning. Many children may also be able to read material in some of these references if they have help initially in locating the information. They are capable also of incorporating the terms *encyclopedia, atlas,* and *almanac* into their vocabularies. Even the youngest of children should be introduced to these reference tools and encouraged to view them as additional sources of information.

Begin by showing children that the information contained in these texts is arranged alphabetically. Some primary children may be able to explore the use of an *index*; however, because this is not common index usage will be discussed for intermediate grade students.

Explore the reference material by

1. introducing the fact that the text contents appear in alphabetical order.
2. selecting a problem.
   a. Who has the greatest batting average in American baseball history?
   b. How did the Academy Awards originate?
   c. Who was the seventeenth president of the United States?
   d. What is the largest body of water in the world?
3. surveying resources with youngsters to determine which is the most suitable for answering each question.
4. making generalizations regarding the use of each resource

If these resource materials are not part of your classroom, you may want to visit the library.

Library Skills. There are several library skills that the child needs to develop at the primary level: proper care of books, appropriate library behavior, and a general understanding of book arrangement in the libraries to which they will have access.

Satisfactory or appropriate library behavior is another way in which children (and all of us) can demonstrate respect for the rights of others. Such behavior does not demand hushed silence on the part of library users and workers. It does require a degree of quietness, however, that allows all library users to do just that—use the library. Therefore, effective instruction on library behavior involves helping children recognize the type of atmosphere that makes their use of the library most pleasant and productive and to realize that they have responsibility in helping create this atmosphere for others, as well as for themselves.

After your primary-grade students have been instructed in care of books and library courtesy, if you feel they are ready to master the card catalog, follow the activity at the end of this chapter. For more specific information on this topic, please refer to a later section of this chapter, "Using a Card Catalog," page 370.

Intermediate Years

At the intermediate level, students need to extend their awareness of locational skills. This may be accomplished by developing a thorough understanding of parts of a book.

Extended Use of Books. In order to use all parts of a book to find and choose material that is suited to their needs, students need to become aware of the parts that give the most information: *title*, *name*(s) of the person(s) or companies responsible for the *production* of the book, and how current the contents are. This, of course, would include surveying cover, title page, copyright and publication date, and acknowledgments. Students need to become competent in uisng the parts of the book which point out its contents, beginning with the table of contents and proceeding to the index, appendixes, and glossaries, on through the headings and subheadings (which do not appear in the table of contents).

Index. Once a general understanding of the table of contents has been developed, you need to explore the use of an index. The index can provide the reader with more in-depth information about the topical relationships within the text that can be found in the table of contents. Children may be encouraged to survey the index first because it synthesizes all parts of the text related to a single topic. The index is also a more precise reference to page numbers. You may want to teach the use of an index in the following way:

1. Provide your students with a set of problems they want to solve.
   a. How did musical instruments originate?
   b. Who is Arthur Fiedler?
   c. Where is the greatest amount of wheat harvested?
   d. Where is the Amazon River located?
2. After developing the problems, encourage the children to delineate the information to be found.
   a. Musical instruments, origins
   b. Arthur Fiedler
   c. Wheat
   d. Amazon River
3. Have students select a text which may contain the information you are seeking. To answer problems *a* and *b* it may be most helpful to select a music text, whereas to answer problems *c* and *d* you may select a social studies text.
4. Once the text has been selected, have students survey the index to determine:
   a. if entries are listed alphabetically.
   b. if topics, symbols, and names are all part of one index.
   c. the meanings of any abbreviations.
   d. the purpose of using commas and dashes in entries.
   e. the meaning of words in italics.
   f. if desired information is contained.

Index

Agriculture
  in Brazil, 102–105, 326, 350, 405–30
  in China, 56–80
  in Egypt, 154, 159, 163, 172–74
  in England, 13, 19–22
  in Germany, 220–35
Airports, 200, 217, 230, 450–80
Amazon River, 80
Balewa, Tafawa, 17, 19
Bedouins, 118–26

While the children are attempting to solve their own problems, they will gain mastery of the index. Activity 5 at the end of this chapter is an aid to further develop this locational skill.

Glossary and Appendixes. Other parts of books that students need to understand are the glossaries and appendixes. They need to realize that a glossary contains words that relate to the special contents of the book. Glossaries and appendixes often do not appear in primary-level books. Appendixes may have varied content, but their purpose usually is to supply, in a condensed form, supplementary information that is related to the textual content. These are listed in the table of contents, and information included is indexed, as is other text information.

Other text sections that should be explained are the preface and foreward. These sections are often overlooked. If children are exposed to these parts of books when they are young, they are more likely to continue to use them. They need to know that a preface includes the author's explanation of his purpose and plan for the book. A foreward is an introduction to the book written by someone other than the author. It usually reflects the writer's interpretation of and reaction to the purpose and plan of the book. Instruction in using the textbook should include discussion of

1. the author's purpose in writing the preface.
2. the author's hope of accomplishment through one's reading of the text.
3. the author's point of view.
4. the intended text use.

Activity 6 at the end of the chapter is designed to aid you in teaching the importance of the glossary.

Extended Dictionary Skills. At the intermediate level, teaching dictionary skills needs to be continually emphasized because the ability to correctly use a dictionary to help unlock word meanings and pronounciation is a skill needed by children at every level. In fact, the individual's mastery of many skills that are usually categorized as dictionary skills will strongly affect his success in using many other reference books. As you attempt to develop this skill, you will need to provide instruction related to the following topics: finding words, word meanings, and word pronunciation.

How to Find a Word. In order to find a specific word in the dictionary a child will have to be able to

a. recognize letters.
b. differentiate between structures of letters.
c. put into sequence the letters of the alphabet.
d. arrange words alphabetically—by first letter and then by second, third, and eventually all letters.

It is helpful to develop a sense of letter locations in a dictionary so that when an unindexed dictionary is being used, words and information can be located as quickly as possible. To help children to develop this skill, you should ask them to open a dictionary in the middle and note which letters are on the pages which fall to the left and right. Next, ask them to divide each half so that they can note the letters in each quarter of the dictionary. Ask them to open the dictionary to the place where the user anticipates finding the first letter and then going forward or backward to the word. Activity 7 at the end of this chapter provides instruction in this area.

Alert children to the use of guide words which can help save time. Once the dictionary has been opened to the approximate location of a word, guide words will help determine whether to turn backward or forward.

Sample Activity

Guide Words

Say to your class:
Look at the sample dictionary page. The words poor and pork are printed at the top of the page to the left. These words are called guide words because they tell you whether a word you are looking for is to be found on this page. The word poor is the first entry on this page. The word pork is the last entry on this page. The words pop, popcorn, and porch are on this page because they occur in alphabetical order between poor and pork.

After the students have a basic understanding of guide words, you may want to teach them how to find each of these sets of words in their dictionary.

| ballet | musical | choreography |
| gnome | scalawag | hectogram |

After they find each word, ask them to write the guide words that are on the same page as the word being pursued.

The child needs to understand that the guide words point out the first and last words on a page. If the word being pursued is alphabetically between the guide words, then the word should be on that page, if it is included in that particular dictionary. You may want to provide children with a list of words and ask them to supply the order in which they could be found in a dictionary.

_____	boy	_____	before	_____	hurry
_____	mansion	_____	today	_____	skip
_____	plane	_____	yesterday	_____	jump
_____	lava	_____	after	_____	amble
_____	apple	_____	always	_____	run

poor / pork

group of people. Dad belongs to a car *pool* in which each person takes a turn driving the others to work. *Noun.*
—To put together for a group to share. The children *pooled* their money to buy a present for their mother. *Verb.*
pool (pōol) *noun, plural* **pools;** *verb,* **pooled, pooling.**

poor 1. Having little money. She is too *poor* to buy a new dress. 2. Below standard; less than needed; bad. He has *poor* health. The farmer had a *poor* wheat crop. He is a *poor* student. 3. Unfortunate. The *poor* boy lost his pet dog.
poor (poor) *adjective,* **poorer, poorest.**

pop 1. To make or cause to make a short, sharp sound. The balloon will *pop* if you squeeze it. He blew into the paper bag and then *popped* it between his hands. 2. To move or appear quickly or without being expected. Aunt Mary *popped* in to see us. He *popped* his head out the window. *Verb.*
—1. A short, sharp sound. The firecracker exploded with a loud *pop.* 2. A soft drink. Jean drank a bottle of *pop. Noun.*
pop (pop) *verb,* **popped, popping;** *noun, plural,* **pops.**

popcorn A kind of corn having kernels that burst open with a pop when heated. The kernels become white and fluffy, and can be eaten.
pop·corn (pop′kôrn′) *noun.*

pope The head of the Roman Catholic Church.
pope (pōp) *noun, plural* **popes.**

poplar A tall, fast-growing tree. It has wide leaves and long, hanging stalks of flowers. The wood of the poplar is soft and is used to make pulp for paper and cardboard.
pop·lar (pop′lər) *noun, plural* **poplars.**

poppy A plant with round, red or yellow flowers. Opium comes from one kind of poppy.
pop·py (pop′ē) *noun, plural* **poppies.**

popular 1. Pleasing to very many people. Baseball is a *popular* sport. The beach is a *popular* place to go on summer afternoons. 2. Having many friends; well-liked. Bill is *popular* at school. 3. Of or for the people. Our country has a *popular* government. 4. Accepted by many people; widespread. It

Poppy

is a *popular* belief that a four-leaf clover will bring good luck.
pop·u·lar (pop′yə lər) *adjective.*

popularity The state of being popular. Gail's *popularity* at school was due to her friendly, happy nature.
pop·u·lar·i·ty (pop′yə lar′ə tē) *noun.*

population 1. The number of people who live in a place. What is the *population* of your city? 2. People. The entire *population* was forced to leave the town because of the flood.
pop·u·la·tion (pop′yə lā′shən) *noun.*

populous Having many people. New York is a *populous* city.
pop·u·lous (pop′yə ləs) *adjective.*

porcelain A kind of pottery. It is very hard, and is thin enough to see through when held to the light. Cups, plates, and other dishes are sometimes made of porcelain.
por·ce·lain (pôr′sə lin) *noun.*

porch A roofed area built onto a house. Grandmother's house has a large front *porch.*
porch (pôrch) *noun, plural* **porches.**

porcupine An animal whose body is covered with sharp quills.
por·cu·pine (pôr′kyə pin′) *noun, plural* **porcupines.**

Porcupine

▲ The word **porcupine** was made from two Latin words that meant "pig" and "thorn."

pore[1] A very small opening in the skin or other surface. Perspiration passes through the *pores* in our skin. ▲ Another word that sounds like this is **pour.**
pore (pôr) *noun, plural* **pores.**

pore[2] To look at, study, or think about carefully. John *pored* over his homework. ▲ Another word that sounds like this is **pour.**
pore (pôr) *verb,* **pored, poring.**

pork The meat of a pig used as food.
pork (pôrk) *noun.*

Word Meanings. The words known and used by children have meaning to them out of their own experiences. Children need to be encouraged to use the dictionary to validate the meanings of their language and to encourage language development.

What a Word Means

The Definition

Say to your class:

You can learn many things about a word from your dictionary. But the question that you will ask most often is, "What does it mean?" That is why we put the meaning right after the entry word itself. The meaning of a word is called its <u>definition</u>. When something is definite, it is very clear. The definition is what makes a word clear to you.

After you find the word you want, you can learn what it means right away. You will not have to read any other information first.

gavel A small wooden hammer. It is used by the person in charge of a meeting or trial to call for order or attention.
gav·el (gav′əl) *noun, plural* gavels.

gay Full of joy and fun; merry; cheerful. The children were *gay* at the birthday party. Ruth wore a *gay* dress with many pink ribbons.
gay (gā) *adjective.*

As you can see from the example for **gavel**, the first part of a definition in your dictionary is short and simple. It is made up of a few words that tell you quickly what you want to know: a **gavel** is "a small wooden hammer."

How to Learn About a Word from a Picture

Say to your class:

"A picture is worth a thousand words." That is an old saying. But even in a dictionary, which is a book of words, a picture can be very important. There are about 30,000 entry words in this book, and more than 1000 pictures—that is, one picture for every 30 words.

Why does a book about words need pictures? Many times a picture can tell you more about something than a definition in words can. Prove this to yourself. Read the following definitions.

metamorphosis The series of changes in shape and function that certain animals go through as they develop from an immature form to an adult. Caterpillars become butterflies and tadpoles become frogs through metamorphosis.
met·a·mor·pho·sis (met′ə·mor′fə sis) noun, plural **metamorphoses.**

bagpipe A musical instrument made of a leather bag and pipes. A person makes music by blowing air into the bag and then pressing the bag so that the air is forced out through the pipes. The bagpipe is often played in Scotland.
bag·pipe (bag′pip′) noun, plural **bagpipes.**

balance 1. The condition of having all the parts of something exactly the same in weight, amount, or force. The two children kept the seesaw in balance. 2. A steady position. He lost his balance and fell down the stairs. The tight-rope walker kept her balance. 3. An instrument for weighing things. The chemist weighed some powder on the balance. 4. The part that is left over. He still has the balance of his homework to do after supper. Noun.
bal·ance (bal′əns) noun, plural **balances;** verb, **balanced, balancing.**

What happens in metamorphosis?
How do you play the bagpipe?
What is balance?

Now look at the picture. Then go back and read the questions over again. Do you have a better idea now of how to answer them?

Here are the pictures of the words.

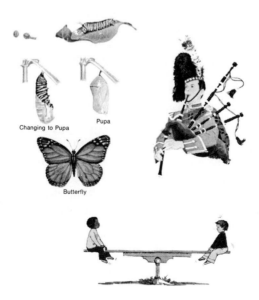

Changing to Pupa

Pupa

Butterfly

Further understanding of word meanings may be developed by studying:
1. synonyms and antonyms.
2. multiple meanings.

Activities 8 through 10 at the end of this chapter are designed to develop these skills.

Pronunciation. The use of the dictionary in providing a key to interpreting spoken language is certainly far more reliable than syllable analysis. To effectively use the dictionary, however, one needs an understanding of phonics and syllabication.

In order to develop pronunciation skills, you will need to provide information regarding the *pronunciation key*. Having located a word, it may be necessary to use a pronunciation key to decide how the word should be pronounced. This requires an understanding of phonetic respellings, the use of accent and diacritical markings, and syllabication. If the reason for locating the word relates to understanding meanings, the user needs to examine the definitions and to select the one that seems to fit the situation in which the word was used. To assist in understanding the meanings of some words, scale drawings are provided. Users need to be able to interpret and use these. Synonyms and antonyms are included as part of the definitions of many words. Before they help with understanding of the meaning of a particular word, the meanings of *synonym* and *antonym* must be understood.

In dictionary pronunciations each pronunciation symbol stands for one sound. To find out which sound each symbol stands for, turn to the full pronunciation key. This key is at the front and at the back of this dictionary.

Look at the symbol a and at the two words that follow it. The words hat and cap are called key words because they tell which sound the symbol a stands for, the vowel sound heard in hat and cap. Perhaps you have learned to call this sound the short a sound.

Now look at the symbols e, i, o, and u. What vowel sound does each of these symbols stand for? How do you know?

Look at the symbol b. What key words are given for this symbol? Where do you hear the b sound in bad? in rob? Look at the symbols d, f, g, and h. What consonant sound does each of these symbols stand for? How do you know? Look at the rest of the single letters that stand for consonant sounds. How can you tell which consonant sound each one stands for?

If you turn to the entry word yacht in your dictionary, you will see the pronunciation (yot) after it. How is yacht pronounced?

Below are the pronunciations of fifteen words. Write the numerals 1 through 15 on a piece of paper. Then say each word from its pronunciation, using the full pronunciation key if you need to. Write the spelling of that word after the numeral. The spellings are given in alphabetical order at the right. Do it this way: 1 half

1 (haf)	4 (laf)	7 (fir)	10 (jim)	13 (hil)	does	have	odd
2 (rek)	5 (rij)	8 (lok)	11 (hav)	14 (ruf)	fear	hill	ridge
3 (fuj)	6 (sez)	9 (nit)	12 (duz)	15 (od)	fudge	knit	rough
					gym	laugh	says
					half	lock	wreck

Students also need to understand the *Schwa* (ə) and *accent marks*. When we say a long word, we say some parts of it more loudly than others. We say the first part of the word *breakfast* more loudly than the second part.

The black marks in the dictionary, called accent marks, show which part of a word is spoken more loudly. The mark comes after the part of the word that is spoken more loudly.

> con·test (kon′test)
> be·gin·ning (bi gin′ing)

In order to develop pronunciation skills, children also need to understand prefixes, suffixes, and plurals. Activities 11 through 15 at the end of this chapter are designed to aid you in teaching pronunciation skills.

Extended Library Skills. Additional library skills to be taught at the intermediate levels include: library organization; use of the card catalog; and extended knowledge of reference resources. Children must be taught that the card catalog is like the index of a book, and that books are located in three ways in most card catalogs: the *author card*, the *subject card*, and the *title card*. Students need to learn how to read each of these types of cards and to develop an awareness of the type of card to look for, depending on the information they have.

Visiting the library and actually using the card catalog will enable children to understand that:

1. Cards are arranged alphabetically by author, subject, or title.
2. Subject, title, and author cards all contain the same information.

You may want to give students the following:

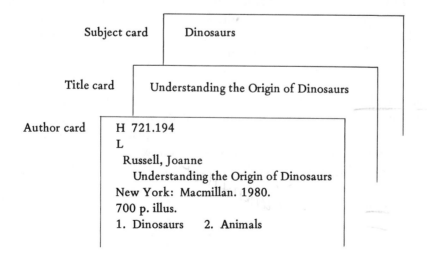

| Subject card | Dinosaurs |

| Title card | Understanding the Origin of Dinosaurs |

Author card	H 721.194
	L
	Russell, Joanne
	Understanding the Origin of Dinosaurs
	New York: Macmillan. 1980.
	700 p. illus.
	1. Dinosaurs 2. Animals

After they have surveyed the information on each of the cards, you may want to explain:

1. how each card is read.
2. the differences among the cards.
3. when each card is used.
4. to what the numbers and letters in the left-hand corner refer.

In an attempt to encourage children to use library and reference materials, their assignment should include:

1. using current events and maps to plan field trips.
2. asking questions that encourage children to consult many sources. For example, "How did Ellis Island reflect the ethnic flavor of many major American cities?"
3. using reference materials to develop the background information for topics currently being studied.

Children need to understand when to choose a particular general reference book. To find the pronunciation and definition of a word, a dictionary is needed. If an extensive explanation of a particular word is desired, an encyclopedia may be the desired reference. If one needs more specialized information related to a geographic area, a type of plant, or a scientific phenomenon, then a specialized reference book is needed. To help children learn to use reference books, such activities as 16 and 17 at the end of this chapter should be part of classroom instruction. The student needs to be aware of the library's resources and how these resources are to be used—whether they are books, tapes, films, filmstrips, records, or artifacts. The librarian has responsibility for assuring that students know about and have access to such media, but the teacher shares this responsibility.

Extended library skills are often needed by the intermediate student who wants to pursue an area of interest or complete a research paper. As well as referring to the card catalog for texts on a particular topic, students should be encouraged to examine the *Reader's Guide to Periodical Literature* to secure magazine articles related to the topic under study. *The Reader's Guide*, which provides references to forty-four periodicals, is used in a manner similar to that of the index. Once the desired text or magazine has been located, the success of interpreting the material will depend on the extent of a student's reading flexibility.

Reading Flexibility. Although the primary attention of the reading program should be directed toward the development of *word recognition* and *comprehension* skills, some specialized attention needs to be placed on the development of flexible reading techniques. Students need to know

1. when to read slowly and carefully.
2. when to read quickly.
3. how to skim materials.
4. how to scan materials.

In order to help children to develop such an understanding, you should provide them with the following information:

1. When reading for study you are attempting to
   a. answer questions.
   b. detect important facts.
   c. develop generalized impressions.
   d. remember details.
   e. reproduce data.
2. When reading for enjoyment, you are not required to engage in these specified activities.
3. The <u>rate</u> of your reading should depend on your <u>purpose</u> for reading. If, for example, you are reading to determine the main idea of a story, you may concentrate on the introductory paragraphs, and your rate of reading may begin more slowly than it would end.

After discussing this information with your students, present them with factual text excerpts and several purposes for reading:

a. for enjoyment.
b. to determine the general study topic.
c. to find a specified bit of information.

After completing a, b, and c, discuss with the students how they have altered their reading rates and techniques according to each new purpose.

Skimming is a useful tool for students. When students use skimming they quickly look over the excerpt to gain a general impression of the content. Skimming encourages very selective reading because it allows one to "get the gist" of the passage. In order to answer detailed questions about a topic, more detailed reading practices have to be used.

Another technique used by the flexible reader is that of *scanning*. Scanning is used to find a specified bit of information. The reader should be encouraged to scan the selection to determine the specific section containing the desired information.

When engaging your students in activities that will develop scanning techniques, you might begin by asking them to determine answers to very simple questions:

1. <u>What</u> color is the dress?
2. <u>In what year</u> did the volcano erupt?
3. <u>How</u> large was the structure?

After asking the questions, refer your students to the excerpt containing the information. Ask the students to quickly move their eyes across each line of information until the clue word for their answer becomes obvious.

1. color, dress
2. date, volcano
3. measurement, structure

When the information has been located, encourage them to read the sentences immediately preceding and following the one containing the pursued information. These sentences may add exactness to the information being secured.

Developing skimming and scanning skills requires *practice* with a *purpose*. As students develop proficiency with these skills, their reading rate will undoubtedly increase because flexibility is inherent in these practices.

Following Directions

Perhaps one of the most difficult tasks facing a person is *following directions*. This is strange when one stops to consider how many things one is directed to do in one's lifetime and the early age at which one begins.

The young child has some maturational limitations that affect his ability to follow directions. As directions are given to him orally or in writing, it should be kept in mind that he is not all at once given directions involving a long string of things to do, which can only lead to confusion. The young child receives most directions orally; therefore, he needs to learn to give his attention to directions to become an effective listener. It should also be kept in mind that the teacher's pattern for giving directions is soon recognized and responded to by children. The teacher who habitually repeats directions three times may soon find that children tune in on round three, if at all, and even then they may listen very ineffectively.

At the intermediate levels, more dependence is placed on written directions. At these levels the child has reached greater maturity and can recall a longer list of things to do for a longer period of time. At these levels, increased ability to reason and see relationships should enable the student to make mental connections that facilitate ability to follow directions.

It is very important that you help the child to develop skill in following directions by organizing directions as clearly and as concisely as possible. The directions themselves should facilitate success in developing the skill rather than serve as an impediment. When you are planning instruction that will enable children to better follow directions, remember to do the following:

1. Give one-step directions:
   a. Circle the correct picture.
   b. Number each item.
2. Move to two-step directions only after the child has mastered the concept of one-step:
   a. Underline all nouns and circle all verbs.
   b. Review the information in the text and then develop a graphic aid to illustrate the data.

3. Introduce three-step directions only after the child has mastered the concept of two-step directions:
   a. Read the story, draw a picture to illustrate it, and share the story and illustration with a friend.
   b. Eat your lunch, clean up the classroom, and go out to play.
4. Introduce activities that involve multistep directions:
   a. Assemble the model.
   b. Complete the experiment.

Children need help in mastering techniques and skills that will enable them to be as successful as possible when they read for study purposes. These skills, like reading itself, are of no particular significance in and of themselves, but they become highly significant when their overall effect on the child's academic success is considered. These skills are developmental in nature. Each child deserves to be introduced to them and to be helped to recognize their purpose and value. He also needs multiple opportunities to develop and refine his command of them. Most of these opportunities will be developed through learning pursuits that interrelate study skills and such content areas as math, science, and social studies.

ACTIVITIES TO DEVELOP STUDY SKILLS: ORGANIZATIONAL SKILLS

1. Classify the Animals

<u>Goal</u>: Developing classificational skills

<u>Grade level</u>: K–2

<u>Construction and utilization</u>: Have students design a bulletin board display. They can divide the board into five sections for a topic such as groups of animals and label them for birds, reptiles, amphibians, insects, and mammals. Then the students look for magazine pictures to illustrate the various sections. Students can also draw a picture for each heading.

2. Scrambled Outline

<u>Goal</u>: Developing outlining skills

<u>Grade level</u>: 1–3

<u>Construction</u>: On oak tag or cardboard, print an outline giving the name and subtopics and four to five supporting details. Cut each line into strips and attach felt tape to the back of them.

<u>Utilization</u>: The student puts the outline back together in the proper order, using a felt board.

ACTIVITIES TO DEVELOP STUDY SKILLS: DICTIONARY AND ALPHABETIZING SKILLS

3. Make a Class Directory

Goal: Alphabetizing and utilizing guide

Grade level: 2–4

Construction: Design a telephone directory by folding a piece of oak tag or construction paper in half and stapling in white paper for the desired number of pages.

Utilization: Have a group of children design a class telephone directory that includes the name, address, and telephone number of each student. The last names of the students must be placed in alphabetical order. Guide words for a page would be the first student's surname and the last student's surname appearing on each page.

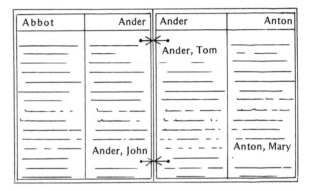

Children need to be introduced to dictionaries at this level also.

USING A CARD CATALOG

4. Find Me a Book

Goal: Using a card catalog

Grade level: 1–3

Construction: This activity can be done in the library or classroom. There should be a good supply of books labeled with call numbers, as well as a card catalog, which could also be constructed by the teacher, if necessary. Put the call number, title, author, number of pages, and a short description on the cards. There should be duplicate cards so that the student can locate the book using the title, author, or subject. Prepare a grab bag containing index cards that say "Fine me a book written by … " or "Find me a book about elephants."

Utilization: Students must use the catalog and then present the books to the scorekeeper, who gives five points for each card done correctly. The first person to complete five cards correctly wins.

ACTIVITIES TO DEVELOP STUDY SKILLS: USING AN INDEX

5. Make Your Own Index

Goal: Using an index

Grade level: 4–8

Construction and Utilization: Each student makes his own index to any book, comic book, or magazine, and then devises questions for a classmate to answer that require the use of the index. Classmates score two points for each question answered correctly (the index maker is the judge), and the first to score 10 wins.

USING A GLOSSARY

6. What Does Burlyboo Mean?

Goal: Understanding the purpose of a glossary

Grade level: 4–8

Construction: During a creative writing activity, have the class make up a science fiction or other type of story using any kind of made-up words, no matter how ridiculous.

Utilization: After the stories are written, have students make up a glossary for the "unfamiliar" words. They should then exchange stories and ask questions about the new words.

ACTIVITIES TO DEVELOP STUDY SKILLS: EXTENDED DICTIONARY SKILLS

7. Who Has the Fastest Dictionary in the West?

Goal: Developing skill in using the dictionary

Grade level: 3–6

Construction: Choose a volunteer who looks up 10 to 15 words in the dictionary and notes the page, column number, and guide words.

Utilization: Have a contest to see who can look up words the fastest. The MC calls out a word and the first person in the group to find the word shouts "I've got it" and reads the page number, column, and guide words he used. Each person to find a word the fastest scores one point. The highest score, when all the MC's words have been used, wins.

8. Can You Answer That?

<u>Goal</u>: Locating words and finding definitions in a dictionary

<u>Grade level</u>: 4–6

<u>Construction</u>: Teacher and children write questions containing unfamiliar words on 3-x 5-inch cards. For example: What does a <u>sloth</u> look like?

<u>Utilization</u>: Children are grouped into two teams. Team A begins by selecting a card, reading it to Team B, and asking "Can you answer that?" Team B must look up the unfamiliar word in a dictionary, answer the question, and verbally state the two guide words taken from the dictionary page on which the answer was found.

9. Ring Around a Guide Word

<u>Goal</u>: Interpreting guide words

<u>Grade level</u>: 1–3

<u>Construction</u>: Acquire a three-walled board and insert small wooden pegs or large nails on it. On each peg, hang a small card with a word beginning with <u>g</u> (or any other letter) written on it. Get small plastic loops (drapery or shower curtain hangers) for a type of ring-toss game.

<u>Utilization</u>: Players, in turn, toss rings around two words and then must name five words that come between those words in a dictionary. Score one point for each correct word. The first player to reach 100 wins.

10. Lace the Shoe

<u>Goal</u>: Reinforcement of word meanings

<u>Grade level</u>: 4–6

<u>Construction</u>: Cut out a piece of cardboard, oak tag, or construction paper approximately 12 x 18 inches. In one column, write several words that are unfamiliar to the student; in a second column, list short definitions of the words. Do not write the correct definition directly across from the word. Punch holes along the right side of each word and on the left side of each definition. Attach a long shoe string or piece of yarn to each hole on the word side.

<u>Utilization</u>: The child threads the yarn into the holes on the definition side, matching the word with the correct definition.

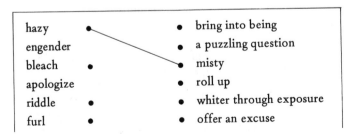

11. "Translation, Please!"

Goal: Pronunciation using diacritical markings

Grade level: 4–6

Construction: Write jokes, stories, or sentences using only diacritical marks.

Utilization: The child translates the joke, story, or sentence and then copies the translation on paper or records it on tape.

> ex: thē flou´ər bloōms
>   thē skī iz sun´ē
>   it iz Sprĩng

12. How Do They Say It?

Goal: Using diacritical markings to phonetically pronounce words in foreign languages.

Grade level: 4–6

Construction: On a 3-x 5-inch card, write a word or phrase from a foreign language. Beside each word or phrase write its phonetic pronunciation, using the diacritical marking of English sounds.

Utilization: In turn, players draw a card and attempt to pronounce it. If the player pronounces the word correctly, he has the opportunity to draw a second card. If the player is incorrect, he does not get the opportunity to draw a second card. His card is simply returned to the deck and the next player draws. The game continues until all cards have been successfully drawn. When this occurs, the player with the most cards wins.

> ex: sayonara   sī ə nar´ə

13. Accent Pronunciation

Goal: Utilizing accents to aid in word pronunciation

Grade level: 4–6

Construction: Make 7-x 4-inch word cards containing words that are spelled the same, but pronounced differently (heteronyms). Be sure to include the accent marks for each word.

cón tent		prés ent
con tent´		pre sent´

Utilization: Flash the cards and ask the children to write sentences correctly using each word.

14. Give the Dog a Bone

<u>Goal</u>: Classification of vowel sounds according to pronunciation keys

<u>Grade level</u>: K–3

<u>Construction</u>: On a bulletin board, hang a picture of a dog. Next, secure three paper plates. Cut one plate in half. Staple one half on each of the other paper plates to form pockets on both of the two remaining paper plates. On the front of one plate write, "I like to eat long vowels"; on the second plate write, "I like to eat short vowels." Now design one-syllable word cards in the shape of bones. The words should not be part of the child's sight vocabulary.

<u>Utilization</u>: Each child selects a bone and checks the pronunciation key in his dictionary to determine where to place his word bone. If it is a short-vowel word bone, he places it in the short-vowel pocket, and if it is a long-vowel word bone he places it in the long-vowel pocket.

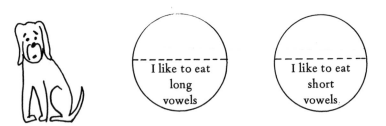

15. Post Office

<u>Goal</u>: Classifying words according to vowel pronunciation keys

<u>Grade level</u>: 4–6

<u>Construction</u>: Place a cardboard box with dividers that held large bottles on one side and label each slot with either $\breve{a}$, $\bar{a}$, $\breve{e}$, $\bar{e}$, $\breve{i}$, $\bar{i}$, $\breve{o}$, $\bar{o}$, $\breve{u}$, or $\bar{u}$. Make word or picture cards of one-syllable words with long or short vowel sounds.

<u>Utilization</u>: Each child sorts the mail by putting the word or picture cards in the proper slots, according to the vowel sound in the word.

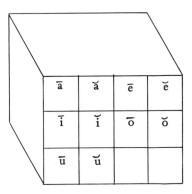

16. How Else Can You Say It?

Goal: Reinforcement of word meanings and utilization of a thesaurus

Grade level: 4–6

Construction: All that is needed is one or more copies of a thesaurus, preferably in dictionary form.

Utilization: Give each child a simple sentence, or one containing new vocabulary words. The child, using the thesaurus, must rewrite the sentence in several different ways, keeping the original meaning.

> The knife can <u>cut</u>.
>
> The knife can <u>carve</u>.
>
> The knife can <u>dissect</u>.
>
> The knife can <u>slice</u>.
>
> The knife can <u>sever</u>.
>
> The knife can <u>separate</u>.

17. Bet You Can't Find This

Goal: Utilizing reference books

Grade level: 4–8

Construction and Utilization: Have students look through reference books to make up five questions to exchange with one another. The more obscure questions, the better. The first person of the pair to correctly answer all five questions, using the reference books, wins.

Activity II — EDCO Based*

Construction: Design a playing board representing a football field, with a goal post at either end. On the board, place the names of various reference books and draw a circle around them, connecting each circle with lines. The circles will represent football passes. Then construct cards asking questions that would necessitate using a particular reference book. For example, What is the annual rainfall in Bloomington, Indiana?

Utilization: Players, in turn, pick a card and decide which reference book would be needed to answer the question. The player then can move to that reference on the board <u>if</u> it is connected by a line to the space he presently is on. If no line connects his present space with the answer, the player loses his turn. The first person to reach the other goal wins.

*This game is similar to one developed by <u>EDCO</u>. Cambridge, Mass.

QUESTIONS AND RELATED READINGS

If at this time you do not feel that you have attained adequate knowledge to successfully answer the following questions, we would like to suggest related readings.

1. What are the major study skills students need to master?
2. Explain why study skills are considered developmental in nature.
3. Explain how study skills might be taught so that students recognize their value and incorporate them into daily study practices.

Goal 1: To aid the reader in understanding the definition of "reading study skills"

Question 1: What are the major study skills students need to master?

Gray, William S. *Improving Reading in All Curriculum Areas.* Supplementary Educational Monographs, no. 76. Chicago: University of Chicago Press, 1952.
Laffey, James L., ed. *Reading in the Content Areas.* Newark, Del.: International Reading Association, 1972.
Thomas, Ellen L., and H. Alan Robinson. *Improving Reading in Every Class.* Boston: Allyn & Bacon, Inc., 1972.

Goal 2: To aid the reader in understanding the awareness of the variance in skills required for successful study at different maturational levels

Question 2: Explain why study skills are considered developmental in nature.

Bruner, Jerome S. et. al. *Studies in Cognitive Growth.* New York: John Wiley & Sons, Inc., 1967.
Davis, Frederick B. "Research in Comprehension in Reading." *Reading Research Quarterly,* 3 (Summer 1968), 439–45.
Karlin, Robert. *Teaching Elementary Reading.* New York: Harcourt Brace Jovanovich, Inc., 1971, p. 218.

Goal 3: To aid the reader in understanding the various ways children can be helped to learn and use study skills effectively

Question 3: Explain how study skills might be taught so that students recognize their value and incorporate them into daily study practices.

Bilodeau, Edward A. *Acquisition of Skill.* New York: Academic Press, Inc., 1966.
Herber, Harold. *Teaching Reading in Content Areas.* Englewood Cliffs, N.J.: Prentice-Hall, Inc., 1970, p. 13.
Robinson, H. Alan, and Ellen L. Thomas, eds. *Fusing Reading Skills and Content.* Newark, Del.: International Reading Association, 1967.

BIBLIOGRAPHY

Bruner, Jerome S. et al. *Studies in Cognitive Growth.* New York: John Wiley & Sons, Inc., 1967.
Chambers, Dewey W., and Heath W. Lowry. *The Language Arts.* Iowa: William C. Brown Company, Publishers, 1975, p. 75.

Courtney, L. "Recent Developments in Reading in the Content Areas." *Conference on Reading,* 27 (1965), 134–44.

Estes, Thomas H. "Reading in the Social Studies: A Review of Research Since 1950." In *Reading in the Content Areas,* ed. by James L. Laffey, Newark, Del.: International Reading Association, 1972, pp. 177–87.

Fay, Leo, Thomas Horn, and Constance McCullough. *Improving Reading in the Elementary Social Studies.* Bulletin no. 33. Washington, D.C.: National Council for the Social Studies, 1961.

Reeves, Ruth. *The Teaching of Reading in Our Schools.* New York: Macmillan Publishing Company, Inc., 1966.

Russell, David. *Children Learn to Read.* Lexington, Mass.: Ginn and Company, 1961, p. 457.

Sheperd, David. *Comprehensive High School Reading Methods.* Columbus, Ohio: Charles E. Merrill Publishing Company, 1973, p. 259.

Witt, Mary. "Developing Reading Skills and Critical Thinking." *Social Education,* 25 (May 1961), 239–41.

11

Reading: The key to content area learning

Reading Is Survival

Books are no substitute for living, but they can add immeasurably to its richness. While life is absorbing, books can enhance our sense of significance. When life is difficult, they can give us momentary release from trouble or a new insight into our problems, or provide the rest and refreshment we need. Books have always been a source of information, comfort, and pleasure for people who know how to use them. This is as true for children as for adults. Indeed, it is particularly true for children.

May Hill Arbuthnot

May Hill Arbuthnot, *Children and Books* (Glenview, Ill.: Scott, Foresman, 1957), p. 2.

GOALS: To aid the reader in understanding
1. the comprehensiveness of the reading process.
2. the processes involved in the act of reading.
3. the skills common to reading in any content area.
4. the interrelatedness of reading and mathematics.
5. the interrelatedness of reading and social studies.
6. the interrelatedness of reading and science.
7. the interrelatedness of reading and music and art.

The Basic Ingredient in All Learning

Reading is a process that is not unique to the mastery of any one content area. This claim can be documented by visiting American classrooms and observing children *reading* social studies, science, and mathematics texts. The same visit may cause you some confusion, however. You may understand that reading is a process *necessary* to the mastery of all content area learning, but you may not see it being taught in any context other than a basal reading program.

Such a visit may cause you to wonder why reading skills are not taught within content area lessons. You may ask: "Is it because classroom teachers do not realize that content area learning is complex and it involves (1) understanding a specified body of knowledge, and (2) understanding a series of strategies for acquiring, interpreting, evaluating, and using the content?"

When you see this phenomenon occurring, you may question the role of university training programs. This question was addressed in a study by Lapp (1976) because she found that universities have espoused teaching reading in the content area for decades, but few satisfactory *models* have been provided to encourage the classroom teacher to emphasize content area reading skills. Lapp found that preservice teachers were only able to implement instructional strategies related to reading in the content areas when the cooperating teacher served as a model to demonstrate the implementation of these strategies. Some universities have attempted to provide in-school models of teaching that emphasize the implementation of reading as a process which is needed by students to master all content area learning. The implementation of these models rests upon a philosophy of thematic teaching which presents reading as an integrated, continuous process rather than as a single, static, isolated 45-minute-per-day basal series activity. In thematic teaching, reading becomes the integrated base of all content area learning. Thematic teaching has been developed from an earlier teaching strategy, referred to as unit teaching. Unit teaching stressed the importance of teaching children to read in one specific *content area* such as reading in science. Thematic teaching, however, broadens the base of reading in the content areas by integrating many content areas and reading skills. Thematic teaching is based on a natural phenomenon, reading about a particular theme. For example, a teacher may introduce a lesson on train transportation in Boston. While studying this unit, children are required to read time schedules and price lists (mathematics), information about department stores, monuments, and inhabitants of particular neighborhoods (social studies), maps (geography), and information on the construction of trains and the mechanics of engines (science).

In the remainder of this chapter, when we refer to reading in the content areas, we are referring to this new concept of thematic teaching; we are not referring to the former concept of unit teaching.

As the classroom teacher engages in thematic teaching, he or she is *encouraged* to retain the successful *word-recognition* and *comprehension* teaching strategies that are commonly identified with the majority of basal reading programs. This is stressed because word-recognition and comprehension skills are needed by the reader who is encountering content area texts. Most basals contain narrative stories. Word-recognition skills enable the student to recognize, as well as analyze, newly encountered lexical items. Regardless of the format of the material, comprehension skills are needed as students recognize literal facts, infer hidden meanings, and evaluate author intent. These basic reading skills which were acquired through basal reading by the first- or second-grade reader will also service the intermediate and the advanced reader who is encountering new content area skills.

After readiness skills such as letter and sight-word recognition have been mastered, the child is ready to include content area texts into his repertoire of reading materials. The inclusion of content area materials should occur in *addition* to the basal reader, not as a *replacement* for the basal. Although the practices encouraged throughout a basal program prepare and support content area learning, one cannot assume that the transfer of learning from the basal to a fact-specific type of content reading will occur without instructional aid. We teachers must not fail to remember that, during the early years of school, various basal as well as language experience programs are utilized to aid children in reading narrative, imaginative materials. Through various methods, children are taught the basic word-recognition and comprehension techniques one employs when reading. Developing the basic skills necessary for learning *how* to read becomes the major focus of the early reading programs.

Although basals are beginning to offer some factual stories, children in the primary grades spend most of their reading time with narrative materials. Even when basals are supplemented by trade books, young children spend most of their time reading narrative stories; not surprisingly this reading is not adequate preparation for content area reading. Many intermediate children who have exhibited little, if any, difficulty when reading narrative materials sometimes demonstrate a limited understanding of content area materials. This occurs because content area materials, unlike basal texts, contain synthesized facts drawn from many areas of life experiences of the reader; and a concisely stated, often terse style of writing.

The following excerpts, taken from intermediate texts, illustrate the differences in writing styles and content which are encountered by the intermediate-age child who is required to read narrative and factual materials. Both excerpts deal with the topic of weather and seasonal changes. Which of the passages would be more difficult for a middle-school child to read? Why?

"Oh boy! It'll snow! And tomorrow is Christmas!" Eddie flipped his furry cap into the air, missing Mom's reading lamp. It landed among the potted plants Willa Mae was watering.

"Cut it, Ed!" she cried. "And be sure to stay right with Jason. Mom said for you boys to be home before the snow gets bad."

"Okay, we'll make it home" Jason promised. "It isn't snowing yet. Come on, Eddie, I've got our money all counted."

Eddie slammed the front door. They clattered down the stairs fast.

"Is there enough money for the lamp shade, Jay?" Eddie asked to make sure. "And what will we get for Willa Mae?"

"We'll find something. There'll be enough."

It wasn't long before they caught their first sight of the fountain in the park.

"It's frozen!" Eddie gasped. He pulled Jason toward it. The water in the fountain must have frozen while it was still bubbling down. Now the statue animals—the turtles, frogs, and swans—had frozen into strange, icy shapes. It was lovely, like fairyland.

"Hm ... snow's starting," Jason said, sniffing the air. A few flakes were blowing lightly over the ice. He looked up at the gray, tumbling sky. "We'd better get downtown for our shopping," he said.

(Clymer, 1970, pp. 42-2)

If you live in a place where the leaves change color, you probably have noticed that the color display is never quite the same from one year to the next. One year the leaves may be very colorful, but the next year their colors may be dull. Several things seem to affect how bright or how dull the color change will be—the amount of water in the ground during the summer, the amount of nitrogen in the soil, the amount of light reaching the leaves, the amount of sugar stored in the leaves, and the night temperatures during autumn. Strong light and cold nights, for example, seem to help certain pigments form in leaf cells.

In some way we do not yet fully understand, toward the end of summer the chlorophyll pigment of the leaf cells begins to break down. As more and more chlorophyll is broken down, the yellow and orange pigments are unmasked. At the same time, new yellow and orange pigments are being made. The leaves begin to change color.

Meanwhile, other pigments are being made in the leaf cells. How much they show up depends partly on weather conditions during the summer. It also depends partly on weather conditions while the leaves are changing. Brown pigments begin to form when the chlorophyll breaks down. So do the flaming red, blue, and purple pigments. When the brown pigments form, they blend with orange and yellow and give oak leaves their typical orange-brown color. The red pigments seem to reach their peak when the outflow of sugar made in the leaves slows down and the sugar then collects in the leaves.

(Gallant and Asimov, 1973, pp. 33-4)

Which excerpt do you think is more difficult for the fourth- or fifth-grade student to read? While both passages are about the same length and deal with the same topic, the second passage contains many more technical, difficult-to-pronounce terms than the first passage. It also contains many familiar words (color, leaves) that are used in unfamiliar ways, and it contains several concepts that are inadequately explained. The terse style of writing found in the second passage is certainly more difficult to comprehend than the narrative, storylike style of the first passage. A child reading either of these selections uses word-recognition and comprehension skills, but the second selection, as well as most content area materials, demands that the child have competence in using many of the following general study skills.

1. Establishing a purpose for reading
2. Locating and verifying information from multiple sources: almanac, atlas, encyclopedia, and *Reader's Guide to Periodic Literature*
3. Considering alternative sources and applying methods of cross-checking
4. Noting simple clues to organization of selection: definitions, context, numbered ideas, cue words indicating order
5. Skimming for general concepts
6. Scanning for minute details
7. Differentiating fact from opinion
8. Recognizing main ideas
9. Interpreting charts, diagrams, and maps
10. Using dictionaries, glossaries, and footnotes to determine meaning
11. Utilizing newspapers as a source of current information and opinion
12. Organizing and summarizing material through outlining
13. Adjusting reading rate to suit reading purpose and type of material
14. Classifying information presented from several points of view

You are probably wondering *how* and *when* to begin developing these study skills. Let us reexamine the preceding list and the two passages. Greater readiness for reading content-specific materials could be developed if a narrative story about weather information was also presented through a factual-type story format. Questions and discussions regarding the different types of stories would enable young children to recognize that they will be experiencing a variety of reading materials.

Language experiences can also be used to help young children to differentiate factual statements from opinion statements. The teacher might engage the children in a discussion of their toys, vacations, or hobbies. Opinion statements that the children might make include:

> "My toys are the nicest in the world."
> "I like to go on vacations."
> "Andy's hobby isn't any fun."

The teacher could encourage the children to realize that these are statements of *opinion*, and through her help the children could change these to *factual* statements:

> "I have three toys."
> "I am going on vacation to Ohio."
> "Andy's hobby is collecting turtles."

The children could then survey their texts to find statements of fact and opinion. Newspapers, encyclopedia, and other reference materials can be used for this activity throughout the primary grades.

The Process of Reading

As we review the processes involved in reading, one is struck by the fact that the reader must be able to *perceive* information, *interpret* information, and *evaluate* information for decision-making situations. What specifically is involved in this three-part learning process? Let us begin by defining our terms:

Perception

Perception involves an act of categorization. Put in terms of the antecedent and subsequent conditions from which we make our inferences, we stimulate an organism with some appropriate input and he responds by referring the input to some class of things or events.

(Bruner, 1957, pp. 123–52)

Perception requires the student to determine symbol-sound associations. The reader perceives a letter or word *symbol*, cognitively compares the symbol to other known symbols, and then associates a sound with the symbol. *Perception*, the base of reading, is a very limited skill if it is viewed in isolation because the reader may not have acquired the concept that is represented by the symbol. A second major step in the reading process is the *interpreting* of symbols.

Interpretation

The reader should not only associate sound with the symbol but also associate meaning with the symbol, drawing on ideas he has developed in relationship to the symbol. If the symbol is a word, he associates it with an experience he has had—real or vicarious—in connection with it. That is his meaning for the symbol. If the symbol is other than a word, perhaps a formula, an equation, a sentence, or a paragraph, the process is the same, differing only in degree of complexity.

(Herber, 1970, p. 13)

After the reader has perceived or *decoded* the symbol, as well as *interpreted* or gained a *general understanding* of the material, he must evaluate the content of the material.

Evaluation

The reader must suppress emotion to become more objective and analytical. In critical reading he must judge. He must compare what the book, newspaper, or magazine says with what he knows from his previous experience or what is stated in another source. The term critical thinking is used in many ways in educational writing, but the essential factors seem to be: (1) an attitude of suspending judgment until the evidence is considered, and (2) skills in clarifying and attacking a specific problem presented in the materials. In some cases, the problem lies outside the materials, as in determining the author's purpose or bias. Sometimes it is stated explicitly with arguments on two sides of the question and an invitation to the reader to make up his own mind.

(Russell, 1961, p. 457)

A sound knowledge base is necessary for evaluative reading to occur. Students must be provided with real and simulated experiences that enable them to form concepts against which they can appraise newly encountered statements and concepts. After this knowledge base has been fostered, the child is ready to formulate a decision base that is necessary for making judgments and for applying newly acquired information to future explorations.

Many of the instructional processes involved in enabling the child to perceive, interpret, and evaluate narrative texts have already been discussed. In this chapter, information will be provided: (1) to enable you to gain an understanding of the processes involved in transferring these skills to the reading of fact-specific content materials, and (2) to develop a thorough understanding of content area reading skills.

Thematic Teaching

You are probably beginning to realize that successful content area reading is dependent on the application and extension of study skills throughout content area reading. Chapter 10 provided you with an understanding of these general skills. The remainder of this chapter will provide you with an understanding of specific processes and activities needed to integrate study skills and content area reading and to provide you with the basic strategies needed to develop a thematic teaching unit.

Information about study skills and content area reading will be pertinent, regardless of the grade you intend to teach, because you cannot assume that all of these skills will be developed and refined in any one grade. The early reading years must provide the child with instruction in the basic study of reading skills. Reading instruction for the student in the middle grades involves:

1. *Refining* basic reading skills.
2. *Extending* comprehension skills throughout the highest levels of evaluative thinking.

3. *Expanding* reference study skills.

4. *Exploring* mathematics, social studies, science, and other content area materials in an attempt to extend concepts and to clarify generalizations.

Planning Reading in Thematic Curricula

The teachers today just go on repeating in rigamorole fashion, annoying the students with constant questions and repeating the same things over and over again. They do not try to find out what the students' natural inclinations are, so that the students are forced to pretend to like their studies; nor do they try to bring out the best in their talents. As a result, the students hide their favorite readings and hate their teachers, are exasperated at the difficulty of their studies, and do not know what good it does them. Although they go through the regular course of instruction, they are quick to leave when they are through. This is the failure of education today.

(Confucius, c. 551–479 B.C.)

As classroom teachers who are trying to remedy the instructional pitfalls described by Confucius nearly 2,500 years ago, we need to consider the following principles when planning for reading in any content area lesson.

Children

1. Children need to have a purpose for learning. This may be accomplished by asking them what, where, when, why, and how questions. It can also be accomplished by helping children to formulate questions about a specific topic. Ask children to state all of the facts they know about a particular topic. Encourage them to ask: What do I still need to know? At that point, they will have a purpose for further reading.

2. Children need to be motivated to learn. Many of the activities provided in this chapter are suggested as motivational devices that may be useful when you begin to explore a specified concept.

3. Children learn effectively when they have a positive attitude. Positive attitudes are developed by children who understand the rationale behind learning experiences and who are presented with interesting, challenging activities.

4. Children need various types of background readiness to learn. Through diagnosis you must determine *how* much a child knows about a particular topic. Your instruction should begin at his level of readiness.

5. Children need word-recognition, comprehension, and study skills to learn through reading.

6. Children learn through a variety of modalities. Some children learn best through activities that involve listening, whereas other children thrive on reading, writing, and language activities.

7. Children learn at different rates. Do not set a time limit unless you intend to measure rate.

8. Children need to be active participants in the learning process. Activities that involve children in planning, as well as participating, are suggested throughout this chapter.

Teachers

1. Teachers need to be familiar with the children they are teaching. (See Chapter 5 for techniques that will enable you to know your children better.

2. Teachers need to understand the practical applications of learning theory: How do children learn? Does their rate of learning coincide with their physical and social growth?

3. Teachers need to be well-versed in evaluative techniques. (See Chapter 15.)

4. Teachers need a thorough understanding of the material they are teaching. (See Chapter 15.)

5. Teachers *must* have a firm understanding of various methods designed to teach reading through content area subjects. (See Chapter 12.)

6. Teachers need to plan activities that are pertinent to the growth of *all* individuals. (Please refer to the activities throughout this text.)

7. Teachers need to remember that there is no set of unique skills related to learning a specific content area.

8. Teachers need to remember that the teaching of reading in a content area implies making proper adjustments for word-recognition, comprehension, and study skills application.

Implementing Thematic Instruction

As an elementary classroom teacher you will most likely be responsible for teaching all of the content areas. In order to integrate and individualize your curriculum, you may want to use thematic teaching, which involves the following steps: (1) selecting a theme or themes, and (2) incorporating all content area and reading objectives within the theme.

Selecting a Theme. The first task of thematic instruction is the selection of possible themes with your children. Themes should reflect the interests of students and the fundamental information required for a specific grade level. Some examples of themes that can be explored throughout the intermediate grades are:

1. Consumerism
2. Dinosaurs
3. American cultures
4. Transportation
5. Physical hygiene

One or more themes can be operating simultaneously in your classroom.

Determining Content Area Skills. Frequently, classroom teachers avoid thematic teaching because they are skeptical about covering content area skills. Step 2 in thematic instruction is specifying the skills you want to cover in math, science, social studies, and the language arts lesson.

Planning Lessons. After you have selected your themes and delineated content area skills, you can begin to develop lessons that relate to the thematic areas and incorporate the skills to be covered. Be sure to include activities within your lessons that encourage the development of functionally literate students. A detailed example of thematic teaching is presented in Chapter 15. Please refer to it to obtain a more complete understanding of the planning, as well as evaluative techniques, of thematic teaching.

In the next few pages we will present several suggestions for the teaching of reading in three key curricula areas: mathematics, social studies, and science. It is extremely important for teachers to understand the standard structures which are used in the written discourse of these three curricular areas.

Reading in Mathematics

The reading and studying of mathematics demands an understanding and development of specific concepts and principles. The dual objective of mathematics instruction should be to enable the child to develop an *understanding* of the patterns that are used to formulate concepts and principles and to solve problems. The accomplishment of these objectives will ensure *both* problem mastery and conceptual understanding.

In order to accomplish these objectives, the child must master the language of mathematics—a language composed of words and symbols $(=, +, -, \times, \div)$. As in the mastery of any other language, the child hears, explores, discusses, experiments, uses, and tests words that might be part of the conceptual framework of this language.

A second step in accomplishing the dual objective of *understanding* and *solving* involves the child's competence in reasoning, a process that involves a student's ability to reorder known data in an attempt to derive new relationships. *Reasoning* is closely related to *comprehension* because both entail ability to detect problematic clues, to hypothesize, and to evaluate conclusions. Finally, in an attempt to accomplish the specified objective of understanding and to solve problems, the child must be able to estimate and to compute.

A review of reading/mathematics literature suggests:

1. Certain intellectual capabilities are essential for mathematical achievement. According to Piaget, these are competence with the concept of conservation of number, quantity, length, volume, and weight; the achievement of the concept of reversibility; and the maturation of logical abilities. Piaget stated that a child must be able to comprehend the fact that a number is the synthesis of two logical entities: class and asymmetrical relations, before he can achieve in mathematics. He contended that these capabilities are achieved when a child has matured sufficiently to comprehend them.

   Bruner, while accepting a developmental sequence in mathematical capability, contended that a child's environment can be changed so that it is consistent with his intellectual development. Piaget allowed considerable age-range for the development of the intellectual behaviors of children, and Bruner believed that environmental factors modify the learning rate of a child. Perhaps these amount to the same concept. In any event, both maturation and environment should be considered by teachers of elementary mathematics.

2. Certain reading skills are necessary for success in solving verbal arithmetic problems. According to Corle and Coulter (1964), the three most important reading skills are vocabulary development, literal interpretation of the problem, and selection of the proper solution process (reasoning). It is also noted that listening skills seem to be related to mathematical ability, primarily through their relationship to reading achievement.

3. Success in mathematical problem solving is greatly influenced by certain mathematical prerequisites and reading skills, but it is also affected by other variables. Among these are motor abilities, verbal abilities, personality characteristics, and physical conditions. It is also influenced by the arrangement of data within a mathematics problem.

4. Textbook readability is a major consideration in a child's mathematical success because in many classrooms textbooks are the only resource provided for mathematics instruction. Therefore, the vocabulary, both general and quantitative, the difficulty of nonverbal items such as symbols and graphs, and the interest level of the text should be evaluated carefully to insure that the material is suitable to the child's ability and grade level.

From "Reading in Mathematics: A Review of Recent Research," Clyde G. Corle in James L. Laffey (Ed.) *Reading in the Content Areas*, IRA, 1972, pp. 87-88. Reprinted with permission of Clyde G. Corle and the International Reading Association.

Interpreting Mathematical Language. The child encounters two types of language when he is studying mathematics. The first type involves an understanding of the *printed word*. The second type involves interpretation of signs and symbols.

Shepherd (1973) states that four types of vocabulary are apparent within the printed language of mathematics.

In mathematics there are four kinds of vocabulary words, any of which can cause difficulty. The first type is the technical word peculiar to some area of the mathematics. For example, *sine* and *cosine* in trigonometry; *polynomials, linear equations* in algebra; and *isosceles, arc,* and *polyhedron* in geometry. The second type is the general word in our language which has a mathematical meaning such as *prime, natural, radical, exponent, square,* etc. A third type is the word which signals a mathematical process. This includes such words as *subtract, times, multiply, difference, column.* Many of these also have other meanings in general language usage. Finally, the fourth type is the general word, which can determine a student's comprehension. Such words as *before, of, compare, increase, least* are examples. (p. 259)

By providing concrete and abstract illustrations and by defining terms and discussing concepts, recognition and understanding of various mathematical terms can be accomplished. This understanding of the printed word is necessary as the child encounters story problems. In order to ensure that the child reads and analyzes the problem, he should be encouraged to:

1. read the problem carefully and begin to conceptualize.
2. reread to decide what problem is posed.
3. reread to detect the clues given for solving the problem.

4. determine procedures for solving the problem.
5. solve the problem.
6. check the results.

For example, if Daryl is 135 centimeters tall and Denise is 145 centimeters tall, how much taller is Denise than Daryl?

1. Difference in height?   (Problem conceptualization)
   Daryl is 135 centimeters.
   Denise is 145 centimeters.

2. How much taller is Denise than Daryl?   (Problem posed)

3. 145 centimeters   (Clues)
   135 centimeters (difference)

4. Subtraction   (Solution)

5. 145 centimeters   (Solve)
   135 centimeters
   _____
   10 centimeters

   Denise is 10 centimeters taller than Daryl

6. 135   (Check)
   +10
   _____
   145

In addition to vocabulary words and story problem concepts, the student of mathematics encounters symbols and signs like $=, \times, +, -, \div$ that represent words such as equal, times, plus, minus and divide.

Activities 1 and 2 at the end of this chapter offer examples of the various ways in which you might introduce and reinforce the mathematics language of words and symbols.

Comprehending Tabular, Graphic, and Pictorial Data. Children who are involved in the study of mathematics are often required to read and to design tables and graphs in order to illustrate *growth, gain, divisions,* and the like in a visual manner. In order to understand and develop these representations, the child must understand that formulas, equations, and symbols are forms of mathematical shorthand. When attempting to read and study these representations, children should be encouraged to:

1. read descriptive phrases that tell what the table or graph represents.
2. carefully study any given numbers or letters or words to determine what has been measured.
3. read any column of data presented to gain a clearer understanding of what is being represented.
4. analyze any pictorial representations and convert them to numbers.
5. compare and draw conclusions, if requested.

Apply these steps to the following illustration: Margaret is a member of the school baseball team. She has been keeping track of the number of home runs made by her team during each game. Margaret's team has played ten games so far.

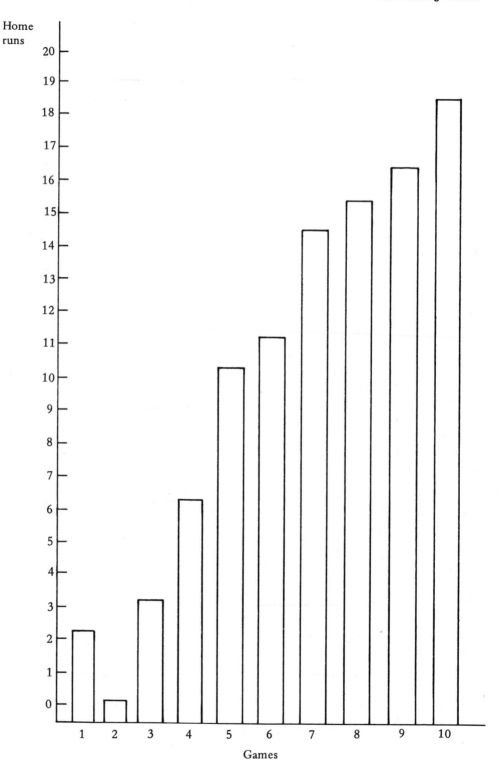

Figure 1. Team Record

1. team games   (Descriptive phrases)
   team home-run scores

2. games and home runs   (Clue words)

3. read bar representations   (Read graph.)

4. 2 home runs = game 1   (Data conversion)
    0 home runs = game 2
    3 home runs = game 3
    6 home runs = game 4
   10 home runs = game 5
   11 home runs = game 6
   14 home runs = game 7
   15 home runs = game 8
   16 home runs = game 9
   18 home runs = game 10

5. Margaret's team continues to increase its home runs.   (Conclusion)

Bar, line, circle, and picture graphs, tables, and histograms all are better understood by children if they are encouraged to follow the preceding five steps of analysis.

Teaching Mathematics.   In pursuing further study, remember that in order to teach mathematics successfully, you need to have a basic understanding of mathematics, and you need to transfer this knowledge while incorporating the following teaching practices:

1. Children need intense practice in *reading, speaking,* and *computing* the succinct language of words and symbols in mathematics.

2. Activities need to be designed to reinforce the technical terms, labeling processes, and symbol representations of mathematics.

3. Children must be encouraged to *read for the purpose* of the problem. Careful reading must be encouraged because the purpose of the problem is intrinsic to solving it.

4. Children must be encouraged to view symbols as mathematical shorthand. Begin by asking children to write formulas in longhand and to restate them in symbols.

5. Children must be encouraged to employ both *analytical* and *computational* processes in solving story problems. Encourage children to read a problem and picture it in their minds. Then ask them to reread the last sentence to determine what they are being asked to do. Next, have them reread and determine the process, estimate an answer, and then attempt to solve the problem.

6. Practice and opportunity must be given children to design tabular, graphic, and pictorial representations. Encourage your children to read the table or graph and determine its purpose. Next, they should analyze the vertical columns to determine their meaning. Finally, they should read all bindings and additional notes. If they are reading a graph instead of a table, they will need help in noting the quantity or units of measurement.

7. Children must be given practice in following directions. Ask children to read or listen to the directions to gain an overview of the task. Next, have them

reread each separate phrase of the directions while thinking about the exact application. Then, they synthesize or combine all parts of the directional task and proceed.

8. Practice in reasoning, estimating, generalizing, and computing are part of a successful math program.

> Teachers who wish to achieve the objective of wide reading in mathematics will plan their work to include the following steps: (1) Review the mathematics courses to find places where time may be saved from content without neglecting the essentials; (2) Select a few topics in connection with which wide reading may be done—i.e., a bibliography including the history of a topic, biographies of mathematicians, and more extended writings or articles related to certain topics or units in the texts; (3) Locate these references, examine and evaluate them, and distribute them to the pupils; (4) Give the pupils time to use these materials and time to discuss the ideas they have gained.
>
> *(Austin, 1961, p. 391-6)*

Activities 3 through 8 at the end of this chapter will encourage your sensitivity to the teaching practices suggested in the preceding eight teaching practices.

Reading in Social Studies

Social studies is a unique discipline whose content is comprised of factual information drawn from geography, anthropology, economics, civics, sociology, and psychology.

For example, the following selection, taken from an elementary social studies text, incorporates history, geography, sociology, government, and language:

> Egyptian Civilization developed in the valley of the Nile River. The civilization which merged with it was brought to the area by Alexander the Great in 331 B.C. Alexander was a Greek; but when he conquered Egypt, he went to the temple of Amun and was recognized as the successor to the Pharaohs. As a result of his conquest, Egyptian Civilization and Greek Civilization blended.
>
> The city called Alexandria, which Alexander built at the mouth of the Nile, became a marketplace for the exchange of goods and learning. Alexander loved Alexandria and asked to be buried there. It was the center of trade and culture for all the countries that bordered the Mediterranean Sea. In 200 B.C., it was the largest city in the world.
>
> If we look at a map of Alexander's empire, it is not hard to see how Alexandria achieved its importance. It was set on the point where the Nile meets the sea. It had good harbors and was connected with overland trade routes across the desert. Alexander's empire spread from Greece to India and included North Africa. Alexandria was its center.
>
> Egyptian and Greek culture flourished in Alexandria. An enormous library was built, and scholars went there to study. Learning was so highly prized that ships that sailed into port were forced to surrender the manuscripts which they carried. The library at Pergamum, in Asia Minor, was brought to Alexandria and housed there, as well. The city was known as the "Capital of Learning."
>
> Two harbors served Alexandria, one on the Nile and one on the Mediterranean. Traffic was heavy. Barges came down the Nile loaded with papyrus and corn for export. Gold, spices, pears, and ivory were brought overland from the Red Sea. Timber, olive oil, slaves, and horses were unloaded from foreign vessels and sold in Egypt.

Alexandria held its position of influence and power for several centuries. The last ruler of Egypt under the successors of Alexander was a queen named Cleopatra. Cleopatra was bold. She was both loved and feared by young Roman leaders who wanted control of her country. When she felt she was no longer in a position to influence those leaders, she killed herself. Egypt then became a Roman province.

(Kenworthy, 1972, p. 177)

This excerpt, which focuses on the plight of a civilization, integrates information from several disciplines. Excerpts with a similar cultural theme are common in social studies materials because the focus of social studies is the *individual* as he interacts in large and small social settings. Social studies encourages the study of the interactions of people.

As you encourage your students' understanding of social studies you must (1) provide the content base needed to explore this vast area of knowledge, and (2) enable each student to acquire the skills needed to become an independent learner of this information. Because this is not a social studies text, we will concentrate on item 2, which is to provide you, the classroom teacher, with a thorough understanding of skills related to the reading of social studies materials and with an understanding of the processes for implementing these skills within your classroom.

Interpreting Social Studies Language. Understanding social studies materials is highly dependent on one's ability to understand a specific set of concepts. As Marksheffel (1966) suggests:

Most textbooks are excellent sources of information, facts, and ideas pertinent to learning in specific content areas. The material is usually of the highest caliber because it is written by experts in the particular area of concentration. The fact that textbooks are written by experts is at once both a major weakness and a major strength. Specialists in subject matter are usually amateurs at writing. They understand so well the materials about which they write that they appear to forget that the student has but a meager knowledge of the vocabulary and concepts necessary for understanding (p. 174)

When the student encounters the social studies text he will experience many *multisyllabic, technical,* and *difficult* terms, e.g.:

Multisyllabic words	Technical words	Foreign words
Hittite	democratic	plateau
Moslem	loyalty	saga
Mississippi	conservation	mesa
monsoon	New Frontier	fief
Arabian	cold war	kriser
Constantinople	Iron Curtain	ballet
manuscripts	Dark Ages	atrium
colonial	dignity	hotelier

In an effort to develop the language/reading skills that are necessary to master social studies vocabulary, it might be useful to:

1. Introduce new words as they appear in context.

Example: Barges come down the Nile loaded for export with papyrus and corn.

2. Use media to furnish background experiences necessary to understand social studies language.
   a. models
   b. globes
   c. maps
3. Discuss word derivations.
4. Discuss any words in the student's life that may serve as a substitute or synonym for the newly encountered word.
5. Categorize words according to historical periods.
   a. pharaohs
   b. whig
   c. democracy
6. Focus attention on terms which involve the concepts of distance, space, time, depression, and evolution.
   a. beyond
   b. age
7. Introduce social slogans and figures of speech and slang.
   a. Beat the Draft.
   b. It's a bummer.
   c. Uncle Sam wants you.
8. Construct new vocabulary through a variety of emotional settings.

   Example: The president declared war!
              The war between the states ...
              In what year was the war ended?

9. Use the dictionary because facility with the dictionary is an underlying study skill on which mastery of the language of any content is dependent.

Comprehending Social Studies Data

Geographic Representations.   In addition to the development of language facility, social studies reading instruction must provide the student with the means to *interpret, analyze,* and *synthesize* pictures, charts, tables, graphs, and maps. The necessity of these skills becomes obvious as you begin to explore a social studies text. You are likely to encounter the following illustrations:

I.

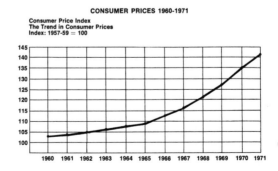

(Jarolimek and Davis, *Web of the World,* 1973, p. 125)

or II.

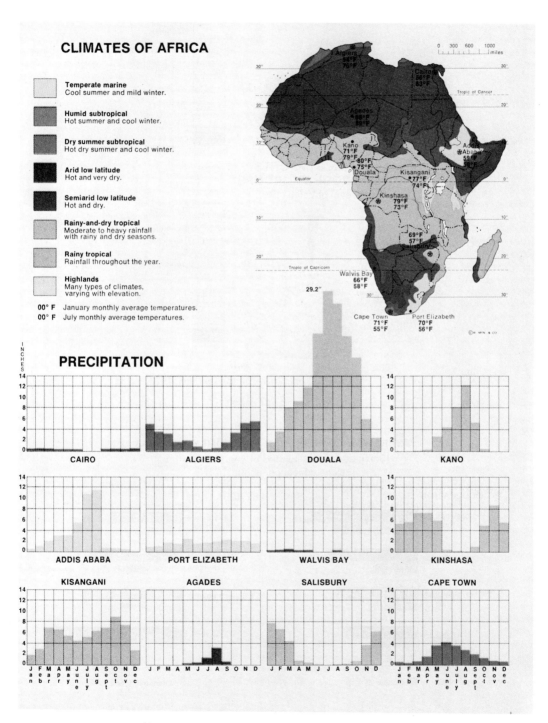

(Jarolimek and Davis, *The Ways of Man*, 1974, p. 512)

or III.

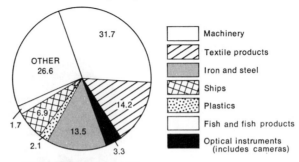

**JAPAN'S EXPORTS
BY PRODUCT GROUPS**
Percent of Value (1969)

31.7

OTHER
26.6

14.2

6.9

1.7

13.5

2.1

3.3

☐ Machinery

▨ Textile products

▨ Iron and steel

▨ Ships

▨ Plastics

☐ Fish and fish products

■ Optical instruments
  (includes cameras)

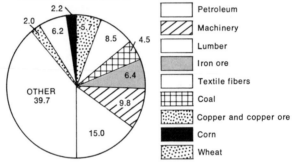

**JAPAN'S IMPORTS
BY PRODUCT GROUPS**
Percent of Value (1969)

2.2

2.0

6.2

5.7

8.5

4.5

6.4

OTHER
39.7

9.8

15.0

☐ Petroleum

▨ Machinery

☐ Lumber

▨ Iron ore

☐ Textile fibers

▦ Coal

▨ Copper and copper ore

■ Corn

▨ Wheat

(Jarolimek and Davis, *The Ways of Man*, 1974, p. 155)

or IV.

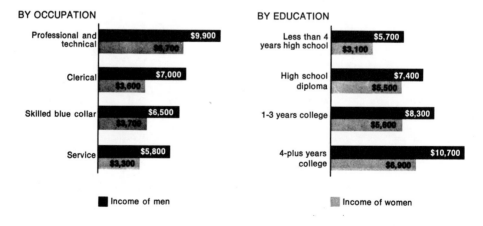

AVERAGE INCOME OF MEN AND WOMEN WORKERS
(Same age, same number of years on the job,
same education, about 1971)

BY OCCUPATION

Professional and technical	$9,900 / $6,700
Clerical	$7,000 / $3,600
Skilled blue collar	$6,500 / $3,700
Service	$5,800 / $3,300

BY EDUCATION

Less than 4 years high school	$5,700 / $3,100
High school diploma	$7,400 / $5,500
1-3 years college	$8,300 / $5,600
4-plus years college	$10,700 / $6,900

■ Income of men   ▨ Income of women

(Jarolimek and Davis, *Web of the World*, 1973, p. 154)

Because you are not a content specialist, you may become anxious about ways in which you can help children to analyze these geographic representations. As a start, you should ask the following questions about each illustration:

1. What is being illustrated?
2. What is the purpose of the illustration?
3. What information is provided by the caption?
4. What information is provided through the key, symbols, or scales?

By reflecting on the answers to these questions, the reader can begin to gain understanding of the concepts that are in the illustration. Through examples and questioning, you can relate the new information to previously acquired information:

1. Do you think our exports are similar to those of Japan?
2. How is our climate similar to Africa's?
3. If you lived in Africa, would you need the same types of clothing you now wear?

Your attempts to draw attention to the information found in the illustrations will serve as an example to be followed when children engage in independent reading exercises. Many texts present graphics but do not require students to use them or fail to explain them sufficiently so that they can be used. Authors often use graphic or pictorial aids in an attempt to lessen the verbal difficulty of newly encountered content materials. Some children who are having initial difficulty with the printed text might find that the graphics provide an additional aid because they often contain few words.

Maps may be the most frequently illustrated graphic material found in a social studies text. When encountering a map, children should be encouraged to:

1. use the scale and key.
2. determine longitude and latitude. (This can be taught by discussing why there are both horizontal and parallel lines on the map.)
3. determine the information being conveyed.
4. determine how directions are portrayed.
5. compare distances.

The exactness of the learning activities are dependent upon the type of map which is being read. Activity 9 at the end of this chapter has been designed to help you when you are teaching map reading skills. In an attempt to further help your children in the development of skills that are necessary for interpreting graphic aids, you should:

1. have them carefully analyze the parts of the map being studied.
   a. What is the author's purpose for including this material?
   b. What type of map is this?
   c. Dates? Parts of map?
2. provide activities that require one to analyze climates, trade routes, currents, and topography.
3. ask students to note relationships between two maps when analyzing a specific population distribution.

4. provide information on interpreting the keys, scales, or symbols that are part of graphic aids.

5. discuss the social realities behind cartoons.

6. discuss the relationship between pictures and their captions.

7. aid children in utilizing pictures, maps, and graphs to present information.

8. encourage students to develop time lines of their lives.

9. aid children in developing bulletin boards or displays illustrating similarities or differences between two governments or countries.

When reading social studies materials, the child is required to draw heavily on several skills of comprehension, such as understanding cause-and-effect relationships, making comparisons, detecting propaganda, differentiating fact from opinion, sequencing chronological occurrences, and conceptualizing time, space, place relationships.

Cause and Effect. Children need skill in detecting cause-and-effect relationships because human interactions depicted in texts are often characterized by a chain of activities. You may design curricula for developing this skill by asking children to:

1. list the causal factors.

2. discuss how each factor was causal.

3. discuss similar situations in their own lives.

4. discuss similar historical situations.

5. make predictions based on their newly learned information.

A second curricular strategy, which integrates reading and social studies, as well as develops the ability to detect cause and effect relationships, involves daily newscasts. While listening to a newscast, encourage your students to analyze it to determine:

1. the causal factors.

2. the sequence of happenings, if more than one cause was involved.

3. the effect.

4. alternative effects that could have occurred.

5. alternate causes that could have resulted in this effect.

6. stated facts to make predictions.

Activity 10 at the end of this chapter is designed to aid you in teaching cause-and-effect relationships.

Making Comparisons. Children should be encouraged to make comparisons between countries, customs, governments, policies, religions, climates, land scales, languages, and people. Making comparisons can be encouraged by asking children to look for similarities and differences when they are reading. You can reinforce comparative analysis by having your children:

1. compare the toys played with by children of different cultures.

2. compare the educational systems of various cultures.

3. compare several countries to determine relationships between climate and occupation, religion and government, and nuclear family design and interactions.

4. compare historical documents between 1800 and 1900.

5. compare travel in 1900, 1950, and 2000.

Activity 11 at the end of this chapter suggests an activity that will encourage children to compare the traits of people campaigning for public office.

Detecting Propaganda.   As we suggested in Chapter 9, the child is greatly influenced by many types of propaganda. Detection of propaganda can be encouraged by using social studies materials as a means of enabling students to:

1. determine an author's purpose.

2. determine key words used to introduce propaganda.

3. evaluate the data provided by the author to convey an issue.

4. introduce types of propaganda.

5. evaluate historical slogans as to their origins, application, and persuasive appeal.

6. analyze various approaches to persuasion used by historical leaders when governing.

Children should be encouraged to detect propaganda when they are listening to a spoken text and when they are reading a written text. Activity 12 at the end of this chapter provides you with a specific propaganda-detection activity for your classroom.

Fact and Opinion.   As we suggested earlier in this chapter, teachers at all grade levels must develop activities that encourage children to differentiate fact from opinion. While this is not an easy task, it may first be illustrated through student language. Encourage your students to express their opinions while telling them that their opinion becomes stronger when it is supported by facts.

As potentially literate consumers and independent decision makers, children need to be able to distinguish between statements based on fact and statements of *conjecture*, based on the author's beliefs. Too often children are encouraged to accept and regurgitate all that is read without evaluating supporting premises. Activity 13, which appears at the end of this chapter, can be used in your classroom to alert children to the need to analyze critically printed information.

The practice of differentiating factual statements from those based totally or partially on opinion can be further encouraged by helping children to:

1. identify clue words that are usually followed by statements of opinion: *perhaps, think, maybe, one possibility, my beliefs suggest.*

2. use bibliographic dictionaries, encyclopedias, and almanacs to check statements that appear to be factual but cause concern to the reader.

3. analyze selected paragraphs for practice in distinguishing fact from opinion statements.

4. detect the point of view of the author.

Conceptualizing Relationships.   Conceptualizing *time, space,* and *place* relationships provides students with an understanding of geographical and historical world developments. Where are they in this time capsule? Most activities that explore time, space, and place relationships encourage the child to develop retrospection while providing an opportunity for predicting future events.

Concepts such as these may be encouraged further by helping the student to:

1. develop his family tree: Where did his family originate? What was the world like at that time and place? What is life like in that country today? How would his life have been different if his family had never immigrated to America?

2. illustrate variations in *life-span* expectancy and *world-time* evolution.

3. illustrate transportation changes that have occurred in the last 100 years.

4. detect similarities and differences in lands and people.

Activity 14 at the end of this chapter will enable you to help children understand time, space, and place relationships.

Sequencing. The concept of sequential ordering underlies historical developments. How did we get where we are as a nation? In using activities 15 and 16 at the end of this chapter, you can continuously encourage children to develop a chronological perspective by:

1. discussing present-day occurrences while identifying historical factors.

2. developing historical time lines.

3. reviewing historical occurrences that have repeated themselves more than once in history: assassination, war, treason. What is the nature of man that he continues to perpetuate these behaviors? What societal factors contribute to his nature?

Teaching Social Studies. Through activities described at the end of this chapter, your students will begin to gain some understanding of the chronological evolution of history. They will appreciate the fluidity with which history has developed, and they will be amazed by the overlap of historical movements.

As classroom teachers who are attempting to integrate reading and social studies materials, you must constantly encourage children to *question* generalizations; to observe *cause-effect* relationships; to *compare* and *contrast* behaviors; to identify historical, social and geographic *sequence*; and to enumerate occurrences through the use of reference materials. Estes (1972, p. 180) supports this when he delineates the reading skill areas which are necessary for one to obtain an understanding of social studies: (1) vocabulary knowledge; (2) comprehension of both a literal and critical nature; and (3) study skills such as map reading, use of references, use of indexes and tables of contents, use of the dictionary, and use of graphs, charts, and tables.

Reading in Science

Elementary science curricula integrates biology, physical science, chemistry, zoology, geology, and botany in a program that emphasizes *involvement* through *observation, inquiry,* and *discovery.* Your role as a reading/science classroom teacher will be to aid children in discovering scientific facts through films, observations, models, pictures, and a variety of reading materials. The child's scientific experiences should include the acquisition of information by observing, smelling, feeling, listening, tasting, talking, and reading.

The child's language and reading skills aid him in discovering scientific data, interpreting factual data, and formulating generalizations. Children need a great deal of guidance in developing the language and reading skills that are necessary for mastering science materials. The materials are often characterized by a multitude of facts and interrelationships. Unlike narrative materials, scientific writings contain: (1) a terse writing style, (2) an extremely high readability level, (3) a great number of facts and details, and (4) a variety of difficult concepts.

As you attempt to teach elementary science, it is important to realize that the child will only experience success in this content area if you provide instruction that enables him to:

1. understand scientific language.
2. synthesize his rate of reading with his purpose for reading.
3. utilize the parts of his text.
4. understand and utilize scientific formulas.
5. read graphic aids.
6. follow directions.
7. evaluate data.
8. make generalizations.
9. apply new data to solve problems.

As you read and reread this list, it will become obvious that many of these practices involve reading and study skills which are relevant to understanding other content area materials. Without belaboring the point, we do want to stress that reading any material involves perceiving, interpreting, and evaluating. In order to make this a workable process the child of any age must develop word-recognition, comprehension, and study skills.

Interpreting Scientific Language. A "hands-on" approach to science has been used in many schools in an attempt to develop basic concepts before children confront the technical language of science. This hands-on approach has been implemented in many schools in an attempt to develop a positive attitude toward the study of science. Before this experience-based approach was used, it was found that the vocabulary of science often negatively affected children's listening comprehension. Children were unfamiliar with both the *technical* and *nontechnical* language. A similar problem occurred when children read scientific materials. Mallinson (1972) suggested that this was true for the following reasons:

1. The level of reading difficulty of many textbooks in science were found to be too high for the students for whom the textbooks were designed.
2. The differences between the levels of reading difficulty of the easiest and the most difficult textbooks analyzed in all the studies were both statistically significant and consequential.
3. In some science textbooks, whose average level of reading difficulty seemed satisfactory, there were passages that would have been difficult even for some college students.
4. Many science textbooks contained nontechnical words that could have been replaced by easier synonyms.

5. Little cognizance seemed to have been taken of growth in reading ability during the school year, since the earlier portions of some of the textbooks were difficult, whereas the latter portions were easier.*

The extent of this language complexity becomes obvious as we explore excerpts from elementary scientific materials.

> About half a billion years ago, one kind of creature very slowly developed something quite unusual. Instead of a shell outside the body, a stiff rod formed inside the body. The rod ran along the creature's back just underneath the nerve cord that carries messages to all parts of the creature's body and keeps the various parts working together.
>
> The rod called the notochord (no tə kord) is present, at some time, in the development of chordates (cor dat'), a large group of animals an early stage in their development— when they are embryos.
>
> *(Asimov and Gallant, 1973, p. 55)*

What type of scientific training have you had? Are you having difficulty with this passage? If so, you probably have the dictionary skills necessary to add meaning to the passage. But what about the intermediate-aged child who is reading this text. Will he fail because he does not possess adequate study skills? And what about this passage?

> The garbage collectors of the sea are the decomposers. Day and night, ocean plants and animals that die, and the body wastes of living animals, slowly drift down to the sea floor. There is a steady rain of such material that builds up on the sea bottom. This is especially true on the continental shelves, where life is rich. It is less true in the desert regions of the deep ocean.
>
> As on the land, different kinds of bacteria also live in the sea. They attack the remains of dead plant and animal tissue and break it down into nutrients. These nutrients are then taken up by plant and animal plankton alike. Among such nutrients are nitrate (ni' trat), phosphate (fos' fāt), manganese (mang' ga nes), silica (sil k), and calcium (kal se m).
>
> *(Asimov and Gallant, 1973, p. 155)*

Did you experience difficulty when you read this passage? Children often have difficulty interpreting the message because they are unfamiliar with words like *decomposers, bacteria, phosphate,* and *nutrients.*

And what about this passage?

> About the same time Empedocles lived, a Greek philosopher named Democritus (di mok r t s) had other ideas about matter. He imagined that all substances were made of tiny particles too small to be seen. Nothing was any smaller. Democritus called his particles atoms. The word comes from two Greek words—*a* which means "not," and *tome* which means "cut" or "separate." Atoms could not be cut apart. They were hard and solid. They came in different sizes and had different masses. Some were heavy, others were light. Some were rough, others were slick and smooth.
>
> *(Asimov and Gallant, 1973, p. 155)*

*Reading in the Sciences: A Review of the Research," George G. Mallinson, in James Laffey (Ed.) *Reading in the Content Areas,* IRA, 1972, p. 139. Reprinted with permission of George G. Mallinson and the International Reading Association.

Although it is very interesting, this type of subject matter is difficult for *Reading process* many children because they lack the skills necessary to perceive, interpret, and evaluate this type of fact-specific data. While the writers of these selections have attempted to use contextual clues as an aid to reading, both the technical language (nutrients, phosphate, fossil, sediments, notochord) and the nontechnical language (matter, particles, substance, decomposers) may not be part of the child's experiential background.

As you realize, science materials differ greatly from the basal reader narratives in both language and concept development. Multiple concepts may be introduced in one scientific selection. When this occurs difficulty often arises for the reader who does not perceive the necessary relationships, classifications, relevance of the materials. A further problem may arise when readers of science are required to interpret charts, tables, graphs, maps, and formulas. Teachers realizing the possibility of language and conceptual difficulty have incorporated first-hand observation through field trips, experiments, films, models, and pictures into their teaching. When attempting to teach scientific data remember to:

1. substitute common terms for technical terms, for example, the common term *balance* may be a substitute for the technical term *equilibrium.*

2. discuss the scientific concept before adding the technical label.

3. define the new words with your students.

4. develop scientific word charts that clarify scientific words.

Seasons	Heat	Climate
tropics	radiation	weather
temperate zones	conduction	polar climates
frigid zones	convection	tropical climates
		desert climates
		mountain climates
		continental climates
		marine climates

5. analyze words parts.

chloro,   oid,   therm,

6. discuss the multiple meanings of scientific words.

7. determine if sentence context provides any understanding of the term.

Remember that a successful reader can interpret as well as perceive the printed symbol. Activities 17–24, presented at the end of this chapter, are designed to aid you in teaching children to understand and read the language of science.

When presenting new material, it is important to introduce the new vocabulary and concepts that will be encountered in the selection. Many words have multiple meanings and each subject area contains a unique vocabulary. As a classroom teacher, you must teach the vocabulary upon which the key concepts rest.

Comprehending Scientific Data. Many children in the primary grades are exceedingly interested in science. However, they sometimes begin to lose this interest during the intermediate years when they are required to read science texts. This loss of interest usually occurs when children do not easily comprehend printed scientific data. As a classroom teacher, you may be able to lessen this difficulty by following these suggested procedures when you are introducing and implementing a unit of scientific study:

A. Planning for unit implementation
   1. Begin by surveying the unit of study to determine the difficult vocabulary.
      a. Which words contain the stems of other words?
      b. Which words may cause multiple meaning difficulty?
      c. Which words present entirely unexplained concepts?
      d. Which words can be associated with objects?
      e. Which words draw on the experiences of your students?
   2. Determine which of these words contain key bits of understanding.
   3. Categorize all of the remaining terms under key terms.

B. Implementing the unit
   1. List the key terms on the board or on a wall chart.
   2. Present an illustration for each word. Illustrations may be made through *pictures, live specimens, slides.*
   3. Ask questions that will help youngsters to use the new words.
   4. As the unit progresses, introduce other categories of terms in the same manner.
   5. Utilize magazines, newspapers, and trade books to supplement textbook reading.
   6. Actively engage students in the unit by having them:
      a. collect specimens or pictures of specimens.
      b. label specimens or picture displays.
      c. draw charts.
      d. develop models.
      e. perform experiments.
      f. plan field trips.

When you are planning for a unit of this type, it is important to remember that you must plan for mastery of the following study skills. Through the following skills the student can collect adequate data to make evaluative judgments:

1. locating information.
2. interpreting formulas.
3. understanding graphic representations.

By now you should be very familiar with these study skills. Their mastery is a key element in content area reading; therefore, we will discuss how these skills relate to the teaching of science.

Teaching Science

Locating Information.   When you are planning a reading/science curriculum, special attention must be directed toward practice in locating and using sources. The development of this library study skill is particularly related to *scientific inquiry*, the basis of many content area science programs.

The use of glossaries, indexes, headings, pictures, and graphs can be easily explored in order to develop and reinforce the mechanics of study skills. After the child has developed basic competency in using these sources, he can be encouraged to explore *Scientific American*, as well as government and scientific publications necessary for the development of a particular concept. When looking for new information, children should be encouraged to survey the materials available in their own classroom. The library should be an alternate source of investigation. When perusing magazines, newspapers, an encyclopedia, or texts for new information the student should:

1. survey the table of contents.
2. check the text index.

After the topic under investigation has been located the child should:

1. survey passages to determine the main idea.
2. note all important details.

Once the specific information has been located, the student will be able to continue his study. The location of new scientific data may call for the interpretation of technical formulas.

Interpreting Formulas.   The short-hand formula abbreviations of scientific language often interfere with the child's comprehension of the materials. Children must be given practice understanding this code. Similar to the study of mathematics, scientific formulas should be viewed as an extension of the technical vocabulary. They should be told that the symbols of the formula are synonyms for the scientific words. A formula, like a sentence, represents scientific thought. The symbols within the formula can be viewed as words. The sentence, "Centripetal *force* is equal to the *mass* times the *velocity* squared divided by the *radius* of a circle" can be represented as:

$$F = \frac{MV^2}{R}$$

The sentence equals the formula. Now let's examine each symbol, or word, within the formula:

$$F = \text{force}$$
$$M = \text{mass}$$
$$V = \text{velocity}$$
$$R = \text{radius}$$

After the reader *interprets* the symbol and the meaning, he is ready to evaluate the message. Activity 25, at the end of this chapter, encourages this development.

Understanding Graphic Representations. Most scientific readings present graphics as supplementary aids to the printed material. Graphic aids are often a great help for students who have difficulty interpreting the printed text. The purpose of graphics becomes obvious to the reader who is encouraged to survey the *title*, as well as the elements of the illustration. Children must be aided in interpreting graphic symbols because many elementary science materials contain the following types of graphic representations:

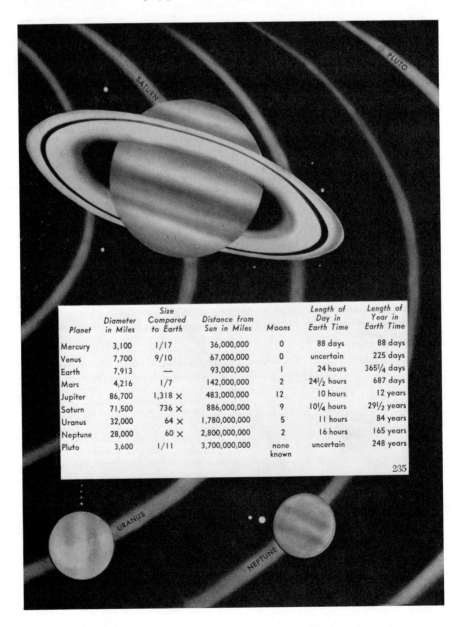

Planet	Diameter in Miles	Size Compared to Earth	Distance from Sun in Miles	Moons	Length of Day in Earth Time	Length of Year in Earth Time
Mercury	3,100	1/17	36,000,000	0	88 days	88 days
Venus	7,700	9/10	67,000,000	0	uncertain	225 days
Earth	7,913	—	93,000,000	1	24 hours	365¼ days
Mars	4,216	1/7	142,000,000	2	24½ hours	687 days
Jupiter	86,700	1,318 ×	483,000,000	12	10 hours	12 years
Saturn	71,500	736 ×	886,000,000	9	10¼ hours	29½ years
Uranus	32,000	64 ×	1,780,000,000	5	11 hours	84 years
Neptune	28,000	60 ×	2,800,000,000	2	16 hours	165 years
Pluto	3,600	1/11	3,700,000,000	none known	uncertain	248 years

235

(Barnard, Stendler, Spock, Beler, 1966, *Science: A Search for Evidence,* New York: Macmillan Publishing Co., Inc. (p. 235).

Yeast cells, magnified 1000 times. Within four hours after the cell farthest left had begun to bud, there were eight cells.

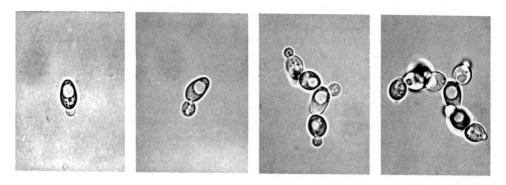

(Barnard, Stendler, Spock, Beler, 1966, *Science: A Search for Evidence.* New York: Macmillan Publishing Co., Inc. p. 375).

or

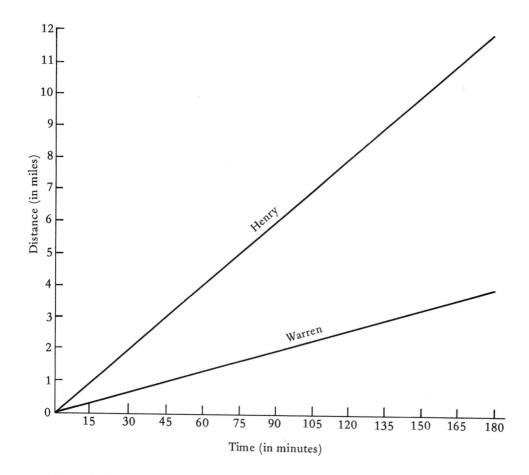

(Barnard and Lavatelli, 1970, *Science: Measuring Things*, p. 35)

Graphic representations such as these are found in most sceintific materials. They are intended to supplement the printed text by providing clues. Some children may find them difficult to read unless they are given careful instruction. Other children may never grasp the importance of such representations unless they are alerted to the functional value. Activities 26 through 28 at the end of this chapter are designed to encourage children to comprehend and use graphic representations as an aid to comprehending the scientific language of their text.

Although all study skills relate to the competent reading of all content areas, we have attempted to enable you to clearly understand the application procedures necessary for implementing these integrated processes within the context of your classroom. Mathematics, science, and social studies have been given prime consideration because they are the content areas in which children seem to have the most difficulty.

As a teacher in a self-contained classroom, you may find yourself responsible for teaching art and music. Let us briefly explore the relationships between reading and the arts.

Reading and Related Areas

Those teachers who are fortunate enough to have music and art specialists as part of the staff sometimes fail to incorporate these areas into content related subjects. They tend to see the role of the humanities specialists as unrelated to the base curriculum. Music and art, like reading and science, are musts in every classroom.

We hope that as teachers you will provide both art and musical activities that encourage lifetime interest, enjoyment, and pursuit; we will attempt to alert you to reading/music/art curricular integrations. Although young children do not become involved with in-depth studies of musical theory, they do encounter new vocabulary and symbols that need to be carefully integrated in the existing curriculum. Teaching reading in the arts is not totally unlike teaching reading in other content areas because children must be helped to:

1. perceive the technical terms and symbols.
2. interpret and understand the symbols.
3. follow performance directions.
4. evaluate music and art criticisms.

In an attempt to avoid the following problem suggested by Tirro (1968), activities 29 through 33 at the end of this chapter are designed to encourage the incorporation of reading/art/music into the curriculum:

> Music theory texts are almost in a class unto themselves. Very similar to an algebra text or a geometry problem book where each letter, number, and sign must be carefully considered, tasted, chewed, swallowed, and rechewed like a cow's cud, it becomes obvious that one does not really read a theory book; one grapples with it in a life-and-death struggle. (p. 105)

Functional Literacy

As you prepare children to critically analyze content area readings, you need to include materials such as: newspaper want ads, job application forms, labels on cans, bank loan applications, tax forms, and insurance policies. The inclusion of these literacy materials as a curriculum component seems both desirable and legitimate because students who can use critical communication skills in order to meet their basic daily needs are functionally literate.

Functional literacy has become a major thrust in educational literature. It has also become the basis of many educational programs because students as adults often encounter difficulty when applying for schooling, housing, health care, and employment. By exploring some of these situations and materials, middle-school-age children often become aware of the reading/language criteria needed for future success in these encounters.

Early classroom activities, which may include "playing store," provide children with an opportuntiy for comparative shopping. The *age* of the children will determine the particular topics to be covered. Primary- and intermediate-grade students may be excited about following toy-assembly directions, whereas children in the upper grades may be interested in reading the *Driver's Education Manual* or Boy Scout-Girl Scout manuals.

Functional literacy programs should be approached as a beginning, rather than a terminal point, in the building of positive educational experiences for students of all ages. A well-planned functional literacy curriculum should provide the study of topics and skill areas that will be of value in encounters outside of school, and in school-related activities. Being able to read and follow recipe directions, for example, may spark interest and competency in projects related to content area knowledge, such as the reading of graphs and measurement techniques.

As a teacher you may view functional literacy programs as a means by which you can provide students with relevant educational experiences. The utility of such a successful curriculum must be viewed as an integrated content area component that extends reading, writing, listening, and speaking skills.

While your goal may be that of developing functionally literate students, your approach cannot be one that only allows fifteen minutes per day for reading insurance forms, recipes, or topical manuals. The functional literacy component must be integrated within a well-planned thematic unit of study. For example, as you study "Our Community" with a group of second-graders you may want to discuss the procedures their parents engaged in when they bought a house or rented an apartment. A question such as the following may be all that is needed to spark a lively conversation: "How did your parents find out that your home or apartment was for rent or sale?" Simulated activities, such as visiting and interviewing a bank teller or a rental agent, may provide all the understanding needed by that age group.

As you can see, the success of the functional literacy program will be dependent on (1) its relevancy to social, economic, political, and cultural aspects of daily living, and (2) its integration within content area units of study.

TEACHING ACTIVITIES THAT INTEGRATE
READING AND MATHEMATICS

1. Another Way to Say It

<u>Goal</u>: Developing an understanding of the language of symbols

<u>Grade level</u>: 2–4

<u>Construction</u>: Write sentences replacing words with mathematical symbols.
<u>Example</u>:
   ÷ the room in ½.
   Two wrongs do not = a right.

<u>Utilization</u>: The student rewrites the sentence substituting the correct word for the symbol. Depending on grade, other symbols may be substituted.

2. Word Hunt

<u>Goal</u>: Developing an understanding of mathematical language

<u>Grade level</u>: 3–6

<u>Construction</u>: Design and mimeograph a chart of math terms placed vertically, diagonally, and horizontally in rows and columns. Extra, nonfunctional letters can be placed in the chart. On a laminated card give definitions of mathematical terms.

<u>Utilization</u>: After reading a definition, the student circles the correct term in the puzzle. Words can be circled horizontally, vertically, or diagonally.

3. The Wall Street Game

<u>Goal</u>: Interpreting information portrayed through graphs

<u>Grade level</u>: 4–8

<u>Construction</u>: Assist students in choosing a particular kind of stock and aid them in keeping track of its losses and gains by reading the newspaper.

<u>Utilization</u>: Students can graph the daily fluctuations by putting the date on the <u>X</u> axis and the losses or gains on the <u>Y</u> axis. The class might also want to have a bake sale or car wash and buy a small share of their own stock.

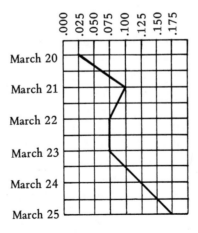

4. Plan Your Own Field Trip

<u>Goal</u>: Designing math tables

<u>Grade level</u>: 4–8

<u>Construction and Utilization</u>: Arrange for the class to go on a field trip. The class is responsible for arranging the transportation, reservations, meals, supplies, and equipment. Each group could be responsible for one aspect of the preparations. This would involve reading bus or train schedules, lists, and tables of the times museums are open; another activity that would involve using tables is figuring out the expenses involved.

5. Mathematical Scavenger Hunt

<u>Goal</u>: Following directions in mathematics

<u>Grade level</u>: 3–8

<u>Construction</u>: Hide a certain object and plant clues around the room that describe tasks to be completed in order to find the object. The clues could say "measure 3 meters from the desk," or multiply 6 × 6 and walk that number of centimeters." Make a different set of clues for each player.

<u>Utilization</u>: The first person to find the object according to his clues wins.

6. Our Town at a Glance

<u>Goal</u>: Understanding picture graphs

<u>Grade level</u>: 5–8

<u>Construction</u>: Assist students in collecting data about the surrounding areas of their homes or school. From the library, chamber of commerce, weather stations, or state house, they can find amount of rainfall in the different areas, location of natural resources, or elevations, for example.

<u>Utilization</u>: From the information gathered, students should choose a color code representing various elevation levels, amounts of rainfall, and so on. Using the color code, the students could design a picture map showing the different elevations or the amounts of rainfall of the selected geographical area.

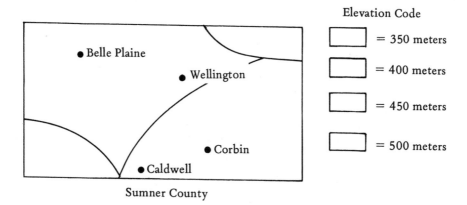

Sumner County

7. Class Favorites

<u>Goal</u>: Constructing math histograms

<u>Grade level</u>: 5–8

<u>Construction</u>: Prepare dittos divided into small squares or give each child a piece of graph paper.

<u>Utilization</u>: Have one student ask one question of other members of the class.
<u>Example</u>:

What is your favorite color?
What is your favorite TV show?
In what month were you born?
On the paper, the student labels the <u>X</u> and <u>Y</u> axis according to the topic (see below). He then marks an <u>X</u> in the appropriate square to show the person's response. A short summary of his results should be written.

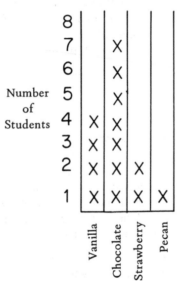

Favorite ice cream

8. Careers

<u>Goal</u>: Developing math tables

<u>Grade level</u>: 3–8

<u>Construction and utilization</u>: Have each group of students choose a topic with which they can survey the rest of the class. One possible topic might be future careers. The group would design survey questions asking, "What would you like to be when you graduate from high school? What skills are required to obtain the desired job?"

TEACHING ACTIVITIES THAT INTEGRATE
READING AND SOCIAL STUDIES

9. Learning Stations—Intermediate Grades and Above—
Wellesley School District
By Diane Scatasti

Goal: To increase proficiency in map reading; to develop alphabetizing; to develop understanding of directionality used in maps

Grade level: 4–6

Construction: Map of midtown New York City
Numbered index of museums in midtown Manhattan, NYC
Written directions.
Activity cards with outlined task and answer key.

Utilization: Provide a map of restaurants, a restaurant index, written instructions, activity cards, and work sheets. Allow students to choose one of five activity cards. Have them read the task outlined on the card and, using the given map and index as references, record the number of the activity card and complete the assignment on the work sheet provided. Upon completion, check their answers by lifting the flap on the activity card.

Sample Activity-Card Tasks

Activity Card A. You are at Rockefeller Plaza between W. 48th St. and W. 51st St. and would like to examine the five restaurants in that immediate vicinity. Locate each of them on the map and list their names and numbers on your paper in alphabetical order.

Activity Card B. Number and list alphabetically all of the restaurants you would encounter on your left-hand side as you stroll on Second Ave. from E. 65th St. to E. 46th St.

Activity Card C. In touring only those streets between 59th and 65th running from west to east as you leave Central Park, number and list alphabetically only those restaurants you would directly encounter along the way.

Activity Card D. Facing west at E. 49th and Second Ave., walk a complete rectangle back to your starting point, listing alphabetically all of the restaurants you would pass on either side along the way.

10. Cause-and-Effect Radio Show

Goal: Understanding cause-and-effect relationships

Grade level: 4–8

Construction: One group of students could prepare a radio newscast for the remainder of the class. The news could be of a serious nature, events around school, or humorous; fictional news stories using teachers, students or political figures. A tin can or microphone from a tape recorder can be used for the radio microphone.

Utilization: The audience listens to the newscast and makes a cause-and-effect chart stating five effects of five causes. The team of newscasters determines if they are correct.

11. Compare Before You Vote

Goal: Making comparisons in social studies

Grade level: 3–8

Construction: Have two or more volunteer students from the class run for political office, assuming the identities of prominent people currently campaigning for president, senator, mayor, or city council. The campaigning students must research their platform, using newspapers, radio, TV, or the campaign headquarters.

Utilization: The class develops a record of the collected information, making a chart of each candidate's positive and negative aspects. At the end of an alloted time period, the class votes on the basis of the charted information, identifying statements of fact and opinion and propaganda, for example.

12. Have I Got a Deal for You ...

Goal: Detecting propaganda

Grade level: 3–8

Construction: A student chooses a topic or item to convince, sell, or persuade classmates. After a selection has been made, an oral presentation is given to the class.

Utilization: The class then tells what motions, words, and propaganda devices the person used. They discuss which devices were most convincing.

13. Fact or Fooling?

Goal: Differentiating fact from opinion

Grade level: 2–8

Construction: Have the class observe TV, radio, and newspaper advertisements for one week.

Utilization: Students then make a list of all the words, techniques, and devices that aren't really fact, but opinion or hearsay. They should then try to write their own advertisements, using only facts, and present them to the class.

14. Another Way to Look at It

Goal: Conceptualizing time, space, and place relationships

Grade level: 4–8

Construction: Have students make a three-dimensional model of their surrounding neighborhood. First, if possible, have drivers take groups of students to survey the area and make general maps of the area showing streets, buildings, and landmarks.

Utilization: The class can then make a three-dimensional model of the area using salt clay or regular modeling clay. (See recipe.) Mark buildings, the students' homes, and the school with small flags, using toothpicks and construction paper. If desired, the students can also make charts stating the number of miles or blocks between two points and how long it takes to travel between the points by walking and by car.

Modeling Mixture for Relief Maps

2 c. salt   (500 gr)   1 c. water   (250 mililiters)
1 c. flour   (150 gr)

Mix the ingredients until they are smooth and pliable. On a piece of plywood, draw the outline to be molded. Apply a thin layer of modeling mixture no more than 1/4-thick to the entire surface. Depress the clay where there are to be rivers and lakes and add additional clay to form mountains.

Away from a radiator the clay takes one week to dry. Paint with temperas and run strings to pinpoint specific locations.

15. How Did You See It?

Goal: Sequencing and making comparisons

Grade level: 5–8

Construction: Arrange with two or three students or members from another class to stage a one-minute totally unexpected event in the classroom. For example, the group could run in, say a few words to each other, pantomime a crime, and run off. Later, have a few members of the class write down exactly what happened in the correct order.

Utilization: Compare the reports with the class and discuss discrepancies in what was seen. Draw a parallel between this experience and that of witnesses at trials.

16. What Happened When?

Goal: Sequencing chronological events

Grade level: 3–8

Construction and utilization: Have students follow a newspaper story for a period of a week or more and make a time line of the events that occur. The time line could be prepared individually or as a class project. Hang a clothesline across the classroom on which events can be hung on cards and chronically sequenced. Events such as Watergate provide many places, people, dates, and events to keep in order. Students could also take one complex article or TV show and make a time line of its events.

TEACHING ACTIVITIES THAT INTEGRATE READING AND SCIENCE

17. Multiple Meanings

Goal: Developing science vocabulary

Grade level: 1–8

Construction: On a large piece of cardboard or oaktag, draw circles with scientific vocabulary written in each.

Examples: mass, energy, work, heat, standard, substance, power

<u>Utilization</u>: The board is placed on a table and players sit about one meter away. Using small plastic or cardboard disks, the player aims for any word. For whatever word the disk lands on, he must give both the technical and nontechnical meaning. A student judge decides if the definitions are acceptable. The players receive five points for each acceptable definition—five points if he only knows one meaning, ten if he knows both. The game ends when each word has been given both a technical definition and a nontechnical definition. No word can receive more than one technical definition and one nontechnical definition.

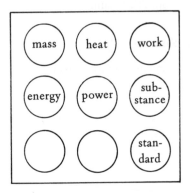

18. Scrambled Animals

<u>Goal</u>: Understanding science vocabulary

<u>Grade level</u>: 1–2

<u>Construction</u>: Divide a sheet of laminated paper in half. Label one side Carnivores and the other Herbivores. Under each heading write the names of appropriate animals, but scramble the letters. Underneath each word, draw small boxes in which students can write the unscrambled words.

<u>Utilization</u>: The student should first try to think of animals that are plant or meat eaters, and then they should try to unscramble the letters. The headings can be changed to reinforce any vocabulary words: reptiles and amphibians, conductors of electricity and nonconductors, and so on.

Carnivores	Herbivores
a b e r	f a b u o l f
b e a r	b u f f a l o
s l w e e a	w c o
w e a s e l	c o w

19. Scientific Squares

<u>Goal</u>: Understanding science vocabulary

<u>Grade level</u>: 3–5

<u>Construction</u>: The game requires 12 participants: one is the MC, two are contestants, and the remaining nine represent a tic-tac-toe board, sitting in three rows of three each. Write words from the science vocabulary on index cards with the definitions on the reverse side and give them to the MC. Write an <u>X</u> on nine large cards and an <u>O</u> on nine large cards. Each of the nine students representing the tic-tac-toe board is given one X card and one O card.

<u>Utilization</u>: One contestant is assigned X and the other contestant is assigned O. The MC reads a science vocabulary word for the first contestant. The contestant selects a student on the tic-tac-toe board to provide a definition. The contestant then states whether he agrees or disagrees with the given definition. To determine if the contestant received his letter, see the chart below:

Student on Playing Board	Contestant	Scores an X or O
Gives correct definition	Agrees	Yes
Gives correct definition	Disagrees	No
Gives incorrect definition	Agrees	No
Gives incorrect definition	Disagrees	Yes

If the contestant scores the X or O, the student on the tic-tac-toe board holds the appropriate letter in front of him. Whoever is the first to score three Xs or three Os in a vertical, horizontal, or diagonal row wins.

20. I Am Thinking of a Word ...

<u>Goal</u>: Understanding science vocabulary

<u>Grade level</u>: 4–6

<u>Construction</u>: Prepare short word-clue games in which 9 to 12 words are presented on dittos. Give approximately five clues so that by the process of elimination the student will be able to pick the correct word.
Example:
The word is not a reptile.
The word is not part of an engine.
The word is not the name of something that floats.

<u>Utilization</u>: The word clues are read to the students. The student crosses out the words eliminated by the clues, which should enable him to tell which word was selected beforehand.

21. Science Crossword

<u>Goal</u>: Understanding science vocabulary

<u>Grade level</u>: 4–8

Construction: Make up a crossword puzzle on a laminated sheet of paper or dittos. If desired, give a list of words to choose from at the bottom of the page. The clues should be worded so that they give a definition or provide context clues.

Utilization: Students complete the puzzle by finding the proper word and writing it in the correct puzzle square.

22. Concentrating Scientists

Goal: Understanding science vocabulary

Grade level: 3–8

Construction: Make paired sets of index cards so that one card is a science vocabulary word and one is a short definition of that word.

Utilization: Cards are scrambled and placed face down in rows. The players take turns turning over two cards. If the word and the definitions match, the player retains them and takes another turn. If they do not match, the cards are turned back over and the other player takes his turn. Whoever has the most pairs when all the cards have been matched wins the game.

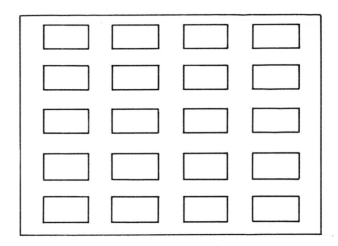

23. Solitaire Roots

Goal: Analyzing word roots (science)

Grade level: 5–8

Construction: Choose four different root words for which there are 12 other words or word combinations.
Example: oat, oats, oat cake, oat like, wild oats, oaten, oatmeal, rolled oats, oat grass, oatmeal cookies, Quaker Oats, Mother's Oats.
Make 52 palying cards with words on them from the four different roots. Number the cards from ace to king (Q, J, 10, 9 ...) with the aces being the root words.

Utilization: Any solitaire rules can be used, with the goal being to get the king through ace all in the same row for each root category.

24. Domino Derivatives

<u>Goal</u>: Analyzing word derivations.

<u>Grade level</u>: 5–8

<u>Construction</u>: Make a domino game using derivatives of scientific words. Cut rectangle dominos measuring 5 cm by 8 cm from stiff cardboard. On one domino write two derivatives of the same word on both ends. This double derivative is to be used as the starting domino. For the rest, write two words of different derivatives on each domino.

<u>Utilization</u>: Play begins by turning all the dominos face down with each player drawing five dominoes. Whoever has the double domino puts it out. If no one has the double domino, all the dominoes are returned face down to the middle, and players draw again. In turn, players try to match one end of their domino to an open end of another domino already played. If a player cannot make a match, he draws up to five dominoes from those remaining, and if he still cannot make a match, he loses his turn. The game ends when one palyer has used up all his dominoes or no one can play. In this case, the player with the fewest number of dominoes is the winner.

Examples:

mitotic	analyze	hydrolosis	evaporate
mitosis	analysis	hydrate	vaporize
osmosis	analytic	dehydrate	vaporous
osmotic			

25. Shoot for the Moon

<u>Goal</u>: Interpreting scientific formulas

<u>Grade level</u>: 4–8

<u>Construction</u>: Make a large board game with a path of squares to follow. The beginning square should be labeled "Blast Off," and the ending square should contain a picture of the moon. The remaining squares should be blank or labeled with "Draw a card", "Lose a turn", "Go back three spaces," etc. For "Draw a card" construct small oak-tag cards stating a scientific formula. One or two dice should be secured for the player.

<u>Utilization</u>: Each player is given four playing pieces. The object of the game is to land all four playing pieces on the moon. Each player rolls one die, moves one of his four playing pieces the specified number of squares, and then follows the instruction on the square. If a player lands on a space that says "Draw a card," he must draw a card and interpret the formula correctly or else lose his turn. The first person to land all four playing pieces on the moon wins the game.

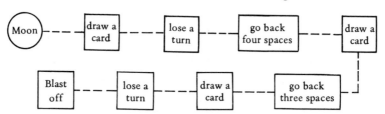

26. Illustrate an Experiment

Goal: Utilizing graphic representations as an aid to understanding scientific language

Grade level: 4–8

Construction and Utilization: Have students make up a simple experiment. When possible, encourage the use of picture diagrams as a substitute for vocabulary. After attempting the experiment, the student should reexamine the diagrams illustrating the aids to understanding unfamiliar scientific language. A diagram is then exchanged with another student. After a second person has performed the experiment, the results should be compared, noting any changes that need to be made in the diagram.
A modification of this activity could involve taking something apart that is not too complex and using diagrams to explain how to put it back together.

27. Find the Experiment

Goal: Utilizing indexes and graphs

Grade level: 5–8

Construction: Give each student a secret message that states a topic discussed in a children's science magazine.

Utilization: The student must use the indexes or table of contents of the magazines to locate an experiment concerning the topic in his secret message. The student repeats the experiment described in the magazine article and graphs the results. He should then compare his results with those of the magazine article. Discuss reasons for any differences and, if desired, repeat the experiment.

28. Teacher for a Day

Goal: Developing location skills involving the glossary

Grade level: 5–8

Construction and Utilization: Have students write a short article concerning any area in science for someone in a lower grade. At the end of the story, the student-author should provide a glossary of the more difficult terms. Perhaps after the younger student has read the article, he can discuss it with the student-author, reviewing the terms in the glossary.

ART AND MUSIC

29. Do, Re, Mi to Reading

Goal: Applying the skills needed to read music textbooks

Grade level: 2–6

Construction: Instruct students in the basics of music reading—in particular, how to tell if a note is a C, B, or G, for example, by the line the note is standing on.

Prepare laminated music sheets, placing notes in such a position that, when interpreted into letters, they will spell out a message.

Utilization: Students write the correct letter next to the note and read the secret message.

c   a   b   b   a   g   e

30. Our Own Puppet Show!

Goal: Incorporating reading and art activities

Grade level: 5–8

Construction: Students choose a play they want to perform with puppets. If they cannot decide on a particular play, assist them in rewriting a favorite story in dialogue form.
Make puppets out of old socks with buttons and other pieces of material sewed on for facial features. If desired, paper bags can be used instead of socks. Decorate with yarn and construction paper.

Utilization: Students present the puppet show to the class, reading from the prepared script during practices. If possible, the students should be encouraged to memorize the lines for the final production.

31. The Greatest Show on Earth

Goal: Combining reading/art/music skills

Grade level: 3–8

Construction and Utilization: Assist the class in planning a small-scale musical. First they must select a play or write their own show about the people or events in school. After the script has been chosen or written, parts should be assigned including those of actors, stage crew, scenery painters, prop collectors, and costume makers. Next, the music for the show should be selected from contemporary songs on radio or TV, or just songs that everyone knows. Everyone should have the chance to help paint the scenery, practice the music, and perform for other classes.

32. Sing and Syllabicate

Goal: Developing reading skills through singing

Grade level: K–3

Construction and Utilization: Simply learning a song is an excellent way to practice rote memorization, rhythm, and proper inflection, accenting and syllabication. For syllabication, in particular, have a group walk and clap the beat of a song, separating the words into correct syllables. Next, just have them sing part of the song, leaving out certain syllables, words, or phrases to develop a hearing for the proper separation of words.

33. What's Your Book About?

Goal: Developing an interest in reading

Grade level: K–3

Construction and Utilization: Have students design a cover for a book they have read, or have them make a diorama using a shoebox and pieces of wood, plastic, and material and doll house furniture, for example. In addition, the students could paint posters advertising a certain book to entice others to read it.

QUESTIONS AND RELATED READINGS

If at this time you do not feel that you have attained adequate knowledge to successfully answer the following questions, we would like to suggest related readings.

1. How is reading related to the learning process?
2. What processes are involved in the art of reading?
3. What skill commonalities are necessary for mastering any content area?
4. How is reading related to the study of mathematics?
5. How is reading related to the study of social studies?
6. How is reading related to the study of science?
7. How is reading related to the study of music and art?

Goal 1: To aid the reader in understanding the comprehensiveness of the reading process.

Question 1: How is reading related to the learning process?

Hill, Margaret K. "Reading in the Content Fields." In *Combining Research Results and Good Practice*, edited by Mildred A. Dawson. Proceedings of the International Research Association, Vol. II, part 2, 1966 (Copyright 1967), pp. 19–28.

Kingston, A. J. "What Do We Mean by Reading in the Content Areas?" *Journal of Reading*, 15 (April 1972), 482–4.

Wiggins, Phyllis W. "The Reading Teacher: Heart of the Curriculum." *Journal of Reading*, 15 (April 1972), 484–4.

Goal 2: To aid the reader in understanding the process involved in the act of reading.

Question 2: What processes are involved in the act of reading?

Rystrum, R. "Listening, Decoding, Comprehension and Reading." *Reading Teacher*, 24 (Dec. 1970).

Sullivan, Joanna. "Receptive and Critical Reading Develops at all Levels." *Reading Teacher*, 27 (May 1974), 796–800.

Wanat, Stanley F. "Language Acquisition: Basic Issues." *Reading Teacher*, 25 (Nov. 1971), 142–7.

Goal 3: To aid the reader in understanding the skills common to reading in any content area.

Question 3: What skill commonalities are necessary for mastering any content area?

Braam, Leonard S., and James E. Walker. "Subject Teachers' Awareness of Reading Skills." *Journal of Reading,* 16 (May 1973), 608–11.

Smith, Nila Banton. "Reading in Subject Matter Fields." *Educational Leadership,* 22 (March 1965), 382–5.

Whipple, Gertrude. "Essential Types of Reading in the Content Fields," in *Improvement of Reading Through Classroom Practice,* edited by J. Allen Figurel. Proceedings of the International Reading Association, 1964, 31–33.

> Goal 4: To aid the reader in understanding the interrelatedness of reading and mathematics.
>
> Question 4: How is reading related to the study of mathematics?

Aaron, I. E. "Readings in Mathematics." *Journal of Reading,* 8 (May 1965), 391–5.

Call, R., and N. Wiggin. "Reading and Mathematics." *The Mathematics Teacher,* 59 (Feb. 1966), 149–57.

Collier, Calhoun C., and Lois A. Redmond. "Are You Teaching Kids to Read Mathematics?" *Reading Teacher,* 27 (May 1974), 804–8.

> Goal 5: To aid the reader in understanding the interrelatedness of reading and social studies.
>
> Question 5: How is reading related to the study of social studies?

Carpenter, Helen McCracken, ed. *Skill Development in Social Studies.* Thirty-third Yearbook. Washington, D.C.: National Council for the Social Studies, 1963.

Johnson, R. E. and E. B. Vardian. "Reading Readability and Social Studies." *Reading Teacher,* 24 (Feb. 1973), 483–8.

McAulay, J. D. "Social Studies Dependent on Reading." *Education,* 82 (1961), 87–9.

> Goal 6: To aid the reader in understanding the interrelatedness of reading and science.
>
> Question 6: How is reading related to the study of science?

Beldon, Bernard R., and Wayne D. Lee. "Textbook Readability and the Reading Ability of Science Students." *Science Teacher,* 29 (April 1962), 20–3.

Ediger, M. "Reading in the Elementary School Science Program." *Science Education,* 49 (1965), 389–90.

Romans, M. J. "Reading and Science: A Symbiotic Relationship." *Education,* 81 (Jan. 1961), 273–6.

> Goal 7: To aid the reader in understanding the interrelatedness of reading and music and art.
>
> Question 7: How is reading related to the study of music and art?

Green, F. "Art Helps Us Read." *Arts and Activities,* 57 (Feb. 1965), 17.

Gump, Patricia L., and Richard R. Muller. "Using Art and Imagery in a Multimedia Center." *Reading Teacher,* 25 (April 1972), 657–62.

Vawter, G. P. "Music Attuned to Reading." *School and Community,* 51 (Nov. 1964), 21.

BIBLIOGRAPHY

Artley, A. Sterl. *Trends and Practices in Secondary Reading.* ERIC/CRIER Reading Review Series. Newark, Del.: International Reading Association, 1968, p. 108.

Asimov, Isaac, and Ray G. Gallant. *Ginn Science Program: Intermediate Level C.* Lexington, Mass.: Ginn and Company, 1973.

Austin, Mary C. "Improving Comprehension of Mathematics." In *Reading in the Secondary Schools,* edited by M. Jerry Weiss. Indianapolis, Ind.: Odyssey Press (Publishing), 1961, pp. 391–6.

Austin, Mary, and Coleman Morrison. *The First R.* Cambridge, Mass.: Harvard University Press, 1963, p. 50.

Bilodeau, Edward A. *Acquisition of Skill.* New York: Academic Press, Inc., 1966.

Board of Education. *Reading and Language in the Elementary School.* Gary, Ind.: Gary Public Schools, 1962.

Bruner, Jerome S., "On Perceptual Readiness." *Psychological Review,* 64 (1957), 123–52.
———*On Knowing.* Cambridge, Mass.: Harvard University Press, 1962.
———et al. *Studies in Cognitive Growth,* New York: John Wiley & Sons, Inc., 1967.

Chambers, Dewey W., and Heath W. Lowry. *The Language Arts.* Dubuque, Iowa: William C. Brown Company, Publishers, 1975, p. 75.

Clymer, Ted. *Ginn 360, 720,* Lexington, Mass.: Ginn Xerox Co., 1970, 76.

Corle, Clyde G. "Reading in Mathematics: A Review of Recent Research." In *Reading in the Content Areas,* edited by James L. Laffey. Newark, Del.: International Reading Association, 1972, pp. 75–94.
———and M. L. Coulter. *The Reading Arithmetic Skills Program—A Research Project in Reading and Arithmetic.* University Park, Pa.: The Pennsylvania School Study Council, 1964.

Courtney, L. "Recent Developments in Reading in the Content Areas." University of Chicago. *Conference on Reading,* 27 (1965), 134–44.

Davis, Frederick B., "Research in Comprehension in Reading." *Reading Research Quarterly,* 3 (Summer 1968), 499–545.

Dechant, Emerald V. *Improving the Teaching of Reading.* Englewood Cliffs, N.J.: Prentice-Hall, Inc., 1964.

Early, Margaret J. "The Interrelatedness of Language Skills." In *Developing High School Reading Programs,* edited by Mildred H. Dawson. Newark, Del.: International Reading Association, 1967, p. 101.

Estes, Thomas H. "Reading in the Social Studies: A Review of Research since 1950." In *Reading in the Content Areas,* edited by James L. Laffey. Newark, Del.: International Reading Association, 1972, pp. 177–87.

Fay, Leo, Thomas Horn, and Constance McCullough. *Improving Reading in the Elementary Social Studies.* Bulletin no. 33. Washington, D.C.: National Council for the Scoial Studies, 1961.

Gallant, Roy and Isaac Asimov. *Ginn Science Program.* Intermediate Level B. Lexington, Mass. 1973, pp. 33–34.

Herber, Harold. *Teaching Reading in Content Areas.* Englewood Cliffs, N.J.: Prentice-Hall, Inc., 1970, p. 13.

Jarolomek, John and O. L. Davis. *Social Studies in the Elementary School.* New York: Macmillan Publishing Co., Inc. 1974.

Joly, R. W., "Reading Improvement in Subjects Other Than English." *High Points,* 47 (Jan. 1965), 22–30.

Karlin, Robert. *Teaching Elementary Reading.* New York: Harcourt Brace Jovanovich, Inc., 1971, p. 218.

Kenworthy, Leonard S. *Eleven Nations.* Lexington, Mass.: Ginn and Company, 1972, p. 177.

Lapp, Diane, and Linda Lungren. "Musical Creativity: Exclusively an Elementary School Concept?" *Massachusetts Music News,* 23 (1975), 31–32.

Lapp, Diane, Anton Lahnston and Richard Rezba. "Is It Possible to Teach Reading Through the Content Areas?" Paper presented at annual International Reading Convention, Anaheim, Calif, 1976.

Mallinson, George G. "Reading in the Sciences: A Review of the Research." In *Reading in the Content Areas,* edited by James L. Laffey. Newark, Del.: International Reading Association, 1972, pp. 127–52.

Marksheffel, Ned D. *Better Reading in the Secondary School.* New York: The Ronald Press Company, 1966, p. 174.

National Society for the Study of Education. *Reading in the Elementary School.* (48th). Chicago: University of Chicago Press, 1962.

Reeves, Ruth. *The Teaching of Reading in Our Schools.* New York: Macmillan Publishing Co., Inc., 1966.

Robinson, Helen M. *Dimensions of Critical Reading.* Reading Study Center, University of Delaware, 1964.

Russell, David. *Children Learn to Read.* Lexington, Mass.: Ginn and Company, 1961, p. 457.

Shepherd, David. *Comprehensive High School Reading Methods.* Columbus, Ohio: Charles E. Merrill Publishing Company, 1973, p. 259.

Tirro, Frank. "Reading Techniques in the Teaching of Music." In *Fusing Reading Skills and Content,* edited by H. Alan Robinson and Ellen Lamar Thomas. Newark, Del.: International Reading Association, 1968, pp. 103–7.

Wallen, Norman E., and Robert M. W. Travers. "Analysis and Investigation of Teaching Methods." In *Handbook of Research on Teaching.* Skokie, Ill.: Rand McNally & Company, American Educational Research Association, 1963, p. 453.

Witt, Mary. "Developing Reading Skills and Critical Thinking." *Social Education,* 25 (May 1961), 239–41.

Section **IV**

Your Reading Program

The purpose of this section is to introduce you to the task of understanding and designing a diagnostic-prescriptive reading program. It is extremely important for you to think about the nature of reading and to attempt to refine, as fully as possible, your concept of the reading process. Within this section you will be provided with a number of interpretations of the reading process. You will be continually encouraged to realize that your own definition is the all-important one on which you will base your entire approach to the teaching of reading.

The historical development of the pedagogy of reading is traced within this section. Several "methods" of teaching reading are also explored.

This section also introduces you to the communication processes of bilingual speakers and the relationship of this language process to the act of reading.

Formal and informal assessment measures are also examined, with emphasis directed toward personalized curriculum planning and management. Simulated programs are explored in an attempt to integrate theory and practice.

Too often, classroom teachers, while well trained in educational theory, are limited in their knowledge of classroom management procedures. The focus of this section is on the integration of theory and practice.

12

Approaches and methods of teaching reading

We find that instruction in handwriting in cities with an extraordinary developed civilization is more proficient, easier, methodically better (than elsewhere) because the colouring (of the craft of writing) is firmly established in them. Thus, we are told about contemporary Cairo (Egypt) that there are teachers there who are specialized in the teaching of calligraphy. They teach the pupils by norms and laws how to write each letter ... .

Writing is not learned that way in Spain and the Maghrib. The letters are not learned individually according to norms the teacher gives to the pupil. Writing is learned by imitating complete words.

The Magaddimah (1377)

GOALS: To help students understand
1. an historical overview of reading instruction in the United States.
2. the need for a personal definition of reading as the basis of an instructional approach.
3. a variety of methods of reading instruction.
4. the strengths and needs of each method studied.

Now that you have learned a great deal of information about the process of reading and the components of reading, you probably want to ask the most important question concerning your own *teaching* of reading: "How do I teach a child to read?" In this seemingly simple question, there are innumerable hidden questions; for example:

1. What approach should I use?
2. What materials are most effective?
3. How can I evaluate the effectiveness of the material?
4. If a child is not progressing, what should I do?
5. When should I change to an alternate method?

These questions could continue for pages, but the point is already clear. Teaching a child to read involves a great deal of psychological and intellectual preparation on the part of the teacher, and it also involves teacher participation in complex decision making within the classroom.

In this chapter, we will present a brief overview of the ways in which reading instruction has taken place in the United States, in order to understand how educators in the past have answered the question: "How do I teach a child to read?" These historical insights will help us to understand the advances made in reading instruction, as well as the progress that has been made in scientific teaching.

Historical Overview

In the colonial period of education in the United States, an alphabet spelling system was the methodology used to teach reading. The two sample pages here are from Noah Webster's *The Elementary Spelling Book*, which was published in 1800. Instruction was given in single-letter recognition; then combined letter-sound correspondences, such as *ab* and *ac*; then parts of words, such as *tab*; and finally, the whole word, *table*. Reading was almost a totally oral process in these early years because it included intensive instruction in pitch, stress, enunciation, gesticulation, memorization, and recitation. Here are some examples from Webster's book:

8   THE ELEMENTARY

ANALYSIS OF SOUNDS
IN THE ENGLISH LANGUAGE.

The Elementary Sounds of the English language are divided into two classes, *vowels* and *consonants*.

A *vowel* is a clear sound made through an open position of the mouth-channel, which molds or shapes the voice without obstructing its utterance; as *a* (in *far*, in *fate*, etc.), *e*, *o*.

A *consonant* is a sound formed by a closer position of the articulating organs than any position by which a vowel is formed, as *b, d, t, g, sh*. In forming a consonant the voice is compressed or stopped.

A *diphthong* is the union of two simple vowel sounds, as *ou* (äŏŏ) in *out*, *oi* (a̤ī) in *noise*.

The English Alphabet consists of twenty-six letters, or single characters, which represent vowel, consonant, and diphthongal sounds—a, b, c, d, e, f, g, h, i, j, k, l, m, n, o, p, q, r, s, t, u, v, w, x, y, z. The combinations *ch, sh, th*, and *ng* are also used to represent elementary sounds; and another sound is expressed by *s*, or *z*; as, in *measure, azure*, pronounced *mĕzh'yoor, äzh'ur*.

Of the foregoing letters, *a, e, o*, are always simple vowels; *i* and *u* are vowels (as in *in, us*), or diphthongs (as in *time, tune*); and *y* is either a vowel (as in *any*), a diphthong (as in *my*), or a consonant (as in *ye*).

Each of the vowels has its regular long and short sounds which are most used; and also certain *occasional* sounds, as that of *a* in *last, far, care, fall, what; e* in *term, there, prey; i* in *firm, marine; o* in *dove, for, wolf, prove;* and *u* in *furl, rude,* and *pull*. These will now be considered separately.

A. The regular long sound of *a* is denoted by a horizontal mark over it; as, ān'cient, pro-fāne'; and the regular short sound by a curve over it; as, căt, păr'ry.

SPELLING BOOK.   9

Occasional sounds.—The Italian sound is indicated by two dots over it; as, bär, fä'ther;—the short sound of the Italian *a*, by a single dot over it; as, fȧst, lȧst;—the broad sound, by two dots below it; as, ba̤ll, sta̤ll;—the short sound of broad *a*, by a single dot under it; as, wha̭t, qua̭d'rant;—the sound of *a* before *r* in certain words like *care, fair*, etc., is represented by a sharp or pointed circumflex over the *a*, as, câre, hâir, fâir, etc.

E. The regular long sound of *e* is indicated by a horizontal mark over it; as, mēte, se-rēne'; the regular short sound, by a curve over it; as, mĕt, re-bĕl'.

Occasional sounds.—The sound of *e* like *a* in *care* is indicated by a pointed circumflex over the *e*, as in thêir, whêre; and of short *e* before *r* in cases where it verges toward short *u*, by a rounded circumflex, or wavy line, over it; as, hẽr, pre-fẽr'.

I, O, U. The regular long and short sounds of *i, o*, and *u* are indicated like those of *a* and *e* by a horizontal mark and by a curve; as, bīnd, bĭn; dōle, dŏll; tūne, tŭn.

Occasional sounds.—When *i* has the sound of long *e* it is marked by two dots over it; as, fa-tïgue', ma-rïne';—when *o* has the sound of short *u*, it is marked by a single dot over it; as, dȯve, sȯn;—when it has the sound of ŏŏ, it is marked with two dots under it; as, mo̤ve, pro̤ve;—when it has the sound of ŏŏ, it is marked with a single dot under it; as, wo̤lf, wo̤'man;—when it has the sound of broad *a*, this is indicated by a pointed circumflex over the vowel; as, nôrth, sôrt;—the two letters *oo*, with a horizontal mark over them, have the sound heard in the words bōōm, lōōm;—with a curve mark, they have a shorter form of the same sound; as, bŏŏk, gŏŏd;—when *u* is sounded like short *oo*, it has a single dot under it; as, fu̇ll, pu̇ll; while its lengthened sound, as when preceded by *r*, is indicated by two dots; as in rṳde, rṳ'ral, rṳ'by.

NOTE.—The long *u* in unaccented syllables has, to a great extent, the sound of *oo*, preceded by *y*, as in *educate*, pronounced ĕd'yoo-kāte: *nature*, pronounced nāt'yoor.

Noah Webster, The Elementary Spelling Book. New York: American Book Company, 1800.

24		THE ELEMENTARY			

BÄR, LÄST, ÇÂRE, FĄLL, WHĄT; HËR, PRĘY, THÊRE; ŒT; BÏRD, MARÏNE; LIŊK;

ăpt	eärt	stärt	hûrt	pást	jĕst
chapt	dart	pērt	shïrt	vast	lest
kĕpt	hart	vert	flirt	dĭdst	blest
slept	chart	wert	eást	midst	nest
erept	mart	shôrt	fast	bĕst	pest

No. 25.—XXV.

rĕst	quĕst	mĭst	eŏst	thĭrst	lŭst
erest	west	grist	fîrst	bŭst	must
drest	zest	wrist	bûrst	dust	rust
test	fĭst	wist	eurst	gust	erust
vest	list	lŏst	durst	just	trust

Fire will burn wood and coal.
Coal and wood will make a fire.
The world turns round in a day.
Will you help me pin my frock?
Do not sit on the damp ground.
We burn oil in tin and glass lamps.
The lame man limps on his lame leg.
We make ropes of hemp and flax.
A rude girl will romp in the street.
The good girl may jump the rope.
A duck is a plump fowl.
The horse drinks at the pump.
A pin has a sharp point.
We take up a brand of fire with the tongs.
Good boys and girls will act well.
How can you test the speed of your horse?
He came in haste, and left his book.
Men grind corn and sift the meal.
We love just and wise men.
The wind will drive the dust in our eyes.
Bad boys love to rob the nests of birds.
Let us rest on the bed, and sleep, if we can.
Tin and brass will rust when the air is damp.

	SPELLING BOOK.			25

MǪVE, SÔN, WǪLF, FŎŎT, MŌŌN, ÔR; RŲLE, PŲLL; EXIST; €=K; Ô=J; Ģ=Z; ÇH=SH.

No. 26.—XXVI.
WORDS OF TWO SYLLABLES, ACCENTED ON THE FIRST.

bā' ker	trō ver	sō lar	wō fŭl	pā pal
sha dy	elo ver	po lar	po em	eō pal
la dy	do nor	lū nar	fo rum	vī al
tī dy	vā por	sō ber	Sā tan	pē nal
hō ly	fa vor	pā çer	fū el	ve nal
lī my	fla vor	ra çer	du el	fī nal
sli my	sa vor	grō çer	erų el	ō ral
bō ny	ha lo	çī der	grų el	ho ral
po ny	sō lo	spi der	pū pil	mū ral
po ker	hē ro	wā fer	lā bel	nā ṣal
tī ler	ne gro	ea per	lī bel	fa tal
eā per	tȳ ro	tī ḡer	lō eal	na tal
pa per	out go	mā ker	fo eal	rų ral
ta per	sā go	ta ker	vo eal	vī tal
vī per	tū lip	ra ker	lē gal	tō tal
bi ter	çē dar	sē ton	re gal	o val
fē ver	brī er	rų in	dī al	plī ant
ō ver	fri ar	hȳ men	tri al	ġi ant

Bakers bake bread and cakes.
I like to play in the shady grove.
Some fishes are very bony.
I love the young lady that shows me how to read.
A pony is a very little horse.
We poke the fire with the poker.
The best paper is made of linen rags.
Vipers are bad snakes, and they bite men.
An ox loves to eat clover.
The tulip is very pretty, growing in the garden.
A dial shows the hour of the day.
Cedar trees grow in the woods.
The blackberry grows on a brier.

Because instruction was directed toward a single purpose (the reading of prayer books and religious and moral books), reading instruction was an extremely simplified process. Only a limited number of people were actually taught to read. Most of these children learned letters of the alphabet from the *Hornbook* and the *New England Primers*, which were among the earliest readers in the United States.

In the early 1800s, Horace Mann introduced a new method of teaching reading, the *whole-word* method. He stressed memorizing entire words before analyzing letters and letter patterns. His approach stressed silent reading and emphasized reading for comprehension. About this time, the *McGuffey Eclectic Reader*, which emphasized a controlled repetition of words, was introduced. Children were beginning to be taught to read through the use of stories, parables, moral lessons, and patriotic selections in an attempt to develop "good" citizens. Although the *McGuffey Readers* were not filled with the most interesting narrative stories, they were definitely an improvement over the existing texts because of their organizational scheme in which sentence length and vocabulary were controlled to match the students' present developmental level.

Selections from the primer and the sixth reader of the *McGuffey Eclectic Readers* (1881, 1879) are included in order to demonstrate the differences between the early and more advanced readers. You will see differences in print size, vocabulary, syntactic control, and content. (See pages 434–437.)

A phonetics method was introduced in the latter half of the nineteenth century; it was a synthetic phonics system, much like the programs explained in detail in Chapter 7. Teachers became dissatisfied with this method because too much attention was placed on word analysis and too little attention was given to comprehension. This method was temporarily abandoned, being replaced sometime around 1910 with the new "look-and-say" method. The look-and-say method was also unsatisfactory to many teachers because the child had to learn every word as a sight word, and children made little progress in learning to read.

About 1920, the silent reading method, much like the earlier program espoused by Horace Mann, emerged as the official reading program in many schools. This method urged the total abandonment of all oral methods of instruction and testing. During the 1920s, which is popularly referred to as the scientific era in United States education, intelligence testing and measurement came into vogue and a great deal of reading research was widely conducted (Gray, 1925–1932, Good, 1923–1953). The results of this research gave rise to the extremely popular method that followed: the basal reading method, launched throughout the United States in the early 1930s.

The basal reading program included a student text and teacher's manual as the base of the reading program. Each basal presented a controlled vocabulary and introduced levels of syntactic complexity that paralleled children's development. The basal method held predominance over other methods until the 1950s and 1960s when there was a return to *phonics*. This occurred because teachers were dissatisfied with the basal as the *only* form of reading instruction.

These selections appeared in the primer of the McGuffey Readers:

LESSON XIV.

hōldṣ   tọ

blīnd   Mā′rў̆

hănd   kīnd

ā   ọ   k   ў̆

This old man can not see.
He is blind.

Mary holds him by the hand.
She is kind to the old blind
man.

LESSON XV.—REVIEW.

I see ducks on the pond; Tom
will feed them.

Tom is blind; he holds a box
in his hand.

Nell is kind to him.

This old hen has a nest.

Mary will run and get the
eggs.

LESSON XVI.

Sūe   dŏll   drĕss   new   hĕr

lĕt

ẽ

ū

ew

Sue has a doll.
It has a new dress.

LESSON XXXVI.

Mĭss   wạnts   wo̞uld   tĕllṣ

rụle

kēep

ḡŏod

thăt

ēach

ụ

The girls and boys all love Miss May; she is so kind to them.

Miss May tells them there is a rule that she wants them to keep. It is, "Do to each one as you would like each one to do to you."

This is a good rule, and all boys and girls should keep it.

LESSON XXXVII.

sehōol   child

chûrch   whĕn

bŏoks

slātes

What kind of house is this? Do you think it is a schoolhouse, or a church?

It looks like a church, but I think it is a schoolhouse.

These selections are taken from the sixth reader of the McGuffey series:

CXV. THE LAST DAYS OF HERCULANEUM.

Edwin Atherstone, 1788-1872, was born at Nottingham, England, and became known to the literary world chiefly through two poems, "The Last Days of Herculaneum" and "The Fall of Nineveh." Both poems are written in blank verse, and are remarkable for their splendor of diction and their great descriptive power. Atherstone is compared to Thomson, whom he resembles somewhat in style.

THERE was a man,
A Roman soldier, for some daring deed
That trespassed on the laws, in dungeon low
Chained down. His was a noble spirit, rough,
But generous, and brave, and kind.
He had a son; it was a rosy boy,
A little faithful copy of his sire,
In face and gesture. From infancy, the child
Had been his father's solace and his care.

                                        Every sport
The father shared and heightened. But at length,
The rigorous law had grasped him, and condemned
To fetters and to darkness.

                                The captive's lot,
He felt in all its bitterness: the walls
Of his deep dungeon answered many a sigh
And heart-heaved groan. His tale was known, and touched
His jailer with compassion; and the boy,
Thenceforth a frequent visitor, beguiled
His father's lingering hours, and brought a balm
With his loved presence, that in every wound
Dropped healing. But, in this terrific hour,
He was a poisoned arrow in the breast
Where he had been a cure.
    6.—26.

V. THE VOICE.

PITCH AND COMPASS.

The **natural pitch** of the voice is its keynote, or governing note. It is that on which the voice usually dwells, and to which it most frequently returns when wearied. It is also the pitch used in conversation, and the one which a reader or speaker naturally adopts — when he reads or speaks — most easily and agreeably.

The **compass** of the voice is its range above and below this pitch. To avoid monotony in reading or speaking, the voice should rise above or fall below this keynote, but always with reference to the sense or character of that which is read or spoken. The proper natural pitch is that above and below which there is most room for variation`.

To strengthen the voice and increase its compass, select a short sentence, repeat it several times in succession in as low a key as the voice can sound naturally; then rise one note higher, and practice on that key, then another, and so on, until the highest pitch of the voice has been reached. Next, reverse the process, until the lowest pitch has been reached.

EXAMPLES IN PITCH.

High Pitch.

Note.—Be careful to distinguish *pitch* from *power* in the following exercises. Speaking in the open air, at the very top of the voice, is an exercise admirably adapted to strengthen the voice and give it compass, and should be frequently practiced.

1. Charge`! Chester`, charge`! On`! Stanley, on`!

2. A horse`! a horse`! my kingdom` for a horse`!

3. Jump far out`, boy`, into the wave`!
Jump`, or I fire`!

4. Run`! run`! run for your lives!

5. Fire`! fire`! fire`! Ring the bell`!

6. Gentlemen may cry peace´! peace´! but there is no peace!

7. Rouse`, ye Romans! rouse`, ye slaves`!
Have ye brave sons´? Look in the next fierce brawl
To see them die`. Have ye fair daughters´? Look
To see them live, torn from your arms`, distained`,
Dishonored`, and if ye dare call for justice´,
Be answered by the lash`!

Medium Pitch.

Note.—This is the pitch in which we converse. To strengthen it, we should read or speak in it as loud as possible, without rising to a higher key. To do this requires long-continued practice.

1. Under a spreading chestnut tree,
The village smithy stands`;
The smith, a mighty man is he,
With large and sinewy hands`;
And the muscles of his brawny arms
Are strong as iron bands.

2. There is something in the thunder's voice that makes me tremble like a child. I have tried to conquer` this unmanly weakness`. I have called pride` to my aid`; I have sought for moral courage in the lessons of philosophy`, but it avails me nothing`. At the first moaning of the distant cloud, my heart shrinks and dies within me.

3. He taught the scholars the Rule of Three´,
Reading, and writing, and history`, too`;
He took the little ones on his knee´,
For a kind old heart in his breast had he´,
And the wants of the littlest child he knew`.
"Learn while you 're young`," he often said´,
"There is much to enjoy down here below´;
Life for the living´, and rest for the dead`,"
Said the jolly old pedagogue`, long ago`.

Teachers began to supplement basals with phonics strategies. Examples of these strategies included: i/+/a and Words in Color, which will be explained later in this chapter. Many basal series now contain a strong phonics emphasis.

The following chart illustrates the changing focus of reading instruction:

Approximate date	Learning system	Materials	Characteristics
1600–1800	Alphabet spelling system	Hornbook New England Primer	Oral reading Memorization Recitation
1800s	Whole-word method		Silent reading Oral reading Reading for comprehension
	Controlled repetition	McGuffey Eclectic Readers	Silent reading Controlled repetition of words
Late 1800s	Artificial phonics system	Basic readers containing tales and excerpts from classics	Word-analysis emphasis
Early	Look-and-say		Sight-word emphasis Testing initiated
	Silent reading method		Elaborate testing and measurement Silent reading emphasis
1930s	Basal method	Student and teacher workbooks Dick and Jane Alice and Jerry	Controlled vocabulary Oral and silent reading, phonics influence

1950s
and 1960s
	Phonics strongly
	  emphasized
	Words-in-color
	Individualized instruction
	Programmed instruction
	Language experience
	  method
		SRA materials	Individualization
			Individual Language
			  patterns
			Personalization

Late 1960s	Linguistic influence	Let's Read	Patterned word units
Mid-1970s	Managed language reading	Use of a variety of methods and materials Ginn 720 Macmillan R	Personalization Individualization Sequential organization

During the decade of the 1960s, in an attempt to meet the individual needs of children, techniques for *individualizing reading instruction* were encouraged. During this period *programmed materials* were developed to provide better classroom management techniques.

The *language experience method*, which was an updating of an earlier practice, was promoted as an effective teaching method in the 1960s. From the late

1960s until the present, linguistic points of view have influenced the structure of many basal readers. Linguists have promoted the teaching of reading through patterned word units—for example:

> Nan ran to the man.

Although most educators agreed with the need for a personalized program for each child, a major problem has been the time factor involved in creating an efficient, well-organized system for managing each child's personalized program. Excellent teachers with the best intentions often found themselves without enough time to plan to teach twenty to thirty different reading programs within the course of a single day. This situation occurred because teachers were not trained in flexible grouping techniques, personalized contracts, and classroom management processes.

In the 1970s an attempt is being made to alleviate many of these management constraints with the newest creation of several book publishers: a *managed language/reading method*, which includes elaborate record-keeping systems, basal readers, teacher's manuals, and criterion-reference and norm-reference tests. These tests will be explained in detail in Chapter 14.

This brief historical overview of reading instruction practices in the United States may shed some light on important considerations that you will have to deliberate on before selecting the best methods of instruction for your students.

If we analyze this body of historical literature by examining the following time line, it becomes apparent that *two* different philosophies of reading instruction have existed throughout the history of reading teaching. The first of these philosophies may be referred to as a *sequential reading approach*, which encourages the use of materials that are systematically designed according to the developmental stages of children. In the following diagram, application of this philosophy is labeled *A*. The second philosophy may be referred to as the *spontaneous reading approach*, which encourages the development of materials related to the organic interest of the child. In the diagram, application of this philosophy is labeled *B*. (See page 438.)

These philosophies are not entirely opposed to one another because the end goal of each is teaching the child to read. However, the process of implementation is quite different for each philosophy. It may be productive to think of these two philosophies existing in a continuum because they encompass almost all of the existing methods and influences of teaching reading.

In fact, these two philosophies exist today and both are probably in operation in every school in the United States. They encompass every approach to reading instruction. We will refer to these two philosophies as the basic approaches to reading instruction that have existed at various points in the educational history of the United States.

Although it seems that the managed language reading system is the most effective method of teaching reading, it should be noted that teachers' personal preferences and experiences sometimes dictate the use of a different method.

In fact, most teachers use a variety of methods in their classrooms in order to personalize each child's instructional program.

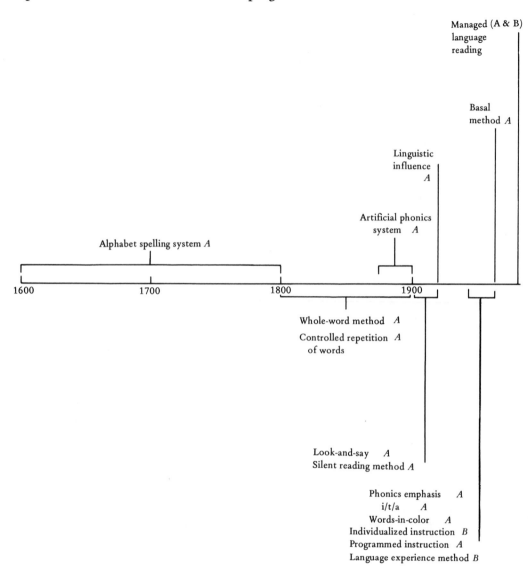

The following diagram illustrates the embedding of existing methods of teaching reading within the sequential and spontaneous reading approaches. The *sequential* reading approach is exemplified in *phonics* and *linguistic basals* and *programmed instruction*. As these methods clearly demonstrate, the sequential development approach emphasizes *decoding* followed by comprehension. The *spontaneous reading approach* is characterized by *language experience* and *individualized instruction*. Reading for meaning from the initial stages of reading instruction is the major emphasis of this program. The diagram also shows the origins of the current *managed language reading approach*, which integrates the strengths of both the sequential and spontaneous developmental approaches.

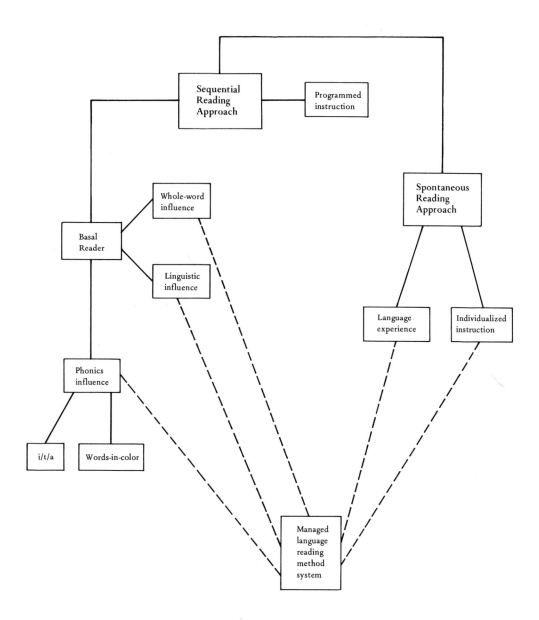

The strengths and weaknesses of each of the two basic approaches are readily apparent, and they can be explained in the following way:

Approaches	Sequential reading development	Spontaneous reading approach
Strengths	Prepared materials Logically organized	Personalized Emphasizes language base
Weaknesses	Lack of personalization	Too time-consuming Lack of manufactured materials Elaborate record keeping

BEGIN

After realizing these strengths and weaknesses, modern educators have developed managed language/reading systems that build on the strengths, as they are listed here, and rectify the weaknesses of each approach. Creators of these new systems acknowledge the logical developmental stages of children, while providing management systems that encourage the incorporation of spontaneous development. The creators fully realize that such systems cannot be effectively implemented without the classroom teacher. They strongly encourage the teacher to use the spontaneous language development of the child as the base of the reading program. The application of the managed language experience approach is thoroughly explained in Chapter 15.

Methods of Teaching Reading

This section of the chapter is designed to explore several of the methods of teaching reading illustrated in the preceding diagram. These methods provide the basis for most of the programs currently available for classroom use.

We will use the following outline in presenting the various methods and their programs:

    I. Sequential Reading Approach
       A. Basal Reading Instruction
          1. Whole-word influence
          2. Phonics influence
             a. i/t/a
             b. words-in-color
          3. Linguistic influence
       B. Programmed Instruction
   II. Spontaneous Reading Approach
       A. Language Experience
       B. Individualized Instruction
  III. Managed Language/Reading Systems

Sequential Reading Approach

The content to be conveyed through the sequential reading approach is objective, tightly structured, and logically organized. The prime focus of this material is directed toward the intellectual dimensions of the student. As suggested in the preceding time line, the earliest attempts to develop criteria for this approach occurred in early Puritan times. A Massachusetts law of 1642 extended this practice because it mandated that all children be taught to read.

The philosophical parameters of this approach rely heavily on the validity of premises similar to Bruner's idea that "knowledge is a model we construct to give meanings and structure to regularities of experience," and on Piaget's suggestion that "intelligence is sequentially related to age." Based on these and similar learning theories, basal readers and programmed materials which emphasize a sequential reading approach have been designed.

Basal Reading Instruction

The basal method assumes that reading is a developmental task involving the acquisition of major skills and that each of these major skills is comprised of many subskills. These subskills vary in difficulty and complexity and, therefore, need to be introduced to the reader in a logical, prescribed order. Not only do the subskills in each major skill area need to be ordered, but plans need to be made for integrating them into an instructional program so that the reader can begin to interrelate them. If this is successfully managed, reading becomes an integrated, meaningful whole.

Basal series are generally developed for the elementary school, grades one through six. They include stories for reading levels from readiness through sixth grade or the equivalent subdivisions used by various school systems. Traditionally, the materials of a basal program have been a collection of reading readiness materials, two or three preprimers, a primer, a first reader, two texts for the second grade, two texts for the third grade, and one text for fourth-, fifth-, and sixth-grade levels. At every level, workbooks, dittoes, work sheets, films and filmstrips, records, and supplementary readers may be included in the package. At the beginning levels, large charts or large editions of the child's book are available.

A teacher's manual is provided for each text in the program. Publishers usually include in these manuals a statement of the philosophy basic to the particular program, a series of story-lesson plans, unit tests, lists of supplementary materials, and other related information.

The program identifies and introduces a controlled vocabulary, new words in isolation and in context. This is followed by silent and oral reading and interpretation of the material that the child has read. Subsequent activities usually involve further skill development (word-recognition, comprehension, and study skills) and enrichment activities designed to relate the topic of the lesson to art, music, dance, or literature.

In examining a typical basal series from beginning to end, certain efforts to adjust to the maturity level of the reader will be noted. In beginning materials, a very limited number of words are introduced. These are used repeatedly in the sentences on the subsequent pages and continue to appear throughout the book. As the child moves upward throughout the series, more words are introduced at each level with fewer repetitions. Some teacher's manuals explain the ratio of new words per page and the number of repetitions planned for each new word. The purpose behind controlled vocabulary and planned repetition is easily understood: too many new words introduced at once, and too few exposures to the word, easily lead to reading difficulties.

In addition to the limited vocabulary and planned repetition of words in primary reading materials, one also notes the adjustment in print size and spacing between letters, words, and lines. These adjustments are designed to help the child who is learning to move his eyes from left to right and swing back to the beginning of the next line on the left.

Other adjustments in the basals include adjusting the ratio of illustration space to print space. At lower levels, illustrations often appear on every page or every other page. These are usually large pictures that are controlled for salient features. By the sixth grade, illustrations may be sparse, small, and quite detailed.

Samples of contemporary basals are presented here. The first two selections are taken from the primary-level 5 basals (grade 1) of the *Ginn 720* series. Note the print size, the illustrations, the repeated vocabulary items, and the controlled syntax. (See pages 443–446.)

Throughout the last decade, basal series have been the focus of much of the criticism directed toward reading programs. It is not at all unusual to hear people speak critically of reading instruction and hurl disparaging remarks toward Dick and Jane, those characters found in the basal series that, at its peak, probably had been purchased and used more widely than any other series ever produced. Poor Dick and Jane became the symbols of the boy and girl found in all beginning materials, and, therefore, had to suffer the insult and injury aimed at many similar basal series.

These are some of the frequent criticisms of basal series:

1. The vocabulary and sentence patterns do not match the spoken language of the children.

2. The content is not interesting to children.

3. The books are developed for graded levels and the child is forced to read in the book for his grade level.

4. The manual is looked on as the last word in instructional guidance and must be followed to the last letter. As a result, the program is not adjusted to individual needs and instruction often becomes sterile and uncreative.

5. Use of a basal leads to a uniform three-achievement-level grouping plan.

6. Children are asked to do workbook pages which they may have mastered.

7. The basal reader provides the sole source of material used in teaching reading skills to children.

8. Basals do not provide for different learning styles or different modes of instruction.

9. Basals are not based on a sound theory of learning.

10. Basal series do not provide instructional procedures.

11. The content often furthers sexual and class stereotypes.

ISABEL

" You can't guess where we are going, "
said David Yee.

" It's going to be a surprise. "

" I like surprises, "
said Isabel.

" I'll let you guess
where we are all going, "
said David.

68

Mr. Pine got up.

" Now where did I put
my glasses? " he said.

Mr. Pine looked everywhere
in the house.

" That's funny! " he said.

" I don't know where
my glasses are. "

110

This selection is taken from level 13 (grade 6) of the *Ginn 720* series. Note the print size, the sophistication of the illustrations, the advanced vocabulary—for example, sullenly—and the complex syntax—for example, "She turned to the blackboard—which is not black, but green, and you're supposed to call it the chalkboard, but only Mrs. Friedman calls it that—and wrote ... ."

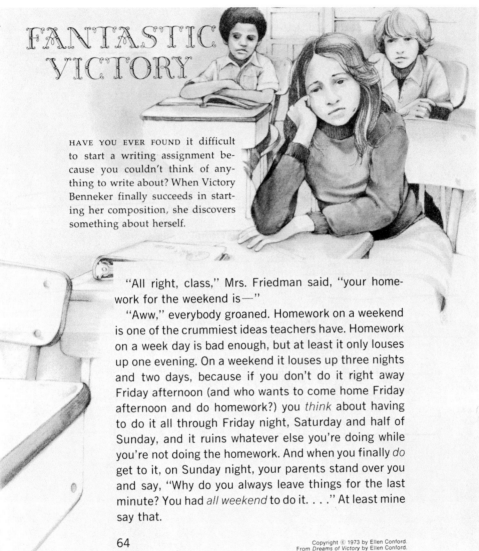

FANTASTIC VICTORY

HAVE YOU EVER FOUND it difficult to start a writing assignment because you couldn't think of anything to write about? When Victory Benneker finally succeeds in starting her composition, she discovers something about herself.

"All right, class," Mrs. Friedman said, "your homework for the weekend is—"

"Aww," everybody groaned. Homework on a weekend is one of the crummiest ideas teachers have. Homework on a week day is bad enough, but at least it only louses up one evening. On a weekend it louses up three nights and two days, because if you don't do it right away Friday afternoon (and who wants to come home Friday afternoon and do homework?) you *think* about having to do it all through Friday night, Saturday and half of Sunday, and it ruins whatever else you're doing while you're not doing the homework. And when you finally *do* get to it, on Sunday night, your parents stand over you and say, "Why do you always leave things for the last minute? You had *all weekend* to do it. . . ." At least mine say that.

64

"Your assignment for the weekend," continued Mrs. Friedman, ignoring the groans, "is to write a composition—"

"Yucch," said Kenny Clark.

"—about one of these qualities."

She turned to the blackboard—which is not black, but green, and you're supposed to call it the chalkboard, but only Mrs. Friedman calls it that—and wrote:

Humor
Intelligence
Imagination
Beauty

"Now what I want you to do is pick the quality that you think is most important, and tell me why."

"I don't get it," Kenny Clark said sullenly. "Most important for what?"

"For whatever you want," Mrs. Friedman replied. "That's up to you to decide."

"I still don't get it."

Anyone who has visited schools where basal series are used would probably recall some situation to support each of the preceding critical statements. It is important, however, to analyze them. How many are actual criticisms of basal series? The crucial question is: How many are critical of the way in which the basal series were *used*?

It is true that the content of beginning levels of basal series does not reflect the extensive oral vocabulary which many beginning readers possess, nor are the sentences modeled after the language patterns of many children. Admittedly, improvement is needed in this area, and changes have been made in some of the more recent series. Although there seems to be a need to loosen the control of the vocabulary in the content of the series, an attempt to match the extensive lexical diversity of the majority of beginning readers may not be possible or desirable when teaching the child *to read*. As a teacher, you must be ready to personalize reading instruction to facilitate the language development of your students. No publisher can print a series that will reflect the oral vocabulary of every child in the United States. As a teacher, you will need to supplement the basal series with the experience of the children you are teaching. Remember, the basal series was designed to be only the *base* of your program rather than the entire program.

Today, all basal series are not the same. There are some (Economy, 1975) that provide a strong phonics program; while others (Macmillan R, 1975, Ginn 720, 1976) purport to be more creative than the average in their content and managed enrichment activities; and others are developed around classical literature for children. The authors and producers of every series have attempted to build into their program activities that give the series unique characteristics. As few as five years ago, some series attained uniqueness by shifting from graded to ungraded levels. Increased difficulty of material was shown by consecutive letters and numbers—for example, J, K, L, M, N. This shift is now a trend among all basal series.

One of the most compelling arguments for use of basal series has been the help provided by the teacher's manuals. These manuals provide continuity for the program, and they provide security and assistance for beginning teachers. In answer to the criticisms that basals have had too strict control over vocabulary, Harris and Jacobson (1972) have found that:

> A much less stringent control over vocabulary than formerly is characteristic of some of the new basal reading programs. ... Thus it may be anticipated that a word list based on readers popular in 1930 may reflect this trend toward less exacting control over basal reader vocabularies. (p. 227)

Answering the criticism that basals tend to reflect the values and mores of white middle-class families, educators have developed *The Chandler Language Experience Readers* by Carillo et al. and *The Bank Street Readers* by Black. While both of these series deal with multiethnic urban environments and contain many illustrations to motivate readers, criticisms have also been raised against them because they illustrate only the mores of one culture: the black inner-city culture. In an attempt to rectify the sociological narrowness of a one-culture text, Ginn 720, Macmillan R, the Laidlaw Reading Series, and many others have attempted to present a culturally diverse content.

These following examples are taken from *The Bank Street Readers*.

But one thing the boys and girls did
wish for. They had never seen snow.
They wished it would snow.

It did!

Snowflakes fell from the dark sky. They
fell slowly at first, then faster and faster.

Cold white flakes of snow fell
on the buildings. They fell on the trees.
They fell on the streets. Soon the city
was white with snow.

Snow was in the parks and on the
buildings. Car wheels threw wet snow
up on the sidewalks and up on the people.
The policeman at the corner looked like a
snowman. There was snow on everything.

132

For ten long years it had not snowed
in River City.

And all the children of River City
shouted and laughed as they played.

"It's snowing!" they shouted.

"It's snowing!"

"Snowing!"

"After ten long years!"

133

I'm All Alone

If you are a boy who is friendly,

Do you have a friend you can send me?

I'm all alone, you see.

No one is here but me.

Do you have a friend you can lend me?

From *My City,* Bank Street Readers, Level 2 — Irma Simonton Black, Senior Editor (© Copyright Macmillan Publishing Co., Inc. 1966), pp. 132–133.

Always Arthur

There was Arthur. He was always there.

Every day when David came home
from school, Arthur was there, waiting
for him.

Arthur was only four. He lived
in the apartment next to David. He waited
for David every day.

Some days he waited on the steps
of the house. Some days he came to the
door of David's apartment. But every day
he was there, waiting for David.

Although all basal series will probably continue to be criticized, it should be noted that basals, when used properly, are an asset to you as a classroom teacher. Publishers, in recent years, have made serious attempts to present relevant stories and to provide technical assistance for teachers. We urge you to avoid being swept away with current propaganda that sounds like this: "Basals are not helpful; I individualize." Examine the basal series for yourself and then decide if it is useful for your purposes. In doing so, you will find that basals used properly will aid you in the process of individualizing and personalizing your curriculum.

Whole-Word Influence. Whole-word instruction is often referred to as the look-and-say method for teaching unfamiliar vocabulary. This process differs from phonics because the children are not engaged in letter-by-letter, sound-by-sound analysis. Rather, they are expected to identify the word immediately upon contact. The whole-word method involves instant identification of the whole word rather than subdividing the word into parts, analyzing the parts, and saying the word. Each time you, as a classroom teacher, turn to your students and say, "What does that word say?" you will be using the whole-word method of instruction.

The whole-word method is one process of instruction which is presented in most basal readers. This occurs because the English language is not a perfectly alphabetic language. Twenty-six letters in the English alphabet represent approximately forty-four sounds. In many instances, it is difficult to predict through phonetic analysis the sound patterns of many irregular words. You will notice this when you are teaching basic sight words like: *saw, was, them, they, it, under, over,* as well as words derived from other languages—*chamois, hors d'oeuvre, depot, choir, vein, suite.* It may also be useful when teaching *homographs*:

> Paul wound the bandage tightly.
> Patty's wound is bleeding.
>
> Bob, please read me a story.
> Daryl read the story today.

or *homophones*:

> Denise loves to sail.
> Mary went to the sale.
>
> Brian is a handsome male.
> Kelly forgot to pick up his mail.

It becomes obvious that advanced knowledge of these whole-word structures would certainly be more productive to the reader than engaging in an analysis of letter-sound relationships.

When you teach children whole words, you are relying heavily on their *visual discrimination ability*. This topic has been discussed in depth in Chapter 8; however, let us reemphasize that studies by Barrett (1965), Durrell (1958),

Samuels (1972), Sivaroli (1965), and others who suggest that the *major* visual discrimination skill highly correlated with reading success is the ability to discriminate letters of the alphabet. The necessity of this skill becomes quite obvious when you are teaching whole words; for example:

> This word is <u>pat</u>.
> It looks like <u>bat</u>, except
> <u>pat</u> begins with <u>p</u> and
> <u>bat</u> begins with <u>b</u>.

After several exposures to these words, they will become part of the students whole-word sight vocabulary. As mentioned before, this is the same procedure that is used when introducing students to the basic sight words found in the Dolch sight vocabulary lists contained in Chapter 8.

The Influence of Phonics. The phonics influence in reading materials and reading instruction began to become apparent in the late 1800s, when educators observed the use of letter-sound relationships as an aid to identifying unfamiliar words. Although the importance of such a process is quite obvious, it is equally important to realize that phonics can only be a partial word analysis process because the English language contains 26 letters representing approximately 44 sounds. The English language, which frequently borrows words of foreign origin does not have an exact one-to-one sound-symbol correspondence in the English language. Even though such limitations are a reality, phonics instruction is quite important and has for decades been part of basal materials. (See Chapter 7 for an in-depth discussion of the content of phonics as well as classroom application strategies.) Let us focus on two teaching materials that educators had once hoped would alleviate phonic inconsistencies.

ITA. ITA, the Initial Teaching Alphabet, is an augmented alphabet. Those who read and write English have long been aware of some of the problems that stem from a 26-letter alphabet and a 44- or 45-phoneme sound system. The fact that some graphemic symbols must represent more than one sound and that several sounds can be represented by multiple spellings may cause confusion for the reader.

A number of years ago, James Pitman (1964), an Englishman, devised an augmented alphabet to alleviate some of the confusion of the English sound-symbol system. This alphabet, or artificial orthography, has 44 symbols. In formulating this augmented alphabet, an attempt was made to illustrate the upper half of the alphabetic letter as it was illustrated in the traditional Roman alphabet. This system was devised in an attempt to aid the student who would eventually have to transfer to the traditional orthography. It was believed that such illustrations would make the transfer easier.

Use of the ITA is not tied to a specific method of reading instruction. The Early-to-Read program (1966) has been circulated throughout America and used in a number of school systems in beginning reading programs. ITA can readily be used in a language experience program. While ITA may be integrated with any other reading program, you need to be aware that the use of ITA has many disadvantages. Researchers have discovered that children who begin reading through an ITA method often have difficulty transfering their reading skills to texts which use traditional orthography. A second criticism of the ITA method is the difficulty that many children experience with learning to spell.

Pitman's alphabet is presented below:

Figure 1. James Pitman's 44 symbol alphabet.

Words in Color. A second material believed to aid children in phonics analysis was _Words in Color_, developed by Caleb Gategno (1962). The material consists of charts of words representing traditional letter configurations. Colors are used to represent an English speech sound. Thirty-nine colors are used on the charts. A single letter or a combination of letters representing an English speech sound is presented on the chart with a visual stimulus of _color_ presented in each sound.

Twenty-one charts contain word illustrations, while letters and letter combinations are presented on six phonic-code charts. For example, the following phonic codes are presented to represent the sound of long $\bar{A}$.

a —	able	eigh —	weigh
ey —	they	aigh —	straight
ay —	hay	ea —	great
ai —	mail		

Whether you pronounce each of these words as a long $\bar{A}$ sound depends upon your dialect. Each time any of these long $\bar{A}$ sounds appear in the word they are coded _green_. Each time the short $\breve{u}$ sound appears in a word it is coded _white_. All letter combinations representing the sound of long $\bar{E}$ are colored _vermillion_. Color codes are presented for 39 English sound combinations.

These materials rely heavily on phonics instruction and may limit children in their selection of reading materials because very few other materials are presented with this colored letter code. As with any phonics program, children rely heavily on letter sounds and word parts rather than on letter names and whole words. Children may also have difficulty with the visual discrimination of colors because the exactness of color is not significant. For example, when observing one series of color shades: dark green, olive green, yellow green, light green, emerald green, and leaf green, the possibility of a discrimination problem becomes obvious.

Linguistic Influences. The linguistic influence on basal reading instruction is relatively new. Linguistics is the scientific study of language. Such study leads to an investigation of the sounds used in language, the words that result from a combination of sounds, and the meanings attached to these sounds. It also involves the structuring of words into meaningful units. Among the linguistic reading programs developed, the influence of the structural linguists seems strongest at the present time.

The first linguistic series to be developed was the Bloomfield-Barnhart _Let's Read_ (1961). Since that time, a variety of "linguistic" reading programs have been developed: the _Merrill Linguistic Readers,_ the _Miami Linguistic Reading_ program, and the _Palo Alto Linguistic Program._ These series use strict vocabulary control in beginning materials. This control facilitates the teaching of certain phonic principles. Students learn the sound-symbol relationships for specified consonants and the short sound of one or two vowels. Then, as many different words as possible are made from the combination of these letters. The following set of sentences illustrates the type of content characterizing the beginning levels of these programs:

Dan is a man.
Dan is tan.
Dan is a tan man.
Is Dan tan?
Fan Dan, the tan man.

In some materials, these stories do not include pictures or illustrations. Some authors support the theory that pictures are an unnecessary crutch and should be avoided. Other authors achieve a compromise between stark reading materials and ordinary illustrations by using very simple illustrations involving one or two colors.

A criticism sometimes launched by linguists toward the basal reading programs is that the language patterns used are unnatural—for example, "See Spot Run." It is also difficult to recognize the naturalness of expression in sentences about "Dan, the tan man." However, as the program moves to more advanced levels, sentence patterns reflect ordinary language usage and, when they are compared with other basal materials on an equivalent level, the sentences in the linguistic readers often appear more complex. (The following example is taken from the *Palo Alto Reading Program*, Book 20.)

TAM AND TAT

I see Tam.

I see Tat.

I see Tam and Tat.

I see Tam, the ram.

I see Tat, the ram.

I see Tam and Tat, the rams.

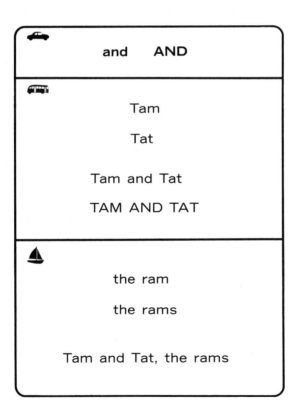

and   AND

Tam

Tat

Tam and Tat

TAM AND TAT

the ram

the rams

Tam and Tat, the rams

From the *Palo Alto Reading Program: Sequential Steps in Reading,* Book 20 by Theodore E. Glim. Copyright © 1968 by Harcourt Brace Jovanovich, Inc. Reprinted by permission of the publisher.

Ham for Nat

Dad had a tin can.

The can had bits of ham in it.

The ham is for Nat.

Dad had to fit the bits of ham
into Nat's tin pan.

Nat ran to look.

He had a bit of ham.

Ham for Dan

A bit of ham is in a tin can.

It's for Dan.

Dan looks into the can.

Rags looks at Dan.

He sits and wags for the ham.

Ham fat is bad for Rags.

The ham in the can is Dan's.

From the *Palo Alto Reading Program: Sequential Steps in Reading*, Book 1 by Theodore E. Glim. Copyrighted © 1968 by Harcourt Brace Jovanovich, Inc. Reprinted by permission of the publisher.

The Dragon That Laughed

Long ago, in the days of King Arthur, there lived a terrible dragon. It lived in a cave in the forest. It was unlucky for any person to be in the forest at nighttime. The terrible dragon might be roaming about looking for victims. Fire and smoke came from its nostrils. Chilling roars came from its mouth. Its long claws tore up the ground. Its huge tail snapped the trees as if they were twigs. Indeed, it was a terrible dragon. And all who lived in King Arthur's kingdom feared the terrible dragon—all but one person, Sir Dunton the Terrible.

It was said that the terrible dragon was once a relative of Sir Dunton. It was said that was why they understood each other. Sir Dunton plotted with the

Charles E. Fries, et al., *Merrill Linguistic Readers*. Reader 2. Columbus, Ohio: Charles E. Merrill Publishing Company, 1966, pp. 16–17. Reprinted by permission.

Linguistic programs have appeared in a variety of formats—including basal series, a series of small paperbacks, and one developmental program stressing a programmed material format. Regardless of format, the programs have attempted to systematically deal with mastery of sound-symbol relationships and to avoid calling special attention to the spelling of irregular words.

The aspect of linguistic programs that has provoked the most unfavorable reactions is the rather monotonous content which results from the patterns of letter substitution and morpheme substitutions. Some teachers find it extremely difficult to generate enthusiasm for "Dan the Tan Man." Other teachers, however, feel that content is of little significance in the initial stages of reading, and that the security which children gain from the contact with these dependable sound-symbol patterns more than compensates for the lack of content substance. This pattern generates dependability and its concomitant success generates its own success.

The selections on pages 456–457 are from different programs illustrating the variety in linguistic reading programs.

Programmed Instruction

A second example of the sequential reading approach is programmed instruction. Basically, programmed instruction of any type takes a specified block of information and divides it into small units that are organized for logical, sequential learning. This organization may be linear or branched.

If a branched arrangement is used, one unit, or frame, of information will be presented to the learner for response. If he responds correctly or accurately, he may bypass several frames and move through several frames designed to teach what he did not know before he can move to the advanced level. This allows for some differentiation of instruction.

If a linear program is used, no frames are bypassed. Each individual using the program moves step by step through each frame. In this type of program, individualization must come through the rate at which the learner moves through the program.

Two of the positive factors related to programmed instruction are the instant feedback provided for the learner and the immediate correction of an error. In programmed instruction, the learner usually completes one frame, or small block, of the program and checks to determine the correctness of his response before moving to the next frame. If the learner's response is erroneous, he is corrected at once, so that he need not continue thinking and using incorrect data.

The program itself comes in a variety of formats. It may be a workbook format or it may be something of a more mechanical nature. In conjunction with the differences in format there may also be differences in mode of response. Whatever these are, they are designed to require individual response, immediate feedback with reinforcement (answer correct), or correction (answer wrong).

There has been some variety in partially programmed programs. However, to date, *Sullivan Programmed Reading* (1963) seems to be the most complete program designed for developmental reading instruction. This is a linear program that reflects a linguistic approach.

The following is an example of a child using programmed instruction.*

> Eric Michaels entered his nongraded school and took his seat at a learning carrel. He keypunched his name onto the empty computer spaces.
>
> Good morning—The punching of his name alerted the computer to the fact that Eric was ready to begin study of the program his teachers had earlier prepared for him.
>
> As the first frame appeared, . . .

---

1. Programmed instruction is a learning experience in which a program replaces a tutor. The student is led through the program by a sequence of learning sets which are structured to teach the student a desired skill.

   _____ _____ is a learning experience that replaces a tutor.

Eric remembered that earlier in the week Ms. Roser, one of his instructors, had mentioned that Eric was interested in computers and he might enjoy learning about programmed instruction. Eric keypunched the words programmed instruction and smiled as frame two appeared.

---

2. Good work, please continue.

   The program, which may be presented to the student in the form of a teaching machine or a programmed textbook, consists of statements, facts, and questions to which a student is asked to respond. The response may be made by filling in short answers or selecting an answer from multiple choices. Correct program responses are made available for the student to compare with his own. Frame one of this program asked you to respond by

        A. filling in a short answer.
        B. selecting from multiple choices.
   _____   C. leaving the space blank.

Eric hesitated and then punched A. and B. Frame three appeared

---

3. Very good thinking, please continue.

   In programmed instruction, large subject areas are divided into smaller thought sequences called frames. Material presented in one frame is related to material presented in preceding frames. Material

> contained in a frame is brief, with generally one question being asked
> about the material. In many programs, the ability of the student to
> answer the questions is a prerequisite for proceeding to the next
> frame. The above discussion of a programmed instruction frame is in
> itself a _____ .

While very interesting to Eric, this was somewhat difficult. He read the frame
again and keypunched the word <u>frame.</u> Immediately frame four appeared.

> 4. Excellent, please continue.
>   B. F. Skinner's demonstration of a practical learning device based on
>   reinforcement drew attention from academicians who began to dis-
>   cuss the educational possibilities of programmed instruction.
>
>   Programmed learning was early applauded by _____ .

Easy, thought Eric as he punched <u>Skinner</u>. Frame five appeared.

> 5. Well done, please continue.
>   While the idea of programmed instruction may have originated with
>   the Elder Sophists of Ancient Greece, Maria Montessori may have
>   been the first to attempt to apply a mechanism to a psychological
>   theory of child development.
>
>   The first person to attempt to apply a theory to a mechanism was
>
>   _____ _____

Eric punched Maria Montessori and wondered who she was.

> 6. Good work, please continue.
>   At the American Psychological Association Convention in 1926,
>   Sidney Pressey, a psychologist from Ohio State, exhibited a teaching
>   machine.
>
>   Sidney Pressey presented a _____ in 1926.

Eric punched <u>teaching machine</u> and thought about those in his classroom:
television; filmstrip projectors; slide projectors, record players and earphones;
talking typewriters and books with recorded stories. He smiled and thought
about the fun he had working with the teaching machines. Frame seven appeared.

---

7. Very well done, please continue.

Industry has also adopted the programmed instruction for many on-the-job training situations. This occurred because programmed instruction could often accommodate daily scheduling better than traditional lectures. Having two or three trainees using machines at one setting seems more practical in industry than stopping production to have the entire office attend one lecture.

For job-training economy, _____ adopted programmed instruction.

As Eric keypunched the word <u>industry</u>, he wondered how many other people were learning through computer-assisted instruction at that exact moment. As frame eight appeared, Ms. Roser put her arm around Eric and asked if he needed any help. He told her his thoughts. She smiled and reminded him that computers were involved in sending people to the moon, in developing new energy systems, and in eliminating disease and famine. She also explained to him that someday he wouldn't have to read to acquire information but that any knowledge he might desire could be obtained from an electronic bank where the information could be directly transmitted to his nervous system by means of coded electronic messages. These several uses of computers made Eric anxious to learn more about his nervous system. As he listened he thought of all the things he would like to learn without reading. Ms. Roser asked if she could listen to Eric read and answer frame eight. Eric began:

---

8. Well done, please continue.

While programmed instruction in many instances successfully supplements both business and educational programs, research suggests that the success of this supplement is dependent on the acceptance level of both instructor and trainee. One weakness of programmed instruction seems to be that students are rewarded when their thinking positively correlated with the programmer.

In some instances programmed instruction is a _____ to both business and educational programs.

Eric keypunched <u>supplement</u>, and Ms. Roser smiled as frame nine appeared.

---

9. You are doing a fine job, please continue.

The program is the most important part of programmed instruction. One type of program which offers the student many answer clues is linear programming. In such a program the student is required to recall information presented to him in a frame by either filling in an answer or selecting one answer from a series of multiple choices. When the child obtains the correct answer, he is positively reinforced as he continues to the next frame. All students working the same program proceed through the frames in the same order.

This frame on programmed instruction has thus far been a ____ program.

Eric keypunched <u>linear</u> and proceeded to frame ten.

---

10. You are doing very well, please continue.

The second major type of programmed instruction program is called intrinsic. Incorrect responses are corrected through a system known as branching. The sequence of frames which the student views is determined by his response to the questions. An incorrect response generally directs the student toward additional frames dealing with the subject with which the student experienced difficulty. A correct response directs the student to skip the additional frames. If you think the above frame is linear, turn to frame eleven. If you believe this frame is intrinsic or branching, turn to frame 13.

Although Eric realized the answer was intrinsic, he pushed number eleven to see exactly what happened with incorrect answers.

---

11. Frame ten is intrinsic because the direction which you took in your program depended on your response. The basis of the intrinsic or branching system is the computer's ability to record performance data and select sequential program frames on the results of previous performance. Branching provides for the individuality of the respondent by designing a program from his correct replies.

A program in which the direction of the program is determined by your response is called an _____ or _____ program.

Eric keypunched <u>intrinsic</u> and <u>branching</u> and continued to frame twelve.

---

12. Good work, please continue.
A linear program is one in which your response does not alter the frame sequence. All frames are viewed by all students.

A program in which all students follow the same frame sequence is called a _____ program.

Eric keypunched <u>linear</u> and frame thirteen automatically appeared.

---

13. Good, please continue.
A third type of program is the combination program. In the combination program, some of the frames are linear while others are intrinsic.

A _____ program combines aspects of both linear and intrinsic programs.

As Eric keypunched the word <u>combination,</u> Mr. Lee, his other instructor, approached and asked if he was enjoying the programmed instruction program. Mr. Lee and Ms. Roser were team instructors who believed that their major function was to work individually with their students. Mr. Lee suggested that when Eric finished his program he might like to join with Mr. Lee and four other students to discuss how computers are programmed. Eric agreed, since he had been discussing this concept with Mr. Martin, the teacher aide, only yesterday. Mr. Lee watched as Eric began frame fourteen.

---

14. Well done, please continue.
    A teaching machine is a device which presents a program. The basic function of all teaching machines is to teach a program frame by frame. Some programs, such as yours, are connected to a computer.

    A teaching machine may serve as a _____ when it presents a program.

Eric hesitated. Mr. Lee reread the frame with Eric and suggested that the teaching machine is often the <u>teacher</u>. Eric laughed and keypunched teacher. Frame fifteen appeared.

---

15. Good work, please continue.
    A program must be reliable. To establish such reliability the porgram must be administered to students and revised according to their responses. Without this data one cannot be sure that the program teaches what it was designed to teach.

    The _____ of the program is important to determine if it teaches what it was designed to teach.

As Eric keypunched <u>reliability</u>, he and Mr. Lee reviewed the term, since they had discussed it early that year. Mr. Lee moved to another student as Eric began frame sixteen.

---

16. Very good, please continue.
    The final step in developing a good program is the development of a multiple-choice or fill-in test which measures student knowledge of the presented material. Success on the test is determined by initial program objectives. If the main points of the program are not learned, the program may be revised through evaluation.
    At this time you are to group with Mr. Lee, who will determine through discussion with you the degree of program competency. Thank you, you did very well.

---

*Lapp, D., et al. *Teaching and Learning: Philosophical, Psychological Curricular Applications.* New York: Macmillan, 1975, pp. 95–101.

The teaching methods and programs that have been presented in this first part of the chapter are all examples of the sequential reading approach.

In the next part of the chapter, we will present several methods that have been used to implement the spontaneous reading approach.

Spontaneous Reading Approach

The content of the spontaneous reading approach is organically related to the students' interests as well as their needs. By developing a curriculum which is of interest to children you will be able to strengthen their competencies and eliminate their needs. The spontaneous reading approach, like the sequential reading approach, is sequentially organized according to levels of cognitive development; however, one major difference between these two approaches is that the spontaneous reading approach is highly dependent upon the *affective* dimensions of the students. Learning is closely related to student interests and cognitive needs throughout the spontaneous reading approach.

The spontaneous reading approach occurred through happenstance in the early decades of reading instruction. Throughout American educational history, attempts to focus instruction on the competencies as well as the interests of children have met with little success. Such limited success can be partially attributed to a lack of understanding about classroom management procedures.

When attempts are made to personalize reading instruction, we commonly discuss two methods: language experience and individualized instruction. Philosophical parameters of these methods rely heavily on the validity of such premises as Dewey's famous statement (1916, p. 125) "to learn from experience is to make a backward and forward connection between what we do to things and what we enjoy or suffer from things in consequence" and Jenkin's (1955):

> Children work hard and long when they choose their own jobs. They move ahead when they have the opportunity to set their own goals. They read with greater enjoyment when they choose the material. In self-selection the teacher works with the individuals and knows their interests and needs more adequately than when a group works on a single book chosen by the teacher. (p. 125)

Language Experience

One example of the spontaneous reading approach is the language experience program. It attempts to integrate listening, reading, and writing skill development with the already existing language of the child. This is not to suggest that training in phonics analysis, structural analysis, or contextual analysis is unnecessary.

The language experience approach to reading instruction is designed to capitalize on the listening and language skills the child has already acquired. Proponents of the language experience approach believe that it has merit because it builds upon the interest of the child and the language that the child has already mastered. Perhaps, more strongly than any other approach, it emphasizes the relationships among thought, oral language, and written language. This is reflected in the points outlined by Lee and Allen (1963) when they describe their definition of language experience:

1. What a child thinks about he can talk about.
2. What he can talk about can be expressed in painting, writing or some other form.
3. Anything he writes can be read.
4. He can read what he writes and what other people write.
5. As he represents his speech sounds with symbols, he uses the same symbols (letters) over and over.
6. Each letter in the alphabet stands for one or more sounds that he makes when he talks.
7. Every word begins with a sound he can write down.
8. Most words have an ending sound.
9. Many words have something in between.
10. Some words are used over and over in our language and some words are not used very often.
11. What he has to say and write is as important to him as what other people have written for him to read.
12. Most of the words he uses are the same ones which are used by other people who write for him to read. (pp. 5–8)

These points are in some sense an elaboration of Allen's (1961) often quoted statement:

> What I can think about, I can talk about.
> What I can say, I can write.
> What I can write, I can read.
> I can read what I write and what other people can write for me to read. (p. 880)

Some proponents of the language experience method maintain that the teacher must help the child to realize that "reading (or written material) is talk written down." Although it is desirable to help children make the connection between talk and reading, this is not a totally accurate conception of the relationship. There are some aspects of talk, such as voice inflection and rate of speech, that will not be recorded when "talk is written down." Therefore, even though it seems highly desirable to help children relate reading to talking, it does not seem desirable to use the idea of "talk written down" in isolation because you will not be dealing with the entire process of reading.

The following example, "Zoo Animals and Me," illustrates materials that have been developed and published in an attempt to encourage language experience programs. The method was not conceived as a method relying heavily on published materials. Rather, it was meant to grow out of the oral expressions of children that were tied to either group or individual experiences. The example on page 469 reflects one type of lesson or series of lessons that might be used in a language experience reading program.

Page 5
Zoo Animals and Me

Suggested time: 3–4 days

Concept to be developed

• The use of comparisons (similes) helps other people picture our thoughts.

Activities with the pupil book

30–40 minutes per day

1. Play a recording, read a story or poem, or show a film about zoo animals.

Let children engage in dramatic play to show movements and sounds of animals.

If possible, play the record "The Carnival of the Animals" by Saint-Saens (Leonard Bernstein and the New York Philharmonic Orchestra, Columbia Masterworks, ML 5768). On the record Mr. Bernstein explains each portion of this wonderful musical trip to the zoo. As the record is played, have children seated on the floor or in a circle of chairs so that they will have ample space to act out movements and sounds of the animals. Since the record is too long for one listening session, choose an actively animated portion of the record or have more than one listening session.

"Let's Go to the Zoo" by Ed Lewis (Magic Key Record, MK-12) is another good record for the study of zoo animals. Some children may be able to bring records from home.

If suitable records are not available, stimulate dramatic play by reading stories and poems about wild animals. A film is also a good way to introduce the topic and invite dramatic play. It is important to show a film to children who have never had an opportunity to see zoo animals.

The following are just a few of the many good poems about wild animals.

218   Animals Everywhere

SUPPER FOR A LION

Dorothy Aldis

Savage lion in the zoo,
Walking by on padded feet,
To and fro and fro and to,
You seem to think it's time to eat.

Then how about a bowl of stew
With jello for dessert? Or would
A juicy bone be best for you?

Oh, please don't stare as though you knew
That I'd taste good!

IF YOU SHOULD MEET A CROCODILE

If you should meet a Crocodile
   Don't take a stick and poke him;
Ignore the welcome in his smile,
   Be careful not to stroke him.
For as he sleeps upon the Nile,
   He thinner gets and thinner;
And whene'er you meet a Crocodile
   He's ready for his dinner.

THE KANGAROO

Old Jumpety-Bumpety-Hop-and-Go-One
Was lying asleep on his side in the sun.
This old kangaroo, he was whisking the flies

("Supper for a Lion," reprinted by permission of G. P. Putnam's Sons from ALL TOGETHER by Dorothy Aldis. Copyright 1925, 1926, 1927, 1928, 1934, 1952 by Dorothy Aldis.)

(The author of "If You Should Meet a Crocodile" is unknown. Reprinted from THE SOUND OF POETRY, by Mary C. Austin and Queenie B. Mills, Allyn and Bacon, Inc., 1963.)

(The author of "The Kangaroo" is unknown. Reprinted from THE SOUND OF POETRY, by Mary C. Austin and Queenie B. Mills, Allyn and Bacon, Inc., 1963.)

Zoo Animals and Me   Name _____

I can run
as fast as
_____ _____

I can eat
as much as
_____ _____

5

I can play like   I can _____ like

as slow as a tortoise
Sue

as big as an elephant
Charles

(8)

(With his long glossy tail) from his ears and his eyes.
Jumpety-Bumpety-Hop-and-Go-One
Was lying asleep on his side in the sun,
Jumpety-Bumpety-Hop!

2. Let children who have visited a zoo or circus tell something about their visit. List animals they saw there.

bear	tortoise
lion	sea lion
tiger	penguin
elephant	deer
giraffe	fox

Ask the children, "What can *you* do like one of these animals? Can you compare something you know to these animals by saying that something is as _____ as a _____?"

3. Explain to the class that we can say we act or sound like a particular animal in order to help our listeners and readers know better what we mean.

Talk about ways in which we compare our own actions with those of animals. Add the comparisons to the list of animals on the board.

as tall as a giraffe
as big as an elephant
as slow as a tortoise
as sly as a fox
growl like a bear
roar like a lion
swim like a sea lion
jump like a kangaroo
strut like a peacock
soar like an eagle

The words *as* and *like* are used many times in

speech and writing. Their use needs to be understood by children although you do not need to use the term *simile*. Your object is to help the children realize that they already use these forms of comparison in their speech and that the same forms are useful in writing.

4. Each child chooses one zoo animal to illustrate with a paper cutout or a crayon drawing.

Help each one select an appropriate simile to write or dictate at the bottom of the picture. Make a bulletin board display of these animal posters (8).

Choose a few of the similes for dramatization. All the children can participate in the dramatization or you can select a few at a time until all children have participated. They can, for example, leap like a kangaroo, growl like a bear, strut like a peacock.

5. Give children Page 5 of the pupil book and help them read the sentences on the front and back of the page.

Direct children to resources in the classroom to help them spell the words they want to complete the sentences. After the children have spelled and written the words correctly, have them do the illustrations to complete both sides of the page.

6. Combine the pages into books.

Read the books with groups of children, helping them read the sentences with meaningful expression. Work to build a sight vocabulary of animal names.

7. Provide animal stories and books for children to read, especially stories about wild animals. Read with a few children each day.

Mrs. Fredericks, a beginning level reading teacher, is working with a group of five children who came to school very excited about a television program they had watched the previous evening. The program had followed a particular bird family from the nest-building stage through the leaving-the-nest stage. Mrs. Fredericks decided to take advantage of their interest and excitement and develop a reading story. She called the group together in one corner of the room near the chalkboard. She invited the children to think of one thing they would like to say or ask about the birds. They knew from previous experience that she would write the things they said. She recorded the following:

> The two birds worked hard to build the nest.
> They used grass and real little sticks.
> The nest was high up.
> Little birds hatched.
> The big birds fed them.
> The big birds pushed the babies out of the nest.

As Mrs. Fredericks recorded each sentence, she repeated what the speaker had said. Then she asked the child to repeat the sentence looking at the written form while the others looked also. She swept her hand from left to right to help the readers follow. When composing had been completed, the group reread the story. Then individual children volunteered to read different sentences. They discussed a name for the story and chose "The Bird Family."

Children in the group already knew some of the words: the, was, of, to, birds, and big. Mrs. Fredericks asked them to identify some words they would like to add to their word banks. (These were individual word files that the children kept. Each file had two compartments: one for words already learned; one for words the child wanted to learn.) Children took turns telling Mrs. Fredericks three words they wanted to put in their files. She wrote the words on individual cards for them. After each child's words were written, he looked at the words and pronounced them. It was understood by each child that he would say the words for her again later in the day.

Each child in the group also made his own copy of the story to put in his personal story book. When he had finished copying the story, he took his copy for Mrs. Fredericks examination and read the story to her from his copy. If any significant errors had been made in copying, the child corrected his work before putting the story in his book folder.

Mrs. Fredericks made two chart copies of the story. One copy she put on a chart board where children who wished might read or refer to it. She asked each child to draw an illustration for the sentence he had contributed to the story. These were placed around the chart as they were completed.

During her next session with this group, Mrs. Fredericks used sentence strips from the second copy of the story. These were distributed to different children who read their sentences to the class. Then they stood in line according to the sentence order in the story. In addition, each child read the words from the "to learn" compartment of his word file to Mrs. Fredericks. When a word had been identified without help during three different reading sessions, it could be filed in the "learned" compartment. Soon Mrs. Fredericks hoped to advance to the individual composition of stories. The words in the word files could be used independently in these stories.

Mrs. Fredericks uses a procedure, or pattern, common to many language experience programs. She encourages oral expression and tries to help children to be more aware of new words they hear and may pick up. She moves into group composition, and then, as children are able, she moves them into individual composition.

As she works with children she learns their interests and selects trade books to bring from the library into the classroom. She reads books to children and encourages them to look at and, if possible, read these books. She also encourages and provides opportunities for children to read their own stories to others.

Mrs. Fredericks recognizes two potential problems in a language experience program. One relates to the teaching of word-recognition skills. Mrs. Fredericks tries to use words that occur in children's stories as a basis for teaching as many phonic principles as possible. She does realize the danger inherent in such a program of limited development of phonics skills.

She also realizes that some children have a wealth of background experiences from which stories can be generated, whereas others have limited story resources. She tries to provide many new and appropriate experiences for her children. She also realizes the necessity of pulling in new vocabulary through these experiences. She encourages children to use new words in communication through conversation and writing.

Mrs. Fredericks is well aware of the factors that need to be developed in an effective reading program. She is adept at learning children's interests and concerns and at getting them to express themselves verbally. She also views the language experience reading program as a stepping stone to another type of program and works to integrate other reading materials into the program. She does not recommend that the language experience approach be used as the major plan for helping children learn to read after the primary levels. She does feel that it can be used well in conjunction with some other approach in the intermediate levels. Perhaps at those levels the emphasis in its use should shift to creative and informative writing rather than reading instruction.

Teachers preparing to use the language experience reading method often ask questions about editing children's oral contributions. Perhaps there is no right answer to this question because children are unique. What works for one child may be disastrous for a second child. Each of you will have to decide what is appropriate for your classroom.

You will have to consider all of the following questions:

1. Is the form of expression used by the child reflective of that used by the group? Do others understand what he is saying?

2. Do you consider the change you would like to be a mechanical, inaccurate choice of words, or a crude/rude expression?

3. Can the child's wording be changed without diminishing him?

Some teachers who use the language experience approach are adamant in their belief that you must record the child's utterance verbatim, e.g., "When I Am Zoo I Want Hats." Other teachers feel they cannot record some errors or expressions that children may use freely. Perhaps the answer lies in adjusting to the needs of the individuals in a group. Sometimes it may be important to record exactly what the child says because doing otherwise would diminish its value for him. On other occasions, the composer/contributor may be confident enough that he will be quite happy to work with you in exploring new ways to express his ideas. It is a wise teacher who keeps in mind that language versatility is a goal to seek. Your aim should not be to erase one language style in order to develop another, more acceptable one in its place, but rather to build on the personal language patterns the child has already acquired.

You might ask: How do I plan a language experience program that interrelates visual, oral, auditory, and kinesthetic experiences? You begin with what each child brings to school—his *language*. You plan oral language experiences about ordinary school group activity: recess games, field trips, topical social events, children's feelings about the present season, art activity, or any other experience that interests them.

Written and oral language can come together as you tape record or make a script recording of each child's statements. As you can see, an understanding of oral language, or the listening-spoken vocabulary, is a prerequisite to the development of a reading vocabulary. After you have recorded the spoken text of your children, you transcribe these same reactions onto large sheets of lined chart paper. While orally reading these statements to your children, you might incorporate some of the activities suggested in Chapters 7 and 8, which are designed to aid the development of phonics skills, thereby using their language to develop basic word-recognition competencies. This will aid you in integrating the sequential and spontaneous approaches to the teaching of reading. We must remember that a word-recognition program is a program involving language. Most children come to school with spoken vocabularies of approximately 1,500 words. Children have learned a great many of these words through interaction with people in their environment. This vocabulary can be expanded through the language experience method. Through this method you can captialize on the spoken language of the child, while using the word-recognition skills needed to develop both a sight and meaning vocabulary. The central theme of this process becomes one of communication, with your charting of the children's expressed ideas. Through the development of these charts, the child sees his language turn to print. In addition to capitalizing on the child's experiences, the teacher has made reading *fun*.

Beginning reading based on language experience stresses the importance of teaching sound-symbol correspondence. Children must be helped to see that print represents ideas and that through reading, they can share these ideas. Through emphasis on the child's language, a sight vocabulary can be built. In conjunction with the establishment of this foundation, phonics and other word-attack skills can be introduced to help the child to identify unknown and difficult words. Through language experience, the child's word-attack skills are not being learned in isolation but are developing through his reading activities, the basis of which is his language. Statements such as,

> Following a readiness program in which the names and sounds of letters have been learned, a child in the first grade acquires a sight vocabulary.
>
> *(Durrell and Murphy, 1963, p. 11)*

can illustrate an integral part of the language reading process that stresses the creative intuitiveness of the child who has already acquired language facility.

In this way, sequential and spontaneous approaches to reading instruction are becoming integrated.

The strength of an eclectic or integrated language reading program is in the incorporation of all methods of teaching the language arts within one program.

> Developing and acquiring a sight vocabulary can be done in a circumstance that rightly simulates the learning to talk stage. Sound and sight are not divorced. Rate of "new" word learning is not paced by some artificial, illogical plan of one or two words per page or one or two words per basic reader "story", even though there are no "stories" in preprimers.
>
> *(Stauffer, 1965, p. 259)*

Based on this process, the child continually expands his sight vocabulary. You are encouraged to help children in noting beginning word differences and similarities because studies of eye movement and miscues have indicated that readers concentrate more on initial and ending portions of words than medial positions.

Initial letters: dog, doll, day
Ending letters: ball, tall, call
Medial letters: took, apple, were

As well as furthering skill development, you may also ask the children to discuss their individual reactions to the experience because we often become so involved with the group product that we lose sight of the individuals involved in the production.

As an extension of their basic lessons, you may give each child a typed copy of his reaction to the experience. Each child is asked to cut his story into words and phrases. He begins to realize that stories consist of words and phrases that he can speak. The child is now asked to match these isolated units with the sentence in its complete form.

You might ask the children to name and spell particular words as they paste them onto a second copy. You might also give paired students envelopes containing the words and phrases of their reactions and ask them to reconstruct their stories for their partners to read. Throughout this experience you may want to stress story punctuation. Ask children to consult a dictionary (with your help) to determine word meanings, pronunciation keys, and word histories. You may want to further this language experience by using the activities suggested throughout this text.

Here again we want to emphasize that through the child's own language, you are teaching many needed *phonics generalizations;* you are developing an extended *reading vocabulary,* and you are introducing many *basic study skills.* This is not an isolated process but one that builds on the already existing language of the child while it moves him into many new learning areas. The result is one of a unified learning experience rather than one involving isolated bits of data.

When you work with small groups or individual students to develop a particular concept, such as cooperation, sharing, or other social studies concepts, in essence, you are redesigning your program on the basis of continuous student evaluation, not only of the language arts, but of all subject areas.

Too often children are required to spend twenty minutes on dictionary skills; thirty minutes learning new vocabulary words; forty-five minutes on phonics; and thirty minutes reading their basals. Although all of these experiences may be necessary, a synthesis of learning never seems to occur because we tend to ignore the language of the children rather than using it as a base foundation. Through a language experience method you can provide the child with an opportunity for synthesizing the independent skills of the reading/thinking process.

Another lesson in this series might involve the child perfecting his writing ability. Have the child lie on a large piece of craft paper while you trace his form. Then ask the child to cut out his form and color in any parts he chooses. He might also paste a photograph of himself onto the form. Now give each child a typed copy of his earlier writing contribution that he will edit. When he is satisfied with his piece of writing he may paste it onto his self-portrait or copy onto his silhouette.

Throughout these experiences, the teacher is obliged to continue helping *each* child's phonics, vocabulary, and comprehension development through *individual* or small-group activities that involve the personal story booklets, basal readers, or other materials of interest to the children. As the speaking, reading, listening, and writing abilities of the children become more complex, so will your language experience program.

A great deal of research (Hall, 1975; Stauffer, 1965; Goodman, 1965; Serwer, 1968; Shuy, 1969; Roach Van Allen, 1961) supports the language experience approach because:

A. Children realize through observation that printed text is their language written down.
B. It develops:
   1. Left-to-right reading
   2. Auditory discrimination
   3. Visual discrimination
   4. Auditory-visual discrimination
   5. Hand-eye coordination
   6. Development of cooperation
   7. Expansion of attention span
   8. Oral language usage
   9. Word recognition
   10. Alphabet recognition
   11. Punctuation
   12. Pronunciation
   13. Word meanings
   14. Word histories
   15. Dictionary skills
   16. Group discussion
   17. Social encounters with peers

There are many profitable experiences that result from the language experience method; however, as the classroom teacher, you are cautioned to use this language structure only as a curriculum base. Do not fall into the same kind of faulty repetitious, uncreative patterns that many teachers use when they misuse a basal reader program. Be careful to incorporate the spontaneous expressions of your children in the initial lessons. Grammar, usage, and punctuation may be the focus of supplementary lessons.

You are further cautioned to move a child into basal and trade books smoothly. The transition should be made in conjunction with topics which the child is interested in discussing. For example, if the class is discussing salads, you could introduce supplementary material on the origin of salads. Language experience charts, which may cover a wide variety of topics, can still be of service to your program after your children have begun to explore the topic in texts. Children are a storehouse of ideas, many of which can become language experience charts.

The following lesson plan is an example of one that you might use in your classroom.

Content: Directions for making a Waldorf Salad

Grade level: K–3

Objective: To help students write and read a recipe after they have
                made a Waldorf Salad in class

Activity: Step 1: Have a group of students make a Waldorf Salad.
                Step 2: Have a student copy the steps of the recipe and
                        print them on a large sheet of tag board.
                Step 3: Place the recipe on the board and ask students
                        in a second group to make a Waldorf Salad fol-
                        lowing the recipe directions.

Recipe for Waldorf Salad

1. Cut up a head of lettuce.
2. Slice three celery stalks into ½-inch pieces.
3. Slice one large green pepper into ¼-inch pieces.
4. Core three applies and slice them into ½-inch pience
5. Sprinkle the salad gingerly with walnut pieces.

Individualized Instruction

Individualized instruction is the base of the spontaneous reading approach. A definition of reading is embedded in the individualized reading method because it is this method that is aimed at substituting interesting student-selected reading materials for the sometimes uninteresting content of the basals.

Like the language experience approach, each student establishes his own pace and sequence for reading instruction.

Within the contexts of the spontaneous reading approach, reading has been described as an individual set of process skills which are learned in social settings as the child works alone or with groups using a wide variety of materials. In this type of individualized/personalized program, the child reads materials of his choice, related to his interests. It is the intent of these programs to allow children to set their own pace for progress in materials that they have selected.

When using this individualized method, you need access to a wide variety of materials covering a range of reading difficulty appropriate to the class. It is recommended that you have three to five choices available for each child at all times. If your school library does not have an adequate supply of texts you may secure materials from the public library for an extended period. After the selections have served their purpose, exchange them for additional books.

In directing such a program, you will need to have knowledge of the following areas:

1. The reading process.
2. Organizational skills.
3. Sequential skill development.
4. Assessment techniques.
5. Reading materials.
6. Classroom management procedures.

In the following paragraphs we have included a description of the way one teacher went about acquiring these areas of knowledge and setting up an individualized reading program.

> Ms. Silver decided to begin the school year with an individualized reading program. She read several chapters in several texts describing the approach and added to her mental outline of the requirements for a good individualized program several notes from her own experience. Still feeling unsure about some points, she obtained permission to visit and observe in classrooms where individualized reading programs were being conducted. With this preparation, she still felt there were some questions that would simply have to be answered as her program evolved.
>
> As soon as Ms. Silver was able to learn which students she would have for reading instruction, she obtained their records and studied them to learn as much as possible about their reading acheivement and to gain some insight into their interests. She was fortunate in finding interest inventories that had been completed by a number of the children. These proved very helpful as she tried to anticipate books and materials that children in her class might find intriguing.
>
> After studying the records available to her, she felt she was able to estimate the range in reading levels that would be represented in her class. Had this not been true, she had planned to administer a reading survey (reading achievement test) soon after school began. She had also planned to choose books on what appeared to be an appropriate instructional level for each child. She planned to hear each child read orally from material on his estimated level. This she felt would either confirm her original estimate or give her a sound basis for reestimating. She felt this would still be a good procedure to follow even though she no longer needed to administer the reading test.

Her next step was to purchase multiple copies of workbooks designed for independent use rather than being tied to any specific program content. She went through these materials, taking them apart and reorganizing them so that she had different categories of exercises for developing word-recognition skills, comprehension skills, and some study skills. Feeling that in some areas her supply of work sheets was inadequate, she developed some additional ones herself. She prepared an index for these exercises so that a work sheet for almost any aspect of reading with which the child might need help could be found quickly.

Her next step was an extensive study of the library to determine holdings on the levels needed at the beginning of school and the levels that would most likely be needed by the end of the term. Because her town had a good children's division in its public library, she also surveyed the holdings there. Not only did she check for books of fiction, she also checked on reference books, magazines, and brochures.

Ms. Silver then consulted her principal and found it would be possible to subscribe to two daily newspapers published in the area. She found she would have some money allocated for the purchase of instructional materials and decided to purchase some reading games and records that could be used for additional skill development by individuals or groups.

Prior to the beginning of school, she selected books representing the interests and reading levels in her group. These she organized in her room by topic, not level of difficulty.

Once school began, she introduced the new program to the class. They worked out cooperatively a schedule whereby Ms. Silver would have individual conferences with five or six of the twenty-five students in her class each day. A block of time was left to work with any students who needed and requested help. This made it possible to request interruption-free conference time.

During conference, the student would talk with her about the material he was reading, expressing his reaction to it. He would also read aloud to her. Sometimes she would choose the portion to be read. At other times, the student would make the selection. While this took place, the rest of the class would read independently or work on skill-development activities.

Ms. Silver showed the class the checklist she had developed and would use to keep record of the progress each individual made in reading from conference to conference. On it she had outlined all the skills she hoped to help them develop. On this checklist she could quickly indicate strengths and areas needing extra work. She could also make notes of worksheets or other activities to which the child was being referred. All of this would give her something to refresh her memory and to build on as she gave the individual needed help. The student was invited to refer to his list whenever he felt it would be helpful.

In addition to keeping records herself, Ms. Silver urged each child to keep a record of the things he or she had read throughout the program. She worked with the class developing a list of types of literature and general topics in which they were interested. Each child took a copy of this and was encouraged to read at least one selection for each category during the year.

Ms. Silver kept careful records not only for each child, but on the total program also. As time passed, she felt that some group activity would be helpful. Because sharing what one has read often enhances the reading, she arranged for children who were reading on the same topic to get together to discuss their books and share portions of them through oral reading. When she first initiated the group discussion sharing sessions she remained with the group to help them get organized and use their time well. Later, she felt the groups were able to work satisfactorily without her participation. This allowed her to work with others while tuning in occasionally to the group's activities. In addition, she organized a similar type of group activity where individuals who had completed a selection might get together. She felt this could lead children to develop new interests, if those having read the materials handled them with enthusiasm. As need occurred, she organized groups to work on a common problem. She felt that an economic use of time required this.

Finding still some further need for group involvement, she selected some plays for children to read in a group. Choral reading was worked into some group session.

The class with which Miss Silver was working was at a level roughly equivalent to fifth grade. Many of the things she tried out with these children could not have been done with younger children, or if done, they would have required a different approach on her part. The individualized reading approach is not recommended as a beginning reading plan. However, as children begin gaining some independence in reading, it surely can be used in conjunction with other approaches. The teacher wishing to do so must gradually phase out the other approach.

As you learned from Ms. Silver one of the strongest arguments for using this method is that only by self-selection would two students be reading the same material at the same time. This dramatically reduces the likelihood of achievement comparisons. The other major advantages of this program are that children select their own materials, and they set their own rate of progress. The obvious disadvantage of this method is that you may experience some initial problems with classroom management procedures which may occur because some children move at a snail's pace when they are allowed to set their own course and rate. Occasionally, there is the child who is an enthusiastic selector but a reluctant finisher. These are problems that may occur in an individualized reading program, and you must deal with each of these problems on an individual basis. Chapter 15 has been designed to help you to develop the techniques you will need to successfully implement an individualized reading program.

In the next section of this chapter, we will present the most current system for teaching reading—the managed language/reading system, which has attempted to incorporate the best features of the sequential reading approach and the spontaneous reading approach.

Managed Language/Reading System

The managed language/reading system capitalizes on the strengths of both the sequential and spontaneous reading approaches. Its content, while logically organized, emphasizes an individualized format of instruction. This system has been developed in an attempt to provide classroom teachers with a manageable program. Many of the "new" programs include basals with stories that are relevant and interesting to students. Many of these systems include filmstrips and tapes of the stories, dittoed work sheets, teacher guides and manuals, criterion-referenced tests, and elaborate easy-to-manage record-keeping systems.

Each of these additions to the basic program is intended to help teachers individualize their programs.

These new systems have attempted to include stories that closely reflect the language of real children in real-life situations. In this way, these new materials are similar to experience stories. Because they attempt to provide the teacher with the opportunity to individualize, and to meet the needs of each of her children, the programs include intensive management systems. These management systems help the teacher *diagnose, prescribe,* and *evaluate* the program for each child.

The following description of a management system has been taken from Ginn's *Reading 720*. Other programs by Macmillan, 1975; Economy, 1975; and Laidlaw, 1975 closely parallel this description.

> The management system for an instructional program is neither the content of that program nor the teaching method by which content is presented to pupils. Rather, it represents a kind of framework or pattern by means of which content and teaching methods can be organized to assure that some specific outcomes occur. Usually, the desired effects of managing instruction are as follows: (1) that pupils are systematically taught at least a core set of specified educational objectives, with the exception of those pupils who have previously become proficient in certain of these objectives, (2) that evidence is generated to show whether pupils learn these objectives at a level of proficiency prespecified as desirable, (3) that provision is made for systematic reinstruction of pupils on any of the objectives for which they have failed to demonstrate proficiency, and (4) that teaching pupils to acceptable proficiency on this set of core objectives is accomplished in the minimum reasonable time.
>
> When the core strands of Reading 720 are taught in the management mode, the foregoing outcomes can be realized. Using a management system, the teacher may select from the rich pool of hundreds of objectives, those specific ones that represent the core skills of Reading 720, drawn from the comprehension, vocabulary, and decoding strands. The teacher may then build lesson plans emphasizing, or even restricted to, these core objectives and teach those children known to need them. Additional Reading 720 components allow the teacher to evaluate with precision the proficiency of pupils on the core objectives. Other Reading 720 resources can then be used to reteach missed objectives to just those pupils who need reinstruction. Because managed instruction focuses so tightly on core essentials and attempts to limit instruction within the core strands to that demonstrably required, whether initial or reteaching, it moves pupils with maximum efficiency toward attainment of the desired outcomes.
>
> Implementing a management system in teaching Reading 720 aids the teacher in the following ways:
>
> > in helping to select what pupils are to learn
> > in systematic planning for and provision of supplementary instruction
> > in individualizing instruction according to pupil needs
> > in establishing an instructional pace that is efficient yet accomplishes desired goals

The components of a successfully managed language/reading system are integrated into the existing basal program. The following example and materials, taken from Ginn's *Reading 720*, emphasize such integration.

COMPONENTS OF READING 720
MANAGEMENT SYSTEM

A management system is integrated or built into Reading 720. All the directions needed for managing core skills instruction are found in this Teacher's Edition. Instructions will be found placed sequentially, as needed, throughout the various sections of the lesson plans and in the manuals accompanying the various components that are essential to managing instruction in Reading 720. All such manuals are supplied with these components when purchased separately, and are also reproduced in this section of the Teacher's Edition.

The following are necessary for managing the instruction of the core skills. These items are also available as separate components.

Activities in Part 4 of the lesson plan

Activities in Part 4 of each plan are designed to introduce and give practice reinforcement of objectives taught in unit.

Unit Criterion Exercises

The Unit Criterion Exercises may be used to assess pupil proficiency on the specified core skills of a unit. Pupils scoring at or above Suggested Criterion Score (SCS) are assumed to have attained acceptable proficiency on the tested objective. The rationale for establishing the SCS is described in the Criterion Exercise manual.

Criterion Exercise Record Sheets (CERS)

The CERS are forms for recording and organizing groups of pupils' Unit Criterion Exercise scores and referencing them to specific supplemental instruction or enrichment resources. The CERS for each unit are found on pages 265–267.
unit are found on pages 265–267.

Booster Activities

Paper-and-pencil instructional activities are designed to give practice or reinforcement to pupils scoring below Suggested Criterion Score on any of the objectives tested in a Unit Criterion Exercise. All the Booster Activities for Level 5 are found on page 271–280 and the manual of directions for their use is on pages 268–270. Instructions for selecting the proper Booster Activity are found in the manual. It is important to note that Booster Activities "boost" marginally performing pupils to an acceptable level. When pupils score *very* low on an objective, especially if they get none of the items right, they need reteaching. After reteaching has been accomplished, the Booster or the other practice activities may be given.

Use of the following component, while not essential, is strongly recommended.

Reading Achievement Card

The Reading Achievement Card is a chart for recording and organizing all of an individual pupil's criterion exercise scores for one level. This component is reproduced in this Teacher's Edition. It is also found on the last two pages of each Unit Criterion Exercise booklet, and, in addition, is available separately printed on tag board.

Several other Reading 720 components are optionally usable with management mode instruction and, except for the Informal Reading Inventory, do not appear in this Teacher's Edition. Each has its own manual or other directions describing its use. These components include the following:

Reading 720   Initial Placement Test

CLASS WORK SHEET

Teacher's Name

School   Date

City   Grade

PUPIL'S NAME	IPT Level	Initial Assigned Level	Assigned Level After 2 Weeks	COMMENTS
1.				
2.				
3.				
4.				
5.				
6.				
7.				
8.				
9.				
10.				
11.				
12.				
13.				
14.				
15.				
16.				
17.				
18.				
19.				
20.				

Reading 720
Reading Achievement Card
Level 2

Pupil's Name_____

School_____

_____

Key: Total = Number of Items; SCS = Suggested Criterion Score; PS = Pupil's Score

Directions: Record in the appropriate box the pupil's score on each part of the Criterion Exercise. At the end of a level, sign and date the card.

Unit 1

DECODING
initial consonants
/b/b, /l/l, /r/r, /h/h

Total	SCS	PS
12	10	

VOCABULARY
Word Recognition

Total	SCS	PS
8	6	

Notes:_____
_____
_____
_____
_____
_____

Unit 2

DECODING
initial consonant / ĵ /j

Total	SCS	PS
4	3	

VOCABULARY
Word Recognition

Total	SCS	PS
10	8	

Notes:_____
_____
_____
_____
_____
_____

Unit 3

DECODING
initial consonant /k/c

Total	SCS	PS
4	3	

VOCABULARY
Word Recognition

Total	SCS	PS
12	10	

Notes:_____
_____
_____
_____
_____
_____

Unit 4

DECODING
initial consonants
/f/f, /y/y, /n/n

Total	SCS	PS
9	7	

VOCABULARY
Word Recognition

Total	SCS	PS
10	8	

Notes:_____
_____
_____
_____
_____
_____

Initial Placement Test

The Initial Placement Test aids in determining the level in which to start pupils new to Reading 720.

Informal Reading Inventory

The Informal Reading Inventory helps in making initial individual placement decisions or in post-instruction diagnosis as a supplement to the Unit Criterion Exercises.

Unit Decoding Pretests

The Pretests are an aid in determining which decoding skills pupils already know before they start a unit.

Level Mastery Tests

Level Mastery Tests may be used for surveying pupil achievement on an entire level, or for providing a cumulative, final check on pupil proficiency on the level's objectives.

Reading Progress Card

The Reading Progress Card serves as a device for recording cumulative reading achievement test and other data for all thirteen levels. It is available in file-folder format.

The following exercise is a comprehension measure found in Ginn 720.

Read the following selection and circle the correct answer to the questions. Continue until you have answered all the questions.

Eddie slammed his locker shut, picked up his jacket and books and walked sullenly toward the subway. His sixth grade class had just had an assembly to discuss graduation to the junior high school. The assembly had had a big impact on Eddie. He had learned that the work would be intensified in junior high and that there would be many more students. He didn't want to leave his school. Here he was one of the oldest pupils. Everyone knew him and looked up to him. He was a good baseball player, strong and agile. Besides that, he knew he did well on his school work. The more Eddie thought about it, the less he wanted to go to a school full of strangers where he would be one of the youngest. No one there would know how good he was.

Eddie brooded as he walked along, trying to think of a way out. "I just won't go," he thought. "I'll defy them all. They can't make me do what I don't want!" He began to scheme and think of ways to stay in the sixth grade. Suddenly, he knew what he would do. He would fail his schoolwork! If he didn't pass his courses, then they would have to keep him back.

Eddie began his campaign the next day. He showed up late for school and he did not prepare his lessons. In the weeks that followed, his work went steadily downward. He stopped answering questions in class and didn't turn in his homework. His customary enthusiasm was gone. Eddie's conscience was bothering him and he became shiftless and irritable.

Mr. Panco, Eddie's teacher, became worried about Eddie's strange behavior and one day asked him to stay after school. When Mr. Panco confronted Eddie with his poor performance record, Eddie was reluctant to say anything. He didn't want to tell the teacher he was scared. But Mr. Panco persuaded Eddie to tell him what was wrong. They talked for a long time and the teacher reassured Eddie that in junior high school things would not change so much. "A lot of your friends are going with you, so you won't be alone," Mr. Panco pointed out. "You can still play baseball too. The junior high has a team. If you just continue to do all the things you've always done, everything will be fine."

After their talk, Eddie felt better about his future. He caught up on all the work he had not done, and even began to enjoy the thought of the coming graduation ceremony. By the time June rolled around, Eddie was looking forward to the fall.

1. What two things caused Eddie to be upset?
   He wasn't able to do his schoolwork.
   He was afraid of leaving his school.
   His conscience bothered him.
   He disliked his teacher.

2. What would Eddie probably have done if he hadn't talked with Mr. Panco?
   Failed all his courses   Transferred to another school   Stayed home

3. Which statement describes the theme of this story?
   People sometimes fear the unknown.
   Junior high schools are frightening places.
   It pays to be shiftless.

4. Which of the following is an example of an opinion?
   Eddie will not do well in junior high school.
   Eddie does his sixth grade work well.
   The idea of going to junior high upset Eddie.

5. Which phrase describes Mr. Panco?
   Uppity and conceited   Concerned and reassuring   Sneering and defiant

6. The main idea of the second paragraph is that Eddie began to scheme about how he could stay in the sixth grade. Which of the following is a detail that might be added to support the main idea?
   Eddie is liked by his peers.
   Eddie's parents want him to succeed in school.
   Eddie thought he might bribe his teachers.

7. Which of the following is an example of a fact?
   "No one there would know how good I was."
   "Here he was one of the oldest pupils."
   "They can't make me do what I don't want."

8. At the end of the story, how are Eddie and Mr. Panco alike?
   They are optimistic about Eddie in junior high school.
   They agree that junior high school will be a disaster.
   They think Eddie should stay in sixth grade.

9. Why did Mr. Panco talk with Eddie?
   He was angry about Eddie's misbehavior.
   He didn't want Eddie to fail sixth grade.
   He wanted to help Eddie to be a better ballplayer.

10. What was the effect of Mr. Panco's discussion with Eddie?
    Eddie became more agitated than he was before.
    Eddie decided to drop out of baseball.
    Eddie overcame his fears about junior high school.

At the completion of this activity the classroom teacher is better able to assess the strengths and needs of the reader in the area of comprehension.

Practice in Defining Reading

After examining these two major approaches to the teaching of reading and the various methods which have evolved from the two philosophical points of view, let us again stress the importance of formulating a personal definition of reading. It is extremely important for you to answer these questions:

What do I think reading is?

What are my objectives in teaching a child to read?

Only after you have answered these questions can you decide on an appropriate program. In the next few pages we will present several definitions of reading which the reading research specialists have devised. As you are reading each of these definitions, try to ask yourself if these definitions reflect your own point of view.

Robinson (1966), completing a refinement of a definition of reading that William S. Gray had begun prior to his death, identified five major components of reading: Word perception, comprehension, reaction, assimilation, and rate, a dimension that Gray had not previously included in his analysis of major components of reading. According to the Gray-Robinson definition, or model, of reading, word perception includes word recognition and the association of meanings with words. The second dimension, comprehension, involves two levels of meaning, literal and implied. The third aspect, reaction, involves intellectual judgments and emotional responses. Assimilation, the fourth aspect, involves fusion of old ideas with new ideas which now have been obtained through reading. Rate, the fifth dimension, is recognized as varying speeds depending on load of new words, the length of the lesson or time one is expected to read, and the concept load of material to be read.

Gray and Reese's (1963) definition examines the importance of reading in life. They maintain that reading is an aid to meeting everyday needs, a tool for vocation, a pursuit for leisure time, an aid to enrichment of experience, a tool of citizenship, and a source of spiritual refreshment.

Spache and Spache (1973), taking a somewhat similar approach to the definition of reading, focus on the process rather than the use of reading. They define reading as skill development, a visual act, a perceptual act, a reflection of cultural background, a thinking process, an information process, and as associational learning process.

Harris (1972) discusses the nature of reading, pointing out that reading is an extension of oral communication that must have listening and speaking skills as its foundation. He says that reading may be defined "as the act of responding with appropriate meaning to printed and written verbal symbols" and that the reasoning side of reading becomes increasingly important as recognition is mastered." (pp. 3–10)

Smith and Dechant (1961) call attention to the fact that the vantage point from which one attempts to define reading strongly affects its definition:

The psychologist is interested in reading as a thought process. The semanticist is concerned with meaning and considers the printed page to be the graphic representation of speech. The linguist concerns himself with the relationships between the sounds of language and its written form. The sociologist studies the interaction of reading and culture, and the litterateur reacts to the artistic nature of the production before him. (p. 21)

They point out that reading includes more than recognition of graphic symbols:

Effective reading includes experiencing, learning, and thinking. It frequently requires reflection, judgment, analysis, synthesis, selection, and critical evaluation of what is being read. The reader is stimulated by the author's printed words, but in turn he vests the author's words with his own meaning. And frequently the reader must select one specific meaning from numerous meanings that he has acquired. (p. 22)

Tinker and McCullough (1968) believe that reading:

involves the identification and recognition of printed or written symbols which serve as stimuli for the recall of meanings built up through past experiences, and further the construction of new meanings through the reader's manipulation of relevant concepts already in his possession. The resulting meanings are organized into thought processes according to the purposes that are operating in the reader. Such an organization results in modifications of thought, and perhaps behavior, or it may even lead to radically new behavior which takes its place in the personal or social development of the individual. (p. 8)

Smith (1973) emphasizes the creative aspect of reading in his definition:

Reading is the ability to recognize and understand the printed symbols of the child's spoken vocabulary. Printed words, as well as spoken ones, are meaningful to the young child only insofar as his field of experience overlaps that of the author of the printed text. The old cliché "You can take from a book only what you bring to it" is, in essence, true. The reader learns from a book only if he is able to understand the printed symbols and rearrange them into vicarious experiences in his mind. His ability to think, to reason, and to conceptualize makes it possible for him to receive new ideas from a printed page without actually experiencing the new idea, *but he must have experienced each symbol that helps him make up the new idea.* (pp. 31-2)

Frank Smith's model (1971) of reading describes the process from the printed words to comprehension as follows:

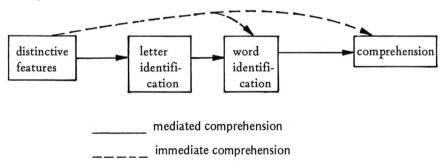

_____ mediated comprehension

_ _ _ _ immediate comprehension

Now that you have considered some of these formal definitions of reading, you should attempt to formalize your own personal defintion of reading and try to establish an effective reading program which logically follows from your definition. In the next few pages, we will describe four classroom situations. As you read each of these, try to determine the definition and the method of reading instruction which each teacher is using.

The four situations which follow may occur in any classroom. Read each of the situations, and answer the questions following each:

1. What is this teacher's definition of reading?
2. What method of reading instruction is this teacher using?
3. To which earlier definition is the teacher's definition most similar?

Situation 1

Mrs. Bellus teaches a class of children who are 9 to 10 years old. If you are grade-level oriented in your thinking, these children would probably be fourth-graders.

Mrs. Bellus's class has expressed a strong interest in the theme of cowboys as an outgrowth of a television program which many of the children watched. After a class discussion, the children voted to do an extended study on cowboys throughout the world. It was decided that much of the information being gathered would have to come from printed material.

Mrs. Bellus is a resourceful teacher who has a good working relationship with both the school and public librarian. She has stocked her classroom with many books, pamphlets, magazines, encyclopedia volumes, some records, and filmstrips (on varying levels of difficulty because of reading levels of students in her class is 2.4 through 8.8).

The selection of nontextbooks materials suggests that Mrs. Bellus believes that any material that displays a written word or idea related to the topic of study is to be viewed as an "instructional material." Instructional materials can be defined as any material that motivates children to read. Such materials are often those related to the private and social lives of children (cartoons, games, magazines).

High-interest, easy-vocabulary books are also found in this classroom. These materials explore topics of interest to older children but contain vocabulary that can be easily read by a child who is having difficulty with grade-level reading. The following references serve as high-interest, easy-vocabulary text sources:

Geisel, T. Seuss. *The Cat in the Hat;* New York: Random House, Inc., 1952.
———. *The Cat in the Hat Comes Back;* New York: Random House, Inc., 1958.

Because many of these materials are ungraded, she has to use a readability formula to determine the approximate grade level of the materials. Readability refers to the difficulty of the material as measured through the use of a simple mathematical formula. Although many formulae are available (Gray (1935), Lorge (1944), Flesch (1943), Dale–Chall (1948), Spache (1973)) we believe the simplest one to use is the Fry (1969).

When selecting materials, Mrs. Bellus keeps the following purposes in mind: she wants to be sure she has a basic understanding of the concepts that the children will be learning; she feels she should have some idea of the vocabulary they will encounter in the books. She wants to keep children motivated and at the same time lead follow-up discussions, after children have completed reading their books. Mrs. Bellus hopes these discussions will not only develop awareness of information, but will provide students with experiences that encourage the development of comparative and evaluative thinking skills. She hopes to encourage her students to question the information they find and to question the qualifications of the authors providing the information. Finally, Mrs. Bellus hopes to help the class synthesize the information they have obtained in an attempt to develop a view and appreciation of cowboys (or their counterparts) that reaches beyond what they may have developed through hours of TV viewing of Western movies or programs.

When planning for <u>some</u> groups, Mrs. Bellus plans to introduce <u>some</u> vocabulary with which she feels <u>some</u> children may have difficulty. She plans to present the written words and then help individual children needing it with the pronounciation of the words. Other words will be analyzed phonetically from the regular spelling, and yet other words that do not adhere to the general phonetic principles of the English language will be introduced through context clues or dictionary aids. Mrs. Bellus views the development of word analysis skills as an important step toward helping children feel comfortable when they meet the words in print. She believes this word knowledge will help with comprehension and rate of reading. She also suspects that it may be helpful in sustaining student interest, because some children are easily discouraged when they meet many unfamiliar words in printed material.

After potentially troublesome vocabulary has been studied, Mrs. Bellus encourages individuals to return to their reading. She circulates among them to note who is reading what, and whether anyone seems to be in difficulty. She pauses here and there to help with a word or to check on an individual's comprehension of whatever he has read. She also makes some mental notes of how rapidly children seem to be reading.

After several periods have been spent reading, the group comes together to share some findings. Individuals in the group are encouraged to respond to what others relate. Mrs. Bellus, too, inserts questions that cause students to relate their findings to those of others. She encourages critical evaluation rather than unquestioning acceptance of what is read.

As summarizing, or concluding, activities, students have an opportunity to compare new images of a cowboy with former images, while explaining the change. This is followed by an enrichment activity that allows students to relate their images of cowboys through art, drama, and music. Children progress through all activities at their own individual rate.

1. What is the teacher's definition of reading?
2. What method of reading instruction is this teacher using?
3. To which earlier definition is this teacher's definition most similar?

Let's see if we agree: We believe that Situation 1 seems to be reflective of the Gray-Robinson definition or model of reading. It gives attention to word recognition, comprehension of words and groups of words, reaction to ideas, fusion of new and already held ideas, and the rate at which some of this can occur. It seems quite likely that Gray and Reese, Spache and Spache, Harris, Smith and Dechant, Tinker and McCullough, James Smith, and Smith and Harris could find their concepts of reading being dealt with in this situation. While each would probably change part or all of the situation or shift some emphasis if he were Mrs. Bellus, each seemingly could accept the situation.

Situation 2

The setting for this situation is a first-year reading group. Children in this group have been taught the names of many of the letters. In some cases, they have also been taught the sound the letter represents. They have mastered the learning of sounds associated with phonograms, such as at, an, and am. They have had experience in blending initial sounds with the sounds represented by these phonograms so that they have worked with a number of words involving one phonogram: bat, cat, fat, hat, mat, nat, pat, rat, sat, tat, and vat. They have also been introduced to a number of sight words. This was repeated until the word was immediately recognized on sight.

Mr. Kavanaugh is the teacher of this group. He believes that his method of reading instruction gives children the key to unlocking words (decoding) and that repeated practice with a phonetic unit helps the child master sound-symbol combinations. He argues that this helps children to develop security in reading.

The phonogram to which the class is now being introduced is ad. They begin with the following list of ad words:

bad	had	pad	dad	tad
lad	sad	fad	mad	

The phonogram ad is examined and discussed; its sound is identified. The blending process is used to add the beginning sounds for the words listed here. Mr. K. spends time with the pronunciation of each of these words. Then the following story is read silently and orally. Mr. Kavanaugh encourages use of correct intonation to indicate statements and questions.

> Tad had been bad.
> He had a pad.
> The pad was Dad's.
> Dad wanted the pad.
> Tad was a sad lad when Dad found the pad.
> Was Tad a bad lad to get Dad's pad?
> Was Dad mad at Tad?

After the story has been read, the students are given copies of the following work sheet and asked to put the right letter in the blank.

> _ad had Dad's _ad.
> Dad was _ad.
> He was mad at _ad.
> _ad found the pad.

The work sheets are collected and checked by Mr. Kavanaugh. Some children who missed specific items are recycled into a second round of similar instruction.

1. What is this teacher's definition of reading?
2. What method of reading instruction is the teacher using?
3. To which of the earlier definitions is the teacher's definition of reading most similar?

We found that Situation 2 is reflective of the kinds of programs linguists have developed. There is definite emphasis on the recognition or association of sound and symbol. Special attention has been given to one linguistic element, the phonogram. It can also be noted that little stress is placed on the comprehension of ideas. This situation is reflective of the philosophy reflected by Fries which emphasized decoding over meaning in beginning reading instruction.

Situation 3

Mr. Hill has an upper-primary class. These children are involved in many exercises designed to sharpen the senses. They frequently have tasting or "sniffing" parties where they try to identify things by flavor and scent.

Today Harold brought some brightly colored leaves that he picked on the way to school. Examination and discussion of these led Mr. Hill to suggest that the entire class go outdoors to examine and enjoy other evidences of the approach of fall. Once outdoors, they noted other types and coloring of leaves and compared shapes, sizes, textures, and shades. They also discussed how the very air seemed to have a softer, gentler feeling than in the past few weeks. Many plants that had previously blossomed now had pods that were bursting and scattering seeds.

Upon returning to the classroom, Mr. Hill and the children discussed the things they saw, heard, felt, and smelled when they were outdoors. Then Mr. Hill gave each child a copy of a poem entitled "Fall" and a story entitled "The Cricket, the Fall, and Me." He read the poem to the children, inviting them to follow along, and then he suggested that they read it with him. Next he called attention to the "word pictures" in the poem. After they had completed this reading, they read the story and looked for "word pictures". When this was over, they were asked to keep their eyes, ears, noses and sense of touch alert as they went home in the afternoon. The impressions which they gathered would be used for discussion and story writing the following day.

1. What is this teacher's definition of reading?
2. What method of reading instruction is this teacher using?
3. To which of the earlier definitions is the teacher's definition of reading most similar?

Situation 3 certainly leaves one wondering how and when children will get to the business of learning to recognize words. There is ample evidence given to sensitizing students to the world through their senses, but it is difficult to understand how and when the teacher gets to the business of recognition of words and the ability to locate information. This situation seems reflective of Jennings definition more than any other. This situation reflects the rudiments of a language experience method. However, Mr. Hill has not yet attempted to deal with each child's needs.

Situation 4

Mrs. DeLeo has a class of 8-year-olds. These might roughly be classified as second-third graders. These students have been introduced to many of the alphabet letters and taught the sounds they represent singly and in clusters. They have also discussed some of the different sounds vowels represent under different circumstances. For example, a vowel in a word that ends with an e can be expected to represent its long sound, whereas a vowel in the middle of a word that ends with a consonant can be expected to represent its short sound.

Today Mrs. DeLeo is working on review and extension of those two vowel "rules." She is using the following list of words:

dim—dime   kit—kite
Tim—time   mill—mile

Each word is analyzed letter by letter and sound by sound.

Situation 4 has some similarity to situation 2 in its emphasis on sound-symbol relationship, but there is a difference in approach. It reflects most of the ideas one would take when using a synthetic approach to phonics. Sounds are analyzed and then blended into words. Flesch (1943) would probably endorse this particular situation and would feel that reading had been satisfactorily achieved when students could "sound and blend" to arrive at pronunciations.

A Final Definition

Reading as it has been considered in this text is the process of perceiving, interpreting, and evaluating printed material. It is one of the four major tools of communication: listening, speaking, reading, and writing. It is usually silent, and it is receptive in nature. Foundations for success in reading lie in the individual's development of skill in listening and speaking.

Reading requires the development of a meaningful vocabulary and a multiplicity of skills. The reader must be able to perceive and recognize written symbols, and he must be able to associate concepts with written symbols. He must be able to understand both concrete and abstract ideas as they are presented in written form.

The effective reader questions that which he has read. He may approach written material on a literal basis, but he must progress to levels of interpretation and critical evaluation. The ability to locate needed material or information and the ability to select materials pertinent to the topic on which one reads are two very important skills in reading. In addition, the effective reader is one who can adjust rate of reading to the purpose for which reading is done.

As you continue to read and think about each of the definitions of reading which have been presented, we hope that you will be able to answer more specifically the probing questions about your individual goals as a teacher of reading. We also hope that you will generate more questions about the specific operations within each definition. Only in this way will you be able to establish an effective, managed language/reading program within your own classroom.

QUESTIONS AND RELATED READINGS

If at this time you do not feel that you have attained adequate knowledge to successfully answer the following questions, we would like to suggest related reading.

1. What are the historical trends in reading instruction?
2. Why is there a need for you to develop a personal definition of reading?
3. Why do teachers need to understand several methods of reading instruction?
4. What are the strengths of each of the methods studied in this chapter?

Goal 1: To aid the reader in the historical overview of reading instruction in the United States

Question 1: What are the historical trends in reading instruction?

Chall, Jeanne S. *Learning to Read: The Great Debate.* New York: McGraw Hill Book Company, 1967.

Karlin, Robert. *Teaching Elementary Reading.* 2nd ed. New York: Harcourt Brace and Jovanovich, Inc., 1975.

Robinson, Helen A., ed. *Reading: Seventy-five Years of Progress. Proceedings of the Annual Conference on Reading.* Chicago: University of Chicago Press, 1966.

Goal 2: To aid the reader in the need for a personal definition of reading as the basis of an instructional approach

Question 2: Why is there a need for you to develop a personal definition of reading?

Aukerman, Robert C. *Approaches to Beginning Reading.* New York: John Wiley & Sons, Inc., 1971.

Harris, Albert J. *How to Increase Reading Ability.* 5th ed. New York: David McKay Co., Inc., 1970.

Vilseek, Plaine C., ed. *A Decade of Innovation.* Newark, Del.: International Reading Association, 1968.

Goal 3: To aid the reader in a variety of methods of reading instruction

Question 3: Why do teachers need to understand several methods of reading instruction?

Aukerman, Robert C. *Approaches to Beginning Reading.* New York: John Wiley & Sons, Inc., 1971.

Hall, Mary Ann. *Teaching Readings as a Language Experience.* Columbus, Ohio: Charles E. Merrill Publishing Company, 1968.

Karlin, Robert, ed. *Perspectives on Elementary Reading.* New York: Harcourt Brace Jovanovich, Inc., 1973.

Goal 4: To aid the reader in the strengths of each method studied

Question 4: What are the strengths of each of the methods studied in this chapter?

Barrett, Thomas C., and Dale D. Johnson. *Views on Elementary Reading Instruction.* Newark, Del.: International Reading Association, 1973.

Hunt, Lyman C., ed. *The Individualized Reading Program: A Guide for Classroom Teaching. Proceedings of the Eleventh Annual Convention.* Vol. II, Part 3, Newark, Del.: International Reading Association, 1967.

Lee, Doris M., and R. Van Allen. *Learning to Read Through Experience.* New York: Appleton-Century-Crofts, 1963.

BIBLIOGRAPHY

Allen, R. Van. *Report of the Reading Study Project,* Monograph no. 1, San Diego, Calif.: Department of Education, San Diego County, 1961.

Allen, R. Van. *Language Experiences in Communication.* Boston: Houghton Mifflin Co., 1976.

Aukerman, R. C. *Approaches to Beginning Reading.* New York: John Wiley & Sons, Inc., 1971.

Barrett, T. C. "Predicting Reading Achievement Through Readiness Tests," *Reading and Inquiry, Proceedings of the International Reading Association.* Newark, Delaware: International Reading Association, 1965, pp. 26–8.

Black, I. S. *The Bank Street Readers.* New York: Macmillan, 1966.

Bloomfield, L., and C. L. Barnhart. *Let's Read: A Linguistic Approach.* Detroit: Wayne State University Press, 1961.

Burmeister, L. E. "Content of a Phonics Program." *Reading Methods and Teacher Improvement,* ed. by Nila Banton Smith. Newark, Del.: International Reading Association, 1971, pp. 27–33.

Calvin, A. D. "How to Teach with Programmed Textbooks." *Grade Teacher,* (Feb. 1967). p. 81.

Carillo, L. W. and D. J. Bissett. *The Chandler Language Experience Readers.* Noble: 1968.

Clymer, T. "The Utility of Phonic Generalizations in the Primary Grades." *The Reading Teacher,* 16 (1963), 252–8.

Clymer, T. et al. *Ginn 720 Reading Program.* Lexington, Mass.: Xerox Co., 1976.

Dale, E., and J. S. Chall. "A Formula for Predicting Readability." *Educational Research Bulletin,* 27 (Jan. 1948), 11–20.

Dallman, M., L. Rouch, L. Y. Chang, and J. J. DeBoer. *The Teaching of Reading,* 4th ed. New York: Holt, Rinehart and Winston, 1974.

Dewey, John. *Domocracy and Eucation.* New York: Macmillan Publishing Co., Inc., 1916.

Durkin, D. *Teaching Young Children to Read.* Boston: Allyn & Bacon, Inc., 1972.

——*Teaching Them to Read,* 2nd ed. Boston: Allyn & Bacon, Inc., 1974.

Durrell, D. "Success in First Grade Reading." *Boston University Journal of Education,* 140 (Feb. 1958), 2–47.

——and H. A. Murphy. "Boston University Research in Elementary School Reading. 1933-63." *Journal of Education,* 145 (Dec. 1963), p. 316–328.

Eller, Wm. et al. *Laidlaw Reading Program.* River Forest, Illinois: Laidlaw Publishing, 1976.

Fisher, J. A. "Dialect, Bilingualism and Reading." *Reading for all,* ed. by Robert Karlin. Proceedings of World Congress of IRA, Buenos Aires, Argentina, 1974.

Flesch, R. F. *Marks of Readable Style: A Study of Adult Education.* New York: Bureau of Publications, Teachers College Press, Columbia University, 1943.

Fries, C. *Linguistics and Reading.* New York: Holt, Rinehart and Winston, 1962.

——. *Reading in the Elementary School.* Boston: Allyn & Bacon, Inc., 1964.

Fry, E. "Programmed Instruction and Automation in Beginning Reading." *Elementary Reading Instruction,* ed. by Althea Beery et al. Boston: Allyn & Bacon, Inc., 1969, pp. 400–13.

Gategno, C. *Words in Color.* Chicago: Learning Materials, Inc., 1962.

Good, Carter V. "Doctoral Studies Completed or Underway." *Phi Delta Kappa.* 1923–53.

Goodman, K. "Dialect Barriers to Reading Comprehension." *Elementary English,* 42 (Dec. 1965), 852–60.

——, ed. *The Psycholinguistic Nature of the Reading Process.* Detroit: Wayne State University Press, 1968.

Goodman, K. "Dialect Barriers to Reading Comprehension." *Elementary English,* 42 (Dec. 1965), 852–60.

———, ed. *The Psycholinguistic Nature of the Reading Process.* Detroit: Wayne State University Press, 1968.

Goodman, Y. M. "Using Children's Reading Miscues for New Teaching Strategies." *The Reading Teacher,* 23 455–9. Feb. 1970

Gray L. and D. Reese. *Teaching Children to Read.* 3rd ed. 1963.

Gray, Wm. S. "Summary of Investigations Relating to Reading." *Elementary School Journal,* 1925–32.

Gray, W. S., and B. E. Leary. *What Makes a Book Readable.* Chicago: University of Chicago Press, 1935.

Hafner, L. E. and Jolly, H. B. *Patterns of Teaching Reading in the Elementary School.* New York: Macmillan Publishing Co., Inc., 1972.

Hall, Mary Anne. Reading Reading as a Language Experience, Columbus, Ohio: Merrill, 1975.

Harris, A. J. *How to Increase Reading Ability.* 5th ed. New York: David McKay Co., Inc., 1970.

Harris, L. A. and Smith, C. B., editors, *Individualized Reading Instruction: A Reader.* New York: Holt, Rinehart and Winston, 1972.

Harris, T. et al. *The Economy Company Readers.* Boston: The Economy Company, 1972.

———, and M. D. Jacobson. *Basic Elementary Reading Vocabularies.* The First R. Series. New York: Macmillan, 1972.

Jenkins, Marion (ed). "Here's to Success in Reading Self Selection Helps." *Childhood Education,* 32 November 1955, 124–131.

Karlin, R. *Teaching Elementary Reading: Principles and Strategies.* New York: Harcourt Brace Jovanovich, Inc., 1971.

Lapp, D. et al. *Teaching and Learning: Philosophical, Psychological, Curricular Applications.* New York: Macmillan Publishing Co., Inc., 1975.

Lee, Doris M. and R. Van Allen. *Learning to Read Through Experience.* New York: Appleton-Century-Crofts, 1963.

Lorge, I. "Predicting Readability." *Teachers College Record.* 45 (March 1944), 404–19.

Mazurkiewicz, A. J. and H. J. Tanzer. *Early to Read Program, Revised Phases 1, 2, 3.* ITA, 1965–66.

McKim, M. and H. Caskey. *Guiding Growth in Reading.* 2nd ed., New York: Macmillan Publishing Co., Inc., 1963.

Pitman, Sir J., A. J. Mazurkiewicz, and H. J. Tanyzer. *The Handbook on Writing and Spelling in i/t/a/.* New York: i/t/a/ Publications, 1964.

Robinson, H. A., ed. *"Reading: Seventy-five Years of Progress.* Supplementary Educational Monographs, no. 96. Chicago: University of Chicago Press, 1966.

Samuels, S. J. "The Effect of Letter-Name Knowledge on Learning to Read." *American Educational Research Journal,* 9 (Winter 1972), 65–74.

Sartain, H. W. "The Place of Individualized Reading in a Well-Planned Program." *Readings on Reading Instruction,* ed. by Albert J. Harris and Edward R. Sipay. 2nd ed., New York: David McKay Co., Inc., 1972, pp. 193–9.

Savage, J. F. *Linguistics for Teachers.* Chicago: Science Research Associates, Inc., 1973.

Schulwitz, B. S., ed. *Teachers, Tangibles, Techniques: Comprehension of Content in Reading.* Newark, Del.: International Reading Association, 1975.

Serwer, B. L. "Linguistic Support for a Method of Teaching Beginning Reading to Black Children." *Reading Research Quarterly,* (Summer, 1969, 449–67.

Shuy, R. W. "Some Considerations for Developing Beginning Reading Materials for Ghetto Children," *Journal of Reading Behavior,* 1 (Spring 1969), 33–44.

Silvaroli, N. J. "Factors in Predicting Children's Success in First Grade Reading." *Reading and Inquiry, Proceedings of the International Reading Association,* 1965, pp. 296–8.

Smith, Carl. *The Macmillan R.* New York: Macmillan Publishing Co., Inc., 1975.

Smith, Frank. *Understanding Reading.* New York: Holt, Rinehart, Winston, 1971.

Smith, H. P., and E. V. Dechant. *Psychology in Teaching Reading.* Englewood Cliffs, N.J.: Prentice-Hall, Inc., 1961.

Smith, J. A. *Creative Teaching of Reading in the Elementary School.* 2nd ed. Boston: Allyn & Bacon, Inc., 1973.

Spache, G. D. "Psychological and Cultural Factors in Learning to Read." *Reading for All,* ed. by Robert Karlin. *Proceedings of the Fourth IRA World Congress on Reading.* Newark, Del.: International Reading Association, 1973, pp. 43–50.

——— and E. B. Spache. *Reading in the Elementary School.* 3rd ed. Boston: Allyn & Bacon, Inc., 1973.

Stauffer, R. G. "The Language Experience Approach." In First Grade Reading Programs, ed. by J. F. Kerfort, *Perspectives in Reading,* no. 5. Newark, Del.: International Reading Association, 1965.

———*Directing the Reading–Thinking Process.* New York: Harper & Row, Publishers, 1975.

———*The Language-Experience Approach to the Teaching of Reading.* New York: Harper & Row, Publishers, 1970.

Strickland, R. G. "The Language of Elementary School Children: Its Relationship to the Language of Reading Textbooks and the Quality of Reading in Selected Children." *Bulletin of the School of Education, Indiana University* 38 (1962), 4.

Strang, R. *Diagnostic Teaching of Reading.* New York: McGraw-Hill Book Company, 1964.

Tinker, M., and C. McCullough. *Teaching Elementary School.* 3rd ed. New York: Appleton-Century-Crofts, 1968.

Wardhaugh, R. "Is the Linguistic Approach an Improvement in Reading Instruction?" *Current Issues in Reading.* ed. by Nila Banton Smith. Newark, Del.: International Reading Association, 1969, pp. 254–67.

13

Understanding bilingual speakers as readers

By the time the native child reaches the age of seven, his cultural and language patterns have been set, and his parents are required by law to send him to school. Until this time he is likely to speak only his own local dialect of Indian, Aleut, or Eskimo or, if his parents have had some formal schooling, he may speak a kind of halting English.

He now enters a completely foreign setting—a Western classroom. His teacher is likely to be a Caucasian who knows little or nothing about his cultural background. He is taught to read the Dick and

Jane series. Many things confuse him: Dick and Jane are two *gussuk* (Eskimo term for "white person," derived from the Russian Cossack), children who play together. Yet, he knows that boys and girls do not play together and do not share toys. They have a dog named Spot who comes indoors and does not work. They have a father who leaves for some mysterious place called "office" each day and never brings any food home with him. He drives a machine called an automobile on a hard-covered road called a street which has a policeman on each corner. These policemen always smile, wear funny clothing, and spend their time helping children to cross the street. Why do these children need this help? Dick and Jane's mother spends a lot of time in the kitchen cooking a strange food called "cookies" on a stove which has no flame in it, but the most bewildering part is yet to come. One day they drive out to the country, which is a place where Dick and Jane's grandparents are kept. They do not live with the family and they are so glad to see Dick and Jane that one is certain that they have been ostracized from the rest of the family for some terrible reason. The old people live on something called a "farm," which is a place where many strange animals are kept: a peculiar beast called a "cow", some odd-looking birds called "chickens," and a "horse," which looks like a deformed moose . . .

So it is not surprising that 60 per cent of the native youngsters never reach the eighth grade.

Bilingual Schooling in the United States, (Washington, D.C.: Office of Education, 1972), p. 72.

GOALS: To aid students in understanding

1. the special needs of bilingual and English-as-a-second-language (ESL) students and the origins of bilingual education in the United States.

2. the linguistic influences in second language teaching and the linguistic differences between several languages and English.

3. the most appropriate methods of diagnosing the reading ability of bilingual and second language speakers.

4. different methodologies of instruction in teaching reading in the native language as well as reading in English.

5. appropriate methods of evaluating the effectiveness of materials for bilingual and ESL students.

Before we begin to discuss the enormously complex task of teaching reading to bilingual and ESL speakers, it is important to present the organization we will follow in this chapter. It will be divided into five major sections:

1. Essential background information for understanding bilingualism
2. Linguistic background information concerning bilingual and ESL Teaching
3. Diagnosis
4. Instruction
5. Evaluation

Teachers of children whose native language is not English need to study the current research on bilingual and second language development, carefully analyzing the contrasting elements of each language and the current research on how to teach these children to read. It probably comes as no great surprise that a very high percentage of non-English speakers never graduate from high school. Although some of the causes of these failures are not language or culture-related, the bulk of them are. Many well-intentioned teachers have taken incorrect steps with bilingual and second language speakers and, inadvertently, have frustrated them to the point of total withdrawal. However, it is not our intention to dwell on horror stories of the past; it is our intention to present a concise body of information about bilingual and English-as-a-second-language students that will help you to teach them to read.

Essential Background Information

Even though it may seem terribly obvious, it is important to underscore the fact that bilingual children are *not* disadvantaged. In fact, they have the privilege of two languages. We, as teachers, have to deal with this abundance when we are teaching reading. Sometimes the situation will call for instruction in the native language, sometimes in English, and sometimes in both languages. Obviously, this instruction will be limited by the teacher's capabilities. The same situation holds for the child whose native language is not English and who is learning English. This child is not disadvantaged; with proper teaching he soon will be able to communicate in two languages. Again, the capabilities of the teachers and the specific situation will dictate the language to be used in reading instruction.

Special Needs of the Bilingual and ESL Student

The bilingual child often encounters difficulty in reading materials written in English. These difficulties arise because he is exposed to a life style and language unlike his own. Frequently, he has special needs in the following areas: ethnic heritage, self concept, and language.

Ethnic Heritage. Zintz (1970) aptly explains some cultural interference problems that teachers and students may experience.

> Too many teachers are inadequately prepared to understand or accept these dissimilar cultural values. Teachers come from homes where the drive for success and achievement has been internalized early, where "work for work's sake" is rewarded, and where time and energy are spent building for the future. Many children come to the classroom with a set of values and background of experiences radically different from that of the average American child. To teach these children successfully, the teacher must be cognizant of these differences and must above all else seek to understand without disparagement those ideas, values, and practices different from his own. (p. 326)

Ching contends that three areas in cultural values need special attention by the teacher of the bilingual child: level of aspiration, often a unique concept for many bilingual children; value orientation, often in direct conflict with the teacher's; and socialization, a concept that varies extensively across cultures.

Self-Concept. Perhaps the most important characteristic of any good teacher is his or her ability to accept each child without prejudice or preconception. Children quickly and thoroughly sense rejection by a teacher. In the case of the bilingual child, the teacher must be quick to accept the child's language because it is the language of his home. Language and self-concept are so closely inter-twined that a child can be made to feel foolish and worthless when his "accent" or dialect is ridiculed by his teacher or peers. Trust and confidence between the teacher and the child must precede linguistic corrections.

Language. Bilingual children need to learn to speak English before they can read English. Obviously, this statement needs qualification. Adults who can read their native language often read English before speaking it. But the young child who does not read his native language probably needs to learn to speak English and to hear English spoken before he can read it or write it.

There are four linguistic "categories" in which bilingual children may need instruction:

a. Experiential-conceptual-informational background. Children often need experiences in English to tap their conceptual knowledge. A child from a farm may find it difficult to read about a bazaar because he has never experienced such an event.

b. Auditory discrimination. Children from language backgrounds other than English will possess a phonemic system which varies considerably from the English phonemic system; for example, Spanish-speaking children often have difficulty discriminating between these minimal pairs:

hit	ship	beat
↕	↕	↕
heat	sheep	bit

Contrastive analysis of several languages and English will be presented later in this chapter.

c. Vocabulary. There are several factors that teachers of bilingual children must take into consideration when teaching vocabulary. First, the child may have an English word for a phenomenon that is culturally determined. This meaning may not be shared by native English speakers. Second, there are many words in other languages which sound like English words, but have different meanings in the first language than they do in English. These words are called *false cognates*; some examples in Spanish are:

liberia   bookstore, not library

chanza   joke, not chance

d. Syntax. Many languages of the world do not have the same syntactic structure as English. The bilingual child needs time and practice to acquire second syntactic structures. Possible difficulties may include:

Reversed/inverted word order:	The white house
	La casa blanca
	I don't know where the boat is.
	I don't know where is the boat.

Copula confusion:	Today he working downtown.
Pluralization:	My foots are sore.
Comparison:	She is more big.
Possession:	The pen of Jim is black.

Differences Among Bilingual Students

To suggest that there is one route, one reading methodology for all bilingual and ESL students is utter folly. The complexity of the situation is often overwhelming for the new teacher. However, the following matrix may help us to understand some of the differences among bilingual and ESL children with regard to their ability to read and write. There are five different combinations represented in the following matrix:

	Student 1	Student 2	Student 3	Student 4	Student 5
SPEAKS	Spanish —	Spanish English	Spanish —	Spanish English	Spanish English
READS	— —	— —	Spanish —	— English	Spanish English

You will note that students 3, 4 and 5 have no problem *per se* because each of them speaks and reads at least one language. Teaching student 3 to read in English or student 4 to read in Spanish depends upon several factors: age, the child's progress in English at the present time, and the need for reading in a second language. The following is an example of a prescriptive approach for teaching each of these students.

Student No. 1. Teach oral English before reading instruction in either language. Begin reading instruction in Spanish.*

Student No. 2. Begin reading instruction in one of the two languages, depending on the following factors:

    a. Student preference
    b. Local expertise
    c. Age
    d. Cultural factors
    e. Family preference

Student No. 3. Begin oral instruction in English. Begin reading instruction in English.

Student No. 4. Begin reading instruction in Spanish (if desired by the student).

Student No. 5. Continue. You are doing an excellent job.

Bilingual Education Terminology

There is terminology used in the field of bilingual and second language education that may not be totally familiar to you. We will define some of these terms which may help you to understand the role of bilingual education in your school.

*Depends on students' concerns and parent's concerns.

Teacher Training Terminology

1. Bilingual education: Teachers are trained to teach in a bilingual setting where the students are often taught in two languages in the course of the day.
2. TESOL or TESL: Teaching English to Speakers of Other Languages; Teaching English as a Second Language. This training usually takes place within the United States.
3. TEFL: Teaching English as a foreign language. This training usually takes place outside of the United States.
4. You will often hear the expressions ESL and EFL; these refer to the field of English as a second language and English as a foreign language. ESL is often a component of a bilingual program, whereas EFL would never be used as a component of a bilingual program in the United States.

General Bilingual Terminology

1. *Bilingualism* is the ability to function in a second language in addition to one's home language.
2. *Biculturalism* is the ability to behave on occasion according to selected patterns of culture other than one's own.
3. *Bilingual schooling* is the particular organizational scheme of instruction which is used to mediate curricula in the home language and in a second language.
4. *Bilingual education* is a process by which the learning experiences provided in the home and other educational and societal institutions enable a person to fulfill total self-development as well as to function in a second language in addition to the home language.
5. *Bilingual/bicultural education* is a process of total self-development by which a person learns and reinforces his or her own language and culture and also acquires the ability to function in a second language.

Program Models Terminology

In establishing a bilingual education program, four different types of programs have been used in the United States.

1. Monoliterate program
   Goals: To develop English literacy and literacy in the native language as a link between home and school.
2. Partial bilingual/dual medium differential maintenance program.
   Goals: To develop a language and cultural maintenance. Native language skills are cultivated in all areas except the technical sciences and math.
3. Transitional bilingual program
   Goals: To assist the child in adapting to school and to progress on a par with his peers in all subject areas while learning English.
4. Full bilingual program
   Goals: To develop language competency in the native language, as well as in the second language in every subject area.

The History of Title VII

Bilingual education was officially sanctioned by the government of the United States with the enactment of Title VII in 1967. A brief description of this history is presented here to acquaint you with the original mechanisms of bilingual education.

A government analysis of the educational achievement of Mexican-American children in the Southwest (*The Unfinished Education: Outcome for Minorities in Five Southwestern States*, 1972) revealed that in Texas, Arizona, Colorado, California, and New Mexico an average of 8.1 years of schooling had been completed by Chicano (Mexican–American) children who were fourteen years of age or older. Julian Zamora (*The Educational Status of a Minority*, 1968) tried with little success to call the educational situation of the Chicano child to public consciousness. However, the situation was ignored and little credence was given to his findings until the United States Government conducted its own analysis of the 1970 census.

In 1966 the National Education Association (NEA) held a conference that focused on the needs of the Spanish-speaking child in the Southwest. As a result of this meeting, the NEA document, *The Invisible Minority*, which recommended bilingual education, was published. The document stimulated a series of conferences in 1967. Participants included local and state educators, and federal and state legislators. As a result of these conferences, participants supported the concept of bilingual education as a major responsibility of the federal government in partnership with the states.

During the conferences, in January 1967, Senator Yarborough (D-Texas) introduced an amendment to the existing (ESEA) Elementary and Secondary Education Act that provided for the creation of bilingual education programs. Because much of Yarborough's constituancy was Spanish speaking, his amendment provided for only the Spanish-surnamed populace. Senator Yarborough, committed to the passage of the legislation, lobbied by heading a special subcommittee on bilingual education. Meetings of this special subcommittee were held throughout the country.

During these early years, the Office of Education was reluctant to accept the concept of bilingual education. Rather, OE policy insisted that the educational problems of the bilingual child could be eliminated through an increase in remedial education programs: Title I and Title III services. ESL programs and reading remediation programs did not correct the basic literacy problems of students who were not native speakers of English.

On July 1, 1967, President Johnson established the Mexican-Affairs Unit as an in-house lobby for Mexican-Americans. This action by the president marked the first governmental commitment to bilingual education. As the Senate hearings progressed, the position of the Office of Education began to change. Other legislators began to introduce similar bills. R. Hawkins and J. Roybal of California proposed a bill that included French speakers, and J. Scheur of New York rewrote Yarborough's bill to include all non-English-speaking children.

Scheur's revision included provisions for teacher-training, materials-development, and demonstration programs. It was this amended bill, HR 13102, which became Title VII, the Bilingual Education Act in January 1968.

Linguistic Background Information
Concerning Bilingual and ESL Teaching

Because reading is a linguistic process, it seems important to discuss several aspects of language that will be helpful for teachers of bilingual children.

Linguistic Influences on Second Language Teaching

The first topic to be considered in this section is an examination of the linguistic influences on instruction in a second language. Effective instruction has changed considerably with the current findings of linguistic research.

The history of second language teaching reflects changes in linguistic theory about the nature of language. Fifty years ago grammarians believed that language consisted of a set of rules that prescribed a best way to form sentences. Dialect differences were viewed only as aberrations from standard English. In the past, second language teachers emphasized both the learning of formal rules about the language to be learned and the memorization of individual lexical items. These were usually studied without the benefit of context. Teachers often taught the formal written language, and they used the students' native language as the language of instruction.

Structural linguists like Leonard Bloomfield rejected the ideas of the traditional grammarians who believed language was a set of speech habits acquired through a series of conditional responses. They eliminated standards of good and bad and proper and improper. They did not consider classroom English superior to nonstandard dialects, and the only criterion for judgment regarding the correctness or incorrectness of an utterance was a native speakers' judgment. Psycholinguists emphasized that children learned language by imitating what they heard. Incorrect utterances and incorrect pronunciation were self-corrected when children failed to effect communication.

Second-language teachers who were influenced by these theories began teaching oral language through patterns of mimicry and memorization. They rejected the notion of teaching the grammatical rules about language; they emphasized phonology and the acquisition of nativelike pronunciation by language learners. The assumption of this approach was that in memorizing enough samples of natural speech, the learner would be able to make proper use of them when the appropriate context arose. Although this approach failed to produce bilinguals, it demonstrated that learners could perfect their accent in a second language even if they learned it after childhood.

The influence of a third group, transformational/generative grammarians, has been most significant. By stressing the unique ability of all children to generate sentences in their native language that they have neither imitated nor memorized, these linguists have changed many of the objectives of second-language teachers. Instead of emphasizing either reading or speaking exclusively, the second-language teacher explores many dimensions of language with the students. The key is to create meaningful contexts that stimulate communication in the new language. Although reading is not to be ignored, in this approach, it has been assumed that one cannot, in the early stages, read what one cannot produce orally. As one moves to a more advanced level in the new language, reading reinforces language and develops it through exposure to new vocabulary, syntactic structures, and cultural contexts.

What the Teacher of Reading Needs to Know About Other Languages

Children from each language group have specific problems with learning to read in English. The second topic to be covered in linguistic background information is the difference between several selected languages and English. We will present some possible sources of difficulty for the second language child, as well as many insights into the contrasts between the child's language and English.

The languages presented here have been randomly selected: Spanish, Chinese, Portuguese, Hebrew, and Sign. You may have the opportunity to work with children whose other language is not one of the languages presented. If this is the case, it is important for you to research the language of your child in order to understand some basic principles of its sound system and syntactic system. This is crucial in order to help your children learn to read.

Spanish

Spanish is the second most frequently spoken language in the United States. It is possible that you will eventually work with a Spanish-speaking child. In the next few pages, you will find information useful for teaching a Spanish-speaking child to read English.

The following rules are presented to introduce you to the phonological and grammatical variations between Spanish and English:

1. Spanish–speaking children will have difficulty pronouncing the following vowels:

i /sit/   ae /cat/   /u/ pull

2. Spanish does not rely on voiced (sit–hit) or voiceless (buzz–bus) sounds for specific contrasting meanings.

3. The speaker of Spanish eliminates or replaces the following sounds in his language:

/v/ voice   /θ/ then   /z/ zone   /j/ juice

4. Words ending in /r/ plus the consonants /d/, /l/, /p/, /s/, /t/ are pronounced by the Spanish speaker without the final consonant.

5. The Spanish language is devoid of the sound of the /s/ blend.

6. The consonant sounds of /t/, /p/, /k/, /f/, /m/, /n/, /l/ do not occur in the Spanish language.

7. The following grammatical differences exist between the two languages:

	English	Spanish
Subject Predicate	The dog sleeps.	The dogs sleeps.
Verb tense	He needed help yesterday.	He need help yesterday.
Negatives	I am not going home.	I no go home.
Omission of noun determiners	He is a dancer.	He is dancer.
Omission of pronouns	She is a doctor.	Is doctor.
Objective ordering	The green dress is beautiful.	The dress green is beautiful.
Comparisons	It is bigger.	Is more big.

The following chart lists comparisons of the pronunciation of certain phonemes in Spanish and English.

SOUNDS OF SPANISH* AND ENGLISH

Phoneme	Initial		Medial	Final
f	(Sp.)	Fuerte	zaFa	—
	(Eng.)	Fine	saFer	LeaF saFe
s	(Sp.)	Seinto	meSa	veS
	(Eng.)	Some	faCing	priCe
p	(Sp.)	Paso	taPa	—
	(Eng.)	Pen	taPer	floP
d	(SP.)	Donde	toDo	—
	(Eng.)	Done	toDay	carD

*Spanish words generally end in l, r, n, s, o, a, o and a. Words in Spanish rarely end in p, t, b, g, f, z.

The following chart lists some sounds in English that are not present in Spanish:

p	point	s	pleasure, zoo	h	hear
t	take	v	vine vote	k	car
k	cock	r	rode	y	yet
j	judge	tt	cotton	wh	what
s	shoe				

This information is useful for you, as a teacher of reading, because you will be able to understand the difficulty which a Spanish-speaking child may encounter when he is trying to read English words which contain these sounds.

Spanish-speaking children may encounter these problems when learning to speak and read English:

PROBLEMS IN THE PRONUNCIATION OF VOWEL SOUNDS

Sound	Example	Possible Error
1. long e	leave, feel	live, fill
2. short i	live, fill	leave, feel
3. long a	mate, bait	met, bet
4. short e	met, bet	make, bait
5. short a	hat, cat	hot, cot
6. short o	hot, cot	hat, cat
7. long o	coal, hole	call, hall

PROBLEMS IN THE PRONUNCIATION OF CONSONANTS/BLENDS IN INITIAL, MIDDLE, AND FINAL POSITION

Sound	Example	Possible Error
1. th	thin, then, path	sin, den, pass
2. sh	shoe, show, wash	sue, choe, bus or bush
3. ch	chew, chop, witch	choe or jew, cash, wish
4. b	bin, beer, tab, rabbit	pin, pear, tap, rapid
5. g	goat, wing	coat, wink, duck
6. w	way, wash	gway, gwash (with more proficiency pronounced gwash or watch)
7. y	yellow, yale	jello, jail
8. v	vote, vail	best, bail

Chinese

The following is a brief overview of selected variations between English and Chinese. This introduction may be useful if you are asked to teach Chinese students.

There are many dialects of Chinese. Mandarin, which is spoken by approximately 70 per cent of the Chinese people, is the national dialect in the People's Republic and Taiwan. Cantonese, another major dialect, is spoken by most of the Chinese families that come to the United States from Hong Kong, Kowloon, or Macao. The Cantonese dialect is the one that is discussed below.

1. The Chinese language does not have as many vowels as English, therefore, a Chinese child learning to speak English may have difficulty with these vowel sounds:

> ay / buy   iy / meat   ey / gait

2. Chinese speakers seldom use consonants in final positions.
3. There is not a direct correspondence between English and Chinese sounds:

> ri<u>ch</u>   <u>sh</u>ed

4. Many Chinese dialects are devoid of the sounds of consonant clusters:

> ca<u>lf</u>   <u>sw</u>i<u>sh</u>

5. Some Chinese dialects do not contain consonant clusters for pluralization:

> calves   swishes

6. Chinese speakers may indicate plurals through the use of numerical designations or auxiliary words:

> three dog = three dogs

7. The Chinese speaker expresses grammatical relationships by auxiliary words and word order:

> She gave me two cars.   (English)
> Yesterday she give I two cars.   (Chinese)

8. Chinese speakers use tone or pitch to distinguish word meanings while speakers of English combine pitch and intonation to present sentence meaning.
9. The Chinese speaker may exclude subjects or predicates if the context is understandable:

> <u>English</u>   <u>Chinese</u>
> It is raining.   It rains.
> The car is shiny.   Car shiny.

10. English speakers invert the noun and verb forms when asking questions. The Chinese speaker does not follow this inversion but instead adds empty words *ma* or *la* to the sentence:

> <u>English</u>   <u>Chinese</u>
> Are you happy?   You are happy ma?

11. Chinese speakers use a time word or phrase to indicate the tense of a verb:

She go "jaw." translates "She went."

In Chinese, there are as many as one hundred spoken dialects, but only one writing system.

Tonal Language. In Mandarin Chinese there are four tones, which can be represented in the following way:

Pluralization.   The *plural concept* in English is developed in the following way:

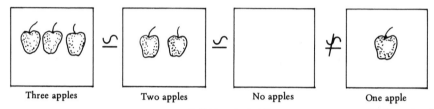

Three apples   Two apples   No apples   One apple

In Chinese, pluralization is similar to the following:

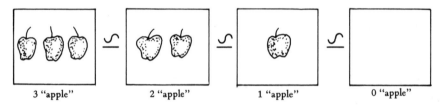

3 "apple"   2 "apple"   1 "apple"   0 "apple"

Portuguese

The sound contrasts of Portuguese and English are presented in the following chart. This information will assist you if you are called upon to teach Portuguese children to read.

Phoneme	Portuguese Example	English Example
/i/	cita	see
/i/	interno	it
/ai/	faixa	fine
/ei/	peito	cake
/e/	Alberto	bet
/e/	pensao	pan
/u/	tu	duty
/u/	bula	boot
/U/	fulano	foot
/ou/	outro	boat
/a/	fado	father
/a/	dona	alone
/au/	auto	about

PORTUGUESE-ENGLISH CONTRASTIVE STRUCTURE PATTERNS

	Structure	Portuguese Examples	Possible Error in English
1.	Negative with <u>do</u>, <u>does</u>, <u>did</u>: John did not go out.	João não saiu	John no go out
2.	Negative imperative: Don't speak.	Não fales	No speak
3.	Present tense third person "s" Mary likes John.	Maria gosta do João	Mary like John
4.	Position of adjectives: The red car.	O carro vermelho	The car red
5.	Nonagreement of adjectives: The small cars.	Os carros pequenos	The car smalls
6.	Position of adverb of time: I went to the movie yesterday.	Ontem, fui para o cinema	Yesterday I went to the movie.
7.	To be to express: age: I am 25 years old. hunger: I am hungry. sleep: I am sleepy. fear: I am afraid.	Tehno 25 anos Tenho fome Tenho sono Tehno medo	I have 25 years I have hunger I have sleep I have fear
8.	The ed past tense ending: Mary wanted to go out yesterday.	Ontem, Maria queria sair	Yesterday Mary want to go out.
9.	It to start a sentence: It is Sunday.	E domingo	Is Sunday
10.	Use of indefinite article: He is a teacher.	E professor	He is teacher
11.	Use of subject pronoun: He can eat.	pode comer	Can eat

Hebrew

The phonological and graphemic system of Hebrew is presented in the following chart. This information will help you to prepare an appropriate beginning reading program in English if you are asked to teach Hebrew-speaking children.

Forms			Name of Grapheme	Graphemic Equivalent in Roman Alphabet	Phonemic Equivalent in English	Cursive Grapheme
	Archaic Grapheme	*Printed Grapheme*				
Consonants	𐤀	א	aleph		glottal	א
	𐤁	בּ ב	bet	b	b, v	בּ, ב
	𐤂	ג	gimel	g	g	ג
	𐤃	ד	dalet	d	d	ד
	𐤄	ה	hey	h	h	ה
	𐤅	ו	vav	v	v	ו
	𐤆	ז	zayin	z	z	ז
	𐤇	ח	het	h	ch (loch)	ח
	𐤈	ט	tet	t	t	ט
	𐤉	י	yed	y	y	י
*used only as	𐤊	כּ כ ך*	kaf	k, h	k (hot)	כ
final letter of	𐤋	ל	lamed	l	l	ל
word	𐤌	*ם מ	mem	m	m	ם*, מ
	𐤍	נ ן*	nun	n	n	ן*, נ
**ayin has two	𐤎	ס	samekh	s	s (hard)	ס
sounds: a weaker	𐤏	ע	ayin		**	ע
general, a Parisian	𐤐	.פּ פ ף*	pey	ph, p	p, f	*ף, פּ
"r"; in modern	𐤑	צ ץ*	toade	ts	s (hiss)	*ץ, צ
pronunciation it is	𐤒	ק	g ef	K (palatal)		ק
not distinguished	𐤓	ר	resh	r	r (palatal)	ר
from alpha.	W	שׁ שׂ	s, in, shin	s, sh	s, sh	שׁ, שׂ
	X	ת	tav	t	t	תּ, ת
	Vowel	(hee) iy ִי	(say) ey ֵי	(eh) e ֶי	(her) a	(aw) o
					(ch) ow וֹ	(w) v וּ

The following is an overview of some syntactic problems that Israelis may encounter when they are learning to read in English:

1. Some verbs that exist in Hebrew as single-word verbs are idiomatic phrases in English:

   to catch a cold, to take a shower, to make friends

2. Hebrew verb forms are inflected for tense, number, and person. In English, one has to examine auxiliaries. Hebrew has no auxiliaries, and a variety of forms does not exist:

   I gave, I was giving, I was given, I give

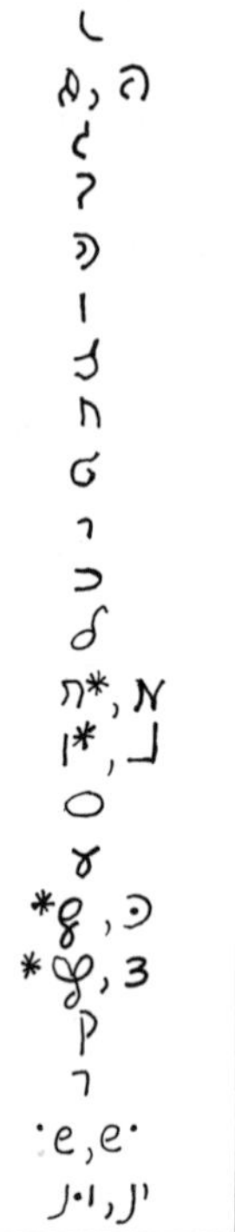

3. Hebrew has only three basic tenses (past, present, future).

4. Adjectives follow the noun in Hebrew—except for numbers:

> The beautiful, new, white, home is expressed as The home, the beautiful, the new, and the white.

5. There is an absence of gender markers in English nouns such as teacher, doctor, lawyer, student, friend. Hebrew nouns are always marked for gender.

Sign Language

Many deaf adults in the United States read at the fourth-grade level and many of them communicate in Sign Language. They can be classified as a linguistic minority. Speakers of Sign Language encounter many of the same problems as bilingual students. In order to help deaf students learn to read in English, you will have to learn some facts about the structure of Sign Language. A very brief overview of selected features of Sign Language is presented below:

Features of Sign Language

1. There are three basic hand shapes which are used when making signs:
    1. Extended
    2. Closed
    3. Y hand shape
2. There are six possible motion features in sign language:
    1. Two hands going in same direction, e.g. follow
    2. Twist: e.g. apple
    3. Alternating, one hand is moving and one hand remains still, e.g. name
    4. Through space: e.g. still
    5. Alternating: e.g. explain
    6. Circular: e.g. around
3. Signs can be made in the following physical ways:
    1. on the face
    2. on the arms
    3. on the hands
4. All signs are made in front of the body.

There is a great deal of research being conducted at the present time in the field of Sign Language. At this point, the most appropriate method of reading instruction for deaf students is still being debated. The rationale for including Sign Language in this Contrastive Analysis section is to expose you to the phenomenon of Sign as a language, and to expose you to the concept of the deaf child as a bilingual student who may experience great difficulty learning their second language, English.

This brief presentation of language differences was intended only as an introduction to the multiple factors which you will need to investigate and understand when you are teaching a bilingual child to read. Although the task seems complex, it is not an impossibility. It is encouraging to note that many Americans are competent readers and speakers of two different languages. With your help, your non-English speakers will soon be reading in English.

Diagnosis

In this section of the chapter, you will be introduced to tests and instruments that are useful for diagnosing student's difficulties and evaluating student progress. It should be pointed out immediately that most norm reference reading tests in English have been standardized on native English-speaking populations. The scores bilingual and second language students receive on these tests must be interpreted with extreme caution and sensitivity.

Where Do I Begin?

The first question you will ask when you are working in English with a second-language child is "How much English does the child know?"

In asking this question you are beginning the process of teaching a bilingual or ESL student to read. The first issue is to assess the child's proficiency in English. It should be emphasized that children have different proficiencies within their language ability. In most cases it may be advantageous for you, as the teacher, to conduct a structured, but informal, nonthreatening interview with the child in order to determine his proficiency and ease in speaking English.

Most tests which have been designed to assess language dominance have ignored the fact that children have many variations in their language abilities. Sometimes their native language is their dominant, preferred language for a particular task, but sometimes it is not. This seems eminently logical because many adults experience the same phenomenon; that is, a Spanish-speaking adult who studies Advanced Statistics in England may prefer to use English when he is discussing statistics. Therefore, before globally assessing a child's language dominance, we need to ask: What is the specific task which the child is being asked to perform? and What is the language of the person to whom the child will speak during the instructional period? The answers to these questions will provide you with a great deal of useful information which will enable you to begin your instructional program.

In determining language proficiency you will want to extract information about several aspects of language so that you can build a program for each student. An example of such a test which gathers information about the reading, writing, speaking and listening skills of the bilingual child is the Maryville Test which is administered in English and Spanish. We have included the reading section of the test. A similar format could be used as the basis for the construction of an instrument for children from language backgrounds other than Spanish.

The Maryville Test

Direction to the Examiner

1. The child should be tested on two separate occasions by separate examiners, unless the teacher is bilingual in English and in the child's native language.
2. The series of questions that follows may be scored as you ask each question.
3. Be certain that you and the pupil are seated in a quiet corner, free from distraction.
4. Make every effort to gain the child's complete attention and tell him that you are going to ask each question only once.
5. Speak in a conversational tone; do not hurry.
6. Do not give emphasis to any of the material that would distort it for the child.
7. Follow the specific instructions for each set of questions.

Administration

Follow the instruction given for each separate page. Use *only* the language of the test. Do not mix Spanish and English.

Scoring

Credit one point for each correct response on each of the four language sections: listening, speaking, reading, and writing.

Test of Reading

Ask the pupil to read the following items. Score correct only an item that is read completely (or letters, characters, symbols of vernacular). Discontinue after three consecutive failures.

1. R. W. X. O. A
2. Me
3. My father
4. Mother and father

Write from dictation:

6. You
7. Did
8. Hands
9. Touch
10. Special

Prueba de Lectura

Digale a los alumnos que lean to siquiente. Califique correcto solamente si el articulo es lendo completamente (o las letras, caracteres, simbolos vernaculos). Descontinuelo despues de tres errores consecutivos.

1. R, W, X, O, A
2. Yo
3. Mi papá
4. Mi mamá y mi papá
5. En el segundo piso de mis casa.
6. El vecindario es bonito.
7. Tengo un amigo muy especial.
8. Antes de que viviera aquí, vivia en Sacremento.
9. Cuando crezca me gustaria ser médico o ser maestro.
10. Deseo que pudiera ayudar a mi mamá, mi papá, mis hermanas, mis hermanos y todos en el mundo entero.

In addition to the Marysville Test of Language Dominance, there are several other tests available for assessing the language proficiency of the bilingual child:

1. Bilingual Syntax Measure, 1973 (grades K–2)
   Harcourt Brace Jovanovich, Inc.
   Testing Department
   757 Third Ave.
   New York, NY 10017
2. Dos Amigos Verbal Language Scales, 1974 (grades 1–4)
   Academic Therapy Publications
   1539 Fourth St.
   San Rafael, CA 94901
3. James Language Dominance Test, 1974 (grades K–1)
   Learning Concepts
   Speech Division
   2501 N. Lamar
   Austin, TX 78705
4. Spanish-English Language Dominance Assessment, 1972 (grades 1–2)
   Professor Bernard Spolsky
   The University of New Mexico
   1805 Roma NE
   Albuquerque, NM 87106

Less Formal Diagnosis of English Language Skills. To date, reliable instruments for measuring the English language competence and performance of nonnative speakers have not been created. Yet, informal diagnosis is vital if teachers are to individualize their objectives to meet the needs of their students. Most traditional diagnostic instruments fail to provide teachers with the specific information necessary to understand the skills a child really lacks.

Some reading selections on these tests reflect the native speakers' knowledge of English syntax, vocabulary, and idioms within specific cultural contexts that are well developed in the young child. Oral selections on these tests can be problematic because non-native speakers may tend to overconcentrate on pronunciation at the expense of comprehension. Silent reading selections tested by oral questioning sometimes reflect a student's ability to understand questions rather than the context of the reading selection. Although word-attack skills tests do provide useful information about the non-native speaker's ability to "break the code," they do not provide information about the student's knowledge of vocabulary.

An evaluation of bilingual children's skills must include assessment of speaking, listening, reading, and writing. Within each of these skills categories, one must be concerned with the following question: How advanced are the student's skills in English? Hirsch's (1976) informal diagnostic assessment provides us with some useful guidelines in assessing a bilingual student's level of English proficiency.

1. *SPEAKING*—Testing should be done individually and the teacher should tape record the students' utterances. Several methods of eliciting free speech are available: Picture description, retelling a story the student has read in his native language, telling about specific things they used to do in their native country, relating differences in lifestyle, telling about their trip to the United States, for example, their first impression of their new school. The sample should be taped and analyzed for syntax, vocabulary, and pronunciations.

2. *LISTENING*—Student should listen to sample conversations of natural speech between two or more native speakers, recordings of simple stories, excerpts from possible class lectures at a more advanced level, or selections from the news. Questions should be asked orally and students should be able to circle the number of the correct response on a paper. Short answers, multiple choice, or true/false questions are most desirable. Selections, as well as questions, should be repeated and instructions should be given clearly and in the native language if possible.

3. *WRITING*—Writing samples can be either structured or unstructured. Students can be asked to complete sentences, fill in punctuation. This can be either open ended or multiple choice. Various tense sequences, pronominal references, can be elicited in this way. Student might be asked to write freely on a given topic suitable to age and ability and this sample can be looked at for overall communication of main idea, as well as specific writing skills.

4. *READING*—Students should be asked to read selections silently. For most students, selections from grade ESL texts are appropriate. Teachers may want to write their own selections or take advanced selections from other sources. The selections should not be on topics that students could answer on the basis of general knowledge. Students should be given as much time as they need to answer questions and to read the selections but the time should be noted. Questions should be read by the student and should be objective in nature.

Scoring and Record Keeping. Score the student's response and write comments in the appropriate box, using the guidelines which are presented below:

	Advanced		Intermediate		Beginner	
	Score		*Score*		*Score*	
Speaking						
Listening						
Writing						
Reading						

Speaking

Advanced. The student is able to express himself appropriately, using complex structures similar to those used by a native speaker of the same age. There is little syntactic interference from the native language. Advanced students use sophisticated vocabulary and are not limited in most subject areas. English pronunciation is good, and the student has few problems with stress, intonation, and overall articulation.

Intermediate. The student is able to express himself in English orally, but may be frustrated on occasion and be unsure about proper choice of words. Although communication is not seriously impeded by poor syntax some misunderstandings may occur; some native language interference is present and the student avoids using structures that really are too advanced. Some errors in word order are made, especially in negative and interogative forms, and some misuse of irregular past tense verbs may be present. Accent does not interfere with communication but is clearly non-native in areas of stress and intonation. Specific phonemes may pose a particular problem for some students at this level.

Beginner. The student often is unable to answer questions accurately because of his lack of experience with English vocabulary and idiomatic expression. Utterances are limited to the present tense. The student omits third person singular inflected forms, and, in general, communication is limited. Accent is strong and acts as a deterrent to clear communication.

Listening

Advanced. The student can comprehend English conversation, as well as television and radio broadcasts. Content classes such as history, math, or science do not cause problems on the basis of listening comprehension. The student may miss some details of a conversation when the speakers are speaking very rapidly or using advanced idiomatic expression.

Intermediate. The student comprehends a speaker in face-to-face conversations when the speaker has slowed down deliberately and altered his use of vocabulary and structures. Lectures, class discussions, and television and radio broadcasts may proceed too quickly, and the student will miss many important details.

Beginners. The student understands only the simplest questions and instructions addressed specifically to him. He lacks experience in listening to spoken English.

Writing

Advanced. The student is able to express his thoughts well in written English without frustration. Errors in vocabulary, syntax, spelling, and punctuation are no greater than one would expect to see in work of a native speaker of the same age.

Intermediate. Errors in syntax, spelling, and vocabulary produce writing that is clearly nonnativelike. Some communication is possible, though, especially if the student limits himself to simple tenses, short sentences, and nonidiomatic expressions.

Beginners. The student may or may not be familiar with the alphabet. His writing ability is limited to answering simple questions in one or two words. Lack of familiarity with spelling and conventions of punctuation make writing very difficult, even for the student with some oral ability.

Reading

Advanced. The student is most likely fluent in reading his native language. His ability to read in English is almost as good as that of native speakers of the same age. Readers of this level are able to figure out words from context. Reading in content areas may be difficult if the tests are very technical, but the student has a strong enough background to do independent reading.

Intermediate. The student concentrates more on literal meaning than critical reading. He cannot usually figure out new words from their context and may have trouble decoding new words if they are long or irregular. Students read at a very slow rate and may or may not be fluent readers in their native language.

Beginners. Student is unable to decode even simple, high frequency English words.

It is important to remember that diagnosis is the first step in the reading instruction process. We should only diagnose students in order to give information that will be useful in establishing an effective instructional program. Bilingual students can become extremely frustrated by grueling testing sessions in English. We must be certain that the information to be gained outweighs the discomfort of the testing session.

The next question is the crucial one if we are to succeed at our task: "Now that I have the student diagnosed, what do I do?"

Instruction

The most useful place to begin to discuss an instructional program for each child is to reemphasize the fact that the child must be able to understand some English before he can begin reading. This leads us to the question: How do I teach ESL? You may quip, "Every teacher of reading has to become an expert in several fields." This is true, and although time limits us from becoming experts, we can become aware of the current issues in teaching ESL. If you find yourself in a situation where it is necessary for you to begin your reading program with ESL instruction, then you will want to feel competent to do so.

Scope and Sequence for ESL

The logical question "What should I teach first?" can be determined by examining the results of your diagnostic testing. After you have analyzed your student's proficiency in English, you may want to begin a structured, sequential program Most linguists will tell you that the order of introducing English grammatical structures does not matter. They will tell you that it is important to contrast each new structure with the previous structure that you taught. For example, if you have already taught present tense verbs and you want to teach past tense, you may introduce your lesson in the following way:

Margarita is eating fruit today. She is also eating a cookie. She eats very quickly.

Yesterday, I _____ fruit. I also _____ a cookie. But today I am <u>not eating</u> fruit because I don't have any to eat.

What <u>is</u> Margarita doing now?

What did I do yesterday?

Why can't I eat fruit today?

This approach is fairly easy to discuss but quite difficult to implement. In the next few pages, we will present a scope and sequence chart for ESL instruction that may help you to find an appropriate starting point and an effective order of instruction for each student.

SCOPE AND SEQUENCE CHART

BEGINNING LEVEL

Syntactic Structures

A. Declarative and question sentence structures.
  1. Word order of declaratives contrasted with different word order of questions with BE verbs. (They are leaving, Are they leaving?)
  2. Use of contracted forms of BE verbs (he's, they're, I'm) Use of pronouns with corresponding form of BE verb (she is, they are)
  3. Use of BE verbs to show action:
     (a) in progress
     (b) of repetitive nature
  4. Use of determiners (THE, A, AN)
  5. Affirmative and negative short answers to questions with BE verbs. (I'm going, He's not going.)

Articulation

A. Contrasted intonation contours of declarative sentences, questions, and short answers.
B. Stress and accent patterns of requests.
C. Articulation of contracted forms of BE with pronouns HE, SHE, WE, YOU, IT, THERE.
D. Articulation of the /S/, /Z/, and /-∂Z/ of third person singular verbs and plurals as in words like EATS, WINS, SMASHES, and contractions such as IT'S, THERE'S.
E. Unstressed forms of A, AN, THE.
F. Articulation of /k/, /g/, /n/. KICK, GO, SING.
G. Stress the accent patterns of compound words.
H. Articulation of /t/, /d/, and -ED endings as in FOOT, WOOD, HUNTED.

Syntactic Structures

B. Verbs other than BE.
   1. Word order for declaratives compared to order for questions with DO and DOES.
   2. Affirmative and negative short answers to questions with DO and DOES.
   3. -S forms of third person singular used with pronouns (he, she, it) and other singular nouns in declaratives, contrasted to plural nouns. (he run<u>s</u>, we run).
C. Expression of Time (tense).
   1. Use of BE in expressions of past tense in statements and questions. (I was walking, Were they singing?)
   2. Irregular verbs which form past tense without-ED (Use of vowel & consonant contrast).
   3. Formation of verbs other than BE to express past tense using regular rule (-ED).
      (a) Past tense forms and placement of verbs other than BE in declaratives and questions.
   4. Forms of short responses to questions asked in past tense (use of BE or DO appropriately.)
   5. Use of BE verbs + GOING TO to express future tense. (She is going to ride home, They are going to sing.)
D. Formation of questions with interrogative words or word order.
E. Negatives.
   1. Use and placement of NOT in declaratives (past, present, future) with verb BE.
   2. Use of NOT in questions with BE.
   3. Use of NOT in sentences (declarative and question) with DO and verbs toher than BE.
   4. Use of ANY, RARELY, SELDOM, FEW, etc.

Articulation

I. Articulation of /p/, and /b/ as in PAY, BOY.
J. Articulation of /f/ and /v/ as in CALF, MOVE.
K. Articulation of /θ/ and /ð/ - THIN, THOSE.
   (a) Contrasting /t/ with /θ/ - BOAT, BOTH.
   (b) Contrasting /d/ with /ð/ - DAY, THEY.
L. Articulation of /s/, /z/, /c/ and /j/ - MASH, PLEASURE, CHOOSE, FUDGE.
M. Articulation of /m/ and /n/ - MOON, NO.
N. Articulation of /l/ and /r/ - LOSE, READ.
O. Articulation of /w/ and /y/ - WOOD, YELLOW.
P. Articulation of front vowels.
   (a) /i/ and /I/ - SEAT, SIT
   (b) /e/ and /ɜ/ - SAY, PET
   (c) Contrast of /ɛ/ with /I/ - SET, SIT.
   (d) Contrast of /I/, /ɛ/, and /i/ - SIT, SET, SEAT
   (e) /æ/ - HAT
Q. Articulation of middle vowels.
   (a) /ə/ and /a/ - NUT, HOT
   (b) Contrast of /a/ with /æ/ - HOT, HAT
   (c) /ai/ - TIE
   (d) /ər/ - HURT
R. Articulation of glides and back vowels.
   (a) /u/ and /U/ - FOOD, FOOT
   (b) /aU/ - COW
   (c) /o/ and / / - Boat, BOUGHT
   (d) /oI/ - TOY

Syntactic Structures	Articulation

F. Frequency words.
  1. Different positions of frequency words with BE contrasted with positions with verbs other than BE (He sometimes walks, He is always late.)
  2. Use of EVER in question patterns; NEVER in declarative sentences.

INTERMEDIATE LEVEL

The following skills should be an extension of a solid foundation in beginning–level materials.

Syntactic structures	Articulation

A. Review of patterns introduced at beginning level.

B. Modification constructions: use of substitute words
  1. How OTHER and ANOTHER can be substituted for nouns, contrasted with their use as modifiers of nouns.
  2. Use of objective forms of personal pronouns in object position.

C. Structures in which ME, TO ME, and FOR ME are used with certain verbs.

D. Patterns of word order when expressing manner. John runs quickly.

E. Modals: Use of MUST, CAN, WILL, SHOULD, MAY, and MIGHT in appropriate place in sentence.

F. Techniques for connecting statements.
  1. AND. . .EITHER contrasted with AND. . .TOO.
  2. Use of BUT.

G. Structures with two-word verbs (verb + particle) CALL UP, PUT ON.
  1. Structures in which they are unseparated.
  2. Structures in which they are separated.

H. Patterns for answers to Why and How questions.

Articulation:

A. Articulation of consonant cluster. /sp/ as in SPECIAL.

B. Articulation of consonant cluster. /st/, /sk/, /sn/, /sm/, /sl/, and /sw/ as in STEP, SKIP, SNAP, SMELL.

C. Articulation of final consonant clusters. Consonant +/s/, consonant + /t/, consonant + /d/, as in CATS, DROPPED, FLAGS, USED.

D. Articulation of final consonant clusters. two consonants + /s/, as in HELPS.

E. Articulation of final consonant clusters. two consonants + /t/, as in JUMPED.

F. Intonation patterns used in comparisons.

Syntactic structures	Articulation

I. Special patterns using TO and FOR.
    1. FOR and TO + other words as modifiers following some terms of quality.
    2. Placement of VERY, TOO, ENOUGH.
    3. Patterns in which nouns or pronouns are used after certain action words.
J. IT or THERE as subject of the sentence.
K. —'S as a contraction and as a possessive marker.
L. Comparisons.
    1. Structures for comparisons with DIFFERENT FROM, SAME AS, LIKE, THE SAME. . . AS AS. . . AS.
    2. Patterns of comparison using -ER THAN and MORE THAN, OF THE. . .-EST, and THE MOST.

INTERMEDIATE-ADVANCED LEVEL

Syntactic structures	Articulation

A. Review structures introduced at earlier levels.
B. Word order pattern and use of relative clauses or embedded sentence to modify nouns.
    1. Words used as subject of the embedded sentence (THAT, WHICH, WHO, etc.).
    2. THAT and related words in other positions.
C. WHAT, WHEN, WHO, etc. in object position.
D. Embedded sentences of different statement pattern type used in object positions.
E. Patterns with HAVE and BE in the auxiliary.
    1. Present-perfect complete HAVE (HAS) + -ED/-EN form of verb.

A. Articulation of final consonant cluster: two consonants + /z/ as in HOLDS.
B. Articulation of final consonant cluster: two consonants + /d/ as in SOLVED.

Syntactic structures   Articulation

   2. BE + ing berb form
     (used with yet, anymore, still, etc.).
   3. HAVE + BEEN + -ing verb
     forms in continuous present-
     perfect structures.
   4. Using BE + -ED/-EN verb forms.
   5. Using BE with -ED/-EN and -ing
     in descriptions.
   6. Special cases:
     (a) BE + two-word verbs and
        -ing form.
     (b) Use of HAD in the above
        structures.

Special structural patterns:

A. Verb modification.
   1. WISH   (that) + declarative
      HOPE   sentence.
   2. TO omitted after certain verbs.
B. Conditionals.
   1. Patterns with SHOULD, MIGHT,
     COULD, MUST.
   2. Cause and effect sentence
     structures.
C. Object Structures and Modification.
   1. Use of -ing endings of verbs.
   2. Patterns for verbs followed by
     an object and one or more
     describing words, and/or an -ing
     form.
   3. Verbs followed by two nouns
     with the same reference.
   4. -ING endings used in subject
     position contrasted to their use
     at the beginning of sentences
     (referring to the subject).
D. Logical order of sentences in
   sequence.
   1. Ordering for sentences related
     by HOWEVER, THEREFORE,
     ALSO, BUT.
   2. Ordering for sentences related
     by terms of time or place (before,
     after that, then).

ADVANCED LEVEL

Syntactic structures

A. Review of all levels above.
B. Review of function words.
    1. Auxiliaries: WILL, MAY, CAN,
        COULD, SHOULD, MIGHT,
        WOULD, MUST, HAVE, BE,
        SHALL, DO.
    2. Preposition adverbs:
        (a) Frequently used: AT,
             BY, IN, INTO, FOR, FROM,
             WITH, TO, ON, OF, OFF.
        (b) Location
        (c) Direction
        (d) Time
        (e) Comparison
C. Conjuntion patterns with BUT
    and OR.
D. Other complement structures.
    1. believe
        want
        think   + declarative sentence.
        expect
    2. Use of appropriate comple-
        mentizer words in the above.

ARTICULATION - Advanced Level

Spelling vowel sounds:

Spelling vowel sounds:
    /I/ and /i/;
    /e/ and / /;
    /I/, / /, and /i/;
    / /, / /, and /a/;
    glides /aI/ and / r/;
    glides /aU/ and /oI/

Intonation and stress patterns used with comparisons, manner and time words, and prepositions.

Intonation patterns for modals: COULD, WOULD, MUST, SHOULD, etc.

Conjunction and intonation pattern with OR and BUT.

Words for degree and for generalizing.

Articulation of TO and TOO.

VOCABULARY DEVELOPMENT

Beginning Level

A basic flexible-content vocabulary should include items relevant to the students' everyday experiences, that is:

eating and cooking utensils
common foods
parts of the body
articles of clothing
furniture
telling time
numbers: cardinal, ordinal
family relationships

colors
name of occupations
days of the week
months of the year, seasons
common animals
various materials: wodd, plastic, etc.
holidays
most important geographic names
words used to ask directions

Pictures and/or objects should be used to explain all of the above.

In addition:

Several basic two-word verbs (verbs + particle) for example, PICK UP, WAIT FOR, HANG UP, GET UP, etc.

Concepts of directionality: IN FRONT OF, BEHIND, BEFORE, AFTER.

Countable and noncountable nouns: CUP as opposed to CEREAL.

Following simple directions

Simple synonyms, antonyms, especially adjectives and prepositions such as GOOD - BAD, ON - OFF.

Intermediate Level

Extension of vocabulary introduced abvove plus:

Shopping expressions

Further occupations and
   responsibilities

Health and health practices

Further synonyms and antonyms

Family names of more distant relatives

Government agencies

Clothing materials

Intermediate-Advanced Level

Daily living skills
   Purchasing suggestions
   Driving
   Traffic regulations
   Postal procedures
   Insurance procedures
Music, literature, the arts
Educational opportunities
Leisure-time activities
Travel
Government

Directions involving choice
Derivations
Structural analysis: prefixes, suffixes,
   hyphenation of words
Synonyms, antonyms, homonyms
   (more advanced)

Advanced Level

Study skills information—locating and organizing information, synthesis of information, and making cross-comparisons

Propaganda techniques—discerning fact and fiction

The human body and its actions
   Evening and morning activities

Special problems: Idiomatic expressions
   Multiple meanings of words

Advanced descriptive terminology
   Attributes of objects (size, shape)
   Attributes of people (including personality)

Buying and selling

Transportation and communication

Personal and professional contacts (job applications)

Further government interaction (law, courts, taxes)

Oral and written reports   (books, movies, trips)

Discussions on American history, geography, climate.

Writing

Beginning Level

In beginning English, writing is quite limited. It should be directly related to the student's understanding and use of vocabulary and structures in the class. At this level, the comma, period, question mark, and apostrophe should be taught in order to develop proper intonation. The use of capital letters at the beginning of sentences should be introduced.

The following is a suggested guide for alloting time for the teaching of language skills at this level: Listening—40 per cent; Speaking—40 per cent; Reading—15 percent; and Writing—5 per cent.

Intermediate Level

As in the beginning, writing should be a direct outgrowth of the student's mastery of the spoken work in class. Simple dictation and writing answers to questions generated by reading and conversation materials can be used as effective exercises.

Reading activities should include silent reading, group oral reading, and individual oral reading, with emphasis on the intonation patterns of language, such as rhythm and stress.

Proportions of time which might be spent in developing skills: Listening and speaking—45 per cent; Reading—35 per cent; Writing—20 per cent.

Intermediate-Advanced Level

At this stage, more time should be devoted to reading and writing. Advanced reading comprehension should be evaluated both orally and in written form, and should include knowledge of literal, interpretive, and critical levels of cognition.

Writing skills should be directly related to the needs of daily living as well as the more formal requirements of education. Reference and study skills should also be emphasized.

Suggested proportions of time: Listening and speaking—40 per cent; Reading—40 per cent; Writing—20 per cent.

Advanced Level

At this stage emphasis should be on the expansion of the material introduced at previous levels. The student should be encouraged to use his reading and writing skills to enable him to gain insight into all realms of our society.

Reading Instruction in the Native Language

All children bring to school many language skills. The task of the reading teacher is to help chidlren develop these skills further and teach them the visual appearance of the language that they already understand. Developmentally, all children learn to listen and to speak before learning to read and write. It is clear that oral language conveys meaning if the speaker and listener share the same set of oral symbols for objects and relationships in their experience. The reading teacher must remember that *oral language is the base of the reading process*, and until it is developed, reading seems a senseless, futile exercise for the child.

Many reading programs being developed for bilingual students take this fact into account. Children are first taught to read their native language while doing oral work in the second language. When the oral base in the second language is strong enough, reading is introduced in that language. As early as 1953, in a survey completed by the United Nations Task Force, the authors concluded that this was the most logical sequence of learning to read and write and cited studies showing that students who first learned to read in the vernacular made better progress even in the second language reading programs than did students who had spent the same length of time working only on second language reading.

Native Literacy Methodologies in Spanish. Thonis (1976) discusses some traditional methods used to teach reading in Spanish to Spanish-speaking students. These methods mirror many of the approaches used to teach reading in English The six most frequently used methods are:

1. *El methodo onomatopoeico.* This method aims at constant auditory associations of letters and sounds, based on children's experiences: for example, the vowel sound /i/ is the same sound as the squeal of the mouse—"iii."

2. *El methodo alfabetico.* Children are taught the names of letters of the alphabet. Instruction begins with vowel letters. One sound is joined to another: ma - no.

3. *El methodo fonico o fonetica.* This method emphasizes the sounds of the letters of the alphabet with little concern for the names of the letters.

4. *El methodo de palabras generadoras.* This is a whole-word method.

5. *El methodo global.* This is a method of teaching both reading and writing using whole words without doing any analysis of component elements, syllables, or letters.

6. *El methodo electico.* This is a method in which phonics and wholeword strategies are used.

Instruction in Reading English

A crucial question arises immediately: What is the best method for teaching reading in English to bilingual students? As we pointed out in the beginning of this chapter, no one program or methodology is foolproof for teaching reading to bilingual students. Every effective teacher uses several methodologies, extracting the best parts of each program in order to help each child.

Language Experience Method

Perhaps the most effective method of teaching reading to bilingual speakers is the language experience method. As you recall, the language experience method elicits language from the child. The teacher or the child, when he is able, transcribes the oral language and the child *reads* what he has spoken. Here is an example of a language experience method that incorporates some of the most frequently used words in English.

Specific Reading Lesson Plan

Topic and Group

The following is a language experience lesson designed to introduce new vocabulary words about SPRING to a full-time ESL primary class where children have different oral and written language skills

Objectives

A. Classroom objective

The teacher will introduce the children to the theme of SPRING, emphasizing SPRING vocabulary.

B. Behavioral objective

Each child will be able to read at least two words related to spring which have been added to their word bank. Each child will read the word spring and any other word(s) of his choice.

Diagnosis

Teacher Observation

While the weather has slowly been changing from winter to spring, the teacher observes how little vocabulary the children are able to use for description. Spring books and pictures placed around the room stimulate the need for SPRING vocabulary development.

Strategies

The theme of SPRING will be introduced by the teacher as she reads a spring picture book to the class. An experience chart will be written by the teacher and dictated by the children. The teacher will ask questions, such as the following, to elicit responses:

> What do you like about spring? What reminds you of spring? What can you see in the spring? What can you smell in the spring? What can you hear in the spring? What can you do in the spring? How do you feel in the spring?

Each child who is able to will dictate a word or phrase for the chart. The anticipated chart would be similar to the following:

THINGS I LIKE ABOUT SPRING

Tania:	Flowers
Sung:	Kite
Angela:	Green leaves
Miguel:	Puddles and worms
Ruby:	Baby animals
Sven:	Nest
Amin:	Warm weather
Young-Mi:	Sunshine
Sasha:	Excited

Each child will be given a word card with spring written on it. The children will be given a piece of drawing paper to illustrate whatever they like best about spring. While the children are drawing, the teacher will go around to each child to write another word card of their choice for their word bank. The more advanced readers could write several of their own word cards.

When each child finishes his drawing, he will label it with a word, phrase, or sentence, or several sentences, depending on level of ability.

Evaluation

A. Formal. Each child will read all the cards he has acquired about spring.
B. Informal. The teacher will observe the use of vocabulary when the children are discussing the weather, spring pictures, books.

Possible Ideas for Further SPRING Vocabulary Development

The more advanced students can write and illustrate a SPRING dictionary, using words from the SPRING blackboard dictionary.

Teaching Individual Words

The question often arises: If I begin to teach individual words, which words should I teach first? An obvious answer is to teach the words that appear most frequently in English. The word list on page 530, supplied by the *Heritage Dictionary*, provides us with useful information about word frequency in English.

The following list, *THE HERITAGE LIST OF SERVICE WORDS*, may serve as a useful supplement for your language experience program. It may help you in some of the following ways:

1. As a diagnostic instrument for determining an appropriate starting point.
2. As a source for the selection of new words.
3. As a reinforcement strategy, using flash cards.

Heritage List

Word Frequency

1. English has a distinctive word frequency distribution.
2. 10 per cent of all the words written and printed in books, magazines, and newspapers for children and for adults are the and of.
3. 20 per cent of all the words written and read are the, of, and, to, a, and in.

Basis of the Heritage Listing

1. The Heritage Dictionary used a computer to find the separate word forms and their frequencies in over a million running words selected from the most technical adult material in all fields.
2. The Heritage Dictionary used a computer to find the relative frequency of 86,761 words in 5,088,721 running words, carefully selected from 1,045 textbooks most commonly used in grades 3 through 9.

Student Usage

1. Knowledge of the most frequently used and common words will allow a student to read any data with increased accuracy.
2. The following list gives the words ranked for frequency by each five-percentage points through 75 per cent, as listed in the Heritage list.
3. One could use mastery for each subdivision as a "celebration point" in reading and in spelling achievement.
4. A pupil might circle known words in a newspaper article, counting them and receiving a note of "celebration" for the family.

HERITAGE LIST OF SERVICE WORDS*

the		all		see		look		read
of	10%	were		time		think		last
and		when		could		also		never
a		we		no	45%	around		us
to		there		make		another		left
in		can		than		came		end
is	20%	an		first		come		along
you		your		been		work		while
that		which		its		three		might
it		their		who		word		next
he		said		now		must		sound
for		if		people		because		below
was		do		my		does		saw
on		will		made		part		something
are		each		over		even		thought
as		about	40%	did		place		form
with		them		back		small		food
his		then		much		every		keep
they		she		before		found		children
at	30%	many		go		still		feet
be		some		good		between		land
this		so		new	50%	name		side
from		these		write		should		without
I		would		our		Mr.		boy
have		other		used		home		once
or		into		me		big		animals
by		has		man		give		life
one		more		too		air		enough
had		her		any		line		took
not		two		day		set	55%	sometimes
but	35%	like		same		own		four
what		him		right		under		

head
above
kind
began
almost
live
page
got
earth
need
far
hand
high
year
mother
light
how
up
out
ever
paper
hard
near
sentence
better
best
across
during
today
others
however 60%
sure
means
knew
it's
try
told
young
miles
sun
ways
thing
whole
hear
example
heard
several
change
answer

down
only
way
find
use
may
water
long
little
very
after
words
called
just
where
most
know
get
through
trees
I'm
lady
upon
family
later
turn
move
face
door
cut
done
group
true
half
sentences
red
fish
plants
living
wanted
black
eat
short
United States
run
kinds
book
gave
order

well
such
here
take
why
things
help
put
years
different
away
again
off
went
old
number
great
tell
men
brought
close
nothing
though
started
idea
call hundred
lived
makes
became
looking
add
become
grow
draw
yet
hands
less
John
wind
places
behind
cannot
letter
among
4
A
letters
comes
able

both
few
those
always
looked
show
large
often
together
asked
house
don't
world
going
want
school
important
until
1
hot
anything
held
state
list
stood
either

shows
tea
fast
seemed
felt
kept
America
notice
can't under
strong
voice
probably
needed
birds 65%
area
horse
Indians
sounds
matter
stand
box
start
that's

parts
country
father
let
night
following
2
picture
being
study
second
eyes
soon
times
story
boys
since
white
days
road
questions
blue
meaning
coming
instead

held
friends
already
warm
taken
gone
finally
summer
understand
moon
animal
mind
outside
power
says
problem
longer
winter
Indian
deep
mountains
heavy
carefully

room	open	dog	class	follow
sea	ground	shown	piece	beautiful
against	lines	mean	slowly	beginning
top	cold	English	surface	moved
turned	really	rest	river	everyone
3	table	perhaps	numbers	leave
learn	remember	certain	common	everything
point	tree	six	stop	game
city	000	feel	am	system
play	course	fire	talk	bring
toward	front	ready	quickly	watch
live	known	green	whether	shall
using	American	yes	fine	dry
himself	space	built	5	hours
usually	inside	special	round	written
money	ago	ran	dark	10
seen	making	full	glide	stopped
didn't	Mrs.	town	past	within
car	early	complete	ball	floor
morning	I'll	oh	girl	Bill
given	learned	person	tried	ice
ship	let's	Tom	rather	soil
themselves	least	energy	length	human
begin	problems	week	looks	trip
fact	followed	explain	speed	woman
third	books	passed	machine	eye
quite	tiny	lost	information	milk
carry	hour	spring	except	choose
goes	B	travel	figure	north
distance	happened	wrote	you're	discovered
although	foot	cities	minutes	houses
added	plant	farm	free	seven
doing	moving	circle	fell	easily
sat	care	cried	suppose	famous
pictures	low	whose	natural	pages
possible	else	bed	ocean	late
names	gold	working	government	rocks
heart	build	measure	lives	flowers
having	glass	straight	trying	pay
writing	rock	base	horses	sleep
real	tail	mountain	the	iron
simple	covered	caught	s	trouble
snow	alone	hair	baby	store
getting	reached	bird	taking	beside
rain	bottom	per	grass	oil
suddenly	walk	wood	plane	modern
easy	forms	running	pieces 70%	filled
leaves	takes	color	sides	fun
lay	check	South	pulled	catch

size	reading	groups	8	growing
wild	fall	war	inches	business
weather	poor	members	street	countries
Mother	map	fly	George	helped
Miss	scientists	yourself	couldn't	gives
carried	friend	decided	reason	exactly
pattern	c	seem	difference	Jim
sky	language	thus	tells	King
walked	job	logs	maybe	reach
6	points	nearly	larger	lot
main	music	square	history	won't
someone	buy	England	mouth	answered
ones	window	moment	middle	case
center	mark	North	step	speak
named	ideas	teacher	thousands	shape
field	heat	happy	steps	eight
stay	grow	changed	cars	edge
itself	listen	products	child	seems
worked	ask	C	opened	soft
boat	changes	bright	thinking	interesting
building	single	sent	strange	watched
question	French	present	eggs	formed
wide	clear	plan	wish	stories
village	material	played	position	works
object	talking	island	hear	busy
stain	isn't	standing	hope	pounds
placed	thousand	there's	song	beyond
Joe	sign	we'll		seeds
age	examples	opposite	missing	Bob
minute	guess	barn	France	produced
wall	begins	sense	heard	fingers
b	forward	cattle	playing	send
meet	huge	million	control	100
record	needs	anyone	spread	love
copy	closed	rule	knows	materials
forest	ride	science	evening	cool
River	regien	helps	brown	laughed
months	largest	farmers	picked	cause
especially	answers	afraid	clean	man's
dogs	nor	women	wouldn't	stands
necessary	period	produce	section	feeling
lower	finished	pull	spent	facts
smaller	blood	son	Dan	please
he's	rich	meant	ring	meat
unit	team	broken	higher	lady
flat	waves	interest	raised	west
7	corner	ends	9	glad
direction	Mary	woods	weeks	British
south	eat	Henry	teeth	action

subject	amount	chance	quiet	divided
skin	liked	homes	ancient	greatest
wasn't	garden	thick	Jack	happens
I've	led	sight	stick	pass
Europe	note	pretty	afternoon	20
New York	various	12	silver	returned
yellow	race	train	nose	adding
ships	developed	sets	century	ears
arms	bit	fresh	saying	soldiers
party	clothes	faster	therefore	type
force	uses	Washington	flying	attention
test	result	drive	level	shouted
bad	greater	lead	you'll	gas
temperature	fields	break	death	World
pair	New	sit	hole	actually
ahead	brother	bought	coast	kitchen
wrong	addition	hundreds	directions	alike
parctice	doesn't	radio	cross	pick
sand	states	method	sharp	scale
tail	dead	gets	fight	basic
wait	weight	king	capital	West
difficult	thin	similar	Old	President
general	stone	return	fill	Uncle
cover	hit	corn	deal	Johnny
areas	wife	decide	patterns	happen 75%
walls	contains	shore		
Africa	row	throughout		
showed	contain	compare		
safe	objects	Sam		
grown	fit	dollars		
cost	students			
wear	turns			
act	clouds			
wings	equal			
Paul	War			
bat	value			
arm	yard			
believe	Americans			
major	beat			
becomes	inch			
gray	walking			
died	sugar			
bones	key			
sitting	product			
wonder	desert			
include	bank			
interested	farther			
describe	won			
electric	total			

sold	wall
visit	wire
15	rose
sheep	cotton
I'd	moves
waiting	spoke
shoes	rope
30	rules
office	four

Using Phonics Strategies With Bilingual Students. Naturally, any reading method includes the use of phonics strategies. We have included an example of an instructional lesson using phonics strategies for teaching bilingual Spanish children some important, but difficult, sound distinctions in English. This lesson is "The IP family and the EEP family."

The "Eeps" and the "Ips"

Procedures

Day one: The teacher, working with small groups (five to ten children) begins by telling the children that this week they are going to meet two new word families. She may ask them to recall other word families they know (the "ake" or "ike" family) and get them to discuss the concept of word families; how all the words sound alike and contain the family name plus another sound or sounds. She then tells the children that the two new word families they will meet this week are the "ip" family and the "eep" family. She may go on to explain that many people think these two are twin families because they sound so much alike, but that the two are very different and that the students should get to know them well enough to tell them apart.

The teacher then introduces the "eep" family. (The long e is the sound the children know and the teacher should move from the known to the unknown). She begins by telling them that the eep family is called the eep family because every one of the family members has an eep in his name. She invites the children to help her find the "eeps" in her pictures.

The first picture (of a boy weeping) is introduced and the teacher asks the children to tell her about it. There is a discussion of the picture, during which the children offer their ideas about what it represents. With the teacher's guidance, the class comes to the conclusion that it is a boy "weeping" (if the children are not familiar with this word, the teacher introduces it). She then asks how we know that weep is a member of the eep family and gets the children to recall the word-family concept again.

This procedure is continued for two more eep words (sheep and sleep), which are also introduced with pictures. The teacher encourages discussion among the children, speculation on why the sheep in sleeping, specualtions on what eep word is represented, and, finally, speculation on why it is an eep word.

To conclude the first lesson, the teacher reviews the pictures, asking which eep words they represent. The teacher might then introduce a sentence that builds on the children's speculation, ties the new words together in a meaningful context, and illustrates the sound similarities: for example, "When the boy weeps, the sheep sleeps in the cave." She encourages the children to remember the sentence.

Day two: The teacher begins with a short review of yesterday's lesson on the three eep words by showing the pictures and trying to elicit appropriate responses, as well as trying to elicit the sentence that tied the lesson together.

She then begins the day's lesson by telling the children that today they are going to meet the ip family. Basic procedures for introducing members of the ip family are the same The teacher shows a picture, asks questions about it, directs students to a given answer (whip, ship, or slip) and encourages them to tell her why the word is a member of the ip family. An added teaching element of great importance for these three words is the use of contrast. The teacher continually adverts to how a given ip word is different from its corresponding eep word. She may do this by asking the children if whipping is the same as weeping and having them show her the appropriate pictures for each word.

Day three: The procedure follows day one and two procedures, but today two final eep words are introduced. These are leap and heap. As before, they are introduced with pictures, and discussed by the students. Conclusions are arrived at with the guidance of the teacher, and students are asked why each word is a member of the eep family. Their meaning and the sound similarity in them are further concretized by putting them in story form via the continuation of the first eep sentence. The new sentence would read: "When the sheep sleeps, the wolf leaps and gobbles down a heap of sheep." Children are encouraged to combine sentences one and two and recall sentence one of the ip family.

Day four: The day begins with a review of the first three days' material and then two final ip words (trip and hip) are introduced. The same instructional procedures are followed: introduction of concept with pictures, student explanation of why the words are ip words, and contrast of the new ip words with yesterday's eep words. The new ip words are tied together with a final "Ship slips, the sailor trips and hurts his hip upon the ship." Students are encouraged to put togehter sentences one and two, and then to compare this ip sentence with the eep sentence.

Day five: The fifth day will be spent on a review of eep and ip words. Now attention will be focused on the two contrasting ip and eep passages ("When the ship slips . . ." and "When the sheep sleeps . . ."). Children are asked to point to pictures that show the boy weeping, the wind whipping, sheep sleeping, ship slipping, wolf leaping, sailor tripping, as well as those that show a heap and a hip. Finally, they are asked to pick out the five pictures described in the passage: "When the boy weeps, the sheep sleeps in the cave. When the sheep sleeps, the wolf leaps and gobbles down a heap of sheep," and the five that are described in the passage: "When the wind whips the ship slips."

Further Suggestions for Teaching ESL in the Bilingual Curriculum. Hirsch (1976) proposes the following suggestions for students in the intermediate grades or junior high school. These ideas may be incorporated into the ESL component of the bilingual curriculum.

1. If a class lesson has stressed the oral use of the structure "used to" and vocabulary related to where people *used to* live, what they *used to do*, what they *used to eat*, where they *used to* work, a reading/writing exercise which followed might include a story about an individual who *used to* live somewhere and do certain things. The teacher may choose to omit key words (i.e., the verbs) and have the students fill them in. Various amounts of structure can be provided and as many details as you like can be included. You might want the student to write about him/herself: i.e., I *used to* _____ *in Puerto*

Rico. I used to _____ at 7:00, _____ at 7:15, _____ at 8:00, and go to _____ at _____ .
Every afternoon I *used to* _____ _____ for lunch and every evening I *used to* _____
_____ for dinner. I *used to* go _____ every night.

Obviously, any amount of detail or any variation of this form would be good practice in
reading and writing and would be based on oral work done in class. At a more sophisticated level, the teacher could relate this practice to content areas.

> That is, kings used to be very powerful. They used to make many decisions every
> day. Everyone used to obey whatever the king said. Nobody used to vote because
> there never used to be elections.

> or: Scientists used to believe the world was flat. (this idea could be developed in
> the same structure based on notions that may be part of the students' science class.)
> The entire format can be adapted to be used with simple past, present, or future, as
> well as conditional tenses—that is, John Smith lost the election. He said, "If I had
> won I would have been a wonderful president." The teacher might ask the students
> what they would do it it rained, what they would have done if they had been king
> a hundred years ago, etc. The vocabulary and structures chosen should reflect the
> level of the class.

2. Stories presented orally should contain information which can be elicited from the
students by purposeful, literal questions. They should be filled with detail and should
emphasize sequence of events. This approach will force students to concentrate and
pay close attention to sequence. In addition, they should compare time, people, or
places: i.e., "*John goes swimming in the summer, plays tennis in the winter, skates in the
fall, and sails in the spring. In Florida, the weather is always warm and everyone sits in
the sun all day long, but in New York it is very cold and everyone goes to work.*" These
kinds of stories are easily reviewed orally and used as reading and writing exercises
later. By including words such as *although, but, since, however,* or *compared to, even
though, in spite of,* the student will learn to recognize words that introduce special kinds
of relationships. For instance, the student should recognize that *although* might signal
unexpected information. "Although I was born in China *I speak only Spanish.*" Students might be asked to complete the sentence with other appropriate responses. Other
structures which elicit comparisons can provide good background to content area work
as well as affective thinking. Students might be asked to compare two cities they have
studied, two pictures, two poems as well as their old homes to their new homes or
themselves to their siblings. (Italics supplied)

3. Along with either of the preceding suggestions the teacher could present a paragraph
and have students unscramble the words in each line to form sentences and then unscramble the sentences to form a paragraph. This could be done as a class exercise, orally
followed by an assignment for the students to do individually. The teacher might ask
why the students would put one word before another or one sentence before another.
In many cases the students will make different choices, all of which are correct. This
could lead to a discussion of style. The students could be asked which form they
prefer, which is better for what purpose.

In addition to this, another exercise that emphasizes the skills of speaking as well as
reading and writing is sentencing combining. The teacher might provide a series of
sentences which are easily combined: i.e., Paris is a city. The city is in France. France
is a country. The country is in Europe. Many people live there [in Paris]. The people
speak French. Again, these sentences can range in topics from things of social interest
to things related to literature or science.

4. A question could be presented to the class for oral discussion, such as, "Who took it?" "Who did it?" "Who found it?" "Who stole it?" "Who lost it?" Students should be asked to use their imagination to make up answers to all the "wh" questions. As much detail as possible should be elicited. "The man who lives in the small apartment in the building on Fifth Avenue found the key in a dark corner of the hallway." The teacher could proceed to ask when he found it, what did he do with it, whose key was it. Such an exercise could be followed by asking students to write their own individual answers to questions. This would also be a good introduction to reading mystery or adventure stories. It could introduce a unit on humor or science fiction.

5. Teachers can encourage students to see the city and can help provide opportunities for them to do so Maps and photographs can be helpful. Students should be asked to make maps of their neighborhoods and discuss what services, streets, places, are important to include. A walk around the neighborhood might refresh their memories. Each student might be asked to focus on a specific area—geographic area—or area of special interests. Maps of the city could be studied, students could talk about how to give directions.

6. A story about five or six different people and the kinds of jobs they do, the names of their professions, îs a good introduction to vocabulary of different careers, as well as an introduction to career education in general. *"John is a carpenter. He decided to become a carpenter because he loved to build things with his hands. He likes to make shelves and cabinets. Sometimes he makes furniture. He makes beautiful things. Susan is a lawyer. She decided to become a lawyer because she loved to solve problems. Sometimes she goes to court. She is a very good lawyer."* A good follow-up to a story prepared by the teacher would be to read the want ads in the paper and examine the qualifications necessary for each job. Many professions supply career materials for students which could be adapted by the teacher into simpler language. Every effort should be made to avoid career stereotyping on the basis of ethnic background or sex. Perhaps trips to various places could be arranged, films of various careers could be shown, and books introducing various careers could be read.

7. At an appropriate point during the year, even beginning students of English will have some familiarity with past, present, and future tenses. The teacher could provide some structured questions or a fill-in form on which the students could write their autobiographies. This unit might provide the students with a personal feeling about what is communicated by various structures. In addition, it is a good introduction to a unit on biography.

In addition to an appropriate teaching methodology and effective learning activities for bilingual students, it is important to have a specific reading program. We recommend an eclectic program for each teacher and a personalized program for each child. All of the activities recommended throughout this book are appropriate for the bilingual student when they are used with sensitivity and understanding of the bilingual child's particular background.

O'Brien has recommended the following program for the early primarly levels, see chart page 539.

At the intermediate and advanced levels, each teacher will want to create her own program, emphasizing the specific components that most directly meet the needs of her students.

A SUGGESTED PROGRAM FOR EARLY PRIMARY LEVELS*

Structured activities	Semistructured activities	Unstructured activities
Large group	*Large group*	*Large group*
Planning time: Teacher-directed discussion of	Total class working on such projects as	Sharing time period provided for
1. plans for the day.	1. social living unit activities (charts, displays, talking murals, bulletin boards, indoor outdoor construction projects, experience charts).	1. show and tell experience.
2. classroom goals.		2. reporting on individual or group activities.
3. preparation for class projects, field trips, social activities, etc.		3. showing art work, reading creative stories, poems, etc. Library period set aside for independent reading or "picture reading" listening to "talking books," etc.
4. classroom rules and regulations.	2. science activities (collections, labeled displays, experience charts, records of experiments, indoor outdoor gardens, science word dictionaries or files).	
5. housekeeping task assignments.	3. a classroom newspaper or news sheet.	
Small group	4. literary experiences, story reading, story telling, poetry, recordings, creative writing.	Demonstration period provided for
Ability-group instruction in beginning language and reading:	5. creative dramatics.	1. creative dramatic presentations.
1. oral language		2. puppet shows.
2. vocabulary building		3. individual talent opportunity.
3. visual and auditory skill building activities		4. choral reading.
4. concept building	*Small group*	*Small group*
5. language experience activity	Groups "cycled" through learning centers for specific learning experiences:	Clusters of children involved in cooperative work or play activity
Individual	1. library center	*Individual*
Teacher-directed individual learning experiences such as	2. listening-viewing station	Free-choice activity in learning center. Playhouse area, toy or game area, art or crafts area, etc
1. programmed instruction in silent reading, and perceptual skill development.	3. reading skills center (games and manipulative devices	Individual-choice work tasks related to plans of the day
2. teacher-constructed tapes and work sheets.	4. creative writing center	
	5. science center	
	Individual	
	Individuals assigned to learning centers for specific learning experiences	

*C. O'Brien, *Teaching the Language Different Child to Read* (Columbus, Ohio: Charles E. Merrill Publishing Company, 1973, p. 57. Reprinted by permission.

Evaluation

In evaluating a program, it is necessary to examine the difficulty and effectiveness of the materials, as well as the progress of each student.

Difficulty of Materials

In addition to the readability formulae that will be presented in Chapter 14, Spaulding (1956) created a readability instrument to be used for assessing the reading difficulty level of materials written in Spanish. He suggests the following for the selection of a sample of content.
1. In long selections, analyze samples of 100 words every ten pages.
2. In shorter selections, analyze samples of 500 words every 1,000 words.
3. In selections of 500 words or less, analyze the entire passage.

Procedures

1. Count the number of words in the sample.
2. Count the number of sentences.
3. Divide the number of words by the number of sentences. Result is average sentence length.
4. Check the words against list I of the Buchanan and Rodriquez "Bou Word List" (page 542) and count the number of words not on the list.
5. Divide the number of words not on the list by the number of words in the sample. The result is the density or complexity of the vocabulary.
6. Using the table, find the number that corresponds to the density.
7. Find the number that corresponds to the average sentence length.
8. Draw a line to connect the two points of density and average sentence length.
9. The point at which the two lines intersect the central column represents the relative difficulty of the sample.

The Index of Reading Difficulty ranges from 20 to 160 and can be divided as follows:

20–40 Primer level	
40–60 Very easy	40–Grade 1
	50–Grade 2
	60–Grade 3
60–80 Easy	60–Grade 4
	70–Grade 5
	80–Grade 6
80–100 Relatively Easy	Grades 6-7-8
100–120 Difficult	Grades 8-10
120–160 Very difficult	Grades 11-12 and above

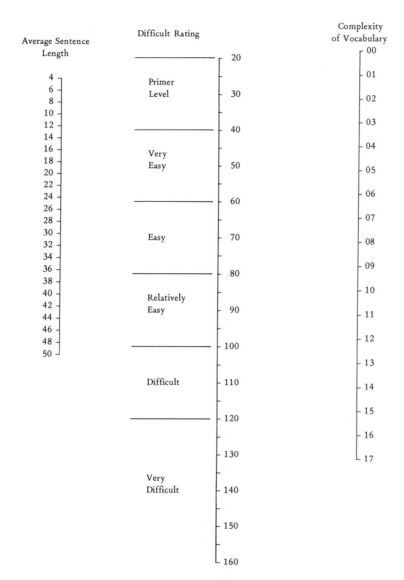

Figure 1. Readability graph. Reprinted with permission from Seth Spaulding. "A Spanish Readability Formula," *Modern Language Journal*, 40:435 (Dec. 1956).

The following word list has been included for two reasons: it is an essential part of the Spaulding formula, and it will provide teachers who decide to begin instruction in Spanish with the basis of their word program. Before moving to more difficult words, teachers should be certain that their children can read the words in this list.

BUCHANAN AND RODRIGUES-BOU WORD LIST I

a	ahogar	año	ave	cabeza
abajo	ahora	apagar	aventura	cabo
abandonar	aire	aparecer	avisar	cada
aborreccer	ajeno	apartar	ay	cadena
abrazar	al	aparte	ayer	caer
abrir	ala	apenas	ayudar	café
absoluto	alcalde	aplicar	azucar	caida
abuelo	alcanzar	apoyar	azul	caia
acá	alegrar	aprender		c(u)alidad
acabar	alegre	apretar	bailar	calma
acaso	alegria	aprovechar	bajar	cajlor
accion	alejar	aquel	bajo	callar
aceite	algo	aquél	balcón	calle
accento	alguien	aqui	banar	cama
acceptar	algun (-o)	árbol	barba	cambiar
acerca	aliento	arder	base	cambio
acercar	alma	ardiente	bastante	caminar
acertar	alrededor	arma	bastar	camino
acompañar	alterar	armar	batalla	campana
aconsejar	alto	arrancar	batir	campaña
acordar	altura	arrastrar	beber	campo
acostumbrar	alumbrar	arreglar	belleza	cansar
actitud	alzar	arriha	bello	cantar
acto	allá	arrojar	benecir	cantidad
actual	alli	arte	bendito	canto
acudir	amable	articulo	besar	capa
acuerdo	amante	artista	beso	capaz
adelantar	amar	asegurar	bestia	captial
adelante	amargo	asi	bien (s.,	capitán
ademas	amargura	asiento	adv.)*	capitulo
adiós	ambos	asistir	blanco	cara
admirable	amenazar	asomar	blando	carácter
admiracion	americano	asombrar	boca	cárcel
admirar	amigo	aspecto	boda	cargar
admitir	amistad	aspirar	bondad	cargo
adonde	amo	asunto	bonito (adj.)	caridad
adorar	amor	atar	bosque	cariño
adquirir	amoroso	atencion	bravo	carne
advertir	anciano	atender	brazo	carrera
afán	ancho	atento	breve	carro
afecto	andar	atrás	brillante	carta
afirmar	ángel	atrevesar	brillar	casa
afigir	angustia	atreverse	buen (-o)	casar
agitar	animal	aumentar	burla	casi
agradable	animar	aun, aun	burlar	caso
agradar	animo	aunque	buscar	castellano
agradecer	anterior	ausencia		castigar
agregar	antes	autor	caballero	castigo
agua	antiguo	autoridad	caballo	causa
aguardar	anunciar	auxilio	cabello	causar
ahi	añadir	avanzar	caber	ceder

celebrar	condicion	costa	deheado	distinguir
celebre	conducir	costar	demas	distinto
centro	conducta	costumbre	demasiado	diverso
cenir	confesar	crear	demonio	divertir
cerca	confianza	crecer	demonstrar	dividir
cercano	confiar	creer	dentro	divino
cerebro	conforme	criado	derecho (-a)	doblar
cerrar	confundir	criar	derramar	doble
cesar	confusion	criatura	desaparecer	doctor
ciego	confuso	cristal	descansar	dolor
cielo	conjunto	cristiano	descanso	dominar
ciencia	commigo	cruel	desconocer	don, D.
cierto (-a-	commover	cruz	describir	donde, donde
mente)	conocer	cruzar	descubrir	doña, Da.
circunstancia	conocimiento	cuadro	desde	dormir
citar	conque	cual, cuál	desear	drama
ciudad	conquista	cualquiera	desco	duda
civil	consagrar	cuando	desesperar	dudar
claridad	consecuencia	cuándo	desgracia	ducño
claro	conseguir	cuanto, cuanto	desgraciado	dulce
clase	consejo	cuarto(s.)	deshacer	dulzura
clavar	consentir	cubrir	desierto	durante
cobrar	conservar	cuello	despedir	durar
cocer	considerar	cuenta	despertar	duro
coche	consigo	cuento	despreciar	
coger	consistir	cuerpo	después	e
cólera	constante	cuestión	destinar	echar
colgar	constituir	cuidado	destino	edad
colocar	construir	cuidar	destruir	edificio
color	consuelo	culpa	detener	educación
columna	consumir	culto	determinar	efecto
combatir	contar	cumbre	detrás	ejecutar
comedia	contemplar	cumplir	dia	ejemplo
comenzar	contener	cura	diablo	ejercer
comer	contento	curiosidad	diario	ejército
cometer	contestar	curioso	dicha	el, el
comida	contigo	curso	dicho (s.)	elegir
como, cómo	continuar	chico	dichoso	elemento
compañero	continuo		diente	elevar
compañia	contra	dama	diferencia	ella
comparar	contrario	daño	diferente	emoción
complacer	contribuir	dar	dificil	empeñar
completo	convencer	de	dificultad	empezar
componer	convenir	dehajo	difunto	emplear
comprar	conversación	deber (v.o.s.)	digno	emprender
comprender	convertir	débil	dinero	empresa
comun	convidar	decidir	dios	en
comunicar	copa	decir	direccion	enamorar
con	corazon	declarar	directo	encantador
concebir	corona	dedicar	dirigir	encanto
conceder	correr	dedo	discreto	encargar
concepto	corresponder	defecto	discurrir	encender
conciencia	corriente	defender	discurso	encerrar
concluir	cortar	defensa	disgusto	encima
conde	corte	dejar	disponer	encontrar
condenar	corto	del	disposicion	encuentro
condesa	cosa	delante	distancia	enemigo

energia	estundiar	format	habutacion	imitar
eniermedad	estudio	formidable	habitat	impedir
enfermo	eterno	fortuna	hablar	imperio
enganar	evitar	frances	hacer	imponer
engano	exacto	franco	hacia	importancia
enojo	examinar	frase	hacienda	importante
enorme	excelente	frecuente	hallar	importar
enseñanza	exclamar	frente	hambre	impossible
enseñar	exigir	fresco	harto	impresion
extender	existencia	frio	hasta	impreso
enterar	existir	fruto	he aqui	imprimir
entero	experiencia	fuego	hecho (s.)	impulse
entomces	experimentar	fuente	helar	inclinar
entrada	explicar	fuera	herida	indicar
entrar	exponer	fuerte	herir	indiferente
entre	expresar	fuerza	hermano	individuo
entregar	expresion	función	hermoso	industria
entusiasmo	extender	fundar	hermosura	infeliz
enviar	extensión	futuro	hervir	infierno
envolver	extranjero		hierro	infinito
época	extrañar	galán	hijo	influencia
error	extraño	gana	hilo	ingenio
escapar	extraordinario	ganar	historia	inglés
escaso	extremo	gastar	hogar	immediato
escena		gato	hoja	immenso
escalvo	facil	general	hombre	inocente
escoger	facultad	género	hombro	inquieto
esconder	falda	generoso	hondo	inspirar
escribir	falso	genio	honor	instante
escritor	falta	gente	honra	instrumento
escuchar	fama	gesto	honrar	inteligencia
escuela	familia	gitano	hora	intencion
ese, ese	famoso	gloria	horrible	intentar
esfuerzo	fantasiä	glorioso	horror	interés
eso	favor	gobernar	hoy	interesante
espacio	favorecer	gobierno	huerta	interesar
espada	fe	golpe	hueso	interior
espalda	felicidad	gota	huevo	interrumpir
español	feliz	gozar	huir	intimo
esparcir	fenomeno	gracia	humanidad	introducir
especial	feo	gracioso	humano	inutil
especie	fiar	grado	humilde	invierno
esperjo	fiel	gran (-de)	humo	ir (-se)
esperanza	fiesta	grandeza	hundir	ira
esperar	figura	grave		isla
expreso	figurar	griego	idea	izquierdo
espiritu	fijar	gritar	ideal	
esposo	fijo	grito	idioma	jamás
establecer	fin	grupo	iglesia	jardin
estado	final	guapo	ignorar	jefe
estar	fingir	guardar	igual	joven
estatua	fino	guerra	iluminar	juego
este, este	firme	guiar	ilusión	juez
estilo	fisico	gustar	ilustre	jugar
estimar	flor	gusto	imagen	juicio
estrecho	fondo		imaginación	juntar
estrella	forma	haber	imaginar	junto

jurar	llegar	mio	nombre	página
justicia	llenar	mirada	norte	pais
justo	lleno	mirar (v.)	mota	pájato
juventud	llevar	misa	notable	palabra
juzgar	llorar	miserable	notar	palacio
		miseria	noticia	pan
la	madre	mismo	novio	papel
labio	maestro	misterio	nube	par
labor	magnifico	misterioso	nuevo	para
labrador	majestad	mitad	número	parar
lado	mal (-o) (adj.,	moderno	numeroso	parecer (v.)
ladrón	s. o adv.)	modesto	nunca	pared
lágrima	mandar	modo		parte
lance	manera	molestar	o	particular
lanzar	manifestar	momento	obedecer	partida
largo	mano	montaña	objeto	partido
lástima	mantener	montar	obligación	partir
lavar	mañana	monte	obligar	pasado
lazo	máquina	moral	obra	pasar
lector	mar	morir	obscuridad	pasear
lecho	maravilla	mortal	obscuro	paseo
leer	marcar	mostrar	observación	pasión
legua	marchar	motivo	observer	paso
lejano	marido	mover	obtener	patria
lejos	mas, más	movimiento	ocasión	paz
lengua	masa	mozo	ocultar	pecado
lento	matar	muchacho	oculto	pecho
letra	materia	mucho	ocupacion	pedazo
levantar	material	mudar	ocupar	pedir
leve	matrimonio	muerte	ocurrir	pegar
ley	mayor	mujer	odio	peligro
libertad	me	mundo	ofender	peligroso
librar	médico	murmurar	oficial	pelo
libre	medida	música	oficio	pena
libro	medio	muy	ofrecer	penetrar
ligero	medir		oido	pensamiento
limitar	mejor	nacer	oir	pensar
limite	mejorar	nación	ojo	peor
limpio	memoria	nacional	olor	pequeño
lindo	menester	nada	olvidar	perder
linea	menos	nadie	opinión	perdón
liquido	mentir	natural	oponer	perdonar
lo	mentira	naturaleza	oracion	perfecto
loco	menudo	necesario	orden	periodico
locura	merced	necesidad	ordenar	permanecer
lograr	merecer	necesitar	ordinario	permitir
lucha	mérito	necio	oreja	pero
luchar	mes	negar	orgullo	perro
luego	mesa	negocio	origen	perseguir
lugar	meter	negro	orilla	persona
luna	mezela	ni	oro	personaje
luz	mi, mi	ninguno	otro	personal
llama	miedo	niño		pertenecer
llamar	mientras	no	paciencia	pesar (v. o s.)
llano	militar	noble	padecer	peseta
llanto	ministro	noche	padre	peso
llave	minuto	nombrar	pagar	picar

pico	proceder	recorrer	rojo	serio
pie	procurar	recuerdo	romper	servicio
piedad	producir	reducir	ropa	servir
piedra	profundo	referir	rosa	severo
piel	prometer	regalar	rostro	si, si
pieza	pronto	region	rubio	siempre
pintar	pronunciar	regla	rueda	siglo
pisar	propiedad	reina	ruido	significar
placer	propio	reinar	ruina	siguiente
planta	propener	reino	rumor	silencio
plata	proporcion	retr		silla
plato	proporcionar	relación	saber (v.)	simple
plaza	proposito	relativo	sabio	sin
pluma	prosequir	religión	sacar	sin embargo
problación	protestar	religioso	sacerdote	sincero
pobre	provincia	remedio	sacrificio	singular
poco	proximo	remoto	sacudir	sino
poder (v. o s.)	prucha	rendir	sagrado	siquiera
poderoso	publicar	renir	sal	sistema
poeta	público	reparar	sala	sitio
politica	pueblo	repartir	salida	situación
politico	puerta	repetir	salir	situar
polvo	puerto	replicar	saltar	soberano
poner	pues	reposar	salud	soberbio
poquito	punta	reposo	saludar	sobre (prep.)
por	punto	representar	salvar	sobrino
porque,	puro	república	sangre	social
porqué		resistir	sano	sociedad
porvenir	que, que	resolucion	santo	sol
poscer	quedar (-se)	resolver	satisfacer	soldado
posesion	queja	respe (c)tar	satisfecho	soledad
possible	quejarse	respec(c)to	se	soler
posicion	quemar	respirar	seco	solicitar
precio	querer	responder	secreto	solo, solo
precioso	querido	respuesta	saguida	soltar
preciso	quien, quien	resto	seguir	sombra
preferir	quienquiera	resultado	según	sombrero
pregunta	quitar	resultar	segundo	someter
preguntar	quizá, quizás	retitar	sequridad	sonar
premio		retrato	seguro	sonido
prenda	rama	reunion	semana	sonreir
prender	rapido	reunir	semejante	soñar
preparar	raro	revolver	sencillo	sordo
presencia	rato	rey	seno	sorprender
presentar	rayo	rico	sensacion	sorpresa
presente	raza	ridiculo	sentar	sospechar
presidente	razon	riesgo	swntido (s.)	sostener
prestar	real	rigor	sentimiento	suave
prentender	realidad	rincón	sentir	subir
primero	realizar	rio	seña	suceder
primo	recibir	riqueza	señal	suceso
principal	recién	risa	señalar	suelo
principe	reciente	robar	señor (-a)	suclto
principio	reclamar	rodar	señorito (-a)	sueño
prisa	recoger	rodear	separar	suerte
privar	reconnocer	rodilla	ser (v. o s.)	sufficiente
probar	recordar	rogar	sereno	sufrir

sujeto	tener	trabajo	valiente	vez
suma	terminar	traer	valor	viaje
sumo	termino	traje	valle	vicio
superior	terreno	tranquilo	vanidad	victima
suplicar	terrible	tras	vano	vida
supóner	terror	trasladar	vapor	viejo
supremo	tesoro	tratar	variar	viento
supuesto	testigo	trato	vario	vino
suspender	ti	traves	varón	violencia
suspirar	tiempo	triste	vaso	violento
	tienda	tristeza	vecino	virgen
tabla	tierno	triunfar	vela	virtud
tal	tierra	triunfo	velar	visión
tal vez	tio	tropezar	vencer	visita
talento	tipo	tu, tu	vender	visitar
también	tirano	turbar	venganza	vista
tampoco	tirar		venir	visto
tan	titulo	u	venta	viudo
tanto	tocar	ultimo	ventana	vivir
tardar	todavia	un, uno (-a)	ventura	vivo
tarde (adv.	todo	unico	ver	volar
o s.)	tomar	unión	verano	voluntad
te (pron.)	tono	unir	veras	volver
teatro	tonto	usar	verbro	voto
tema	torcer	uso	verdad	voz
temblar	tornar	usted	verdadero	vuelta
temer	torno	útil	verde	
temor	toro		vergüenza	y
templo	torre	vacio	verso	ya
temprano	total	vago	vestido	yo
tender	trabajar	valer	vestir	

*s. = substantivo (noun), adv. = adverbio, adj. = adjectivo; v. = verbo; prep. = preposición; pron. = pronombre.

Materials

In planning a bilingual program you will need to purchase a variety of materials. If you are in a position to purchase materials for use in your own classroom or in your school, you will probably want to establish criteria for their selection.

1. Teacher Competency

	Yes	No
A. Must you be a content specialist to successfully use the materials?	___	___
B. Must you be bilingual to use the materials?	___	___
C. Are the materials usable by inexperienced teachers?	___	___
D. Does the publishing company or the school system provide consultants to instruct you in the use of the materials?	___	___

2. Learners
   A. Do the materials provide for student differences in intelligence, experience, and language fluency? _____ _____
   B. Do the materials contain stories of equal interest to both males and females? _____ _____
   C. Do the materials contain high interest, low vocabulary selections? _____ _____

3. Program Sequence
   A. Does the developmental sequence of the program closely parallel the natural development of language learning ? _____ _____
   B. Does the program build on the natural language strengths of the student? _____ _____
   C. Does the program make provisions for the development of all of the language arts? _____ _____
   D. Does the program provide for content area skill development? _____ _____
   E. Do the materials provide for individualizing instruction? _____ _____
   F. Are the materials free from cultural stereotyping? _____ _____
   G. Can the materials be integrated within an existing program? _____ _____

4. Program Packaging
   A. Do the materials contain charts, filmstrips, flashcards, and other supplementary materials? _____ _____
   B. Are the supplementary aids easily used by children? _____ _____
   C. Are materials provided for reinforcement, review, and evaluation? _____ _____
   D. Are the costs consistent with available program funds? _____ _____
   E. Are program time constraints consistent with time allowances for classroom implementation? _____ _____

Student Progress

Most educators agree that literacy is measurable, but they do not always agree upon the most appropriate instruments for measuring student progress. We cannot "protect" our students or ourselves from accountability. The argument about standardized tests is not whether to use them, but which ones should be used, "Which instruments adequately assess the abilities of bilingual students at their present stage of development in English?" If a student, age five or fifteen is just beginning English instruction, let us be absolutely certain that our tests take into consideration this level of limited exposure to English. By way of example, let me present the following fictional test item.

Instructions: Read this brief passage and answer the two questions that follow:

> "There he is up around the bend;
> "Come on down over here," Ian said.
> "We will box him in and ambush him
> like Butch Cassidy used to do with the Sundance Kid."

Answer the following:

> 1. To whom is Ian talking?
> 2. What is Ian's suggested plan of action?

There are very few polysyllabic words in the passage; most of the words are monosyllabic. The only word to be counted as a difficult word, using the Dale-Chall readability formula, would be *ambush*. Almost any young native English speaker would be able to comprehend this passage, but it would be extremely difficult for someone just learning English for the following reasons:

> Syntax: The syntax is complex, <u>used to</u> is a sophisticated structure.
>
> Idioms: This brief selection uses two idioms that the bilingual student may not be able to understand, "<u>up around the bend</u>" and "<u>Come</u> on down <u>over</u> here."
>
> <u>Cultural/Experiential Background</u>: The child needs to have some knowledge of Butch Cassidy to fully appreciate the passage.

There are many items in this short passage that would be impossible for a bilingual student to interpret. A second example may further illustrate the point:

> Had he gone to the dentist on time, his mother wouldn't have yelled at him.

Again, a young antive English speaker probably would be able to interpret this utterance, but a bilingual child, recently exposed to English, would have an extremely difficult time comprehending this complex English syntactic pattern.

We urge extreme caution when using any standardized test to measure the reading growth of bilingual children. We urge you to analyze the test thoroughly and to interpret it in light of the student's present level of functioning in English. If test items are based on complex syntactic structures, English idioms, and English lexical items demanding a specific cultural experience, make a note of the items and interpret your student's scores according to your knowledge of his level of English proficiency.

Clinical Reports

After considering the theoretical information presented in the Evaluation Section of this chapter, it may be useful for you to analyze two separate case reports of bilingual children who have begun to learn to read in English.

The first example is the case of Gladys Sanchez, age thirteen. We will present the entire case including the diagnosis and planned strategies. After reading it, we would like you to answer these questions:

1. Is this diagnosis adequate?
2. Do the strategies meet the needs that were discovered in the diagnosis?
3. Would you eliminate any of these suggested strategies?
4. Would you include any strategies that have not been mentioned in this report?

The second example is the case of David Chu, age twelve. After reading David's case study, it may be useful to answer the same set of questions.

NAME: Gladys Sanchez*
AGE: 13

OVERVIEW OF TEST SCORES

Skill	Test	Score
Listening Comprehension	1. Durrell Listening and Reading	2.8
	2. Durrell Analysis	Grade 3
	3. Maryville Test	Average 3
Oral Reading	1. Durrell Analysis	High School grade
	2. Gray Oral Reading Test	3
Silent Reading	1. Spire	Low second
	2. Durrell Analysis	High second
	3. Stanford Diagnosis (literal)	2.8
Word-attack skills	1. Durrell Analysis	Grade 6
	2. Spire	Grade 6
	3. San Diego Quick Assessment	Grade 7
	4. Botel Test	7.2
Sight vocabulary	1. Durrell Analysis	Grade 6
	2. San Diego Quick Assessment	Grade 6
	3. Peabody Picture Vocabulary Test, English	100

Note: The scores of these tests must not be interpreted in the same way as they are interpreted for a native English speaking child. This student is in the process of learning English.

STRATEGIES AND MATERIALS

Objectives	Strategies	Materials
1. To use the simple past tense of regular and irregular verbs orally and in written English	The student will be helped to discriminate between sounds of present and past— that is, look, looked, bake, baked, by taping several combinations and having her circle the correct response from choices presented in print. Secondly she will be asked to write words she has heard. She will be given no visual cues. She will be given much	Teacher prepared taped materials, ditto sheets, informal stories to be retold in the past.

Objectives	Strategies	Materials
	practice repeating sentences with past and present tense verbs. She will also be asked to retell stories in the past that had been presented in the present.	
2. To use adjectives in the comparative and superlative forms both orally and in writing	With the student we discussed questions about family and school such as, "Who is the smallest one in your class?" "Who is the youngest one in your family?" Also involve student in completing cloze written work such as: He is the --- one in the class, She is --- than he is, etc.	Several ESL texts contain these drills but informal teacher-prepared materials may also be used.
3. To learn to write English sentences with the proper SVO word order in declarative and interrogative sentences.	Play sentence games and do some structured work with scrambled sentences.	Sentence Cubo, Scrabble, informal work sheets of disarranged sentences.
4. To listen to the structure, 'used to' and to use it in structured responses, free speech, and written	Elicit student responses about a story written in the 'used to' form and discuss the things she used to do before coming to the U.S.	Simple teacher-prepared story utilizing this structure.
5. To listen to the conditional structures, 'if I were. . . I would. . . and 'If I had seen. . . I would have. . .' and to use these structures in speech and in writing.	Using the same technique as #4 discuss questions such as What would you have done if you had done, seen, travelled, etc.	Informal stories and written exercise sheets.
6. To follow the details and sequence of events in stories more carefully.	Through detailed elicitation (oral) of details in stories provide student with support and contextual clues for remembering sequence.	Informal stories used in above exercises as well as short newspaper articles.
7. To read stories independently for personal enjoyment.	Discuss newspaper articles and books she has read and ask her to report on the books in writing upon completing them.	News for You Laurback Literacy Association, newspaper in easy English and Scholastic Reading series.

Objectives	Strategies	Materials
8. To understand and be able to accurately use the conjunctions; but, because, although, so, since.	Through oral exercises, consisting of incomplete sentences, and through stories using these words, try to distinguish one from another and then ask Gladys to complete structured written drills.	Teacher-prepared materials such as: I was born in Paris although (a) I do not speak English, (b) I do not speak French (c) I live in Paris (d) I like life in France.

SUGGESTED READINGS FOR GLADYS

1. *Achieving, Venturing, Searching.* Encounters Series, Reality in Reading and Language, Cambridge Book Co., 1971.
2. Fitzhugh, Louise. *Harriet the Spy.* New York: Harper & Row, Publishers, 1964.
   An award-winning novel of a teenage girl written simply enough for Gladys to enjoy reading it.
3. Pringle, Laurence. *City and Suburb: Exploring an Ecosystem.* New York: Macmillan Publishing Co., Inc., 1975.
   A good introduction to reading in the content areas. Some difficult vocabulary but much valuable content material of particular interest to someone who has had both urban and rural experiences.
4. Stoltz, Mary. *Fredou.* New York: Harper & Row, Rublishers, 1962.
   A human interest story of a teenager, done in large print and well written.
5. Zevelle, Emily Chevey. *Garden of Broken Glass.* New York: Delacorte Press, 1975.
   An illustrated novel dealing with the problems of an urban teenager, especially in regard to his family.

Now, let's try to answer the original questions:

1. Is this diagnosis adequate?
2. Do the strategies meet the needs that were discovered in the diagnosis?
3. Would you eliminate any of these suggested strategies?
4. Would you include any strategies that have not been mentioned in this report?

As a bilingual teacher you may have to plan instruction for several children all of whom speak different languages.

The second case report is about David Chu, age twelve. David is a Chinese boy from a middle-class working family who immigrated to the United States approximately two years ago.

NAME: David Chu
AGE: 12

OVERVIEW OF TEST SCORES

Skill	Test	Score
Listening Comprehension	1. Durrell Analysis	3
	2. Durrell Listening and Reading	3.1

Skill	Test	Score
Word Recognition	1. Spire	2
	2. Durrell Analysis	3.0
Oral Reading	1. Gray Oral	2.5
	2. Informal Inventory	3.0
Silent Reading	1. Durrell Analysis	3
	2. Spire	2
	3. Durrell Listening and Reading	3.1

NOTE: David's test scores fall within a range of limited proficiency with reading in English. They should be interpreted, however, within the framework that his exposure to the English spoken word and written form has been of very short duration. In the course of instruction it was apparent that David has an extremely accurate visual memory and a high daily learning rate. Therefore a number (10–20) of vocabulary words can be successfully introduced and retained.

As a note of caution, it should be pointed out that all of the standardized tests which David took were normed on native speakers, therefore, the scores are not necessarily appropriate for a bilingual student.

STRATEGIES AND MATERIALS

Objective	Strategy	Material
1. To improve listening and speaking	Given a short story read orally with repetitive syntax and vocabulary, the student will listen and respond in complete sentences to posed questions.	Teacher-prepared passage based on ESL principles.
	Given a story or poem read orally by the teacher, the student will listen and produce a drawing of what he heard.	Six Blind Men & the Elephant, drawing materials
2. To improve reading	Given a news article, the student will be able to identify basic facts— i.e., who, what, when, where, why.	Boston Globe, work sheet, pencil
	Given an atlas, the student will be able to identify and locate (a) his homeland, (b) his present locale; later provided with a map of Boston, he will locate his exact address and indicate it with a map pin.	Atlas, map of Boston, map pins
	Given a series of everyday consumer materials, the student will read and answer critical-thinking questions orally or in written form.	Instructions for washing clothing, candy bar wrapped in medicine labels, teacher-prepared questions.

Objective	Strategy	Material
	Given an oral presentation on using a camera, the student will be able to (1) fill in a diagram labeling its parts, (2) follow a series of written directions and take a picture.	Teacher-prepared diagram and written instructions, 35mm camera.
3. To improve writing	Given a sample of humorous headlines, the student will write the opening paragraph of a printable news article.	Teacher-prepared headlines, paper, pencils.
	Given exposure to a slide or photograph, the student will describe in written form what he sees.	Photographs, slides, paper, pencil, chalkboard

Recommendations

(a) Referral to any and all of the below is advisable.
   (1) Bilingual program
   (2) ESL classes
   (3) Remedial reading instruction, daily
(b) Classroom teacher suggestions:

Objective	Strategies	Materials/Sources
1. To increase oral language	Engage in frequent, informal conversation.	
	Introduce structured speaking activities based on ESL exercises.	New Horizons (Addison-Wesley)
2. To improve reading skills	Review phonic skills with special attention given to vowels.	Phonics in Proper Perspective, (Merrill)
	Teach structural analysis skills— i.e., affixes, syllabication, contractions.	Phonics in Proper Perspective, (Merrill)
	Build vocabulary through discussion of everyday concepts— i.e., geography, government, science, art, etc. Introduce new words; student makes index cards. Review often.	
	Increase comprehension especially beyond literal meaning. Ask questions on critical/ creative level.	High-interest, low-vocabulary readers. (Allyn Scholastic, Noble & Noble, etc.)
	Make lessons from consumer materials, labels, directions, recipes, applications.	Survival Learning Materials (College Reading Assoc.)

Objective	Strategies	Materials/Sources
	Teach lessons on study skills—i.e., outlinging, note taking, using references, etc.	Student's texts from content areas
3. To improve writing skills	Provide visual or auditory stimulation—i.e., photos, paintings, sculpture, music. Devise open-ended assignments that allow for free expression.	The Language-Experience Approach to the Teaching of Reading (Harper)
	Expose students to new subject matter, possibly through field trips; write individual or group reactions.	The Language-Experience Approach to the Teaching of Reading (Harper)

SUGGESTED READINGS FOR DAVID

Asimov, Isaac. *Fantastic Voyage.* Boston: Houghton Mifflin Company, 1966. (Bantam).
  Sci-fi thriller about miniature crew traveling through a scientist's bloodstream.
Carson, John F. *The 23rd Street Crusaders.* New York: Farrar, Strauss & Grioux, Inc.,
  1958. A street gang becomes an accomplished basketball team under the direction of a
  gifted coach.
Heinlein, Robert. *Farmer in the Sky.* New York: Charles Scribner's Sons, 1950. (Dell)
  Frontier life in outer space.
Lewellen, John. *Understanding Electronics.* New York: Thomas Y. Crowell Company, 1957.
  Readable, basic text with definitions and diagrams.
Zindel, Paul. *The Pigman.* New York: Harper & Row, Publishers, 1968. (Dell). Teenagers
  relating to an eccentric old man.

SUGGESTIONS FOR TEACHER RESOURCES

Professional Books

Ashton-Warner, Sylvia. *Spearpoint.* New York: Vintage, 1972.
  A chronicle about using the language-experience approach in a Colorado school.
Dorry, Gertrude. *Games for Second Language Learning.* New York: McGraw-Hill Book
  Company, 1966.
  Lots of practical ideas.
EDCO. *A Manual of Diagnostic Tests and ABilities, Reading K–3, 4–6.* Boston: EDCO
  Reading Learning Center Publication, 1972. Comprehensive and readable.
Heilman, Arthur W. *Phonics in Proper Perspective.* Columbus, Ohio: Charles E. Merrill
  Publishing Company, 1974.
  Covers sample exercises on all aspects of phonic instruction.
Heilman, Arthur W. and Homes, Elizabeth Ann. *Smuggling Language into the Teaching
  of Reading.* Columbus, Ohio: Charles E. Merrill Publishing Company, 1972.
  Seeks to introduce ideas about linguistics and psychology into a practical series of activities
  that can be used in the classroom.
Kohl, Herbert. *Reading, How to.* New York: Bantam, 1974.
  Popular paperback with several practical ideas, especially useful for the reluctant or older
  beginning reader.

Nilsen, Don L. F., and Alleen Place Nilsen. *Pronunciation Contrasts in English.* New York: Simon & Schuster, Inc., 1971.
Provides examples of the sounds that may cause language and reading difficulty, particularly useful for bilingual teachers.

Stauffer, Russell G. *The Language-Experience Approach to the Teaching of Reading.* New York: Harper & Row, Publisher, 1970.
Theoretical and practical analysis of this useful teaching technique, especially good for bilingual students.

Thonis, Eleanor Wall. *Teaching Reading to Non-English Speakers.* New York: Macmillan Publishing Co., Inc., 1970.
A basic text that provides theory and some practical material.

Wilson, Robert M., and Marcia M. Barnes. *Survival Learning Materials.* York, Pa.: Strine Publishing Co., 1974.
A series of practical activities based on consumer and functional needs.

Professional Journals

English Language Teaching Journal, Oxford University Press, Press Road, Neasden, London NW 10

Journal of Reading, International Reading Association, 800 Barksdale Rd., Newark, Del.
For teachers of secondary reading

Language Learning—A Journal of Applied Linguistics, 2001 North University Building, University of MIchigan, Ann Arbor, MI 48109

TESOL Quarterly, School of Languages and Linguistics, Georgetown University, Washington, D.C.

The Reading Teacher. International Reading Association, 800 Barksdale Rd., Newark, Del.
For teachers of elementary reading.

Classroom Games

Milton Bradley
1. Password

Parker Bros.
1. Scan
2. Spill & Spell

Scrabble
1. Scrabble
2. Scrabble Junior
3. Sentence Cube Game

Again, let us review the four questions which were presented at the beginning of these two case studies:

1. Is this diagnosis adequate?
2. Do the strategies meet the needs that were discovered in the diagnosis?
3. Would you eliminate any of these suggested strategies?
4. Would you include any strategies which have not been mentioned in this report?

You may want to change this diagnosis and instructional report by adding to it or deleting certain elements of the program to meet your specific needs. You will always want to plan your program to help your children without frustrating them or embarrassing them.

QUESTIONS AND RELATED READINGS

If you do not feel that you have attained adequate knowledge to successfully answer the following questions, we would like to suggest related readings.

> Goal 1: To aid students in understanding the special needs of bilingual and ESL students and the origins of bilingual education in the United States

> Question 1: Explain how the needs of the bilingual student are being met by bilingual education.

Alatis, James E. "The Compatability of TESOL and Bilingual Education." *English as a Second Language in Bilingual Education,* ed. by James E. Alatis and Kristie Twadell. Washington, D.C.: TESOL, 1976.

Hines, Mary. "A Critique of the U.S. Commission on Civil Rights Report on Bilingual Bicultural Education. In *English as a Second Language in Bilingual Education,* ed. by James E. Alatis and Kristie Twadel. Washington, D.C.: TESOL, 1976.

Thonis, Eleanor Wall. *Teaching Reading to Spanish-Speaking Children.* Newark, Del.: International Reading Association, 1976.

> Goal 2: To aid students in understanding the linguistic influences in second language teaching and the linguistic differences between several languages and English

> Question 2: Explain the linguistic factors involved in teaching bilingual students.

Eskey, David E. "A Model Program for Teaching Reading to Advanced Students of English as a Foreign Language." *Language Learning,* 23,

MacNamara, John. "Comparative Study of Reading and Problem Solving in Two Languages." *In English as a Second Language in Bilingual Education,* ed. by James E. Alatis and Kristie Twadell. Washington, D.C.: TESOL, 1976.

Smith, Frank, Ed. *Psycholinguistics and Reading.* New York: Holt, Rinehart and Winston, 1973.

> Goal 3: To aid students in understanding the most appropriate methods of diagnosing the reading ability of bilingual and second language speakers.

> Question 3: How do you diagnose the reading problems of a bilingual student?

Ching, D. *Reading and the Bilingual Child.* Newark, Del.: International Reading Association, 1976.

O'Brien, C. *Teaching the Language Different Child to Read.* Columbus, Ohio: Charles E. Merrill Publishing Company, 1973.

Thonis, Eleanor Wall. *Teaching Reading to Non-English Speakers.* Newark, Del.: International Reading Association, 1976.

> Goal 4: To aid students in understanding different methodologies of instruction in teaching reading in the native language, as well as reading in English

> Question 4: Explain several methodologies of teaching reading to bilingual students.

Been, Sheila. "Reading in the Foreign Language Teaching Program." *TESOL Quarterly,* 9. (Sept. 1975).

Pierce, Mary Eleanor. "Teaching the Use of Formal Redundancy in Reading for Ideas." *TESOL Quarterly,* 9,

Thonis, E. *Teaching Reading to Spanish-Speaking Children.* Newark, Del.: International Reading Association.

> Goal 5: To aid students in understanding appropriate methods of evaluating the effectiveness of materials for bilingual and ESL students.

> Question 5: Describe the evaluation component of a bilingual program.

Ching, D. *Reading and the Bilingual Child.* Newark, Del.: International Reading Association, 1976.

O'Brien, C. *Teaching the Language Different Child to Read.* Columbus, Ohio: Charles E. Merrill Publishing Company, 1973.

Thonis, Eleanor Wall. *Teaching Reading to Non-English Speakers.* New York: Macmillan Publishing Co., Inc., 1970.

BIBLIOGRAPHY

Ching, D. *Reading and the Bilingual Child.* Newark, Del.: International Reading Association, 1976.

Hirsch, S. "Informal Diagnostic Instruments of English Language Skills". In *Proceedings of the Boston University Bilingual Reading Laboratory,* ed by J. Flood. Boston: Boston, University School of Education, 1976.

National Education Association. *The Invisible Minority*, Washington, D.C., 1966.

O'Brien, C. *Teaching the Language Different Child to Read.* Columbus, Ohio: Charles E. Merrill Publishing Company, 1973.

Ruddell, Robert. *Reading-Language Instruction.* Englewood Cliffs, N.J.: Prentice-Hall, Inc., 1974.

Spaulding, S. "A Spanish Readability Formula." *Modern Language Journal,* 40, (Dec. 1956) 435.

Thonis, E. W. *Teaching Reading to Spanish-Speaking Children.* Newark, Del.: International Reading Association, 1976.

____. *Teaching Reading to Non-English Speakers.* New York: Macmillan Publishing Co., Inc., 1970.

Unfinished Education: Outcome for Minorities in Five Southwestern States. Washington, D.C.: 1972, U.S. Government Printing Office.

Zamora, J. *The Educational Status of a Minority*, Washington, D.C.: Office of Education, 1968.

Zintz, M. *The Reading Process.* Dubuque, Iowa: William C. Brown Company Publishers, 1975.

Understanding student progress

Teacher-Constructed Tests

Name _____ Number _____
Grade _____ Date _____
Subject Matter _____ Level _____
Textbook _____

| | | Selection and Evaluation of Information | | Organizing Information | | Reading Pictorial Aids | |
| Location of Information | | | | | | | |

| | Use of Index | | | Identifying Answers | | | | | |
Table of Contents	Key Words	Find Pages	Find Answers	Topic	Main Idea		Outline	Sentence Summary of a Paragraph	Charts	Graphs
3	3	3	3	3	3	3	3	3	3	3
2	2	2	2	2	2	2	2	2	2	2
1	1	1	1	1	1	1	1	1	1	1
0	0	0	0	0	0	0	0	0	0	0

Possible criteria:
3 correct = excellent.
2 correct = adequate.
1 correct = marginal.
0 correct = inadequate.

NOTE: Whether these criteria ...
questions used in the inventory.

A form such as this may be used for written tests:

Name _____ Date _____

Grade _____ School _____

Examiner _____ City _____ State _____

PHONIC READINESS

Visual Discrimination Test

Directions: There are three words in each part of the test. One word is different from the other two. Draw a line under the different one. [Do the first three with the pupil(s). Make sure the pupil(s) understand how to do the test before proceeding with the remaining items.]

A. cat cat bee
B. shop milk shop
C. fat flake flake
1. best am best
2. buy tree tree
3. pouch teach teach
4. reading reading ridden
5. purpose porpoise purpose
6. scare scare share
7. capacity capacity capacitor
8. considerable consideration consideration
9. interpretive interpretative interpretative
10. beep deep deep

Name _____ D _____
Grade _____

CAPACITY ... story is based and the difficulty of the

| | Language and Conceptual | | | | Percent |
Grade Placement	Listen. Comp.	Vocab. Comp.	Gen'l. Info.	Aud.-Voc. Assoc.	Aud. Blend.
	S* I+	S I	S I	S I	S I
13.0+					
12.0-12.9					
11.0-11.9					
10.0-10.9					
9.0- 9.9					
8.5- 8.9					
8.0- 8.4					
7.5- 7.9					
7.0- 7.4					
6.5- 6.9					
6.0- 6.4					
5.5- 5.9					
5.0- 5.4					
4.5- 4.9					
4.0- 4.4					
3.5- 3.9					
3.0- 3.4					
2.5- 2.9					
2.0- 2.4					
1.5- 1.9					
1.0- 1.4					

Names of Standardized Tests Used:

Listening Comprehension _____
Vocabulary Comprehension _____
General Information _____
Word Recognition _____
Comprehension Level _____
Comprehension Accuracy _____

*S = Standardized Test I = Informal Test

Conversion Tables for Changing Raw Test Scores to Grade Placement Scores

| Vocabulary | | | Information | | Auditory Digit Span | |
Grade Placement	Raw Score	Grade Placement	Raw Score	Grade Placement	Raw Score	Grade Placement
10.0	31	4.9	22	–	14	–
9.0	30	4.6	21	–	13	–
8.6	29	4.3	20	–	12	–
8.0	28	4.0	19	10.0	11	8.7
7.7	27	3.7	18	8.0	10	5.7
7.5	26	3.4	17	7.0	9	4.0
7.2	25	3.1	16	6.7	8	2.0
7.0	24	2.9	15	6.4	7	1.5
6.8	23	2.6	14	6.0	6	1.0
6.6	22	2.3	13	5.3	5	–
6.3	21	2.0	12	4.5	4	–
6.0	20	1.7	11	3.7	3	–
5.8	19	1.3	10	3.0	2	–
5.5	18	1.0	9	2.4	1	–
5.2	17	–	8	1.7	0	–
	16	–	7	1.0		
			6	–		

Just as every student is not ready to begin formal reading instruction at the same time, every student is not to be confined to the reading difficulty of his assigned grade. In order to make correct reading placement, it is imperative that teachers find each pupil's reading achievement level, whether it be below, on, or above grade level. (p. 83–84)

Guszak, Frank J. *Diagnostic Reading Instruction in the Elementary School* (New York: Harper & Row, 1972).

GOALS: To aid the reader in understanding
1. student diagnosis as one step in the evaluation process.
2. the range of reading levels within a group or classroom.
3. processes for determining the readability of texts.
4. differences between criterion and norm referenced testing.
5. informal assessment of students' achievement.
6. the concept of levels of intellectual functioning.
7. reading expectancy level.

Evaluation is a continuous process that you as a classroom teacher will use
as you:
1. set goals
2. diagnose the strengths and needs of your students
3. plan programs to enable children to accomplish goals
4. determine appropriate instructional programs.
The purpose of this chapter is to introduce you to the formal and informal
measures frequently used to diagnose the strengths and needs of students.

Range of Reading Levels

Think about your ideal classroom. Where is it? How many children are there?
What are the cultural backgrounds of the children? What age range of children
are you teaching? How are your students alike? What obvious differences can
you recognize among your students? Did you know that within your classroom
there may be a wide range of reading abilities?

If your ideal classroom contains third-graders, you will find a range of reading
abilities from grade 1.5 to grade 4.5. Interesting? How can you determine this?
Goodlad (1966) offers an answer to this question when he states:

> The broad spread from high to low achiever steadily increases with the upward movement
> of heterogeneous classes (relatively homogeneous in chronological age) through the school.
> In the intermediate grades, this spread is approximately the number of years designated
> by the number of the grade level: that is, by the third grade, three years; by the fifth
> grade, five years. However, since the spread in achievement accelerates slightly faster
> than a year-per-year of schooling, the overall range in junior high school classes is approx-
> imately two thirds the median chronological age of the group.
>
> In subject areas, such as reading and language arts, where children can readily proceed on
> their own in a variety of out-of-school situations, the spread from high to low achiever
> frequently is one and one half to twice the number of the grade level. Hence, in the
> fifth grade, there frequently is an eight-year spread in reading achievement between the
> best and the poorest readers. Differentiation in classroom group stimuli to provide for
> varying levels of accomplishment does not encompass this range, but the encouragement
> of self-selection of materials for supplementary reading at home and school facilitates
> highly individualized rates of progress. (p. 34)

As Goodlad suggests, the spread of high to low reading achievement can possibly range from one and one half to twice the number of the grade level. In a fourth-grade class, the reading ability range might be computed as follows:

Grade 4:

$4 \times 1.5 = 6$	Grade level (4) times a spread of 1.5 for each grade level.
$6 \div 2 = 3$	Dividing spread by 2 determines the spread on either side of the grade level.
$4 + 3 = 7$ (high) $4 - 3 = 1$ (low)	Adding and subtracting spread (3) from grade level (4) determines the range of reading ability and grade level.

$$\boxed{1} \quad 2 \quad 3 \quad \boxed{4} \quad 5 \quad 6 \quad \boxed{7} \quad 8$$

$$\underset{-3}{\qquad} \qquad \underset{+3}{\qquad}$$

Therefore, in the fourth grade, a teacher might be expected to teach a class of students ranging from first-grade to seventh-grade reading levels.

Now pretend that you are a third-grade teacher and determine the range of reading levels that your children may have.

Grade 3:

$3 \times 1.5 = 4.5$	Grade level (3) times a spread of 1.5 for each grade level.
$4.5 \div 2 = 2.25$	Dividing total spread (4.5) by 2 determines the spread on either side of the grade level.
$3 + 2.25 = 5.25$ (high) $3 - 2.25 = .75$ (low)	Adding and subtracting spread (2.25) from grade level (3) determines the range of reading ability grade levels.

$$\boxed{1} \quad 2 \quad \boxed{3} \quad 4 \quad \boxed{5} \quad 6 \quad 7 \quad 8$$

$$\underset{-2.25}{\qquad} \qquad \underset{+2.25}{\qquad}$$

The reading-ability range in the third grade might vary from first-grade level to fifth-grade level.

Goodlad's statement also suggests that the range of reading achievement in intermediate classrooms equals 2/3 times the chronological age (CA). The following chart reflects the CA for each intermediate grade level.

Grade	CA
6.0	11.2
7.0	12.0
8.0	13.2
9.0	14.2
10.0	15.2
11.0	16.2
12.0	17.2

Now pretend that you are an eighth-grade teacher. What range of reading would be possible according to Goodlad's statement?

Grade 8:

Grade 8 chronological age = 13.2	Information from the chart
$13.2 \times 2/3 = \dfrac{26.4}{3} = 8.8$ or 9	Chronological age times 2/3
$9 \div 2 = 4.5$	Dividing total spread (9) by 2 determines the spread on either side of the grade level.
$8 + 4.5 = 12.5$ (high) $8 - 4.5 = 3.5$ (low)	Adding and subtracting spread (4.5) from grade level (8) determines the range of reading ability grade levels.

$$1 \quad 2 \quad 3 \quad 4 \quad 5 \quad 6 \quad 7 \quad (8) \quad 9 \quad 10 \quad 11 \quad 12$$

In an attempt to accommodate these reading differences you will need reading materials that cover an adequate range of readability.

Readability

Many classroom teachers estimate text readability levels by considering *word difficulty* and *sentence length* within a given passage. The incorporation of such words in sentences, with embeddings and transformations, tends to indicate an advanced readability level. Several readability formulae exist; they include Gray and Leary (1935), Lorge (1944), Flesch (1943), Dale–Chall (1948), Spache (1953), Fry (1968), and Aukerman (1972). These authors have attempted to design and measure the factors that cause children to have difficulty with reading materials. Vocabulary and sentence length appear to be the two factors most commonly agreed on as determinants of reading difficulty.

Readability research conducted by Guidry and Knight (1976) indicated that when the Dale–Chall, Flesch, Fry, and Lorge formulas were used to determine readability levels of the same materials, "the Dale–Chall method seems consistently to be high in its grade-level readability and that a more valid determination can be made by subtracting −0.891 from the final answer, . . . the Fry formula tends to yield a consistently low readability." (p. 556) When using the Fry formula, you will need to add +0.865 as an adjustment grade-level factor. When employing the Flesch and Lorge formulas, the adjustment factors of +0.299 and −0.285 are suggested by Guidry and Knight. With the application of these adjustment factors, it may be possible to use any of these formulas with greater confidence.

One must remember that readability levels are only *approximations* of material difficulty because it is almost impossible to hold constant all of the factors (text organization, concept difficulty, semantics, syntax, reader interest) that can affect one's mastery of a given material.

The Fry Formula

The Fry readability graph is presented here because the score is quickly and easily computed, and it is comparable to the other formulae in terms of reliability.

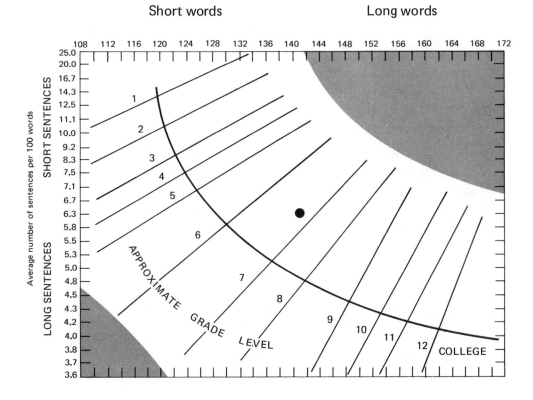

Figure 1. The Fry Graph.*

*Edward Fry, "Readability Formula That Saves Time," *Journal of Reading,* 11: 513-16; 575-577 (April 1968). Used with permission of the author and the International Reading Association.

How to Use the Fry Graph

1. Select three 100-word passages from near the beginning, middle, and end of the book. Skip all proper nouns.

2. Count the total number of sentences in each hundred-word passage (estimating to the nearest tenth of a sentence.) Average these three numbers (add together and divide by 3).

3. Count the total number of syllables in each hundred-word sample. There is a syllable for each vowel sound; for example: cat (1), blackbird (2), continental (4). Do not be fooled by word size; for example: ready (2), stopped (1), bottle (2). I find it convenient to count every syllable over one in each word and add 100. Average the total number of syllables for the three samples.

4. Plot on the graph the average number of sentences per 100 words and the average number of syllables per 100 words. Most plot points fall near the heavy curved line. Perpendicular lines mark off approximate grade-level areas.

Example	Sentences per 100 words	Syllables per 100 words
100-word sample, p. 5	9.1	122
100-word sample, p. 89	8.5	140
100-word sample p. 150	7.0	129
Divide total by 3	3) 24.6	3) 391
Average	8.2	130

Plotting these averages on the graph, we find that they fall in the fifth-grade area; hence, the book is about fifth-grade difficulty level. If great variability is encountered either in sentence length or in the syllable count for the three selections, then you should randomly select several more passages and average them in before plotting.

Cautions When Using Readability Formula

When you are using a readability formula, you must be aware that it should be used *only* as an approximation of the difficulty of the material. In the following list, you will find the most frequent criticisms of readability formulas.

1. The resulting level is only an approximation of difficulty.
2. Varying degrees of reading difficulty may be found within one text.
3. The introductory chapters of a text are often the most difficult.
4. Content area materials often do not evidence a gradation of difficulty.
5. It is virtually impossible to hold constant all of the factors that affect the difficulty level of reading materials; for example:
   a. Metaphorical and poetic words
   b. Semantics
   c. Syntax
   d. Tone, mood, author's style
   e. Context

Be extremely cautious when using readability formulas to determine grade level. Readability cannot possibly take experience or interest into consideration, and this is a serious problem in determining the difficulty level of the materials which your children will have to read. This problem is illustrated in the following exercises. Please read each of the following passages and answer the six questions which succeed each passage.

Passage 1

Christmas always meant going to Grandma's house. On Christmas Eve the entire family tramped out to the woods. Dad was in charge of bringing back the tree, and the rest of us cut fir branches for house decorations. That evening Grandma would distribute the homemade ornaments. We hung up a cookie universe: suns, stars, moons, and unearthly men with raisin eyes. Mom arranged candles in silvery paper on the branches. With dignity and care, Grandpa chained the tree with yards of cranberries and popcorn. We decorated the tree the way Grandma had when she was young; we were learning tradition.

Questions

1. Who cut the Christmas tree? _____

2. What was Grandpa's job? _____

3. Who was in charge of decorating the tree? _____

4. Why did the author of this paragraph go to the woods? _____

5. What does the phrase "cookie universe" mean? _____

6. How did the author of this paragraph learn tradition? _____

Passage II

One of the oldest drinks known to man is milk. Man requires liquids as well as solids to remain healthy because he is a mammal, a warm-blooded being. Prehistoric man did not consume as much liquid as modern man. He devoured fruit from the trees he inhabited. However, man had to change his habits to exist on the arid plains. No longer a fruit-eater, he soon began to hunt plains animals. This new activity required much energy; man perspired and needed to drink liquids directly. To this day man needs liquids such as milk to be able to exist.

Questions

1. What does man need to remain healthy?_____

2. Where did prehistoric man live? _____

3. What is a mammal? _____

4. Why did ancient man not have to drink liquids directly? _____

5. What made man change his eating habits? _____

6. What happened to man's body as he hunted animals?

Did you find one passage more difficult than the other? Did you score equally on each passage? If you found one passage more difficult, it will be interesting for you to ask yourself: What factors within the passage created the difficulty? Both passages, according to readability formulas, are extremely similar. The statistics on each of the passages are the following:

	Christmas	Milk
Number of words	100	100
Number of sentences	8	8
Average sentence length	12.5	12.5
Number of syllables	146	146

This chart demonstrates some of the pitfalls of relying exclusively on readability formulae to determine passage difficulty. If your score was significantly higher on one of the passages, it may have been because you found that passage more interesting than the other passage. You may have performed better on one passage than the other because of your experience; you may have celebrated Christmas in the same way as the people in the passage. On the other hand, you may have performed less well because of a lack of experience; you may not have celebrated Christmas at all, and therefore, you would not have been able to read the passage from an experiential point of view.

From a psycholinguistic point of view, you may have found more difficulty reading the "Milk" passage than the "Christmas" passage. On the surface, the two passages are similar (number of words, syllables, etc.), but if you carefully analyze the two passages, using some of the recent findings from linguistic and information processing research, you will discover the following facts about the "Milk" passage.

It contains several instances where the reader has to *double* process, that is, the reader has to unravel the sequential encoding of contrastive semantic features in order to extract the appropriate feature of the second semantic element. In order to process information about the habitat of later-day man, the reader has to distinguish between prehistoric and later-day man and the habitat of each (prehistoric man, trees; later-day man, dry plains). However, the complexity of double processing is compounded in this passage because the contrastive semantic features are interrupted by the addition of an unrelated element. "However, man had to change his *habits.*"

A second example of the necessity for double processing which occurs in this passage is entwined with a cognitive overloading phenomenon. The reader is forced to encode a negative transformation, "No longer a fruit eater," and he/she is forced to store that information while processing a positive proposition, "he soon began to hunt plains animals." While not dependent on the negative transformation, the positive elements of the proposition may be affected by cognitive overloading and/or by the inclusion of contrastive semantic features within the same proposition.

An additional consideration in the analysis of the differences between the Milk passage and the other passage is a question of complexity of cognitive functioning. The reader is required to sort "prehistoric man" from "man" and the habitats of each by processing inferred relationships between the concepts;

e.g., the reader has to extrapolate unwritten relationships. For example, the following facts are not stated explicitly: (1) man moved from the trees, (2) the dry plains did not have fruit, (3) he needed to gain food and liquid supply from a source other than fruit, (4) fruit was the source of liquid, (5) gathering fruit did not force man to exert himself.

Student Diagnosis

As you can see, your task is extremely complex. You have been presented with instruments for determining the range of your students' reading abilities and interest, and you have been presented with selected instruments for determining the readability of your materials. Now that you realize that success in reading depends on understanding the difficulty and complexity of the passage and the experience and interest of the child, you must also realize that your task has just begun. You must attempt to meet the personal, individual needs of each of your students. In order to accomplish this complex task, your first step is to evaluate your students to determine their strengths and needs. Through diagnosis, you will be better able to plan prescriptive programs to develop their individual skills. Do not be alarmed; although we are suggesting that you will need to develop the skills of individual students, we are not suggesting that you must work with each child in isolation. Chapter 15 is designed to aid you in understanding and implementing flexible grouping techniques which are necessary for prescriptive teaching.

In order to begin a diagnostic process, you must answer the following questions:

1. How can I determine the strengths and needs of my children?
2. What is the role of diagnostic evaluation in my classroom? Remember, evaluation is a process of testing that can be used to diagnose and plan a curriculum.
3. What do my children know about a specific topic?
4. What skills do my children need in order to pursue the study of this topic?

In attempting to answer such questions, you are evaluating the competencies of your students.

While a reemphasis on the processes of diagnostic evaluation may seem somewhat contemporary, the topic is ageless. Early norms of colonial school evaluation consisted of oral recitation because the major goal of most colonial educators was to train students to recite from memory. As written materials became more readily available, measures of evaluation began to include essay or problem-solving tests. Standardized testing became part of educational evaluation at the turn of the century when Alfred Binet and Thérèse Simon (1905) developed standardized intelligence tests in an attempt to differentiate formal from retarded children. They eventually broadened their studies to include the measurement of intelligence of all children.

The IF Factor

Intelligence tests, as they are currently designed, do not measure *intellectual potential* (IQ). Instead, they measure one's present level of *intellectual functioning* (IF). Intellectual functioning is a measure of one's cultural experiences and information which are acquired through daily interactions with a variety of stimuli in an environment ranging from significant others to tangibles. If the child has been exposed to cultural experiences which are measured on a given intelligence task, he often performs well on such a measure. If the tasks are outside his range of experience, he is often considered intellectually inferior when he may only be missing daily exposures to such tasks or interactions.

Cultural exposures, coupled with *biological factors,* determine the potential of one's mental development (intelligence). One's inherent biological characteristics determine *potential*, while environment encourages the full or partial development of this potential. Because existing intelligence tests measure only one's present intellectual functioning (IF), electronic devices such as the *ERTL Index** may prove to be our only means of measuring one's brain potential or intelligence (IQ).

When a child is born, his intellectual *potential* is determined by biological structures. In certain cases brain damage, chromosone abnormality, or other physical factors may affect potential academic or scholastic achievement. The degree of fulfillment of normal potential is realized through environmental exposures and daily experiences. Thus, IQ should be defined as normal intellectual and biological potential plus present intellectual functioning. Biological functioning is innate (it occurs through the development of the human organism), whereas present intellectual functioning is developed through daily experiences.

Available intelligence tests are unable to measure innate intellectual potential (IQ); however, they do report data regarding one's present intellectual functioning (IF) as a result of environmental exposures. This fact was confirmed by Wechsler (1950, p. 78) when he stated, "General intelligence cannot be equated with intellectual ability however broadly defined, but must be regarded as a manifestation of the personality as a whole."

Currently existing IQ tests are used to:
1. measure and compare mental endowment.
2. measure one's capacity for learning.
3. measure lack of mental capacity.
4. measure the presence of special abilities.

*The ERTL Index is an electronic device that attempts to analyze neural efficiency. Neural efficiency is processed in a period of fewer than three minutes. A helmet equipped with electrodes that are supposed to collect brain waves is placed on the person being tested. A flashing light stimulates the brain, while a computer analyzes the efficiency with which the brain processes the light flashes. An oscilloscope, on which the waves can be monitored visually, and a device to amplify the waves are also parts of the machine. For more detailed information see William Tracy, "Goodbye IQ, Hello EI (ERTL Index), *"Phi Delta Kappan",* 89–94 (Oct. 1972). J. Trout, G. Packwood, and Barry Wilson, "Ertl's Neural Efficiency Analyzer: Still Promising—But What?" *Phi Delta Kappan,* 448-51 (March 1976).

5. measure the presence of mental disabilities.
6. determine school placements.
7. determine a need for vocational guidance.
8. determine those in need of counseling.
9. predict life adjustment abilities.
10. predict tendencies for juvenile deliquency.
11. predict college success.

Assuming that intelligence tests are useful in all of the above situations, one begins to question exactly how the term "intelligence" is being defined. Thorndike (1975, p. 5) helped us to develop such a definition when he stated, "There is not just *one* unique, but *several* different kinds of intelligence, namely *abstract, social,* and *practical.* The first is manifested by the individual's ability to work with symbols, the second by his ability to deal with people, and the third by his ability to manipulate objects." Many existing measures seem to assess one's present functional level in the first area, that of *abstraction*. While other measures of intelligence may also include verbal, spatial, and numerical factors, all existing IQ tests measure one's present cognitive functioning on a specified set of items. What has been measured is intellectual functioning (IF) rather than intellectual capacity (IQ).

There are certain social, emotional, and cultural influences (affective dimensions) which may affect one's IF. However, you, as a classroom teacher, must also be aware that the IF is influenced by one's drive, persistence, will, and sense of preservation. These psychological factors may be studied within the context of the conative domain. In order to better understand the IF of the student, you will need to study the *affective* and *conative* dimensions of learning as well as the child's *cognitive* skills. This triadic emphasis is needed to understand one's IF since, as Wechsler (1950, p. 81) states, " ... factors other than intellect contribute to achievement in areas where, as in the case of learning, intellectual factors have, until recently, been considered uniquely determinate, and ... other factors have to do with functions and abilities hitherto considered traits of personality."

As educators who are attempting to determine the strengths and needs of children, we must be cautious not to confuse what is being measured by intelligence tests. When such confusion occurs, inferior instruction may also occur. We too often erroneously label children as dull or retarded learners. Once labeled, children are treated as though they are dull or retarded. When one is treated as an intellectually inferior person, his learning potential may stagnate. Unfortunately, teachers confuse cultural exposures (readiness for a given task) with biological composition.

Because existing tests do not measure intelligence (intellectual potential + cultural experiences) but instead measure one's present level of intellectual functioning (IF), we believe that the term *IQ testing* should be replaced by *IF testing*. Perhaps the realization and understanding of the need for this substitution will enable us to avoid erroneous, inappropriate labels. We cannot measure intellectual potential (IQ), but we do have some measures that begin to assess one's *present* level of *intellectual functioning* (IF) on a given task. Examples of tests that measure IF and not IQ are the *Stanford-Binet Scale* and the *Weschsler Scale for Children.* In the next few pages, we will use the term *IF* to refer to what has previously been called IQ.

MA + IF.   In addition to being interested in a child's IF score and his reading level score, teachers are often anxious to determine a student's *mental age.* Why? Because many tests are scored according to the age at which a majority of the population succeeds at a given task. For example, a student who succeeds on the items at the eleven-year level and fails at the twelve-year level has a mental age of eleven. If his chronological age is less than eleven, the child may be considered to be very competent in behaviors being measured by the test. If his chronological age is greater than eleven, he may need instruction or exposure to the behaviors measured by the test.

Mental age (MA) refers to one's level of mental development as compared with others on a given set of standardized tasks. MA is one's IF (present intellectual functioning level) expressed in units of age.

One's MA is easily determined through use of the following formula.

$$MA = \frac{IF}{100} \times CA$$

Thus, if a child's IF is 80 and his CA (Chronological age) is 8 his MA is 6.4.

$$\frac{IF\ 80}{100} \times MA\ 8 = \frac{640}{100} = 100\overline{)640} \quad 6.4$$
$$\frac{600}{400}$$

Or, a child whose CA is 10 who has an IF of 140 has an MA of 14.0.

$$\frac{140}{100} \times 10 = 14.0$$

If we accept that an IF of 120 means that a child has intellectually grown at the rate of 1.2 years for each chronological year until age fifteen, while an IF of 80 means that the student has advanced intellectually at the rate of 0.8 for each chronological year, the commonly used formulae (MA = IF × CA) and (IF = $\frac{MA}{CA}$ × 100) become easier to interpret.

Reading Expectancy or Instructional Level

Knowledge of the student's IF, MA and CA is very helpful in determining his reading expectancy or instructional level. As teachers we are interested in helping each student achieve at or near his capacity level. Students often have the ability to achieve above or below their chronological grade placement level because the chronological grade level is not an achievement criterion. American educators for decades have grouped children homogeneously according to age levels, assuming that grouping would occur within each grade level because of the teacher's sophisticated knowledge about personalized curricula that emphasize individualized student progress. As you attempt to implement such personalized groupings within a given grade level, remember that the actual achievement level of each student should be compared with his learning capacity, not his grade placement.

The following formulae have been designed to aid you in determining your students' reading expectancy level.

Bond and Tinker (1967)

$$\text{Reading expectancy level (REL)} = \frac{\text{IF}}{100} \times \text{years in school}) + 1$$

This formula, which is based on the fact that the child has never failed in school, is interpreted as follows: David, who is an eight-year-old in the second-grade, has an IF of 120. David's REL is 3.4. $(\frac{120}{100} \times 2) + 1 = \frac{240}{100} = 2.4 + 1 = 3.4$ (measured in grade levels).

Harris (1970)

$$\text{REL} = \frac{2\text{MA} + \text{CA}}{3}$$

Can you refer to the statistics on David and determine his REL using Harris' formula? First we must determine his MA.

$$\text{Remember:} \quad \text{MA} = \frac{\text{IF}}{100} \times \text{CA}$$

$$\text{Thus:} \quad \text{MA} = \frac{120}{100} \times 8 = 9.6$$

Now that we have David's MA we can proceed:

$$\text{REL} = \frac{2\text{MA} + \text{CA}}{3} = \frac{2(9.6) + 8}{3}$$

$$= \frac{19.2 + 8}{3} = \frac{27.2}{3} = 9.1 \quad \text{(Reading expectancy measured in years)}$$

The REL, as well as the MA, CA, and IF, is a rough estimate of a child's ability employed with great discretion in your classroom. One must note that the formula of Bond and Tinker (1967) reports the reading expectancy level (REL) in *grade-level units,* whereas the Harris formula (1970) reports the REL in *chronological age units.* The importance of these two formulae is the following:

1. It is useful for you to know the approximate level of a child's current capacity for reading so that your expectations are realities for *every* child.

2. It is useful to know both the Bond and Tinker formulae and the Harris formula because children are often in grades that do not reflect their current ages, e.g., some ten-year-olds are in the third grade and some ten-year-olds are in the fifth or sixth grade.

3. It is useful to know both formulas because some schools have an ungraded system.

Criterion and Norm Referenced Testing

Instruments that enable the teacher to determine a student's IF are referred to as norm referenced tests because they assess one's performance in relation to the achievement levels of others on the same test. In contrast, criterion-referenced instruments are tests which are used to ascertain a student's performance with respect to a given criterion. When using a criterion referenced instrument, the teacher is able to determine the tasks which the student can accomplish, rather than how he compares with others on the given task.

Norm referenced testing became prominent in the 1930s as only one dimension of the process of evaluation. As the concept of evaluation has expanded, educators have begun to encourage alternate methods of testing because the wide array of instructional outcomes that you want to test are seldom incorporated within a single standardized test. Testing should not be viewed as an end in itself, but rather as the first step in diagnostic-prescriptive teaching.

Norm and criterion referenced measures differ in the ways in which they are designed, as well as in the type of information conveyed through student responses. (See Figure 2). Items on a criterion referenced achievement test must be a representative sample of the competencies identified by instructional objectives. If the competencies are stated in specific behavioral terms, the problems of assessing the degree of demonstration on the part of the student are minimized. The scoring of the criterion referenced instruction should be designed to provide information about the developed skills and existing needs of a student. For example, the end product of a criterion referenced measure should provide descriptive information regarding an individual's degree of competence on a specified task. A criterion might be "Can Linda recite her ABCs?" The criterion is clear, and the assessment is relatively simple. Here Linda is compared to an established criterion; that is, she can or cannot recite her ABCs. The test is criterion referenced.

The criterion referenced instrument may be designed to aid the classroom teacher in assessing individual competencies and designing alternate programs based on individual needs. The norm referenced tests can also look at the individual's competency, as he or she is related to others in the group: the question which is being asked is: "How do the various students rank on the ABC test?" Each of these measures assesses the same behaviors, but each has a different purpose. Therefore, when you are selecting or developing an instrument for use in your classroom, you need to specify your reasons for testing, and you need to specify the criterion being tested. Whether you use criterion or norm referenced evaluation, you will need to select your instrument very carefully.

A Comparison of Norm Referenced and Criterion Referenced Tests

Test Feature	Norm referenced	Criterion referenced
Test design	Design is related to subject matter information and process skills.	Design is related to specific instructional behavioral objectives.
Item preparation	Designed to determine variances among students.	Designed to measure individual competency on a given task.
Item types	Many types are used (multiple choice, true-false, completion).	Many types are used (multiple choice, true-false, completion).
Item difficulty	Moderate; designed to determine a middle range.	Wide variance, but with adequate instructional preparation, responses are generally correct.
Interpreting results	A student is compared to the accomplishments of a norm group by computing his subscore or total test score.	A student's performance on a specified behavioral item is determined by comparing his response to the correct question.
Test availability	Consult Oscar Buros's Mental Measurement Yearbook to ascertain information about norm referenced tests.	The tests, which are often designed by teachers for use in their classrooms, may now also be maintained as part of the management systems of many basal reading programs.
Test use	To determine a comparative score between one pupil and a normative group and to determine global student achievement.	To diagnose student strengths and needs and to evaluate an instructional program.

Figure 2

Until recently, the practice has been to evaluate students against some norm group, whether his own or an arbitrarily chosen group. This has at least two disadvantages: (1) it makes the same children fall at the bottom in every situation and (2) it encourages the development of curriculum unrelated to the needs of the children. Because of these and other disadvantages, the use of criterion referenced tests is encouraged by educators. Two advantages of criterion referenced tests are: (1) Comparison problems are minimized because a child is being evaluated *only* against *himself* and (2) Criterion referenced tests may be informally designed by the classroom teacher to measure a specific behavior.

A test which a classroom teacher devises is often called an informal test. It can be either norm or criterion referenced. A standardized test can also be either norm or criterion referenced. The distinction between informal and standardized testing is that the latter has been administered to many students and "standardized" before being used in an actual situation. Whether you are using an informal or standardized test, it is essential that the test have the following characteristics.

Validity. The basic question to be answered is: "Does the test measure what you think it is measuring?" For example, if a college instructor announces a test and says it will measure understanding and application and then she asks five questions related to details on a footnote on page 47, is it measuring what she thinks (or says) it is? Obviously not. We say the test has no content validity. If, as a teacher, you want to measure problem-solving ability through story problems and you proceed to give a page of fifty long-division examples, your test will have no content validity.

Content validity must be established for achievement tests. This may be accomplished by first deciding what it is you intend to measure and then deciding if your test (or the standardized test) gives a representative sample of the entire field you are interested in testing. If it does, your test has content validity.

Researchers often discuss three other kinds of validity: *predictive validity, construct validity,* and *concurrent validity.* Predictive validity determines how successful the test is at predicting success or achievement at a future time. Most informal measures in the elementary or secondary level are not concerned with this aspect of validity. Construct validity refers to the relationship between test scores and other criteria of behavior which logically relate to the test. It examines an ability, aptitude, trait, or characteristic that is hypothesized to explain some aspect of human behavior. Concurrent validity compares the outcome of a test at approximately the same time as the predictor test is taken. For instance, a vocational interest test may be compared to interests exhibited by members of the vocation already. Designers of elementary school measures which are formal or informal are more concerned with content validity than they are with the other types of validity.

Reliability. Another factor that must be determined is the stability of your test (informal or standardized). If you give a reading comprehension test on Monday and again on Friday, and the scores are not similar for each student, then the test may not be reliable. Ambiguous test items are not reliable because students are guessing at answers, for the most part, and students seldom guess twice in the same way. Long tests and very difficult tests are often unreliable because students tend to guess from fatigue; very short tests are seldom reliable because the sample of work is so limited that you may or may not have selected the items that the student knows.

A *correlation coefficient* indicates the reliability of a test. The coefficient of correlation represents the relationship between two specific behaviors of a group of students. The tendency of the students to have systematic similar or dissimilar relative positions in the two distributions is reflected through computing a correlation coefficient. A positive correlation exists between the two measures if students who are high or low in one distribution are also high or low in a second distribution. For example, if Catherine receives a high score on each of two measures and Todd receives a low score on each of the same two measures, the correlation coefficient is positive. If $\frac{r}{tt}$ = .00 (read: the correlation equals zero), the test is completely unreliable. If $\frac{r}{tt}$ = 1.00 (read: the correlation equals 1) the test is completely reliable. Unfortunately, tests are never completely reliable, but a correlation of .75 to .99 is usually acceptable as a measure of reliability.

If a test is both reliable and valid and you want to use it as a criterion referenced test, you have no further concerns. However, if you want to use it as a norm referenced test, you must investigate appropriate norming procedures.

Norms. Norms are as important to the teacher as they are to the doctor. If you took a child to be weighed and measured, and the doctor told you that the child was greatly overweight, you would ask, "Overweight compared to whom?" If you felt the comparison was inappropriate, you would reject the doctor's statement.

The same is true for achievement tests. The score which the child receives may be accurate, depending on the validity and the reliability of the test, but the comparisons you make may be totally inappropriate. A child can *only* be compared with his own group—that is, a ten-year-old urban child should be compared with other ten-year-old children in similar urban environments. To make the wrong comparisons is totally misleading and provides no helpful information. In fact, the information may be considered destructive if the child is labeled intellectually inferior because of his score on measures with which he has had no preparation.

A test can also be used if the appropriate norms are not supplied. For example, you may wish to use the score in the context of the child's own classroom group, use the test for a diagnostic purpose, or establish a set of norms for your own school. It really is not a difficult process. Farr (unpublished), a leading reading evaluator, suggested the following procedures for norming your informal reading test:

1. Administer a standardized silent reading test to a group of students (a sample size of 100 is usually best). Several teachers may cooperate on the project.

2. Develop an informal reading test based on the instructional reading materials used in the classes. Use appropriate questions (as described above) and decide on criteria for establishing instructional reading levels.

3. Use the results of the standardized test (number 1 here) to rank the students from highest to lowest. Use a composite reading score (not subscores) for this ranking.

4. Randomly select three students from each decile of the ranking. That is, select three students from the top ten, select three students from the second ten, etc., until you have selected 30 of the total 100 students.

5. Administer the informal reading test to these students.

6. From this procedure you can develop equivalency (IRI reading levels) for students scoring at various points on the standardized reading test.

Let us assume that the students who are being tested are fourth graders. After you have completed the administration of the standardized test and selected your deciles, you should study the test manual and recode the scores into reading grade levels. The next step is to assume that the scores are accurate for each decile, that is, that students who score at seventh grade level are capable of performing on other tests at a seventh grade level. Now you are ready to administer the informal reading test with test questions you have developed. The scores of each of your groups will establish norms for your informal reading test. The following chart illustrates this procedure.

| Group | Standardized Test | | Mean Informal Reading Test Scores (highest = 10 pts. | Estimated Grade Level |
	Mean Raw Score	Mean Reading Grade Level		
Group A	85	7.0	9	7.0
Group B	50	4.0	6	4.0
Group C	30	1.0	3	1.0

From this chart you can see that the scores for your informal reading test are easily correlated with estimated reading levels. However, these scores should probably be used only to determine grade level criteria. In this case, a score of 6 out of 10 will approximate a reading level score of 1.0. There are several cautions which we would like to point out if you intend to use this procedure:

1. This procedure only *approximates* a reading level.

2. It is assumed that the objective of your informal reading test conforms to the objectives of the standardized reading test. Your informal reading test may have an entirely different purpose than the standardized reading test, and therefore, the score may not accurately reflect reading level ability for this particular task.

3. There is a statistical concern with this procedure. If one student in group A scores two out of ten and most of the other students score nine or ten and if the mean is equated at eight, then a score of eight may not accurately reflect the group's scores. Therefore, you may want to use the median score as the norm instead of the mean score.

In addition to examining reliability, validity, and norming samples when you are choosing a test, you should also consider the following:

1. When was the test first published?
2. Has it been revised recently? Remember that words and concepts change with each generation. Many children today have never heard of an "outhouse" or an "icebox."
3. Is this an individual or group test?
4. Can the test be hand or machine scored? If it is scored by the testing company, remember to request that the student answer sheets be returned. You can plan instruction if you know the consistency of errors made by the students. An IQ score of 103, or a reading score of 6.2, tells you nothing that will aid your planning.
5. How many test forms are available? If you plan to retest after instruction you will need twice as many forms.
6. How long does it take to administer the test? Be careful to measure desired behavior rather than rate.
7. Does your budget afford the cost of this test?
8. What subtests are available? Perhaps one or two of the subtests of a standardized test measure the desired behavior.* If this is the case, then why administer the entire test? Sometimes one subtest is so highly correlated with all of the other subtests in a specific test, that you need only to give one subtest to ascertain reading achievement information for a child. In order to determine if you can use one subtest as a valid predictor of overall achievement, you should consult the statistics provided in the manual for each standardized test.
9. Are tables, maps. or graphs included? If so, be sure that they can be read easily.

Directions. The teacher must be careful to use the same directions in administering the test that were used in standardizing the test. Are the directions clear to all of the children? Lack of clarity in giving directions often measures one's ability to interpret directions, as well as, or instead of, the previously desired behavior. Are the directions written in vocabulary appropriate to your grade level? Would it invalidate the test if you explained the directions to your children?

Some of this information will be found in the manual. However, keep in mind that the manual is written by an author or a publisher, whose major intent is to sell the tests. A less biased review of most tests can be found in the *Mental Measurement Yearbook*, edited by Buros (1972). This reference should be consulted before investing time and money in a testing program.

To avoid misuse of facts, it is very important that you state your reason for testing: What do I want to know about this child? How will this knowledge help me in planning better activities for him or her? After answering these questions, carefully select your instrument, using the previously stated criteria. After scoring, diagnose and plan your curriculum accordingly. No one has to pass or fail as he is only competing with himself.

Go one step farther and explain to your principal that the standardized tests being given to your class at the beginning of the year are really of little instructional value if you only have a list which supplies you with a single grade level

---

*Behavior is used in the sense of desired cognitive or affective outcome or performance. Behavioral objectives are explained in detail in Chapter 15.

score for each child. Ask for a breakdown of the test by category/components, for example, vocabulary score and syllabication score.

As you attempt to further analyze student assessment, you may want to use a *diagnostic test;* an instrument of this type is designed to provide you with a more thorough analysis of individual skill competency. For example, a standard reading survey test will provide you with general information regarding student skill in *vocabulary, comprehension,* and *rate,* whereas a diagnostic instrument provides scores in *knowledge of consonant sounds, blending, syllabication, morphemes, comprehension, study skills,* and *reading rate.* A more thorough analysis of information is provided through the diagnostic test.

Diagnostic tests are often individually administered and require administrative and scoring skills because interpretation may be a complex task. Whichever type of test you use, if it is computer scored, remember to remind the publishing company to return the individual answer sheets so that *continuing diagnosis* can take place.

Standardized achievement test results, which can be used to diagnose and plan instructional needs, can be correlated with informal test results to acquire a more valid understanding of individual student skills. Correlation of standardized and informal tests, if correctly used, will provide a reliable and accurate assessment of student growth.

Informal measures, teacher checklists, textbook tests, and interest and attitude inventories are easily constructed if the teacher is aware of the behavior he or she wants to measure. Do you want to know if the child has map-reading skills or dictionary skills? Do you want to gain some knowledge about Tom's reading vocabulary? The behavior to be measured must be clearly stated so that appropriate materials can be prepared to measure this behavior. Too often, teacher tests are not correlated with material that has been taught. The need for accurate measurement cannot be overemphasized because student growth is the single most frequently used basis for evaluating teaching methods, teacher effectiveness, curriculum, instructional procedures, and grouping practices.

Assessing the growth of the student is essential for making decisions related to the individualization of his program. Student evaluation must be continuous so that program changes can be made in accordance with the progress of the student. Correct use of test results helps the teacher in planning for both group and individual instruction. The process of *diagnosing* the strengths and needs of your students forms your instructional base. Whether your measure has been standardized or informally designed, your instruction should center on the elimination of error, which alters the comprehension of what is read. (Learning to use relevant test instruments effectively requires practice and critical evaluation as to the best application purposes.)

Appendix A is designed to acquaint you with standardized reading tests, publishers, and reading skills being measured. It is included to provide you with the comparative information you need to adquately select a test.

Informal Criterion Measures

As a classroom teacher you will find that you cannot rely solely on standardized tests in a diagnostic-prescriptive curriculum. You will find that informal assessments also provide you with valuable information regarding the reading competencies of your students. Informal instruments differ from standardized measures because they do not involve the formalized procedures for constructing, administering, and scoring. The quality of the informal measures used in your classroom will depend on *your competency* to design, implement, and evaluate them.

Informal measures that will be useful to you as a reading teacher are *informal reading inventories, reading miscue inventories,* and the *cloze readability technique.*

Informal Reading Inventory

The informal reading inventory (IRI) is used by the classroom teacher to determine a student's *independent reading level, instructional reading level,* and *frustrational level.* The independent level is believed to be the one in which the student can read successfully with little or no aid because fluency and comprehension are developed well enough to master materials at this level. The student's instructional level is the level at which he requires teacher assistance. At this level, the student's fluency and comprehension skills are not as well developed as when he reads at the independent level. The frustrational reading level signals an area of difficulty to be avoided by the student. The level of the book at the student's frustrational level is too difficult.

IRIs may be designed to provide you with information related to both the oral and silent reading competencies of your students. For detailed information regarding the development of IRIs we refer you to:

Silvaroli, Nicholas J. *Classroom Reading Inventory.* Dubuque, Iowa: William C. Brown Company Publishers, 1973.
Potter, Thomas C., and Kenneth Rae. *Informal Reading Diagnosis.* Englewood Cliffs, N.J.: Prentice-Hall, Inc., 1973.
Johnson, Marjorie S., and Ray A. Kress. *Informal Reading Inventories.* Newark, Del.: International Reading Association, 1965.

Interpretation of Oral Reading Test. Kress and Johnson (1965) maintain that the child is reading at his independent reading level if he scores 99 to 100 per cent (one error) in his oral reading word analysis skills in a 100-word passage. If the child averages two to five errors, or 95 to 98 per cent, he is considered to be reading at his instructional reading level. The child has reached his frustrational reading level when he cannot master at least 94 per cent of the text.

Administration of an Oral Reading Test

1. Select a 100-word passage from the material you wish the child to read.
2. Child is asked to orally read the passage.
3. The teacher records the following types of errors. The teacher may record the reading and score the child afterward.

Types of errors

Mispronounciation:	Record the incorrect response above the word missed.
Substitution:	Record the substituted word above the one missed.
Omission:	Circle the omitted word or words.
Insertion:	Caret ∧ in the extra word.
Hesitations:	Supply the needed word and write Ⓗ if the child pauses for longer than five seconds.
Repetitions:	Draw a wavy line under repeated words.

Record Keeping

(big) Ⓗ
Pablo Torres and his family lived on a hacienda owned by a very rich Latin American. The village had ⓝⓞ electricity. No paved roads led to it. Some of the people had heard about telephones, and television sets, and radios, but nobody in the village owned *(one)* one. Only a few of the village people knew how to read because *(wasn't)* there was no school.

(many)
Like Pablo's family, most of the people were Indians ⓦⓗⓞ worked as farmers
Ⓗ
and herdsmen. In return for farming the hacienda owner's land and taking care of
(the)   *(not)*
his animals, they were given a part of the harvest. But it was never enough to carry
(the)   *(bad)*
a family through the winter. So Pablo's father, along with many others, had to
borrow from the owner. He was ⓝⓔⓥⓔⓡ able to pay what he owed. Each year he
Ⓗ
sank a little further into debt.

Jarolimek and Davis (1974, p. 476)

Administration of a Silent Reading Test

1. Prepare questions that determine the student's ability to use various parts of the text (index, glossary, etc.):
   a. On what pages will you find information about prehistoric man?
   b. How does the author define prehistoric?
2. Prepare questions that measure both the vocabulary and comprehension of what has been read:
   a. Where did prehistoric man originate?
   b. Define the word skeletal used by the author in the following sentence.
3. When preparing these questions, you must be careful to provide items that assess the many operations of comprehension skills. Please refer to Chapter 9 for practice in developing a complex range of questions necessary to assess the comprehension competencies of your students.

4. Direct the students to read the selection.
5. Students can be timed if you are interested in measuring reading rate.

Record Keeping. You may want to devise a chart that will help you to determine student need at a quick glance.

Name	Parts of book	Vocabulary	Recall	Main ideas	Recognition	Translation	Inference	Evaluation	Details
Deering, Michael									
Hill, Beverly									
Burnce, Bess									
Ramirez, Sadie									
Kavanaugh, Denise									
Houlden, Marilyn									
Jones, Jeff									
Cunningham, Mary									
Hess, Pearl									
Rivera, Juan									
Chu, Gin									
Ryan, Colleen									

Figure 3. Record-Keeping Chart

Interpretation of Silent Reading Test. On the silent reading test, the child is believed to be reading at his independent reading level if he is able to correctly answer 90 to 100 per cent of the questions. If 70 to 90 per cent of the questions are correctly answered, the child is believed to be reading at his instructional level. His instructional level is now planned.

Careful planning of instructional procedures will eliminate any areas of weakness which were evidenced at this level. The frustrational reading level has been reached if the child cannot answer at least 70 per cent of the posed questions.

Informal Reading Inventory Standards

Level	Oral reading	Comprehension
Independent	99–100%	99–100%
Instructional	95–98%	70–90%
Frustrational	Below 94%	Below 70%

Figure 4

These criteria are presented to guide you in determining student reading levels. Be flexible in using them, because a student may differ only slightly from one of the stated standards and still be reading at one of the levels. Remember, all instruments are designed to facilitate *your* decision making about student's needs and competencies. The final decision is yours; therefore, we encourage you to judge wisely and flexibly, remembering that *you*, not an *instrument*, are the trained teacher.

Consider precautions when employing IRIs:

1. The type of error may be more important than the number of errors.
2. Inventory accuracy may be hampered by teacher inexperience in construction, administration, and scoring.

Reading Miscue Inventory. A second informal measure that can be easily used by classroom teachers is the Reading Miscue Inventory (RMI) designed by Goodman and Burke (1972). The focus of this inventory is on the *type* of error being made, rather than on the *number* of errors. The term *miscue* refers to any oral reading response that does not match the expected response.

Example:

Text reads: Wait a moment.
Reader responds: Wait a minute.
Text reads: Please pass some cake.
Reader responds: Please pass me the cake.
Text reads: One day at dinner . . .
Reader responds: One day at the dinner . . .
Text reads: Mildred gulped the biscuits.
Reader responds: Mildred gulped down the biscuits.
Text reads: May ran into the store.
Reader responds: Mary ran in the store.

Administration of Reading Miscue Inventory

1. Select a passage above your student's independent level of reading.
2. Ask student to read the selection orally.
3. Use a recorder to tape the child's reading.
4. Have the child retell the story and answer questions about portions of the story which have been omitted from his retelling.
5. If the child has comprehended the story well enough to be able to retell it, he is believed to be reading successfully.
6. If the child cannot successfully retell the story, you must now code the miscues by using the taxonomy.
7. After you have coded the miscues, determine existing patterns and plan appropriate instructional strategies to alleviate student needs.

When a miscue has occurred, it must be analyzed further, using the following taxonomy, which has been suggested by Goodman, Burke and Lindberg (1972).

use for miscues

Question	Example	Possible interpretation
1. Graphic similarity: How similar are the words in appearance?	Home for hone	Inaccurate decoding; lack of familiarity with the word.
2. Sound similarity: Do the words sound alike?	Dark for park	Faulty decoding; lack of familiarity with the word.
3. Is dialect variation involved in the miscue?	Jill be at school. for Jill is at school.	Ability to use oral language as a reading aid.
4. Does the miscue occur as a result of a change in intonation?	The mínute hand of the clock was painted silver. for The minuté hand of the clock was painted silver.	Unfamiliarity with the author's language structure.
5. Syntactic acceptability. Does the miscue occur in a sentence that is syntactically (grammatically) acceptable?	The violence happened about a piece of land. for The violence hinged on a piece of land.	Oral language competency has been exhibited.
6. Semantic acceptability: Does the miscue occur in a sentence that is semantically (meaning) acceptable?	House for home.	Oral language competency has been exhibited.
7. Meaning change: Does the miscue result in a meaning change?	Beth sat in the dark room. for Beth sat on the park bench.	Unfamiliar language situation.
8. Correction and semantic accountability: Do student corrections make the sentence semantically acceptable?	The mother clapped for the banana. The monkey clapped for the banana. for The monkey clawed for the banana.	High level of comprehension.

When these questions are answered and scored, decisions are made with regard to the student's reading strategies, knowledge, and language usage. Scores are based on graphic, syntactic, and semantic difficulties.

Cloze Readability Technique

A third informal measure of reading is the cloze readability technique, which primarily measures a student's ability to comprehend a given text. Bormuth (1968) designed the following cloze instrument.

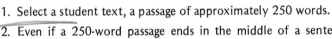

Administration

1. Select a student text, a passage of approximately 250 words.
2. Even if a 250-word passage ends in the middle of a sentence, just use the 250 words.

Lon Leonard was eighteen years old when he first saw the prairie lands in eastern Kansas. The oldest of eight children, Lon had moved there with his family from southern Virginia. His father had sold his Virginia farm because he had no hope of finding farm land for his children in his home state. It was 1876 when the family arrived at the 160-acre farm, about forty miles south of the modern city of Wichita, Kansas. The farm was on open grassland about three miles from the nearest stream.

Lon and his father brought wood from a lumber dealer and hauled it dozens of miles to the new farm. Just before winter began, they finished building a three-room house.

With winter starting, Mr. Leonard needed wood for fuel. He went to the farmers who had settled along the stream to the west of him. Their land had trees on it. He would cut wood for them, Mr. Leonard said, if they would let him cut some wood for himself. Two farmers agreed to this, and Lon and his father cut wood most of that winter.

During the winter they saw a 160-acre piece of land along the stream that looked as if someone had settled there and then left. There was a small sod house on it, but no one was living in it. Lon and his father thought this land would make a good farm. There was the stream, some woods along the stream, and acres of gently rolling grassland.

Lon wanted that land. He and his father went to the closest General Land Office, and Lon put in a claim for the farm. The land could be his, he was told, if the first settler did not come back for the rest of the year. To make it his to keep, he would have to live on it and make it a working farm. This he did.

Lon and his father worked very hard during the next five years. By 1882 they had crops growing on eighty acres of Mr. Leonard's farm and almost ninety acres of Lon's farm. The woods along the stream had supplied wood for both farms. Small barns had been built on both farms. Each farm had a small pasture fenced with osage orange hedge. Lon had planted the hedge all around the boundary of his farm.

Three years later Lon had one-hundred-twenty acres of his farm plowed and planted. He had a large barn by then. He had dug a well near his house, but he used the stream for water for his horses and cattle. It took too much time and work to haul enough water for them, bucket after bucket, out of the well.

By this time Lon was sick of living in the little sod house. And he was lonely. Even though his family lived nearby, he lived and worked alone most of the time.

3. Delete every fifth word and substitute a straight line in place of each missing word.

4. A passage should contain approximately fifty straight lines after deletions have been made.

Example:

Lon Leonard was eighteen _____ old when he first _____ the prairie lands in _____ Kansas. The oldest of _____ children, Lon had moved _____ with his family from _____ Virginia. His father had _____ his Virginia farm because _____ had no hope of _____ farm land for his _____ in his home state. _____ was 1876 when the _____ arrived at the 160 _____ farm, about forty miles _____ south of the modern city _____ Wichita, Kansas. The farm _____ on open grassland about _____ miles from the nearest _____ .

Lon and his father _____ wood from a lumber _____ and hauled it dozens _____ miles to the new _____ . Just before winter began, _____ finished building a three _____ house.

With winter starting, _____ Leonard needed wood for _____ . He went to the _____ who had settled along _____ stream to the west _____ him. Their land had _____ on it. He would _____ wood for them, Mr. _____ said, if they would _____ him cut some wood _____ himself. Two farmers agreed _____ this, and Lon and _____ father cut wood most _____ that winter.

During the _____ they saw a 160 _____ piece of land along _____ stream that looked as _____ someone had settled there _____ then left. There was _____ small sod house on _____ but no one was _____ in it. Lon and _____ father thought this land _____ make a good farm.

_____ was the stream, some _____ along the stream, and _____ of gently rolling grassland.

_____ wanted that land. He _____ his father went to _____ closest General Land office, _____ Lon put in a claim _____ the farm. The land _____ be his, he was _____ if the first settler _____ not come back for _____ rest of the year. _____ make it his to keep, _____ would have to live _____ it and make it _____ working farm. This _____ did.

Lon and his _____ worked very hard during _____ next five years. By _____ they had crops growing _____ eighty acres of Mr. _____ farm and almost ninety _____ of Lon's farm. The _____ along the stream had _____ wood for both farms. _____ barns had been built _____ both farms. Each farm _____ a small pasture fenced _____ osage orange hedge. Lon _____ planted the hedge all _____ the boundary of his _____ .

Three years later Lon _____ one hundred twenty acres _____ his farm plowed and _____ . He had a large _____ by then. He had _____ a well near his house, _____ he used the stream _____ water for his horses _____ cattle. It took too _____ time and work to _____ enough water for them, _____ after bucket, out of _____ well.

By this time _____ was sick of living _____ the little sod house. _____ he was lonely. Even _____ his family lived nearby, _____ lived and worked alone _____ of the time.

(Jarolimek and Davis, 1974, p. 280)

5. If you are unsure of standardization of text difficulty, select 12 250-word passages that are approximately eight pages apart. This wide range of passages will ensure a representative sample of text difficulty. If you have previously selected a passage that represents difficulty, administer it.
6. Give every student all of the passages.
7. Students are asked to insert the missing words. No time limits are set.
8. Responses are correct even if misspelled.
9. Each correct closure is worth two points.

Interpretation of Cloze Test

1. If a student scores 58 to 100 points, the material being read is at his independent level. When a score of 44 to 57 occurs, the material being read is at the child's instructional level. A score below 43 indicates that the material is at the child's frustrational level.

2. Determine mean scores for each passage. When you retest, you will then be able to use only the passage that most closely approximates the mean difficulty of the text.

QUESTIONS AND RELATED READINGS

Now that you have some understanding of the criterion and norm referenced measures and processes available to aid you in assessing student competency, we refer you to Chapter 15, "Creating and Managing a Reading Program," which is designed to aid you in *planning* and *managing* the instruction that will facilitate student growth in prescribed areas.

If at this time you do not feel that you have attained adequate knowledge to successfully answer the following questions, we would like to suggest related readings.

1. Why is student diagnosis viewed as a continuous process?
2. What would be the range of reading levels in a fourth-grade class?
3. What cautions would you employ in utilizing readability formulas?
4. How does a criterion-referenced test differ from a norm referenced test?
5. What considerations would you employ in test selection?
6. Compare and contrast two standardized reading readiness measures.
7. What standardized achievement tests have subtests that measure the study skills of children in grades 4 to 6?
8. Discuss some differences between the IRI and the RMI.
9. Explain the Cloze readability technique.
10. Why have children often been erroneously labeled dull or retarded?

11. What does IF mean?

12. How does one compute a reading expectancy level?

Goal 1: To aid the reader in understanding student diagnosis as one step in the evaluative process

Question 1: Why is student diagnosis viewed as a continuous process?

Chall, Jeanne. "How They Learn and Why They Fail." *Improvement of Reading Through Classroom Practice.* Conference Proceedings. Newark, Del.: International Reading Association, 1964, pp. 147–8.

Downing, John. "A Gap Has Two Sides." *Reading Teacher,* 25 (April 1972), 534–8.

Robinson, Helen M. *Why Pupils Fail in Reading.* Chicago: University of Chicago Press, 1946.

Goal 2: To aid the reader in understanding the range of reading levels

Question 2: What would be the range of reading levels in a fourth-grade class?

Emans, Robert. "Teacher Evaluations of Reading Skills and Individualized Reading." *Elementary English,* 42 (March 1965), 258–60.

Mason, George E., and Norma J. Prater. "Early Reading and Reading Instruction." *Elementary English,* 43 (March 1965), 258–60.

Rankin, Earl F., Jr., and Robert J. Tracy. "Residual Gain as a Measure of Individual Differences in Reading Improvement." *Journal of Reading,* 8 (March 1965), 224–33.

Goal 3: To aid the reader in understanding processes for determining readability

Question 3: What cautions would you employ in utilizing readability formulas?

Koenke, Karl. "Another Practical Note on Readability Formulas." *Journal of Reading,* 15 (Dec. 1971), 203–8.

McLaughlin, G. Harry. "SMOG Grading—A New Readability Formula." *Journal of Reading,* 12 (1969), 639–46.

Tibbetts, Sylvia-Lee. "How Much Should We Expect Readability Formulas To Do?" *Elementary English,* 50 (Jan. 1973), 75–6.

Goal 4: To aid the reader in understanding differences between criterion and norm referenced testing

Question 4: How does a criterion referenced test differ from a norm referenced test?

Question 5: What considerations would you employ in test selection?

Question 6: Compare and contrast two standardized reading readiness measures.

Question 7: What standardized achievement tests have subtests that measure study skills in children in grades 4 to 6?

Cox, Richard C. "Confusion Between Norm-Referenced and Criterion-Referenced Measurement." *Phi Delta Kappan,* 56 (Jan. 1974), 319.

Ebel, Robert L. "Educational Tests: Valid? Biased? Useful?" *Phi Delta Kappan,* (Oct. 1975), 82–8.

Frankel, Allen A. "A Substitute for Tests." *Phi Delta Kappan,* 50 (Feb. 1969), 345.

Gage, N. L. "The Causes of Race Differences in IQ: Replies to Shockley, Page, and Jensen." *Phi Delta Kappan,* 53 (March 1972), 422–7.

Green, Robert L. "Tips on Educational Testing: What Teachers and Parents Should Know." *Phi Delta Kappan,* (Oct. 1975), 89–93.

Hill, Walter R. "Reading Testing for Reading Evaluation." In *Measuring Reading Performance,* ed. by William Blanton, et al. Newark, Del.: International Reading Association, 1974, pp. 1–14.

Humphrey, Jack W., and Sandra R. Redden. "Encouraging Young Authors." *Reading Teacher,* 25 (April 1972), 643–51.

Jenkins, William A. "Developing Reading Competencies Through Social Studies and Literature." In *Reading as an Intellectual Activity,* ed. by J. Allen Figurel. Proceedings of the International Reading Association, 8 (1963), 107–10.

Ladas, Harold. "Grades: Standardizing and the Unstandardized Standard." *Phi Delta Kappan,* 56 (Nov. 1974), 185–6.

Lane, Patricia K., and Margery S. Miller. "Listening: Learning for Underachieving Adolescents." *Journal of Reading,* 15 (April 1972), 488–91.

Livingston, Myra C. "Children's Literature—In Chaos, a Creative Weapon." *Reading Teacher,* 27 (March 1974), 534–9.

Manzo, Anthony, and Deanna C. Martin. "Writing Communal Poetry." *Journal of Reading,* 17 (May 1974), 638–43.

Pittman, Grace. "Young Children Enjoy Poetry." *Elementary English,* 43 (1966), 56–9.

Saraceno, J., and A. Piscitello. "A Play! A Homemade Play!" *Journal of Reading,* 17 (Oct. 1973), 44–6.

Sieger, Frederick, J. "Literature and a Concern for Human Values." *Journal of Reading,* 15 (Nov. 1971), 139–42.

Steinacher, Richard. "Reading Flexibility: Dilemma and Solution." *Journal of Reading,* 15 (Nov. 1971), 143–50.

Sullivan, Howard. "Effects of Systematic Practice on the Composition Skills of First Graders." *Elementary English,* (May 1974).

Sullivan, Joanna. "Liberating Children to Creative Reading." *Reading Teacher,* 25 (April 1972), 639–42.

Thorndike, Robert L. "Mr. Binet's Test 70 Years Later." *Educational Researcher,* 4 (May 1975), 3–7.

Torrance, E. P. *Encouraging Creativity in the Classroom.* Dubuque, Iowa: William C. Brown Company, Publishers, 1970.

Way, G. J. "Teaching Listening Skills." *Reading Teacher,* 26 (Feb. 1973), 477–82.

Goal 5: To aid the reader in understanding informal assessment

Question 8: Discuss some differences between the IRI and the RMI.

Question 9: Explain the Cloze readability technique.

Bormuth, John. "The Cloze Readability Procedure." *Elementary English,* 45 (April 1968) 429–36.

Goodman, Kenneth S. "Miscue Analysis: Theory and Reality in Reading." In *New Horizons in Reading,* ed. by John E. Merritt. Newark, Del.: International Reading Association, 1976, pp. 15–26.

Gray, William S. "The Value of Informal Tests of Reading Performance." *Journal of Educational Research,* 1 (1920), 103–11.

Pyrczak, Fred, and Jerome Axelrod. "Determining the Passage Dependence of Reading Comprehension Exercises: A Call for Replications." *Journal of Reading,* 19 (Jan. 1976), 279–83.

<u>Goal 6</u>: To aid the reader in understanding the concept of present level of intellectual functioning

<u>Question 10</u>: Why have children often been erroneously labeled dull or retarded?

<u>Question 11</u>: What does <u>IF</u> mean?

Cleary, Anne T., et al. "Educational Uses of Tests with Disadvantaged Students." *American Psychologist,* (Jan. 1975), 15–41.

Davis, Allison. *Social Class Influences upon Learning.* Cambridge, Mass.: Harvard University Press, 1948.

Eells, Kenneth. *Intelligence and Cultural Differences.* Chicago: University of Chicago Press, 1951.

McNeil, Nathaniel D. "IQ Tests and the Black Culture." *Phi Delta Kappan,* (Nov. 1975), 209–10.

Ornstein Allan. "IQ Tests and the Culture Issue." *Phi Delta Kappan,* 57 (Feb. 1976), 403–4.

<u>Goal 7</u>: To aid the reader in understanding reading expectancy level

<u>Question 12</u>: How does one compute a reading expectancy level?

Harris, Albert J. *How to Increase Reading Ability.* 5th ed. New York: David McKay Co., Inc., chaps. 9, 10, 11.

Spache, George D. "Estimating Reading Capacity." In *The Evaluation of Reading,* ed. by Helen M. Robinson. Supplementary Educational Monographs, no. 88. Chicago: University of Chicago Press, 1958, pp. 15–20.

BIBLIOGRAPHY

Aukerman, R. C. "Assessing the Readability of Textbooks." *Reading in the Secondary School Classroom.* New York: McGraw-Hill Book Company, 1972, pp. 19–45.

Binet, A., and T. Simon. *The Development of Intelligence in Children.* Baltimore: The Williams and Wilkins Co., 1915.

Bond, G. L., and M. A. Tinker. *Reading Difficulties: Their Diagnosis and Correction.* New York: Appleton-Century-Crofts, 1967.

Bormuth, John. "The Cloze Readability Procedure." *Elementary English,* 45 (April 1968), 429–36.

Bormuth, J. R., ed. *Readability in 1968.* Champaign, Ill.: National Council of Teachers of English, 1968.

Buros, O. K. *Mental Measurement Yearbooks.* Highland Park, N.J.: Gryphon Press, 1965.

Dale, E., and J. Chall. "A Formula for Predicting Readability." *Educational Research Bulletin,* 27 (1948), 11–20.

Farr, Roger. *Reading: What Can Be Measured?* Newark, Del.: International Reading Association, 1969.

———, ed. *Measurement and Evaluation of Reading.* New York: Harcourt, Brace & World, Inc., 1970.

Flesch, R. F. *Marks of Readable Style: A Study of Adult Education.* New York: Bureau of Publications, Teachers College Press, Columbia University, 1943.

Fry, E. "Readability Formula That Saves Time." *Journal of Reading,* 11 (April 1968), 513–16; 575–78.

Goodlad, J. I. *School, Curriculum, and the Individual.* New York: John Wiley & Sons, Inc., 1966.

Goodman, Kenneth S. "Miscue Analysis: Theory and Reality in Reading." In *New Horizons in Reading,* ed. by John E. Merritt. Newark, Del.: International Reading Association, 1976, pp. 15–26.

Goodman, K. S. "Analysis of Oral Reading Miscues: Applied Psycholinguistics." *Reading Research Quarterly,* 5 *(Fall 1969), 9–30.*

Goodman, Y. M. "Reading Diagnosis—Qualitative or Quantitative?" *Reading Teacher,* 26 (Oct. 1972), 32–37.

Goodman, Y. and Burke,   *Reading Miscue Inventory.* New York: Macmillan Publishing Co., Inc., 1972.

Gray W. S., and B. E. Leary. *What Makes a Book Readable?* Chicago: University of Chicago Press, 1935.

Guidry, L. J., and F. D. Knight. "Comparative Readability: Four Formulas and Newberry Books." *Journal of Reading,* 19 (April 1976), 552–6.

Harris, A. J. *How to Increase Reading Ability.* New York: David McKay, 1970.

———. "Some New Developments on Readability." In *New Horizons in Reading,* ed. by John E. Merritt. Newark, Del.: International Reading Association, 1976.

Jarolimek, J. and B. Davis. *Lands of Promise.* New York: Macmillan Publishing Co., Inc., 1974.

Johnson, M. S., and R. A. Kress. *Informal Reading Inventories.* Newark, Del.: International Reading Association, 1965.

Lorge, I. "Predicting Readability." *Teachers College Record.* 45 (March 1944), 404–19.

Potter, T. C., and G. Rae. *Informal Reading Diagnosis.* Englewood Cliffs, N.J.: Prentice-Hall, Inc., 1973.

Silvaroli, N. J. *Classroom Reading Inventory.* Dubuque, Iowa: William C. Brown Company, Publishers, 1973.

Spache, G. "A New Readability Formula for Primary-Grade Reading Materials." *Elementary School Journal,* 53 (March 1953), 410–13.

Thorndike, R. L. *Reading Comprehension Education in Fifteen Countries: An Empirical Study.* New York: Wiley, 1973.

15

Creating and managing a reading program

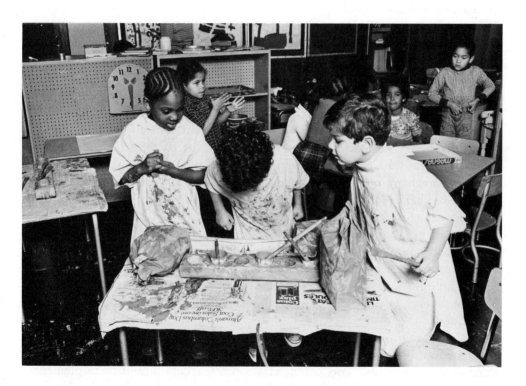

Classroom management is that set of activities by which the teacher promotes appropriate student behavior ..., develops good interpersonal relationships and a positive socioemotional climate, and establishes and maintains an effective and productive classroom organization.

Weber, Wilford, "Classroom Management," in *Classroom Teaching Skills: A Handbook.* James M. Cooper (ed). Lexington, Mass.: D.C. Heath Co., 1977, p. 286.

GOALS: To aid the teacher in
    1. understanding the value of classroom management.
    2. understanding the process of thematic teaching.
    3. developing and utilizing behavioral objectives.
    4. understanding the techniques of grouping.
    5. utilizing educational materials.
    6. utilizing a process of continuous evaluation and understanding the value
of sequencing instruction.

"School is fun this year!" seven-year-old Shannon was overheard telling her
younger brother Eric. "We get to read fun books and we don't just have to
read our readers. This year I like reading as much as science!"

Shannon's parents were somewhat surprised by these accolates because lauda-
tory comments about the Castle Rock Elementary School Reading Program
were never uttered by Shannon. They were anxious to understand Shannon's
change of attitude, so they called Ms. Cunningham, Shannon's teacher, and
arranged to visit the school.

During their visit with Ms. Cunningham, Shannon's parents realized that the
way in which the classroom was managed contributed greatly to the success of
the reading program. Ms. Cunningham explained that she believed learning
environments should include provisions for:
    1. giving *all* children specific information regarding their competencies.
    2. encouraging student participation in the planning of program goals.
    3. having all students participate in evaluating their own progress.
    4. encouraging students to make decisions about participation in alternate
learning activities designed to accomplish the specified goals.

Ms. Cunningham further explained that these beliefs were best accomplished
if she viewed herself as a classroom manager, because in this role she could work
alone or with children to determine:
    1. reading program goals
    2. student competencies
    3. procedures for individual or group progress.
    4. techniques and materials needed to implement appropriate procedures
    5. continuous evaluation of the goals, student competencies, processes, and
techniques.

Ms. Cunningham realized that once she had developed a working philosophy
of education, she had to determine specific means for helping her students
accomplish their goals. Too often, classroom teachers intend to implement a
very personalized model of education but are unable to do so because they lack
the skills needed to manage one. The use of management systems in educational
planning is expanding. Through such a system, the teacher is able to compare
student growth with stated objectives and reschedule or recycle student programs according to exhibited competencies. Many textbook companies have
begun to develop basal reading series that provide the teacher with a management system model: for example, *Ginn 720* (1976), *Macmillan R* (1975), *The
Laidlaw Reading Program* (1976).

Management Systems

We have encouraged you, throughout this text, to develop a definition of reading, as well as to determine the teaching strategies you believe best facilitate teaching a child to read. With the hope that you have completed these tasks, this chapter is designed to help you to understand the procedures for assessing your students and implementing your program. This process of continual evaluation is best accomplished through an educational management system.

System management has become widespread because of the increased use of technology during the 1950s and 1960s. Looking toward business management as a model, educational technologists have designed curriculum which is dependent upon an interactional base. This interactional base involves the working together of parents, students, teachers, administrators, school boards and community leaders. The type of complimentary interaction desired is dependent on well- correlated goals.

Let us further explore the processes of defining and developing a management system by focusing our attention on Shannon's classroom. Where is it located? What is the socioeconomic stratification? How old are the children in Ms. Cunningham's class? How many children are in this classroom?

As we attempt to answer these questions about the children who are served by the use of a management system, we may find it helpful to refer to Figure 1, on page 594, an educational management system, as an organizational referent point. Who exactly are the individuals in Ms. Cunningham's classroom, and what existing curricular and societal structures predetermine classroom interactions?

Awareness of Existing Structures and Individuals

Consideration must be directed toward the existing structures that directly affect the happenings within your classroom. Although some of these structures may be governed by you (philosophy and psychology), others (societal influence, budget allocations) may be outside your range of authority, and still other areas (curricular requirements, time schedules) may have been established before your arrival, but can be changed.

You need to be familiar with all the structures in your environment and the extent of your decision-making power regarding each. You may gain initial insights into this area through social and professional interactions with colleagues and administrators. A review of existing school policies, as well as curriculum guides, will offer you some insights into the parametric structure of the existing curriculum. As you begin to collect information about existing structures, remember to ask the following questions:

1. How is the day divided?
2. Is the time schedule predetermined? By whom?
3. Is your classroom self-contained?

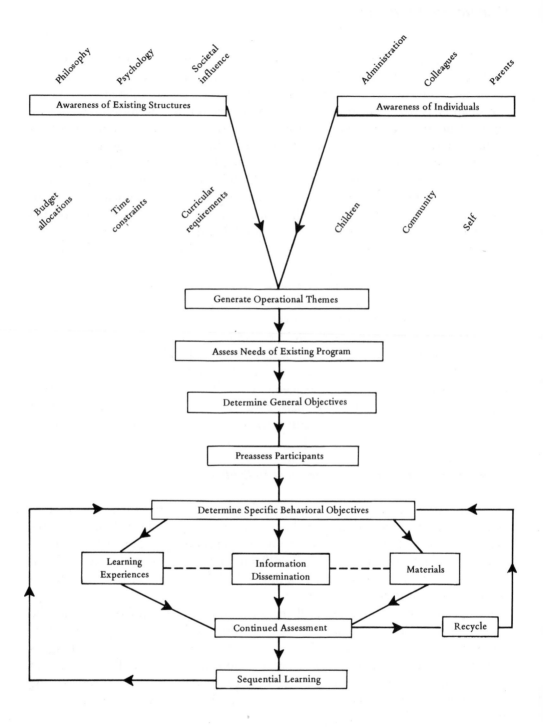

Figure 1. Educational Management System.

4. What special teachers (music, art) or special services (gym, theater) are provided?
5. Is there an organized curriculum committee? If so, how can you join?
6. What funds are available to you?
7. How are text materials adopted?

Questions such as these may be asked during an early interview. Always attempt to compare the answers you receive with your philosophy of teaching. Is there compatibility? If so, you will avoid conflict later on. If not, can alterations (compromises) be made by you?

Awareness of Individuals

Who am I? Who am I working for? Who am I working with? Answers to these questions may be found through your interactions with the administration, colleagues, parents, community, children, and yourself.

Administration

1. What appears to be the major objectives of the administration?
2. How are these objectives related to education?
3. How is their apparent philosophy similar or different than mine?
4. What are the line-staff relationships (line of command) within this administration?
5. What decisions are made by whom?

Colleagues

1. Who are my colleagues?
2. Do there appear to be any major educational beliefs shared by the majority of this faculty?
3. What are the faculty's initial impressions of me?
4. What will be my role as a member of this educational community?
5. What decision-making responsibilities are mine?

Parents

1. Who are the parents of my children?
2. What are their values with regard to the educational training of their children?
3. Are they heavily involved with the decision-making processes of this school?
4. How do they view the existing faculty and administration?

Community

1. Is the surrounding community well represented (economically, socially) by the family make-up of the children within my classroom?
2. What segment of the community controls school-board decision making?
3. What are the apparent and less apparent feelings of the school board with regard to the administration, faculty, and education?

Children

1. Who are my children?
2. What have been their life exposures thus far?
3. What may be their projected life goals?
4. Are their life exposures similar or dissimilar to mine?
5. What will be their projected view of me?

Self

1. What will be my function in this educational community?
2. Do I harbor my prejudices or fears with regard to the people within the community?
3. Are there any barriers that may interfere with my functioning effectively?
4. If so, how is it possible to alter these barriers?

As a veteran or as a beginning teacher, you continually need to pursue answers to these questions. When Ms. Cunningham made these inquiries, she found that the children in Shannon's class were like students in most primary grades: multi-ethnic and culturally diverse, with various dialects, levels of cognitive development, levels of sensory and perceptual readiness, degrees of physical health, degrees of social and emotional development, various interests and attitudes about learning, and a great variety of oral and silent reading skills.

Ms. Cunningham realized that if she were to attempt to meet the learning needs of each of her twenty-six children, she would have to acquaint herself with the existing *program structures* in her school. She began by:

1. reviewing the specific sequence of reading skills covered in the school basal reading program. Because she realized that the levels of student reading ability within a primary grade might range from readiness to intermediate, Ms. Cunningham designed a scope and sequence checklist of reading skills, ranging from preprimer to sixth grade, that included skills in areas such as visual and auditory perception, blending, phonics analysis, and structural and contextual analysis.

2. reviewing specific terms such as *independent, instructional,* and *frustrational reading levels.*

3. surveying school libraries and closets to determine the range of available reading materials.

4. reacquainting herself with her principal's and colleagues' philosophy about reading instruction.

5. surveying community attitudes toward reading instruction.

Generate Operational Themes

After Ms. Cunningham had collected some general understanding of the existing structures and individuals within her educational community, as well as their decision-making effects on the management of her classroom, she began planning her classroom curriculum. She thought about general student interests and needs in order to determine the *topics* she hoped to share with her children. Although she added to and altered this list to accommodate her students' interests, she never confused her role with her students. She was employed to prepare, manage, manipulate, evaluate, and replan the educational environment. You may intend to share in the decision-making situations with your children, but never lose sight of the fact that your experiences are broader and more far-reaching than those of your children. These differences are, however, of *degree,* not *exclusion*. Many of these themes will be provided through the management system of the basal program you are using.

At this point, let's brainstorm to determine the general themes you may plan to share with your students.

> Coping with Change (social, cultural)
> Propaganda (spoken, written)
> Exploring Your Environment (geographically, emotionally)
> Life Today Versus Life Long Ago (family, environment, economic structures)
> New England Trade (waterways, economy, vessels)

As you add to this list of themes, keep in mind the fact that themes may be operating simultaneously because some of your students will not have the same interests or the same levels of readiness. Your intent in any theme will be to convey the basic skills of communication as well as the skills and areas of information that eventually will result in the development of independent learners.

> Students need to learn far more than the basic skills. Children who have just started school may still be in the labor force in the year 2030. For them, nothing could be more wildly impractical than an education designed to prepare them for specific vocations or professions or to facilitate their adjustment to the world as it is. To be practical, an education should prepare a man for work that doesn't yet exist and whose nature cannot even be imagined. This can be done only by teaching people how to learn, by giving them the kind of intellectual discipline that will enable them to apply man's accumulated wisdom to new problems as they arise, the kind of wisdom that will enable them to *recognize* new problems as they arise.
>
> *(Silberman, 1970, pp. 83–4)*

It may be helpful to select themes which facilitate the incorporation of science, math, and social studies lessons. Think of your themes as topics which may be expanded to become an integrated curriculum unit.

In order to aid in the development of an independent learner, you must remember that the student will have difficulty venturing beyond the sphere of indoctrination while developing independent learning skills if he cannot read, write, or engage in problem-solving activities. Your task is to introduce basic communication and study skills in a practical, useful, synthesized, interesting manner.

That's some task! But whoever told you that the effective teacher's job was easy? Through the selection of topical themes, you have begun the process of *thematic teaching*, which is simply the process of integrating content area learning, language arts, and study skills into a manageable, practical, interesting learning endeavor.

Assess the Needs of the Existing Program

Once Ms. Cunningham had selected some general themes, which she altered after assessing student interest, she attempted to assess the needs of the existing program. In making this program assessment, she asked questions such as these:

1. What previous themes have been explored at this grade level?
2. Do these themes apply to the objectives of the system?
3. Am I infringing on material that my colleagues may cover?
4. What resources are available to me?

After thinking about the existing curriculum, Ms. Cunningham attempted to develop general program objectives.

Determine General Objectives

Based on the general survey of the existing program, the following general objectives were designed. Objectives were to be mastered through the programmatic themes Ms. Cunningham had selected.

Theme	General objectives
I. Propaganda	1. Introduce students to the various forms of propaganda.
	2. Develop an understanding of the term propaganda.
	3. Develop an understanding of syllogistic reasoning.
	4. Incorporate syllogistic reasoning into verbal interactions.
	5. Detect propaganda.
	6. Evaluate the effects of propaganda.
II. Exploring your environment	1. Develop an awareness of self.
	2. Identify significant others.
	3. Identify geographic boundaries.
	4. Identify cultural boundaries.
	5. Compare strengths and weaknesses of boundary limitations.
	6. Evaluate social change you can affect.

As Ms. Cunningham planned these general thematic objectives, she became more aware of the interrelatedness of the content areas and of the basic skills each child would need in order to study this topic successfully. For example, within the thematic study of "exploring your environment," the child encounters geography, history, sociology, and mathematics, as well as reading, writing, and speaking. Through the integration of these areas, the learner explores standard, basic content skills while he explores areas of practical self-interest.

> The statement that individuals live in a world means, in the concrete, that they live in a series of situations. And when it is said that they live in these situations, the meaning of the word *in* is different from its meaning when it is said that pennies are "in" a can. It means, once more, that interaction is going on between an individual and objects and other persons. The conceptions of situation and of interaction are inseparable from each other. An experience is always what it is because of a transaction taking place between

an individual and what, at the time, constitutes his environment, whether the latter consists of persons with whom he is talking about some topic or event, the talked-about being also a part of the situation; or the toys with which he is playing; the book he is reading (in which his environment conditions at the time may be England or ancient Greece or an imaginary region); or the materials of an experiment he is performing. The environment, in other words, is whatever conditions interact with the personal needs, desires, purposes, and capacities to create the experience which is had. Even when a person builds a castle in the air he is interacting with the objects which he constructs in fancy.

(Dewey, 1938, pp. 43–4)

Ms. Cunningham realized that because children enter a given learning theme with varying amounts of readiness for the experience, it is important to assess entering competencies when you are planning to individualize the instruction.

Preassess Participants

In order to determine individual needs, Ms. Cunningham began the process of diagnosing student competencies. Through *formal* measures, such as standardized reading tests, and *informal* measures, such as observation scales, teacher-made checklists, and textbook placement exams, Ms. Cunningham assessed each child's:

1. sensory and perceptual developmental needs.
2. emotional and social needs.
3. knowledge of oral reading, noting each child's difficulties with sight words and knowledge of vowel situations, consonant elements, and structural and contextual clues.
4. silent reading comprehension skills, focusing her attention on inferential and evaluative comprehension skills.

Based on this initial diagnosis, groups were designed according to student interests and student needs. Correlation of student needs and interests became possible because Ms. Cunningham first determined the reading needs of each child; then she was able to accommodate student interests through alternate activities.

Planning Groups.   Once instructional levels have been determined through informal and standardized testing, it is possible to group students for instruction according to their skill-development needs, their achievement, their interests, purposes for reading, and attitudes toward reading. The practice of grouping allows for individualization of instruction and provides for economy of teacher effort and increased student participation. It is more efficient for a teacher to instruct a group of children with similar needs, interests, and purposes than it would be to work with a total classroom of separate individuals. Grouping allows materials to be matched to the learner more effectively than would be possible if instruction were geared to a class. Grouping according to individual assessment is beneficial to the learner because the instruction is matched with interests, needs, purposes, and skills. With this in mind, Ms. Cunningham began her program by creating the following grouping patterns.

Reading level	Number of students	Needs	Grouping plans
P	1	Has difficulty understanding concepts of space, time, color, number and value	Group A: Utilize child's interests to employ language experience activities to further conceptual development, as well as introduce and reinforce basic beginning reading word-recognition and comprehension skills.
1^1	1	Has a limited sight vocabulary, which decreases minimal literal comprehension	
1^2	1		
2^1	3	Has difficulty with patterns of organization, comparison, contrast, cause and effect.	Group B: Develop organizational skills that effect reading comprehension.
2^2	6		
3^1	6	Reads at grade level in basal text	Group C: Reinforce basic oral and silent reading skills while extending fluency and mastery of study skills.
3^2	4		
4^1	2	Reads independently above grade level	
4^2	1		Group D: Develop study skills and aid child in transferring and applying them to content area situations.
5^2	1	Reads independently well above grade level	

Although there are four groups that have various reading levels within this classroom, it should not be taken to indicate that there may be only four groups within any given class, or that there must be at least four groups.

First, there may be individuals who already possess the reading behaviors that have been set as the terminal outcome of instruction prior to the initiation of instruction. The teacher has two options for proceeding with the instructional program for these students; they may be allowed to advance to a new and different program, or they may proceed with the original program independently with minimal teacher guidance.

Second, other individuals may emerge who are unable to handle the materials required in the instructional program because they lack the skills which are necessary for dealing with the content. They would be totally incapable of benefiting from the instructional program as it is now planned. These children would be considered to be functioning on the frsutrational level. To make instruction meaningful for them, the program would have to be revised to begin with the skills that the students already possess and build the skills that are needed to master the original program.

Finally, another group of students may emerge, a group who can handle the materials and the instructional program but who still require teacher guidance and instruction. These students can be considered to be functioning at the instructional level, and they may proceed with the program as it was originally devised. There can be as many groups as necessary to meet the needs of the learners, but teacher energies must be taken into consideration. It may be that, in a given class, there are no students at the frustrational level when working within a certain theme; however, at the same time, students may be at various points within the instructional level. A teacher may form two, three, four, or five groups within the instructional level, each with different skills, interests, and purposes.

Because grouping is intended to increase participation for students, materials used for instruction are not necessarily uniform for all groups. For instance, the practice of grouping elementary school readers into "red," "blue," and "yellow" birds has often been the extent of grouping. Having each group use the same materials, purposes, and teaching methods, but at differing rates, is highly questionable because purpose, teaching methods, and materials should be modified, changed, and geared to meet the needs of the learners in a specific group in accord with the various themes being pursued.

It should be remembered that grouping must be based on students' thematic interests whenever possible, and groups will have to change accordingly. Groups are also modified according to specific instructional objectives. As a child progresses through the program and fulfills the objectives, the group for which that program has been formed may become unnecessary for all the learners because each student does not necessarily progress at the same speed. If the objective has been met or if it is determined to be unrealistic, the group may be dissolved. New objectives may then be formed for different purposes and different instructional objectives. The same individuals may or may not be part of both groups. Also, children who progress faster than others may profit from working independently. For grouping to be effective, not only do specific instructional objectives need to be defined, but constant evaluation of student progress is necessary to maintain the validity of the group.

The fact that children's skills constantly develop as a result of instruction emphasizes the need for continual evaluation, regrouping, and elimination of some groups and formation of new groups. Groups should be viewed as temporary and changing. At the same time, it should be recognized that not all students need to be included in groups all the time. This is especially true of students capable of functioning at the independent levels.

The testing instruments that can be used in grouping are much the same as those that are used in determining reading levels: standardized tests, informal tests, textbook tests, and teacher observations. The standardized reading tests can be used to provide evaluations of reading levels to determine groups if the skills measured by the test are the same as those included in the instructional program and are tested in the same manner as the skills to be taught. Informal tests also provide reliable indications of reading levels for the creation of groups, because they are constructed from the actual materials used in the programs and contain questions related specifically to instructional goals. The validity of the informal test for groups and for determining reading levels is often dependent on the competence of the teacher who devises it. Finally, teacher observations and textbook tests are especially useful in grouping. Such measures can provide a readily available means of assessing student progress toward attaining the objectives of the program.

In summary, successful grouping practices are contingent on the definition of what is to be taught, how it is to be taught, and the anticipated terminal behavior. It is also dependent on continuous assessments of student behavior, on flexibility of established groups, and on changing the instructional program to meet the needs of the students. In general, the following steps should be followed in using tests for grouping:

1. Define the objectives of the instructional program and the methodology for teaching the objective.

2. Preassess student reading behavior by using a standardized test (if it matches the objectives and definitions established for the instructional program), an informal test, a teacher checklist, and/or any combination of the three.

3. Form groups according to preassessment (for example: reading levels, thematic interests, purposes for reading, content of instruction, and student attitudes).

4. Evaluate student progress continuously by using informal tests, teacher checklists, or standardized tests (which match the instructional objectives) with the intent of moving students to independent activities if possible, or regrouping on the basis of new instructional goals where the original ones have been met. Prepare to eliminate groups when they are no longer necessary.

Once Ms. Cunningham had determined group composition and needs, she had to determine specific behavioral objectives for each learner or for each learning group.

Determine Specific Behavioral Objectives*

Although the relevance of behavioral objectives to thematic program planning continues to be debated, a review of the literature on this topic (Lapp, 1972) suggests that acceptance or rejection is based on speculation that has often been a replacement for research.

Unfortunately, the training of prospective teachers, which includes instruction in writing behavioral objectives, often is not accompanied by training in the utilization of such objectives. The teacher is never sure of the value of behavioral objectives in thematic curricular planning and evaluation. According to Gilpin (1962), an adequately prepared teacher can develop instructional objectives more effectively if the following questions and procedures are followed:

---

*A behavioral objective is composed of three criteria: (1) the operational *conditions* existing when the behavior occurs, (2) the terminal *behavior* occuring as a result of planned instruction, and (3) the level of *performance* needed for mastery.

1. What is it that we must teach?
2. How will we know when we have taught it?
3. What materials and procedures will work best to teach what we want to teach? (p. viii)

Guidelines such as these may encourage you, as a teacher, to define objectives before beginning to teach a lesson. Mager (1962), for example, specified five steps to follow in the development and use of behavioral objectives:

1. A statement of instructional objectives is a collection of words or symbols describing one of your educational intents.
2. An objective will communicate your intent to the degree you have described what the learner will be doing when demonstrating his achievement, and how you will know when he is doing it.
3. To describe terminal behavior (what the learner will be doing):
   a. Identify and name the overall behavior act.
   b. Define the important conditions under which the behavior is to occur (given and/or restrictions and limitations).
   c. Define the criterion of acceptable performance.
4. Write a separate statement for each objective: the more you have, the better chance you have of making clear your intent.
5. If you give each learner a copy of your objectives, you may not have to do much else. (p. 52)

There are many instances when a general objective is contrived and then designed into a behavioral objective. For example, a classroom objective may be to introduce children to the theme of community helpers. The following example is a behavioral objective derived from such a broad objective:

Given a lesson which introduces the topic of community helpers, the child will be able to name at least one such community helper and describe his role in the community with complete competency.

Why is an objective of this type needed or used by the teacher? When the teacher is asked to state in specific behavioral terms what he or she wants to accomplish by a specific lesson, she will be able to determine:

1. if the accomplishment of the stated objective is really of any value to the total development of the child.
2. if the child has accomplished the objective.
   a. If there are related objectives within the theme that are to be designed and utilized at this time.
   b. Methods of instruction and performance level needed for implementation of related objectives.
3. if the child has not accomplished the objective:
   a. Whether the objective can be accomplished by this child at this time.
   b. Whether the performance level of the objective was too difficult.
   c. What new methods of instruction are needed to better enable the child to accomplish the objective.

Curricular program evaluation depends on a clear explanation and explication of the behaviors that you are attempting to measure. While the teacher may choose from a variety of evaluative models, she must be careful not to base her total evaluation on a few specified behaviors which have been previously outlined in behavioral terms. We should never be so naive as to believe that measured behaviors are the only positive occurrences within classroom settings. The teacher must be so aware of her children and their programs that she can intelligently estimate growth that has not yet been planned and/or objectively measured.

When the classroom teacher becomes skilled at using behavioral objectives, an abbreviated system may be used, and once the terminal behavior has been clarified, the rest becomes relatively simple. The reluctance to use objectives is quite similar to the reluctance of many educators to use instructional technology, such as teaching machines and audiovisual equipment.

Many educators believe that if children are in a classroom setting that allows technology to "dehumanize" them, it is the fault of technology rather than the person determining the objectives and the procedures for meeting the objectives. Television sets, radios, phonographs, programmed machines, and other such technological hardware serve only as mechanical teacher aids. The planning does *not* come from the machine. The hardware is value-free. The teacher must distinguish between reality and fraud. If we consider textbooks and chalkboards as teacher aids, perhaps we could say that technology has always been part of the classroom. Materials and objectives *should not dictate* curricula. Teachers should plan thematic curricula using aids that facilitate the learning process.

The following frames are presented in an attempt to help you to develop skill in writing behavioral objectives.

Frame 1

Behavioral Objectives

A behavioral objective is a statement that describes the

1. setting under which a specified behavior will occur.

External conditions

2. type of behavior that is to occur.

Terminal behavior

3. level of success that must be achieved.

Acceptable performance

Frame 2

External conditions: The setting under which a specified behavior will occur

Examples of correct statements of external conditions are
1. Given a list of basic sight words ...
2. Following a lesson on vowel digraphs ...
3. After discussing various English words borrowed from German ...
4. After comparing the basal and linguistic methods ...
5. Given a simulated phonic rule ...
6. Following a discussion of the history of standardized readiness tests ...

An acceptable statement of external condition is one that describes the exact settings or conditions that will exist during or precede the learner's display of the terminal behavior.

Frame 3

Examples of incorrect statements of external conditions are
1. To be able to ...
2. To have knowledge of ...
3. To enjoy ...
4. To learn by ...
5. To discuss ...

These examples are incorrect because they do not state the exact conditions under which the terminal behavior will occur.

What must precede the occurence of the desired behavior?

Frame 4

Terminal behavior: The type of behavior that is anticipated

Examples of correct statements of terminal behavior are
1. The student will be able to identify ...
                                        (Verbally, visually)
2. The student will be able to recite ...
3. The student will be able to list ...
                                        (In writing, verbally)
4. The student will be able to read ...

An acceptable statement of terminal behavior is one that describes the anticipated behavior with such specificity that it cannot be misinterpreted.

Frame 5

Examples of incorrect statements of terminal behavior are

1. The student knows ....
2. The student will enjoy ....
3. The student appreciates ....
4. The student believes ....

These examples are incorrect because the behaviors are not stated in a manner that can be adequately interpreted and measured.

What type of behavior will be accepted as evidence that the learner has achieved the stated objective?

Frame 6

Acceptable performance: The level of performance that must be evidenced before a specified behavior can be accepted

Examples of correct statements of acceptable performance are

1. .... at least ten of the following sight words.
2. .... both initial phonemes.
3. .... five vocabulary words in three minutes.
4. .... 40 per cent of the basic sight words.
5. .... all of the addition Cloze problems on page 000.

An appropriate statement of acceptable performance is one that describes how well the learner must perform before his behavior will be accepted.

Please complete the following activities. If you have difficulty, refer to frames 1 through 6.

ACTIVITIES

Activity 1: Developing a Behavioral Objective—Reading

You are preparing a unit of study that attempts to facilitate understanding of hypothesis and supporting details. Throughout this unit you plan to rely heavily on the language experiences of the children.

Attempt to develop a statement of external conditions (the setting under which a specified behavior will occur) for the preceding brief unit description.

External conditions (Refer to frames 2 and 3.)

Now can you add a statement of terminal behavior (a type of behavior that is to occur as a result of planned instruction)?
Terminal behavior (Refer to frames 4 and 5.)

Finally, add a statement of acceptable performance (degree of competency).
Acceptable performance (Refer to frame 6.

Now put your sections together and decide what role this behavioral objective has in curriculum planning.

Activity 2: Developing a Behavioral Objective—Poetry

You are preparing a unit of study that attempts to facilitate the language process by introducing children to haiku. Throughout this unit you plan to rely heavily on the language experiences of the children.
Please attempt to develop a statement of external conditions (the setting under which a specified behavior will occur) for the preceding brief unit description.
External conditions (Refer to frames 2 and 3.

Now can you add a statement of terminal behavior (a type of behavior that is to occur as a result of planned instruction)?
Terminal behavior (Refer to frames 4 and 5.)

Finally, add a statement of acceptable performance (degree of competency).
Acceptable performance (Refer to frame 6.)

Now put your sections together and decide what role this behavioral objective was in curriculum planning.

As suggested in Figure 1 on page 594, after determining your behavioral objectives, you can begin the process of designing instruction that will enable the implementation of your objectives.

Learning Experiences, Information Dissemination, and Materials

Once Ms. Cunningham had determined group composition, needs, and objectives, she had to determine *methods of instruction* for each group. Although she reinforced reading and language arts skills whenever she taught content specific subjects, she had also decided to allot one hour each morning for reinforcing through basal programs the processes and skills of reading. Because Ms. Cunningham realized that she would not be able to meet with each group for the entire period, she decided to develop methods of instruction that could be operationalized without her immediate physical presence. She would *manage* the entire program, but she would not be involved verbally with the direct instructional input of each activity.

Ms. Cunningham realized that this was possible because the development of specific behavioral objectives enabled her to determine the nature of the learning experience, as well as the method and materials which would be used to convey the information. To better enable you to understand this procedure, let's look at the following behavioral objective.

Behavioral Objective. After having completed a unit of study dealing with the topic of dinosaurs (external condition), the child will be able to exhibit the following behaviors without error (acceptable performance):

1. List the time periods in which dinosaurs lived (terminal behavior).
2. Discuss the various types of dinosaurs (terminal behavior).
3. Evaluate scientific methods employed to gain information about dinosaurs (terminal behavior).

The nature of the learning experience is the study of dinosaurs:

1. Types
2. Habitat
3. Relationship to man
4. Methods of data collection

The information regarding dinosaurs can be conveyed to the student through a variety of ways, some of which are: (1) the teacher, (2) the text, and (3) technology. When we refer to technology we want to include the following materials:

1. Reference books
2. Trade books
3. Magazines
4. Maps
5. Models
6. Films
7. Records

We have attempted to classify the materials as classroom aids in order to better enable you to understand their total utilization. A program designed and managed by the classroom teacher, with activities which do not require direct verbal input on the part of the teacher, becomes possible through the use of instructional technology. In this way, instructional technology is logically defined as classroom aids.

Classroom Aids

Audio Aids. Audio equipment primarily includes record players, radios. language laboratories, telelectures, and tape recorders. The portability and relatively low cost of the record player and radio increase their classroom utility. The tape recorder is another very versatile device because special sounds can be kept and replayed whenever the user wishes. The tape recorder can be used to highlight developmental language creativity by designing a *sound collage* which involves collecting environmental or commonplace sounds on tape, camouflaging these sounds through speed modification and tape loops, and then organizing and combining the sounds to form new combinations of sounds.

The sound collage can be used in a variety of ways: as a composition of its own, in a study of sound classification, or as a stimulus for creative writing. In addition, the composition can be used to introduce twentieth-century art forms or as a background sound effects for an original dramatic production.

The *language laboratory* is used primarily to offer students instruction in foreign languages. Students listen to a recording and then verbally model the sounds they have heard. The teacher is able to monitor this experience through a mechanical device that enables her to listen to the conversation. The idea of the language laboratory has been incorporated within many technological reading programs for elementary school children because of its ability to provide specialized individualized attention for children in developing language and listening skills.

The *telelecture* enables groups of students to listen to prearranged conversations with renowned speakers. For example, a class studying the undersea world might greatly desire to speak personally with Jacques Costeau.

Audio devices can be used in isolation or in conjunction with visual aids to create the setting necessary for one to totally experience pictorial representations. For example, music by Palestrina would enhance one's learning about the Renaissance. A similar experience might involve one's listening to Debussy while studying Impressionism. Audio devices not only offer the means to reach large groups, but they also provide an opportunity for a great variety of individual student tutoring. The role of the teacher becomes less burdensome because she is freed from repeating lessons.

Visual Aids. Visual aids primarily include chalkboards, bulletin boards, opaque projectors, filmstrip and overhead projectors, teaching machines, and textbooks. Of all visual aids, the *textbook* is the one most frequently used. In many classes the textbook is the major information source, and teachers are viewed as extensions of textbooks. However in some classrooms the teacher actually serves as the central factor synthesizing information from many textbook sources. The chalkboard is closely identified with this process because it has been used in learning situations for decades as a tool by which information can be transmitted.

Another long-time classroom material utilized as a means of transmitting information has been the display or *bulletin board*. Two-dimensional demonstrations are often found on felt, bulletin, or display boards. Through these sources, information can quickly be either conveyed or reinforced.

The *filmstrip* projector is certainly the most commonly found projector in American schools. Filmstrips, made from 35mm film, can be used by individuals or groups of students. This instructional device also serves to free the teacher for working with individuals who are having difficulty with particular concepts.

Optical reflection is the principle on which the *opaque projector* operates. A darkened classroom is required for use because light is reflected off the projected material. This projector is widely used by students who wish to view photographs, drawings, documents, or other such materials. The opaque projector, like many other visual and audio aids is a means of transmitting information without the total aid of the classroom teacher.

The overhead projector is another device found in many school environments. It is used to transmit information to both large and small groups and presents tables, graphs, and lists with considerable clarity.

Teaching machines that convey information on just about every subject are found in many classrooms. Although automated features may be characteristic of some teaching machines, this is not standard. Teaching machines differ primarily in their presentation of information and questioning.

Many educators look askance at programmed material and teaching machines because of their early use as review, drill, and testing. Although today's programs do still serve these objectives, they are also being designed to *individualize* programs for *independent* study.

Educational programs completing and supplementing visual devices use the student's sense of sight. Visual aids can be employed in tutorial situations because they can be used to recreate the past, provide three-dimensional effects, present abstract information, represent microscopic life, and utilize natural color.

Through audio, as well as visual, aids the following positive educational results are made available: *individualized instruction* becomes a reality because the classroom teacher is aided with instructional implementation; curriculum materials based on *sequential development* are made available; students are matched with materials according to their strongest *learning modality*; and, the classroom teacher is provided with *planning time*.

Multisensory Aids. Technological materials involving more than one sense in the learning experience are commonly referred to as multisensory aids. Motion pictures, television, sandtables, sandpaper cutouts, indented objects, and felt or velvet boards are the most common multisensory aids found in educational settings.

The use of motion pictures primarily involves the senses of hearing and sight, as well as the extension of emotional and other human experiences. Simplicity of operation and a vast range of personal involvement have been two prime factors in encouraging motion picture adoption as a teacher aid. Students can explore their own world and those of others through film.

Television is a medium that has advantages similar to those of film. While offering children the possibility of exploring the lives of others, television also capitalizes on the present, providing students with an opportunity for involvement in events as they happen.

Cognitive and psychomotor development are possible through the use of technological materials that involve the tactile and visual senses. Learning involving multisensory aids is strongly encouraged for young children in the process of developing reading readiness skills. Multisensory aids can be inexpensive and adaptable to a variety of learning experiences. Whenever you employ technology, continuously evaluate its effectiveness for a particular subject area or goal accomplishment.

Computer Aids. Computers in their simplest form have been part of the educational scene since the 1950s. The first educational computer, the analog, was limited in implementation accuracy because of its restrictive measurement potential. The analog was followed by the digital computer, which can be used for addition, subtraction, multiplication, and division and for drawing pictures and doing language translations. Through the use of computer-assisted instruction the interests, motivation, and range of information provided to students can be greatly expanded.

The use of technology in an educational setting must be carefully implemented, and educators must be fully aware of the following concerns:

1. Who prepares the materials?
   a. Goals
   b. Programs
   c. In-service training
   d. Research
   e. Evaluation
   f. Funding

2. Who is responsible for program control?
   a. Administration
   b. Faculty
   c. Community
   d. Materials
   e. Funds
   f. Values transmitted

3. What is the role of the teacher?
   a. Developer
   b. Diagnostician
   c. Implementer
   d. Evaluator
   e. In-service model

4. How are students affected?

5. What are the community relations?

When it is used _correctly_, technology can help you personalize your learning environment. Ms. Cunningham found that her students had to take a very _active_ part in the learning process. Ms. Cunningham was able to use all of these resources by designing prescriptive learning packets for each student.

Learning Prescriptions. Each packet contained the daily learning assignments as well as grouping arrangements for each student. Assignments and grouping arrangements were determined through _formal_ and _informal assessment techniques_. Ms. Cunningham had developed this program very deliberately because her purpose was to _meet the various needs_ of all her students, while _maintaining a manageable program_. Classroom arrangement facilitated the development of individual needs and accommodated short-term grouping situations. Grouping arrangements were reassigned as student skills developed and changed.

Grouping patterns also varied according to the content area being studied at any given time, as well as the changing interests of the students.

The particular reading class that Shannon's parents saw included:

1. Four students who were members of group D and one child from group C reading directions, discussing plans, and building science incubators. These children were working in the *building production area.*

2. Three youngsters from group C discussing their answers to a set of story questions that involved their ability to *sequence* information, as well as *predict,* and *hypothesize* future similar events. These children were working in the *committee meeting area.*

3. Five children, also from group C, working independently on their assignments. These children were dispersed throughout the *independent study area,* as well as the *library,* because their learning prescriptions required use of the card catalog and reference books.

4. Two children from group B sitting together in the *independent study area* reading a newspaper story and developing a time line. This activity aided the children in understanding sequential development, which is essential for total comprehension.

5. One child also from group C and three from group B were in the *listening area* listening to a newscast. All of these children were interested in media and social-political events. Their assignment was to listen for cause-effect social happenings presented by the newscasters. After the newscast these children were asked to survey the morning newspaper to determine if they had accurately interpreted the newscast.

6. Four other children from group B were in the *independent study area* completing work sheets taken directly from their basal program.

7. One student from group A was in the *listening area* equipped with a headphone set. He was listening to and reading a primer. This activity reinforced basic sight-word reading skills.

8. Two other children from group A were with Ms. Cunningham in the *private conference tutorial area* discussing a basal story they had just finished reading.

"How does everyone know what to do?" Shannon's parents asked Ms. Cunningham. She told them that she used a system of management through learning prescriptive contracts. She explained that this approach enabled children to take responsibility for their work tasks. The prescriptive contract was simply a note to each child that specified (1) daily goals, (2) assignments and time schedule, and (3) grouping arrangements. Each child's prescriptions were kept in a manila folder for easy reference. The following prescriptive contracts appeared in Shannon's file:

> Good Morning Shannon!
>
> How is Duchess? You're lucky to have such a nice dog. Did you have fun with her on Saturday? Tell me about it when you and I have some free time.

When Shannon's parents visited her classroom, they saw the following architectural structure.

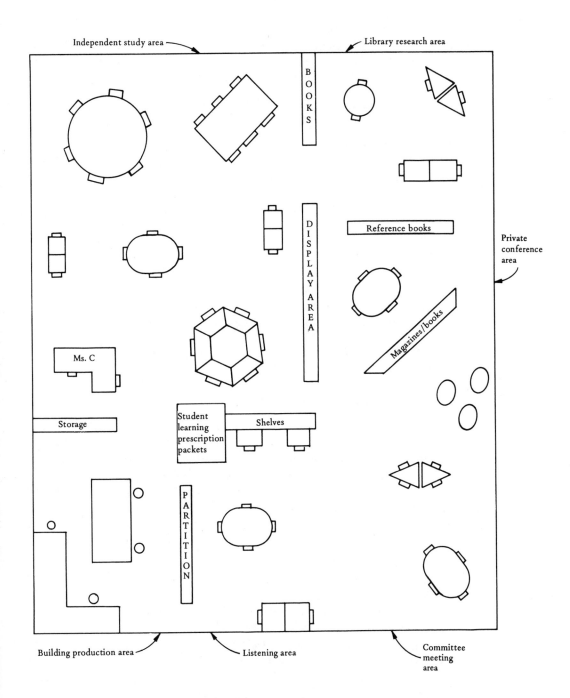

Figure 2. Shannon's classroom.

Please work on the following:

9:00–10:30

    1. Reading level 9, p. 32, End-of-Unit Test

    2. After the test, you may do any <u>two</u> of the following:

       a. Work on a crossword puzzle in the library.

       b. Go to the listening area and select a book about an American inventor. Put on headphones and listen to the tape and read your book. After listening and reading, write three character traits you share in common with the inventor.

       c. Browse through the library and select and read a book you might enjoy.

Shannon, as soon as I have a free moment, I'll help you check your test and give you further reading assignments for Tuesday and Wednesday.

10:30–10:45 Recess—Have a nice break.

10:45–11:30

<u>Math</u>—Complete your math assignment from last Friday. If you have trouble with the multiplication problems please ask Denise, Mary, or Harold for help. Also, finish lesson 6 in your math text. Continue to work on this task on Tuesday and Wednesday.

11:30–12:15

<u>Science</u>—(Monday–Wednesday)
Work with your group on the science experiment we discussed last Thursday. Refer to contract sheet no. 23 for specific instructions.

12:15–1:15 Lunch

1:15–2:00

<u>Social Studies</u>—Meet in the independent study area. Complete your project. I'll assign new groups on Tuesday.

2:00–2:15 Recess

2:15–2:30

On Monday please meet me in the private conference area. We'll talk about your work. On Tuesday and Wednesday you may use this time to finish a task of your choice, or you may choose a new area of interest. You might like to read the new <u>Ranger Rick Science Magazine</u>.

2:30–3:00

Complete the unfinished tasks or engage in

    1. reading your library book.

    2. working crossword puzzles.

    3. reading a magazine.

    4. selecting and completing an art activity listed in the art activity file.

    5. resting and reflecting on your day.

Shannon, if you have anything you want to share with me, please write it on the attached sheet. Have a good day and I'll see you tomorrow.

Although each child's tasks were clearly stated in the prescriptive learning packet, Ms. Cunningham continually mingled with groups of children, as well as individuals, to determine if any immediate issues needed to take precedence over the prescriptive task. Each child had many individual encounters with Ms. Cunningham during any given day.

While observing Shannon's class, her parents realized that individualized prescriptive learning packets did not mean that every child in the class was working on a different task in a different subject area. Students were *grouped* by needs and interests. The program was very *manageable.*

Shannon's parents asked about the time constraints of evaluating the learning prescriptions. Ms. Cunningham explained that she had initially been overwhelmed by the evaluation component of this program; but, she had decided to make her program succeed by devising a manageable plan for evaluating everyone's learning prescriptions. She knew that although she was a dedicated teacher, she also had many personal responsibilities and was, therefore, unable to devote *entire* evenings or weekends to school management.

She explained that continuous evaluation was an essential part of this program because succeeding assignments were based on the competencies and needs of each child as they completed their tasks. From her initial attempts at evaluating the learning prescriptions, Ms. Cunningham concluded that approximately ten to twelve minutes were required to review a student's completed prescription. Because Ms. Cunningham was responsible for developing and evaluating learning prescriptions for twenty-six students, she decided to develop each prescription for three-day periods. She was only required to review seven to nine folders daily. Ms. Cunningham believed that this one- to two-hour process required no more of her time than had the daily grading of individual workbooks and work sheets that accumulated before she attempted to individualize her instruction.

Ms. Cunningham explained that during the day she made minor evaluations whenever time permitted. Immediately after school, she continued the process of evaluating and grading student's work. Evaluations not completed during the day were finished during the evening or the next morning before school.

When developing, evaluating, and replanning a child's prescriptive program, Ms. Cunningham asked herself the following questions:

1. Is the child successfully completing the learning task?
2. How can I continue to motivate this child?
3. Does the child work better at long or short assignments?
4. How can I best reinforce each student's learning successes?
5. What type of materials are most meaningful and interesting to this child?
6. How can I encourage the child to take more responsibility for his learning?
7. What learning techniques encourage the effective development of memory skills?
8. How can I best help this child to transfer what has been learned in one subject area to other areas?
9. How can I best encourage the child to synthesize and generalize the information being learned?
10. How can I best encourage the child to make evaluative decisions about the validity of the information being learned?

By answering these questions, Ms. Cunningham was able to continually evaluate *what* had been mastered and to *plan* the next step for each child. You may also want to pursue these questions if you are interested in implementing Ms. Cunningham's program strategies.

Continued Assessment, Recycling, and Sequential Learning. Once the specific objectives have been designed and information has been conveyed, we must determine varying means of disseminating information for those students who have not reached mastery, as well as develop sequential learning for others who have achieved the prescribed competency level.

A classroom plan would look like this:

Theme

To introduce a group of second-grade students to the earth as a planet.	To introduce a group of children to the concept of propaganda in written text.	To introduce a group of third-graders to the concept of measured length.

Objectives

1. Develop knowledge of the conditions that are needed for life on the planet earth. 2. Gain an understanding of the movement and size of the planet earth.	1. Develop an understanding of the various types of propaganda. 2. Gain an ability to detect written bias and the underlying viewpoint of the bias.	1. Develop an understanding of the following terms: meter, centimeter, millimeter. 2. Gain an understanding of the use of the meter stick to measure length.

Student Preassessment

Informal or formal measures to determine each student's knowledge of the planet earth, as well as his ability to read the available topical materials.	Informal or formal data collection in an attempt to determine each student's knowledge of propaganda, as well as the ability to read the available topical materials.	Informal or formal data collection in an attempt to determine each student's knowledge of measuring length, as well as the ability to read the available topical materials.

Behavioral objectives

1. After a discussion of the sizes and movements of the planets, the student will be able to draw and correctly discuss the dimensions of the planet earth.	1. After completing a unit of study dealing with propaganda, the student will be able to circle all the sentences in a paragraph that reveal bias and tell which viewpoint the author holds.	1. After a discussion of standard and informal measures of length, the student will be able to correctly measure, to the nearest meter or centimeter, all presented objects of various lengths.

Behavioral objectives

2. At the conclusion of a unit of study focusing on living conditions of earth, the student will discuss, with average competency (allow individual criteria), how air, water, light, warmth, and soil make life possible on earth.

2. Given several sample advertisements or paragraphs, the student will be able to label all those evidencing the following types of propaganda: bad name, bandwagon, testimonial, card stacking.

2. Having completed a unit of study dealing with the terms meter, centimeter, millimeter, the student will be able to verbally or in writing correctly define each.

Procedure

1. Teacher directed (lecture)
2. Student-teacher directed (plays, games, discussions)
3. Student directed (reports, panels)

After having planned and implemented the theme, you must continue to evaluate.

Evaluation

Through informal and formal measures, one must make the following decisions:
1. Determine if the objective has been met.
    a. Determine if there are related objectives to be designed and utilized at this time.
    b. Determine procedures for implementation of new objectives.
2. Determine if the objective has not been met.
    a. Determine if the objective should be terminated at this time because it is unrealistic.
    b. Determine which criterion of the stated objective has failed (acceptable performance level, external conditions, terminal behavior).
    c. Develop new procedures or external conditions or acceptable performance levels to meet the initial objective if you have determined that the objective is relevant to your situation.

After making decisions related to the mastery of materials, you may regroup and proceed. Thus, through the aid of an educational management system, we have surveyed, planned, implemented, reimplemented, or sequenced an integrated theme. Continuous evaluation is the prime ingredient for success in a program of this type. A system of management enables you, as a teacher, to clearly state desired terminal behaviors, evaluate instructional effectiveness, and determine sequential learning.

Mastery of instruction may be affected by the amount of instructional time utilized for topical presentation, background readiness of your students, manner or method of presentation, complexity of material, and student interest. As suggested in earlier chapters, instruction needs to be carefully sequenced in order to encourage the children to *formulate* the concept, *interpret* the information, and *apply* the learned principles and facts. The work of Piaget (1959), Gagné (1965), Bloom (1967), Taba (1967) offers many insights into the educational procedures which should be used when you are sequencing instruction.

As you review the effectiveness of your simulated classroom, we encourage you to consider the following facts:

1. Sequencing instruction through the aid of a management system enables you to avoid a hit-or-miss, ineffectual type of teaching.

2. Sequencing instruction through the use of a management system enables children to proceed according to their developing competencies.

3. Sequencing instruction through the aid of a management system enables you to better manage complex skills by presenting them in smaller, subordinate parts.

4. Sequencing instruction through the aid of a management system enables you to develop a clearer understanding of *how children learn*.

You must remember that a program of this type is certainly not a "new idea." You will be able to succeed in your attempts if you always remain cognizant of the following facts:

1. Students are not "on their own" in learning. The degree of decision-making responsibility shared by the student must be commensurate with his experience and ability. It is *the teacher's* responsibility to plan the program and thus guide each student's independence and initiative in learning situations. The learner will, however, have a new role in the individualized program. A child will no longer be found resting contentedly in a program where all of the decisions are made for him. You will provide each with options, and from these options he will choose what, where, when, and how to pursue the learning task. Children in your classroom will no longer know the frustrations of being tagged a "slow learner." Through individualized learning prescriptions, children will no longer pursue learning in a lockstep fashion.

2. The degree of program individualization must depend on the *task* to be accomplished, the readiness exposures of the child for the given task and your abilities to manage multiple methods for accomplishing a given task. You may be more successful in your attempts to individualize your program if you start with only one content area. Once you are successful with initial attempts, you may want to expand the program. You are the program manager. Be careful not to design a program you are unable to manage.

3. Use the materials you currently have to individualize your program. Do not use a lack of materials as an excuse for not individualizing your curriculum. Your *incentive* is the prime factor in the success of these initial attempts.

4. The major portion of your time will be spent in *planning* instructional procedures that may be independently executed by your students. This will be difficult for you in the beginning because you have previously spent as much time *implementing* as *planning*. Your planning of learning prescriptions will be based on what the child has previously accomplished. You may want to develop anecdotal file cards or checklists to enable you to assess the competencies as they are acquired by each individual student.

5. Students will be involved with both the *implementing* and *correcting* responsibilities of their learning. Because each learning prescription will be designed with the learner as the central focus, students will feel that their efforts have been worthwhile.

6. As a teacher you are responsible for the individual development of *each* child. Your professional expertise must be conveyed in a variety of ways if each child is to intellectually and emotionally grow from the encounter. You cannot teach children only today's body of literal facts and expect them to be critical decision makers tomorrow. Your curriculum must encourage this growth by being custom tailored to each learner.

This program will become a reality only if you believe that there is no *one best way* to learn. If this is your belief, select a small portion of your curriculum and begin the process of designing a manageable individualized program. You may be most comfortable following Ms. Cunningham's model by attempting to personalize your reading program. Whatever your choice is, good luck in your endeavors.

QUESTIONS AND RELATED READINGS

If at this time you do not feel that you have attained adequate knowledge to successfully answer the following questions, we would like to suggest further readings.

1. How does a classroom management system aid you in individualizing your educational program?
2. How does thematic teaching affect the interrelatedness of the curriculum?
3. Of what value are behavioral objectives in planning and evaluating your curriculum?
4. How do you plan to utilize grouping within your classroom?
5. What types of educational materials do you plan to utilize in your instructional program?
6. How is individualized instruction facilitated through continuous evaluation?

Goal 1: To aid the reader in understanding the value of classroom management

Question 1: How does a classroom management system aid you in individualizing your educational program?

Barth, Roland S. "So you Want to Change to an Open Classroom." *Phi Delta Kappan,* 53 (Oct. 1971), 97–9.

Gregory, Robert J. "Management Games for Enlightenment." *Educational Leadership,* 28 (April 1971), 743–6.

Petrie, Thomas A. "To Improve Instruction, Supervision, and Evaluation." *Educational Leadership,* 26 (May 1969), 772–7.

Goal 2: To aid the reader in understanding the process of thematic teaching

Question 2: How does thematic teaching affect the interrelatedness of the curriculum?

Arena, John E. "An Instrument for Individualizing Instruction." *Educational Leadership,* (May 1970), 784–7.

Joyce, Bruce R. "Learning Strategies for Learning Centers." *Educational Leadership,* 32 (March 1975), 388–91.

Rubin, Louis. "Curriculum, Affect, and Humanism." *Educational Leadership,* 32 (Oct. 1974), 10–15.

Goal 3: To aid the reader in developing and utilizing behavioral objectives

Question 3: Of what value are behavioral objectives in planning and evaluating your curriculum?

Clegg, A. A., Jr. "The Teacher as Manager of the Curriculum?" *Educational Leadership,* 30 (Jan. 1973), 307–10.

Rosner, Benjamin, and Patricia Kay. "Will the Promise of C/PBTE Be Fulfilled?" *Phi Delta Kappan,* 56 (Jan. 1974), 290–5.

Smith, Philip G. "On the Logic of Behavioral Objectives." *Phi Delta Kappan,* 53 (March 1972), 429–31.

Goal 4: To aid the reader in understanding the techniques of grouping

Question 4: How do you plan to utilize grouping within your classroom?

Allen, R. V. "Grouping Through Learning Centers." *Childhood Education,* (Dec. 1968), 200–3.

French, R. L. "Individualizing Classroom Communication." *Educational Leadership,* 28 (Nov. 1970), 193–7.

Springfield, Charlotte A. "Learning Centers—Stations—Places." *Educational Leadership,* 30 (May 1973), 736–7.

Goal 5: To aid the reader in utilizing educational materials

Question 5: What types of educational materials do you plan to utilize in your instructional program?

Aspy, David N. "Toward A Technology Which Helps Teachers Humanize Their Classrooms." *Educational Leadership,* 28 (March 1971), 626–32.

Brudner, Harvey J. "Computer Managed Instruction." *Science,* 162 (Nov. 29, 1968), 970–76.

Thatcher, David A. "Ask Not What You Can Do for the Machine ..." *Phi Delta Kappan,* 53 (April 1972), 509–11.

Goal 6: To aid the reader in utilizing a process of continuous evaluation

Question 6: How is individualized instruction facilitated through continuous evaluation?

Guba, Egon G., and Danile L. Stufflebeam. *Evaluation: The Process of Stimulating, Aiding, and Abetting Insightful Action.* Monograph Series in Reading Education, no. 1. Bloomington: Indiance University Press, 1970.

Kirschenbaum, Howard et al. *Wad-Ja-Get? The Grading Game in American Education.* New York: Hart Publishing Company, 1971.

Salz, Arthur E. "The Truly Open Classroom." *Phi Delta Kappan,* 55 (Feb. 1974), 388–9.

BIBLIOGRAPHY

Alkin, M. C. *The Use of Behavioral Objectives in Education: Relevant or Irrelevant.* Los Angeles: University of California, Los Angeles Center for the Study of Evalaution (May 9, 1968), 27 pp. EDO35067 Microfiche.

Ammons, M. "The Definition, Function, and Use of Educational Objectives." *The Elementary School Journal,* 62 (May 1962), 432-6.

Barrett, Thomas C. "Taxonomy of Cognitive and Affective Dimensions of Reading Comprehension," unpublished paper.

Binet, Alfred, and Therese Simon. *The Development of Intelligence in Children.* Baltimore: The Williams and Wilkins Company, 1916.

Bloom, Benjamin S. (ed.) *Taxonomy of Educational Objectives: Handbook I: Cognitive Domain.* New York: David McKay Co., Inc., 1967.

Burnett, Richard W. "The Classroom Teacher as a Diagnosticain." In *Reading Diagnosis and Evaluation,* ed. by Dorothy L. De Boar. Vol. XIII, Part 4, Proceedings of the Thirteenth Annual Convention. Newark, Del.: International Reading Association, 1970, p. 4.

Clymer, T. et al. *Ginn 720.* Reading and Management Program. Lexington, Mass.: Xerox, 1976.

Combs, Arthur W. *The Professional Education of Teachers.* Boston: Allyn & Bacon, Inc., 1965.

Dewey, John. *Experience and Education.* New York: Macmillan Publishing Co., Inc., 1938.

Eller, Wm. et al. *The Laidlaw Reading Program.* Illinois: The Laidlaw Pub. Co. 1976.

Gagné, Robert M. *The Conditions of Learning.* Chicago: Holt, Rinehart and Winston, 1965.

Gilpin, J.G. "Forward." In *Preparing Instructional Objectives,* ed. by R.F. Mager. Palo Alto, Calif.: Fearon Publishers, 1962.

Hammond, R. L. *Evaluation at the Local Level.* Miller Committee for the National Study of ESEA Title III, U.S. Pffice of Education, 1967, EDRS.

Lapp, Diane. "Behavioral Objectives Writing Skills Test." *Journal of Education,* 154 (Feb. 1972), 13-24. (This test may be secured from Educational Testing Services, Princeton, N.J.)

——— . *The Use of Behavioral Objectives in Education.* Newark, Delaware: International Reading Association, 1972.

———. "Can Elementary Teachers Write Behavioral Objectives?" *Journal of Education,* (Feb. 1973).

———. "Individualized Reading Instruction Made Easy for Teachers. *Early Years.* February, 1977. Vol. VII, N. 6 p. 63-67, 73.

Lipton, Aaron. "Miscalling While Reading Aloud: A Point of View." *Reading Teacher,* 25 (May 1972), 759-62.

Mager, R. F. *Preparing Instructional Objectives.* Palo Alto, Calif.: Fearon Publishers, 1962.

Piaget, Jean. *The Language and Thought of the Child.* 3rd ed. New York: The Humanities Press, Inc., 1959.

Smith, Carl et al. *The Macmillan Reading Program.* New York: Macmillan Publishing Co., Inc., 1975.

Silberman, Charles. *Crises in the Classroom.* New York: Random House, 1970.

Taba, Hilda. *Teacher's Handbook for Elementary Social Studies.* Palo Alto, California: Addison-Wesley Publishing Co., 1967, pp. 91-117.

Tests

Guide to Reading Tests and Measurements

The following is a listing of reading tests currently in print. It is designed to be a quick reference for teachers and other practitioners in deciding which tests are appropriate for their use. This listing is similar in format to an earlier list compiled by Roger Farr in "Reading: What Can Be Measured?" ERIC/CRIER Reading Review Series, 1969 For example, if a tester wants to identify a student's abilities in comprehension, he simply looks at those tests marked *x* under the comprehension column.

The tests have been divided into seven categories: (1) readiness, (2) general reading survey tests, (3) diagnostic, (4) oral reading, (5) study skills, (6) special fields, such as content area skills, and (7) miscellaneous. Only those tests that are published in the United States are included. The tests are listed alphabetically by name and include the following information:

1. *Title of test.* This is the title listed on the front cover of the test. The date on which it was first published and the most recent revision are given below the title. If an asterisk precedes the test title, it indicates that the test is known to be an individual test.

2. *Grade.* This is the suggested grade level for use of the test as indicated by the publisher. In some cases, only the age levels are supplied. However, these have been converted to the nearest grade-level equivalents.

3. *Number of forms.* Some tests have alternate forms available for pre- and post-testing of the examinees.

4. *Approximate time (in minutes).* The approximate time required to administer the test is listed, according to information given by the publisher.

5. *Publisher.* The publisher's name has been abbreviated in the interest of conserving space. An index listing the complete name and address of each

publisher follows the test guide. Many times the test publisher is very willing to send sample tests on request, or there may be samples available at a college of education library.

6. Author(s). These are the names found in the test booklets.

7. *"Designed to assist in the evaluation of . . ."* This information was obtained through the listing of subtests provided by the publisher and also from *Tests in Print* by Oscar Buros. Any skills that do not belong under the given categories are listed under "other."

8. *Volume and test number in Mental Measurement Yearbooks and page in Reading Tests and Reviews.* This provides a quick index to the critiques compiled by Buros in *Mental Measurement Yearbooks* (Highland Park, N.J.: Gryphon Press, 1968).

These reviews written by professionals throughout the country should be studied before any test is selected. Although the critiques in *Reading Tests and Reviews* are identical to those in *Mental Measurement Yearbooks,* they are both listed for those situations in which the tester has access to only one of the references.

The first column gives the volume number of the *Mental Measurements Yearbook* and the number of the test as it appears in that volume. The number of the most recent review of the test is listed. *The Reading Test and Review* column gives the page number on which description and critique of the test appears. Some tests are not described in either volume.

To give an example, the entries for the California Phonics Survey are 7:714 and 338. The first set of numbers indicates that a critique of the test can be found in Buros's *Seventh Mental Measurement Yearbook* and is the 714th test listed in that volume. The second number stands for page 338 in *Reading Tests and Reviews* where a critique of the test can also be found.

READINESS TESTS

Name of Test	For Grades	No. of Forms	Approx. time (in min.)	Publisher	Author(s)	Speed	Vocabulary
ABC Inventory to Determine Kindergarten and School Readiness	K-1	1		RC**	N. Adair		x
Academic Readiness and End of First Grade Progress Scales, 1968	1	1	5-10	AP	H. Burks		x
American School Readiness Test, 1941; rev. 1964	K-1	1	45	BM	W. E. Pratt R. V. Young C. A. Whitmer S. Stouffer		x
Analysis of Readiness Skills: Reading and Mathematics, 1972	K-1			HM	M. Rodrigues W. Vogler J. Wilson		
*Anton Brenner Development Gestalt Test of School Readiness Test for Kindergarten and First Grade, 1945; rev. 1964	K-1	1	3-10	WPS	A. Brenner		
Assessment Program of Early Learning Levels, 1969	Pre K-1	1	40	EC	E. Cochran J. Shannon		
Barclay Early Childhood Skill Assessment Guide, 1973	Pre K-1			ESD	L. Barclay J. Barclay		
*The Basic Concept Inventory, field research edition, 1967	Pre K-1	1	15-15	FEC	S. Engelman		

**The publisher's full name and address follow this listing: e.g., RC is an abbreviation for Research Concepts.

Compre-hension	Word recog-nition and attack	Spelling	Auding	Other	Vol. and Test No. in Mental Measurement Yearbooks	Pages in Tests and Review (Buros)
				Readiness skills-draw a man, characteristics of objects, number and shapes	7:739	15
x				Perceptual motor, memory, number recognition, word recognition, emotional aspects	7:741	
				Alphabet, word matching, discrimination, memory of geometric forms, following directions	5:675	219
				Visual perception of letters and identification, counting, identification of numbers		
				Number recognition, ten-dot gestalt sentence, gestalt draw-a-man		
				Visual discrimination, letter names, premath skills, language, nouns, verbs	7:740	
				Sensory tasks, motor perceptual skills, environmental explora-tion, visual and auditory imitation, self-concept, task-order skills, social interaction		
				Basic concepts, pattern awareness, statement repetition	7:743	

READINESS TESTS

Name of Test	For Grades	No. of Forms	Approx. time (in min.)	Publisher	Author(s)	Speed	Vocabulary
Binion-Beck Reading Readiness Tests for Kindergarten and First Grade, 1945	K-1	1	40	APC	H. S. Binion R. L. Beck		
A Checklist for the Evaluation of Reading Readiness	Pre K			JS	J. Sanacore		
*Childhood Identi-fication of Learn-ing Disabilities, 1974	Pre K+			WLC			
CIRCUS: Pre-liminary, 1974	Pre K			ETS			x
Clymer-Barrett Pre-reading Battery, 1966; rev. 1967	K-1	2	90	PPI	T. Clymer T. Barrett		
*The Contemporary School Readiness Test, 1970	K-1	1	105	MRCP	C. Sauer		
Delco Readiness Test, 1970	K-1	1		DRT	W. Rhoades		
Diagnostic Reading Tests—Reading Readiness, 1947; rev. 1972	K-1	1	un-timed	CDRT	F. Triggs		x
Early Detection Inventory	Pre K	1		FEC	F. McGahan C. McGahan		

Compre-hension	Word recog-nition and attack	Spelling	Auding	Other	Vol. and Test No. in Mental Measurement Yearbooks	Pages in Tests and Review (Buros)
				Picture vocabulary and discrimination, following directions, memory for story, motor control	3:514	128
			x	Visual discrimination, left-to-right orientation, oral language development, concept development, social and emotional development, motor coordination		
				Visual motor, speech, visual abilities, hearing, fine and gross motor skills, psychological perceptual abilities		
			x	Visual discrimination, perceptual motor coordination, letter and numeral recognition, comprehension of oral language, problem solving		
			x	Visual discrimination, visual motor performance	7:744	15
			x	Colors, science, health, social studies, numbers, handwriting, listening comprehension, reading		
				Visual motor, visual discrimination		
				Relationships, coordination, left-to-righ approach, visual discrimination	4:5331	160
				School readiness tasks, social-emotional behavior responses, motor performance	7:746	15

READINESS TESTS

Name of Test	For Grades	No. of Forms	Approx. time (in min.)	Publisher	Author(s)	Speed	Vocabulary
Evanston Early Iden-tification Skill, Field Research Edition, 1967	K-1	1	10-45	FEC	M. Landsman H. Dillard		
*First Grade Screening Test, 1966-69	K	2	30-45	AGS	J. Pate W. Webb		
Gates–MacGinitie Reading Tests—Readiness Skills, 1939; rev. 1969	K-1	1	120	TCP	A. I. Gates W. MacGinitie		
Harrison–Stroud Reading Readi-ness Profiles, 1949; rev. 1956	K-1	1	80-90	HM	M. L. Harrison J. B. Stroud		
Initial Survey Test, 1970; rev. 1972	K	1		SF	M. Monroe J. Manning J. Wepman G. Gibb		
*An Inventory of Primary Skills, 1970	K-1			F	R. Valett		
Keystone Ready to Read Tests, 1954	K	1		KVC			
Kindergarten Evalu-ation of Learning Potential, 1963; rev. 1969	K-1	1		CTB	J. Wilson M. Roebuck		
Lee-Clark Reading Readiness Test, 1931; rev. 1962	K-1	1	20	CTB	J. M. Lee W. W. Clark		

Compre-hension	Word recog-nition and attack	Spelling	Auding	Other	Vol. and Test No. in Mental Measurement Yearbooks	Pages in Tests and Reviews (Buros)
				Identifying children expected to have school difficulties	7:747	
				Intellectual deficiency, central nervous system dysfunction, emotional disturbance		
x	x		x	Visual discrimination, following directions, letter recognition, visual-motor coordination	7:749	15
			x	Using symbols, visual discrimination, using context, names of letters	5:677	265
			x	Language meanings, visual ability, letter recognition, sound-letter relationships, mathematics		
				Administered by parent: body identification, alphabet, numbers, draw-a-man, mathematics, class concepts, paragraph reading		
				Readiness skills		15
				Association learning, conceptualization, self-expression	7:751	
				Letter and word symbols, concepts	7:752	373

READINESS TESTS

Name of Test	For Grades	No. of Forms	Approx. time (in min.)	Publisher	Author(s)	Speed	Vocabulary
Lippincott Reading Readiness Test (Including Readiness Checklist), 1965	K–1	1		JLC	P. H. McLeod		
The Macmillan Reading Readiness Test; rev. ed., 1965–70	K–1	1	90	MC	A. Harris L. Sipay		x
*Maturity Level for School Entrance and Reading Readiness, 1950; rev. 1959	K–1	1	20	AGS	K. Banham		
McHugh–McParland Reading Readiness Test, 1966; rev. 1968	K–1	1		CSB	W. McHugh M. McParland		
Metropolitan Readiness Tests, 1933; rev. 1969	K–1	2	65–75	HBW	G. H. Hildreth N. L. Griffith M. E. McGauvran		
Monroe Reading Aptitude Tests, 1935	K–1	1	30	HM	M. Monroe		
Murphy-Durrell Reading Readiness Analysis, 1949; rev. 1965	K–1	1	80	HBW	H. A. Murphy D. D. Durrell		
PMA Readiness level, 1974	K–1			SRA	T. Thurstone		
*Parent Readiness Evaluation of Preschoolers, 1968; rev. 1969	Pre K–3	1	60–90	PII	A. E. Ahr B. Simons		

Compre-hension	Word recog-nition and attack	Spelling	Auding	Other	Vol. and Test No. in Mental Measurement Yearbooks	Pages in Tests and Review (Buros)
				Readiness skills	7:753	15
	x		x	Visual discrimination, rating scale, letter names, visual motor	7:755	
				Maturity level, behavior	6:847	374
			x	Visual discrimination, identifying letters, rhyming words, beginning sounds	7:754	15
			x	Alphabet, numbers, matching, copying, draw-a-man, word meaning	7:757	194
			x	Visual, motor, articulation,	3:519	133
			x	Sound recognition, learning rate, letter names	7:758	268
			x	Verbal meaning, perceptual speed, number facility, spatial relations		
x			x	Administered by parent: verbal associations and descriptions, motor coordination, visual and auditory memory	7:759	

READINESS TESTS

Name of Test	For Grades	No. of Forms	Approx. time (in min.)	Publisher	Author(s)	Speed	Vocabulary
Prereading Assessment Kit, 1972	K-1			CTB	Ontario Institute for Studies in Education		x
Prereading Expectancy Screening Scales, 1973	K-1			PEI	L. Hartlage D. Lucas		
Preschool and Kindergarten Performance Profile, 1970				EPA	A. DiNola B. Kaminsky A. Sternfield		
Pre-Reading Screening Procedures, 1968; rev. 1969	1		40	EPS	B. Slingerland		
Preschool Screening Instrument, 1973	K-1			FW	V. Kurko L. Crane H. Willemin		
Primary Academic Sentiment Scale, 1968	Pre K-2	1	50	PII	G. Thompson		
Reading Inventory, Probe I, 1970; rev. 1973	1-2			ATC	Diagnostic Reading Committee S. Warner W. Myers		x
Reading Readiness Form A, 1953; rev. 1960	K-1	1	30-45	STS	O. Anderhalter R. Colestock		

Compre-hension	Word recog-nition and attack	Spelling	Auding	Other	Vol. and Test No. in Mental Measurement Yearbooks	Pages in Tests and Review (Buros)
x			x	Symbol perception		
			x	Predicting reading problems: visual sequencing, letter identification, visual/auditory spatial awareness		
				Social, intellectual, and physical abilities		
			x	Visual discrimination, visual perception memory, letter knowledge	7:732	
			x	Memory-auditory and visual, understanding language, motor skills, closure		
				Motivation for learning, level of maturity, and indepen-dence from parent	7:760	
x			x	Visual discrimination		
			x	Uses of things, likenesses in words, listening for "c" and "d" sounds		

READINESS TESTS

Name of Test	For Grades	No. of Forms	Approx. time (in min)	Publisher	Author(s)	Speed	Vocabulary
*Riley Preschool Developmental Screening Inventory, 1969	Pre K–K	1	3–10	WPS	C. Riley		
*School Readiness Behavior Tests used at the Gesell Institute, 1964; rev. 1965	K–5	1	20–30	PE	F. Ilg L. Ames		
*School Readiness Checklist, research ed. 1963	K–1	1	10–20	RC	J. Austin J. Lafferty F. Leaske F. Cousino		
*School Readiness Survey, 1967	K–1	1	15–30	CPP	F. Jordan J. Massey		x
School Readiness Test, 1974	K–1			STS	O. Anderhalter		
Screening Test for the Assignment of Remedial Treatments, 1968	Pre K–1	1	60	PII	A. E. Ahr		
Screening Test of Academic Readiness, 1966	K–1	1	60	PII	A. Ahr		x
Steinbach Test of Reading Readiness, 1963	K–1	1	45	STS	M. Steinbach		
*Valett Developmental Survey of Basic Learning Abilities, 1966	Pre K–1		60–70	CPP	R. Valett		

Compre-hension	Word recog-nition and attack	Spelling	Auding	Other	Vol. and Test No. in Mental Measurement Yearbooks	Pages in Tests and Review (Buros)
				School readiness: design, draw a boy or girl	7:761	
				Readiness to start school	7:750	16
				Checklist to be used by parents	7:762	16
				Number concepts, discrimination of form, color naming, symbol matching	7:763	16
x	x		x	Handwriting and number readiness, letters, visual discrimination		
			x	Visual memory, discrimination, copying	7:764	
				Letters, picture completion, copying, picture description, human figure drawings, relationships, numbers	7:765	16
			x	Identifying letters, memory of word forms, language ability		16
			x	Physical development, tactile discrimination, visual discrimination, language development and fluency, conceptual development	7:767	16

READINESS TESTS

Name of Test	For Grades	No. of Forms	Approx. time (in min.)	Publisher	Author(s)	Speed	Vocabulary
*Van Wagen Reading Readiness Scales, 1933; rev. 1958	K–1	2	30	VW	M. S. Van Wagenen		x
Watson Reading Readiness Test, 1960	K–1	1	50–60	HC	G. Watson		

Compre- hension	Word recog- nition and attack	Spelling	Auding	Other	Vol. and Test No. in Mental Measurement Yearbooks	Pages in Tests and Review (Buros)
				Range and perception of information, opposites, memory open for ideas, word discrimination	3:520	134
				Subjective, objective (teacher's ratings), physical, social, emotional and psychological readiness	6:851	377

READING SURVEY TESTS

Name of Test	For Grades	No. of Forms	Approx. time (in min.)	Publisher	Author(s)	Speed	Vocabulary
Academic Promise Tests, 1959; rev. 1961	6–9	2	90	PC	G. Bennett M. Bennett D. Clendenin J. Doppelt J. Ricks, Jr. H. Seashore A. Westmon		
Advanced Reading Test, 1933; rev. 1971	7–9	3	46	HBW	W. Durost H. Bixler G. Hildreth K. Lund J. Wright-stone		x
American School Achievement Tests: Part I							
Reading Primary Battery, 1941; rev. 1955	2–3	4	35	BM	W. E. Pratt R. V. Young C. E. Cockerville		x
Reading Intermediate Battery, 1941; rev. 1958	4–6	4	35	BM	(See Reading Primary Battery)		x
Reading Advanced Battery, 1941; rev. 1958	7–9	4	40	BM	(See Reading Primary Battery)		x
American School Reading Tests, 1955	10–13	2	80	BM	W. Pratt R. Young C. Whitmer	x	x
Brown-Carlson Listening Comprehension Test	9–16+	2	50	HBW	Brown Carlson		

Compre-hension	Word recog-nition and attack	Apelling	Auding	Other	Vol. and Test No. in Mental Measurement Yearbooks	Pages in Tests and Review (Buros)
				Verbal, numerical, and abstract reasoning; language usage	7:672	
x					7:696	311
x					6:783	290
x					6:783	290
x					6:783	290
x					5:621	219
					5:621	219
				Immediate recall, following directions, recognizing transitions, word meanings, lecture comprehension		

READING SURVEY TESTS

Name of Test	For Grades	No. of Forms	Approx. time (in min)	Publisher	Author(s)	Speed	Vocabulary
Buffalo Reading Test for Speed and Comprehension, 1933; rev. 1965	9–12	2	35	FSC	M. Wagner	x	
Burnett Reading Series: Survey Test							
Primary I 1966, rev. 1967	1.5–2.4	1	47	STS	R. W. Burnett		x
Primary II, 1966	2.5–3.9	1	55	STS	(See Primary 1)		x
Intermediate, 1967	4.0–6.9	1	45	STS	(See Primary 1)		x
Advanced, 1967	7.0–9.9	1	38	STS	(See Primary 1)	x	x
Senior, 1968	10.0–12.9	1		STS	(See Primary 1)	x	x
California Achievement Tests, 1957; rev. 1972							
Lower Primary	1.5–2.5	2	23	CTB	E. Tiegs W. Clark		x
Upper Primary	2.5–4.5	2	40	CTB	(See Lower Primary)		x
Elementary	4–6	2	50	CTB	(See Lower Primary)		x
Junior High Level	6–9	3	68	CTB	(See Lower Primary)		x
Advanced	9–12	3	68	CTB	(See Lower Primary)		x
California Achievement Tests: Reading, 1970							
Level 1	1.5–2.0	1	46	CTB	E. W. Tiegs W. W. Clark		x

Comprehension	Word recognition and attack	Spelling	Auding	Other	Vol. and Test No. in Mental Measurement Yearbooks	Pages in Tests and Review (Buros)
x					3:477	86
x	x				7:682	2
x	x				7:682	2
x	x				7:682	2
x					7:682	2
x					7:682	2
x		x		Math	7:5	290
x		x		Math	7:5	290
x		x		Math	7:5	290
x		x		Math	7:5	290
x		x		Math	7:5	290
x	x				7:683	290

READING SURVEY TESTS

Name of Test	For Grades	No. of Forms	Approx. time (in min.)	Publisher	Author(s)	Speed	Vocabulary
Level 2	2–4	1	40	CTB	(See Level 1)		x
Level 3	4–6	1	45	CTB	(See Level 1)		x
Level 4	6–9	1	50	CTB	(See Level 1)		x
Level 5	9–12	1	50	CTB	(See Level 1)		x
California Sruvey Series: Survey of Reading Achievement, 1959							
Junior High Level	7–9	2	45	CTB	E. W. Tiegs W. W. Clark		
Advanced	9–12	2	45	CTB	(See Junior High Level)		
*The Carver-Darby Chunked Reading Test, 1970; rev. 1972	9–16+	2	25	RP	R. Carver C. Darby, Jr.	x	
Cormerce Reading Comprehension Test, 1956; rev. 1958	12–16+	1	65	DPS	I. Halfter R. McCall		
Comprehensive Reading Scales, 1948; rev. 1953	4–12	1	un-timed	VW	M. Van Wagenen		
Comprehensive Tests of Basic Skills: expanded ed. 1968; rev. 1973							
Level A	K.5–1.5	1		CTB			
Level B	K.5–1.9	1		CTB			

Compre-hension	Word recog-nition and attack	Spelling	Auding	Other	Vol. and Test No. in Mental Measurement Yearbooks	Pages in Tests and Review (Buros)
x	x				7:683	290
x	x				7:683	
x	x				7:683	
x	x				7:683	
					6:815	334
					6:815	334
				Efficiency, accuracy	7:684	
					5:624	221
			x	Prereading skills, language acquisition, elementary math concepts	7:685	
x	x			Language, mathematics letter sounds	7:685	

READING SURVEY TESTS

Name of Test	For Grades	No. of Forms	Approx. time in (in min.)	Publisher	Author(s)	Speed	Vocabulary
Level C	1.5–2.9	1		CTB			x
Cooperative English Tests, Reading Comprehension, 1940; rev. 1960	9–12 13–14	4	45	ETS	C. Derrick D. P. Harris B. Walker	x	x
Cooperative Primary Tests: Reading, 1965; rev. 1967	1.5–2.5	2	10–15	ETS			
Davis Reading Tests, 1956; rev. 1962							
Series I	11–13	4	40	PC	F. B. Davis	x	
Series II	8–11	4	40	PC	(See Series I)	x	
Delaware County Silent Reading Test, 1965	1.5–8	1	45–90	DCRA	J. Newburg N. Spennato		x
Durrell Listening-Reading Series 1969–70	1–9	2	140– 195	HBJ	Durrell		x
Emporia Reading Tests, 1964							
Primary	1	4	36	BEM	M. Barnett M. Sanders A. Seybold D. Carline E. Eaton S. Studer		x
Elementary	2–3	4	20	BEM	(See Primary)		
*Intermediate	4–6	4	30	BEM	D. Carline A. Seybold E. Eaton M. Sanders		

Compre-hension	Word recog-nition and attack	Spelling	Auding	Other	Vol. and Test No. in Mental Measurement Yearbooks	Pages in Tests and Review (Buros)
x		x		Language expression and mechanics, math, science, social studies	7:685	
x					6:806	321
	x		x		7:10	
x					6:786	291
x					6:786	291
			x	Interpretation, organization, structural analysis		
			x	Vocabulary listening and paragraph listening and reading	7:728	
	x		x	Matching objects, like words, phonetic recognition		3
	x			Sentence and paragraph reading		3
	x			Paragraph reading		3

READING SURVEY TESTS

Name of Test	For Grades	No. of Forms	Approx. time (in min.)	Publisher	Author(s)	Speed	Vocabulary
*Functional Readiness Questionnaire for School and College Students, 1957	1–16	1	5	RSSC	E. Taylor H. Sloan		
Gates-MacGinite Reading Tests							
Primary A, 1926; rev. 1965	1	2	45	TEP	A. I. Gates W. MacGinitie		x
Primary B, 1938; rev. 1965	2	2	45	TCP	(See Primary A)		x
Primary C, 1938; rev. 1965	3	2	55	TCP	(See Primary A)		x
Primary Cs, 1926; rev. 1965	2–3	2	12	TCP	(See Primary A)	x	
Survey D, 1939; rev. 1965	4–6	6	50	TCP	(See Primary A)	x	x
Survey E, 1964; rev. 1965	7–9	6	49	TCP	(See Primary A)	x	x
Survey F, 1969; rev. 1970	10–12	2	49	TCP	(See Primary A)	x	x
Gilliland Learning Potential Examination, 1966, rev. 1972	K+	1		MRCP	H. Gilliland		
Gray-Votaw-Rogers General Achievement Test, 1934, rev. 1963							
Level 1	1–3	4	70–80	SV	H. Gray D. Votaw J. Rogers		x
Level 2	4–6	4	170	SV	(See Level 1)		x

Compre-hension	Word recog-nition and attack	Spelling	Auding	Other	Vol. and Test No. in Mental Measurement Yearbooks	Pages in Tests and Review (Buros)
				Physical readiness, emotional	6:835	360
x					7:689	301
x					7:689	301
x					7:689	301
x				Accuracy	7:689	301
x				Accuracy	7:689	301
x				Accuracy	7:690	
x				Visual memory, nonreading and noncultural	7:351	13
x		x		Arithmetic reasoning and computation	6:10	
x		x		Arithmetic, science, language literature, social studies, health safety	6:10	

READING SURVEY TESTS

Name of Test	For Grades	No. of Forms	Approx. time (in min.)	Publisher	Author(s)	Speed	Vocabulary
Level 3	7–9	4	170	SV	(See Level 1)		
The Illinois Test of Psycholinguistic Abilities, 1961; rev. 1968	Pre K-5	1	45–60	UI	S. Kirk J. McCarthy W. Kirk		
Individual Placement Series—Reading Adequacy "READ" Test, 1961; rev. 1966	12+	1	10–15	PRA	J. Norman	x	
*Individual Pupil Monitoring System-Reading, 1974	1–6			HM			x
Instruction Objectives Exchange: Objective Collection in judgment: Analyzing Fallacies and Weaknesses in Arguments, 1974	.7–12			IOE	R. Morrow		
Inventory-Survey Tests							
Intermediate	4–6			SF	M. Monroe		x
Upper Grades	7–8			SF	M. Monroe		x
IOWA Silent Reading Tests							
Elementary, 1953; rev. 1942	4–8	4	60	HBW	H. A. Green	x	x
Advanced, 1927; rev. 1942	9–14	4	60	HBW	H. A. Green A. N. Sorgensen V. H. Kelley	x	x

Compre-hension	Word recog-nition and attack	Spelling	Auding	Other	Vol. and Test No. in Mental Measurement Yearbooks	Pages in Tests and Review (Buros)
x		x		Arithmetic, science, language, literature, social studies, health safety	6:10	
			x	Visual Motor association, auditory and visual decoding, motor encoding	7:442	
x					6:805	321
x	x			Discrimination study skills		
				Fallacies of relevance, insufficient evidence and ambiguity, arguments that compare context and soundness of arguments		
x	x			Dictionary skills		
x	x			Dictionary skills		
x				Directed reading, alphabetizing, use of index	6:794	307
x				Directed reading, poetry, com-prehension, use of index, selection of lay words	6:794	307

READING SURVEY TESTS

Name of Test	For Grades	No. of Forms	Approx. time (in min.)	Publisher	Author(s)	Speed	Vocabulary
IOWA Silent Reading Tests, 1973 ed.							
Level 1	6–9	1		HBJW	R. Farr		x
Level 2	9–14	1		HBJW	R. Farr		x
Level 3	11–16	1		HBJW	R. Farr		x
Junior High School Reading Test, 1964	7–8	4	55	BEM			x
Lee-Clark Reading Test, 1931; rev. 1965							
Primer	1	1		CTB	J. M. Lee W. Clark		
First Reader	1–2	1		CTB	(See Primer)		
McGrath Test of Reading Skills, 2nd ed., 1965; rev. 1967	1–13	1	5–10	MRC	J. McGrath	x	x

Compre-hension	Word recog-nition and attack	Spelling	Auding	Other	Vol. and Test No. in Mental Measurement Yearbooks	Pages in Tests and Review (Buros)
x				Directed reading and efficiency	6:794	307
x				Directed reading and efficiency	6:794	307
x				Reading efficiency	6:794	307
			x	Visual stimuli, following directions	6:795	308
			x	Visual stimuli, following directions, completion, inference	6:795	308
	x				7:692	4

READING SURVEY TESTS

Name of Test	For Grades	No. of Forms	Approx. time (in min.)	Publisher	Author(s)	Speed	Vocabulary
McGraw Hill Basic Skills System: Reading Test, 1970	11–14	2	66	CTB	A. Raygor	x	
McMenemy Measure of Reading Ability, 1965; rev. 1968							
Primary	3	1	45	RM	R. A. Mc-Menemy	x	x
Intermediate	5–6	1	50	RM	(See Primary)	x	x
Advanced	7–8	1	65	RM	(See Primary)	x	x
Maintaining Reading Efficiency Tests, 1966; rev. 1970	7–16+	2	20	DRD	W. Peeples	x	
Mastery: An Evaluation Tool, 1974	3–8			SRA			x
Metropolitan Achievement Tests: Reading, 1932; rev. 1971							
Primary 2	2	2	79–84	HBW	W. Durost H. Bixler G. Hildreth K. Lund J. Wright-stone		x
Elementary	3–4	3	43	HBW	(See Primary)		x
Intermediate	5–6	3	46	HBW	(See Primary)		x
Minimal Reading Proficiency Assessment, 1972	12			TM	T. McDonald		

Compre-hension	Word recog-nition and attack	Spelling	Auding	Other	Vol. and Test No. in Mental Measurement Yearbooks	Pages in Tests and Review (Buros)
x				Skimming, scanning, flexibility, retention	7:704	
x					7:693	4
x					7:693	4
x					7:693	4
x				Reading efficiency	7:694	4
x	x			Study skills and math objectives		
	x				7:696	311
x					7:696	311
x					7:696	311
				Minimal reading proficiency for graduating seniors		

READING SURVEY TESTS

Name of Test	For Grades	No. of Forms	Approx. time (in min.)	Publisher	Author(s)	Speed	Vocabulary
Minnesota Reading Examiniations for College Students, 1930; rev. 1935	9–16	2	55	UMP	M. Haggerty A. Eurich		x
Monroe's Standard- ized Silent Read- ing Test, 1919; rev. 1959	3–5 6–8 9–12	8	4–5	BM	W. S. Monroe	x	
Municipal Tests: National Achieve- ment Tests: Read- ing, 1938; rev. 1957	3–8	2	37–38	APC	R. K. Speer S. Smith	x	
National Achieve- ment Tests: High School Read- ing Test, 1939; rev. 1952	7–12	2	40	APC	R. K. Speer S. Smith		x
National Achieve- ment Tests: Read- ing Comprehension Test, 1953; rev. 1957	4–9	1	35	APC	L. D. Crow M. J. Kuhl- mann A. Crow		
Nelson-Denny Reading Test, 1924; rev. 1973	9–16+	2	35	HM	M. J. Nelson E. Denny J. Brown	x	x
Nelson Silent Read- ing Test, rev. ed. 1931; rev. 1962	3–9	2	35	HM	M. J. Nelson		x
New Developmental Reading Tests— Intermediate Tests	4–6	2	60	LC	G. Bond B. Balow C. Hoyt		x
*Peabody Picture Vocabulary Test, 1953; rev. 1968	Pre K–12	2	10–15	AGS	L. Dunn		
Pressey Diagnostic Reading Tests, 1929	3–9	1		BM	S. L. Pressey L. C. Pressey	x	x

Compre-hension	Word recog-nition and attack	Spelling	Auding	Other	Vol. and Test No. in Mental Measurement Yearbooks	Pages in Tests and Review (Buros)
x					3:491	59
x					6:798	312
x				Following directions	5:648	232
x	x			Noting details	5:634	225
x					5:647	231
x					6:800	315
x					6:802	320
x				Reading for information relationships, interpretation, appreciation	7:697	295
				Verbal abilities	7:417	
x						5

READING SURVEY TESTS

Name of Test	For Grades	No. of Forms	Approx. time (in min.)	Publisher	Author(s)	Speed	Vocabulary
Primary Reading Survey Tests, 1973							
Early Primary	2			SF	A. Schiller J. Wepman E. Glibb		
Late Primary	3			SF	(See Early Primary)		
Primary Reading Test: Acorn Achievement Tests, 1943; rev. 1957	2–3	2	40	APC	W. Stayton F. Ransom R. Beck		x
Public School Achievement Tests: Reading, 1928; rev. 1959	3–8	2	45	BM	J. S. Orleans		
Insert 1.) Pupil Placement Tests 1970	1–9		Varies	HM		x	x
Basic Reading and Word Test, 1968; rev. 1969	Disadvantaged adults	1	25–30	RBH			x
RBH Reading Comprehension Test, 1951; rev. 1962	12+	1	25	RBH	Richardson Bellows Henry		
RBH Scientific Reading Tests 1950; rev. 1952	12+	1		RBH	Richardson Bellows Henry		
Reading: Adult Basic Education Survey, Parts 1 and 2, 1966; rev. 1967	16+	1		FEC	E. Rasof M. Neff		x
Reading Comprehension Test	College entrants			WM	W. McCartney		
The Reading Progress Scale, 1970; rev. 1971	3–12			RP	R. Carver		

Compre-hension	Word recog-nition and attack	Spelling	Auding	Other	Vol. and Test No. in Mental Measurement Yearbooks	Pages in Tests and Review (Buros)
x	x			Word opposites	5:642	230
x	x		x	Oral reading accuracy	6:807	324
					7:700	
					7:701	337
						17
x						17
x						

READING SURVEY TESTS

Name of Test	For Grades	No. of Forms	Approx. time (in min.)	Publisher	Author(s)	Speed	Vocabulary
Reading for Understanding Placement Test Junior and general ed., 1963; rev. 1967	3–9 5–16	1		SRA	T. Thurstone		
Senior ed., 1963; rev. 1965	8–12	1		SRA	T. Thurstone		
SRA Achievement Series: Reading Hand Scored Edition							
Level 1, 1954; rev. 1968	1–2.5	2	120	SRA	L. Thorpe D. Lefever R. Nasbund		x
Level 2, 1954; rev. 1968	2–4.3	2	90	SRA	(See Level 1)		x
Multilevel ed., 1963; rev. 1969	4–9	2	70	SRA	(See Level 1)		x
SRA Reading Record, 1947; rev. 1959	6–12	1	30	SRA	G. T. Buswell	x	x
STS Analysis of Skills—Reading, 1974	1–8			STS	O. Anderhalter		
Schrammel–Gray High School and College Reading Test, 1940; rev. 1942	7–16	2	30	BM	H. Schrammel W. Gray	x	
Stanford Achievement Test: Reading Tests, 1922; rev. 1974							
Primary 1	1.5–2.4	1	95	HBW	T. Kelley R. Madden E. Gardner H. Rudman		x

Compre-hension	Word recog-nition and attack	Spelling	Auding	Other	Vol. and Test No. in Mental Measurement Yearbooks	Pages in Tests and Review (Buros)
						6
						6
x				Verbal pictorial association language perception	7:706	
x					7:706	
x					7:706	
x				Everyday reading scales	4:550	177
x	x			Study skills		
x					3:500	112
x	x			Word-study skills	7:708	331

READING SURVEY TESTS

Name of Test	For Grades	No. of Forms	Approx. time (in min.)	Publisher	Author(s)	Speed	Vocabulary
Primary 2	2.5–3.4	1	85	HBW	(See Primary 1)		x
Primary 3	3.5–4.4	1	85	HBS	(See Primary 1)		x
Intermediate 1	4.5–5.4	1	48	HBW	(See Primary 1)		x
Intermediate 2	5.5–6.9	1	50	HBW	(See Primary 1)		x
Advanced Paragraph Meaning	7–9.5	1	35	HBW	(See Primary 1)		x
Stanford Achievement Tests: High School Reading Test, 1965	9–12	1	40	HBW	E. Gardner J. Merwin R. Callis R. Madden		
Sucher-Allred Reading Placement Inventory, 1968; rev. 1971	1–9			BYP	F. Sucher R. Allred		
Tests of Reading; Inter-American Series, 1950; rev. 1973							
Level 1 Primary	1	4	18	GTA	H. Manuel		x
Level 2 Primary	2–3	4	23	GTA	(See Level 1)		x
Level 3 Elementary	4–6	4	41	GTA	(See Level 1)		x
Level 4 Intermediate	7–9	4	41	GTA	(See Level 1)		x
Level 5 advanced	10–13	4	41	GTA	(See Level 1)		x

Compre-hension	Word recog-nition and attack	Spelling	Auding	Other	Vol. and Test No. in Mental Measurement Yearbooks	Pages in Tests and Review (Buros)
x				Word-study skills	7:708	331
x				Word-study skills	7:708	331
x				Word-study skills	7:708	331
x				Word-study skills	7:708	331
x				Word-study skills	7:708	
						7
x						
	x			Oral reading, independence,		
	x			instructional, and frustrational reading levels		
x				English and Spanish Language forms	7:711	
x				English and Spanish Language forms	7:711	
x				English and Spanish Language forms	7:711	
x				English and Spanish Language forms	7:711	
x				English and Spanish Language forms	7:711	

READING SURVEY TESTS

Name of Test	For Grades	No. of Forms	Approx. time (in min.)	Publisher	Author(s)	Speed	Vocabulary
Survey of Primary Reading Development, 1957; rev. 1964	1–4	4	30–60	ETS	S. Harsh D. Solberg		
Survey Tests of Reading, 1931; rev. 1932	3–13	2		PI	L. J. O'Rourke	x	
Survey Test of Vocabulary, 1931; rev. 1965	3–12	2		OP	L. O'Rourke		x
Tests of Academic Progress: Reading, 1964; rev. 1966	9–12	1	60	HM	H. Smith D. Scannell		
Traxler High School Reading Test, 1938; rev. 1967	10–12	2	55	BM	A. Traxler	x	x
Traxler Silent Reading Test, 1938; rev. 1969	7–10	4	55	BM	A. Traxler	x	x
Van Wagenen Analytical Reading Scales, 1953; rev. 1954	4–6 7–9 10–12	1	Un-timed	VW	M. Van Wagenen		
Van Wagenen Comprehensive Primary Reading Scales, 1956; rev. 1965	1–3	1	Un-timed	VW	M. J. Van Wagenen M. A. Van Wagenen M. Klaeger		x
Wide-Range Achievement Test, 1936; rev. 1965	1–12	1	20–30	GTA	J. F. Jastak J. R. Jastak		
Williams Primary Reading Test, 1926; rev. 1953							
Primary 1	1	2	25–35	BM	A. Williams		
Primary 2	2–3	2	25–35	BM	A. Williams		
Williams Reading Test for Grades 4–9, 1926	4–9	1		BM	A. Williams		

Compre-hension	Word recog-nition and attack	Spelling	Auding	Other	Vol. and Test No. in Mental Measurement Yearbooks	Pages in Tests and Review (Buros)
x	x			Form comparison, pictorial-narrative reading	7:709	332
x				Accuracy		7
					7:234	
x				Making inferences and evaluations	7:710	7
x					4:559	187
x						
x						
x	x					
x	x	x		Oral reading, arithmetic	7:36	391
					5:658	246
					5:658	246

DIAGNOSTIC TESTS

Name of Test	For Grades	No. of Forms	Approx. time (in min.)	Publisher	Author(s)	Speed	Vocabulary
California Phonics Sruvey, 1956; rev. 1963	9–16	2	40–45	CTB	G. M. Brown A. B. Cottrell		
Classroom Reading Inventory, 1965; rev. 1969	2–8	2	12	WBC	N. Silvaroli		
Cooper-McGuire Diagnostic Word Analysis Test, 1970; rev. 1972	1–5	1		CES	L. Cooper M. McGuire		
Cooperative Primary Tests: Word Analysis, 1965; rev. 1967	1.5–3	1	10–15	ETS			
*The Denver Public Schools Reading Inventory, 1965; rev. 1968	1–8	1	30–40	DEN			
*Monroe Diagnostic Reading Examination for Diagnosis of Special Difficulty in Reading	1–4			ST	M. Monroe		
Diagnostic Examination of Silent Reading Abilities	4–6 7–9 10–12	1	Un-timed (Except Rate Test)	VW	A. Dvorak M. Van Wagenen	x	x
*Diagnostic Reading Scales, rev. ed., 1963; rev. 1972	1–8	1	45	CTB	G. D. Spache	x	

Comprehension	Word recognition and attack	Spelling	Auding	Other	Vol. and Test No. in Mental Measurement Yearbooks	Pages in Tests and Review (Buros)
				Vowel confusion, blends,	7:714	338
	x	x		Independence, instructional frustration, reading levels, hearing capacity	7:715	
	x					
	x				7:10	
				Instructional, independence and capacity reading levels	7:716	
	x			Oral reading, mirror reading		
x				Range of information	3:480	89
x	x		x		7:717	339

DIAGNOSTIC TESTS

Name of Test	For Grades	No. of Forms	Approx. time (in min.)	Publisher	Author(s)	Speed	Vocabulary
Diagnostic Reading Tests, 1957; rev. 1963, 1966	K–4	2		CDRT	F. Triggs		
Lower Level, 1947; rev. 1972	4–8	2		CDRT	F. Triggs		
Upper Level, 1947; rev. 1971	7–13	2		CDRT	F. Triggs	x	x
Diagnostic Reading Test, Pupil Progress Series Primary Level I, 1956; rev. 1957	1.9–2.1	2	40–60	STS	O. Anderhalter R. Gawkowski R. Colestock	x	
Primary Level II, 1956; rev. 1957	2.2–3	3	40–60	STS	O. Anderhalter R. Gawkowski R. Colestock	x	
Elementary Level, 1956; rev. 1957	4–6	2	65	STS	O. Anderhalter R. Gawkowski R. Colestock	x	x
Advanced Level, 1956; rev. 1960	7–8	2	65	STS	O. Anderhalter R. Gawkowski R. Colestock	x	x
Doren Diagnostic Reading Test of Word Recognition Skills, 1973 ed., 1956; rev. 1973	1–4			AGS	M. Doren		
*Durrell Analysis of Reading Difficulties, 1937; rev. 1955	1–6	1	30–90	HBW	D. D. Durrell		

Compre- hension	Word recog- nition and attack	Spelling	Auding	Other	Vol. and Test No. in Mental Measurement Yearbooks	Pages in Tests and Review (Buros)
	x				6:823	342
	x				6:823	342
x	x				6:823	342
x	x			Work-content relation, words in use, recalling information, locating information, reading for descriptions	7:718	340
x	x			Following directions, words in use, recalling information, reading to locate informa- tion, reading for description.	7:718	340
x				Study skills; table of contents, selection of best source, read- ing for directions	7:718	340
	x	x	x	Letter recognition, sight words	5:659	246
x	x	x	x	Naming letters, visual memory, learning rate, oral reading	5:660	248

DIAGNOSTIC TESTS

Name of Test	For Grades	No. of Forms	Approx. time (in min.)	Publisher	Author(s)	Speed	Vocabulary
*Gates-McKillop Reading Diagnostic Tests, 1926; rev. 1962	2-6	2	30-60	TCP	A. I. Gates A. McKillop		x
Group Diagnostic Reading Aptitude and Achievement Tests-Intermediate Form, 1939	3-9	1	60-70	NPC	M. Monroe E. Sherman		x
Group Phonics Analysis, 1971	1-3	1		DES	E. Fry		
LRA Standard Mastery Tasks in Language, 1970							
Primary I	1	1		LEA	D. Smith J. Smith R. Cabot		
Primary II	2	1		LEA	D. Smith J. Smith R. Cabot		
McCullough Word Analysis Tests, 1960; rev. 1963	4-6	1	90	PPI	C. M. Mc Cullough		
McGuire-Bumpus Diagnostic Comprehension Test, 1971; rev. 1972	2.5-3 4-6			CES	M. McGuire M. Bumpus		
Monroe-Sherman Group Diagnostic Reading and Aptitude Achievement Tests, Intermediate, 1939	3-9	1	60-70	NPC	M. Monroe E. E. Sherman	x	x

Compre-hension	Word recog-nition and attack	Spelling	Auding	Other	Vol. and Test No. in Mental Measurement Yearbooks	Pages in Tests and Review (Buros)
	x	x	x	Alphabet, oral reading, syllabication	6:824	345
	x	x	x	Visual and motor abilities, arithmetic	6:825	348
			x	Numbers, letters, alphabetiz-ing, syllabication, final e rule		
			x	Letter Matching		
	x		x	Letter naming, writing, word naming and writing		
				Phonetic and structural analysis (7 tests)	7:719	348
				Literal, interpretive, analytical, and critical reading		
x	x	x	x	Arithmetic, visual ability, motor ability	6:825	

DIAGNOSTIC TESTS

Name of Test	For Grades	No. of Forms	Approx. time (in min.)	Publisher	Author(s)	Speed	Vocabulary
Ohio Diagnostic Reading Test (a special form of Stanford Diagnostic Reading Test), Level I, 1966	2.5–8.5	1	133	OTS	B. Karlsen R. Madden E. Gardner		x
Level II, 1966	4.5–8.5	1	100	OTS	B. Karlsen R. Madden E. Gardner	x	x
Phonics Criterion Test, 1971	1–3			DES	E. Fry		
Phonics Knowledge Survey, 1964	1–6	1	10–30	TCP	D. Durkin L. Meshover		
Phonics Proficiency Scales, 1966; rev. 1973	1–12			EPS	A. Gillingham B. Stillman S. Childs		
Phonovisual Diagnostic Test, 1949; rev. 1973	3–12	1	15	PHI	L. D. Schoolfield J. Timberlake		
Prescriptive Reading Inventory, 1972							
Level A	1.5–2.5			CTB			
Level B	2.0–3.5			CTB			
Level C	3.0–4.5			CTB			
Level D	4.0–6.5			CTB			
Interim Tests: Experimental ed., 1973	1.5–6.5			CTB			

Compre- hension	Word recog- nition and attack	Spelling	Auding	Other	Vol. and Test No. in Mental Measurement Yearbooks	Pages in Tests and Review (Buros)
x			x	Syllabication, beginning and ending sounds, sound discrimination, blending		350
x			x	Syllabication, beginning and ending sounds, sound discrimination, blending		350
				Vowels, consonants, blends, and diagraphs		
				Names of letters, consonants and vowel sounds, syllabication	7:720	350
		x		Letter-sound correspondence, reading and spelling words, consonants, vowels, other phonetic units		
		x		Phonetic weaknesses	6:829	350
x	x			Sounds and symbol recognition, phonic analysis		
x	x			Sound and symbol recognition, phonic analysis		
x	x			Phonic analysis and translation		
x	x			Phonic analysis and translation		
x				For use after obtaining results of Prescriptive Reading Inventory		

DIAGNOSTIC TESTS

Name of Test	For Grades	No. of Forms	Approx. time (in min.)	Publisher	Author(s)	Speed	Vocabulary
Primary Reading Profiles, 1953; rev. 1968	1–2 2–3	1	95–100	HM	J. B. Stroud A. N. Hierony- mous P. McKee		
Reading Diagnostic Probes, 1970							
Probe 1	2–5	1		ATC	S. Warner W. Myers		
Probe 2	3–9	1		ATC			
Probe 2	3–9	1		ATC	S. Warner W. Myers		
Insert 2.) Reading Miscue Inventory 1972	All levels		Varies	Mac- millan	Y. Goodman C. Burke		
Reading Skills Diagnostic Test, 1967	1–8	1		EP	R. Bloomer		
*Roswell-Chall Diagnostic Read- ing Test, 1956, rev. 1959	2–6	2	5–10	EP	F. Roswell J. Chall		
Silent Reading Diagnostic Tests, 1965; rev. 1970	2.5–6	1	90	LC			

Comprehension	Word recognition and attack	Spelling	Auding	Other	Vol. and Test No. in Mental Measurement	Pages in Tests and Review
x	x		x		5:665	252
			x	Consonants, blends, vowels		
				Compound words, contractions, syllabication, prefixes, suffixes		
				Psycholinguistically analyzes where miscues are made as reader extracts meaning; qualitative as well as quantitative analysis.		
				Letter-sound identification, phonetic words and sounds, inconsistant words and phrases, letters and words in context		11
	x			Syllabication	6:831	255
	x		x	Word analysis, synthesis, word parts	7:722	

DIAGNOSTIC TESTS

Name of Test	For Grades	No. of Forms	Approx. time (in min.)	Publisher	Author(s)	Speed	Vocabulary
*Sipay Word Analysis Tests, 1974	1+			EPS	E. Sipay		
SPIRE Individual Reading Evaluation, 1969							
Spire 1, rev. 1970	1–6			NDE	H. Alpert A. Kravitz		
Spire 2, rev. 1971	4–10			NDE	H. Alpert A. Kravitz		
*Standard Reading Inventory, 1966	1–7		30–120	KUC		x	x
Stanford Diagnostic Reading Test, 1966							
Level 1, rev. 1971	2.4–4.5	2	162	HBW	B. Karlsen R. Madden E. Gardner		x
Level 2, rev. 1971	4.5–8.5	2	162	HBW	B. Karlsen	x	x

Compre-hension	Word recog-nition and attack	Spelling	Auding	Other	Vol. and Test No. in Mental Measurement Yearbooks	Pages in Tests and Review (Buros)
				Letter names, visual, and phonic analysis and visual blending (16 tests)		
x	x			Oral reading, instructional, frustration, and independence reading levels		
				Oral reading, isntructional, frustration, and independence reading levels		
x				Oral reading	7:723	
x			x	Syllabication	7:725	12
x			x	Syllabication, blending	7:725	12

DIAGNOSTIC TESTS

Name of Test	For Grades	No. of Forms	Approx. time (in min.)	Publisher	Author(s)	Speed	Vocabulary
Level 3, rev. 1974	9–13			HBW	B. Karlsen R. Madden E. Gardner	x	x
Test of Individual Needs in Reading, 1961, rev. 1966	1–6	2		MRCP	H. Gilliland	x	
Test of Phonic Skills, 1971	K–3			HR	K. Smith H. Truby		
Wisconsin Tests of Reading Skill Development: Word Attack, 1970; rev. 1972							
Level A	K–2			NCS	W. Otto E. Askor K. Kamm P. Miles D. Stewart V. Van Blaricom M. Harris		
Level B	1–3			NCS	(See Level A)		
Level C	2–4			NCS	(See Level A)		
Level D	3–6			NCS	(See Level A)		
Woodcock Reading Mastery Tests, 1972; rev. 1973	K–12			AGS	R. Woodcock		

Compre- hension	Word recog- nition and attack	Spelling	Auding	Other	Vol. and Test No. in Mental Measurement Yearbooks	Pages in Tests and Reviews (Buros)
x	x			Decoding	7:725	12
x				Oral reading, word analysis	7:726	12
		x	x	Phonics rules—vowels, consonants; blends, diagrams		
			x	Readiness skills—rhyming, shapes, letters, and numbers, consonants		
				Consonants, vowels, rhyming, diagraphs, contractions, possessives, compound coordination, plural		
				Consonant blends and variants, vowels, diphthongs, plurals, homonyms, antonyms, synonyms		
				Three-letter blends, silent letters, syllabication, accent, possessives		
x	x					

ORAL READING TESTS

Name of Test	For Grades	No. of Forms	Approx. Time (in min.)	Publisher	Author(s)	Speed	Vocabulary
*Flash-X Sight Vocabulary Test, 1961	1–2	1	10	EDL	G. Spache S. Taylor		x
*Gilmore Oral Reading Test: new ed., 1951; rev. 1968	1–8	2	15–20	HBW	J. Gilmore V. Gilmore	x	
*Gray Standardized Oral Reading Check Tests, 1963; rev. 1967	1–16+	5	1–3	BM	W. S. Gray	x	
*Neal Analysis of Reading Ability, 1957; rev. 1958	1–7	3	10–15	SMP	M. Neale	x	
*Oral Reading Criterion Test, 1971	1–7			DFS	E. Fry		
*Reading Miscue Inventory, 1972	1–7			MC	Y. Goodman C. Burke		
*Slosson Oral Reading (SORT) Test, 1963	1–12	1	3	SEP	R. Slosson		
Standardized Oral Reading Check Tests, 1923; rev. 1955	1–8	5	1–3	BM	W. Gray	x	
*Standardized Oral Reading Paragraphs, 1915	1–8	1	5–15	BM	W. Gray		

Compre-hension	Word recog-nition and attack	Spelling	Auding	Other	Vol. and Test No. in Mental Measurement Yearbooks	Pages in Tests and Review (Buros)
				Sight and experience vocabulary	6:841	367
x				Accuracy	7:737	257
					6:842	367
x		x	x	Blending and recognition of syllables, accuracy, names and sounds of letters	6:843	370
				Independence, frustration, and instructional reading levels		
				Grammatical and meaning dueing systems		
				Oral reading	6:844	373
				Accuracy	2:1570	71
				Oral reading	2:1571	72

TESTS OF STUDY SKILLS

Name of Test	For Grades	No. of Forms	Approx. time (in min.)	Publisher	Author(s)	Speed	Vocabulary
College Adjustment Study Skills Inventory, 1968	13–16		15–20	PGP	F. Christensen		
Comprehensive Tests of Basic Skills: expanded ed., 1968; rev. 1973							
Level 1	2.5–4.9	1		CTB			x
Level 2	4.5–6.9	1		CTB			x
Level 3	6.5–8.9	1		CTB			
Level 4	8.5–12.9	1		CTB			
The Cornell Class-Reasoning Test, 1964	4–12			UI	R. Ennis W. Gardiner R. Morrow D. Paulus L. Ringel		
The Cornell Conditional-Reasoning Test, 1964	4–12			UI	R. Ennis W. Gardiner J. Guzzetta R. Morrow D. Paulus L. Ringel		
The Cornell Critical Thinking Test, 1961; rev. 1971	7–12	1	50	UI	R. Ennis J. Millman		
The Cornell Learning and Study Skills Inventory, 1970	7–12			PEI	W. Pauk R. Cassel		

Compre-hension	Word recog-nition and attack	Spelling	Auding	Other	Vol. and Test No. in Mental Measurement Yearbooks	Pages in Tests and Review (Buros)
				Taking notes, exams, class participation, personal adjustment, time distribution	7:777	
x		x		Reference skill, science, math, social studies, language expression and mechanics	7:778	
x		x		(See Level 1)	7:778	
				(See Level 1)	7:778	
				(See Level 1)	7:778	
				Deductive logic		
				Deductive logic	7:779	
				Critical thinking	7:779	
				Goal orientation, lectures, textbook, examination mastery		

TESTS OF STUDY SKILLS

Name of Test	For Grades	No. of Forms	Approx. time (in min.)	Publisher	Author(s)	Speed	Vocabulary
Evaluation Aptitude Test, 1951; rev. 1952	12+ 16+	1	55	PA	D. Sell		
IOWA Every Pupil Test of Basic Skills, Test B, Elementary Battery, 1940; rev. 1947	3–5	4	55	HM	E. Lindquist H. Spitzer E. Horn M. McBroom H. Green		
IOWA Tests of Basic Skills, Test 9, Use of Sources of Information, 1942; rev. 1967	9–12	2	35	SRA	E. F. Linquist		
A Library Oreintation Test for College Freshmen, 1950; rev. 1961	13			TCP	E. Feagley D. Curtiss M. Gaver E. Greene		
Library Tests Library Survey Test (Test 1), 1967; rev. 1972	7–8	1		PFC	Perfection Form Co.		
Library Sources and Skills (Test 2), 1967; rev. 1972	9–10	1		PFC	Perfection Form Co.		
Library Sources and Uses of Information (Test 3), 1967; rev. 1972	11–12	1		PFC	Perfection Form Co.		
Logical Reasoning Test, 1955	9–16+	1	25	SSC	A. Hertzka J. Guilford		

Compre-hension	Word recog-nition and Attack	Spelling	Auding	Other	Vol. and Test No. in Mental Measurement Yearbooks	Pages in Tests and Review (Buros)
				Neutral syllogisms, emotionally toned syllogisms, emotional bias, indecision	5:691	275
				Study skills: map reading, use of references, use of index and dictionary, graphs	4:558	210
				Use of sources of information	6:858	381
				Library skills	6:859	382
				General information, periodicals, oral and written reports, Dewey Decimal System, dictionary, reference books		
				Reader's Guide, scholarly terms, Dewey Decimal System, research organization, encyclopedia, card catalog		
				Alphabetizing, Dewey Decimal System, card catalog, reference books, using sources of information		
					5:694	279

TESTS OF STUDY SKILLS

Name of Test	For Grades	No. of Forms	Approx. time (in min.)	Publisher	Author(s)	Speed	Vocabulary
National Test of Library Skills, 1967; rev. 1971	2–4 4–12				F. Hatfield I. Gullette W. Myers		
Nationwide Library Skills Examination, 1962; rev. 1963	4–12			ES	D. Honz		
OC Diagnostic Dictionary Test, 1960	5–8	1	20	OPC	K. O'Connor		
Peabody Library Information Test							
Elementary Level, 1940	4–8	1	35	ETB	L. Shores J. Moore		
High School Level, 1940	1–12	1	35	ETB	(See Elementary Level)		
College Level, 1938; rev. 1940	13–16	1	37	ETB	(See Elementary Level)		
SRA Achievement Series: Work-Study Skills, 1955; rev. 1969	11–14	2	80	SRA	L. Thorpe D. W. Lefever R. Naslund		
Study Habits Checklist, 1957; rev. 1967	9–16	1		SRA	R. Preston M. Botel		
Study Habits Inventory, 1934; rev. 1941	12–16	1	10–20	CPP	C. Wrenn		
Study Habits and Methods Survey, 1972	9–16			EITS	W. Michael J. Michael W. Zimmerman		

Compre-hension	Word recog-nition and attack	Spelling	Auding	Other	Vol. and Test No. in Mental Measurement Yearbooks	Pages in Tests and Review (Buros)
				Arrangement and parts of a book, card catalog, reference books, indexing		
				Library skills	6:860	382
				Dictionary skills	6:861	382
				Library study skills	3:538	148
				Library study skills	3:538	148
				Arrangement of books, dictionary, encyclopedia, periodicals, reference books, bibliography	3:538	148
				References, charts	7:780	
				Study skills		19
					3:540	150
				Academic interest, study methods, alienation from authority		

TESTS OF STUDY SKILLS

Name of Test	For Grades	No. of Forms	Approx. time (in min.)	Publisher	Author(s)	Speed	Vocabulary
Study Performance Test, 1934; rev. 1943	9-16	1		WL	H. Toops G. Shover		
Study Skills Counseling Evaluation, 1962	7-16	1	10-20	WPS	G. Demos		
Study Skills Test: McGraw Hill Basic Skills System, 1970	11-14	2	56	CTB	A. Raygor		
Survey of Study Habits and Attitudes (SSHA), 1953; rev. 1965, 1967	7-14	2	25-35	PC	W. Brown W. Holtzman		
Test on the Use of the Dictionary, 1955; rev. 1963	9-16	1	30-40	RCL	G. Spache		
The Uncritical Inference Test, 1955; rev. 1967				ISGS	W. Haney		
Watson-Glaser Critical Thinking Appraisal, 1942; rev. 1964	9-16+	3	50-60	HBW	G. Watson E. Glaser		
Wisconsin Tests of Reading Skill Development: Study Skills, 1970; rev. 1973							
Level A	K-1			NCS	K. Kamm D. Stewart V. Van Blaricom		

Compre-hension	Word recog-nition and attack	Spelling	Auding	Other	Vol. and Test No. in Mental Measurement Yearbooks	Pages in Tests and Review (Buros)
						19
				Study time distribution, study conditions, taking notes, taking exams, habits and attitudes	6:865	384
				Problem solving, library information, study skills and habits		
				Study habits and attitudes (efficiency, attitude toward teachers, educational objectives)	7:782	378
		x		Pronunciation, meaning, usage derivation	6:886	386
				Inference, recognition of assumptions, deductions, interpretation, evaluation of arguments	7:783	386
				Position of objects measurement		

TESTS OF STUDY SKILLS

Name of Test	For Grades	No. of Forms	Approx. time (in min.)	Publisher	Author(s)	Speed	Vocabulary
Level B	1–2			NCS	K. Kamm D. Stewart V. Van Blaricom		
Level C	2–3			NCS	K. Kamm D. Stewart V. Van Blaricom J. Allen M. Ramberg		
Level D	3–4			NCS	K. Kamm D. Stewart V. Van Blaricom J. Allen M. Ramberg E. Weible J. L. Marshall D. Sals		
Level E	4–5			NCS	(See Level D)		
Level F	5–6			NCS	(See Level D)		
Level G	6–7			NCS	(See Level D)		
Work-Study Skills: IOWA Every-Pupil Tests of Basic Skills, Test B, 1940; rev. 1947							
Elementary	3–5	4	55	HM	H. F. Spitzer E. Horn M. McBroom H. A. Greene E. F. Lindquist		
Advanced	5–9	4	90	HM	(See Elementary)		

Compre-hension	Word recog-nition and attack	Spelling	Auding	Other	Vol. and Test No. in Mental Measurement Yearbooks	Pages in Tests and Review (Buros)
				Picture symbols, measurement, graphs		
				Measurement, graphs, tables, alphabetizing color keys		
				Scales, graphs, tables, index, table of contents, dictionary, fact and opinion		
				Directions, scales, graphs, dictionary, references		
				Maps, scales, graphs, schedules, dictionary, library skills		
				Maps, graphs, schedules, out-lining, references		
				Map reading, use of references, index, dictionary, alphabetizing	4:15	
				Map reading, use of references, index, dictionary, graphing	4:15	

SPECIAL AND CONTENT AREA TESTS

Name of Test	For Grades	No. of Forms	Approx. time (in min.)	Publisher	Author(s)	Speed	Vocabulary
Adult Basic Reading Inventory, 1966	Functionally illiterate adolescents or adults	60		STS	R. Burnett		x
ANPA Foundation Newspaper Test, 1972 ed., 1969; rev. 1972	7–9			ETS	American Newspaper Publishers Association		
Iowa Tests of Educational Development							
Test 5: Ability to Interpret Reading Materials in the Social Studies, 1942; rev. 1961	9–12	2	70	SRA	E. F. Lindquist		
Test 6: Ability to interpret Reading Materials in the Natural Sciences, 1942; rev. 1961	9–12	2	70	SRA	E. F. Lindquist		
Reading/Everyday Activities in Life, 1972	9–16+			CP	M. Lichtman		
Robinson-Hall Reading Tests, 1940; rev. 1949	13–16	5		OSU	E. Robinson P. Hall		x
Tests of General Education Development							
Test 2: Interpretation of Reading Materials in Social Studies, 1944; rev. 1970	9–16	1	120	VTS	Examination Staff of the U.S. Armed Forces Institute		

Compre-hension	Word recog-nition and attack	Spelling	Auding	Other	Vol. and Test No. in Mental Measurement Yearbooks	Pages in Tests and Review (Buros)
			x	Context reading, sight words	7:769	17
				Newspaper reading ability	7:768	
				Reading materials in social studies	7:771	378
				Reading materials in the natural sciences	7:770	378
				Functional literacy	7:773	
x				Reading ability for art, geology, history, and fiction	4:575	197
					7:771	270

SPECIAL AND CONTENT AREA TESTS

Name of Test	For Grades	No. of Forms	Approx. time (in min.)	Publisher	Author(s)	Speed	Vocabulary
Test 3: Interpretation of Reading Materials in the Natural Sciences, 1944; rev. 1970	9–16	1	120	VTS	Examination Staff of the U.S. Armed Forces Institute		

Compre-hension	Word recog-nition and attack	Spelling	Auding	Other	Vol. and Test No. in Mental Measurement Yearbooks	Pages in Tests and Review (Buros)
					7:770	270

MISCELLANEOUS READING TESTS

Name of Test	For Grades	No. of Forms	Approx. time (in min.)	Publisher	Author(s)	Speed	Vocabulary
*Auditory Discrimination Test, 1958; rev. 1973	K–3	2		LRA	J. M. Wenman		
Basic Reading Rate Scale, 1971	3–12	2		RP	R. Carver M. Tinker		
*Botel Reading Inventory, 1961; rev. 1970	1–12	2		FEC	M. Botel C. L. Holsclaw G. C. Cammarata		
Composite Auditory Perception Test, 1973	1–3			AC	B. Witkin K. Butler D. Hedrick C. Manning		
Cumulative Reading Record, 1933; rev. 1956	9–12	1		NCTE	M. M. Skinner		
Dolch Basic Sight Word Test, 1942	1–2	1	35	GP	E. W. Dolch		
Durrell Listening- Reading Series							
Primary Level, 1969	1–2	1	80	HBW	D. D. Durrell		

Compre-hension	Word recog-nition and attack	Spelling	Auding	Other	Vol. and Test No. in Mental Measurement Yearbooks	Pages in Tests and Review (Buros)
			x			
					5:687	
	x			Phonics skills, opposites	7:727	359
			x	Attention span, short-term memory, following directions, integrating information, recognizing language units and structure		
						12
	x			Basic sight words		12
			x	Sentence reading	7:728	

MISCELLANEOUS READING TESTS

Name of Test	For Grades	No. of Forms	Approx. time (in min.)	Publisher	Author(s)	Speed	Vocabulary
Intermediate Level, 1969	3-6	1	80	HBW	D. Durrell		x
Advanced Level, 1969	7-9	1	80	HBW	D. Durrell		x
Durrell-Sullivan Reading Capacity and Achievement Tests, 1937; rev. 1945	2.5-4.5 3-6			HBW	D. Durrell H. Sullivan		x
*Diplexia Schedule, 1968; rev. 1969	1		20-25	EPS	J. McLeod		
+Frostig Developmental Test of Visual Perception, 1961; rev. 1966	Pre K-3	1	30-45 40-60	FEC			
Harris Test of Lateral Dominance, 1947; rev. 1958	1- adult			PC	A. Harris		
Individual Reading Placement Inventory, Field Research Edition, 1969	1-7		10-35	FEC	E. Smith W. Bradt-mueller		
The Instant Word Recognition Test, 1971	1-4			DP	E. Fry		

+Both group and individual administration

Compre-hension	Word recog-nition and attack	Spelling	Auding	Other	Vol. and Test No. in Mental Measurement Yearbooks	Pages in Tests and Review (Buros)
			x	Paragraph listening and reading	7:728	
			x	Paragraph listening and reading	7:728	
x		x		Written recall		
				Questionnaire to be completed by parents	7:729	
				Eye-motor coordination, spatial relations, perceptual abilities	7:871	
				Hand, eye, and foot dominance	5:761	
				Present language potential, in-dependence, instructional, and frustrational levels	7:730	
	x					

MISCELLANEOUS READING TESTS

Name of Test	For Grades	No. of Forms	Approx. time (in min.)	Publisher	Author(s)	Speed	Vocabulary
Jordon Left– Right Reversal Test, 1973	1–5			ATP	B. Jordon		
*Keystone Visual Survey Tests, 1933; rev. 1971	Pre K– adult	1		KVC			
Learning Methods Test—Mills, 1954; rev. 1955	K–3	1	85–100	MCI	R. E. Mills		
Merterns Visual Perception Test, 1969–74	K–1			WPS	M. Merterns		
Michigan Speed of Reading Test, 1932; rev. 1937	6–16	2	7	PC	E. Greene	x	
Minnesota Speed of Reading Test for College Students, 1936	12–16	2	15	UMP	A. Eurich	x	
*Mott Basic Language Skills Placement Test, 1967	1–3	1	15	AEC			
National Test of Basic Words, 1970	1–5			ATC	S. Halpern		
OC Diagnostic Syllabizing Test, 1960; rev. 1962	4–6	1	15–20	OPC	K. O'Connor		
*Ortho–Rater, 1942; rev. 1958	16+	1		BLI			
Perceptual Forms Test, 1955; rev. 1969	K 1	1	10	WHLR	Publication Committee, Winter Haven Lions Club		

Compre-hension	Word recog-nition and attack	Spelling	Auding	Other	Vol. and Test No. in Mental Measurement Yearbooks	Pages in Tests and Review (Buros)
				Relative frequency of letter and number reversals		
				Visual functions, necessary individual reading	5:780	
	x			Learning methods, training and testing	6:836	13
				Spatial recognition, visual memory, visual perceptions related to reading-design production and completion		
					3:523	136
				History, geography, economics, government, psychology, science education	2:1555	61
x				Sentence completion, initial consonant recognition		
	x			Service words		
				Syllabizing skills	6:827	350
				Visual discrimination, per-ception of depth, color discrimination	5:783	
				Visual motor coordination	7:872	374

MISCELLANEOUS READING TESTS

Name of Test	For Grades	No. of Forms	Approx. time (in min.)	Publisher	Author(s)	Speed	Vocabulary
Pictographic Self-Rating Scale, 1955; rev. 1957	9–16	1	35	APC	E. Ryden		
Reader's Inventory, 1963	9–16+	1		EDL	G. D. Spache S. Taylor		
*Reader Rater With Self-Scoring Profile, 1959; rev. 1965	10–12+	1	60–120	BRP		x	x
*Reading Eye, 1959; rev. 1969	1–16+	8	4	EDL	S. Taylor H. Fracken-pohl J. Pettee	x	
Reading Versatility Test—Reading Eye Edition, 1961; rev. 1962							
*Basic Level	6–10	2	35	EDL	A. McDonald M. Alodia S. Taylor	x	
Intermediate Level	8–12	1		EDL	(See Basic Level)	x	
Advanced Level	12–16	4	30	EDL	G. Zimmy J. Byrne	x	
Reading Versatility Test—Paper and Pencil Edition, 1961; rev. 1968	5–8	4	30	EDL	A. McDonald M. Alodia	x	
*Roswell-Chall Auditory Blend-ing Test, 1963	1–4	1		EP	F. Roswell J. Chall		

Compre-hension	Word recognition and attack	Spelling	Auding	Other	Vol. and Test No. in Mental Measurement Yearbooks	Pages in Tests and Review (Buros)
				Attitude toward classroom and study activities	6:701	280
				Attitude	7:733	13
x				Reading habits, summarizing, skimming	6:837	363
				Fixations, regressions, span recognition, grade level of reading skills, efficiency, visual adjustment, directional attack	7:734	363
x				Span of recognition, fixation, apparent number of lines, regressions and fixations per 100 words	7:735	365
x				Skimming and scanning rate and comprehension	7:735	365
x				Skimming and scanning rate and comprehension	7:735	365
x				Skimming and scanning rate and comprehension	7:735	365
	x				6:830	352

MISCELLANEOUS READING TESTS

Name of Test	For Grades	No. of Forms	Approx. time (in min.)	Publisher	Author(s)	Speed	Vocabulary
SRA Tests of Educational Ability							
Level 1, 1958; rev. 1963	4-6	1	52	SRA	L. Thurstone T. Thurstone		
Level 2, 1958; rev. 1963	6-9	1	67	SRA	T. Thurstone		
Level 3, 1957; rev. 1963	9-12	1	45	SRA	T. Thurstone		
SRA Tests of General Abilities, 1957; rev. 1960	K-2 2-4 4-6 6-9 9-12	1	35-45	SRA	J. Flanagan		
Screening Test for the Assignment of Remedial Treatments, 1968	Pre K-1	1	60	PII	A. Ahr		
Screening Tests for Identifying Children with Specific Language Difficulty 1964; rev. 1970	1-2.5 2.5-3.5 3.5-4	1	56	EPS	B. H. Slinger-land		x
Sequential Tests of Educational Progress-Reading, 1956; rev. 1972	4-6 7-9 10-12 13-14	2	45	ETS			
*Spache Binocular Reading Test, 1943; rev. 1955	1-adult			KPC	G. D. Spache		
Understanding Communication (Verbal Comprehension), 1956; rev. 1959	9-16	1	20	EITS	T. Thurstone		

Compre-hension	Word recog-nition and attack	Spelling	Auding	Other	Vol. and Test No. in Mental Measurement Yearbooks	Pages in Tests and Review (Buros)
				Language, reasoning, quantitative	6:495	411
				Language, reasoning, qualitative	6:495	411
				Language, reasoning, qualitative	6:495	411
				Information, non-cultural reading	6:496	411
			x	Visual memory, visual copying and discrimination	7:764	16
			x	Visual perception and memory, kinesthetic memory	7:969	13
				Recall ideas, translate ideas and make inferences; analyze motivation and presentation; ability to criticize	6:810	
				Eye preference in reading	6:959	
x					6:840	365

MISCELLANEOUS READING TESTS

Name of Test	For Grades	No. of Forms	Approx. time in (min.)	Publisher	Author(s)	Speed	Vocabulary
Wide Range Vocabulary Test, 1937; rev. 1945	3-16	2	10	PC	C. R. Atwell F. L. Wells		x
Word Discrimination Test, 1958	1-8	2	15-20	MUAA	C. Huelsmanor		
Word Preference Inventory, 1972	K-6			PDR	P. Dunn-Rankin		

Compre-hension	Word recog-nition and attack	Spelling	Auding	Other	Vol. and Test No. in Mental Measurement Yearbooks	Pages in Tests and Review (Buros)
					5:241	
	x					
					7:736	
				Maintaining letter order, partial word retention, misperception versus rotation, minor letter order changes versus major letter permutations		

List of Publishers

AC	Alameda County School Dept. 224 W. Winston Ave. Hayward, CA 94544
AEC	Allied Education Council P.O. Box 78 Galien, MI 49113
AGS	American Guidance Service, Inc. Publishers' Building Circle Pines, MN 55014
AP	Academic Press 111 Fifth Ave. New York, NY 10003
APC	Acorn Publishing Company Psychometric Affiliates 1743 Monterey Ave. Chicago, Ill. 60643
AR	Arden Press 8331 Alvarado Dr. Huntington Beach, CA 92646
ATC	American Testing Company 6301 S.W. Fifth St. Fort Lauderdale, FL 33317
ATP	Academic Therapy Publications 1539 Fourth St. San Rafael, CA 94901
BEM	Bureau of Educational Measurements Kansas State Teachers College Emporia, KS 66801
BLI	Bausch and Lomb, Inc. Rochester, NY 14602
BM	The Bobbs-Merrill Company, Inc. 4300 West 62nd St. Indianapolis, IN 46206
BP	Brador Publications, Inc. Livonia, NY 14487
BRP	Better Reading Program, Inc. 230 East Ohio St. Chicago, IL 60611
BYUP	Brigham Young University Press 205 UPB Provo, UT 84601

CDRT	Committee on Diagnostic Reading Tests, Inc. Mountain Home, NC 28758
CES	Croft Educational Services, Inc. 100 Garfield Ave. New London, CT 06320
CP	CAL Press, Inc. 76 Madison Ave. New York, NY 10016
CPP	Consulting Psychologists Press, Inc. 577 College Ave. Palo Alto, CA 94306
CSB	Cal-State Bookstore 25776 Hillary St. Hayward, CA 92542
CTB	California Test Bureau/McGraw-Hill Del Monte Research Park Monterey, CA 93940
CTD–ETS	Cooperative Test Division Educational Testing Service 20 Nassau St. Princeton, NJ 08540
DCRA	Delaware County Reading Consultants Associations c/o Nicholas A. Spennato Delaware County Public Schools Court House Annex Media, PA 19063
DEN	Denver Public Schools 414 Fourteenth St. Denver, CO 80202
DES	Drew Educational Systems, Inc. 320 Raritan Ave. Highland Park, NJ 08904
DPS	Department of Psychological Testing DePaul University 25 E. Jackson Blvd. Chicago, IL 60604
DRD	Developmental Reading Distributors 1944 Sheridan Ave. Laramie, WY 82070
DRT	Delco Readiness Test 111 Linda Lane Media, PA 19063

EC	Edcodyne Corporation 1 City Blvd. West Suite 935 Orange, CA 92668
EDL	Educational Developmental Laboratories, Inc. 294 Pulaski Rd. Huntington, NY 11744
EITS	Educational and Industrial Test Service P.O. Box 7234 San Diego, CA 92107
EMH	E. M. Hale Co., 1201 S. Hastings Way Eau Claire, WI 54701
EP	Essay Press P.O. Box #5 Planetarium Station New York, NY 10024
EPA	Educational Performance Associates, Inc. 563 Westview Ave., Ridgefield, NJ 07657
EPS	Educators Publishing Service 301 Vassar St. Cambridge, MA 02139
ERB	Educational Records Bureau 21 Audubon Ave. New York, NY 10032 Cooperative Tests and Services
ES	Educational Stimuli Telegram Building Superior, WI 54880
ESD	Educational Skills Development, Inc. 431 S. Broadway Suite 313 Lexington, KY 40508
ETB	Educational Test Bureau Publishers' Building Circle Pines, MN 55014
ETS	Educational Testing Service 20 Nassau Street Princeton, NJ 08540
F	Fearon Publishers Lear Siegler, Inc. Educational Division 6 Davis Dr. Belmont, CA 94002

FEC   Follett Publishing Company
       1010 W. Washington Blvd.
       Chicago, IL 60607

FSC   Foster & Stewart Publishing Corporation
       c/o M. E. Wagner
       500 Klein Rd.
       Buffalo, NY 14221

FW   Fort Worth Independent School District
       3210 W. Lancaster
       Fort Worth, TX 76107

GC   Ginn and Company
       Waltham, MA 02154

GP   Garrard Publishing Co.
       1607 N. Market St.
       Champaign, IL 61820

GTA   Guidance Testing Associates
       6516 Shirley Ave.
       Austin, TX 78756

HBW   Harcourt Brace Jovanovich, Inc.
       757 Third Ave.
       New York, NY 15017

HC   C.S. Hammond and Company
       515 Valley St.
       Maplewood, NJ 07040

HM   Houghton Mifflin Company
       110 Tremont St.
       Boston, MA 02107

HR   Harper & Row Publishers, Inc.
       10 E. 53rd St.
       New York, NY 10022

IOE   The Instructional Objectives Exchange
       Box 24095
       Los Angeles, CA 90024

IPAT   Institute for Personality and Aptitude Testing
       16020-04 Coronado Dr.
       Champaign, IL 61820

ISGS   International Society for General Semantics
       PO Box 2469
       San Francisco, CA 94126

JFP   John Hopkins Press
       Homewood
       Baltimore, MD 21218

JLC   J.B. Lippincott Company
       E. Washington Square
       Philadelphia, PA 19105

JS	Joseph Sanacore Reading Coordinator Hauppauge School District 600 Town Line Rd. Hauppauge, Long Island, NY 11787
KPC	Klamath Printing Company 320 Lowell Klamath Falls, OR 97601
KVC	Keystone View Company Meadville, PA 16335
LC	Lyons and Carnahan, Inc. 407 E. 25th St. Chicago, IL 60616
LEA	Learning Research Associates, Inc. 1501 Broadway New York, NY 10036
LRA	Language Research Associates 950 E. 59th St. Chicago, IL
MC	Macmillan Publishing Co., Inc. Front and Brown St. Riverside, NJ 08076
MCI	Mills Center, Inc. 1512 E. Broward Blvd. Fort Lauderdale, FL 33301
MRC	McGrath Reading Clinic 15944 W. McNichols Rd. Detroit, MI 48235
MRCP	Montana Reading Clinic Publications 517 Rimrock Rd. Billings, MT 59102
MUAA	Miami University Alumni Association Muskin Alumni Center Miami University Oxford, OH 45056
NCS	NCS Interpretive Scoring Systems 4401 W. 76th St. Minneapolis, MN 55435
NCTE	National Council of Teachers of English 508 S. Sixth St. Champaign, IL 61820
NDE	New Dimensions in Education, Inc. 160 Dupont St. Plainview, NY 11803

NPC   C. H. Nevins Printing Company
311 Bryn Mawr Island
Bradenton, FL 33505

OPC   O'Connor Reading Clinic Publishing Company
Box 447
Roscommon, MI 48653

OSU   University Publications Scales
Ohio State University
242 W. 18th St.
Columbus, OH 43210

OSUP   Ohio State University Press
Columbus, OH

OTS   Ohio Testing Service
Division of Guidance and Testing
State Department of Education
751 Northwest Blvd.
Columbus, OH 43212

PA   Psychometric Affiliates
1743 Monterey Ave.
Chicago, IL 60643

PC   The Psychological Corporation
304 East 45th St.
New York, NY 10017

PDR   Peter Dunn-Rankin
University of Hawaii
Education Research & Development Center
1776 University Ave.
Honolulu, HI 96822

PE   Programs for Education
Box 85
Lumberville, PA 18933

PEI   Psychologists and Education, Inc.
Suite 212
211 W. State St.
Jacksonville, IL 62650

PFC   Perfection Form Company
214 W. 8th St.
Logan, IA 51546

PGP   Personal Growth Press, Inc.
Box M
Berea, OH 44017

PHI   Phonovisual Products, Inc.
4708 Wisconsin Ave. N.W.
Washington, D.C. 20007

PI	Psychological Institute P.O. Box 1118 Lake Alfred, FL 33850
PII	Priority Innovations, Inc. P.O. Box 792 Skokie, IL 60076
PPI	Personnel Press, Inc. 20 Nassau St. Princeton, NJ 08540
PRA	Personnel Research Associates, Inc. 1435 South LaCienega Blvd. Los Angeles, CA 90035
PRF	Purdue Research Foundation Personnel Evaluation Research Service Division of Educational Reference Purdue University Lafayette, IN 47907
PSP	Public School Publishing Co. Division of the Bobbs-Merrill Co., 4300 W. 62nd St. Indianapolis, IN 46268
RBH	Richardson, Bellows, Henry and Co. 355 Lexington Ave. New York, NY 10017
RC	Research Concepts 1368 East Airport Rd. Muskegon, MI 49444
RLC	Reading Laboratory and Clinic University of Florida Gainesville, FL 32601
RM	R. A. McMenemy 3028 N. E. Brazee St. Portland, OR 97212
RP	Reviac Publications 1535 Red Oak Dri. Silver Spring, MD 20910
RSSC	Reading and Study Skills Center, Inc. c/o Taylor Center for Controlled Reading and Research 75 Prospect St. Huntington, NY 11744
SEP	Slosson Educational Publications 140 Pine St. East Aurora, NY 14052

SF	Scott, Foresman & Co. 1900 E. Lake Ave. Glenville, IL 60025
SHTS	State High School Testing Service for Indiana Purdue University Lafayette, IN 47907
SMP	St. Martins Press, Inc. 175 Fifth Ave. New York, NY 10010
SPS	Seattle Public Schools Seattle, WA
SRA	Science Research Associates, Inc. 259 E. Erie St. Chicago, IL 50511
SSC	Sheridan Supply Company c/o Sheridan Psychological Services, Inc. P.O. Box 837 Beverly Hills, CA 90213
ST	C. H. Stoelting Co. 424 N. Homa Ave. Chicago, IL
STS	Scholastic Testing Service, Inc. 480 Meyer Rd. Bensenville, IL 60106
SUP	Stanford University Press Palo Alto, CA 94305
SV	Steck-Vaugh Co. P.O. Box #2028 Austin, TX 78767
TCP	Teachers College Press Teachers College, Columbia University 525 West 120th St. New York, NY 10027
TM	Thomas F. McDonald, Director, Reading Program Phoenix Union High School Program 2526 W. Osborn Rd. Phoenix, AZ 85017
UI	University of Illinois Press Urbana, IL 61801
UMP	University of Minnesota Press 2037 University Ave., S.E. Minneapolis, MI 55455

VTS	Veterans' Testing Service c/o General Educational Development Testing Service of the American Council on Education 1785 Mass. Ave. N.W. Washington, D.C. 20036
VW	Van Wagenen Psycho-Educational Research Laboratories 1729 Irving Ave. South Minneapolis, MI 55411
WBC	William C. Brown Book Company 135 South Locust St. Dubuque, IA 52001
WHLR	Winter Haven Lions Research Foundation, Inc. P.O. Box 1045 Winter Haven, FL 33881
WL	Wilbur L. Layton 3604 Ross Rd. Ames, IA 50010
WLC	Westinghouse Learning Corporation 100 Park Avenue New York, NY 10017
WM	McCartney, William A. P.O. Box 507 Kaneohe, HI 96744
WPC	Webster Publishing Co. Division of McGraw-Hill Book Co. Manchester Rd. Manchester,MO 63011
WPS	Western Psychological Services Box 775 Beverly Hills, CA 33881

Appendix B

Objectives

Behavioral Objectives Writing Skills Test (BOWST)*

Diane Lapp, Associate Professor, Boston University, Copyright 1970

Outline

I. General Information
    A. Test Construction
    B. Test Development Studies
       1. Validity
       2. Reliability
II. Directions for Administering and Scoring
    A. Test Materials
    B. Time Requirements
    C. Test Administration
    D. Scoring the Test

General Information

The Behavioral Objectives Writing Skills Test (BOWST) was designed to provide an estimate of the elementary teacher's ability to write behavioral objectives.

This instrument, which requires the teacher to develop three behavioral objectives for each of four hypothetical classroom settings, has wide utility as a teacher training tool. It may be administered as both a pre- and post-test in either inservice or preservice programs which attempt to measure the ability of teachers to write behavioral objectives.

The BOWST has the following advantages as a measuring instrument: (1) extensive preparation is not needed for its administration or scoring; (2) it is untimed and therefore is not a speed test; (3) no oral response is required; and (4) alternate forms of the test are provided to facilitate repeated measures.

Test Construction

For the purpose of assessing elementary teachers' abilities to write behavioral objectives, the *Behavioral Objectives Writing Skills Test* (BOWST) was developed. The BOWST was composed of a total of four hypothetical class settings, one in each of the four following curriculum areas: reading, arithmetic, science, and social studies. The teachers were asked to develop three behavioral objectives for each of the four hypothetical settings. Successful completion of a behavioral objective was dependent upon the inclusion of the following specified criteria: (1) terminal behavior, which describes the type of behavior that is to occur as a result of a planned instruction; (2) external conditions, which tell the setting under which a specified behavior will occur; and (3) acceptable performance, which tells the level of performance that will be accepted.

Test Development Studies

The following studies were conducted to determine the validity and reliability of the BOWST.

Validity Studies

Test validity, which is the extent to which a test measures what it is purported to measure, was studied in the following manner:

1 The first test development study attempted to determine the content validity of the BOWST. The assessment of this type of validity is based on an analysis of the relationship between the content that a specific test is said to cover and the actual content and abilities that it does cover. In order to establish content validity, the following materials were mailed to thirty-four persons who have evidenced through articles, lectures, etc., knowledge in the areas of measurement and behavioral objectives: (1) copies of both forms of the BOWST; (2) test and scoring directions; and (3) a test development explanation sheet. These specialists were asked to complete and return a test evaluation questionnaire in order to offer critical reactions to the content validity of this instrument. Upon receiving the returned evaluation questionnaires, a careful analysis was made of these opinions. Several revisions were based on the judgments of the surveyed group.

2. Another test development study to examine the content validity of the BOWST was also carried out. It was hypothesized that this instrument could measure teacher ability to write behavioral objectives. In order to assess the content validity of the BOWST, it was administered to two populations differing in ability to write behavioral objectives. The population for this study consisted of fifty-four persons: seventeen graduate students trained in writing behavioral objectives and thirty-seven elementary teachers who had no prior training in the writing of behavioral objectives. It was hypothexized that there would be a relationship between prior training and ability to write behavioral objectives. After the tests had been scored, a one-way analysis of variance was computed between the mean scores of trained and untrained persons to determine if the BOWST did indeed measure the ability to write behavioral objectives. Results of this one-way analysis of variance appear below.

TABLE 1: MEAN SCORES OF TRAINED AND UNTRAINED PERSONS*

Variable	Group Means	
	Trained	Untrained
Terminal behavior	11.6471	0.8919
External conditions	11.7059	4.5404
Acceptable performance	8.9412	2.343
Total BOWST score	32.2941	13.7027

*Trained = 17 subjects; untrained = 37 subjects

Results indicated that there were highly significant differences between trained and untrained persons in their abilities to develop the total behavioral objective and highly significant differences between trained and untrained persons in their abilities to develop each of the three criteria of a behavioral objective: i.e., terminal behavior, external conditions, and acceptable performance.

TABLE 2. ONE-WAY ANALYSIS OF VARIANCE BETWEEN MEAN SCORES OF TRAINED AND UNTRAINED POPULATION*

Variable analysis	Source	Mean square	D.F.	F-ratio	P
Terminal behavior	Total	17.2610	53		
	groups	263.3834	1	21.024	0.0001[†]
	error (G)	12.5279			
External conditions	Total	24.4072	53		
	groups	598.0407	1	44.507	0.0000[†]
	error (G)	13.4369	52		
Acceptable performance	Total	21.0384			
	groups	509.9878	1	43.830	0.0000[†]
	error (G)	11.6356	52		
Total BOWST score	Total	155.1950	53		
	groups	4026.0742	1	49.855	0.0000[†]
	error (G)	80.7550			

*Trained = 17 subjects; untrained = 37 subjects

[†]significant < .05 level

Concurrently with the validity studies, the following test development studies were conducted to determine form and rater reliability:

Reliability Studies

Test reliability, or consistency, was studied in the following manner:

1. The first reliability study was conducted to determine if: (a) different scorers arrived at the same scores; and (b) training in writing behavioral objectives is needed to reliably score the tests.

After the BOWST had been completed by the fifty-four persons in the second validity study described earlier, it was scored by four raters and the researcher. Two of the raters had previous training in the development and utilization of behavioral objectives, and two raters had no such prior training. The four raters who scored the tests were doctoral students in various fields of Education at Indiana University.

After the scores were compiled, correlations were computed between the scores assigned by each rater and the researcher. Correlations appear in the following table.

TABLE 3. CORRELATIONS OF RATER SCORES

		1	2	3	4	5
Total BOWST scores						
	1	1.0000	0.9948	0.9957	0.9970	0.9947
	2		1.000	0.9958	0.9957	0.9947
	3			1.0000	0.9988	0.9981
	4				1.0000	0.9980
	5					1.0000
Means		19.6111	19.8148	19.3519	19.4630	19.5556
Terminal behavior scores						
	1	1.000	0.9897	0.9685	0.9767	0.9744
	2		1.0000	0.9787	0.9822	0.9816
	3			1.0000	0.9876	0.9796
	4				1.0000	0.9783
Means		8.4259	8.6111	8.3704	8.5000	8.3889
External conditions scores						
	1	1.000	0.9878	0.9859	0.9850	0.9847
	2		1.0000	0.9872	0.9862	0.9837
	3			1.0000	0.9958	0.9928
	4				1.0000	0.9949
	5					1.0000
Means		6.6296	6.6111	6.7037	6.6852	6.7963
Acceptable performance scores						
	1	1.0000	0.9830	0.9856	0.9861	0.9789
	2		1.0000	0.9752	0.9758	0.9681
	3			1.0000	0.9945	0.9920
	4				1.0000	0.9919
	5					1.0000
Means		4.5556	4.5926	4.2778	4.2778	4.4074

*1 = Expert rater; 2 = nonexpert rater; 3 = expert rater, 4 = nonexpert rater; 5 = researcher.

2. The fourth test development study was conducted to determine the reliability of forms A and B of the BOWST. A total sample of fifty-four subjects previously described was administered either form A or B of the BOWST.

Twenty-five subjects completed form A, while twenty-nine subjects completed form B. A one-way analysis of variance was computed between the total test scores for each form and also on the total scores for each criteria level: terminal behavior, external conditions, and acceptable performance. Results of the one-way analysis of variance are included in Table 4.

TABLE 4. MEAN SCORES OF PERSONS COMPLETING EITHER FORM A OR B
OF THE BOWST*

| Variable | Group Means | |
	Form A	Form B
Terminal behavior	9.0400	7.8276
External conditions	7.6000	6.1034
Acceptable performance	4.4400	4.3793
Total BOWST score	21.0800	18.2414

*Form A = 25 subjects; form B = 29 subjects

Results indicated that there were no significant differences on either total terminal behavior or total external condition scores for either form of the test. However, this analysis of the data did indicate that there were significant differences between the total mean acceptable performance scores of elementary teachers having completed form A or B of the BOWST. There were also significant differences found between teachers' total mean scores on the BOWST.

TABLE 5. ONE-WAY ANALYSIS OF VARIANCE BETWEEN MEAN SCORES
ON FORMS A AND B*

Variable analysis	Source	Mean square	D.F.	F-ratio	P
Terminal behavior	Total	17.2610	53		
	groups	19.7354	1	1.147	0.2892
	error (G)	17.2134	52		
External conditions	Total	24.4672	53		
	groups	30.0696	1	1.234	0.2710
	error (G)	24.3594	52		
Acceptable performance	Total	21.0384	53		
	groups	0.0495	1	0.002	0.9608[†]
	error (G)	21.4421	52		
Total BOWST	Total	155.1950	53		
	groups	108.1830	1	0.693	0.5861[†]
	error (G)	156.0990	52		

*Form A = 25 subjects; form B = 29 subjects
[†]Significant < .05 level

The researcher was cognizant of the possibility that in randomly assigning the total population to either form of the test, the group of trained persons might not have been evenly distributed. Therefore, a two-way analysis of variance was computed between examinees and forms. The total sample of fifty-four persons was now divided into groups of trained and untrained participants, with designation being made to which form of the test they had completed.

This study was conducted to determine if there were significant differences between forms A and B or merely between trained and untrained participants' abilities to complete the forms.

Results of this two-way analysis of variance indicated that there was no significant difference found between forms A and B when the populations completing the forms were classified, respectively, as trained or untrained participants. This two-way analysis of variance indicated that the reason for variance found between forms of the earlier one-way analysis was that more trained persons had taken form A than form B of the BOWST.

Results of the two-way analysis of variance appear in the following table:

TABLE 6. TWO-WAY ANALYSIS OF VARIANCE BETWEEN FORMS AND EXAMINEES

Variable analysis	Source	Mean square	D.F.	F-ratio	P
Terminal behavior	Total	16.967	53		
	A*	252.402	1	19.7570	0.0002
	B	4.322	1	0.3383	0.5703
	AB	3.753	1	0.2938	0.5967
	Error (G)	12.775	50		
External conditions	Total	23.948	53		
	A	578.277	1	42.8524	0.0000
	B	3.033	1	0.2248	0.6426
	AB	13.177	1	0.9764	0.6711
	Error (G)	13.495	50		
Acceptable performance	Total	21.283	53		
	A	512.551	1	44.8477	0.0000
	B	13.708	1	1.1995	0.2783
	AB	30.284	1	2.6498	0.1060
	Error (G)	11.429	50		
Total BOWST score	Total	153.078	53		
	A	3935.803	1	48.5768	0.0000
	B	0.078	1	0.0010	0.9739
	AB	126.160	1	1.5571	0.2156
	Error (G)	81.022	50		

*A = Examinee; B = Form; AB = Interaction

Directions for Administering and Scoring

The administration and scoring of the Behavioral Objectives Writing Skills Test (BOWST) requires no special preparation other than familiarity with the scoring procedure. If the scoring key is strictly observed, the test does not necessarily have to be scored by only persons with training in writing behavioral objectives.

Directions for administering and scoring forms A and B of the BOWST are identical.

Test Materials

The test kit includes: (1) forms A and B of the BOWST, (2) scoring key procedure, (3) scoring sheet.

Time Requirements

Approximately 55 minutes are required for completion of this untimed test. After the examinee receives either form A or B of the BOWST, he works at his own speed until completion.

Test Administration

Test administration of the BOWST is realtively simple. Upon receiving the test kit, the administrator dispenses the test form to the examinee who, in essence, self-administers his own test. This occurs by the examinee's reading of the directions and proceeding at his own pace until the test is completed.

Scoring the Test

The highest possible socre for this test is thirty-six points. This score can be achieved by writing three behavioral objectives for each of the four lesson plans.

Each behavioral objective is scored as follows: One point is given for each of the three criteria included in the behavioral objective. These criteria are external conditions, terminal behavior, acceptable performance.

A. *External Conditions*

One point is given for each correct statement of the external conditions which tell when the acceptable behavior will occur.

Examples of correct statements of external conditions are:
1. Given a set of criteria . . .
2. Given a list of . . .
3. Given a specific . . .
4. Without the aid of . . .

These statements are correct because they describe the exact settings or conditions that will be present when the learner exhibits the terminal behavior.

The following examples are statements of incorrect external conditions:

1. To be able to . . .
2. To have knowledge of . . .
3. To learn by . . .

These examples are incorrect because they do not state the *exact* conditions under which the behavior will occur. The statement of *external condition* should answer the following question:

When will the desired behavior occur?

B. *Terminal Behavior*

One point is to be given for each correct statement of terminal behavior which tells what type of behavior will be accepted as evidence that the learner has achieved the stated objective. Examples of correct statements of terminal behavior are

1. The learner is able to identify . . .
2. The learner is able to list . . .
3. The learner is able to recite . . .

An accepted statement on terminal behavior will be one that describes the behavior in such a way that it cannot be misinterpreted. It states the exact behavior that will be exhibited: i.e., list, identify, recite It must clearly state some behavior to be displayed by the learner when he has reached the goal.

Examples of incorrect statements of terminal behavior are

1. The student knows . . .
2. The student will enjoy . . .
3. The student appreciates . . .
4. The pupil believes . . .

These are incorrect statements of terminal behavior because they cannot be adequately measured. The teacher must designate more specifically how the child may exhibit what he knows, appreciates, or believes. The statement describing what the student will be doing when he is exhibiting a specified skill is the statement of terminal behavior.

The statement of terminal behavior should answer the following question:

What type of behavior will be accepted as evidence that the learner has achieved the stated objective?

C. *Acceptable Behavior*

One point is to be given for each statement of acceptable performance, which indicates how well the learner must perform a specified task for it to be considered acceptable. Some examples of correct statemnts of performance are

1. . . . at least ten of the following problems . . .
2. . . . those appropriate to the discussion . . .
3. . . . the five elements in three minutes . . .
4. . . . 40 per cent of the basic sight words . . .
5. . . . all of the addition problems on page 206 . . .

These statements are correct because they tell how well the learner must perform before his behavior will be acceptable. Exclusion of the acceptable performance will occur more often than will incorrect statements. The acceptable performance may be better illustrated within a behavioral objective. For the purpose of further clarity, the following behavioral objectives are stated and the acceptable performance measures are underlined.

Given a list of basic sight words, the child will be able to identify <u>at least three words that rhyme with "can."</u>

Given fifty spelling words orally presented by the teacher, the child will be able to write down, with correct spelling, <u>at least 80 per cent of the words.</u>

The statement of acceptable performance should answer the following question: *How* well must a learner perform a specified task for it to be considered acceptable?

Each form of the BOWST is composed of a total of four hypothetical class settings, one setting in each of the four specified curriculum areas. Persons taking the test are asked to develop three behavioral objectives for each of the four settings. Each objective is then examined for the inclusion of the three criteria necessary for developing a behavioral objective. The maximum number of points for an examinee is, therefore, thirty-six. This is arrived at by multiplying the number of behavioral objectives to be written for each setting (3), times the number of curriculum areas (4), and then multiplying this product times the number of criteria included in each developed behavioral objective (3). This would result in $3 \times 4 \times 3 = 36$.

The following table outlines the two basic dimensions of the BOWST.

TABLE 1. DIMENSIONS OF THE BOWST

Curiculum areas

Reading	3 points possible	3	3	9
Arithmetic	3	3	3	9
Science	3	3	3	9
Social studies	3	3	3	9

Criteria:

T E R M I N A L	B E H A V I O R 12	C O N D I T I O N 12	P E R F O R M A N C E 12 =	36 total points

From this test it is possible to determine each teacher's ability to write behavioral objectives in each of the four curriculum areas. The total possible score for these four areas would be nine points. This is arrived at by multiplying the number of behavioral objectives to be written for a specific curriculum area (3) times the number of criteria for rating each behavioral objective (3). This would result in 3 X 3 = 9.

In addition, it is possible to determine each teacher's ability to write behavioral objectives which include each of the three stated criteria. The total possible score for each of these three areas is twelve points. This is arrived at by determining whether each of the twelve behavioral objectives met one of the three specific criteria. A maximum score of twelve points is possible for each specific criteria area. This would result in 12 X 1 = 12.

Finally, it is possible to determine each teacher's ability to write behavioral objectives in each of the four curriculum areas according to one of three criteria. The total possible score for each of these two dimensional areas would be three points. This is arrived at by assessing the three behavioral objectives according to one of the three criteria. This would result in 3 X 1 = 3.

The BOWST, therefore, is composed of a total score of thirty-six points and nineteen subscores ranging from three to nineteen points. The following table presents a detailed outline for the BOWST.

TABLE 2. OUTLINE FOR THE BEHAVIORAL OBJECTIVES WRITING SKILLS TEST

	Number of Objectives	Criteria Criteria	Subscore Subscore	Total
A. Developing behavioral objectives in:				
1. Reading	3	3	9	
2. Arithmetic	3	3	9	
3. Science	3	3	9	
4. Social studies	3	3	9	
				36
B. Developing behavioral objectives to meet specific criteria:				
1. Terminal behavior	12	1	12	
2. Conditions	12	1	12	
3. Performance	12	1	12	
				36
C. Interaction between subject matter area and criteria:				
1. Reading—Terminal behavior	3	1	3	
Reading—Conditions	3	1	3	
Reading—Performance	3	1	3	
2. Arithmetic—Terminal behavior	3	1	3	
Arithmetic—Conditions	3	1	3	
Arithmetic—Performance	3	1	3	
3. Science—Terminal behavior	3	1	3	
Science—Conditions	3	1	3	
Science—Performance	3	1	3	
4. Social Studies—Terminal behavior	3	1	3	
Social Studies—Conditions	3	1	3	
Social Studies—Performance	3	1	3	
				36

Behavioral Objectives Writing Skills Test[*]

Form A

Diane Lapp, copyright 1970

Test Directions

The following test consists of hypothetical class situations and procedures that could be utilized in developing a lesson or unit of study for a class session or sessions. A total of four situations are presented, consisting of one in each of the following subject areas: reading, arithmetic, social studies, and science. For *each* general situation you are asked to develop three behavioral objectives, or a total of twelve behavioral objectives in all. This does not mean that you would necessarily plan to accomplish all three of these objectives within the same class period.

Please utilize the following definition of a behavioral objective in each of your twelve responses: *A behavioral objective is a statement that tells the conditions under which a specified behavior will occur, the type of behavior that is to occur as a result of planned instruction, and the performance level that will be accepted.*

After reading the content of each situation, write three behavioral objectives that you feel could be accomplished for an individual pupil or a group of pupils. No predetermined objectives or grade levels have been developed for these plans, so as to be easily adaptable to any grade level. This test is untimed.

---

[*]This test may not be reproduced without permission of the author, but it may be obtained from *Educational Testing Services*, Princeton: New Jersey.

Science

You need to increase your students' knowledge and practice of good oral hygiene habits. It's Dental Health Week and time for an all-out campaign for increased oral hygiene. You wish to promote your students' regular brushing and dental visits. Record keeping will play an important role. Children will record not only their toothbrushing habits, but also keep records of between meal snacks and amounts of water consumed.

You feel that a historical prologue can lead the children to list modern dental aids from the electric drills to striped toothpaste. They should be able to role play a visit to the dentist and give demonstrations as to proper brushing techniques. The children can draw and label parts of the mouth, as well as apply labels to all teeth. They should be able to distinguish the function of various kinds of teeth such as incisors, molars, etc.

Through recognition of the functions of various kinds of teeth, the child should realize the importance of proper care and maintenance of teeth.

Please write three behavioral objectives for this lesson. If adequate space has not been provided, use the back side of this page.

1. _____

   _____

   _____

2. _____

   _____

   _____

3. _____

   _____

   _____

Form A

Reading

Even though your reading group will approach completion of their basal text, you feel that many of the children have not mastered their new vocabulary words. This, of course will interfere with their comprehension of the text. You will review these new words with the children, allowing them to identify the words in a contextual setting; that is, you will want the group to recognize new words in phrases or sentences.

Another of your broad goals will be for the children to identify a synonym or offer a simple definition of the new vocabulary words. Perhaps those children requiring less practice with word identification will be able to form their own new word lists by combining words into compound words. They may also add prefixes and suffixes to the already known root word. All of this practice, you believe, will increase the group's readiness for the next-level text.

Please write three behavioral objectives fot this lesson. If adequate space has not been provided, use the back side of this page.

1. _____

_____

_____

2. _____

_____

_____

3. _____

_____

_____

Form A

Arithmetic

You will develop a unit on percentages and their relevance to the child's daily life. The majority of examples and problems will be posed by the life situations of the child rather than by a textbook.

You will have decided that the first lesson will involve a discussion of the students' pets. The total number of students having pets will be the basis for the percentage problems. After obtaining this total, the students will be calculating the percentages of specific varieties of pets owned by the students themselves.

You will have decided that the children will conduct a poll of the pets in the entire school. The class will be divided into several groups with a certain percentage of the class in each group It will be the responsibility of the group to go to two other classrooms and collect the information for the poll. They will also compute the percentages in the same manner as you will have indicated earlier. At the end of a given length of time, each of the groups will report their findings to the rest of the class and will chart the percentages on a graph.

An extension of this unit could include a categorization of the pets into specific breeds and then computation of the percentages. Through the lessons planned for this unit, you feel the children will gain a practical understanding and knowledge of percentages.

Please write three behavioral objectives for this unit. If adequate space has not been provided, use the back side of this page.

1. _____

_____

_____

2. _____

_____

_____

3. _____

_____

_____

Form A

Social Studies

"Living in Japan" is the title of the unit you will select to present to your social studies class. The first lesson will deal with very basic information about Japan; its location and size in relation to the United States.

Since involvement will be so essential to the learning atmosphere of the child, you will have decided to arrange the room environment to include aspects of Japanese homes, people, clothing, food, or geographical settings.

A wealth of materials will be available on Japan because of Expo '70. The students will be encouraged to keep notebooks of the numerous clippings they will be seeing in the papers and magazines You plan that through this experience each child will have an opportunity to gain information and have something to share and discuss with the class.

You will ask the Junior Red Cross to supply you with the name of a school in Japan so that your school can correspond with a type of sister school. The children will also be encouraged to write to the Japanese students as pen pals if they wish. You will speak to several room mothers about the possibility of having a Japanese tea time at the conclusion of your unit.

Such an experience will help your students to think more realistically about the life experiences of the people they will be reading about in Japan.

Please write three behavioral objectives for this unit. If adequate space has not been provided, use the back side of this page.

1. _____

_____

_____

2. _____

_____

_____

3. _____

_____

_____

Scoring Sheet

Place a score of "1" in each square if the behavioral objective includes the criteria for the column. If it does not include the criterion, leave the square blank. Total the columns and the rows.

Lesson plans	Terminal behavior	External conditions	Acceptable performance	Totals
Reading Behavioral objective #1				
Behavioral objective #2				
Behavioral objective #3				
Arithmetic Behavioral objective #1				
Behavioral objective #2				
Behavioral objective #3				
Social studies Behavioral objective #1				
Behavioral objective #2				
Behavioral objective #3				
Science Behavioral objective #1				
Behavioral objective #2				
Behavioral objective #3				
Totals				

Behavioral Objectives Writing Skills Test

Form B

Diane Lapp, copyright 1970

Test Directions

The following test consists of hypothetical class situations and procedures that could be utilized in developing a lesson or unit of study for a class session or sessions. A total of four situations are presented, consisting of one in each of the following subject areas: reading, arithmetic, social studies, and science. For *each* general situation you are asked to develop three behavioral objectives, or a total of twelve behavioral objectives in all. This does not mean that you would necessarily plan to accomplish all three of these objectives within the same class period.

Please utilize the following definition of a behavioral objective in each of your twelve responses: *A behavioral objective is a statement that tells the conditions under which a specified behavior will occur, the type of behavior that is to occur as a result of planned instruction, and the performance level that will be accepted.*

After reading the content of each situation, write three behavioral objectives that you feel could be accomplished for an individual pupil or a group of pupils. No predetermined objectives or grade levels have been developed for these plans, so as to be easily adaptable to any grade level. This test is untimed.

Form B

Science

With the coming of spring, your class will decide to plant a garden. Each child will be given the responsibility of bringing two varieties of seeds from home. Many of the seeds will be labeled when they are planted.

After the plants have sprouted, the children may begin to notice how rapidly some of the plants grow. Each student will be expected to keep a daily log of each plant variety's general growth rate, while also noting the different colors and shapes of each sprout.

Within a few days, the children will begin to learn the parts of the plants and identify flowers, leaves, stems, and roots. Books placed in the classroom will aid children in learning these identifications. Leaves can be grouped and organized according to shape, size, or other schema. You will plan to have the children develop classification schemas of their own and record them in their progress logs. Roots will be extracted and examined under a microscope. Student class reprots will be given about the function and nature of plant roots. Charts, drawing, and graphs, as well as the daily logs, could result from systematic observation.

Please write three behavioral objectives for this lesson. If adequate space has not been provided, use the back side of this sheet.

1. _____

_____

_____

2. _____

_____

_____

3. _____

_____

_____

Reading

"Squanto and the Pilgrims" will be the title of a story in your reading group. The historical nature of this lesson will allow for the opportunity to teach and reinforce study skills.

Rather than confine the lesson to the classroom, you will take the children to the library and teach them to use the card catalog and encyclopedias to find further information about this period in history   Here will be a good opportunity to refresh alphabetization skills. This will also offer the students an indirect opportunity to digest, organize, or classify information about the Pilgrim forefathers.

You will find that an aid to accomplishing these skills will be through the preparation of written or oral reports using several sources. You will hope that the children read broadly, will note and evaluate discrepancies in accounts, and will be able to discuss their findings. In short, you will hope that this lesson provides an opportunity for involvement through reading.

Please write three behavioral objectives for this lesson. If adequate space has not been provided, use the back side of this page.

1. _____

_____

_____

2. _____

_____

_____

3. _____

_____

_____

Form B

Arithmetic

Rather than isolate your presentations in math and social studies you will correlate these two areas into a unit dealing with several aspects of Japanese culture.

After discussing the types of houses in Japan, you will decide that the children should design Japanese houses using multiples of 3×6 for room construction.

Since you will have discussed time tables in math, you will decide to use time tables for computing the transportation times between the school and a principle city in Japan. This will include transportation by airplane, train, and boat.

The children will be asked to think of other aspects of Japan and its culture to compare and calculate. An example of this might be to compare Japan's area and population with that of the United States. Since you will have discussed an aspect of the population, perhaps the children could also learn about the Japanese currency and compare its value to American currency. Watching the interactions of disciplines in a foreign culture may better enable the student to be able to discover the interactions of disciplines within a familiar situation.

Please write three behavioral objectives for this lesson. If adequate space has not been provided, use the back side of this page.

1. _____

_____

_____

2. _____

_____

_____

3. _____

_____

_____

Social Studies

"Pueblo Indians" is the title of the unit you will have selected to use with your social studies class. The first lesson will deal with the life style of the Pueblo Indian.

You will ask a guest speaker who is familiar with the activities of the Pueblo Indians to discuss the type of work done by various tribe members. After such an experience the children will be able to role play various experiences—i.e., preparing corn to be dried, grinding corn for piki bread, and baking bread.

The music teacher will cooperate with you by teaching the children several Pueblo Indian songs. You will plan to present records which will give the children insight into the type of music and dances enjoyed by these people. You will secure a film which deals with the family relationships of the Pueblo Indian. During one class session several of the students will act out a short drama portraying the vamily they have just studied.

Through these experiences, you feel the children will be able to compare the music, working conditions, and family relationships of the Pueblo Indians with similiar situations in their home.

Please write three behavioral objectives for this lesson. If adequate space has not been provided, use the back side of this page.

1. _____

_____

_____

2. _____

_____

_____

3. _____

_____

_____

Scoring Sheet

Place a score of "1" in each square if the behavioral objective includes the criteria for the column. If it does not include the criterion, leave the square blank. Total the columns and the rows.

Lesson plans	Terminal behavior	External conditions	Acceptable performance	Totals
Reading				
Behavioral objective #1				
Behavioral objective #2				
Behavioral objective #3				
Arithmetic				
Behavioral objective #1				
Behavioral objective #2				
Behavioral objective #3				
Social Studies				
Behavioral objective #1				
Behavioral objective #2				
Behavioral objective #3				
Science				
Behavioral objective #1				
Behavioral objective #2				
Behavioral objective # 3				
Totals				

Materials

Materials and Resources for Reading Instruction

Readiness, Perception and Language

Allied Education Council
The Fitzhugh PLUS Program
Perceptual training and spatial organization books for reading

American Book Company
Dandy Dog's Early Learning Program
A readiness program

American Guidance Service
Peabody Language Developmental Kits
Kits of puppets, pictures, and lesson plans to develop oral skills

Appleton–Century–Crofts
Matric Games Package
Games for reading

Benefic Press
Experimental Development Program
A readiness program

Educational Teaching Aids
Learning Aids for Young Children in Accordance with Montessori
Material and equipment for readiness, perception, and motor development
Montessori-Type Teaching Aids
Materials patterned from the Montessori program

Follett
The Frostig Program for Development of Visual Perception
Workbooks for training visual perception

Holt, Rinehart and Winston
Children's World
A kit of multisensory materials for early childhood and readiness

Macmillan Publishing Co., Inc.
Early Childhood Discovery Materials
Readiness program

Mafex Associates
I Can Do It
Visual-motor activity exercises

Noble and Noble Publishers, Inc.
Try Experiences for Young Children
Visual–perceptual tasks

Science Research Associates, Inc.
Detect
A sensorimotor approach to visual discrimination

Distar Language I and II
(Preschool and Primary) A structured program designed to teach basic language concepts
and to build vocabulary

Webster
Developing Learning Readiness
A motor and perceptual development program

Materials, Games, Aids, and Equipment: Readiness, Perception, and Language

Continental Press
Preprinted masters for liquid duplication; readiness, perceptual, and visual-motor material

Creative Playthings, Inc.
Toys and games for perception and motor activities

Developmental Learning Materials
Manipulative materials for the development of perception, motor coordination, and handwriting

Garrard Publishing Co.
Dolch Teaching Aids; teaching aids and games for phonics and reading

I. L. Hammet Co.
Aids for reading

Ideal School Supply Co.
Reading aids

Instructo Corp.
Instructive Aids to Education; materials for early childhood; transparencies and flannel-board
visual aids

Kenworthy Education Service
Games and phonic games

J. B. Lippincott Company
Readiness activities

Milton Bradley Co.
A variety of TV–related reading games

Parker Bros., Inc.
TV–related reading and spelling games

J. A. Preston Corp.
Material for motor assessment and teaching; eye-hand coordination and perception

Teachers Publishing Corp.
Reading aids and games

Teaching Resources
A variety of programs for visual–motor, perceptual–motor, and eye–hand coordination.

Visual Products Division, 3M Company
Readiness and oral language activities

Beginning reading, phonics, word analysis, and decoding

Allied Education Council
Mott Basic Language Skills Program
Reading program for adolescents; levels 1–3 and 4–6; text-workbooks

American Book Co.
The Reading Experience and Development Series (READ)

American Guidance Service
Peabody Rebus Reading Program
The use of rebus pictures for teaching beginning reading
Weekly Reading Practice Books
Beginning reading phonics program

Appleton–Century–Crofts, New Century Pub.
Write and See
Self-correcting phonics materials with reappearing ink process (1–4)

Behavioral Research Laboratories
Sullivan Remedial Reading Program
Series of programmed workbooks

Continental Press
Wordland Series
A phonics program on preprinted ditto masters

Economy Company
Phonetic Keys to Reading
A phonic approach to beginning reading; books, cards, charts (1–4)

Educator's Publishing Service
Developmental and Remedial Reading Materials

Encyclopaedia Britannica Education Corp.
Language Experiences in Reading Program
Language experience approach to beginning reading

Ginn and Company
Ginn Word Enrichment Program
Seven workbooks for word recognition skills

Harcourt Brace Jovanovich, Inc.
Durrell-Murphy Phonics Practice Program
Self-directing phonics picture cards
The Palo Alto Reading Program: Sequential Steps in Reading
A programmed and linguistic approach to beginning reading
Speech-to-Print Phonics
Cards and manual for developing phonics skills

Houghton Mifflin
Get Set Games
Games to teach decoding skills

Initial Teaching Alphabet
i/t/a Early-to-Read Program revised
I/t/a as a medium for beginning reading

Instructo Corp.
First Experiences with Consonants. First Experiences with Vowels
Materials to teach consonants and vowels

Learning Research Associates
Michigan Language Program
Individualized program for beginning reading books for listening and reading words, word
    attack, and comprehension

J. B. Lippincott Company
Reading with Phonics
Workbooks and phonics cards for teaching phonics skills (primary)

Lyons and Carnahan
Phonics We Use
A series of phonics workbooks (1–8)

Macmillan Publishing Co., Inc.
Decoding for Reading
Audiovisual program for older nonreaders

McCormick–Mathers
Phonics Skill Builders
Set of six workbooks for teaching phonics skills (1–6)

McGraw Hill Book Company
Programed Reading
21 books of programmed instruction in reading

Charles E. Merrill Publishing Company
Merrill Linguistic Readers
A linguistic-approach basal reader

Open Court Publishing Co.
Open Court Correlated Language Arts Program
Basal reader series stressing phonics

Phonovisual Products
The Phonovisual Method
A series of books, charts, manuals, and cards for teaching phonics (primary)

Science Research Associates
Distar Reading I and II
(K–2) Highly structured program to teach beginning reading; emphasis on decoding
Lift-Off to Reading
A programmed beginning reading approach
Reading in High Gear
A programmed reading program for adolescent nonreaders
SRA Reading Program
A basal reading series with a linguistic emphasis (1–6)

Teaching College Press
Word Attack Series
Three workbooks to teach word-analysis skills

Webster
Conquests in Reading
Review of phonics and word-attack skills

Webster Division, McGraw-Hill Book Company
Magic World of Dr. Spello
Phonics and spelling book (4–8)

Xerox Education Division
Words in Color
Uses of color to teach initial reading

Reading Comprehension and Reading Improvement

Benefic Press
The Thinking Box
Designed to develop critical thinking skills; boxed material individualized to teach 12 thinking skills (upper intermediate–junior high)

The Bobbs–Merrill Co., Inc.
Developmental Reading Test Workbooks
Six workbooks to give training and practice in several reading skills (K–6)

Burgess Publishing Company
Developing Reading Efficiency
A workbook for junior high levels containing lessons for a variety of reading skills

Charles E. Merrill Publishing Company
Diagnostic Reading Workbooks Series
Workbooks designed for developmental or remedial programs in reading (K–6)
Gaining Independence in Reading
Three hard-covered textbooks (grades 4 and up)
Improve Your Reading Ability
Text-workbooks for development of comprehension skills and rate (intermediate level)
Reading Skilltext Series
Reading comprehension workbooks (1–6)

Continental Press
Reading-Thinking Skills
Preprinted masters for liquid duplicating (PP-6)

Croft
Croft Skill Package
Sequential process of comprehension skills

Dexter & Westbrook Ltd.
Barnell-Loft Specific Skill series
Exercise books designed for practice in specific reading comprehension skills: locating the answer, following directions, using the context, getting the facts, working with sound, drawing conclusions, getting the main idea (1–6)

Educational Developmental Laboratories, Division of McGraw-Hill Book Company
Study Skills Library
Reading skills focusing on content subjects; material boxed by subject area and difficulty level (4–9)

Globe Book Co.
Effective Reading
Exercises and materials for levels 4–8

Houghton Mifflin Company
The Reading Skills Lab Program
Nine workbooks for teaching specific comprehension skills (4–6)

J. B. Lippincott Company
Reading for Meaning Series
A series of workbooks designed to improve comprehension skills: vocabulary, central thought, details, organization, summarization (4–6 and 7–9)

Macmillan Publishing Co., Inc.
Macmillan Reading Spectrum, Reading Comprehension
Six workbooks for improvement of reading comprehension (3–8)

My Weekly Reader
Reading Success Series
Six booklets of high interest level to teach basic reading skills

Prentice-Hall, Inc.
Be a Better Reader
Reading improvement in the content areas (Junior high)

Be a Better Reader, Foundations
Designed for practice in reading in content areas (4–6)

Reader's Digest Services
Reading Improvement Material
Workbooks for reading improvement at advanced levels (7–10)

Reading Skills Builders
Magazine format with short reading selections and accompanying comprehension questions (1–8)

Science Research Associates Inc.
Reading for Understanding
Boxed multilevel selections, graduated in difficulty; designed to develop comprehension skills (5–12)

SRA Reading Laboratory
Boxed materials consisting of multilevel and color-cued reading matter with questions and answer keys; materials for improving rate as well as comprehension (1–12)

Scott, Foresman and Company
Basic Reading Skills for Junior High School Use
Workbook for developing reading skills; designed for remedial reading for pupils at junior high level

Steck-Vaughn
New Goals in Reading, Reading Essentials Series
Reading workbooks (3–4)

Teachers College Press
Gates-Peardon Reading Exercises
Reading exercises to develop the ability to read for general significance, to predict outcomes, to understand directions, and to note details
McCall-Crabbs Standard Test Lessons in Reading
Paperback booklets with short reading selections and comprehension questions (3–7)
Study Type Reading Exercises
Reading exercises at the secondary level (high school)

Webster Division, McGraw-Hill Book Company
New Practice Readers
Reading selections and questions designed to improve comprehension skills in reading (2–8)
Step Up Your Reading Power
Five workbooks designed for remedial reading students to improve reading comprehension

Multimedia Equipment and Teaching Machines

Bell & Howell
Language Master; an audiotape system for teaching language, phonics and vocabulary

Benefic Press
Reading multimedia kits; a multimedia reading program for adolescents

Borg-Warner Educational Systems
System 80; an individualized audiovisual programmed approach to teaching beginning reading

Bowmar
Coordinated books, photographs, sound filmstrips, and records for the readiness level
Reading Incentive Program; books, records, filmstrips, junior high school interest level

Craig Corp.
Craig Reader: machines for reading-rate improvement, multitrack recording tape equipment

Educational Developmental Laboratories
Audiovisual reading improvement equipment; tapes and workbooks for listening skills

Educational Projections Corp.
Self-instructional reading readiness program; film lessons for reading readiness; multichoice viewer

Electronic Future, Inc.
Wireless Reading Systems; Audio Flashcard system

General Learning Corp.
Phonoviewer system; combination film-slide record units; self-instructional for young children

Hoffman Information Systems
Audiovisual reading improvement program

Imperial International Learning
Audiovisual equipment; spelling, reading, speech, and mathematics program

Keystone View Co.
Overhead projector, tachistoscope

Perceptual Development Laboratories
Reading-rate improvement equipment

Psychotechnics
Remedial reading filmstrips, tachistoscope, reading laboratories, shadowscope reading pacer

Readers Digest
Young Pegasus Packet; related storybook and games for readiness

Rheem Califone
Multimedia reading program, tape lessons, books, and manuals

Scholastic Magazine
Multimedia kit of posters, records, paperbacks for reading improvement (Reading levels, 2–4;
 interest, junior high)

Science Research Associates, Inc.
Reading accelerator; pacer for improvement of reading rate

Viking Press
Viking Sound Filmstrips; coordinated record, filmstrip, and user's guide for presentation of
 literature to children

Glossary

Ability grouping The practice of organizing students into groups having similar levels of achievement or needs. The groups may be formed on the basis of reading skills or competencies in other subject areas.

Abstract thinking The skill of comprehending and identifying relationships. It also includes the skill of understanding abstract symbols and concepts.

Accelerator A device used to improve reading rate through utilization of a shutter, line maker, or shadow. Examples of such mechanical devices include the reading pacers, controlled readers, rate controllers, skimmers, and rateometers.

Achievement age The age at which a previously determined level of performance is reached by the average child. Also known as the educational age.

Achievement test An instrument designed to measure the level attained in some academic area.

Acuity Sharpness, usually of vision or hearing.

Adjustment inventory An instrument used to assess an individual's personal problems or social maladjustments.

Agraphia The type of aphasia involving the inability to translate thoughts into written language.

Allograph A dictionary pronunciation key in which a form of a letter is changed, as a result of its position in a word. An example is the combination of *a* and *e* to form *ae*.

Allophone Sounds that comprise the total members of a phoneme class. They are phonetically the same: such as the *f* at the beginning of *fix* and the *f* at the end of *if*. Both are allophones of the phoneme /f/.

Alternate test forms Tests that are equivalent to another form of a given standardized test. They are used to ensure reliability in test results, as comparable scores should be obtained.

Ambidexterity The ability to use both hands with equal proficiency.

Ambilateral The ability to use bodily parts (arms, ears, legs, arms) on both sides with equal facility.

Analytic methodology An approach to teaching reading in which whole words and meaning segments are presented. The wholes are examined so that conclusions or generalizations about parts can be made.

Anecdotal record A means of reporting observations of classroom occurences and behavior using diary form.

Anomaly Anything that deviates from the common rule; an abnormality.

Anthology A collection of poems, stories, essays, etc., extracted from various sources and combined into one volume.

Antonym A word opposite in meaning from another. For example, *big* is an antonym of *little*.

Anxiety level The degree of apprehension or nervous excitement present at a given moment, or in a particular situation.

Aphasia The inability to use language, resulting in either sensory (through process) or motor (speech) impairment.

Aptitude An ability or trait that may give an indication for future success in a particular skill.

Aptitude test A predictive measurement composed of items that are thought to correlate with scholastic achievement.

Articulation The production of speech sounds resulting in the formation of words.

Ascending letters Letters, such as b, d, f, k, l, that extend above the lines in printing or writing. They can, therefore, be used as configuration clues in reading.

Asemia The inability to use such communication symbols as figures or words, either spoken or written.

Association grouping The formation of groups on the basis of the members feeling free to join together for a common purpose.

Associative learning A means of acquiring knowledge by reintegrating ideas, and words or stimulus and responses from past experiences.

Atomistic methodology Any method of teaching reading involving the decoding of small parts that are combined to form whole words. The alphabet and phonics approaches belong in this category.

Attention span The extent of ability a person has to concentrate on a certain activity, usually involving listening, reading, or writing.

Attitude inventory An instrument designed to assess students' attitudes toward reading.

Auding A deeper level of hearing that involves listening with comprehension and critical interpretation.

Auditory discrimination The ability to differentiate between various sounds, including differences in direction, rhythm, volume, or tone. It is also used to describe the ability to perceive parts of a word and to then identify and produce those sounds in the proper order.

Auditory memory span   The extent to which a person can recall and reproduce a number of sounds after hearing them only once.

Auralize   To make use of the sounds acquired through hearing for the purpose of thinking, creating, etc. To express as an analogy: auralize is to hearing as visualize is to seeing.

Automatization   A behavior that can be done without effort or conscious thought: i.e., performed automatically.

Avoidance tendencies   Behaviors that imply a negative attitude, resulting in a withdrawal from a situation or an object.

Balanced reading program   A reading instruction program in which all types of reading materials and practices are used: trade books, fiction and non-fiction, study skills, references, and recreational, oral, and silent reading.

Basal reader method   A method of reading instruction in which a series of graded reading textbooks are used in conjunction with a student workbook and teacher's guide.

Behavioral objectives   The expected outcome or instructional goal a student is expected to attain after instruction has been presented. The outcome should be performable and, therefore, able to be observed and measured. Objectives can be categorized under the following domains:

Affective—Those skills involving emotions, feelings, and values.

Cognitive—Those skills involving thinking, interpreting, or memory.

Activity psychomotor—Involving fine and gross motor skills, or any physical activity.

The affective, cognitive, and psychomotor domains can include the following "subdomains." These are used as alternate ways to evaluate the skills that were taught.

Consequence objectives—Those objectives used in teacher training in which the success of the trainer's instruction is determined through evaluation of the *pupils* the student teachers taught. It is necessary to both pre- and post-test the pupils.

Performance objectives—A means of evaluating the skills taught through observation of an action or performance.

Bibliotherapy   The use of books or other readings for the purpose of improving a person's outlook, attitude, or behavior. It is most commonly used with children experiencing personal, emotional, or mental problems.

Biculturalism   The ability to behave, on occasion, according to selected patterns of culture other than one's own.

Bilingual   A term used to describe the ability to speak more than one language fluently.

Bilingual Education   A process by which the learning experiences provided in the home and other educational and societal institutions enable a person to fulfill total self-development, as well as to function in a language in addition to the home language.

Bilingualism   The ability to function in another language in addition to one's home language.

Binaural The function of using both ears together.

Binocular The function of using both eyes together.

Blend The combining of two or three letter sounds such that no one sound is unidentifiable. Examples are *gr* as in *grips* or *str* in *straight*.

Breve A diacritical mark used to indicate the short sound of a vowel for pronunciation: for example, făt.

Cancellation test A measurement usually employed in readiness tests in which the code must cross out the symbol that does not belong in the same category as the other symbols presented.

Case study The practice of collecting all necessary data in order to diagnose and prescribe for a student. This could include health reports, test results, and teacher and parent evaluation.

Central dominance The existence of one dominant hemisphere of the brain controlling bodily activity. If there is some neurological impairment or brain damage present, it will result in confusion of this control.

Chronological age The actual number of years a person has lived, usually used in comparison with mental or developmental age.

Cloze procedure A measurement of comprehension or readability in which a reading selection is given and certain words are deleted. The student must then provide closure by inserting the proper words according to context clues.

Cognition The act or process of becoming knowledgeable of ideas or objects. This process involves recall, reasoning, evaluating, interpreting, translation, and application.

Comprehension level The level of understanding a person can attain in response to the combination of meanings and word symbols. Comprehension involves understanding of both oral and written language.

Concept The result of forming generalizations concerning events, objects, or ideas that can be representative of other similar entities.

Concept load An analysis of the number of new concepts, difficulty of ideas, and organization complexity in a selected reading passage.

Configuration clues An aid in word recognition that makes use of the shape and pattern of the letters in a particular word. It mainly relies on the presence of ascending and descending letters.

Content analysis The practice of examining reading materials for the presence or absence of previously determined items, concepts, or ideas.

Content word In linguistics, a term used to identify those morphemes that have a semantic meaning, as opposed to words having functional meanings. For example: the words *boat* and *cloth* would be content words, as contrasted with *the* or *if*, which would be considered functional words.

Context clues An aid used in word recognition in which the surrounding word or sentences are used to pronounce or gain meaning from the word or words in question.

Controlled vocabulary A listing of words introduced in a beginning reading program at a set rate and pattern.

Copula A linking verb: *is, are, was, were, have, had,* etc.

Corrective reading The use of individualized remedial reading instruction to assist in the prevention of a persons' reading retardation in the regular classroom.

Craig Reader A teaching aid used in remedial classes in which a controlled reader is used in conjunction with a tachiscope using strips of material mounted in plastic envelopes with small windows.

Creative reading The level of reading characterized by the ability to interpret, predict, and understand symbolic or indirect shades of meaning.

Criterion In regard to testing, those concepts or ideas used in evaluating the content of a test, etc., and estimating its validity.

Criterion test A test used to determine whether students have mastered a particular unit of instruction. It is often used to determine if a student is able to progress to the next level of instruction.

Critical reading A high level of comprehension in which the reader can differentiate between fact and opinion, fact and fantasy, fiction and nonfiction and determine what propaganda techniques are being used or judge the accuracy and completeness of information given.

Curricular Reading Program Instruction used to develop reading skills in all subject areas, particularly social studies, math, and science. Also known as reading in the content areas.

Censory reading A rapid scanning of reading material for the purpose of gaining an idea of the main topic or general facts.

Decoding The process of attaching words in reading that are not recognized as sight vocabulary.

Denotation The specific meaning of a word.

Descending letter Letters in print or handwriting that extend below the line, gjpqy. They can, therefore, be used as configuration clues in reading.

Development age A stage of growth used in comparison with age equivalents. It describes a combination of such characteristics as height, weight, growth factors, and muscular control.

Development Reading Program A plan of reading instruction that utilizes all approaches and skills necessary for the student to progress at his own learning rate. It purports to help the child master the broad spectrum of skills needed for effective, efficient reading.

Dextrality A term used to describe the preference of the right side of the body for the performance of most functions.

Diacritical mark Symbols used above a word to serve as a guide for pronunciation.

Diagnosis The methods used to assess an individual's specific strengths and weaknesses in reading. This information is then used to prescribe a program of instruction tailored to the person's individual needs. A diagnostic reading test is just one aspect of a complete diagnosis.

Diagnosis–informal Any method of analysis that does not include a formal, standardized reading test. The methods commonly employed are checklists, criterion referenced tests, anecdotal records, or inventories of a person's skills.

Diagnostic reading test An instrument used to assess a person's specific strengths and weaknesses in reading. Results can provide a basis for developing to assist the learner in overcoming reading difficulty.

Dialect The particular form of a language used by a particular group of people. Its variations in pronunciation, accents, grammar, and vocabulary are influenced by geographic location, cultural heritage, and socioeconomic level.

Dictionary skills Those functions necessary to make use of all aspects of a dictionary. They include using guide words, pronunciation keys, syllabication, word meanings and usage, parts of speech, derivations, etc.

Digraph The combination of two or more letters that form only one speech sound. For example, the *gh* in *rough* and the *oa* in *boat.*

Diphthong A blending of two vowel sounds that begin with the sound of the first vowel and then glides into the sound of the other: for example, the vowel sounds in toy or oil.

Directional confusion A disability in reading in which the individual makes reversals, substitutions, and regressions as a result of left-to right perceptual difficulties.

Dominance The preference an individual has for one side of the body when performing tasks using eyes, ears, or limbs.

Dyslexia A disability in reading in which the person cannot recognize or decode words.

Eclectic approach An approach to reading instruction that combines what the user deems to be strengths of different approaches.

Educational age The age at which a particular level of performance is reached. It is used in comparison with the norms of the person's chronological age.

Encoding The translation of speech into a written code.

Equivalent form See alternate test forms.

Etiology The study of the causes or origins of a particular disorder. In reading, this could include physiological or psychological dysfunctions, deficient early stimulation, or poor instruction.

Etymology The study of the origin and derivation of words. It involves the tracing of the history of a word from its first usage through modifications in various languages.

Experience chart A story or statements dictated by children and recorded by the teacher. One particular strength of experience charts is that they allow the child to read his own language, expressing ideas about his own interests.

Families in reading A term used to describe the combination of letters that is common to certain words. For example, the distinguishing of *it* in *bit, sit, fit, mit* can be a device used in word recognition. The term is also used to describe any groups of words that contain a rhyming ending.

Figure-ground perception The ability to perceive that certain figures are indistinct from their backgrounds.

Figures of speech Words or phrases that are composed of figurative language. The metaphor, simile, personification, paradox, and hyperbola can be used when "speaking figuratively."

Finger writing A technique using the kinesthetic sense, in which the child uses his finger to make an image on paper, a desk top, or in the air.

Fixations Brief, momentary pauses in eye movement during the reading act.

Fluency A reading term used to describe smoothness of speech in oral reading, speaking, or writing skills.

Frustration level The stage of reading at which the student's word-recognition abilities fall below 90 per cent, and comprehension abilities are below 75–60 per cent. The student may also react with anxiety or difficulty in vocalization. The teacher should then realize that easier reading material is necessary.

Generalization A judgment of what one might usually expect in a certain type of situation after data and other information have been accumulated and studied.

Global methodology A method of reading instruction in which whole words, phrases, and sentences are introduced. The sight-word or language experience can be categorized under this methodology.

Grade equivalent The grade level for which a given test score is considered average.

Grade norm The average test score achieved by students of a given grade.

Grapheme The written symbol of a particular sound. The phoneme /g/ is represented by the grapheme *g*.

Haptic A term used to describe those abilities and modalities associated with the kinesthetic and tactile modes of instruction and learning.

Holistic methodology A philosophy of teaching in which importance is placed on the child as an entire being, rather than on single aspects. He is dealt with as a meaningful whole, rather than the sum of his parts.

Homograph Words that are spelled alike but have more than one meaning. For example, charge can mean to attack and also to buy on credit.

Homonym Words that sound the same but are different in spelling and meaning. For example, *to, too, two* or *tow* and *toe*.

Homophone Another term for homonym, meaning words that are identical in sound but have different meanings.

Ideogram Characters in some forms of writing in which symbols stand for a word or idea. An example would be hieroglyphics.

Independent reading level The stage of reading in which the individual's word-recognition abilities are 98–99 per cent accurate and comprehension is at least 90 per cent. The student needs no teacher assistance and can use this reading level when selecting books for recreational reading.

Informal reading inventory A method of evaluation in which the teacher uses a checklist and a series of passages to record the number, type, and frequency of reading, word-recognition, and comprehension errors.

Instructional reading level The stage of reading in which word-recognition abilities are 95 per cent accurate and comprehension is at, or above, 75 per cent. The student needs to make use of teacher guidance or other material aids at this level.

Interest inventory A questioning device used to gain knowledge of an individual's personality, interests, attitudes, and favorite activities.

Intonation Patterns of stress within a spoken language.

IQ (Intelligence quotient) An attempt to measure the level of mental growth a person has attained by dividing the mental age obtained from the test score by his chronological age and then multiplying that quotient by 100. A synonym for IF (Intellectual Functioning).

ITA (initial teaching alphabet) An alphabet sometimes used in beginning reading and writing instruction. It consists of 44 phonemes, utilizing all of the traditional symbols except *x* and *q* and adding twenty others.

Joplin plan A grouping plan in which students from various grades are brought together and grouped according to their achievement level.

Juncture In real language, pauses that are used to separate like words, distinguish phrases or clauses or to indicate the completion of a sentence.

Kinesthetic methodology A sensory approach to reading instruction in which the student traces letters or geometric forms in order to strengthen learning. Sandpaper or felt letters are often used to increase the tactile awareness.

Kinesics A term used in linguistics to describe all forms of nonverbal communication, such as facial expressions, bodily gestures, shrugs, and nudges.

Kinetic reversals A type of mirror reading in which the letters of a word are reversed: for example, *bat* is read as *tab* and *won* is read as *now*.

Language experience method A method of reading instruction in which the child's own interests, speech, and past experiences are utilized in a sight-vocabulary approach.

Lateral dominance The use of one side of the body for most actions as a possible result of cerebral dominance.

Learning modality (style) The channels through which an organism learns to use the senses. For example, some individuals learn best through the visual modality, others through the aural modality, and some through the haptic modality.

Lexicon The body of meaningful units acquired by a person for use in his language: e.g., a word or a bounded morpheme (ed, ly).

Linguistics The study of the structure, nature, and changes of human language. This would include such aspects as accent, grammar, phonetics, semantics, syntax, function, and correlations between speech and written language.

Linguistic method of reading An approach to teaching reading in which word families are introduced rather than individual letter sounds.

Local norms In standardized testing, the use of data collected in a particular school or system in place of national norms, in order to evaluate test results.

Macron The straight line placed over a vowel in pronunciation keys to indicate a long vowel sound.

Maturation The normal person goes through stages or levels of physical, mental, social, and emotional development. The nature of the individual and the nurture of the environment are strong affecting factors.

Memory span A measurement of the number of forms, letters, pictures, or words a person can retain, given a certain amount of exposure to the items.

Mental age The level of intellectual development is sometimes interpreted from achievement of a particular score on a scholastic ability test. This score related to a specific age is considered average for that chronological age. Mental age is also found by multiplying chronological age by I.Q.

Methodology The branch of education that deals with the analyzation and evaluation of teaching methods and curriculum.

Mirror reading A reading disability in which the person views letters, words, or sentences in a right-to-left order. For example, *p* is read as *q* and *tip* is read as *pit*.

Mixed dominance Absence of lateral dominance, which may seemingly result in confusion. Mixed-hand dominance, mixed-key dominance, or cross dominance are all types of this disability.

Modality See learning modality.

Morpheme The meaning of a unit of language. There are two kinds of morphemes: free, consisting of whole, one-syllable words: and bound, which applies to prefixes and suffixes. Both types contain no smaller meaningful parts.

Morphology The study of structures in language: e.g., plurals /z/, /s/, /es/; tense markers /ed/, /s/.

Motivation The activation of a person's interest in or the ability to sustain a particular activity.

Multisensory approach A method of teaching reading that makes use of several learning modalities involving the senses. This could involve visual, aural, kinesthetic, and tactile learning activities.

National norm In comparing the results of a standardized test, this norm is based on the results of a national sampling.

Norms Test scores that describe the performance of a particular group of examinees. They should not be viewed as necessary levels of attainment.

Objectives See *behavioral objectives.*

Objective-instructional The expected behavioral outcome of any unit or lesson plan that the instructor considers necessary for the students to attain.

Observational methodology Techniques such as charts, graphs, anecdotal records, and recordings that a clinician uses in observing behavior.

Organismic age The stage of development for which the test scores are combined to yield the mental, functional, and physical growth stage. This process is sometimes used to define the best age for beginning reading.

Paradigm A pattern or example of a conjugation showing the word in all its forms.

Parallel tests See *alternate test norms.*

Perception Processes such as discrimination, awareness, and sensation through which an individual is able to organize his environmental experiences into an interpretive response.

Performance test A measurement device in which the examinee must use and manipulate objects as a test of his physical and motor skills.

Phoneme The smallest unit of speech, which distinguishes one sound from another: for example, *fit* vs. *fat,* or *top* vs. *tip.*

Phonemic language A type of language in which each letter has only one sound. The initial teaching alphabet (ITA) is a phonemic alphabet.

Phonic analysis A method of teaching word recognition in which word elements are matched with their corresponding sounds. This involves analyzing consonants, vowels, blends, digraphs, and diphthongs.

Phonogram A letter or symbol that represents a word, syllable, or sound. It can also refer to a combination of letters or symbols that have the same sound in a family of words. For example the *ame* in *game, blame, tame,* and *same.*

Phonology The study of the sounds of a language.

Pitch Includes the specific aspects of spoken language, which are called tone and volume.

Power test A type of measurement in which the items are arranged in increasing difficulty for the purpose of measuring knowledge and accuracy, rather than speed.

Pragmatics A component of linguistics; the study of the usage of language, appropriateness conditions, and speech acts.

Profile chart A listing showing a comparison between a person's strengths and weaknesses and the normal levels expected for various reading skills.

Programmed reading method A method of individualized reading instruction in which sequenced lessons are presented using a teaching machine, student workbooks, or activity cards. The material is presented in small amounts, followed by questions for which the correct answers are given for immediate reinforcement.

Prosody The elements of spoken language, which include stress, pitch, and intonation.

Psycholinguistics The study of language involving knowledge of cognitive development and the structure of language.

Raw score The original test score, usually consisting of the number of correct answers or number of points achieved on a previously determined scale.

Readability The level of reading difficulty of a particular piece of reading material. The level is ascertained by the use of a readability formula scale in which the vocabulary load, word structure, and sentence composition and length are analyzed.

Reader's theater Students read prepared scripts to an audience that does not have copies of the scripts. Few gestures and almost no costumes are used. The reader is supposed to convey the setting, time, and tone through the reading of the script.

Reading age The level of reading ability a person has attained stated in terms of age. For example, if an individual reads as well as a nine-year-old is expected to read, his reading age would be considered as nine, despite his chronological age.

Reading Miscue Inventory An informal measure of the *type* of reading error made, rather than the *number* of errors.

Reading readiness A term used to refer to the necessary level of preparation a person should attain before formal reading instruction is begun. Factors considered in determining readiness include emotional and intellectual maturity, age, vision, hearing, environmental experience, language development, and cognitive development.

Reading vocabulary A reading sight vocabulary needed for effective comprehension in both recreational and content area reading.

Rebus story A reading exercise in which certain words in a story are replaced by pictures.

Reference books Books and resources used for locating information such as textbooks, encyclopedias, almanacs, dictionaries, and atlases.

Regression Those brief, reverse eye movements performed in order to reread words or sentences already covered.

Reliability The consistency of a test as determined by whether it yields the same score when given more than one time using an equivalent form or the retest method.

Remediation The individualized diagnosis and prescriptive reading program administered to an individual experiencing reading difficulty. It is usually carried out by a reading specialist outside the regular classroom setting.

Reversals The practice of reading letters, words, or sentences in a right-to-left order as a result of visual impariment. There are two types of reversals: static reversals, in which the person confuses single letters such as *b* and *d,* and kinetic reversals, in which the whole words are confused, as in reading *pan* for *nap.*

Root word A meaningful word entity form which other words are formed by adding prefixes, suffixes, or inflectional endings.

Schwa A form of a vowel sound most often located in an unaccented syllable of a word. The pronunciation is similar to the *uh* sound as in *motion* and is diacritically recorded as mō shə n.

Semantics The body of lexical meanings within a language.

Sight reading The act of orally reading a selection that has not been previously reviewed by the reader.

Sight word A word that is learned using the configuration as a whole. No structural or phonetic analysis is used in this type of word recognition. It can also be defined as any word recognized on sight.

Sight-vocabulary approach A method of reading instruction in which configuration clues rather than phonetic or structural analysis of letters, syllables, and words are utilized.

Sinistrality A term used to describe the preference of the left side of the body for the performance of most functions.

Scanning The rapid viewing of columns, charts, lists, or other materials in order to acquire specific information.

Skimming The rapid viewing of reading material for the purpose of gaining the main idea of general tone of the passage.

Snellen chart The printed card used for testing visual acuity in which the person stands 20 feet from the chart and reads, or points out the direction of, the letters or symbols.

Syntax The word order of a specific utterance.

Standardized reading test A measurement that has been administered to various groups under the same conditions and for which norms have been calculated.

Stress The degree to which a syllable or sound is emphasized in a word.

Structural analysis A method of decoding in which such parts of a word as prefixes, suffixes, compounds, and syllables are separated and analyzed.

Study skills Proficiency in such reading skills as skimming, scanning, outlining, reference book use, map reading, note taking, and memorizing.

Subtest A set of items in a test that are included to measure more specific areas of general ability. for example, vocabulary could be a subtest of a complete reading test.

Subvocal reading An inefficient reading habit in which the reader moves his lips, tongue, or throat muscles in a slight whisper during silent reading. This slows down the reading rate.

Survey test A measurement of general achievement in a given subject area that is more concerned with general knowledge than specific details or diagnosis. it is usually a group-administered test.

Sweep The movement of the eyes returning to the beginning of the next line during the reading process.

Syllabication The method of dividing words into parts, having at least one vowel in each syllable. They should roughly correspond to the syllables of spoken languages and are used as pronunciation guides or to divide a word at the end of a line.

Syllable The smallest divisible unit of a word. A syllable usually contains at least one vowel sound.

Tactile A term used to refer to the sense of touch. In reading instruction, the tactile kinesthetic approach is utilized by having the learner touch, trace, or write words and letters as an additional reinforcement.

Trade books Books written and sold for recreational reading as opposed to textbooks or reference tools.

Transfer The application of knowledge previously learned to a new situation or a higher level or learning.

Unvoiced sounds A speech sound made using the breath rather than the vocal cords.

VAKT A method of learning that utilizes the visual, auditory, kinesthetic, and tactile senses in multisensory instruction. For example, in learning a word or letter, the student sees its form, hears the sound and pronounces it himself, writes the word or letter, and traces it with his finger.

Validity The degree to which a test measures what it supposed to be capable of measuring. There are several different kinds of validity according to the different types of evidence used. Some examples are

> *Concurrent validity*—The extent to which a person's test results can predict his ability to perform on any other kind of criterion not associated with that test.

> *Construct validity*—The extent to which particular explanations or concepts affect performance on the test.

Content validity—The extent to which the test items sample the subject matter from which conclusions will be drawn.

Predictive validity—The extent to which the predictions made from test results are confirmed by results obtained at a later time.

Verbal test   A measurement that contains items requiring the use of language, either oral or written.

Visual acuity   Sharpness and clearness of vision. Normal vision is considered to be 20/20; that is, the ability to read at 20 feet what a person with normal vision can read at the same distance.

Visual discrimination   The ability to perceive similarities and differences in and to differentiate between geometric symbols or words and letters.

Vowel cluster   Another name for vowel diphthong.

Word analysis   A method of decoding using phonetic analysis, structural analysis, or meaning guides for word recognition.

Word attack   The use of any reading skill to recognize words. This would include the use of phonics, configuration clues, structural analysis, sight-word knowledge, picture clues, and context clues.

Word calling   The pronunciation of a word or words without knowledge of its meaning. It is also used to describe a halting, step-by-step way of reading.

Word load   The number of different words appearing in a particular reading selection. It is performed in order to ascertain the vocabulary load, reading level, or reading material.

Word count   The total number of words appearing in a reading selection.

Word families   A group of words that rhyme because of a like element. For example *map, cap, gap,* and *lap.* The linguistic method of teaching reading introduces various word families rather than assigns a sound to individual letters.

Words in Color   A program for teaching reading in which every sound of the English language is categorized into a particular color regardless of spelling. For example, for the "long" *a* sound *ae, ay, a, ey, eigh,* etc., would all be the same color on the charts. Basal readers are used in conjunction with this program after various sounds and words have been introduced.

Word wheel   Word parts are written on two concentric cardboard circles attached in the center. The student or teacher can spin the wheel to form new words.

Index